1990

# COMMUNICATING
# IN BUSINESS
# TODAY

# COMMUNICATING IN BUSINESS TODAY

## RUTH G. NEWMAN

*with*

### MARIE A. DANZIGER
*Massachusetts Institute of Technology*

*and*

### MARK COHEN
*Digital Equipment Corporation*

### D. C. HEATH AND COMPANY
*Lexington, Massachusetts          Toronto*

*Acquisitions Editor:* Paul Smith
*Developmental Editor:* Holt Johnson
*Production Editor:* Holt Johnson
*Designers:* Victor A. Curran, Bruce Terzian
*Production Coordinator:* Michael O'Dea
*Photo Researcher:* Martha Shethar
*Text Permissions Editor:* Margaret Roll

## Acknowledgments

Russell Baker, "Little Red Riding Hood Revisited." From *The New York Times*, January 13, 1980. Copyright © 1980 by The New York Times Company. Reprinted by permission.

Dianna Booher, "You Are What You Write— Model Memos for All Occasions." *From Send Me A Memo* by Dianna Booher. © 1984 by Dianna Booher. Reprinted by permission of Facts on File, Inc., New York.

Jerr Boschee, "The Anatomy of an Interview." *From IABC Communication World*, April 1985. Reprinted courtesy of The International Association of Business Communicators and Jerr Boschee.

David W. Ewing, "A Sinister Disease Invades the Business World." *Los Angeles Times*, January 12, 1979. Reprinted by permission.

Gail Godwin, "The Watcher at the Gates." *New York Times Book Review*, January 9, 1977. Copyright © 1977 by The New York Times Company. Reprinted by permission.

Carol A. Gosselink and Suzanne J. McKinley, "What You Don't Say." From *Communicator's Journal*, March/April 1964.

Carole Howard, "When A Reporter Calls . . ." From *Communicator's Journal*, May/June 1984.

Terry Marotta, "Speechless." From *The Boston Globe*, April 17, 1985. Reprinted by permission of Terry Marotta, a syndicated columnist whose work appears in newspapers throughout New England.

Eugene McCarthy and James Kilpatrick, "The Gobbledegook." From *A Political Bestiary* by Eugene McCarthy and James Kilpatrick. Copyright © 1978 by McGraw-Hill Book Company. Reprinted by permission.

Jonathan Newman, "Today, Tomorrow, and Always: Office Automation." Reprinted by permission.

Ruth G. Newman, "Case of the Questionable Communiqués." From *Harvard Business Review*, November/December 1975. Reprinted by permission.

Herbert Popper, "Six Guidelines for Fast, Functional Writing." Reprinted by special permission from *Chemical Engineering*, June 30, 1969. Copyright © 1969 by McGraw-Hill, Inc., New York, NY 10020.

Ralph Proodian, "A Strong Voice Is a Valuable Managerial Asset." Published in *The Wall Street Journal*, January 31, 1983. Copyright © 1983. Reprinted by permission of Ralph Proodian, Ed.D., Assistant Professor of Speech, Brooklyn College, CUNY.

Carl B. Rogers and Richard E. Farson, "Active Listening." The University of Chicago, Industrial Relations Center.

The Royal Bank of Canada, "Imagination Helps Communication." The Royal Bank of Canada 1960. Reprinted with the permission of the Royal Bank of Canada.

Susan E. Russ, "A Bureaucrat's to Chocolate Chip Cookies." Special to *The Washington Post*.

William Safire, "The Fumblerules of Grammar." From *The New York Times Magazine*, November 7, 1979. Copyright © 1979 by The New York Times Company. Reprinted by permission.

Paul S. Swensson, "Keys to Good Writing." From Women in Communications Journal, *Matrix*, fall 1977. Reprinted with permission of Women in Communications, Inc. from the *Matrix* magazine.

Marvin H. Swift, "Clear Writing Means Clear Thinking Means . . ." From *Harvard Business Review*, January/February 1973. Reprinted by permission.

To David and Anne, Jon and Pam, and Debby

# PREFACE

During the past twenty years or more, I have been a student, a teacher, a writer, manager of several communication functions within business firms, and more recently an entrepreneurial consultant in business communication. For most of my professional life, therefore, while preoccupied with words and their effects, I have shuttled between two separate worlds. The first of these is the academic world of students, teachers, and scholarship; the second is the world that students, and even some teachers, call the "real world" — the marketplace where business transactions take place.

For most students and for many employees, however, the latter world is not very *real* at all. They harbor an abiding and contagious suspicion that business has a special mystique. They expect that the business environment will require them to put on hold their commonsensical perceptions about how to make people respond well to their ideas and words. If they are industrious and ambitious, they are prepared at the outset to master a whole new set of rules about writing, speaking, and even thinking. For the most part, they are wrong in this expectation.

The first breakthrough in learning to communicate well is achieved with the perception that communication begins with knowing who one is, whom one is addressing, and what one hopes to accomplish. Further success is almost guaranteed if one aims to be as logical, persuasive, and personable as one's personal endowments permit . . . and then some.

A basic premise of this text is that all writers must work hard to master the traditional tools of their trade. And even when they have the requisite knowledge in place, the writing process is always highly individualized, filled with starts and stops, and pressing endlessly towards a moving goal. In a real sense, writers must rediscover a successful writing process with each new effort to communicate.

*Communicating in Business Today* makes no bones about the fact that confidence and skill in communicating are acquired through study, strenuous effort, and constant practice. And it makes it clear that for student writers, adding to their arsenal can be a strenuous and time-consuming enterprise. But, through many realistic cases and examples, it also strongly implies that the business environment rewards those individuals who possess these skills in abundance.

# Key Features

In designing this text we have aimed to provide students with pathways to learning that, while strenuous, are also interesting and compelling. We have tried to challenge and motivate students to discover their best selves and to exert their individual powers to resolve problems that they typically will encounter in the workplace. Moreover, because *Communicating in Business Today* avoids cookbook solutions and stresses the uniqueness of each writer and each business situation, it challenges instructors to help students develop their special abilities.

Among the text's distinctive features are the following:

**Process/Product Case Method.** A new approach to the case method stimulates rapid learning:

- Although many opportunities are provided for students to think independently, they are first carefully trained in audience and situation analysis. At frequent intervals, both an appropriate process for resolving the case problem and examples of the resulting memo, letter, or report are discussed in detail.
- Cases mirror real workplace tasks; moreover, they place readers in roles that are appropriate to the professional aims and aspirations of entry-level employees across a broad spectrum of industries and business functions.

**Readability and Accessibility.** This text is written in a style that aims to emulate what it teaches:

- We have tried to speak directly to our readers in a clear, candid, conversational style.
- Both style and content reflect a close analysis of our reading audience; an important objective has been to help our readers perceive that they are in touch with an instructor who understands and to a great extent shares their attitudes and perspectives.

**Exceptionally Broad Coverage.** Along with close attention to all aspects of business writing, the text provides extensive coverage of the following critical topics:

- *The job campaign*, from preliminary brainstorming, résumés and cover letters, through the acceptance letter.
- *The preparation and use of graphics* for business writing and speaking, with multiple examples.
- *Collaborative writing efforts*, in a full chapter devoted to "The Politics of Report Writing."
- A detailed list of *business research sources*, with discussion of available on-line data bases.

- *Planning, preparing, and delivering the spoken presentation.*
- *Business meetings*, from the perspective of both leader and participant.
- *International communications.*
- *Office automation technology* and its benefits.

**Realistic, Practical Discussion Problems and Tasks.** The text includes an extremely broad selection of chapter-end exercises.

- *Discussion Problems*
  These do not simply invite students to regurgitate the chapter's content. Many are case related; others help students to share their own communication strategies with their peers.
- *Tasks*
  Many are related to the preceding discussion problems—allowing students to implement the strategies they have defended in discussions. Others provide opportunities for practicing the techniques demonstrated in the chapter.

**Innovative Approaches.** Although there are many innovations in our text, the following are perhaps most notable:

- *The Dialogues*
  Four dialogues, or short plays, vividly reveal how writers tackle business communication. Based on actual recorded transcripts, they show a group of students analyzing each other's writings. Their discussions provide exceptional insights into the minds of writers and editors. Each dialogue is based on an interesting and challenging case. Each is followed by additional student letters or memos to discuss and revise.
- *Dynamic Treatment of Proposals and Reports*
  In confronting an important contemporary issue, an entry-level employee helps resolve a critical problem at his company. As he masters essential communication skills, the text covers in detail research techniques (including use of on-line data bases), letter proposals and formal proposals, formatting, and all topics relevant to preparing a major report.
- *Unique Application of Rhetorical Modes to Business Writing*
  The "Patterns of Relationship" chapter provides new insights into methods by which writers create logical structure. Using real-world examples, the text clearly shows that the relationships we deal with most frequently in business writing are natural and familiar: space, time, comparison, analysis, cause/effect, and problem/solution.
- *Traditional and New Techniques for Prewriting and Planning*
  Not only the traditional outline but also modern methods taught to executives by business consultants and trainers are explained. Students are helped to see planning as a natural and inevitable part of the writing process.

# The Authors

*Communicating in Business Today* reflects the experience of three authors who are actively employed in business or academic administration. In addition, all of us have spent a major portion of our professional careers in the teaching and training of writing, speaking, and interpersonal relationships.

Marie A. Danziger is currently Assistant Dean for Academic Support at the Massachusetts Institute of Technology. In this capacity, she is responsible for developing and implementing programs to coordinate the efforts of various academic departments and to provide counsel to students on their academic progress and career issues. Prior to holding this position, she was Assistant to the President of Bentley College. There she was responsible for administering, writing, and editing many critical communications, including reports, correspondence, and speeches to faculty and trustees, students and parents, the community-at-large, and government officials. In the past, she has been coeditor of a popular English-language monthly periodical for German readers, and has taught writing and other subjects at both American and European universities.

Mark Cohen has designed and taught communications and management development courses at four major Boston-area firms engaged in manufacturing, retailing, financial services, and information technology. At Digital Equipment Corporation, where he is currently employed, he is Human Resource and Development Manager of New Product Operations, a position that focuses on ensuring high productivity and job satisfaction for the Digital workforce. At Digital in 1985, he received the "Instructor Excellence Award" for innovative and successful course design. He has also developed training programs for a variety of government and business clients. Early in his career, he was a teacher within the Massachusetts public school system.

My own professional career has been propelled by a love for teaching and writing. Chance and opportunity brought me into the business community, and I became deeply interested in business communication.

I have taught writing to students and business people at many levels and in varied environments. While a graduate student, I spent summers at Emerson College in Boston teaching students with severe writing problems. At Boston University and at the University of Massachusetts, I taught a variety of traditional composition courses. Later, at the Open College at Pine Manor College and at Boston University's Metropolitan College, I worked with women reentering the job market and men and women needing communication skills to improve their job status. At the Harvard Business School, I had my first encounter with business majors. During the six years I spent there, I was given the opportunity to head up the first-year Written and Oral Communication program; I also designed and taught the seminar from which the *Dialogues* were taken.

Since 1979, I have worked within the consulting industry. For six years,

I concurrently directed the communications function at three Boston-area management consulting firms, supervising internal communications, marketing communications, public relations, and quality control of client letters, memos, and reports. I also designed and taught writing and presentation workshops for employees and clients. Working across a broad spectrum of industries, I helped executives and their employees to build their communication skills in workshops tailored to their needs. In late 1985, I decided to buckle down to the task of completing *Communicating in Business Today*, which had been sporadically in progress for over four years. Simultaneously, I launched my own communications consulting business.

## Acknowledgments

As the preceding sketch of my career may imply, although I have loved writing this book, without the encouragement and help of many people the project would likely have foundered.

First of all, I owe thanks to my two co-authors. Without Mark Cohen's enthusiasm and assistance, the book would not have been started. Without Marie Danziger's support and hard work, it is unlikely that it could have been finished.

Next, I would like to thank my two editors at D.C. Heath. For nearly four years, from his first encounter with the proposed manuscript, Paul Smith believed in the project and kept it on course. Holt Johnson understood and shared my commitment to making this a text that would speak to students in my own voice, and he expertly supported my effort to write it that way.

All of us who worked on the book owe a special note of gratitude to Mary Silva, who did much more than merely type the manuscript with professional elegance. She unstintingly gave her nights and weekends to the project, assisted us greatly with early copyediting and formatting, and even enlisted her husband, Joe, for delivery service.

Lois DuBois, Director of Planning, Sonoco Products Company, and David Ewing, author and former Managing Editor of the *Harvard Business Review*, both reviewed large portions of the manuscript and contributed excellent suggestions. We also owe thanks to Howard Dinin, Vice President and Account Supervisor of Rizzo, Simons, Cohn Inc., for sharing his knowledge of the field of advertising and graphic arts, and to Wayne Grincewicz, illustrator, who supplied us with two fine illustrations for Chapter 6. In addition, the text benefited greatly from the advice of the following reviewers: J. Douglas Andrews, University of Southern California; Stephen A. Bernhardt, Southern Illinois University at Carbondale; Joseph F. Ceccio, The University of Akron; Susan Currier, California Polytechnic State University—San Luis Obispo; Birt Fischman, Bryant College; Robert Guiselman, University of Illinois; Carol Hartzog, University of California—Los Angeles; Barbara Hunt, Columbus College; Donna Kienzler, Iowa State

University; Wayne Losano, University of Florida; Patrick Parzarella, St. Bonaventure University; David Ramsey, Southeastern Louisiana University; C. Gilbert Storms, Miami University of Ohio.

Not only individuals but also organizations supported this project. At Temple, Barker & Sloane, Lexington, Massachusetts, Carl Sloane, President, generously permitted the entire manuscript to be typed into the firm's computer system. In addition, Larry Prusack, Director of Information Services, provided us with comprehensive information on business research sources. At Index Systems, Cambridge, Massachusetts, Tom Gerrity, then President and now Chairman, invited us to make use of the firm's copying and mailing facilities; also, Patrice Rafail provided us with a number of excellent exercises for on-line research projects, and Ann Hewitt, Senior Editor, also provided us with innovative research problems. The chapters on proposals and reports were greatly strengthened because Milton Cooke, Vice President and General Manager of The Management Consulting Division of The Austin Company, Chicago, Illinois, gave me access to training materials belonging to the firm.

Finally, I owe my thanks to the students who participated in my communications seminar at the Harvard Business School and gave permission to publish the writings and discussions that appear in the *Dialogues*. They certainly taught me as much as I taught them. I will do my best to let them know that this book did get written, as promised.

Ruth G. Newman

# CONTENTS

## 15 Report Writing II, Process & Product: The Report    380

## 16 Graphic Aids for Reports and Presentations    428

# SELECTED READINGS

# A NOTE ON GIVING
# AND RECEIVING CRITICISM

"Criticism" can be positive as well as negative. You can learn as much from a compliment as a complaint.

In this course, you may spend a considerable amount of time reviewing and criticizing the work of other students. On each such occasion you will have had the opportunity to analyze a case and you frequently will have prepared your own memos or letters in response. And chances are that while working out your own solution you will have developed some strong opinions about the best way to tackle the problem.

It's right to have established your own viewpoint; in fact, it's the *only* way you can begin to understand someone else's effort to travel the same route. But remember, they are *not* you. Their judgments will be swayed by their individual experiences—just as yours are. And their assessment of the case facts may surprise or trouble you. How can you deal with your misgivings and be most helpful to other writers?

## Giving Criticism

Rather than deciding if a fellow student's solution is "correct," step aside from that judgment for a moment and ask yourself the following questions:

- What is the writer trying to achieve?
- What is the writer's personal style?
- How does the writer envision the recipient of the writing?
- How does the writer perceive his or her own role?

**Empathy.** Truly helpful criticism responds to the writer's needs, not to your own. In a class where you frequently play the role of both contributor and instructor, you must be able to produce a superabundance of *empathy*, or sympathetic understanding, for the writer's perception of the task—even though that perception may not agree with yours.

On the other hand, your own effort to analyze the problem and to grasp the facts at hand will help you to perceive both the strengths and weaknesses of another's presentation. You will be able to make some helpful observations about

- What he or she has *included.*
- What he or she has *omitted.*
- How he or she has *ordered* the presentation.
- The personal *image* he or she has tried to project.

But all such judgments must follow your initial effort to empathize.

**Specificity.** Good criticism needs to be specific. If you tell a writer that his or her introduction is weak, you may have a valid point. But you will be far more helpful if you suggest, "You probably should omit the first sentence and begin the letter with the second because . . . ."

**Usefulness.** Criticism needs to be useful: it should help the writer to better his or her performance. You may be correct in saying, "You don't seem to have any real conception of whom you are writing to." But the student receiving your criticism would be able to make much better use of this sort of comment: "I feel you are writing to a hostile audience; actually Jones is pretty receptive to your plan."

By learning to empathize and to give useful and specific criticism, you not only will help your fellow students to improve their writing but also you will strengthen your own business writing skills. Furthermore, you will soon discover that, in all ways, you have become a far better communicator.

## Receiving Criticism

When receiving criticism from others, you may wonder how to know if it is valid. There are two ways to test the validity of criticism. Neither is foolproof, but both deserve your consideration.

*Self-evaluation* allows you to reexamine your work with new insight.

Probably, like most writers, you have had vague feelings of dissatisfaction with certain passages even as you were writing them. Perhaps you struggled to resolve the problem but were frustrated, or perhaps time constraints forced you to move on.

Later, if a discerning critic zeroes in on that problem and offers you a workable solution, you may hear an audible "click" in your mind. In conscientious writers this sensation usually provides a keen sense of satisfaction. A similar and even more gratifying experience is to hear what you have already happily suspected—that your work is absolutely on target and that you have achieved your purpose with noticeable skill.

*Group consensus* can also provide an excellent way to measure the validity of criticism.

When the group entirely agrees or disagrees with criticism, you should give its opinion some hard thought. If the critic appears to be in error, you might want to force him or her to be more specific. You might also ask the other members of the group to specify their reactions in detail. Criticism that is slightly aslant can often be put into proper perspective through open-minded discussion. Often, after a brief dialogue with the writer, another member of the group can clarify the original critic's point or suggest a good way to alleviate the problem.

When receiving criticism, remember that your goal is not to defend yourself; nor is it to please everyone in the room. Your aim is to discover how to use their criticism as a positive force for improving your written document.

# COMMUNICATING
# IN BUSINESS
# TODAY

# BUSINESS COMMUNICATION TODAY

## 1

ompany X is a large manufacturer of computer software products. If today you were to stroll through its lengthy corridors, you would see employees at every level—from technicians to senior executives—putting their thoughts down on paper. Systems analysts are writing instructions to programmers, who are laboring to distill their thoughts into neat, compact phrases. Marketing people are presenting surveys to product managers. People in technical communications are compiling information for a new product brochure. The company president and the chief financial officer are tearing apart a ten-page rundown of company finances. A network of communication, much of it written, extends from employee to employee, upwards, downwards, and sideways. This network also reaches beyond headquarters to Company X's West Coast subsidiary, to customers and potential customers, to suppliers, the media, and government agencies, and to many other people who this day are the audience for the ideas, messages, and explanations important to the company's operations.

Company Y does not manufacture a product, but it does have something to sell. It is a successful service organization, and its business is employment. On this day, counselors and recruiters are spending a great deal of time on the phone contacting potential employers and setting up interviews to screen job candidates. They are also participating in interviews and conferences. Nevertheless, in offices up and down the halls, at any odd minute when people are alone, you will probably spot them writing—jotting memos to each other about new clients and rumors of job opportunities, corresponding with employers, and drafting reports to senior members of the firm about potential growth markets, new ideas for attracting clients, and the many other subjects that preoccupy them.

Company Z is not a large firm. It is a family-owned enterprise that rents and sells uniforms to hospitals, laboratories, and other medical facilities. Its office and management staff includes about 30 people, and virtually half of them are "jacks-of-all-trades." Today Carol Taylor is out of the office, visiting a new bio-tech facility where she believes many new kinds of protective uniforms will be required. When Carol returns to the office, she will file a trip report to be read by her co-workers and retained in the company's active file. Her regular officemate, Peter Jones, is at his desk putting the finishing touches on a lengthy report about the company's current public relations and advertising tactics. This report is important to

Peter because he knows that Bob and Joan Green, the firm's owners, will be reviewing his ideas about how to get the company's name mentioned in the newsletters of several of the city's larger hospitals.

In these three settings we catch a glimpse of some of the activities that in our system of free enterprise we call *business*. But if we ourselves are not part of the daily business scene (and often even if we are) business may be only an abstraction. Economics textbooks tell us: "Business is the production of goods and services to be sold for a profit." And, of course, business is precisely that. But it is also the daily reality of the people who produce those goods and services, men and women who get up in the morning with specific ideas and tasks on their minds and head out their doors bent on "making a living"—exchanging time, energy, skill, and insights for wages or salaries. To perform effectively throughout their workday, they must share information, ideas, and opinions with one another. In short, they must communicate.

If anything is obvious about today's business environment, it's that words have more importance and power than ever before. If we had started with A and described a different firm for each letter of the alphabet, we still would not have exhausted the almost limitless number of verbal interactions that businesses require of their employees during a single day of normal operations. Business people communicate to describe ideas, processes, products, and services.

The size and intricacy of our business organizations have made communication more essential than ever before, and our technology has made it more abundant. Even a simple instrument like the telephone offers communications options that once would have seemed astonishing—messages relayed to new locations, conference calls across great distances, and many other possibilities. Today, when a manager has something to say, the means to say it quickly are almost always at hand.

Even though spoken communication has increased, today's technological revolution has diminished neither the volume nor the frequency of written communication. The written word, whether typed onto paper or entered onto a terminal screen, continues to lie at the heart of business communication. As in the past, the operation of a business continues to demand that people express their ideas in words and transmit those words in a form that can be retained if necessary, usually with some degree of permanence. For most employees, this requirement makes writing a critical skill.

Rather than decreasing the amount of writing and reading that employees face, modern technology has added to its abundance by increasing the ease and speed with which we can collect, store, and transmit data. The copying machine alone has revolutionized the way business communication is handled—not just the author of a document but anyone with access to a copier can easily retain or transmit the information that document contains. And the computer has, of course, made information management a whole new business discipline. Even small companies are likely to have memory typewriters and word-processing equipment, and large establishments commonly make use of terminal-to-terminal electronic mail and desktop computers that allow managers and employees to access enormous pools of information.

No wonder that effective communication (and especially effective writing) is given such a high priority in today's business environment. Brevity and clarity are watchwords, and the favorite edict of programmers—"garbage in, garbage out"—can be taken as an admonition to all business people. Mangled ideas, snarled sentences, and muddy verbiage are wasted effort. Moreover, if sent to the wrong person or badly timed or tactless, even a clear and succinct message can be counted as waste.

## ■ Business Writing: How Is It Different?

As human beings, we think with words, and our thoughts move so swiftly that it is difficult to be conscious of the words that contain them. But writing alters this state. As we write, we make our thoughts visible and accessible; we can refine, revise, or expunge them. All writers, whether business writers or poets, are engaged in this process of capturing thoughts by carving them into words. Nevertheless, people put their thoughts into writing for very different reasons, and these differences are rooted in the writers' feelings about potential readers.

For instance, people who write in their diaries are capturing memories and impressions, perhaps to savor them later but rarely to share them. Poets and novelists normally hope for an audience, but with or without one, they generally feel compelled to write. Two groups of writers, however, write exclusively to be read: journalists and business writers. For both of these, the effect their words have on an audience is critical. This similarity can provide some provocative insights into the pressures and challenges that confront business writers. Because they write for an audience, both reporters and business writers are greatly concerned about clarity; they know that their readers have limited time and many distractions. Furthermore, as writers, both reporters and business people are working under severe time constraints; they know the importance of deadlines. And finally, despite the pressures on them, both groups are highly accountable for their accuracy.

It is interesting to compare the *lead* of a news story to the tightly constructed opening of a well-written business memo. Both are digests of critical information that cater to the reader's need to know what will follow. And, in a sense, both are contracts between the writer and reader—

promises that the indicated information will be the writer's primary focus. The lead can, for the same reasons, also be compared to the *executive summary*, which introduces a long report and provides a capsule of its contents for executives who must set priorities concerning what documents to read, how thoroughly, and in which order.

Despite such similarities, there is an important difference in the outlooks of reporters and business writers. For reporters, events and their own reactions to those events provide the primary motive for writing. But for business writers, concern for the reader's response is usually paramount. If you ask business people why they write, nine times out of ten the answers you receive will focus on the reactions of prospective readers. The reason for writing will be described in words such as these:

"Because I want to persuade *them* to . . . "

"Because I need to ask *them* to . . . "

"Because I want to sell *them* a . . . "

"Because we want *them* to understand our . . . "

"Because we would like *them* to explain their . . . "

"Because we would like *them* to attend our . . . "

More than any other kind of writers, business people try to know as much as possible about their readers. A simple profile generally will not suffice; they must have information about their readers' particular situations, interests, and needs. And since they write to people inside and outside their own organizations, to people they supervise, to peers, and to superiors, business writers do not always have easy access to this information. For instance, to plan an ad campaign or design a sales letter for a specific audience, a marketing specialist will spend time and resources learning about that audience's concerns. Similarly, almost any business writer will usually need to appraise his or her intended reader before writing.

## ■ The Spoken Word at Work: Changes and Choices

Just as the importance of writing has increased in today's business environment, so has the importance of speaking. In a typical workday, business people use speaking and listening skills in a wide spectrum of activities. A list of the most obvious and important might include interviews and conferences (face-to-face and by phone), meetings (work sessions and formal gatherings), speeches, and formal presentations. It's also true that in the compressed schedule of a busy workday even casual conversations can contain nuggets of important ideas or signals concerning the way people feel

*Duffy* by Bruce Hammond © 1985, Universal Press Syndicate. Reprinted with permission. All rights reserved.

about projects or problems. Therefore, although our primary focus in this text is on written communication, we will not disregard the spoken word.

Today, selecting the right medium for sending a message can be an extremely important decision. The age-old practice of dictating a letter to a secretary who transcribes it and sends it off to the mailroom is losing ground. First of all, the cost of this traditional method of communicating has skyrocketed. In 1930, the cost of preparing such a letter was approximately 30¢; ten years ago, it was $3.31; in 1984, it had reached $7.60.* Making a long-distance phone call today will therefore often be less expensive than writing a letter. Moreover, new technologies are now available that make oral communication especially attractive. Conference calls are regular events in most companies, and in large companies teleconferences that provide not only audio but also video reception are frequently used to disseminate information among large numbers of employees, sometimes over great distances.

Writing and speaking in a business setting have much in common: both are audience-centered, task-related, and purposeful. But they are not equally effective in all situations. Sometimes written communication serves best, and at other times a form of oral communication is more appropriate; frequently both must be used in tandem.

The two primary factors that business people consider when deciding whether to write or to speak are *spontaneity* and *permanence*. At times, business communication needs to be spontaneous and immediate; at other times, it should be carefully considered and controlled. On some occasions, a permanent record of the transaction is essential; on others, permanence may be undesirable.

*Reported in *The Boston Sunday Globe Magazine*, January 1, 1984, this cost survey was done by the Darnell Institute of Business, a Chicago-based publishing and subscription service founded in 1917.

Compare, for instance, the relative benefits of a letter and a phone call. If expressing yourself powerfully is your main concern and you need to choose your words with great care, a letter will certainly serve you better. On the other hand, if your main concern is to see how the other person will react or to draw a prompt response, a phone call can provide immediate feedback and allow you to revise on the spot. It is important to remember, however, that any benefits are available to both parties. Although a copy of a letter provides the writer with a permanent record, the letter itself is a permanent record for the recipient. Therefore, to offer a preliminary idea or a tentative conclusion, a phone call (or face-to-face conference) is often the best option.

Let's see how you might choose to handle some specific situations.

1. You want to recommend a new piece of office equipment to your manager. Do you write an explanatory note outlining your rationale and giving cost estimates before meeting with her to propose the purchase? Or do you call first to see if she shows any initial interest before taking the time to research costs?

2. Harry Black from marketing is late with his report on a new ad campaign for your group's product, and your manager has asked you to see why marketing has been giving the group such poor support. Do you phone Harry or go see him in person? Do you drop him a line first to let him know what's on your mind? Are there other people you should contact before getting in touch with Harry?

In the first instance, if you have a close working relationship with your manager and if you feel that she is likely to share your belief that the equipment is needed, then you probably can simply phone her for a quick okay before preparing your cost estimates. On the other hand, if you feel that your suggestion is likely to surprise her, you might want to document your rationale and the likely costs in a written report, giving her a chance to consider it before you request a meeting.

In the second instance, your course of action depends a great deal on your assessment of Harry and what you know about his current behavior. Has he been really busy—or is he simply stalling? If the report is late because he has been busy, a friendly memo may be enough of a push. If he ignores the memo, you might have to try to arrange a face-to-face meeting. And if he refuses to meet with you, a formal memo on which you copy your own manager might be the best strategy—and you certainly would keep a permanent copy of that memo on file.

*There is no absolutely right procedure in either of these cases.* The lesson to be learned is that one does have alternatives and it is important to consider them carefully.

The issues of spontaneity and permanence are significant even when selecting among the available modes of oral communication. One might, for instance, prefer a face-to-face conference to a phone conversation because the conference will allow the audience to be monitored more closely. Not only voice signals but also facial expressions and body language (posture, gestures, etc.) will suggest feelings and attitudes, thereby helping the speaker to know precisely when to clarify ideas or revise an approach. As a further illustration, suppose that you have the choice of disseminating information through either an informal meeting or a videotape presentation. The meeting would provide a freewheeling forum for communication, but the presentation would allow you to choose your words carefully and to retain a clear record of how you stand on the issue examined.

Although strategic considerations should be given the most weight, time and cost factors must also influence decisions about the most appropriate mode of communication. These two factors depend heavily on available technology. As we have already pointed out, given today's wage scale, the time-consuming process of dictating and transcribing a letter can be extremely costly; on the other hand, in many large companies an employee can compose a memo on a terminal, press the "send" key, and distribute the message throughout the firm or even across the country. Also, companies of all sizes use the Postal Service's Express Mail or overnight delivery by private couriers to expedite written correspondence. All of this suggests that if time or cost is an important issue, it is best to do some investigation and make comparisons. The results are often surprising.

For most business people, writing and speaking tasks intersect throughout the day. To carry out a single project often requires phone calls, correspondence, and meetings. At the beginning of this chapter, we looked through a wide-angle lens at a panorama of communications at several different firms. Now we will zoom in on two other companies to follow two employees as each moves through a fairly typical workday.

---

At a large, well-known financial service and investment house, Tod Andrews, a recently hired marketing researcher, arrives at work to hear the phone ringing in his cubicle. The person on the other end is his boss, Frieda Barrymore, who manages the marketing research function. "I have a new project for you, Tod, " she says.

**Tod Andrews**

Frieda explains to Tod that she had a long meeting the previous afternoon with several of the company's senior officers. A large part of the discussion centered on a tax-exempt bond fund that the company is currently offering in 13 states. The issue was whether or not to distribute the fund nationally, as proposed by the fund manager. "Tod, you will have to do some solid research on this one. We need to know how the fund is doing and to examine the pluses and minuses of offering it nationally. You'll want to talk to Herb Zolski, the fund manager; but, of course, keep in mind that he's really eager to see its distribution expanded. And maybe there are some tax wrinkles here—I'm wondering why we originally limited this one to only 13 states."

Tod takes some notes as he talks with Frieda and then suggests that he can have his preliminary report ready in about a week. She feels that he ought to be able to get back to her sooner on this, but when he explains that he feels he needs to talk with all the district managers who currently handle the fund, she agrees that a week is an appropriate amount of time.

Tod heads for a centrally located terminal and logs on; in a matter of minutes he has the names, addresses, and telephone numbers of all the district managers. Next, he drafts a letter to them explaining that he will be contacting them by phone for pertinent information about the bond fund. In addition, he contacts the fund manager to set up an appointment at the earliest opportunity, which turns out to be later the same day. Tod also takes one more step. He's heard through the grapevine that Herb Zolski, an old-timer in the company, can be somewhat of a dragon to deal with and is especially impatient with younger employees who don't appear to know the lay of the land. Tod therefore telephones David Ames, a senior researcher with whom he frequently works, and arranges a business lunch. He hopes to be briefed on some of the ins and outs of managing tax-exempt funds.

For the remainder of the morning, Tod holes up in his cubicle with a copy of the bond fund's prospectus, a legal document that describes the features and mechanics of a fund to customers.

---

| Analysis | Let's list some of the communication tasks that fill up Tod's workday: |
|---|---|

- He talks to his boss on the phone and takes notes on the conversation.
- He studies the prospectus, takes notes on the main features of the fund, and lists points to discuss with the district managers and fund manager.
- He has a lunch meeting with David Ames to help prepare himself for the conference with the fund manager.
- He participates in that conference, takes notes, and later dictates a quick review of the meeting into his personal tape recorder.
- He writes a memo to the district managers to let them know he will be calling them in a few days. (The memo is transmitted by electronic mail and is received at the outlying offices the same day.)

By the time Tod leaves the office at the end of the day, he has spent more than 75 percent of his time in tasks that require communication skills. And this proportion is not due solely to the nature of his job. As we look over the shoulder of Joan Fisk, an employee who holds an entirely different kind of position in a very dissimilar company, we will see that communication plays an equally crucial role in her workday.

---

At 8:30 in the morning Joan Fisk is driving down the highway heading for her office. She is a quality control supervisor at a large Midwestern manufacturing company whose major product is plastic sheeting. **Joan Fisk**

As Joan's car heads toward the plant, she is thinking about the presentation that she will be giving at 2:30 that afternoon to her boss, several other members of the department, and three of the division's senior executives. She has been preparing this talk on "the costs and benefits of quality assurance" for a full week. Yesterday she made the final corrections on the graphic displays she will be using, and now she is bothered by the thought of one more detail she wishes she had added.

On the way to her office, before crossing the plant floor to the east wing, she stops at the cafeteria for a cup of coffee. With the Styrofoam cup in her hand, she enters her office, and before she can put the cup down, sees a pink slip taped to her phone: "Call Rudy in Baltimore. Urgent!" She wriggles out of her coat and reaches for the phone.

Rudy Denby is a wholesaler who distributes the sheeting manufactured by Joan's company. He tells her that one of his largest customers, Bondex, has notified him that an entire shipment is defective and that it will be returned to the plant. Rudy says Bondex has enough sheeting to last until the replacement order is received, but if that order is defective, then "goodbye customer." Furthermore, Rudy feels that a letter of explanation should be sent immediately to Hugh Morley, Bondex's purchasing manager, to assure him that there will be no further problems with the product.

Joan promptly makes two more phone calls. First, she telephones Seth Ordway, the product manager in charge of the particular kind of sheeting that was shipped to Bondex. This is the second complaint that she has received about a shipment of this product. She knows the news she has to impart will not be happily received, but the problem has to be handled promptly. She believes an informal talk over lunch might be a good way to open the discussion, so she sets up an appointment to lunch with Seth at noon. Her second phone call is to her boss, Ted Stein, manager of quality control; he listens to her story and (as she expected) asks to see the preliminary draft of the letter going to Bondex. In the time remaining before lunch, Joan puts the finishing touches on her afternoon presentation and starts drafting the letter.

When Joan's workday comes to an end, she has engaged in the following communication tasks: **Analysis**

- She has talked to Rudy Denby regarding the Bondex fiasco.
- She has also talked to her boss, Ted Stein, about the same situation.
- She has had a lunch meeting with the product manager, Seth Ordway.

- She has polished her costs/benefits presentation and checked the order of the graphics.
- She has drafted a letter to Hugh Morley, the Bondex purchasing manager, reviewed it with her boss, and begun a new draft.
- She has delivered her presentation, and then returned to her office to take notes on the follow-up discussion and to sketch out an action plan based on the suggestions she received.

Like Tod Andrews, Joan Fisk has spent most of her day communicating. Although they work in different parts of the country, in very different companies, and at very different jobs, these two people cannot carry out their responsibilities with any degree of success unless they are proficient communicators. Few business people today can.

## ■ Summary

In today's business environment words have more importance and power than ever before. Modern technology, rather than decreasing the amount of writing and reading required of employees, has added to it. Whether writing or speaking, most business people cannot carry out their job responsibilities successfully without the ability to communicate effectively.

Two groups of writers—business writers and journalists—write exclusively to be read. Both groups strive for the utmost clarity. Both are also held accountable for their accuracy. Both must meet deadlines imposed by others. But while reporters deal with their own reactions to events, business writers are primarily concerned with the response of their readers. They need to know as much as possible about their intended audience.

In the business arena, the importance of the spoken word may equal that of the written. Business people use speaking and listening skills in a wide spectrum of activities throughout the workday. Speaking, like writing, should be audience-centered, task-related, and purposeful. In determining whether a message is to be spoken, written, or both, communicators weigh the advantages of spontaneity versus the need for permanence. Time and cost considerations may also influence the choice of medium.

## ■ Discussion Problems

**1.1** Consider an actual job that you or someone you know well holds or has held. (It could be a summer job or a college internship.) Describe the kinds of communication most frequently needed and the methods used. Describe ongoing kinds of communication that are important to running the business.

**1.2** John McClintock supervises Lewis Bantam. In the last few months John has observed that Lewis's performance on the job has been slipping. Lewis's projects are frequently behind schedule, and he is often late arriving at work. If you were John, would you arrange a conference with Lewis or send him a carefully written memo? Would you do both? Explain.

**1.3**   Barbara Whitman has to tell the five employees she supervises about several new and fairly complex procedures that will change the department's method of doing inventory. How should she handle this responsibility? Explain.

**1.4**   Would Tod Andrews be wiser to prepare a questionnaire for the district managers rather than attempting to confer with them by phone? Explain your answer. Can you think of alternative procedures that Tod might use?

**1.5**   Do you think that Joan Fisk's plan to discuss a difficult problem at lunch is a good strategy? Explain your answer. If you feel that another option would be better, describe it.

# STRATEGY AND
# THE BUSINESS WRITER

## 2

*1* n business, you pave the way to your objectives with words, but you are unlikely to get there without a strategy. Often that strategy will be almost intuitive: if you know *who you are* (you), *to whom you are writing* (your reader), and *what you want to accomplish* (your purpose), you will instinctively proceed in the right direction. Unfortunately, however, there will be a number of times when one of the first two categories of information will be difficult to come by, unclear, or missing entirely. For instance, you may not have a clear picture of who you are because you are writing for someone else's signature or are wondering whether to be your formal or your informal self. You may not know precisely to whom you are writing because your audience is large and diversified or is composed of people whose attitudes and opinions are unknown to you. On those occasions, writing an effective letter, memo, or report may require not only a great deal of thought but also some careful research and perhaps some advice from someone who is better informed or more experienced than you are.

## ■ Purpose: The Key To Strategy

The third component of strategy—purpose—is the only one that lies within your control. When you write, you must know what you hope to accomplish. Only when your purpose is clear can you begin to select your medium, gather the information you need, and work to present it in a form that will appropriately engage the attention and interest of your audience.

Probably the chief reason why so many senior executives ask their secretaries to screen their phone calls, or why they shudder before opening their morning mail, is that a great many people expect to be heard (or read) before they have considered what they want their words to accomplish. Purposeless communication is a great waste of time for the receiver, and for the originator it can cause even more serious losses. Not only has time been misspent, but the misguided effort has probably also left a residue of disinterest, confusion, or perhaps even bad feeling.

Defining your purpose, however, is not always easy. Frequently you'll have more than one goal in mind. Often what you want to accomplish at the outset appears too difficult, so you are forced to pull back and establish an easier goal. Many times as you work on a project your purpose changes. Nevertheless, despite these difficulties, if you hope to be effective, you must take the time to think through your intentions and keep your purpose before you.

In Chapter 1, you saw that the initial decision faced by business communicators often concerns what medium to use, and that their choice usually is dictated by whether they most desire immediate interaction or time to prepare a careful and persuasive document. Of course, decisions about how to communicate ultimately must rest on what the person who initiates the communication wishes to accomplish—that is, on the purpose for communicating.

## Purpose versus Task

Many people fail to identify their purpose clearly because they are unable to distinguish between purpose and task.

Suppose you've been asked to announce a meeting to form a team to write and produce a department newsletter. Your task is to select six capable people and get a memo off to them. Your purpose, however, is not so simple.

You know that your six associates are busy on other projects that have high priority. They'll be less than eager to add another meeting to their schedules. Also, you're afraid that a number of them might greet the idea of a newsletter with skepticism. You therefore have at least two clear and interrelated purposes for writing: to persuade the six people that the meeting will be orderly and brief, and to get them thinking about the value of a newsletter.

As you can see from this example, your *task* is what you have been asked to do; your *purpose* is what you hope to accomplish. In the above scenario, a memo that simply announces, "A meeting to discuss the department newsletter will be held on Wednesday at 3:00 p.m." might be met with a good deal of passive resistance. But if you tackle such a problem strategically, you can devise ways to accomplish your purpose. Perhaps you could contact people individually beforehand to tell them why they have been selected and to exchange ideas about a newsletter. Perhaps you could attach an agenda to your memo to show that the meeting will be worth attending. Or you might have a different strategy in mind. But whatever your course of action, you'll want to think about all the alternatives before reaching for your memo pad, grabbing the phone, or crossing the hall.

## ■ Business Writing as Persuasion

During a typical business day, you'll often have reason to make comparisons, describe procedures, or explain your rationale. Chances are that your motive in doing these things will be to get someone to think or to say "Yes, you are right, that machine will do the job better" or "that procedure is the smoothest" or "that decision makes good sense." And as your responsibilities and authority increase, you will find yourself looking not only for agreement but also for action. You'll want your audience to think or to say "Yes, we'll take that step—and soon." Whether hidden or obvious, the intent of most business communications is to get ideas approved or actions started. Persuasion is the name of the game. And when we step back to consider the matter, it's pretty clear why this is so.

Being in business means persuading someone to part with money in exchange for your products or services. To perform successfully, you need to get someone to allocate time, money, or resources to help you achieve your goals. In fact, employment doesn't even begin until you can persuade an employer that your potential contribution is worth the company's commitment to you of salary, office space, supervision, training, and so forth.

In Chapter 9 we will look closely at the strategies that underlie memos and letters whose overriding purpose is to overcome a reader's misgivings or objections and persuade him or her to accept an opinion or to take an action. But even daily correspondence on matters to which no great sensitivity or controversy is attached needs to be persuasive. Bear in mind that whenever you find yourself writing "Let's meet Tuesday morning" or "Let's purchase a new word processor" or "Let's hire Sam Jones" you are actually attempting to persuade someone. To see how this is so, we'll look at an example illustrating the third situation—a memo recommending that a specific candidate be selected to fill a position.

You have been asked to interview the three finalists from a series of applicants for a technical editing position in your department and to select the best candidate. Deciding on Sam Jones, you write the memo in Figure 2.1 to your boss.

---

TO:   Wendy Wasserman               DATE: March 5, 198-
FROM:
RE:   Opening for Supervisor of Technical Editing

     Although I was favorably impressed with all three people I interviewed this week, Sam Jones is unquestionably the best person to fill the slot of Supervisor of Technical Editing.

     As you and I discussed, the job needs someone entirely familiar with the software for the Panther-M Desktop, aware of the needs of the managers who are its primary users, and capable of strong technical writing.

     Sam Jones is an internal candidate--he's been a technical writer for the department for the last eight months. In that time he's done documentation for several Panther-M user's manuals and is, I believe,

**Figure 2.1**
A memo recommending a job candidate.

entirely familiar with the full range of software. Before joining the company, Sam managed his own word-processing business for two years at the University of Michigan student co-op. That experience, plus his business major, suggests that he has a sound grasp of the managers' needs. Finally, our personnel department has informed me that Sam's scores on the editing test far outranked those of all the other contenders.

Not only does Sam meet the criteria we have established, but also he tells me that he feels eager to play a supervisory role. I have watched him work with the other writers and observed that he is able to be simultaneously assertive and tactful. I'm sure that he'll do a fine job leading the editing team.

And with this memo you persuade her to hire Sam. By doing so, you complete your task (to locate the best candidate) and accomplish your purpose (to get Wendy to okay Sam's promotion to the supervisory position).

## ■ Scope: An Integral Part of Strategy

When college students receive an assignment, their instructors usually give some indication concerning its scope: "Write three to five double-spaced pages on the subject of . . . ." In a business situation, however, how much to write is a much trickier question. The task you have been assigned may come with specifications, such as "Check out the three major competitors" or "Get opinions from John, Ben, and Sam" or "Review the price increases from May through September," but such instructions constitute only a beginning. Unless you focus on why you are checking out the competitors or gathering opinions or looking over the numbers, you will not have a good idea as to how much information you need to gather or how much to cover in your memo or report.

Like many other problems related to communication strategy, the issue of scope leads directly back to purpose. Let's look at a specific case to see more clearly why this is so.

**The Case**   Pam Donaldson is a trainee for the position of credit analyst in a program at New England Mutual Bank. The program requires her to prepare preliminary analyses of the credit-worthiness of prospective loan candidates. Mike Hartt and Glenn Burns of Mike and Glenn's Town Hardware have applied to New England Mutual for a $450,000 loan to open a second store in a neighboring city. What should be the scope of Pam's report?

Consider the purpose of Pam's report. Although Pam is a trainee, once her report is approved by Diane Kelly, her supervisor, it will be turned over to a senior analyst, who will further refine it and then send it on to a department vice president for final dispensation. Naturally, as a trainee, Pam's own purpose is to show her supervisor that she has done a careful client interview and a careful analysis. On the other hand, she knows that Diane will be especially impressed if the report saves time and effort for everyone else concerned with the loan application. If Pam supplies all the facts she has uncovered, she may show that she has been thorough, but chances are her report will be many stages away from its final destination—the vice president's desk. Diane will quickly zip it back for revision.

Pam's best strategy is to be as meticulous as she can be in collecting her information, and then to stop and take a hard look at the data. *Are there any significant issues concerning the application?* Perhaps in the last six months the original store has shown a noticeable drop in sales. Perhaps Glenn Burns has a large outstanding loan at another bank. To feel confident that she has been thorough, Pam will want to interview the applicants carefully. But the purpose of her report is to recommend approval or rejection of the loan: she has to focus on the issues that will pertain directly to her recommendation. For instance, if she's ready to recommend that the loan application be turned down, the fact that the site selected for the new business is a good location will not have much significance and will not require detailed documentation.

Like Pam Donaldson, you may frequently face assignments for which you have to decide how much information to include in a document you are preparing. You may, on the other hand, be asked to complete tasks for which you receive preliminary instructions about scope. For instance, you might be told at the outset how many people to interview or how many sites to visit or how many reports to read. But even with such guidance, you will not be able to escape the necessity of giving careful thought to your purpose before deciding exactly what to include. As we saw, Pam had to focus on why she interviewed Mike Hartt and Glenn Burns.

Similarly, if you were asked to compare two sites, you would need to know why. If you were trying to establish a selling price for the properties, you would normally not include a great deal of historical data. And, to take another example, if your task were to compare the employee health plans offered by two major insurance companies, you would need to know the reason for that comparison. If your purpose were to help your employer select the best plan, you would almost certainly devote most of your report to any significant differences between the two programs and treat the similarities much more briefly.

# ■ Structure and Style: Strategy Made Visible

Once you have decided to communicate in writing, you must determine what to put into your document (and, equally important, what to leave out); furthermore, you must select an appropriate sequence for everything you plan to include.

If we analyze the organization of letters, memos, and reports, we find they are constructed of smaller and smaller components: sections, subsections, paragraphs, sentences, phrases, and words. As we compose a business document, the choices we must make become more narrowly focused. At first, we are concerned with what topics to cover and the general arrangement of larger segments; as the document evolves, however, we must make choices (often half-consciously) about what words and phrases to use and in what order to arrange them.

The choices that focus on the larger blocks—the sections, subsections, and paragraphs—relate to what we are calling *structure*; those that focus on sentences, phrases, and words relate to what we term *style*. Here are formal definitions of structure and style:

**Structure:** the division of information or ideas into units of sections, subsections, and paragraphs, as well as the way those units are ordered.

**Style:** the projection of information and ideas into words, phrases, and sentences, as well as the way words are arranged within sentences and the way sentences are ordered within paragraphs.

Even the simplest thought, once expressed in writing, leaps into existence with *both* structure and style; the structure and style may not be effective, but they are there. Since structure and style are simultaneously the visible outcome of each writer's decisions about what to include and how to order it, the distinction between them (as you may have recognized) is artifical. And yet, to write effectively, we must at the outset force them apart. We must fracture our thought processes and learn to work separately with the components of structure and style. Here we will concentrate on understanding how each can be dealt with in its own right and how they both relate to a writer's strategy. In Chapter 5 we will give our full attention to structure, and in Chapter 10 we will focus on style.

Let's first step back and view structure in the making. Imagine for a moment that you need to write a lengthy memo to announce that your firm will inaugurate a student intern program and to ask managers to suggest appropriate three-month assignments for the interns. As you consider your purpose, you recognize that you must not only generate interest in the program but also ensure that the internships will provide students with a genuine learning experience.

This dual purpose at first suggests a two-part structure for the memo: one section to focus on the managers' needs, and a second to focus on the students' needs. But which of these sections should come first? And how can you connect them smoothly? As you study these questions, you may begin to feel that you want to write about the benefits of the program as well as about each group's needs. The memo may have to have four parts. And since the managers are the people you want to convince, you may decide to focus on them first.

Suppose that you draft a tentative outline for your memo about the proposed program. You decide to start with four major headings: "Needs of Managers," "Needs of Students," "Benefits to Managers," and "Benefits to Students." Before long, you've enumerated three managerial needs and three student needs. So far, your outline is clear and symmetrical, and you're pleased with the structure taking shape on your notepad.

Next, you begin to outline the proposed benefits of the internship program, both for managers and students, and here you run into an unexpected problem. (See Figure 2.2.) You find that the needs and benefits

---

Proposed Internship Program

A. Current Needs

    1. Needs of Managers
       a. Maximum workforce with minimum capital outlay
       b. Increased creative input from junior staff
       c. Pool of experienced candidates from which to choose permanent staff members

    2. Needs of Students
       a. Practical training from proven professionals.
       b. On-the-job experience to add to their résumés
       c. Business contacts to expand their networking capabilities

B. Proposed Benefits

    1. Benefits to Managers
       a. Maximum workforce with minimum capital outlay
       b. Increased creative input from junior staff
       c. Pool of experienced candidates from which to choose permanent staff members

    2. Benefits to Students
       a. Practical training from proven professionals
       b. On-the-job experience to add to their résumés
       c. Business contacts to expand their networking capabilities

**Figure 2.2**
An outline for a persuasive memo.

you've described are identical! Your outline clearly is redundant. So where do you go from here?

The solution, you decide, is to turn the apparent problem to your advantage by using it to achieve your purpose. You have realized that in meeting the needs of the managers and students the program will provide the very benefits that each group seeks. Therefore, you can use this important point to persuade the managers to inaugurate a strong internship program. In fact, it occurs to you to make this contention the opening statement of your memo. You write the following tentative opening sentence: "For both our managers and the prospective student interns, a strong internship program will provide precisely the benefits that each group seeks."

As you can see, until this moment you have been focusing solely on the structural elements of your memo. Furthermore, thinking about structure has helped you to refine your strategy; in fact, your thoughts on structure and strategy have been completely interdependent. The process went like this: as you began to think about the purpose of your memo, a preliminary structure occurred to you; then, the effort to make that structure more effective helped you to devise a more appropriate strategy.

With the bold outline of your structure now established, you are ready to deal with style—that is, to search for the right words to contain your ideas. Your object is to find the particular words and sentences that will help you to achieve your purpose.

You decide that you need to be very clear. If the managers don't understand your meaning, all could be lost at the outset. To achieve clarity, you try to avoid writing tangled or ungrammatical sentences and to reach for words that convey your precise meaning. You also attempt to be reasonably interesting, to compel the managers' attention by using vigorous language. For instance, instead of writing "Many factors make it evident that an internship program might offer a number of benefits," you vigorously assert "A practical, well-designed training program for student interns will address some of our most pressing current needs at minimum cost." Finally, striving to be as concise as possible so as not to waste the managers' time, you reread the memo and edit out all unnecessary verbiage.

*Clarity, vigor,* and *conciseness* are the three key elements of business writing style. Perfecting them is an unending task. Nevertheless, after reviewing your completed memo, you feel reasonably confident that you have come close enough to expect to achieve your purpose in writing to the managers.

In Chapters 3 and 4, we will focus more closely on the writing process. You will learn a great deal about yourself as a writer, the importance of your audience, and the components of the message you are sending. In Chapter 5, we will examine the process of building structure into a business document as well as some practical methods of organizing information and ideas. After studying the most common forms of business letters in Chapters 7, 8, and 9, we will focus on the components of business writing style in Chapter 10.

# ■ Summary

Effective business writing demands a carefully conceived strategy; a good strategy, in turn, requires a clearly defined purpose. Make certain to distinguish *purpose* (what you hope to accomplish) from *task* (what you have been asked to do).

Most business writing entails persuasion: getting ideas approved or actions started.

The scope of a business assignment (what information to include and what to omit) is directly related to purpose.

Once you have decided on the content of your document, you must determine the appropriate sequence of its larger components (structure) and the ideal choice and arrangement of words and sentences (style).

# ■ Discussion Problems

**2.1**  Can you distinguish between the task and the purpose in the following situations? What are the goals you wish to accomplish in each case? What role will the power of persuasion play in achieving those goals? Can you suggest a writing strategy to achieve each purpose?

- You're an administrative assistant to the vice president for resource development at a major university. Your boss's major responsibility is to raise funds for the university through contacts with alumni and other leaders of the business community. He has asked you to draft a letter of congratulation to be sent to ten alumni who have recently been promoted to senior-level positions in major corporations.

- As office manager of a rapidly expanding software development firm, you find that you can no longer handle your colleagues' informal verbal requests for stationery and supplies. You decide to initiate a new system requiring all supply requests to be written on standard order forms. To introduce the new procedure, you must write a memo to the entire staff, to be sent with a copy of the new order form attached.

- You're the assistant manager of a university bookstore that extends charge privileges to faculty members. One of the store's most regular customers, Professor Wilchfort, has charged over $200 in small purchases over the past ten months, and so far all bills have remained unpaid. Even though you added a note to his last bill requesting full payment of all past due accounts, there has been no response. You must draft a letter informing the professor that unless he pays his outstanding balance in full, his charge privileges will be suspended.

**2.2**  Imagine you are the copyeditor/proofreader for a small publishing firm. You are sure that a word processor would significantly improve the speed and accuracy of your work, but the company's budget is relatively small, and you know it won't be easy to persuade your boss to buy one. Can you suggest a tentative structure for a persuasive memo to the firm's vice president? Give examples of the main headings and subheadings that would outline your strategy. Which heading should come first?

**2.3**  Val Green is a personnel intern at a large university. She has interviewed three candidates for the position of secretary of the French Department, and now she must write a memo comparing the three applicants and recommending one of them, Jean Littleton, for the job. How much information should she include about each candidate? Why?

**2.4**  Have you ever had the experience of turning a supposed difficulty into an advantage? What was the sudden insight that enabled you to see the problem in a new light? Is the ability to turn difficulties into advantages a skill that could be developed?

**2.5**  Suggest ways in which the following structural problems might lead you to develop a better strategy for your letter or memo. Be creative!

■ Your report on the leading competitor's product range is far too long. You've described each of eight products, including price, sales figures for the past five years, and positive and negative characteristics vis-à-vis your own company's comparable product. Even *you* aren't sure where this report is leading. Help!

■ You've been asked to outline the pros and cons of switching a medium-sized textile mill to "flextime" (employees work an eight-hour day but can choose their work hours from several available schedules). But you find that for every convincing pro, you come up with an equally indisputable con. As a result, your report has no focus, and you are completely unable to make a recommendation. What now?

## ■ Writing Tasks

**2.1**  Draft the memo about the internship program described on pages 20–22.

**2.2**  Draft the letter of congratulation described in Discussion Problem 2.1. Make up the necessary details.

**2.3**  Draft the letter to Professor Wilchfort described in Discussion Problem 2.1. Add any details you feel are necessary.

**2.4**  Draft the opening paragraph of Val Green's memo, described in Discussion Problem 2.3.

**2.5** Ann LaCava is Manager of Marketing Communications for a large insurance company. She is responsible for producing all major product brochures, the company's annual report, and a short monthly employee newsletter. At this point she is under enormous pressure to meet her various deadlines. Ann has just learned of the new internship program described earlier; she quickly decides that the employee newsletter is an ideal project for a promising intern. Draft a memo from Ann to Mike Murphy, Assistant Director of Human Resources, in which she tries to persuade him to assign one of the first new interns to her department.

# YOU AND YOUR AUDIENCE

## 3

*riting* means getting words down on paper—perhaps only to please yourself. *Business writing*, however, implies a much more complex process. In business writing, *a writer with a definite purpose in mind selects information and shapes it into a form that allows it to be communicated effectively to a specific audience*. In this chapter we will look closely at the writer and the audience; in Chapter 4 we will focus on the message that links them. As a starting point, however, we will step back and consider the business writing process as a whole.

## ■ The Process Begins

A good way to understand how the writing process begins is to picture how a business writer might approach a difficult writing task. Although the sequence of steps may alter as circumstances or situations change, the following scenario illustrates what you might experience from the moment you face an assignment, through the tentative sorting of information, to the audience analysis that provides you with a focused idea and a well-defined purpose.

---

**The Case**

Imagine your desk piled high with notecards and news clippings. At first the raw data lie there, disorganized and untouched. But then you stroll into the room, head for your desk, and begin to sort and arrange the materials, at the same time jotting down words on a large yellow notepad. You are trying to make sense of the data, but at this stage your thoughts are random and your purpose is vague. You are simply experimenting in putting ideas together, with no real intention of communicating them to anyone.

Gradually, however, you realize that an idea that will greatly interest your supervisor is taking form. You rearrange the materials on your desk with much more decisiveness. Now you are absolutely certain that your concept will help attract new business. You tear off a clean sheet of paper and begin to write a memo to your supervisor. You have established your purpose. You focus on the data that you believe will persuade your supervisor that you are right, and you choose your words with care. Your writing has become a *message*—a bridge between your mind and your reader's. Your next task will be to refine and strengthen that message.

---

In this brief scenario you faced a particularly difficult challenge. The only instructions you received from your supervisor took the form of a rather terse query: "Could you spend a little time and try to make some sense out of this stuff?" The writing task was only hazily defined, and your purpose was not specified. Usually (especially as an entry-level employee)—you can expect to receive more specific instructions.

Even when you are faced with a task that seems clear-cut, defining your purpose can take effort and thought. Let's consider such a case from your perspective.

**The Case**

You are an entry-level human resources specialist at a large metropolitan department store, and you have just attended a day-long workshop on employee benefits (health and life insurance, vacation time, and the other means by which companies compensate employees beyond their basic wages). Your manager, Mike Adams, has requested a written report on the program. On your desk is a pile of materials distributed at the five sessions you attended, as well as a fairly lengthy summary of the company's current benefits program. You're sure you are familiar with all the data in front of you, but you're having trouble getting your report started.

Your thought process perhaps goes something like this: "Well, I could just dash off a note to Mike telling him the workshop was pretty good—maybe it could have been a bit more focused in spots, but it was really a pretty good day. Still, I was pleased that he picked me to go; I'd better give him something worth reading so I'll be selected again . . . but *what*? Hmmm. Maybe I'd better take some time and really give this the full treatment.

"I could take this summary report of the company's program and walk Mike through it, item by item, and mention what the workshop had to say about each area. What a pain *that* would be to write. And why would Mike want to read all that stuff anyhow? It would just be an expanded version of the summary he's already got. Well, what would be useful to him?

"He's asked me to take a hard look at that summary; I bet he'd like to know how our current benefits match up with those of other firms. I could start out by giving him a picture of what we do here now, just an overview, and then focus on some features that I heard about at the workshop. Yeah, and I'll go into some detail on the pros and cons of a dental plan since the company has really been looking hard at that option."

**Analysis**

If you followed this monologue fairly closely, you must have seen that *purpose* fuels the whole thought process. First, there is your own purpose—to persuade your manager that you were the right person to send to the workshop. Second, your understanding of *his* purpose—to appraise the present benefits program—comes into play. Next, you might have noticed that, on both counts, your decision about what to write depends to a great extent on how you picture Mike's reaction. As you think about *him*, you begin to pick and choose from the assorted ideas that come to you. If you continue to imagine the process of preparing this report, you will picture yourself thinking about Mike as you arrange your points and even as you select the words to express them.

## ■ Relating Purpose to Audience

In the preceding scenario, you were the writer and your manager was your audience. The finished report would be the message that links the two of you. Although your task was clearly described, to define your purpose you had to think carefully about what you wanted to accomplish. As you did so, you were forced to make choices; although those choices were somewhat guided by your own needs, they were most heavily influenced by the needs of your audience.

To understand better why purpose depends so much on audience, let's change the scenario and consider how you might write a similar report for someone other than Mike.

Suppose that you are asked to be a last-minute substitute at the benefits workshop for your officemate, Jean, who suddenly became ill. Assume that you had previously been told that she would be going to all workshops on employee benefits, and since you were involved in many other projects, you were not at all disappointed. You are happy to stand in for her at this one meeting, however. When you return from the workshop, you settle down to write a report for Jean. **The Case**

How will you focus such a report? What will be your primary purpose in writing it? **Analysis**

Your main purpose under these circumstances probably will be to help Jean catch up with all that was covered at the workshop, and you therefore will try to provide her with a great deal of factual detail. Perhaps you will also refer her to the department's existing summary report and help her to make connections between it and what was covered at the meeting. Perhaps you also will include your own assessment of the workshop. Alternatively, you might make your report a simple step-by-step narrative of what was covered in each session, and you could suggest that she review the summary report to make her own comparisons. Unquestionably, before writing to Jean you have some options to think about. But one thing is certain—your report for Jean would be different from the one written for Mike in the preceding scenario.

Now, for further practice in relating purpose to audience, let's alter the circumstances one last time.

**The Case**    Suppose now that you are the one who regularly attends the benefits workshops each month. Because your schedule is overloaded, Mike has selected Jean to stand in for you at the next meeting. He's asked you to brief her by writing a short instructional memo to her. He's also stipulated that Jean give you a written report on her return from the workshop. Mike has pointed out that your instructions to Jean will determine the focus and content of her report to you.

**Analysis**    In this case you have become Jean's audience. And fortunately you have the opportunity to explain your needs to her. Perhaps you will ask her to pay particular attention to one specific issue or a special section of the program. Perhaps you will request a simple rundown of the entire day. But, whatever you decide they are, your needs will determine the purpose of Jean's report.

As we have seen, when audience changes, purpose also shifts, because the new audience almost always has different needs. Later in this chapter we'll see how to analyze audiences to determine their needs. But first it is essential to analyze the complex individual who controls the writing process—*you*, the writer.

## ■ YOU, the Writer: Your Many Personalities

If immediately after lunch one day this week, as you are heading into a meeting or a lecture, you stop in your tracks, turn swiftly, and catch your image in a mirror, you will see someone who appears to be a very different sort of person from the one who just drank your coke and ate your sandwich in the cafeteria. And the person in the mirror will display many characteristics that differ from those of the individual who will be sitting in your chair at dinner tonight.

Appearances aside, all three of these people are, of course, you. Underneath the facade of differences lie *your* abilities, brains, judgment, values, and experience. However, with each new occurrence during your day, you dip into this pool of possibilities and discover a comfortable and appropriate combination of characteristics. You shift your identity in response to the people and situations that confront you. For instance, if you were to see the president of your company in the parking lot at the end of a workday, you probably would not call out "So long, Sam!" Similarly, bidding goodnight to your friend and officemate, Bob Jones, you almost certainly wouldn't say "Have a pleasant evening, Mr. Jones." Such choices are not only a matter of the other person's preferences; they also stem from your sense of what is natural and appropriate to your own personality.

In business writing, the process of adapting to your circumstances is much the same, or at least it should be. The personality you adopt should be one that feels right for you: it should not be phony; it should not violate any of your principles or infringe on your value system. The point to remember, however, is that you do have flexibility and choice, to a greater degree than you might imagine. In writing, just as in other aspects of life, you have the opportunity to control the way you come across and to create an appropriate impression.

For instance, the salutation of a letter (e.g., Dear Ms. Smith:) is a simple greeting, and the complimentary close (e.g., Sincerely yours,) is a way of saying goodbye. As you will see in Chapters 7, 8, and 9, even in formal business writing you have a good deal of latitude when selecting the way to close a letter; you also have some options in choosing a salutation. And there are other much more difficult and complex choices to make—key decisions concerning structure (Chs. 5 & 6), format (Chs. 7, 14 & 15), tone (Ch. 4), and style (Chs. 10 & 11).

It is a curious fact that many business writers either forget that the element of personality in the writing process exists or else do their very best to make it disappear. These people often display their own personalities openly and vigorously during interviews and phone calls, and yet they insist that all business writing should sound alike. Either by neglect or intent they relentlessly banish humanity from their correspondence and reports.

Such people find themselves writing atrocities like "as per our last conversation" instead of "when we last spoke" or "in regard to yours of March 31" instead of "concerning your letter dated March 31." They stubbornly avoid using the first person (I or we) in their reports, thinking that "it is recommended that" is somehow more convincing than "I recommend." The result of such writing is that, in spite of efforts to conceal it, a personality does emerge—but it is a stilted and irksome personality. Frequently the problem with heavy-handed, stuffed-shirt writers is that they mistake pomposity for formality. The contemporary business environment offers many opportunities for formal writing and (as we'll demonstrate later in our discussions of tone and style) many good ways to project formality. On the other hand, it's difficult to imagine any occasion when a business person would want to appear pompous.

No matter what impression you make, your writing is stamped with the imprint of your presence: *you* are there. And, of course, this inescapable fact makes it imperative that you show your personality to advantage. Usually you can do so by asking yourself: "Does this sound like me? If this person were here before me, would I use these words?" Let's examine a simple illustration of how circumstances affect the writer's personality.

**The Case**

Assume that, as the assistant business editor for a community newspaper, you are trying to interest some of the local merchants in placing ads by calling on them in person at their establishments. You approach Don Bloom, who owns a thriving plant boutique. Don is close to your own age, and he meets you with a handshake and a warm smile. He's wearing a flannel shirt and jeans because he's been working in his greenhouse. After the two of you talk for a while about your mutual enthusiasm for tropical plants, he suggests that you send along a sample layout for an ad that would capture the spirit of his store.

When you write to him the next day, even though you have only met him once, you begin the letter "Dear Don" and follow this salutation with a comma, as you would when writing to a personal friend. Something about the way your meeting went makes informality seem appropriate: you know that if you were to meet again, you and he would certainly use one another's first names. On the other hand, Don is not the only person you called on the previous day. You had also met with Margaret Pilton, the owner of Pilton's Pharmacy. Although she too had agreed to place an ad, the interview had been very brief and to the point. Instinctively, you feel that you should address her with some formality.

Figures 3.1 and 3.2 are samples of possible letters to Don Bloom and to Margaret Pilton.

Relying on feelings and instincts rather than on established rules to tell you what to write does, however, have some hazards. If you misjudge when speaking face to face, you often see your mistake right away and are able to do your best to remedy it. But when you write, you not only record your words permanently on paper but you also must wait for a response— or, if you've erred very badly, for no response at all. Mistakes in writing are usually much harder to correct than mistakes in speech. Therefore, in correspondence it is exceedingly important to think about the way you deal with people and to choose your words carefully.

1234 Brown Street
Anytown, OH 00000
January 7, 198-

**Figure 3.1**
Informal follow-up
letter to client.

Mr. Donad Bloom
The Greenery
10 Morgan Street
Anytown, OH 00000

Dear Don,

After meeting with you yesterday, I knew your ad for The Greenery had to be something special. Therefore, I spent a good deal of time talking to Perry Bond, who designs our ads, explaining the qualities that make your plant boutique so unusual. He will be submitting his layouts to me in a few days, and I'll send them on to you. After you receive them, I'll call you so that we can review the options we discussed about the size of your ad and related costs.

I'm sure you know how much I enjoyed meeting you yesterday, Don. I am going to take your suggestion about moving my yucca to a sunnier location, and I'll let you know in a few weeks how it's doing.

Cordially,

[Your Signature]

1234 Brown Street
Anytown, OH 00000
January 7, 198-

**Figure 3.2**
Formal follow-up
letter to client.

Ms. Margaret Pilton
Pilton's Pharmacy
103 Main Street
Anytown, OH 00000

Dear Ms. Pilton:

We are very pleased that Pilton's Pharmacy plans to place ads in our February, April, and June issues. As you specified yesterday, the ads will appear on the last page and will occupy a two-column spread (dimensions: 4 inches by 4 inches). The cost of the ads will be $300 for the first appearance and $150 for each subsequent run. I will send you a layout early next week for your approval. When the first ad appears in print, you will receive our invoice.

Thank you for this expression of your confidence in our ability to attract customers to your excellent establishment.

Yours truly,


[Your Signature]

---

Such a commitment to excellence in business writing asks a lot of you. But in return it gives you the privilege of maintaining as much of your individuality in your correspondence as you do in person or on the phone. One word of caution, however. Never use your right to be yourself as an excuse for careless or ineffective writing. When you receive notice of weaknesses in your writing, guard against the urge to be defensive. Ineffectual writers have been known to dismiss helpful criticism with a pained cry of "That's my style. . . . That's the way *I* write." The sad truth about such writers is that we know they are not lying to us. That *is* the way they write. But we certainly hope they will make an effort to change!

## ■ Writing for Someone Else's Signature

Business people frequently are asked to draft a letter to be signed by their boss or by a high-level executive in the firm. This is one occasion when the writer's preferences must take a back seat to those of another person. Writing for someone else is never easy. Even if the business writer knows the signer well, the task can cause anxiety. If the writer scarcely knows the signer at all, the obstacles to success can be formidable. Therefore, let's consider how to make this difficult task as easy as possible.

When you write a letter for someone else, he or she is likely to have preconceived notions about what that letter is to accomplish—and even about how it is to sound. Therefore, if at all possible, try to arrange for an exchange of ideas before you begin to write. Request a conference, or at least confer by phone. Gather as much information as you can about the signer's dealings with and attitude toward the intended reader and about the purpose of the letter; also note any problems that might be associated with the situation being addressed. Unless there are severe time constraints, ask whether you may submit a first draft for comments and suggestions before writing the final version. By following this procedure, you will have an opportunity to test your initial ideas, and you will ultimately feel much more confident about the quality of your work.

As you compose your first draft, strive to achieve as clear and direct a style as possible rather than to imitate the signer's way of writing. On the other hand, do allow yourself to be influenced by that person's usual demeanor. If, for example, he or she is friendly and informal, consider using first names in the letter and an informal closing such as "Cordially." Try to empathize with how the signer feels about the situation at hand. For example, if you sense that respect for the particular audience is important to the purpose of the letter, consider how you might inject that attitude. Or if an ongoing problem is causing the signer to feel anxiety or irritation, let the letter reflect the feeling in a low-keyed way. But before you inject any strong feeling into a letter, discuss this strategy with the signer to be certain that he or she approves.

If you are to write a letter for a senior executive at some distance above you in the organization and you will have no opportunity to confer with him or her, you'll just have to buckle down and do your best on your own. Know, however, that your first draft will almost surely not be accepted, and be ready for a strenuous round of reviews and frequent requests for revisions or for entirely new drafts. If you are attentive and receptive and try to understand the executive's perspective and goals, you will move the project along quickly, with a high probability of success.

## ■ Coming Across to Your Audience

Good business writers are self-aware. They understand that it is important to be in touch with their own needs and to feel secure about the personality they exhibit in their writing. They know that to be themselves in their business correspondence gives them both freedom and responsibility because it requires making choices. But self-awareness can carry business communication only half the distance; *audience-awareness* is essential for completing the journey. As you face a business writing assignment, *you should never write without a sense of the human being who will read your words.*

If a writing task seems at all complex, you may (like most writers) feel reluctant to get started. Even writers who are skilled and experienced find themselves sorting and resorting notes, writing sporadically if at all. On the other hand, after they've digested the facts and figures, writers are just as likely to be overpowered by the need to say a great deal and to get words down on paper fast; they are often, in fact, bedazzled by the light of their own insights. Still, this state of agitated enthusiasm is certainly better than its opposite—feeling frustrated and blocked. But after that initial rush of ideas and words, if writers are wise, they will sit back, try to read objectively, and ask "How am I coming across?" Carried a bit further, this question contains the crux of the matter—"coming across" to where and to whom?

The proper answer is, of course, "coming across to the intended audience." A piece of business writing should bridge the gap between the writer and the reader; it should carry facts, ideas, attitudes, and opinions from one mind to another. In other words, it should communicate.

Even when the information to be conveyed is simple and factual, the writer has definite obligations to the reader. Before writing, you should know why your reader might want that information, or at least how it could be used. Moreover, you should try to communicate the information clearly and succinctly so that it can be comprehended easily. And when you are not only transmitting factual information but also offering ideas, opinions, and attitudes, you should try very hard to understand and to empathize with your reader's needs and concerns.

In the next chapter, in which we focus on the message, we will examine some of the complexities associated with distinguishing between facts and opinions, but for a preliminary understanding, consider the two short memos in Figures 3.3 and 3.4.

---

**Figure 3.3**
Memo containing solely factual information.

TO:    List A                        DATE: February 10, 198-
FROM:  D. Wong
RE:     Energy Costs

     John Sharp of Minneapolis Electric will speak to all first-level supervisors on "Cutting Energy Costs" on Tuesday, April 14, at 4:30 in the East Conference Room.

---

**Figure 3.4**
Memo containing opinions in addition to factual information.

TO:    List A                        DATE: February 10, 198-
FROM:  D. Wong
RE:     Energy Costs

     I strongly recommend that all first-level supervisors plan to attend a talk entitled "Cutting Energy Costs" to be given at 4:30 on Tuesday, April 14, in the East Conference Room. The speaker, John Sharp of Minneapolis Electric, has proven expertise in reducing energy costs by eliminating waste.

---

The writer of the memo in Figure 3.4 certainly has an opinion about the scheduled talk.

To understand your reader's needs and concerns, you must give careful thought to his or her stake in your communication. This does not mean forgetting your own concerns or casting your opinions to the winds. It does, however, mean working hard to express your views in ways that are both acceptable and highly persuasive. And frequently there is a further complication—to achieve understanding, you may even have to decipher *who your reader really is.*

We have been using the singular noun *reader*, as though the audience were inevitably composed of just one person. In business writing, an audience of several or even many people is more typical. When there are several readers of like disposition and with similar needs, there is no problem. But what do you do when you recognize that some of your readers have more background information than others or that some will need more persuading?

The best answer to this question is not perfect, but it will help you a great deal: choose a *key reader* (the person whom you most need to persuade) and design your letter or report for him or her. Next, figure out what you can do to make it easier to reach and to persuade other important readers.

For instance, you might attach an executive summary* to a long progress report aimed primarily at co-workers in your own department but also requiring the approval of the senior vice president whose name appears first on the distribution list. Or, if a report addressed to a key executive is also to be read by an influential co-worker, you might attach an informal, personal memo similar to the one shown in Figure 3.5.

By sending this memo to Sam, Sandy shows that she respects his position and his opinions. Furthermore, had she not included the note, Sam might have resented having a long report concerning one of his key projects plunked on his desk without explanation.

Even trickier than appealing to multiple readers is trying to affect a hidden audience. A *hidden audience* is a reader (or readers) whose name does not appear on the heading of a document. (It is even possible for the hidden audience to be the key reader. For instance, you might write a letter addressed to the manager of another department at the request of your own manager, who has explicitly told you his objectives for the correspondence. Knowing that your manager will review your draft closely, you should probably keep him or her foremost in your mind as you write.)

When you want someone other than the person addressed in the heading to read a document, you should, of course, send a copy to that person. If you want the addressee to know that another person will be

---

*Executive summaries will be discussed in detail in Chapter 14.

**Figure 3.5**
Personal memo to
accompany a copy
of a report.

TO:   Sam Kincaid                          DATE:   April 19, 198-
FROM:   Sandy Donahue
RE:   Attached Report on Marketing of Product 78075

    Dale Baldwin asked me to prepare this report for him and to
pass along a copy to you. I predict he's now giving a good deal of
thought to releasing 78075 to the market. Since I know how much
work you have put into preparing for this product release, Sam, I'm
sure you will be glad to see that my analysis of our competitors' offerings shows that we are more than ready to enter this market.

    I'm looking forward to receiving your comments. Feel free to
call me if you have any questions concerning the data.

*Sandy*

reading it, you should note on the document that a copy has been sent by
using the abbreviation cc: (see the format for letters on page 149). On the
other hand, if you don't want the addressee to know that you have sent
someone else a copy, you can eliminate the cc: notation and mark your
own file copy bcc:, which stands for "blind carbon copy."

As you can see, audience analysis is a fairly complex process, and mis-
judging your audience's needs or expectations can ruin your chance of
achieving your purpose. For instance, consider a case in which a writer
neglected to give thought to the needs of his key reader:

**The Case**

Barry Owens is Production Manager at TKO Industries, publishers of periodicals and newspapers for the trucking industry. Recently, at the request
of the editor-in-chief and the managing editor, Barry spent a great deal of
time working out a revised production schedule for *Transportation Topics*, a
monthly newspaper for dealers. *Transportation Topics* had been beset by a
series of significant copy errors and complaints from advertisers. The new
schedule allowed the advertisers time to verify their copy, but it called for
the press room to operate on one Saturday each month. Barry had
promised the two editors that he'd try to get the new production schedule
in operation by the next issue.

As he wrote his report, Barry worried that he might have some trouble
getting the approval he needed from Shirley Benson, TKO's Chief Financial Officer. He therefore documented his findings carefully and included a
good deal of detail; he even attached a flow chart of the day-by-day schedule of activities.

*Duffy* by Bruce Hammond © 1983, Universal Press Syndicate. Reprinted with permission. All rights reserved.

Shirley found Barry's report on her desk when she arrived on Friday morning, but she was on her way to an all-day meeting of the board of directors. She decided to take the report home to review over the weekend, but on Sunday evening the 20 pages began to look like a better project for Monday morning. On Monday at 9:15 a.m., just as she was reaching for the report, her secretary called to tell her that the two senior editors from *Transportation Topics* were outside her door, requesting an interview.

"I better see what Barry's worked out for these people before I meet with them," Shirley thought. Barry had not prepared an executive summary, so she quickly flipped to page 20 to review his conclusions. "Saturday overtime? . . . No way! We can't afford that." That afternoon Barry's report was back on his desk with the suggestion that he come up with a more cost-effective plan. Barry was visibly annoyed when he read Shirley's criticism. After all, his flow chart *was* carefully footnoted to show that the expenditure on overtime in the press room would be more than offset by the new schedule's eliminating the need to hire another full-time copyeditor.

---

**Analysis**

It's hard not to sympathize with Barry—Shirley probably should have read the whole report before jumping to a conclusion. But the truth is, what happened to him is not really unusual. Busy executives frequently scan reports to see whether they merit close study. Suppose, instead of burying a critical point in a footnote, that Barry had attached an executive summary to the front end of the report, pinpointing the chief advantages of the new schedule and showing *immediately* that there was a cost advantage to the plan. We can be almost certain that Shirley would have read the complete report and given it the consideration it deserved.

Barry lost his case because he failed to think about Shirley's needs. First, he should have realized that as Chief Financial Officer her primary concern is not a smooth production schedule but rather cost control. Second, he should have anticipated the strong possibility that, because of the pressures of her high position in the company, she would need to extract the key information quickly. An executive summary would have filled both needs. It would have immediately supplied her with what was the most significant information *from her perspective*, and it would have helped her to conserve time.

# ■ Performing an Audience Analysis

Although your immediate, intuitive assessment of your audience can have much validity, a rigorous audience analysis is never wasted effort and is often essential to communicating successfully. The amount of time you devote to an audience analysis should be influenced by the importance of the communication and the size and complexity of the audience. The best way to appraise the importance of a piece of writing is to consider its purpose. Even a brief memo announcing a meeting can be very important if you know that the meeting is urgent or controversial. And as we have stressed, to communicate with a large group of people who have varying viewpoints or objectives, you must carefully select a key reader and plan how to appeal to both the key reader and other parties. With the following case as a focal point, we'll describe how a thorough audience analysis can be conducted.

**The Case**

You are an assistant to the vice president of administration for a small but growing manufacturing company. Your boss has spent the last few months dealing with the problem of diminishing space because of the large number of new hires, and he has finally retained a consultant to replan the use of the firm's office space.

Since the consultant selected represents a company that deals in open offices, the replanning will result in many people moving from enclosed offices to partitioned space or open cubicles. Your boss knows that there are bound to be strong feelings about these changes. Your task is to draft a memo from your boss to all of the company's managers announcing the decision and informing them that the consultant will be calling on them soon for information and suggestions.

**Analysis**

To proceed with a systematic audience analysis, you should first ask yourself these three critical questions:

- Who is the key reader?
- Who else will or might read this document?
- Is there a hidden audience?

Choosing a key reader in this case is very difficult. The managers are the ones you most need to persuade; therefore, from our definition of key reader they are the obvious choice. But your boss is also a very important reader. After all, if he disapproves of your draft and decides not to sign the memo, the managers will never see it! Therefore, it would probably be very wise for you to begin your audience analysis by carefully considering his purpose. What does he want to accomplish with this memo? Without doubt, he wants to reduce the managers' anxiety about the new office design and to get them to cooperate wholeheartedly with the consultant.

With a clear understanding of the memo's purpose, you can turn your thoughts to the managers—your key readers. What are their concerns? If you try to imagine what it would be like to expect that you will be asked to trade a roomy, private office for less desirable quarters, you can guess their state of mind; and you may begin to think of ways to appeal to them. For example, you might reassure them that the move will not occur until an audit has been taken of everyone's most essential needs. And you might explain that the consultant will be carefully noting how they interact with their staffs and with other departments, so that their work will be facilitated rather than impeded by the change.

You might conclude that the consultant is either a hidden or a secondary audience. She will probably have an opportunity to read the memo; in fact, it might be a good idea to copy her on it to ensure that she does read it. Before talking with the managers, she will certainly need to know what they have been told about the impending changes and about her reasons for interviewing them.

You would be wise to expect that sooner or later the content of the memo will be revealed to the company's employees. They are definitely a hidden audience. And their reactions will be likely to influence the way the plan is received by their managers. Therefore, for the sake of the employees, the memo might also touch on the necessity that the managers think carefully about the needs of their staffs.

A second set of questions will help you to analyze your audience's needs in detail and to present your case persuasively. In particular, these questions will help you to decide what information to include. You should first ask each question in reference to the key reader and then ask the entire list consecutively in reference to each secondary and hidden audience.

- What does this reader already know?
- What else does this reader need to know to follow my reasoning?
- What is the reader's present attitude toward this subject? Is it indifference? acceptance? antagonism?
- What are the reader's current needs in reference to this subject?
- What do I want the reader to believe after reading this document?
- What do I want the reader to do after reading this document?

For our example, we will answer these questions first in terms of your boss and then in terms of the managers.

Your boss knows that there is a problem concerning office space and that most of the managers understand the situation. On the other hand, he knows that they will probably be unenthusiastic about any plan that appears to take away conveniences they already have. He, of course, favors the plan highly. Furthermore, although he has confidence in the consultant's abilities, he knows that she will need the managers' cooperation to come up with a genuinely effective office design. He will certainly want the memo to show that he has made his decision, but he will also want to be seen as fair-minded. In addition, he will want the managers to understand that he considers it very important for them to spend time with the consultant.

After your boss reads your draft, you hope he will perceive that you understand all the issues well and that you have responded to them effectively. You also hope that he will approve the memo and sign it.

Like your boss, the managers know that a space problem exists. Some of them will probably be aware that a plan is in the wind, but most will not know specifically what it is. They will therefore have to be told the facts clearly and tactfully: the decision has definitely been made, and the consultant will be calling on them for information. The managers' responses to this announcement will undoubtedly vary from concern to outright disfavor. They need to be reassured that the renovation offers them at least as much as it takes away. After they have read the memo, you hope that they will believe an open office design can succeed and that they will forthrightly and honestly discuss their needs with the consultant.

There is one more set of questions that you should use as part of a thorough audience analysis. These questions will help you to establish the *tone* of your document. They explicitly deal with the relationship of the writer to the reader. If reader and writer work for the same organization, the writer should ask:

- Is the reader my supervisor? Am I his or her supervisor?
- Are we in the same department? Are we well acquainted?

If reader and writer work for different organizations, the writer should ask:

- Do we work for competing organizations?
- Is the reader or the reader's organization a client or customer?
- Are we peers, or does one of us have a higher job status?
- Is our relationship distant and formal, or are we close associates or friends?

For the case we have been analyzing, it is important that these questions be answered as though your boss were the writer, because he will sign the memo. You will try to develop a tone that is appropriate for him to use in communicating with his managers. Certainly it will be a tone of authority; on the other hand, since he and his managers work closely together, it should also relfect that relationship.

We will look closely at tone in the next chapter, but for some immediate insight consider the different effects of these three possible opening statements for the memo from your boss to the managers:

1. John (each manager's first name), we all know that space is currently a big problem.
2. I would like to call your attention to our pressing need for additional space.
3. Please be prepared to relinquish your present office quarters in six months, at which time we will be instituting an open office arrangement.

You can see that these openings become increasingly authoritative and impersonal as we move from the first through the third. If you were drafting the memo, would you select any of the above sentences for your opening? If you believe that none is appropriate, take a moment to draft one that you feel would be more effective.

## ■ Summary

In Chapter 1 we noted that business comprises the transactions of many people bent on producing and exchanging goods and services for money.

In this chapter we have stressed the *human* perceptions and interactions that bring about and support these transactions. We have seen that effective business writers do not ignore the fact that they and those with whom they communicate are human beings. On the contrary, they make every effort to share the perceptions and understand the motivations of all who have a stake in the transaction—including themselves. They use this understanding to gain their own and their company's ends; but—because they are mature, ethical human beings—they do so with consideration, good judgment, tact, and courtesy.

## ■ Discussion Problems

**3.1**  Suppose that you are the assistant manager of a college bookstore that sells textbooks, popular books, stationery and office supplies, records, nonprescription health aids, and sundries. You have been asked to take the preliminary steps to prepare a report that will evaluate the store's product offerings. You recognize that this is probably going to be a time-consuming assignment, which you might be able to simplify and expedite if you can get a line on what the primary purpose of the report ultimately will be. Therefore, you try to make some educated guesses about the main purpose of the report. What might the report's purpose be if it has been requested by your manager? by the dean of the College of Science and Engineering? by a large supplier of stationery goods? by the chairperson of the Committee for Student Minorities? In each of these cases, how would you go about getting the information you will need to have before the report can be written?

**3.2** Figure 3.6 consists of two brief letters. Could both have been written by the same writer? Explain.

---

**Figure 3.6**

Dear Sir:

> At your request, I am enclosing payment for work completed at our establishment on January 5, 198-. We thank you for a job well done and will call upon you for assistance again in the future.

> Yours truly,

> [Signature]

Dear Bob:

> The enclosed check is for the work you did for us on January 5. We all thought you did a great job. You can count on us calling on you again when we need help.

> Best regards,

> [Signature]

---

**3.3** The following are examples of three openings for the same letter. Which one do you feel is most effective? Why?

- Enclosed is a questionnaire we are sending to all our retail stores in this area. We would appreciate an answer as soon as possible.
- The enclosed questionnaire was designed to give us information so that we can make this year's sales training program most useful to you and your sales force.
- To make this year's sales training program as useful as possible to you and your sales force, would you please answer the enclosed questionnaire?

**3.4** You have just completed a summer business internship that you found especially challenging and enjoyable. You hope that after you graduate next year you will be invited to join the firm. Before returning to your college program, you plan to write a thank-you letter to the manager who supervised your internship. What personal qualities might you try to communicate by the content and tone of your letter? What do you need to consider in making a decision about how you would like to come across in your letter?

**3.5** Students in business writing classes sometimes feel concerned about the ethics of audience analysis. If we try to "psyche out" an audience, they ask, aren't we really trying to figure out how to manipulate that audience? And is this really a fair way to sell our ideas or products? Think carefully about this issue, and be prepared to share your ideas with your fellow students. To what other aspects of modern living does this issue seem to apply?

# ■ Writing Tasks

**3.1** Draft a brief cover memo for the report you are to write for Jean (page 29) when you return from the benefits workshop. Assume that you found the workshop very productive.

**3.2** Draft a memo from your boss, the vice president of administration, telling the managers about the new office design and the consultant's impending conferences with them. Review the audience analysis on pages 40–43 before drafting your memo.

**3.3** The town in which your firm is located has just passed new legislation regarding the rights of nonsmokers in business establishments located within town boundaries. The result is that, although employees may continue to smoke in their own offices, smoking will no longer be permitted in common areas such as the cafeteria and conference rooms. Also, any employee requesting a smoke-free environment must be assigned to an office with other nonsmokers. There are a significant number of heavy smokers in the firm, among them three senior vice presidents. You report directly to the director of human resources, and she has asked you to draft a formal memo to all employees telling them that the company will, of course, adhere to the new law. Draft the memo.

# MESSAGE: THE BRIDGE BETWEEN WRITER AND READER

## 4

With your purpose in mind, you, the writer, sit down and try to find an effective way to communicate your thoughts to a particular audience. With effort and care, you build a bridge of words and sentences to carry your ideas across to these readers. And a persuasive message can, in a very real sense, bring about a meeting of minds. In fact, even when the message transmits information of only slight importance, its effects are observable. For example, suppose the message is "The product demonstration will interest you. It will take place in Conference Room A on Tuesday at 9 a.m." The reader stops to consider and, if persuaded, makes a note to attend.

But what about less-than-effective, hastily composed messages? Don't they sometimes carry the day too? Quite truthfully, if your reader thinks a message might be important, he or she may be willing to take time to decipher it. But since getting the message across is probably even more important to you, it is a mistake to count on the reader's dedication to see you through. Most readers will construe an obscure message to mean what they want to believe.

As an example of the pitfalls of writing an unclear message, consider the following case:

**The Case**

Scott Carter is Assistant Buyer for the luggage department of Branson's Department Stores. Early in September, the department had placed an order for a shipment of 100 pieces of Flightware, a lightweight line of luggage, to arrive at the store on November 1, in time for both Christmas and the midwinter vacation season. Unfortunately, by November 8 the luggage shipment had not arrived. Scott's boss suggested that they quickly let Flightware's wholesaler know what's what, and that this had better be done in writing, since they would need a permanent record. About half an hour later Scott dashed off the letter shown in Figure 4.1, and sent it by express mail.

**Figure 4.1**

November 8, 198-

Dear Sirs:

    We recently placed an order with you for a luggage shipment. Since the order involved a major part of our Christmas inventory, we counted on its prompt arrival. Assuming that you received our order, it has not arrived on time. It is necessary, therefore, to request that our order be canceled unless you can promise immediate delivery.

Yours truly,

*Scott Carter*

Scott Carter
Assistant Buyer

**Analysis**

When the shipment arrived two weeks later without further explanation, Scott was startled and annoyed. What had gone wrong? Had the wholesaler stubbornly decided to ignore his letter?

No, the truth was that because of a strike at the luggage manufacturer, all shipments were reaching the wholesale outlet far behind schedule. The rush to fill orders was intense and somewhat disorganized. At the wholesaler's the supervisor did not check Scott's letter against Branson's original purchase order. He merely scanned the letter hastily, saw that it said that the order had been placed "recently," and obligingly followed through with "immediate delivery." He interpreted Scott's words as meaning that Branson's was assuming that the purchase order had never reached the wholesaler; he therefore decided that no other explanation concerning the delayed shipment was needed.

Looking at Scott's letter, we can see why it was misinterpreted. First of all, it lacks important specific facts. Second, stylistic weaknesses and grammatical errors make it vague and ambiguous. And finally, the letter's tone does not communicate Scott's feelings of urgency. Figure 4.2 is a revised version of the letter.

**Figure 4.2**

November 8, 198-

Dear Sirs:

On September 3, 198—, we ordered 100 pieces of Flightware luggage (copy of purchase order #29986 is attached) to be delivered to our main store no later than November 1, 198—. As of today, we have not received the shipment. Since these items are intended for our Christmas inventory, we cannot accept the luggage after November 15. If you cannot meet this deadline, please cancel our order immediately.

Yours truly,

*Scott Carter*

Scott Carter
Assistant Buyer

By specifying the exact date that the order was placed and having a copy of the order attached, this revised letter immediately establishes the accuracy of Branson's claim that the order is late. It also gives exact instructions concerning what is to be done now. In this revision there is also much less room for misinterpretation. Not only has the vague word "recently" been replaced by a specific date, but also the glaring grammatical error in the third sentence of the original letter has been eliminated. (From the original version, the reader would have a hard time deciding whether the purchase order or the shipment "has not arrived on time." Also, although the first version does communicate that something is bothering the writer, the seriousness of the situation is obscured by the flabby language and muffled tone.

To rectify the muddle caused by the poorly written letter, Scott was forced to make several phone calls to people within his own company and also to send the wholesaler a second letter. As is often the case, the time spent straightening things out far exceeded the time it would have taken to write an effective letter at the outset.

Scott's original letter suffers noticeably from a lack of clarity. But clarity is only one of the attributes of an effective message. The letter's omission of important details (lack of development) and its inappropriate tone are also problems. We will focus on clarity in Chapter 10 when we study style. Here we will concentrate on *development*, *tone*, and *order*—the three elements of message that are directly related to the writer's strategy.

## ■ Development

Development is a straightforward matter. When we talk about how a message has been developed, we simply mean how much the writer has chosen to say about the subject, or how many details he or she has supplied. Development is, of course, closely related to scope, which we discussed in Chapter 2. In fact, the only difference between the two concepts is that you should begin to think about *scope* at the most preliminary stages of your planning—even as far back as when you are establishing the limits for your initial research. *Development*, on the other hand, is an ongoing process. Every time you put an idea or thought into words, questions about how much to say surface: Is the idea self-evident? Does it need support? Should you supply details?

For instance, when Scott Carter wrote "We recently placed an order," he should have realized that recency is a concept whose meaning depends on the reader's vantage point and inclinations. To Scott, recent meant a few weeks ago; to the wholesaler, it meant a few days ago.

Sometimes the problem is not a lack of clarity but a need to establish more credibility. Your readers may like you, respect you, and want to believe you; but if your ideas are undeveloped, you may leave them longing for more information. The writer who doesn't say enough will often protest: "Hey, what else was there? I told you what I thought!" But when readers feel that nothing of any consequence has been said, they are frequently right.

As a simple illustration, consider the reactions of those who receive a memo containing this undeveloped idea: "The talk was very interesting."

- What was said?
- Why was the talk of interest?
- Did it cause the writer of the memo to formulate any questions?
- Did the writer agree with the speaker?

These are just a few of the many questions that might occur to frustrated readers, who haven't the slightest notion why the memo concerns them.

Here's another undeveloped idea: "Karen is an outstanding leader." Suppose you were an employer and found this unembellished statement in a letter of recommendation. How much would this statement mean to you without answers to the following questions?

- What qualities make Karen a good leader?
- When was she observed leading?
- What did she do on those occasions?
- Who else admires her leadership?

And here is still another statement that whets the appetite for more information: "The project was completely successful."

- What was the project's objective?
- What was accomplished?
- Why is this accomplishment important?

As you can see, all of the above undeveloped ideas are *opinions*, and the answers to the questions would constitute support for those opinions. If you describe an event factually in a report, such as by writing "The talk began at 9:10 a.m. and ended precisely at noon," you don't usually need to supply detailed documentation; but as soon as you comment on the *value* of the event—its interest or usefulness—you had better be ready to develop your ideas further.

To understand the trick of developing an idea, consider this statement about an unfortunate, but common, experience: "My car was damaged in an accident." One person's fact may be another's opinion. "Damaged" may seem like an unvarnished fact to you, the car's owner, as you contemplate the aftermath of the impact. But the driver of the truck that bashed your car might heartily disagree. Eyeing your car, he might mutter that, actually, he only sees a small dent in the fender and a few cracks in a tail light.

Later, when completing the accident report, you try to be both accurate and specific. Here is what you write: "The left tail light was shattered and the rear left fender dented when a tractor trailer truck struck the rear of my 1983 Ford Mustang on Commonwealth Avenue at 9:15 a.m. last Thursday morning."

Usually, when an opinion is backed up with factual information, it becomes far more persuasive. With sufficient information, the reader can fully comprehend the point being made; more often than not, this understanding allows the reader to react the way the writer intended.

If you have any doubts about development, let your overriding concern be your reader's needs. *Empathize*. Consider precisely how much your reader needs to know. For instance, suppose your task is to describe a physical object, let's say a new copying machine just ordered for your department. If the reader is going to be your boss, you will probably prepare a statement of the machine's cost and the new capabilities it offers over the old equipment; you will probably not provide information about its size, shape, or specific components. On the other hand, if you are describing the machine to the maintenance people who will be moving it into its alcove, you will focus on the machine's exact size, including all of its dimensions and its weight. And, if your reader is to be the office manager whose job is to brief the secretarial staff on how to use the machine, you will be likely to include complete information about all its capabilities and working parts, focusing on its specific functions and on any special features or limitations. You might also include a few instructional diagrams for additional clarity.

Development is, of course, an issue not only when describing objects but also when handling many other business writing tasks. Let's consider just a few:

- Explaining a process: how many steps should you include? When instructing an employee, should you write instructions such as these?

  First enter the customer's name, address, and phone number; then the object purchased, date of purchase, and price; then the particular complaint; and finally, your specific response, the resolution, and the date.

  Or should you merely state the following?

  First enter all pertinent information about the customer; then describe the object purchased and the complaint; and finally, document the resolution of the problem.

- Arguing a case: How many issues should you cover? How much data should you supply to address those issues? If you are trying to persuade your department manager to drop a line of merchandise, do you simply mention this month's poor sales record?

Or should you also allude to the fact that several top-notch fashion magazines called this line a passing fad? Should you include hard numbers or specific quotations to support your contentions?

- Writing a technical report: how completely should you define your terminology? In a report about computers, should you include a formal definition like the following?

  Microprocessor: all of the components of a central processing unit on a single integrated circuit.

  Or should you include a simple definition in the context of your introductory remarks, for example:

  The microprocessor is the fundamental component of today's personal computers.

Preliminary decisions about these and similar matters should, of course, be made when you are determining the scope of your document—before you write a single word. Nevertheless, if you are like most writers, a steady stream of ideas will occur to you while you are writing. You should therefore anticipate the need to exercise careful judgment about which ideas to include and, even beyond that, which to enlarge upon.

What about writers who overload every report, letter, or memo with extraneous comments and information? The undeveloped idea quickly vanishes, but the idea that is subjected to explanation after explanation or expanded in infinite detail is usually lost from sight, buried under piles of mental debris.

For example, consider the following unfortunate case of overdevelopment:

**The Case**

Peter Brandon is the owner and operator of a small printing and design firm. The firm produces brochures, flyers, and other mailers. Peter has always taken pride in meeting his customers' deadlines. Recently, however, he moved his offices and plant to larger quarters and acquired much more modern equipment. To explain to customers why their current projects would be delayed, he composed the letter shown in Figure 4.3.

**Figure 4.3**

Dear (Name of Customer):

During the last two years, our firm, Peter Brandon, Printers, increased our customer base from 50 to 135 loyal customers, of which you are one. We have always tried to give our customers state-of-the-art printing, but even though you apparently have been satisfied, we have often wished that we could offer you greater variety in typography and design and more rapid service.

You will be pleased to know that, although you will probably be experiencing a two-to-three-day delay in receiving your current shipment, from now on you can expect a far more rapid turnaround. Three months ago we decided to switch from hot type to phototypesetting. We therefore purchased a photounit.

A major investment, this equipment was purchased from Panographic, Inc., and provides us with a combination of photographic, electronic, and mechanical components to set type. We can now achieve automatic font changes and can simultaneously hold four fonts on-line. Also, although previously we could only supply you with Helvetica for sans serif type effects and Times Roman for serif ones, we now can offer you three more type families: Bodoni, Optima, and Garamond. Furthermore, we now have the capacity for new and better methods of letter spacing, including kerning to reduce space between characters.

We know that you will be patient with us through this transition period. The slight inconvenience this month will be offset by the best service possible in the future.

Sincerely,

*Peter Brandon*

Peter Brandon

---

**Analysis**

Peter Brandon's letter is greatly overdeveloped. Customers discovering that their orders will be delayed are unlikely to be in the mood to learn about the wonders of a new photounit. It is understandable that Peter feels the need to explain the reason for the delay, but the details about the capabilities of the new equipment should be saved for a more suitable occasion (and perhaps some of the more technical details will never be of much interest to this audience). Once the crisis is past, Peter might send out an attractive direct-mail flyer to his customers, clearly describing and illustrating the new typesetting capabilities. The purpose of that mailing would be to market the firm's new services and capabilities; the purpose of this letter is to explain the delay. As written, Peter's letter merges these two discrete objectives in a hodgepodge of detail.

Some writers overdevelop their messages because they feel a need to qualify every assertion. Such people signal that they have very little confidence in their own judgment or that they are too timid to commit themselves to an out-and-out opinion. Similarly, some writers provide unneeded or redundant explanations; they seem to imply that they have little confidence in their readers' ability to understand. For example, consider the memo in Figure 4.4, which displays these faults.

---

**Figure 4.4**
A memo whose message is overdeveloped.

TO:   Distribution                                          DATE: December 15, 198-
FROM:  Karl Davidson
RE:   January Meeting, Ad Hoc Committee on
       Customer Service

    I would like to recommend that, since Chuck Wilson will be on vacation in Bermuda the week of January 8, we cancel our January meeting, if this is no great inconvenience to any member of the group. As you know, Chuck is an extremely valuable member of the committee. For instance, he provided us with a survey of customer reactions to our new return policy. He was, of course, to have presented his report on the frequency of customer complaints in the last six months. There's no need to point out that this report is vital to our work.

    If everyone is in agreement, therefore, I would like to suggest that we hold our next meeting on February 10 at 4:00 p.m. in Conference Room 2.


Distribution:   Jim Dowd
                Sandy Jones
                Bart Steinberg
                Beverly Zinn

---

The needs of the readers of this memo are simple and clear: they must learn that, for good reason, the January meeting has been canceled; they also need to know when and where the February meeting will be held. But surely they all remember that Chuck's report was vital and that he previously prepared a survey. Karl Davidson, the memo writer, is essentially correct in using the phrases "as you know" and "there's no need to point out." Yet despite his protestations, the profusion of detail broadcasts that he has little faith in either his readers' powers of recollection or his own judgment. The version of Karl's memo in Figure 4.5 reflects a writer with more self-confidence and a more positive feeling about his readers.

Figure 4.5
An improved ver-
sion of the memo
in Figure 4.4

```
TO:    Distribution                DATE: December 15, 198-
FROM:  Karl Davidson
RE:    January meeting, Ad Hoc Committee on
       Customer Service
```

      Since Chuck Wilson will be on vacation January 8, I recommend that we postpone our next meeting until February 10. At that time Chuck will be able to present his vital report on customer complaints during the last six months.

      If this rescheduling causes you inconvenience, please call me by 5:00 p.m. Tuesday. Otherwise, we will meet promptly at 4:00 p.m. on February 8 in Conference Room 3.

```
Distribution:  Jim Dowd
               Sandy Jones
               Bart Steinberg
               Beverly Zinn
```

Since achieving the right degree of development is not easy, all writers will sometimes make mistakes. Our egos may impel us to pour out more information than our readers need, or time constraints or fatigue may tempt us to be overly brief. But the best strategy is to be guided by the readers' needs, tempered, of course, by your intent to achieve your own purpose.

Your readers' *response* to your message may also prove helpful in evaluating whether a piece of writing was developed appropriately. If your message was not sufficiently developed, you may receive a number of phone inquiries or be asked to write a follow-up memo. If your work regularly receives this sort of reception, it's time to take the hint and begin to supply more detail. On the other hand, if people often seem to miss the main point of your message or if they respond by harping on one of your minor points, you may need to cut back.

As we have stressed, development is an ongoing process of deciding how much detail to supply in order to support or explain your ideas. Too little development leaves your audience confused or unable to retain your ideas. Too much development results in ideas that are buried in detail. Again, consider your readers' needs while keeping your own purpose firmly in mind.

## ■ Tone

The following three messages in Figure 4.6 were all written by the same person.

**Figure 4.6**

*Message I* (Fred Cain is Vice President of Marketing at Widgets, Inc. Franklin T. Adams is a senior project manager):

Dear Mr. Cain:

It pleases me greatly to tell you that Acme Industries has accepted our recent proposal (June 5, 198–) to supply them with 20,000 micro-widgets. Copies of our proposal and their letter of acceptance are attached.

Yours truly,

*Franklin T. Adams*

Franklin T. Adams

*Message II* (Susan is Frank Adams's manager).

Dear Susan,

I'm happy to tell you that Acme has given us a green light on the micro-widget order.

Cordially,

*Frank Adams*

Frank Adams

*Message III* (Pat is Frank Adams's co-worker and friend).

Pat,
It's in the pocket—they've given us the order!
Frank

---

Acme Industries has placed an order, and Frank Adams is pleased. All three of his letters quickly convey this information, but it's apparent that their similarity stops there. Frank clearly has a different attitude toward each person and has indicated this by varying the *tone*—the letters do not *sound* at all alike. And it's perfectly reasonable to expect that they would not, because Frank has a very different relationship with each of the three people. Furthermore, if we give it some thought, we can see that he also has a different purpose for writing to each of them.

Toward Mr. Cain his attitude is formal and respectful; his purpose is to communicate new information, to formalize the sale, and perhaps to draw attention to the good work represented by the attached proposal. To Susan, who is aware that the proposal was submitted to Acme, he explains very little; he uses a respectful tone mingled with a note of friendliness and informality to emphasize their cordial working relationship. And to his friend Pat, who has worked beside him to get the contract and who has also been eagerly awaiting Acme's decision, he uses a completely informal tone to communicate his pleasure and excitement.

The tone of writing communicates the way you feel about the person you are writing to; it may also convey your attitude about your subject and even about the situation at hand. To be able to hear the sound of *unspoken* words is a rather awesome human capability, and it's even more impressive that our written messages are able to carry so many nuances of meaning.

What techniques do you have at your disposal to create the proper tone?

First, and most obvious, is your *choice of words*. In writing as in speaking, if you have a good sense of who you are and whom you are addressing and what you both have at stake, you will find that some of the right words come to mind almost automatically. But the trickier the situation or the more you have at stake, the more effort you will need to exert. After all, English is a particularly rich language, supplying us with an almost infinite number of ways to express even the simplest idea. For example, the words *explain*, *inform*, and *assert* all describe the act of conveying information, but each will affect a reader differently. And that kind of difference can matter a great deal.

Suppose, for example, that you have just interviewed a job applicant—a 21-year-old female, 5 feet 2 inches tall weighing 110 pounds, who wore a dark gray suit. She spoke rapidly and frequently leaned forward in her chair. If your response to her is positive, you might use the following words in your evaluation: "The applicant is young, petite, well-tailored, articulate, and eager." But if your attitude is unfavorable, you might describe her like this: "She is immature, small and thin, severely dressed, talkative, and aggressive." Here, your tone is determined by your attitude toward your subject. To some degree, it is also determined by your situation; you are writing a formal report. An informal note would probably sound very different. For example, you might write this as your positive response: "She is attractive, spunky, and a great talker."

Of all the words that have a direct and immediate effect on tone, perhaps the most powerful are the personal pronouns *I*, *we*, and *you*. There was a time in the past when several generations of teachers sternly preached against the use of the first person in business writing or, for that matter, in expository or technical writing. Both *I* and *we* were considered marks of egotism—a sort of distracting and unneeded intrusion of the writer's personality. But today we recognize that the relationship between the writer and his or her reader is not intrusive; rather, it is the lifeblood of communication. Therefore, why shouldn't business writers use *I* and *we*? If a business writer, speaking for himself or herself, says "it is recommended that" instead of "I recommend" or "it is understood that" instead of "I understand," it creates a tone so formal that the tone itself is an intrusion or at least a distraction. Such extreme formality is appropriate to modern business communication only in those exceptional cases when a writer wishes to create a sense of austere distance or impersonal authority. Similarly, when a writer speaks for his or her company or group, the natural and appropriate wording is "we recommend" or "we understand."

Although there is no need to avoid using *I* or *we*, you should keep in mind that *you* is the most powerful pronoun for furthering communication. The *you attitude* is a writing strategy that suggests the writer is genuinely concerned about the readers' needs and concerns. For example, "We believe that our program is extremely beneficial" conveys a different attitude than does "We believe that our program will benefit you." Most compelling of all, however, is "You will find that our program is extremely beneficial." Similarly, a subscription renewal acknowledgment expressed in the following way obviously projects a *we attitude*:

> We want to take this opportunity to express our appreciation for your continued interest in our magazine. We are proud to publish Dateline, the country's leading weekly. In the coming year, we intend to increase our efforts to provide complete coverage of worthy events at half the newsstand price.

The following revision is far more effective from the standpoint of both tone and development:

> Thank you for deciding to renew your current subscription to Dateline. Now you will continue to keep up with the latest happenings in politics, business, science, and the arts—while saving half of the newsstand price for the country's leading weekly.

If you always perform the close audience analysis called for in Chapter 3, the "you attitude" will almost spontaneously begin to permeate your writing. When you are trying to see things from your readers' point of view, your words and your tone tend to reflect that effort. You often find yourself "talking" to your readers, demonstrating that you have thoroughly considered their perspective, even while making it clear that you know precisely where you stand.

Along with choice of words and use of personal pronouns, *punctuation and certain visual signals* (for example, underlining and italics) can help you to establish your tone. For instance, look back at Figure 4.6 and compare

Frank Adams's note to Mr. Cain with the one he wrote to his friend Pat. Both the dash and the exclamation point convey Frank's excitement to Pat, and, of course, the first-name-only salutation followed by a comma indicates informality. Also, just like music, prose has *rhythm* that affects the feelings and reactions of the audience. In comparing Frank's two notes, also observe the difference in rhythm, which is mainly accomplished through phrasing and sentence length. The long, flowing sentences add formality to the letter to the vice president; the staccato beat of the short sentences meant for Pat conveys a very different impression.

Writers cannot raise or lower their voices or inflect their words to communicate attitudes and feelings. But, as you see, they *can* use emphasis, pause, rhythm, and word choice in almost the same ways that speakers do. And, with skill and effort, writers can convey even the most subtle shades of feeling or differences in attitude. You will learn more about these techniques in Chapter 10, when you study style.

## ■ Order

Where do I begin? How should I end? Which issue should I discuss first? Should I put my main conclusion up front?

Like development and tone, *order* is a strategic element of the writing process. The answers to the above questions generally require much thought. For instance, your first instinct will often be to tell your reader where you stand, so a clear statement of your position is frequently the most appropriate opening. But suppose you know that your viewpoint is likely to surprise your reader or arouse his or her resistance. In such a case, you would be wiser to build your arguments carefully, exploring each issue that is important to your reasoning process before announcing your conclusions.

Suppose, for instance, that you own your own business, a small, regional moving and storage operation. After graduating from college, you started this entrepreneurial venture with very little capital and have built a small but solid customer base by offering highly personalized service at very low rates. It has now become obvious to you, however, that you need to increase your hourly charges or the business will not survive. You must immediately inform all customers who are scheduled for moves that there will be an increase of $5.00 per hour over the prices originally quoted them.

Do you open this letter to your customers by stating "As of February 1, all moves will be handled at an increased rate of . . ."? Not if you hope to keep their goodwill and to maintain your reputation as a moving firm that cares about its customers! Your strategy in informing them should be to outline the reasons for the cost increase first. Perhaps your letter would read something like the one shown in Figure 4.7.

**Figure 4.7** A letter explaining a rate increase.

Dear (Name of Customer):

Metropolitan Movers is now exactly three years old. In this brief time, we have earned a reputation for providing you with the kind of service that your valuable possessions deserve. Our estimates have been accurate, and our packers and delivery people careful and professional. But, unfortunately, our costs have been skyrocketing in the meantime.

You are aware that the price of fuel has risen considerably in the last few years; however, you may not realize that the prices of paper goods and high-quality cartons for packing have also shot up dramatically. Furthermore, to continue to provide our increasing numbers of customers with the timely service we take pride in, we have had to purchase a second moving van.

To support these new expenses, we must increase our hourly rates for packing and moving. If your move is scheduled to take place after September 1, you will be charged an additional $5 per hour over the rate quoted in our original estimate. Of course, we will understand if you choose to notify us that you wish to negotiate with another mover. On the other hand, we expect that very few of our loyal customers will do so. Please do not hesitate to call me personally if you wish us to submit a new estimate of your moving expenses or to answer any questions concerning our new pricing policy.

Yours truly,

[Your signature]

There are also many occasions when subjects that are not controversial need to be introduced with background information. Instead of presenting your solution at once, you may want to orient your readers by describing the problem you are attempting to resolve. Also, there may be times when you suspect your readers might be baffled by technical terms, and you will need to define these terms at the outset.

Efforts have been made to come up with established patterns, or models, for certain kinds of messages. In practice these models must be used with great care and discretion (see Chapter 9). For instance, perhaps you've read or heard that you should *never* put "bad news" up front in a letter, but should always use a buffer to cushion the blow. Depending on your purpose, this strategy may or may not be sound. To see clearly why this is so, consider the following situation.

Suppose your manager has asked you to prepare for internal distribution a policy letter stating that, as a result of customer complaints, a new and far more rigorous quality control system will soon be instituted throughout the department. Your first instinct might lead you to begin "Since we have been receiving an inordinate number of complaints. . . . "

Actually, if you know that your manager wants the letter to shake people up and get them to feel really concerned about the quality problem, this aggressive opening may not be a bad idea. On the other hand, if the letter's purpose is to launch the new system smoothly, without getting people upset, you will have a much better chance of succeeding with an opening like this: "Since the recent upturn in sales, all of us have had to increase our productivity, and the pressure is really on this department. Perhaps understandably, there have been some slip-ups. The only way we can avoid these lapses in the future is to. . . . " By walking the readers through your logic before mentioning the sensitive issue, you hope they will be able to accept the bad news more easily. As your purpose changed, so did your opening—and the "bad news" moved further down in your letter.

In the preceding case the recipients of the unwelcome message were other people. But picture another situation, in which the bad news has come to your own doorstep. Imagine for a moment that you have recently applied for a higher-level job at your company, and the letter you have just opened and begun to read is a rejection notice. If the first sentence of this letter is a truly relevant explanation that will help to ease your disappointment (perhaps a mention that you are being considered for a different position of equal status), you will be likely to feel inclined to plunge ahead. But would you be soothed if the opening of the letter contained a series of bland platitudes about "many qualified applicants" and "your excellent potential"? Probably not. Probably, like most people, you would feel patronized, and your eyes would quickly leap to the paragraph containing the meat of the matter.

As you can see, although we can attempt to make a few generalizations about recurrent types of correspondence (see Chapter 9), there is no one "right" way to deliver bad news . . . or good news . . . or any message at all. An order that is strategically appropriate will always be derived from the writer's willingness to empathize with the reader's mind-set, situation, or needs and to devote care and thought to analyzing purpose. Finding the proper balance is not always easy, but the following guidelines should help:

- Unless you have a good reason for doing otherwise, put your main point or conclusions near the beginning of your document.
- If your reader will need background information to understand your main point or conclusion, respond to that need first.
- If your reader is doubting or is likely to be hostile, try to resolve those doubts or misgivings before stating your conclusions.

- The things you say first and last will have the most impact; so if you wish to deemphasize or "bury" information, place it in a middle section of your document.
- In a short memo the thing you say last will generally be remembered longest.
- In a long report the things you say first will gnerally get the most attention.

Remember that these are not rules: they are *guidelines*. They will not provide you with ready answers, but they will help you to assess your alternatives and to get moving in the right direction.

Again, establishing a sound strategic order in your document requires a close analysis of your readers' needs and your own purpose. Mediating between what your readers desire or expect and what you wish to accomplish should provide you with a sense of priorities and order. In this chapter, you were given some useful guidelines to get you started and to help you avoid mistakes. In the next chapter, you will learn some practical methods to help you sort out your ideas and to make your structure clear to your readers.

## ■ Summary

In this chapter we have examined three elements of message that are directly related to the writer's strategy: development, tone, and order.

Development refers to the amount of detail necessary to support your thought. It is an ongoing process of choice as you write. In deciding how much information to include, let your overriding concern be the needs of your reader.

Tone communicates how you feel about your audience and your subject. Choice of vocabulary and visual signals such as punctuation, underlining, and the pronouns *I*, *we*, and *you*, are powerful influences on tone. Most important of all is the pronoun *you*, which conveys empathy for your reader's point of view.

There is no one "right" place in a document for bad or good news. To determine the best sequence of topics, balance your own purpose with the desires and expectations of your reader.

## ■ Discussion Problems

**4.1** Which of the following statements require further development? Why?

- Today's meeting is very important.
- Your flight leaves at 5:15 p.m. on Wednesday, April 9.
- She always meets her deadlines.

- The report required more documentation.
- He completed the accounting procedure in two hours.
- This product does not perform well.
- We are currently dissatisfied with this product's performance.

**4.2**   Supply appropriate details to amplify the statements in Discussion Problem 4.1 that you feel require futher development.

**4.3**   Cliff Hayes is the manager of The Tasty Taco, one of a chain of fast-food Mexican restaurants. It is late June, and after a slow winter business has suddenly begun to boom. With a busy summer ahead, Cliff would like to increase his staff of servers by at least four. He decides to write a letter to the Chicago headquarters to convince his superiors that the new hires are essential. What arguments might he include in the letter to bolster his case? How much detail should he supply?

**4.4**   Select a process to describe to a classmate or friend. For instance, you might describe one of these processes: starting a car with a standard transmission, baking a loaf of bread, or warming up before jogging. How much detail should you include, and what sort of information would help you to make this decision?

**4.5**   Describe the situations and attitudes that you believe might underlie the following statements. (Each statement may reflect more than one attitude.)

- Send payment at once!
- Thank you for your time and consideration.
- Have it here by 9:00 a.m. sharp.
- Our establishment meets the highest standards.
- Perhaps our last inquiry did not reach you.
- Let's not let this one slip between the cracks.
- We take pleasure in announcing that we have achieved our goal.

**4.6**   Taking the first statement from Discussion Problem 4.5 ("Send payment at once!"), revise the wording so that the tone of the statement becomes increasingly diplomatic. Try to supply four or more revisions, each more tactful than the preceding one.

**4.7**   Discuss how changes in emphasis (italics) or in punctuation alter the tone (and sometimes the meaning) of the following statements. Describe the attitude of each writer.

- Don't change a *single word*.
  *Don't* change a single word.

- Men and women never agree on *this* subject.
  Men and women *never* agree on this subject.

- The bad news was delivered by telephone.
  The bad news was delivered by telephone!

- This procedure was not done correctly, so make the necessary changes.
  This procedure was not done correctly; make the necessary changes.
  This procedure was not done correctly. Make the necessary changes!

**4.8**  Have you ever been advised not to use *I* or *we* in a a written report? What were the circumstances? How did you handle this problem? Do you still feel somewhat uncomfortable about writing in the first person? Why or why not?

**4.9**  If you believe that you can improve the tone of the following messages, do so. Explain why you have made your revisions, and be prepared to defend them by providing details about the circumstances, the reader(s), or the writer.

- *Note tacked to the wall of a self-service coffee room:* People using this facility should be responsible for returning all materials to their proper places.

- *Memo from management to first-level supervisors:* It is intended that no one feel discriminated against by this policy.

- *Memo from a department manager to his staff:* We believe that this schedule will assist you in meeting assigned deadlines.

- *Memo from an administrative vice president to all employees:* It is essential that all employees refrain from parking in the spaces designated for handicapped persons.

- *Memo from a chairperson to her committee:* There is no reason to feel responsible for the failure of the plan to achieve its objectives.

**4.10**  Imagine that you have a list of points to cover in a letter or memorandum. All of these are more or less neutral in content, but some are more important than others, and one point is particularly complicated. In general, what order would you choose for presenting this information: important news first, last, or in the middle? Where would you place the complicated point? Can you think of situations that would require special consideration in establishing the order of this material?

**4.11**  Marian Hansen, Personnel Administrator at Emco, Inc., is writing a memo to inform employees of several recent developments:

- It will no longer be possible for employees to buy Emco stock at the very favorable rate that has been available up to now.

- Arrangements have been made with Bodybuild, a local health spa, to offer a free six-month trial membership to all Emco employees. A sign-up form is attached.

- Because of severe personnel shortages last summer, it will be necessary to require employees to request specific vacation dates in writing at least three months in advance. Unfortunately, it will not be possible to guarantee that the particular dates requested will be available. In some cases alternative dates will be suggested by the Personnel Department.

Suggest ways in which Marian could highlight the good news and make the bad news less offensive. What could Marian say in her introductory paragraph to make her audience more receptive to what follows? What tone would be most effective? Can you think of approaches to the bad news that would cushion the blow?

**4.12**  In the following situations where in the letter or memo would you place your main point? What strategies could you use to make each communication either less offensive or more persuasive?

- You have to explain to all owners of the 1986 two-door sedans (Model 710Y) manufactured by your company that their vehicles must be returned to the dealers because of a technical flaw in the exhaust system.

- As the business manager of a small trade publication, you have carefully researched comparative printing costs and have found that a printer in the next state can provide quality service for considerably less than you are currently paying. You decide to write a memo to your staff to persuade them to change printers. You know they will not be enthusiastic, since they have dealt with the same local printing firm for several years and there are obvious disadvantages to dealing with an out-of-state printer.

- As a consultant on organizational design, you are preparing a report about the organizational structure of a client's company. In your opinion, much recent conflict among the firm's middle management has been caused by an overlap of responsibilities, resulting in part from hazy job descriptions in several departments. Your report is 30 pages long and is addressed to the firm's president and three vice presidents.

# ■ Writing Tasks

**4.1** Write out the description of the process you selected in Discussion Problem 4.4. Pay particular attention to your choice of details—those you include and those you decide to leave out.

**4.2** Draft Cliff Hayes's letter to Tasty Taco headquarters, as described in Discussion Problem 4.3.

**4.3** Reread Peter Brandon's overdeveloped letter to his customers (Figure 4.3). We indicated that this letter might have been better had it been separated into two different kinds of communications: a letter explaining the delay, followed at a later date by a flyer describing the firm's new typesetting capabilities. Write a briefer, more appropriate letter explaining the delay.

Describe the design and appearance of the flyer in a brief statement. Then, using the details in the original letter and inventing any others you need, draft the content of the flyer. Your work will not be judged on artistic ability, but you should try to be creative. What clever techniques might Peter use to illustrate the potential of his new equipment?

**4.4** Is the following message appropriately concise or rudely abrupt? If you have any misgivings, compose your own version.

Your subscription expires as of 3/7/8-. Kindly fill out the enclosed renewal form and return it within ten days, accompanied by your check for the appropriate amount.

**4.5** Kate Maloney is a successful young attorney who has lived for the past six years in a luxury high-rise in Manhattan. Recently she moved to a slightly larger apartment on a different floor. She loves her new apartment but is constantly upset about the loud rock music played at strange hours by her upstairs neighbor,

Mac Lewis. Studying the building's standard lease with her sharp lawyer's eye, she ascertains that the music is shaking her ceiling fixtures at an hour well after the building's "noise curfew." She has called Mac several times to complain firmly and courteously, but there has been no noticeable reduction in the noise level. (Mac no doubt feels that she is hopelessly straightlaced and incapable of appreciating good music.)

Kate next notifies the building's security officer, asking him to call Mac on her behalf. The security officer does so, but the problem still remains. As a last resort, she decides to write a letter to the building management to explain the situation. Her immediate purpose is to enlist their action. She also realizes she will probably have to continue to live with Mac and his stereo; therefore, she wants to be reasonably tactful and open-minded.

Draft Kate's letter to the management company, paying particular attention to tone and development. Can you suggest an especially tactful opening? Should she include *all* the relevant details? Where in the letter should she place her strongest statements? What should be included in her request for action? Should she send a carbon copy to Mac, and if so, should she add an accompanying note? What tone would be appropriate for such a note? Draft the note as well, if you think sending it is a good idea.

**4.6**  You're a senior technical consultant specializing in transportation systems, and you've just been notified that your team's recent proposal to study the feasibility of a new airport has lost out to that of your major competitor. You're disappointed, of course, but you're also convinced that your team did a fine job and you're concerned about keeping up their morale. At the same time, you have to break the news to the vice president who is your own boss and provide her with a brief account of the probable reasons why you didn't get the assignment.

Write the following brief memos, choosing a tone appropriate to the occasion and to your relationship with each recipient:

- To Dr. Joan Scranton, Vice President, Transportation Division, advising her of the situation and offering a possible explanation.

- To your team members, Marsha Lanscomb and Phil Berger, giving them the bad news but praising them for their good work and team spirit.

- To Dick Blount, your long-time colleague and close friend at the competing firm, congratulating him on his team's success.

**4.7**  Improve the tone of the following examples by changing the focus from *I* or *we* to *you*.

- We appreciate your order, and we hope that our product will give you complete satisfaction. At Madewell, Inc., we realize that happy customers are our key to continued success.

- To facilitate our renewal process, we ask you to fill out the enclosed form and submit it with your payment.

- I am sure you will understand our delay in considering your recent application. We have heard from several hundred interested candidates, and our search committee will therefore require at least three more weeks to produce a short list of applicants to interview.

- I am very enthusiastic about the position you describe. I feel sure that it will offer me the opportunity to acquire valuable high-tech experience while allowing me to put my writing and editing skills to good use.

**4.8**  As an assistant acquisitions editor for the fiction department of a paperback publisher, your job is to evaluate submitted manuscripts and recommend the best ones for eventual publication. You have just received a marvelous first novel, written by a 26-year-old teacher at a community college in a small, isolated town in the mountains of Kentucky. After two years in your entry-level position, you feel you have spotted the novel that will help you to move up in the company and probably also make a small fortune for the firm, which badly needs a big success. The novel has everything: unforgettable characters, a quaint historical setting, passionate romance, intrigue, idealism, and a wonderfully lively sense of the absurd.

You have two immediate objectives: first, to make sure that the author will eventually agree to sign with your company, despite the relatively low royalty rate it usually offers to first novelists; and second, to convince your company's senior editors that this manuscript is a rare opportunity that should be snatched up without hesitation. With these objectives in mind, do the following:

- Draft a letter to the author, Dr. Mary Margaret O'Brien, expressing your serious interest in her novel and offering to have a definite answer for her within three weeks.

- Write a memo to senior editors Hal Praeger and Bob Malin, conveying your confident enthusiasm that *Teach Me to Love* will be next year's runaway best-selling romance. Supply enough detail to be convincing. They are exceedingly busy editors, however, so don't overdo it!

- Write a brief note to your friend and mentor, Professor Emily Delano, telling her of your find and sharing your excitement.

**4.9**  Draft Marian Hansen's memo to Emco employees informing them of the recent personnel developments described in Discussion Problem 4.11.

# PATTERNS OF
# RELATIONSHIP

## 5

**W**hen a piece of writing has an inherently logical structure, the reader feels drawn along a clearly charted route toward an explicit destination. Even if unenthusiastic about the journey or uncomfortable with the terrain, he or she is propelled forward and is persuaded to examine the ideas encountered along the way.

When something you have written has a clear and discernible structure, you often feel a sense of mastery and control. You have given yourself reason to believe that your reader will be able—perhaps even be compelled—to follow your logic.

The power to organize effectively depends on how well you can perceive and depict patterns of relationship. To describe, to compare and evaluate, to explain, and to argue effectively, you must discover and establish logical relationships among facts, ideas, and opinions and make your readers see them as clearly as you do.

## ■ Unity and Coherence

To convince yourself how important patterns of relationship are to comprehension, try this simple test. Quickly look at Figure 5.1, and without counting them, give an immediate guess as to how many dots you see. Now—just as quickly—glance at Figure 5.2, and do the same. Whether or

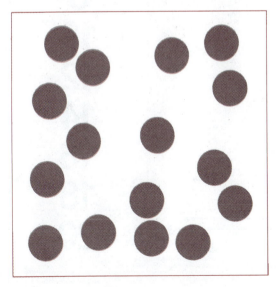

**Figure 5.1**  Dots that lack a unifying pattern.

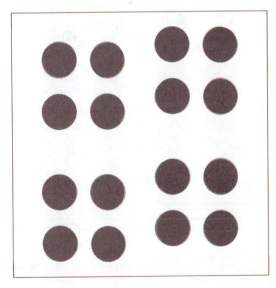

**Figure 5.2**  Dots arranged in a unifying pattern.

not your two answers are alike, you undoubtedly had a much easier time counting the dots in Figure 5.2. That figure exemplifies the principle of *unity*: the four groups each represent a unified whole. If you will imagine that the dots represent information, you can picture each cluster in Figure 5.2 as a group of related ideas or facts that were positioned together to make their kinship immediately apparent to a reader.

An equally simple test can be used to illustrate the effects of *coherence*. First, glance quickly at the list of numbers in Figure 5.3, making no attempt to study them. With your book closed, jot down the sequence as you remember it. Now, look at Figure 5.4. Doubtlessly, if asked to, you could immediately repeat this list. It has coherence because each number follows the preceding one for a discernible, logical reason; furthermore,

**Figure 5.3**
A list of numbers
without coherence.

**Figure 5.4**
A list of numbers
with coherence.

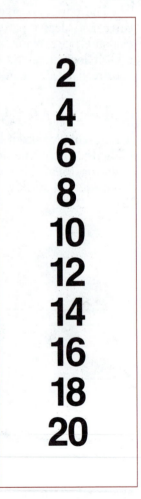

the numbers move in a clear direction from start to finish. In a coherent document, ideas are ordered so that each can be seen to be logically related to those that precede and follow it. All of these connected ideas carry the reader toward a logical conclusion.

You can comprehend and retain information better when it is unified and coherent, and so can your readers. Unless your readers discern clear relationships between your ideas and sense a steady movement toward your conclusion, they may not feel up to the challenge of trying to decipher your meaning.

## ■ Six Patterns of Relationship

The relationships that we deal with most frequently in business writing are those of *space, time, comparison, analysis, cause/effect,* and *problem/solution.* Let's now briefly consider how and when each is used.

It is nearly impossible to describe where an object is located without dealing with *spatial relationships.* For a very simple illustration, suppose that a co-worker has asked you where the president sat at a recent meeting you attended. Your response might be something like this: "The president sat between the chairman and the guest speaker and across the table from Harry Jones, the Director of Planning." Or supposes that you are asked about the location of the site for the company's new store. You might answer: "It is five blocks from the center of town, across the street from the First National Bank." Even if you are asked to establish a location in the most precise terms, your measurements will all depend on distances from one point to another.

As well as spatial relationships, *chronological relationships* are critical to people's ability to think and to communicate. In business, gathering historical data, scheduling, planning, and describing processes all call on one's ability to perceive sequences in time. "The committee will reconvene when Charlie returns from Europe" is a fairly typical example of the simplest kind of chronological relationship. But items of overriding importance, such as econometric forecasts or multimillion-dollar acquisition programs, are also explained wholly or partially in terms of the order of events.

Here, for instance, is an economist's report on the state of the economy: "As the expansion, which began in late 198-, moves beyond the 18-month mark, the rise in general business activity is notable. It roughly matches the average increases in comparable stages at seven earlier expansions. In the first year of the latest upturn, for instance, real GNP rose 6.2 percent. Most forecasters project a further rise in real GNP of 4 to 5 percent in the second year of the upturn." And, as a further example, here is the key sentence in an acquisition proposal: "We plan to initiate our search for a suitable acquisition in the forest products industry early in fiscal year 198-, to commence negotiations by mid-year, and to complete the purchase before fiscal year 198- is well underway."

We rely on relationships just as heavily when we are *comparing*, or *evaluating*. In a business atmosphere charged with a constant need to make quick and rational decisions, the ability to evaluate existing alternatives can be crucial. Comparison (finding similarities) and contrast (finding differences) are often at the heart of the decision-making process in many of business's major functions. To mention just a few examples, we might cite marketing, in which alternative modes of selling or advertising must be considered; manufacturing, in which alternative processes or equipment need to be examined; and organizational development, in which different patterns of human interrelationships must be taken into account.

To make a valid comparison, you first need to establish a *basis*. For instance, in speaking about a business's performance, you might use profitability as your basis and compare profits in two years. Here, as often happens, you are combining patterns—relating the profits chronologically as well as by comparison. Looking back at the economist's report, you can see that the growth of the economy is the basis for comparison. And there, too, a writer was working with chronology and comparison simultaneously: not only did the report relate events over time; it also compared the GNP at different points. As a final example, suppose that you are asked to evaluate an employee's performance. You might use productivity as the basis and compare his or her current performance to that of a previous year. Alternatively, you might compare the employee's performance to that of other employees with similar responsibilities.

*Analysis* requires that something be broken into its component parts. As with comparison, you must select a basis by which to break the parts down. A chemist and a botanist, for instance, will each use a very different basis in analyzing an apple. Where the botanist sees skin, pulp, and seeds, the chemist will discover a variety of chemical compounds. Business people perform analyses just as frequently as scientists. A business person may need to identify the component parts of a machine, an organization, a system, a plan, or an event. An information system might be analyzed according to the benefits it provides for the people it serves. An organization might be analyzed according to the types of positions people hold, such as senior executives, managers, supervisors, staff people, etc.

Just as the ability to depict relationships is one of the strongest assets you can have in describing, evaluating, and analyzing, so too is it essential in explaining a point or arguing persuasively. Here the critical relationship often is that of *cause and effect*. To show why something has occurred or is likely to occur, you must relate it to its cause. You begin with a fact or an observation and explain either its origin in the past (cause) or its influence in the future (effect). Cause/effect relationships can be as simple as "Bad weather caused the flight to be delayed," as controversial as "His error caused us to lose the contract," or as complex as "Without a clear understanding of the market (cause), we cannot successfully introduce this product (effect)."

Causes and effects can be multiple. For instance, *both* bad weather and mechanical difficulties could have caused a delayed flight. And the effects of misunderstanding the market could be both the failure to introduce the product and the loss of ground to one's competitors. Whenever you deal with multiple causes or effects, you need to order them according to your specific priorities, perhaps from most significant to least significant or from most probable to least probable.

The relationship that business people probably deal with most frequently can be described as *problem/solution*. Someone, usually your supervisor, complains about a problem, and you are asked to resolve it. The problem may originate from doubt or confusion, or it may be a case of something gone wrong. You may be told "I don't think Joe is the right person for the job," or "I thought they wanted a full-page ad," or "We aren't likely to meet that deadline." Then you will be expected to propose a solution, and often to explain it carefully in a written memo. The best way to structure such a memo is to first restate the problem and then, if necessary, explain how it originated. Next, clearly state your solution. Finally, support that solution.

For instance, taking the first example as a case in point, you might write: "Since Joe's frequent absences have made it impossible for him to supervise the group, I propose that Harry be selected to replace him. Harry is a strong leader, extremely knowledgeable, and is almost never absent from the office." As you can see, Harry's qualifications constitute the support for your solution to the problem. Alternatively, the support could have been a cause/effect explanation or even a comparison. You might have written, for example: "Harry is our choice because his excellent attendance will ensure good and consistent supervision." Or you might have said: "Compared to Joe, Harry has shown a far more consistent attendance record."

## ■ A Closer Look at the Patterns: Case Examples

In a business document of any complexity, we typically need to rely on several kinds of relationships to carry the message to the reader. For instance, a long report might include a close analysis, an examination of cause and effect, and several comparisons. In Chapter 15 we'll consider such reports, but now let's examine some case examples and memos that rely on one predominant kind of relationship.

# Space

In Chapter 3 we considered the case of a rapidly growing company that retained a consultant to create a new plan for the use of available office space. We left the case at the point where the consultant was about to interview the senior managers and submit a design for an open office plan. There, the role you played was that of an administrative assistant to the vice president of administration. Now, put yourself into the role of the consultant. Assume that you have completed the initial interviewing and have drawn up a preliminary plan for each department. The first of a series of memos that you are writing is addressed to the head of the Marketing Department, Benjamin Phillips, a senior vice president. A copy of the memo will go to the vice president of administration; a copy will also be sent to the hard-working, clear-headed administrative assistant who helped out before (see Chapter 3). Because this memo is long and detailed, we reproduce only a portion of it in Figure 5.5.

**Figure 5.5**
A memo that relies on spatial relationships.

TO:   Benjamin Phillips                    DATE: May 7, 198-
        Senior Vice President, Marketing
FROM: [Consultant]
SUBJ: Marketing Department Office Design
CC:   [Vice President, Administration]
        [Bright Administrative Assistant]

Attached you will find a schematic diagram showing the precise dimensions of the preliminary office plan for the Marketing Department. In this memo, I will explain some of the details of the plan and the underlying rationale for the design.

Because Marketing is such a busy, high-intensity area, people are constantly interacting within the department and they need to be able to move about freely. On the other hand, because vigorous open discussions do require guarantees of uninterrupted privacy, there is an obvious need for enclosed meeting spaces. The plan therefore calls for an open work area with 20 spacious, well-lit cubicles and two enclosed focal points for private meetings.

The first of these two focal points is your own office, located at the extreme corner of the southeast wing, with doors opening into both the main work area and a small enclosed conference room. By enabling you to use either your own office or the adjoining conference room, this arrangement will guarantee your privacy in conferences and meetings. Furthermore, it will allow you and your staff easy access to one another for frequent informal conferences.

The second focal point is the large enclosed conference room, located diagonally across from your office and also opening into the main work area. . . .

As you can see, the description cannot proceed without showing how each part of the design is spatially related to the others. It is also important to note that in business or technical descriptions emphasis is normally placed on relating the object's placement to its *function* within the whole. Not only does the reader need to know where the object is located, he or she must also understand *why* it occupies that particular space. For this reason, cause/effect relationships can be extremely important to such descriptions.

This principle certainly holds true in the memo in Figure 5.5: the consultant must explain the rationale for the entire plan before the vice president can understand the functions of all the interrelated parts. If you picture how the vice president might react to the description without this orientation, you can see why cause/effect relationships are normally a critical part of business and technical descriptions. To understand this principle even better, try to imagine how you might describe a new building site to a management group, the location of a new machine to members of the department who will use it, or the parts of the machine itself to a new operator.

Therefore, when you are faced with organizing a memo or report that relies on spatial relationships, a good plan is to proceed in this way:

- Describe the overall function of the object or the underlying rationale for its placement.
- If appropriate, describe the relationship of the parts to the whole in regard to their function (why) and placement (where).
- If appropriate, describe the relationship of the parts to each other in regard to their function (why) and placement (where).

## Time

Chronological relationships are extremely important in business writing—first, in planning and establishing timetables, and second, in describing processes. For instance, still in the role of the consultant, imagine that you have to send the vice president of administration a detailed plan establishing a timetable for implementing the new office designs for the various departments. Again, only part of this memo is reproduced in Figure 5.6.

Note that it is much easier to describe a process if you first segment it into stages. If the memo in Figure 5.6 were presented as a longitudinal listing of steps from beginning to end (" . . . and then, and then, and then . . ."), the reader would be less likely to understand and retain the information. In fact, if a listing of each step in the procedure were all that was required, a memo would not be needed; the timetable alone would be sufficient.

**Figure 5.6**
A memo that relies
on chronological re-
lationships.

TO:   [Vice President, Administration]    DATE: March 2, 198-
FROM:   [Consultant]
SUBJECT:   Moving Timetable
CC:   [Vice President, Marketing]
      [Bright Administrative Assistant]

Our three-phase process for implementing the new office plan
will be accomplished at the rate of one department every two weeks
over an eight-week period. The four departments include Marketing,
Administration and Finance, Product Engineering, and Telephone
Sales and Service.

Attached you will find a timetable describing in detail the
specific procedures to be accomplished on each date. Here I would
like to give you a general overview of each phase and its implications for the respective staff.

The three phases of the process include (1) dismantling the
existing inner walls and painting and refurbishing the outer walls,
(2) building the new enclosed office spaces, and (3) assembling and
fine-tuning the open workspace cubicles.

Marketing Department

As the timetable indicates, phase one for the Marketing Department will commence on April 3. Members of the department
will need to occupy temporary quarters until April 12, when both
phase one and phase two will be completed. At that time, Mr.
Phillips's office can be refurbished.

On the morning of April 12, we will assemble the ten cubicles
to be occupied by the Marketing Research staff; during the afternoon of that day, we will complete the ten cubicles intended for
Marketing Communications. Although cubicles can be occupied as
soon as they are assembled, we suggest that the staff can expect a
good number of bugs to need attention in the few days following assembly. We will plan to spend the remainder of that week eliminating problems and adding features to meet the specific needs of the
occupants.

Administration and Finance

The initial step in transferring . . . .

To prepare a memo that describes a process or a time sequence, therefore, you should take the following steps:

- Provide an overview of the entire process and its purpose.
- Segment the steps into a number of integrated phases.
- Describe each phase and its purpose.

As you have perhaps perceived, in taking the above steps you are *analyzing* the process. In this respect, just as the cause/effect relationship is critical to description, analysis is critical to presenting chronology.

## Comparison

When you are asked to deal with seemingly unrelated or overabundant facts, figures, and tangential considerations, comparing or contrasting can help you to generate meaning. By discovering the similarities and differences between alternatives, you can make a rational choice among them or recommend different courses of action for each of them.

But, as we discovered earlier, every comparison that you make must be based on clearly defined criteria. Creating a clear, logical pattern of comparison can be extremely difficult, so we will look rather closely at the preliminary sorting process.

As a simple case, suppose that you are faced with the happy prospect of buying a new car, and you have narrowed the field to either a Rambo XR or a Blitz GL. They both offer many attractive features. How can you select the better car for you? You cannot know which features to compare until you decide on your criteria; moreover, you need to set some priorities. If you are looking for reasonable price, luxury, and performance, you will probably have to decide which of the three is most important to you. The Rambo XR has front-wheel drive, a high-quality stereo cassette system, and a higher price tag. The Blitz GL offers two more cylinders and special rustproofing. Which of these features are comparable? And which interest you the most?

Let's assume that you decided that for you luxury counts least and performance most. You might then organize your evaluation as follows:

   I. Performance
     A. Blitz GL (6 cylinders, rustproofing)
     B. Rambo XR (front-wheel drive)
  II. Price
     A. Blitz GL ($9,350)
     B. Rambo XR ($10,050)
 III. Luxury
     A. Blitz GL (standard features only)
     B. Rambo XR (stereo cassette system)

Using this plan to write a letter explaining why you finally selected the Blitz GL, you might offer a preliminary judgment after each subsection; alternatively, you could state your conclusion at the very end.

A second structural pattern that often works well when making a comparison is to consider the objects (or ideas) being compared one at a time and discuss each in relationship to the selected criteria. For example, your car evaluation could be organized lke this:

I. Blitz GL
   A. Performance (6 cylinders, rustproofing)
   B. Price ($9,350)
   C. Luxury (standard features only)
II. Rambo XR
   A. Performance (front-wheel drive)
   B. Price ($10,050)
   C. Luxury (stereo cassette system)

You will need to decide which of the two basic patterns best suits your purpose in a given situation. The first makes the comparison more explicit; the second is tidier and more compact. Furthermore, as you become more adept at handling structure, you will find ways to vary these patterns to match your specific aims.

**The Case**

Let's now examine a more complex case of comparison. Pete Linton has been asked to research the relative merits of two major car rental companies and to get a memo off to his boss, Dave Winthrop. Pete and Dave work for a busy consulting firm, and it has fallen to their lot to develop a travel convenience plan for the firm's consultants. Dave has told Pete that he is most concerned that they select the company whose special features more closely match the needs of their firm. Not surprisingly, he is also interested in the cost differential. After studying the two companies' brochures and phoning their downtown offices for additional information, Pete drafts the memo shown in Figure 5.7.

**Figure 5.7**

TO: Dave Winthrop         DATE: November 3, 198-
FROM: Pete Linton
RE: Car Rentals

    As you requested, I have compared the special features and rates of two major car rental agencies. For the reasons outlined below, I feel our choice clearly is Atlas rather than Firtz.

    Although Firtz offers subcompacts at a particularly low rate, Atlas has consistently better rates for full-size cars. Since our car rental records for the past six months show that our consultants have preferred to use full-size cars, Atlas scores higher here, particularly since Firtz does not even guarantee the availability of subcompacts.

    Both companies offer comparable special weekly rates; but Firtz requires reservations seven days in advance for their special low rate, whereas Atlas needs only two days' notice. Our consultants are inclined to take advantage of low weekly rates but frequently must travel on exceedingly short notice. Again, Atlas offers the better deal for us.

Although Atlas charges an additional drop-off fee for cars not returned to the point of origination and Firtz offers free drop-off privileges at any major airport, our people almost always return their cars to the point of origin.

Since Atlas offers better rates for the cars we prefer to use and better terms with regard to notice on reservations, that company will provide us with more convenient and cost-effective service. If we contract with Atlas, however, we will need to remind consultants to continue to make an effort to return their cars where they picked them up. I certainly don't see this as a major drawback. Let's contract with Atlas for this fiscal year.

---

**Analysis**

Pete's memo more closely resembles the first of the two organizational patterns described earlier: his criteria constitute its architectural framework. But he does shape that pattern to his needs; for instance, he firmly states his conclusions in the opening paragraph.

---

Effective comparisons almost always require careful sorting and weeding out of the available data. It's easy to lose your reader's interest and understanding in a maze of detail; more often than not, genuinely persuasive comparisons are built upon the mounds of debris eliminated from preliminary drafts. For instance, Pete learned that Atlas recently initiated a "Shuttle Express" service enabling commuters between major cities to pick up the rental agreement at the point of departure before their flights. But since the agreement had to be secured at one end of the flight or the other, Pete decided this point was not relevant, and in his final draft he opted not to mention it.

One more aspect of Pete's memo merits attention. Note that he frequently uses certain linking words in communicating his observations. Words such as *although, but, whereas, both*, and *however* signal that alternatives are being examined. The following are some additional examples of this kind of usage:

- *Although* Company X offers a discount, Company Y has lower list prices.
- We certainly need more clerical support, *but* our office space is severely limited.
- *Whereas* Plan A could be put into effect immediately, Plan B would require a six-month waiting period.

- *Both* applicants are qualified for the job; *however*, the first has a more impressive educational background.

The point is not that you should try to use these particular words but that you recognize that both your word choice and your sentence structure help to indicate that you are evaluating alternatives.

To summarize, in making a comparison in order to choose between alternatives, you should take the following steps:

- Establish criteria that provide a clear basis for the comparison.
- Set priorities.
- Decide on an appropriate organizational pattern.
- Evaluate the relevant data in light of the criteria you have established.

## Analysis

When business people take something apart, whether it is an idea or an object, they generally have a specific objective. For example, you might be asked to look at the internal organization of your department and analyze it on the basis of the salary and wage structure; alternatively, you might be requested to analyze it according to the report system, that is, how many employees report to each manager or supervisor.

Analysis and classification are really two sides of the same coin. When you analyze an object or idea, you partition or disassemble it according to a particular principle or basis. When you perform a classification, you assemble and relate objects or ideas that formerly were separate, grouping together those that are similar according to a specified basis. For instance, you might classify the employees in your department according to exempt (salaried) and nonexempt (hourly wages), according to their marital or educational status, or according to any number of other bases.

A market study is an example of an extremely important and complex kind of analysis and classification. In such a study, using whatever bases are relevant, you look at the number and kinds of competitors, customers, existing distributors, outlets, etc. Even fairly routine matters, however, can require careful analysis and classification, as in the following case:

**The Case**

Marcia Wheeler is Customer Service Supervisor for a mail-order sporting goods firm. Janette Smith, Vice President of Sales and Marketing, is concerned about the high volume of customer complaints received in the last quarter, and she has asked Marcia to analyze the situation and come up with some concrete recommendations. Marcia decides that the only way to tackle the problem is to classify all the written complaints received during the past quarter according to the nature of the customers' problems. She will then describe how to resolve each separate category of problems. Figure 5.8 is a copy of Marcia's memo to Janette.

Figure 5.8

TO:   Janette Smith                    DATE: Oct. 18, 198-
FROM: Marcia Wheeler
RE:   Complaint Analysis and Recommendations for Customer
      Service Improvements

During the period from July 1 to September 30, 198-, I have processed 143 written complaints. Below, I have classified these complaints by their general type and have followed each category with recommendations for procedural changes that should improve customer service.

Case 1: Late Deliveries (83 complaints). On our new order form, we state that shipments will arrive within three weeks of receipt of customer payment. We are receiving an unusual number of complaints about delayed deliveries. In 76 out of 83 cases, the delays were due to warehouse shortages. These stockouts could be replenished within two weeks from the date of the discovery of the shortage.

Recommendations:

o   Change the promised three-week delivery to a more realistic five weeks.
o   Consider overstocking on selected popular items, to be determined by further analysis of order data.

Case 2: Wrong Size, Color, Style, Model Number, etc. (27 complaints). We had 27 complaints that concerned delivery of merchandise that didn't conform to buyers' (alleged) specifications. However, 17 of these 27 customers had failed to fill in the necessary details regarding size, color, etc. The other 10 customers were sent items that really did not correspond to their specifications.

Recommendations:

o   Print a highly visible reminder on the order form stating that all details must be specified.
o   Design a simple form letter to be sent out by the Order Department when necessary order information is missing.
o   Institute a double-check system in the Order Department to ensure that only correct merchandise is shipped.

Case 3: Inferior Quality (23 complaints). Of these 23 complaints, 20 concerned one of these two items:

o   Item No. 88-230NT, a four-person nylon tent manufactured by Acme

o   Item No. 606-724LS, a polyester-filled sleeping bag manufac-
    tured by Mountaineers, Inc.

    Recommendation:

o   Discontinue both items, and replace them with similar mer-
    chandise of better quality.

    Case 4: Damaged Item (10 complaints). Since it was impossible
    to ascertain whether these items were damaged before, during, or
    after shipping, no particular problem could be isolated. (All dam-
    aged items were quickly replaced.)

    Recommendation:

o   The number of complaints about damage was relatively small,
    and damaged items were efficiently and courteously replaced. I
    therefore recommend that we maintain our current procedures
    for handling such cases.

**Analysis**

Many business problems can be handled effectively by identifying the most
relevant data and then sorting that body of data into meaningful categories. For Marcia, the complaint letters from the last quarter contained a
wealth of information, but that information became useful only when she
discovered relationships between specific items and classified them accordingly.

Marcia's method in essence reflects the following general process for
analyzing and classifying:

- Identify an appropriate body of data for analysis.
- For a simple analysis, decide on a principle or basis for breaking the
  data into components.
- If classification is called for, establish categories that will reflect the re-
  lationships within groups of components.
- Classify the data accordingly.
- For problem solving, treat each category as a separate unit. (See the
  later section entitled "Problem/Solution.")

# Cause/Effect

**The Case**

Suppose that you are a brand-new employee trying to do well at your first
job. In fact, you have been trying so hard that you have overloaded your
schedule and taken on more responsibilities than you can possibly handle
effectively. Your boss, Greg Martin, is a manufacturers' representative

whose primary product lines are personal computers and related software. Greg, a great guy, selected you from a large number of applicants. After watching your performance during your first three months, he's a bit worried, and he therefore decides that he wants to have a conference with you. As a preamble to your meeting, he writes you the memo shown in Figure 5.9.

Figure 5.9

TO: [Brand-New Employee]     DATE: June 22, 198-
FROM: Greg Martin
RE: Performance Assessment

    Since you joined our staff as sales coordinator three months ago, we have all been impressed by your willingness and enthusiasm. Unfortunately, despite your strong skills and excellent attitude, your record of achievement has lately been somewhat disappointing.

    I am virtually certain that the overriding reason for your difficulties is your failure to allocate your time effectively. Although I don't want to dampen your urge to pitch in and help wherever you spot the need, I believe your not setting priorities is causing you serious problems. A number of your projects were completed after the deadlines you and I established, and, as you know, I found some serious omissions in your monthly report on retail vendors in the New England area. Perhaps most disturbing of all is that in the past few weeks I have noticed that you appear to be tense and a little demoralized.

    As a new employee who really is doing a good job of learning the ropes, you should not be disheartened about receiving this memo. To some degree, I blame myself for not giving you more specific help in deciding how to allocate your time. I would like to make amends by working with you now on precisely that. We'll put our heads together tomorrow and decide where your skills and time can be most effectively used, and then we'll set up feasible timetables to get those specific things done. Call me when you have read this, and we'll schedule a two-hour meeting.

**Analysis**

Although Greg Martin opens his memo with a tactful sentence to cushion his bad news (see Chapter 8), he quickly gets to his main point—his observation that your performance has not been meeting expectations. The remainder of his memo deals first with the effects and then with the cause of this lapse. To explain his concern, he examines the effects first. Had the effects been *predicted* rather than real, he might have chosen to deal with their cause first, stating that *if* you don't learn to budget your time (cause), the *results* are likely to be missed deadlines and poorly prepared projects (effects).

Note how Greg's memo carefully orders the effects to build to a climax. Through unmistakable verbal signals ("serious omissions," "most disturbing of all"), Greg indicates the mounting importance of each effect. If the circumstances had been somewhat different, he might have selected an alternative principle for his order. For instance, if he felt all of the effects were equally important, he might have decided to list them chronologically, according to when they occurred. Or, once again, if he were predicting rather than stating what already happened, he might have listed the effects from most likely to least likely (or, alternatively, from least likely to most likely).

In working with a cause/effect relationship, your objective may resemble Greg Martin's: to state the likely cause of one or more effects. On the other hand, you may need to predict the likely consequences of an action or event. In the latter case, the event or action may have taken place already or it may be under consideration. To mention just a few such predictions that business people are called upon to make, explain, and defend, we can cite the following: predicting the outcome of a particular investment, of dropping a product line, of promoting an employee, of changing a deadline, or of lowering a price.

To review, the best way to deal with the exceedingly common structural pattern of cause and effect is as follows:

- Decide whether your primary observation is a cause or an effect.
- If you are dealing with a cause, list the likely effects in order of an assigned priority (importance, likelihood, chronology).
- Similarly, if you are dealing with an effect, assign priorities to the likely causes.

## Problem/Solution

In a general sense, the large majority of business memos represent solutions to problems. Certainly, our examples of memos explaining the office plan and its implementation represent solutions to problems, and so do the decision about the best car-leasing plan, Marcia Wheeler's analysis of how to cut down the number of customer complaints, and Greg Martin's memo setting up a meeting to help his new employee to allocate time more effectively. In some cases the primary aim of a piece of writing is to explain a problem in some detail and to offer support for a particular solution. The main objective then is to present evidence that this solution will work well and that it is the best answer to the problem. A good example of such a case is the following:

**The Case**

Carlos Alvarez is the travel director for Morgan Standard, a large manufacturer of consumer household products whose home offices are in Dallas,

Texas. For the last five years, the company has offered its executives the convenience of a company-run airline on which to make the many trips they must take to branch offices in Chicago, Minneapolis, and Detroit. In the past two fiscal quarters, Morgan Standard's sales have fallen off rather badly, and the company is planning a widespread cost-cutting program, which will mean eliminating this much-appreciated luxury. Carlos has however, come up with what he believes is an innovative and appropriate way to retain the service. He writes the memo shown in Figure 5.10 to Walter Forma, Senior Vice President of Personnel.

---

Figure 5.10

TO:   Walter Forma                    DATE:  October 10, 198-
FROM: Carlos Alvarez
RE:   Company Airline

Although it is clear to us all that Morgan Standard's airline is a great convenience to our company executives, no one disputes that it is also a great expense. Therefore, in line with the current cost-cutting program, we have had to agree to discontinue the service. I believe, however, that the airline can be saved and can even become a profitable venture for Morgan Standard.

In the current deregulated transportation environment, company carriers can be used for profit-making ventures. As you know, we recently have been leasing space on our fleet of trucks to other shippers in the Midwest. I propose that we also offer available space on our planes to executives from other companies who seek flights between Dallas and the three major cities in which our branch offices are located. I suggest that we continue to offer the same conveniences that are now available on our flights— plenty of space, good food, and excellent service—and that we charge a competitive rate. We could reserve four seats per flight for our own use and assign all others according to normally accepted reservation procedures, with no exceptions made for our own personnel.

Walter, I believe my plan will work because, as we all know, there is a great demand for comfortable and reliable air service—especially between Dallas and Detroit. We will certainly fill enough seats to cover our expenses. Furthermore, as the attached cost estimates indicate, if we consistently fill our planes and add two more flights to Detroit per day, we should come out far ahead.

I would like to contact the 20 major corporations who are obvious candidates to use this service and ask if they would commit themselves to recommending it to their people. I have attached a draft of a letter that I could send as part of a preliminary inquiry. I would, of course, follow up by phone.

I look forward to hearing your response to my idea.

---

**Analysis**

The pattern for dealing with a problem/solution relationship is at first glance simple and straightforward. But frequently, showing why your solution is sound or proving that it is the best of all options will require you to use one or more of the previously described patterns of relationship. You may want to compare your solution to those suggested by other people, or your solution may entail describing a complicated process. If you look closely at Carlos Alvarez's memo, you can discern that he presents his solution in a cause/effect pattern: if space on the company airline is sold, the effect will be sufficient revenue to continue the service and perhaps to make it a profit-making operation.

The following suggested steps for writing about a problem and solution should, therefore, not blind you to the real complexity of the task. In writing a problem/solution memo, you should proceed as follows:

- State the problem, and provide any needed background information.
- Explain your solution.
- Show why the solution is sound.
- If appropriate, show why it is the best solution of all the possibilities.

The pattens of relationship that we have examined in this chapter are modes of organizing information into unified segments and meaningful sequences. These patterns are natural and familiar to writers and readers, and they therefore provide clear pathways for communication.

In the next chapter, we will consider some practical techniques for sorting, classifying, and arranging abundant or complex information into a coherent and persuasive written presentation.

## ■ Summary

When a piece of writing has a clear and discernible structure, the reader is drawn—perhaps even compelled—to follow its logic.

Effective organization depends upon the writer's skill in perceiving and depicting patterns of relationship. Ideas need to be organized into unified wholes that are coherently linked to one another.

This chapter has discussed the six patterns most useful in business writing: space, time, comparison, analysis, cause/effect, and problem/solution. Several of these patterns may be combined in a business document of any complexity.

## ■ Discussion Problems

**5.1** Study the following groups of words, and try to discover a meaningful pattern or relationship that would organize each one into unified sub-groups.

- skill, crime, happiness, sin, knowledge, rule, achievement, love, order, temptation, power, poverty
- active, mandatory, comprehensive, strict, naive, sedentary, obvious, elective, suspicious, obscure, partial, loose
- wide, eventual, periodic, eastern, farther, prehistoric, lower, perpendicular, antiquated, previous, frequent, high

**5.2** The order of the sentences in the following paragraph has been scrambled. Study the relationships between the sentences, and reconstruct the sequence of the original paragraph. Be prepared to supply reasons to support your sentence order.

(1) As a matter of fact, four different principles are involved here: sex, type of vehicle, quality of driving, and state of sobriety. (2) If one of your classes is determined by color, all the other classes at this level must also be determined by color. (3) Automobiles may be classified according to age, manufacturer, color, maximum speed, horsepower output, number of cylinders in the engine, and so on—but only according to one of these considerations at a time. (4) A member of any one of these classes might also at the same time be a member of the other three. (5) As a result, the classes overlap, and the classification is therefore meaningless. (6) An attempt to classify motor vehicle drivers into women drivers, truck drivers, good drivers, and drunken drivers is obviously illogical because the principle of classification is not consistent.

**5.3** Describe your typical weekday in detail, first from a spatial perspective and then from a chronological point of view. Make sure each narrative is unified and coherent from beginning to end.

**5.4** The student body of a college or university might be classified in many different ways. For instance, the registrar, the financial aid office, the student health center, the chaplain, the security force, and the athletic department all might have reason to perform an analysis. Determine the basis that each of the preceding entities might use for analyzing a student body, and explain why or how each might use such a classification system. Mention at least three other ways to analyze a student body, and explain who would find each of these analyses useful and why.

**5.5** To show how often we all rely on patterns or categories when we are describing or explaining, ask an unsuspecting friend to describe the last person he or she dated. Can you detect any implied or actual comparisons or classifications in your friend's description?

**5.6** Have you ever been accused of trying to "compare apples to oranges"? Try to think of a typical business situation that might tempt an inexperienced analyst to compare or contrast data that are generically different. Why is it tempting to make such an effort? Can you think of an example of the use of this illogical (sometimes unscrupulous) technique in advertising?

**5.7** Suggest a pattern—spatial, temporal, comparative, analytic, or causal—that will organize each of the following kinds of information into an effective memo. Don't hesitate to combine two or more patterns.

- Statistical data covering college enrollment figures over a two-year period, including breakdown of student body by sex, race, rank in class, home state, and major field of study.

- Results of a customer satisfaction survey commissioned by an encyclopedia publisher, followed by recommendations for revisions of the next edition.
- Outline of possible reasons for the recent decrease in your company's automobile sales in three major cities.
- Discussion of factors contributing to an unusually high employee turnover in the sales division of a major computer manufacturer.
- Description of your relevant background and qualifications for a job described in a recent advertisement.
- Reassessment of your company's standard procedure for ordering office supplies.
- Review of the three lowest bids for construction of the company's new cafeteria, with your recommendation for a decision.

**5.8**  Assume that each of the following business situations can be interpreted as either cause or effect. Suggest two underlying causes for each effect and two effects for each cause.

- The deadline for the first draft of the annual report has been changed from July 26 to August 30.
- As of July 1, we will discontinue production of our A62 toaster oven.
- For the third straight quarter, insurance salesman Jack Burns has failed to meet his recommended minimum sales quota.
- Starting Monday, June 21, all requests for stationery supplies must be submitted in writing to Carol Jensen using the form attached; informal verbal requests can no longer be processed.
- The employee cafeteria has been enlarged and divided into two separate sections: one for secretarial and support staff, and one for managers, clients, and senior-level administrators.

**5.9**  Use your imagination to generate two or three alternative solutions to each of the following business problems, and then decide which of your solutions would probably be most effective. Defend your choice by using one or more of the thought patterns described in this chapter.

- Your secretary complains that she's overworked, specifically that she has too many assignments. She's a great secretary; you don't want to lose her, but your funds are limited and so is your office space.
- Your firm's latest model of pocket camera simply isn't selling. Competition is enormous, and you're afraid that, contrary to the findings of your market research department, the market for this particular type of camera might just be flooded this year.
- You run a small printing company that produces quality work for slightly above-average prices. Although business has been brisk for the past three years, you now find that nine of the last ten bids you submitted have been turned down because they were too high.

# ■ Writing Tasks

**5.1**  Write out careful descriptions of the geometric patterns shown in the box below emphasizing spatial relationships. Hand your descriptions to a friend, and see if he or she can reproduce the patterns correctly just from reading your descriptions.

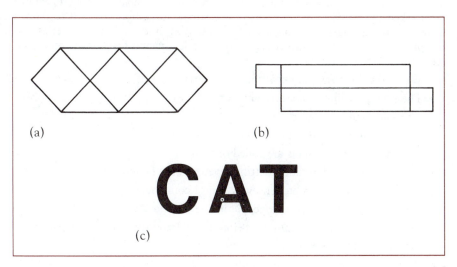

(a)        (b)

**CAT**

(c)

**5.2**  Deborah Patton, an office manager for a law firm, has accepted a position at another company and will be vacating her office to make room for her successor. Unfortunately, the new office manager will not arrive until several weeks after Deborah has left. Write a detailed memo from Deborah describing where needed articles are kept in her office as well as in the surrounding office complex.

**5.3**  Describe in detail the process followed in carrying out a domestic task, such as washing a car, following a particular recipe, starting a charcoal fire, or cleaning out a drawer. Then underline every word or phrase that indicates a chronological relationship between one step and the next.

**5.4**  Your department's budget has been cut considerably for the new fiscal year. Consequently, one of the two department secretaries must be let go. Draft a memo to your boss comparing and evaluating the performance of the two secretaries. You should discuss most of the following qualifications: initiative, punctuality, knowledge of spelling and grammar, typing speed, telephone skills, interpersonal skills, and business knowledge. Give special thought to how you should organize the criteria for your comparison.

**5.5**  In a recent letter Ms. Sally Rhodes, Office Manager, Best Products, Inc., requested further information about your company's two available copying machines. Write a response, explaining both the similarities and the differences between the models. Finally, suggest which model would be most appropriate for Ms. Rhodes's purposes as outlined in her letter.

**5.6**  Write a formal memo analyzing either one department of a company or a small entrepreneurial business on the basis of salary structure. Include at least five employees, listing the salary of each, along with his or her job description (invent the necessary facts and figures). Your memo should recommend one or more salary increases based on your analysis.

**5.7**  As the new assistant manager of a large discount department store, you've been asked to evaluate the contents of the store's suggestion box and to draft a memo to the manager outlining your findings. Classify the following queries and complaints into several categories, and then draft a memo that draws some concrete conclusions.

- Why isn't the cosmetic department self-service?
- The checkout lines are unbearably long.
- The sale items run out too soon.
- I got the wrong change three times.
- Too many clothing items are soiled or torn.
- The cashiers stand around chatting, even at busy periods.
- The automatic door is broken every time I come here.
- There are never enough salespeople in the camera section.
- I walked around for ten minutes before I could find the hardware department.
- Where are the rest rooms?
- Why aren't baby carriages allowed?
- There's not enough space between the aisles to move my shopping cart.
- The check-cashing system is too complicated.
- It's stifling in here!
- There are never enough salespeople on Sundays.
- Too many items don't have price tags.
- There's always a crowd of tough kids hanging around the refreshment stand.
- Why can't we listen to a record before buying it?
- The whole place is depressing.
- I couldn't find one helpful salesperson.
- All the sizes are mixed up in the kids' clothing department.
- Why is the sale stuff always sold out?
- The floors are filthy!
- I can't tell the salespeople from the shoppers.
- Many items have two different prices attached.
- I can't find the specials.
- Why are there so many damaged housewares?
- The salespeople fool around among themselves instead of being helpful.
- Why don't you have a Lost and Found?
- I stood for 15 minutes at checkout #8!

**5.8**  Choose one of the business situations described in Discussion Problem 5.8, and draft a brief memo explaining the implied cause/effect relationship in some detail. (You decide whether the given situation is a cause or an effect.) The heart of this memo should be your attempt to convince your reader of the necessity of the cause/effect relationship.

**5.9**  Write letters of apology to the dissatisfied customers who submitted the following complaints. In each case explain the cause behind the unsatisfactory goods or services.

- Your repairman arrived on two separate occasions without the replacement part I had specified beforehand by phone. Now he tells me that the digital clock on my two-year-old stove cannot be fixed at all!

- I ordered your four-person nylon tent, no. TX472, and found that the zipper door won't close completely, the seam around the door leaks even in a light rain, and there are two small holes in the roof. This is definitely inferior merchandise.

- While a patient in Room 227 of your hospital, I repeatedly called for assistance during the night of March 18 and was completely ignored. Fortunately, my case was not critical, but I did spend an extremely uncomfortable night, with no sleep whatsoever. It was an awful experience.

**5.10**  Stella Joseph, Assistant Production Manager for her company's Laserman robot toy, has been told by her boss that unless each Laserman can be produced for $.85 less than the current production cost of $4.25, the product will have to be discontinued. Stella studies the cost of each step of the production process and becomes convinced that a combination of substituting cheaper materials and making a minor simplification in Laserman's body parts will solve the problem. She realizes, however, that her boss would prefer to drop the product, so she will have to be persuasive. Draft Stella's memo to her boss.

# PREWRITING: THE PROCESS OF CREATING STRUCTURE

# 6

*I* n most cases a writer's thoughts and insights do not arrive in neatly organized bundles; rather, they come forth sporadically and piecemeal. Moreover, each new idea calls out others in its wake—some to be quickly discarded, others to lie dormant but expectant among the waiting pile of data. When a project requires research, facts and figures and technical information also need sifting and sorting. Before long, objectives, constraints, impressions, opinions, facts, and figures begin to seem like so many pieces of a jigsaw puzzle dumped helter-skelter onto a table.

If you have ever worked on a large, intricate jigsaw puzzle, you probably recollect that you began by looking for pieces that seemed to share a common theme, perhaps of color or line. You may also recall that the task was much easier if you had a fairly good idea of what the finished picture was to look like. Furthermore, once the framework was completed, the rest of the work probably proceeded with much greater speed.

Let's extend this puzzle analogy a bit further. An acquaintance who is a camera buff often begins teaching a management workshop on structure by plopping a dismantled camera onto a table and asking the participants to put the "object" back together. As soon as people determine that the object is a camera and locate the framework, they begin to feel more confident about their ability to reassemble it. They quickly discover other familiar parts and begin to make piles of the smaller pieces that they believe will ultimately go together.

Similarly, the main purpose of a memo or a report often supplies the writer with a preliminary framework for the ideas the document will contain. If you know what you want a document to accomplish, you can begin to chart the terrain you will need to cover and to mark off boundaries beyond which you should not stray. Next, as you consider the various elements you plan to include, you will begin to perceive their relationships to the whole and to one another.

## ■ Sorting and Ordering Ideas

When doing a jigsaw puzzle whose picture you have seen or when looking at the parts of a familiar object, you can easily call to mind the finished product. But the final shape of a complex piece of writing is usually much harder to envision. The image of the finished document is annoyingly elusive; it teases you with the sense that you almost have it and then fades rapidly. Your only recourse is a good, workable *prewriting* technique. Such a technique helps you to make your ideas tangible and accessible so that you can give them a place in the total design. It helps you to identify irrelevant information that should be discarded and to recognize where artful transitions will be needed. Prewriting can also help you to envision paragraphs and subsections, and even to detect where subheads, italics, bullets, or enumeration will effectively accentuate your logic.

Because prewriting is such an important and time-consuming part of the writing process, many experts suggest that it should occupy close to 25 percent of the time allocated to a writing project. For most situations, prewriting begins when you have established your purpose and have on hand all the data you expect to include. If done effectively, prewriting will help you get started and will save you a great deal of agonizing later on. It will also prevent you from unwittingly writing yourself into a corner, like the painter who meticulously varnished a floor, stroke after immaculate stroke, with no idea where he was headed.

Below are seven suggested prewriting techniques. The object is not for you to mimic them laboriously. You may already know how to use one or more of these methods, or you may have developed a good method of your own. Don't abandon a technique that works well, but do experiment. See if any of these seven methods suggests a way to improve the process that you currently use; test them in different situations. Time constraints or the complexity of a writing task can make one method preferable to another. Of course, if you do not use *any* prewriting method, you should try each of these to see which one suits you best for most occasions and which ones work well under special circumstances.

## Method 1: On the Analyst's Couch

If you are at all familiar with modern psychotherapy, you know that psychoanalysis relies heavily on free association. The patient relaxes on the analyst's couch and lets his or her mind freely wander, with each new thought evoking the next. Although the doctor will sometimes focus the patient's thoughts on a particular topic, more frequently he or she will neither interrupt nor interpret the stream of ideas until the end of the session. The first and perhaps most rigorous of the prewriting methods described here resembles this technique.

The method begins after you have carefully researched your topic and reviewed all the relevant data. You know who you are and what you want the document to accomplish. But the data in front of you are awash in detail, and the thought of organizing this pile of facts and figures leaves your mind paralyzed. Through free association and interpretation, you can begin to turn all this information into an orderly piece of writing.

To use this method, you perform the following six steps:

1. State your *position* (or the problem) as a complete sentence.

2. Using free association, list your ideas in the order in which they occur to you.
3. Identify your main ideas.
4. Identify the supporting data for each main idea.
5. Order your main ideas.
6. Order your supporting data.

These steps are more completely described below with the aid of a case example.

**State Your Position.** Believing that you have spotted an inequity, you plan to propose that your company institute paid paternity leave for new fathers. You have done some intensive research, and you are ready to assert that this policy should be incorporated into the company's standard benefits package. Your position statement might read like this:

> Acme should grant paid paternity leave to all new fathers.

Like the one above, a position statement must be expressed as a complete sentence. Moreover, it must not be a "This paper is *about* . . ." kind of sentence. You should not, for instance, write "This proposal is about paid paternity leave for new fathers." Nor should you allow yourself to write a fragment, such as "Paternity leave for new fathers." "About" sentences and fragments are static; they do not push your thoughts forward.

A position statement shows you where you stand and also supplies the impetus for launching your argument. It is a working tool. Although it represents your main conclusion, it often will not appear in your finished document—at least not in its original form. Its purpose is to force you to say to yourself, "This is what I believe," and to define your reasons for that belief. If at any time you begin to feel that the statement contradicts your opinion or doesn't grow naturally from the data, you have a clear signal that something is very wrong. You must either revise the statement or eliminate the conflicting points from your list.

Rereading your position statement, you should feel ready and perhaps eager to provide a number of follow-on "because" clauses, such as "*because* such leaves would improve morale among our employees" or "*because* we must offer new fathers the same benefits as new mothers" or "*because* our three major competitors all have begun to offer this benefit to their employees."

Even when your intention is to describe a problem rather than to propose a solution, your statement should be expressed as a sentence. If your aim is to be objective rather than persuasive, your problem statement should read something like this: "Personnel has recently received a number of requests from new fathers for paid paternity leave." In being objective, you will then try to think of as many "*becauses*" in favor of paternity leave as against it.

**List Your Ideas.** Having defined in writing either your position or the problem, you are ready to relax. Grab a pencil and a sheet of paper, find yourself a quiet, comfortable spot, and prepare to free-associate. You are now "on the analyst's couch." Don't worry about the order in which your ideas arrive or how they relate to one another; don't try to decide which points are major or minor. Just keep glancing back at your position or problem statement whenever you feel stuck, and write down everything that comes to you.

You don't need to write your thoughts down in complete sentences, but do write something for each one. It's a fatal mistake at this stage to think that you can remember your ideas without recording them. All too often a good idea surfaces, drifts away, and then reappears much later when you have nearly completed your final draft and have neither the time nor the inclination to revise in order to insert it where it belongs. Even tape-recording your ideas doesn't work as well as writing them down. Speaking tends to lessen your concentration; furthermore, you will need a written list for the next step of this method.

It is a good policy however, to limit the number of ideas you write down. Too many points will ultimately make the task of organizing more difficult. If you know the approximate length of the final document, you can quickly determine the number of ideas to write: your list should include from five to ten ideas for each double-spaced typed page.

Assuming you intend the paternity leave proposal to be two or three typed pages, your list of ideas might look something like this:

1. Another request for a paternity leave today.
2. Attitudes are changing.
3. Many two-career families.
4. Fatherhood: a hot topic today.
5. Professor Isherwood's article in *The Sun Times*.
6. Could get us some pretty good publicity.
7. Legal department says no real danger of law suits yet.
8. SPAR, Denton, Ltd., and Canton Chemical all offer paternity leave now.
9. How long? Who qualifies? Cost?
10. Major turnover problem this year.
11. Requests for day-care facilities also multiplying.
12. Baby boomers have come of age.
13. Reversal in declining birth rate.
14. Older, better-educated parents.
15. Charlie Corelli said he'd quit if he didn't get his leave next month.
16. Didn't have such problems when the boss's kids were born.
17. Fairness a major issue.
18. My own feelings may count here, too.
19. Dual-care options could attract high-grade employees.

**Identify Main Ideas and Identify Supporting Data.** Once you have your list in hand, it is time to head back to your desk. While brainstorming for ideas, it is to your advantage to allow thoughts to wander. Afterwards, you must stare hard at your list and force yourself to think rigorously about what you have written and how it relates to your position or problem statement. Furthermore, you must decide how the ideas relate to one another.

Looking closely at the list, you first observe that a number of items represent problems that the firm is currently having, probably because it lacks a paternity leave program. You then note that item 2 is in itself one of your main reasons for proposing the program. Next, you realize that, in one way or another, items 6, 8, and 19 suggest some specific benefits the program could offer. Finally, you take into account that several items point to the need for careful planning before instituting such a program. Again using complete sentences, you record the main ideas you have defined:

1. Evidence suggests that this issue is causing problems within the company.
2. Attitudes are changing.
3. There are obvious advantages in instituting this program.
4. The details of the program must be carefully planned.

Going back to your list, you can now extract the supporting data related to each of these major ideas. You don't need to record these data in sentence form, but you should try to cluster those points that seem to relate to one another. When you begin to write, such clusters will become subsections or paragraphs. For example, your grouping of ideas might look something like Figure 6.1.

---

1. Evidence suggests that this issue is causing problems within the company.
   —Major turnover problem this year
   —Charlie Corelli's case

   —Legal problems down the road? Isherwood's article describes law suit in Michigan
   —Fairness an issue, too
2. Attitudes are changing.
   —Proliferating requests from baby boomers
   —Birth rate now increasing again

   —Older, better-educated parents aware of importance of fathering
   —Fatherhood a hot topic today

**Figure 6.1**
A list that identifies main ideas and supporting data.

3. There are obvious advantages in instituting this program.
   —Competitors have such programs
   —Options for two career families could attract superior employees
4. The details of the program must be carefully planned.
   —Cost factors
   —Timing
   —Eligibility

   —Ad hoc committee needed

**Order Main Ideas and Order Supporting Data.** You have identified your main ideas and selected the data to support each of them. But you have not thought about the *order* of your ideas. Which should come first? Why?

As always, your strategy depends to a large extent on your appraisal of your audience. You know that your boss, who raised his family in a very different world, is likely to be skeptical about this proposal. To launch into this subject with a discussion of current problems and the issue of fairness seems rather aggressive—even tactless. You decide it would be better to lay some groundwork by opening with a discussion of why paternity leave has become an important issue. Accordingly, you renumber your list to indicate the new order. When you are satisfied that the major sections are ordered correctly, you look closely at the supporting points for each to see if they, too, are ordered properly. You reorder these items whenever it seems necessary. Your original list has become a blueprint for your first draft (see Figure 6.2). After subsequent drafts, the structure of the proposal may not be absolutely identical to this plan; but if you have done your prewriting work well, the final structure will resemble this blueprint in most respects.

**Figure 6.2**
A blueprint for a first draft, showing the ordering of main and supporting points.

1. Attitudes are changing.
   —Proliferating requests from baby boomers
   —Birth rate now increasing again

   —Fatherhood a hot topic today
   —Older, better-educated parents aware of importance of fathering
2. Evidence suggests that this issue is causing problems within the company.
   —Charlie Corelli's case
   —Major turnover problem this year

   —Legal problems down the road? Isherwood's article describes law suit in Michigan
   —Fairness an issue, too

3. There are obvious advantages in instituting this program.
   —Competitors have such programs
   —Options for two-career families could attract superior employees
4. The details of the program must be carefully planned.
   —Cost factors
   —Timing
   —Eligibility

   —Ad hoc committee needed

# Method 2: The Deck of Cards

The second prewriting method is very similar to the first. However, you record your ideas and data on index cards rather than in the form of a list. Cards allow you to sort and reorder your ideas quickly, without having to rework or rewrite a list, as called for in Method 1. On the other hand, the final list gives you a nice bird's-eye view of the entire structure, but your cards will show you the big picture only if you spread them out on an accommodating table, wall, or floor. (Some writers substitute "post-it" notes for index cards. These small slips of yellow paper adhere to most surfaces, come in several sizes, and are sold as notepads.)

You can buy index cards in a variety of sizes and colors; and by exercising your ingenuity, you can use both of these features to your advantage. For instance, once you have decided on your major categories, you can record those items on cards of a distinctive color or size. Another alternative is to use a distinguishing color for each group of subsections. Or you could go gung-ho for order and combine the two methods, indicating subsections by color and major headings by size.

No matter how much use you make of size and color, cards provide greater flexibility than lists. This flexibility can be a real benefit, but it can also tempt you to stray beyond the boundaries of your purpose or to lose sight of your position. Therefore, as when working with a list, you should discipline yourself at the outset.

Before you begin to sort your cards, force yourself to write a clear position or problem statement. A good technique is to print the statement boldly on a large card and tack it up where you can frequently glance at it while ordering your ideas. If at any time you begin to believe that the statement does not properly capture your main drift, stop whatever you are doing and think deeply. Where did you get off the track? Have you misjudged the implications of your data? You may have to reframe the statement, or you may decide that either your structure or subordinate points are inappropriate.

# Methods 3 and 4: Picture Gallery

Some writers need to be able to *see* exactly what their structure looks like. Lists hardly help these people at all; cards are better because they can be spread out in patterns, but even they do not provide the needed visual sustenance. Such people prefer a prewriting method that allows them to depict their thinking process in a diagram or schematic drawing. Two of the more popular graphic techniques are building pyramids and creating a wheel with spokes around the hub. Let's look closely at each method, first seeing how it might work for organizing a simple shopping list, and then noting how it might be used to depict the structure of the memo recommending paternity leaves.

**Building Pyramids.** * All of us have had the experience of hastily jotting down a list of things that we need to purchase, or perhaps picking through such a list that has grown in bits and pieces over a week's time. Before heading out to shop, your normal instinct is to try to order your list in some way to make the ordeal a bit easier. For instance, a typical shopping list might start out looking like this:

### SHOPPING LIST
Hammer
Milk
Laundry soap
Smoke detector
Dog food
Cereal
Apples
Ladder
Lettuce

To order the list, you have to do a bit of thinking. Where are you headed? What stops will you be making and in what order? You chart your route—hardware store, supermarket, farmstand—and then you classify the items under the appropriate categories:

### SHOPPING LIST
Hardware Store
Hammer
Ladder
Smoke detector

*The first use of the pyramid-building method is credited to writing consultant Barbara Minto, who uses it as the core theory in her training courses for major corporations.

Supermarket
    Laundry soap
    Dog food
    Cereal
    Milk
Farmstand
    Lettuce
    Apples

If you tend to be fairly meticulous, you may even arrange the sequence of individual items in each category in some special way, perhaps (given your limited funds) according to importance, or perhaps according to their location in the stores you will visit.

This shopping list is converted to a pyramid diagram in Figure 6.3. In examining this figure, observe that at the apex of each pyramid stands the general heading for that group. From top to bottom, we move from general to specific; under each of the headings, the items are sequenced from left to right. "Ladder" is *meant* to follow "Hammer," and "Smoke detector" to follow "Ladder." Finally, observe that all the items on any given level are equivalent in specificity. You do not, for example, find "Hardware store" and "Laundry soap" on the same level.

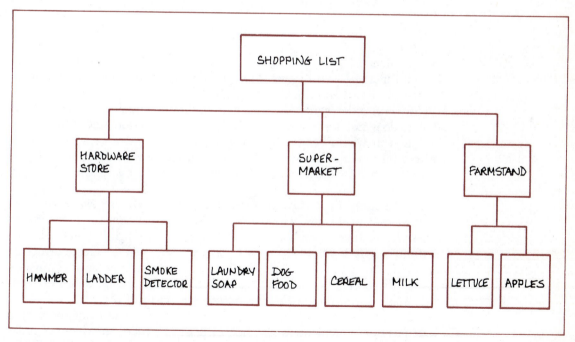

**Figure 6.3** Pyramid diagram of a shopping list.

If you think of the shopping list as a stand-in for the list of ideas you jotted down in preparing to write the paternity leave proposal, you will begin to see how this method can be used to sketch the structure of a memo or report. Your position statement will stand at the apex, the four main points of the proposal (see Figure 6.2) will occupy four boxes at the next lower level, and the subpoints will fill the lowest level of boxes. Of course, to handle a great deal of complicated data, you will have to develop a shorthand system for your entries. Figure 6.4 shows how the paternity leave proposal might be structured using pyramids.

The lower the level, the more specific becomes the item within each box. Each lower level partitions the box that forms the apex of its pyramid. In Figure 6.4, for example, "Costs," could be further divided into "Immediate costs" and "Future costs."

Once you get comfortable with displaying your ideas in pyramids, you will probably come up with a few innovations of your own. If you keep in mind that at any given level the items must be equivalent, you can embellish your diagram any way you choose. The object is to map out the progression of your ideas and their underlying logic, not to create pyramids. If at one level you find that simply partitioning the element doesn't satisfy you because you have uncovered two items that are cause and effect, draw an arrow from the cause box to the effect box. Or, if you are planning to compare two items, insert a double arrow like this:

Add numbers, letters, names, or notations where they will help you. The pyramid method works best for people who remember that the schematic diagram is a tool and not the main event!

As with index cards, the pyramid-building method's main weakness is that it does not force you to compose a clear position statement at the outset. You would be wise to do so anyway. Furthermore, if your ideas seem a bit muddled at *any* level, force yourself to write them out as complete sentences and then return to your abbreviated box entries.

**Free-wheeling (and Other Useful Art Forms).** Free-wheeling is a method that works best when you are trying to envision the organization of a short document, such as a memo or letter. Although it won't help you perform an in-depth analysis, it is an excellent way to create structure rapidly. Not surprisingly, free-wheeling diagrams and similar art forms are frequently spotted on placemats in executive dining rooms, and they regularly appear as intriguing doodles on office memo pads.

To achieve an authentic free-wheeling diagram, start out by placing your position statement in the hub of a wheel; then, in whatever order

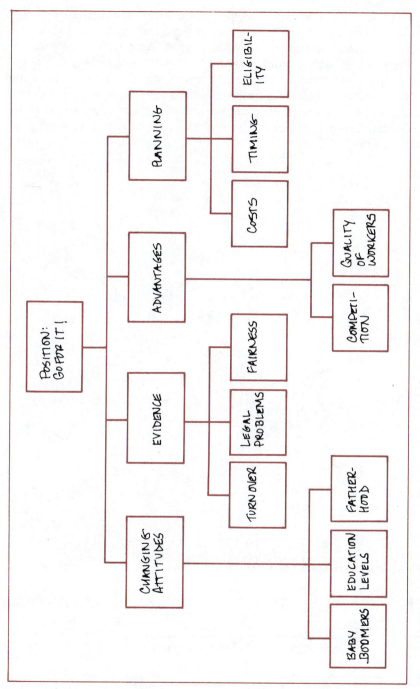

**Figure 6.4** Pyramid diagram of the structure of the paternity leave proposal.

they occur to you, quickly record your main ideas on the spokes of the wheel. Next, go back and number the spokes to suggest their correct sequence. Any major spoke can be made to grow mini-spokes that contain subordinate ideas, whose order should also be indicated. Figure 6.5 is an example of a free-wheeling schematic diagram, again using the paternity leave proposal. As you can see from the illustration, a free-wheeling drawing is apt to become extremely complex in a very short time, and it lacks the precision of a pyramid chart. Nevertheless, for rapid brainstorming, it works beautifully.

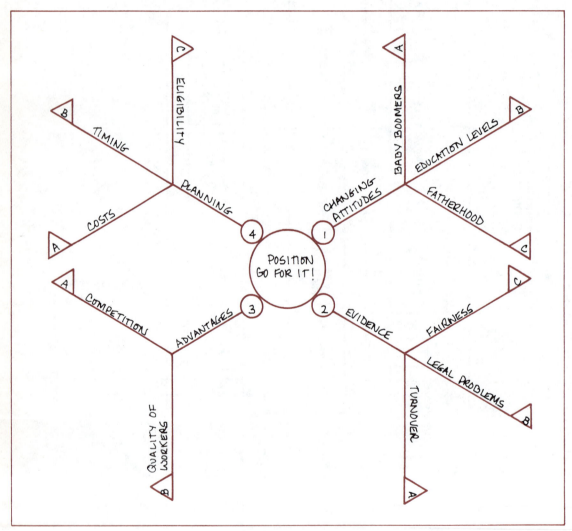

**Figure 6.5**   A free-wheeling diagram of the structure of the paternity leave proposal.

Whether you choose to draw authentic free-wheels or indulge your creativity with another form of artwork, your objective is to be able to step back and view the way your ideas are related to one another and to the whole document. We've seen business writers gleefully jot their ideas down inside small squares on a rectangular grid; we have also seen them work effectively with intriguing systems of interlocking circles. In all cases they were exploring how their ideas fit together and how their data could be used to support major topics or assertions.

A note of caution is necessary here: Don't be seduced by your own artistic ingenuity. A neat little diagram cannot substitute for careful analytical thinking. Although it will help to generate ideas and to identify any flaws in your classification system, a diagram can only be as logical and show as much insight as the thinking that produced it.

## Method 5: The Tried-and-True Outline

The old-fashioned, tried-and-true outline has been something for teachers and students to reckon with since our grandparents' schooldays, and presumably their parents and grandparents also had to learn to use it.

To many of us, the thought of outlining revives not-too-fond memories of an arid exercise performed in a junior-high-school classroom under the stern tutelage of an uncompromising and determined English teacher. Yet, even if learned under duress, the method worked well for some of us. We took comfort and even pleasure in seeing our thoughts neatly laid out in outline form—Roman numerals standing imposingly beside major premises, capital letters marking the next level, Arabic numbers signaling further subordination, and so on down the ranks. On the other hand, for a large number of students, outlining represented the deathblow to creativity. At the mere mention of an outline, their creative juices dried up. If you were of that persuasion, you very likely recollect many times when you wrote a composition and then furtively created an outline representing the *fait accompli.*

If you outline speedily and enjoy the discipline and order that an old-fashioned outline provides, don't force yourself to switch to a new-fangled technique. Why learn how to create elaborate pyramids when a traditional outline works well for you? However, you shouldn't totally reject the newer prewriting approaches. The kind of free association provided by the analyst's couch technique can be useful in getting ideas to surface. Similarly, if you find yourself in a situation where you need to sketch out your thoughts and order them swiftly, Free-wheeling diagrams can be an enormous help.

On the other hand, even if you have always disliked planning your structure with an outline, you might consider openly using the ploy we referred to above—outlining after the fact. To test your report's structural soundness, you might attempt to outline your *completed* first draft. Are there any missing elements? Are there places where topics overlap or lack unity? Should you try to incorporate some clear transitions or emphasize categories by adding subheads? Don't let the outline boss you around, but do think about any warning signals it provides.

Figure 6.6 is a traditional outline of the structure of the paternity leave proposal. It is interesting to compare it to Figure 6.2, the final list developed using the analyst's couch method. Although the outline is much more rigorous in its logical and careful partitioning of topics, the listing method has brought the writer much closer to the finished memo. Looking at Figure 6.6, one finds it difficult to imagine how the proposal will ultimately read; but Figure 6.2 is just a short step away from the finished document. Even tone and attitude are foreshadowed; we seem to hear the writer's voice.

**Figure 6.6**
A traditional outline for the structure of the paternity leave proposal.

PROPOSAL FOR PATERNITY LEAVE

  I. Changing Attitudes
    A. Growing Concern
      1. Baby boomers now of age
      2. Increasing birth rate
    B. Heightened Awareness
      1. Fatherhood a hot topic
      2. Older, better-educated parents

 II. Surfacing Problems
    A. Employee Turnover
      1. Statistics for 1986
      2. Charlie Corelli's situation
    B. Potential Legal Problems
      1. Law suits
      2. Fairness issues

III. Advantages for Company
    A. Competitors
    B. Superior Employees

IV. Planning Process
    A. Issues
      1. Costs
      2. Timing
      3. Eligibility
    B. First Steps
      1. Memo
      2. Ad hoc committee

As you might guess, the actual memo will never be as strictly logical as the traditional outline implies. But, whatever it lacks in strict logic, the list in Figure 6.2 maintains a strong insistence on the writer's defining the real content and flow of the finished piece. It forces the writer to *write*! Therefore, for most people, the analyst's couch method is less inhibiting to creativity and more stimulating to self-awareness.

## Method 6: Free-Writing

Professional writers know that when they are confronted by a stubbornly blank piece of paper, they can ultimately produce a decent piece of writing if they begin to record whatever comes to mind, writing rapidly and without pausing to organize or to edit. After writing freely for about 10 or 15 minutes, they then review the result, separate the wheat from the chaff, and begin to sort and refine their output. For business writers, this technique can serve two purposes: first, it can shake loose ideas and half-forgotten data lying dormant just beneath your level of awareness; second, it can provide unexpectedly clear or new insights into how to focus or order very complex or seemingly unrelated information.

The free-writing technique can be used effectively in combination with any of the other methods we have described above. Even the free association that produced the first list by the analyst's couch method might be preceded by a free-writing session. The advantage of doing so is that rapid nonstop writing achieves a very different result from the stop-and-go listing of ideas. Although listing helps to compile existing ideas and data in a form that makes them accessible and manageable, free-writing uncovers *new* ideas and previously unsuspected ways to synthesize them. Furthermore, free-writing forces writers to use their own voice and if they have a clear perception of the audience, to hear themselves "speaking" to that audience.

In a "dry season," when ideas are scarce, creative writers often exercise their imagination with a session of totally unfocused free-writing. They start out with no particular subject in mind and keep writing. For business writers a better technique is one that Peter Elbow, an innovative teacher of writing, has called *loop writing.*[*] This is almost-free-writing in which you focus at the outset, write freely for a period of time, and then bend back to select, organize, and revise parts of what you have written.

To use the loop writing method effectively, begin by thinking deeply about your purpose and audience. Don't write a word; just allow yourself to think and feel. If the audience is a large group of undefined people, try to imagine one or two of them. If your audience is someone whose image immediately stifles your ability to think creatively, picture yourself writing

[*]See especially *Writing with Power*, Oxford University Press, New York, 1981.

to someone else who is more open-minded and receptive. Or take a different approach—imagine that *you* are someone else (such as your boss) writing to that troublesome audience. Once you have primed your imagination, you should select an appropriate pathway for your thoughts and then begin to write steadily. If your words and ideas are ready to leap onto the page, let them come. Otherwise, one of the following techniques might help you get started.

Begin by telling your audience how you feel about the problem or issue at hand. You might describe what went wrong or project future consequences. If you don't have strong feelings about the issue, picture yourself talking to someone who does. Or if you are of a divided mind, attempt a one-person debate about the pros and cons (picture yourself actually speaking the words of each of the opposing proponents).

Alternatively, you might begin by describing a relevant incident or case. Begin with the magic word *once*, and launch into the story: "*Once*, three people walked into personnel on the same day and . . ." or "*Once*, we announced a new product too early and. . . ." If you can't imagine the details of a particular incident, try briefly narrating a series of incidents. Sometimes they come readily to mind if you force yourself to think about specific people: a face or a voice will appear to you in the context of a memorable occurrence.

There's no way to tell you precisely what to do with your pages of free-writing. To align your thoughts and integrate them into a coherent whole, you will probably need to use one of the five preceding prewriting methods. A quick free-wheeling sketch may be all that is needed, or you may want to create a detailed traditional outline. At the very least, your free-writing will bring to the surface some new ideas or give you a better sense of priorities. If you are an especially talented or fortunate free-writer, you may discover that you have actually developed large chunks of your first draft.

## Method 7: Terminal Fever— Prewriting with the Computer

Today, in many offices and in an increasing number of homes, business people are doing their composing at computer terminals. Using a word processor, writers type their text and immediately see it appear on a screen. In addition, a simple command quickly produces a good-quality typescript (or hard copy, as it is termed).

The computer has opened up not only a whole new world of opportunities for furthering communication with others but also an intriguing new pathway for communing with oneself. Writers addicted to composing at a terminal report that the word processor (or text editor, as it is sometimes called) maximizes all the benefits of free-writing, in regard to both structure and self-discovery. These writers explain that the ease of making corrections on work stored in the computer's memory allows them to suspend judgment about their immediate output. They work swiftly, capturing each idea at the moment of awareness, producing two or three versions of the same thought for later comparison, and ignoring any rough spots and simple textual errors. Knowing that passages can be corrected, refined, and moved to new positions without tedious recopying or cutting and pasting, these writers feel free to take risks. They can experiment with innovative structural arrangements and abandon them without penalty. Furthermore, they assert that the responsiveness of the computer gives them the sensation of composing for an alert, attentive, and totally nonjudgmental audience.

If you have the opportunity to learn to compose at a terminal, you would be wise to take a deep breath and plunge in. You may find that you take instinctively to writing at a terminal. (This is generally true *if* you are at least a semi-proficient typist and *if* mechanical objects do not on first encounter inevitably look like the enemy.) But even if you are not a natural, you may yet become a word-processing enthusiast. You will find that once you can type with some equanimity and once you have mastered the ins-and-outs of your software package, the improvement in the quality of your work becomes addictive. You magically see your thoughts transformed into words and—with a brief command—your words turned into neatly typed copy. You can edit in an instant; you may even have immediate access to a spelling check system or a thesaurus. You no longer need to pay for a typist (if you are a student) or wait for your turn to use the services of the typing pool. Perhaps most important of all, once you have gotten over your initial jitters and find yourself master of the genie that inhabits your word processor, you may for the first time feel entirely in *control* of the quality of your business documents. You are now in charge of the entire process from the inception of your first idea, through composing, editing, proofing, to the final appearance of the letter, memo, or report.

If you are already doing your writing at a terminal or are thinking seriously of taking this route, you should, however, exercise a bit of caution. The computer's potential benefits are fully realized only if you take the time to assess your own style of composing—particularly in reference to how you create structure. Although a marvel for expediting free-writing, the computer does not do away with the need to work from a plan. Futhermore, since normally only part of a page can be seen on a terminal screen, most writers find that to execute a coherent draft they *must* begin to work with hard copy fairly early in the process. There are clear advantages to being able to see the effects of varying the length or position of a sequence of paragraphs. Bullets and subheadings often need to be viewed in the context of a major subsection or of the whole report. These and many other subtle impressions are not available when small bits of the document are scanned on a terminal screen.

Chances are that computer terminals will soon become as commonplace in business offices as typewriters are today. At this time, rudimentary software is already available to help writers improve their structure, style, and spelling.* For business writers, learning to take full advantage of this dynamic new technology will require much more than an elementary understanding of computers and some new clerical skills. It will be up to all of us to learn to use this technology innovatively for very different kinds of tasks, and especially to adapt it to those subtle and often idiosyncratic needs and attitudes that writers possess in abundance.

As you have seen, prewriting techniques vary from those that help you to sort and structure large amounts of information to those that lead you to discover fresh ideas and approaches. Moreover, different tasks and situations generally call for different prewriting methods.

In the heat of inspiration of or under the pressure of time, you may feel tempted to dismiss the need for any kind of prewriting at all. But to speed ahead towards your final draft without prewriting is usually a perilous course, leading almost inevitably to the need to go back and fill in gaps or to reorganize a muddled, incoherent presentation.

## ■ Summary

Prewriting activities, which may occupy as much as one-fourth of the time devoted to a major writing project, help immensely in sorting your ideas and in building a sound, logical structure.

The seven prewriting techniques discussed in this chapter are included not as formulas to be strictly and laboriously followed but as devices to experiment with. What works best varies with individual writers and with different types of writing tasks.

## ■ Discussion Problems

**6.1**  Do you have a preferred method for organizing your written work? Why does it work well for you? Are there times when it does not work particularly well? Explain.

**6.2**  Read the following passage *only once*.

> The procedure is actually quite simple. First you arrange things into different groups. Of course, one pile may be sufficient, depending on how much there is to do. If you have to go somewhere else due to lack of facilities, that is the next step; otherwise you are pretty well set. It is important not to overdo things. That is, it is better to do too few things at

*See "Today, Tomorrow, and Always: Office Automation," page 599.

once than to do too many. In the short run this may not seem important, but complications can easily arise. A mistake can be expensive as well. At first the whole procedure will seem complicated. Soon, however, it will become just another fact of life. It is difficult to foresee any end to the necessity for this task in the immediate future, but then one never can tell.

After the procedure is completed, you arrange the materials into different groups again. Then they can be put into their appropriate places. Eventually, they will be used once more, and the whole cycle will then have to be repeated. However, this is a part of life.

Now close your book and try to restate the passage as accurately as possible.

Undoubtedly, you found that the passage was almost impossible to reconstruct. Now read the footnote on page 112. If you then reread the passage, you will find that it has become far more comprehensible and therefore easier to recollect. Discuss why this is so and its implications for business writing.*

**6.3** Have you ever tried to use a traditional outline to organize your thoughts for a term paper or examination? Judging from your own experience, what are some of the advantages and disadvantages of this method? What sorts of data are most resistant to the traditional outline? Why?

**6.4** Can you suggest another systematic method of prewriting (other than those presented in this chapter)? Explain your method, and demonstrate it to your fellow students. You may use the paternity leave case as the basis of your demonstration or create a different case and position statement.

**6.5** As an intern in the public relations department of your college, you've been assigned the project of generating more publicity for the school in local newspapers. Think about recent newsworthy developments on campus (the school paper and a central bulletin board could be good sources of ideas) and then discuss ways in which you might proceed to organize your thoughts for a report to the college's public relations director. You might also study a few local newspapers. What sort of college news might interest local residents? In what sections of the local papers would school news be most likely to be printed?

**6.6** Imagine that you are the assistant manager of the discount department store described in Writing Task 5.7 in Chapter 5. Your boss has asked you to write to the store's personnel director suggesting specific improvements in the quality of customer service provided by the salespeople.

First, study the contents of the suggestion box listed in that writing task. Next, write out a concise position statement that focuses on your view of the situation and the needed improvements. Use one of the prewriting techniques described in this chapter to structure your memo. You will be expected to reproduce your outline, lists, free-wheeling design, or pyramid diagram on the chalkboard for class discussion.

*John D. Bransford and Nancy S. McCarrell, "A Sketch of a Cognitive Approach to Comprehension." This exercise was suggested in *Problem-Solving Strategies for Writing*, Linda Flower, Harcourt Brace Jovanovich, Inc., New York, 1981.

**6.7**  Using the suggestion box data from Writing Task 5.7 again design a memo to the physical plant director at the discount store where you are assistant manager. This time, focus on those suggestions concerning the physical condition of the store. Once again, write out a position statement and then be prepared to sketch your structure on the chalkboard for class discussion. *Do not use the same prewriting technique that you used in Discussion Problem 6.6.*

# ■ Writing Tasks

**6.1**  Turn back to page 77 in Chapter 5, and study the two outlines comparing the advantages of two cars. Convert each of the outlines into a separate pyramid diagram. Briefly describe three other instances in which you would have to decide between two or more alternative purchases, and display your thought processes in pyramid diagrams.

**6.2**  Simone DuBarry is the office manager for the Boston office of Belle Jour Cosmetics, Inc., an international manufacturer of a line of fine cosmetics. One of her current problems concerns where to locate four new copying machines that the company just acquired. The office arrangement is such that each of five department managers has his or her own secretary located in a different area on the two floors that the company occupies in the John Hancock Tower. Each of the managers would like to see one of the machines placed in his or her own area. The secretaries for the most part feel that it would be best to put all four machines into one central copying room. Simone herself somewhat favors placing two machines on each floor. Even if she follows this plan, however, she has to decide whether the two machines on each floor should be located far apart or in a copying center. Before making her recommendation to Damon Cartier, the administrative vice president to whom she reports, Simone has decided to do some hard thinking about all the alternatives.

Imagine that you are Simone. Using the free-writing technique, brainstorm about the pros and cons of each arrangement. You may invent facts about the responsibilities of the managers and their secretaries or about the physical arrangement of the offices on the two floors.

When you have finished brainstorming, select a method of structuring your thoughts into a memo. You need not write the memo, but be prepared to show your instructor your free-writing, your position statement, and your structuring notes. You may use any structuring method—lists, cards, schematic diagram, or an outline.

**6.3**  Larry Davidson is the personnel director for Valley Medical Services, a full-service hospital with five outlying clinics, operating in Appalachia for the benefit of the people in this traditionally undeveloped area. The hospital operates a visiting nurse service staffed by six dedicated home health nurses. The Home Health Service is now facing a crisis because a replacement has not been found for its talented director, who resigned three months ago; furthermore, it is highly unlikely

*Note for Discussion Problem 6.2: The task described is the process of doing your laundry at a laundromat.

that a director will be found in the near future. Larry is faced with choosing from among three imperfect alternatives:

- Break up the Home Health Service, and disperse the six nurses among the five clinics.
- Let the group remain together, administered by the head of one of the clinics.
- Promote one of the six nurses to the position of director.

With these three alternatives in mind, Larry has done some focused free association and has come up with the following list of thoughts:

1. Nursing staff is already stretched too thin.
2. Group of six is very cohesive and cooperative.
3. Brett Nolan at Graypond runs a fine clinic.
4. Catfish Bay is the most centrally located clinic.
5. Nurse Michael Kennedy shows great potential for leadership.
6. Kennedy prefers hospital nursing.
7. Nolan has been with Valley Medical for four years.
8. Morale of nurses is highly important.
9. Smooth-running administration is a necessity.
10. Graypond is our busiest clinic.
11. Director's position is extremely demanding.
12. It takes time to develop a good visiting nurse.

Imagine that you are Larry Davidson. Decide what course of action you will recommend to the hospital board and write a position statement that reflects your decision. Using the analyst's couch method, create a second list showing the primary issues and the supporting data that will substantiate your position. Based on that list, write a memo to the board.

**6.4** Yet another problem has come to the desk of Larry Davidson, Valley Medical Services' Personnel Director. This issue concerns the hospital staff nurses and orderlies. Traditionally, the nightshift workers have received a half-hour of overtime pay because they work eight and a half hours without a dinner break; in contrast, the day-shift workers receive a half-hour lunch break. (The night people can't have a meal break because the hospital is extremely short-staffed at night.) At their last meeting, the hospital board members decided to discontinue the practice of paying the night staff overtime. Instead, the supervisor will cover while each person takes two 15-minute breaks at regulated intervals.

Larry recognizes that the proposed solution is not going to be well received. Nevertheless, it is his responsibility to write a persuasive memo to the night staff, getting them to swallow this bitter medicine with a degree of equanimity and good humor.

Using any method you choose, carefully structure Larry's memo, and then draft it to reflect that structure. (You may invent circumstances or data to strengthen your argument.) Your instructor will want to review both your prewriting notes and your memo.

**6.5** Helen Selenski, a business major at Georgia State University whose career focus is retailing, is spending the summer between her junior and senior years as an assistant to the floor manager of the toy department of the Atlanta branch of Marcus Leaman, a prestigious nationwide chain of department stores. During her junior year, Helen served as an intern at the store in November and December, working in the toy department during the hectic pre-Christmas season. Now Michael Hedstrom, the floor manager, has asked Helen to complete a special project for him. He wants Helen to research the problems encountered by the toy department during the Christmas season and to recommend procedures for correcting them in the coming year.

After searching her memory, conferring with other employees who worked in toys last Christmas, researching the records of Customer Relations, and interviewing Michael, Helen compiled the following list of complaints and problems to be addressed:

1. A stockout of Countdown, the season's hottest electronic game, occurred on November 30 and again on December 5, 12, and 24.

2. Fifteen complaints about the extremely warm temperature of the department were received on December 22.

3. Two complaints about the extremely cold temperature of the department were received on December 23.

4. Because they had not been instructed properly, salespeople were unable to demonstrate Robby-the-Robot or Laserman.

5. The balloons distributed by Santa were of poor quality: most deflated within ten minutes.

6. A stockout of Micro Minnie, the season's most wanted doll, occurred on November 18 and on December 3 and 10.

7. There were five complaints about discourteous salespeople.

8. There were twelve complaints that salespeople could not locate specific merchandise that had been advertised.

9. Three employees walked off the job on December 22 because they felt ill from the exceedingly warm temperature in the department.

10. Space Santa, the department's spectacular electronic display, created an overload on the store's electric circuits and was declared inoperable for the first three shopping days after Thanksgiving.

11. There were fifteen complaints from customers about having to wait too long to be served.

12. Adult electronic games and electronic games intended only for children were sold at the same counter. Ten adults complained about the adult games being located in the toy department. Fifteen parent complained that adults monopolized the childrens' games.

13. There was a stockout of these Micro Minnie wardrobe items: Minnie's Mink, Pinstripes for Minnie, and Minnie's Bikini. All were unavailable after November 30. Reorders did not arrive until January 5.

In the role of Helen, write a coherent, tightly structured memo to Michael Hedstrom, summarizing the problems that the department encountered last

Christmas and recommending appropriate steps for the coming season. When you have completed your memo, prepare a traditional outline that mirrors its structure. Submit the outline with your memo. If you have difficulty creating the outline, redraft the memo to correct the structural problems, and submit the outline and both drafts to your instructor.

**6.6**   Draft the memo to the discount store's personnel director that you outlined for Discussion Problem 6.6.

**6.7**   Draft the memo to the store's physical plant director that you outlined for Discussion Problem 6.7.

**6.8**   Write the report to the director of public relations that you planned in Discussion Problem 6.5. Limit yourself to two or three substantiated suggestions, even though the full report would probably be longer.

**6.9**   As the assistant station manager at Channel 2, you have been asked to analyze and criticize the Tuesday night prime-time program selection (from 7:30 to 11:00 p.m.) in preparation for scheduling the new season's programs. After studying your local TV listings for Tuesday evenings, use one of the prewriting techniques to generate a report that prepares the way for some difficult decisions. Your memo should make specific observations without actually recommending a course of action.

# AN INTRODUCTION
# TO THE DIALOGUES

On the following pages, you will find the first of four dialogues which are transcriptions of the discussions of a group of students in a business writing seminar.* The dialogues show real writers hard at work, bent on improving a business letter or memo. They offer you an intimate look at the writing process and a new way to understand it—perhaps better than ever before. They also provide insights into how to become a better editor of both your own writing and the work of others who rely on your judgment. You can begin to use your improved editing skill in the classroom; later, in your business career, it will be an invaluable asset.

The seminar from which these dialogues were taken can be viewed almost as a laboratory experiment. Rarely have such gifted students come together voluntarily to fasten their attention on business writing and speaking. These students asked for this seminar, lobbied to make it happen, and sparked its success.

Although these students were gifted in many ways, they were not uniformly good writers, and even the most able among them believed that they had weaknesses to overcome. Several of the students had engineering degrees and subscribed to the view that "engineers just can't write." Three confessed that they had never before had a college-level writing course and had until that time avoided courses that demanded a great deal of written work. One student came straight from three years in the Navy, and he informed the group that if he had ever been able to write, he had forgotten how. One had been a history major and wrote in a stilted academic style that was both pompous and affected. Some suffered from an inability to find enough to say; others could not seem to stem their flow of words. In short, these students had a great deal to learn about writing, and they freely admitted it. And probably most important of all, they were determined to learn from each other.

Observing these students at work, you will learn a great deal. Obviously, you will refresh some of the theory you have learned in your own

*The course referred to was an experimental one offered as an elective to MBA students at the Harvard Business School.

writing course, but there is something even more important. The unique quality of the dialogues is that they allow you to empathize with both a writer and an editor almost simultaneously. You will understand the writer's perspective because you will have had an opportunity to familiarize yourself with the case problem and to hear that particular writer's strategy for resolving it. You will perceive how the writer has struggled to embody his or her insights in words, sentences, and paragraphs. And as you "listen" to the students analyze and discuss the results of that effort, you will share each of their perspectives. You will see where—and why—the writing has succeeded or misfired.

The dialogues show the students responding not only to the original piece of writing but also to each other's comments and revisions. By following along as the class hones and refines a rough piece of writing, you can get a close look at the process by which good writing "happens." You will see an enactment of a writer's mind at work, because (as you may already know) good writers *do* engage in a silent dialogue with their inner editors. They debate with themselves about the nature of their audience; they struggle to clarify their own objectives and to decide which are the most relevant issues and the best arguments. They add and delete ideas and experiment with structure. As words come to mind, they grapple with them and test them for shades of meaning; they perhaps even try to judge how their words and sentences sound.

The dialogues graphically depict this drama, and they bring home the truth that writing that seems natural and easy was probably very hard to accomplish. As you read each script, you will see each writer and editor struggle with words and ideas. But you will also sense the students' pleasure and excitement as they watch a clear and persuasive document take shape.

Below are listed the components of all the dialogues except the first. (Dialogue I, which is purely a discussion of the strategic issues that underlie the development of a particularly difficult memo, is an analysis of the writer's approach. It therefore does not include student writings.)

- A brief introductory statement about the case problem and the focus of the discussions
- A case or problem, plus an assignment that asks the students to design a communication strategy and prepare the documents needed to carry it out
- One or more writings by students, each followed by the group's response to it
- A suggested revision to each of the writings, based on the preceding discussion
- Additional student letters and memos based on the same problem, presented for you to discuss and revise

# I

# THE CASE OF THE SMOKE-FREE COMPANY

A forward-looking company is seriously contemplating adopting a policy that potentially could cause conflict among its employees. As part of the process of evaluating and perhaps implementing that policy, a sensitive memo must be written to a senior executive.

The students in the business writing seminar were not asked to write this memo. Rather, they were asked to consider all the strategic implications of developing it—factors such as timing, hidden audiences, tone, content, the order of the arguments, etc. Following the case is their discussion.

## ■ The Case

The Bendell Corporation, one of the nation's leading manufacturers of high-quality women's fashions, is studying the feasibility of implementing a comprehensive clean air policy, consisting of a totally smoke-free work environment at their corporate headquarters in La Sola, California. Headquarters occupies a five-story downtown building, which houses approximately 500 employees.

Bendell is nationally recognized as a liberal, benefits-oriented company. Bendell's employee association is particularly active. Recently, three employees filed complaints about cigarette smoking in the offices and company cafeteria—no doubt spurred on by La Sola's new city ordinance outlawing smoking in public buildings and requiring nonsmoking sections in all restaurants. These complaints led to the formation of an ad hoc committee of concerned employees. After several heated meetings, chaired by Barbara Langley—Bendell's Employee Benefits Specialist, the committee convinced management to hire a consultant to study the situation in detail, with a view toward making recommendations. This consultant, Rita Benson, founder and president of her own business (Pure Air, Inc.), has consistently been a leader in the nonsmokers' rights movement, and she believes wholeheartedly in her cause. Having campaigned successfully to achieve smoke-free environments in hospitals and government offices, she is now eager to see progress made in private industry as well.

One of Rita's first recommendations to Bendell was a companywide survey to measure employee opinions about the possibility of establishing a smoke-free environment at headquarters. Barbara Langley was personally in favor of such a survey, but she guessed (rightly, as it turned out) that her boss, Kent Patterson, Director of Human Resources, would have strong reservations. This would be a real stumbling block, since the survey had to be conducted through Kent's office.

Kent previously had been completely supportive of opening a day-care center at Bendell. That was the sort of employee benefit that he believed would attract potential employees (a large majority of Bendell's employees are women), increase productivity, and do wonders for the company's corporate image. The women's fashion industry in the United States is under ever-increasing pressure from foreign competition, and Kent could clearly see the relationship between high employee morale and optimum productivity. But since child care is a relatively conflict-free issue, there had been almost no employee opposition to establishing a day-care center. Although Kent is known as a strong and fair manager, he does not enjoy dealing with conflict; he hates to be forced to take sides. Recently he had to deal with several unpleasant employee confrontations on the smoking issue. He managed to smooth things out, but only with great difficulty. To complicate matters further, Kent is himself a heavy smoker and has very little innate sympathy for proposals that limit a smoker's personal freedom.

Barbara Langley knew all this, and yet she was also aware that Bendell's Chairman of the Board, Henry Mandile, is a gentle, nonsmoking health nut. In his late sixties, Henry is politically left of center and always open to new ideas.

After careful consideration of the situation, Barbara decided to arrange a meeting between Rita and Henry. As she predicted, Henry was impressed by the persuasive rhetoric of this highly committed consultant. He gave his support to the employee survey, subject to Kent's approval. Kent, with no real alternative, reluctantly agreed to the survey. He signed the cover letter accompanying it, but ardently hoped that the overall employee response to the prospect of outlawing smoking throughout the building would be negative.

Everyone at Bendell—even Rita—was surprised by the survey results: almost 80 percent of Bendell's employees were strongly in favor of creating a smoke-free environment, both in public areas of the building and in private offices. Kent felt that he'd been pushed into a corner, and he was angry. He disliked Rita, sight unseen, but until recently he'd had real respect for Barbara, whom he had hired two years ago. As he saw it, Barbara had lost her usual calm objectivity in dealing with this issue; this was especially evidenced by her support for the hiring of the fanatical Rita.

This was the uncomfortable situation when Kent called Barbara into his smoke-filled office to discuss the implications of the survey outcome:

KENT: Barbara, I don't have to spell out how I feel about this. I don't even want to talk about it. What do you and your ad hoc committee propose to do now?

BARBARA: I'm as surprised as you are about the survey. But I think we have no reason to be upset about this. At this point, the whole issue becomes a corporate-level decision. All we can do is propose that it be put on one of the Management Committee's upcoming agendas.

KENT: Oh, sure. And who is going to make that proposal? Miss Fresh Air herself?

BARBARA: Stay calm, Kent! You know as well as I do that you're the one to approach Dick [the Vice President of Finance, Kent's boss] with the survey results. We've done our job. Now we'll put the ball into top management's court.

KENT: It's not that simple. Everything depends on *how* I present the situation. Dick will want me to interpret the available data and to predict the probable employee response to a total ban as well as the probable external reaction to Bendell's going smoke-free—all the messy implications of your survey. And frankly, I'm not sure where I stand. This business of prohibiting smoking in private offices is the worst of it. It'll cause an uproar.

BARBARA: But Kent, you know why that's necessary. If we're going to do it at all, we have to make an across-the-board ruling. It just wouldn't be fair to exempt middle- and upper-level managers from the ban just because they have closed offices, when 90 percent of the staff work in open cubicles.

KENT: Barbara, I can't believe you're willing to politicize this office to such an extent. I thought you had more common sense.

BARBARA: I'm not *creating* the issues, Kent. I'm merely trying to cope with the consequences: Rita's smoke pollution statistics and the figures on the cost to the company of employing smokers are undeniable—and the great majority of our staff agree.

KENT: Okay, Barbara. I'm not going to play the heavy on this issue. You and I both know where Henry stands. But, as I indicated before, I'm not at all sure what the public reaction will be on this. I want *you* to write the memo to Dick, and then we'll both sign it. And I want you to be as objective as you know how. Present the overall situation, and then ask Dick if he wants to recommend action by the management team. But handle this carefully, Barbara. I don't want to create enemies over this. And you and your committee had better come up with some plan that allows smoking *somewhere* in the building!

## ■ Discussion Problems

Imagine that you are Barbara Langley. You are preparing to draft the memo from you and Kent to Dick LaSalle, Vice President of Finance. You hope to be able to convince Dick that this is an appropriate agenda item for an upcoming Management Committee meeting.

You have before you a copy of the survey results, Rita's smoke pollution statistics, and the chart on additional annual costs shown in Figure I.1.

**I.1** Specifically, what arguments will you include in this memo? What will you say in your opening paragraph? Explain your underlying strategy.

**Figure I.1** Additional Annual Cost of Employing Smokers and Allowing Smoking at the Workplace.

| Source | Annual Cost per Smoker |
| --- | --- |
| Absenteeism | $ 220 |
| Medical care | 230 |
| Morbidity and early mortality (lost earnings) | 765 |
| Insurance (excluding health) | 90 |
| On-the-job time lost | 1,820 |
| Property damage and depreciation | 500 |
| Maintenance | 500 |
| Involuntary smoking | 664 |
| Total cost per smoker per year | $4,789 |

A reprint from Management World, the monthly magazine of the Administrative Management Society, Willow Grove, PA 19090.

**I.2**   Will your memo propose a specific plan of action? If so, how detailed will that plan be? Do you think you should suggest alternatives?

**I.3**   Will you include attachments with the memo? What will they be? What purpose do you hope they will serve?

**I.4**   By what process will you develop this memo? Should you, for instance, try to meet with the ad hoc committee again to seek their advice?

**I.5**   If Dick decides not to propose the smoke-free environment for top management's consideration, do you think you should take further steps? If so, what might they be?

## ■ Optional Writing Tasks

**I.1**   Having read "The Case of the Smoke-Free Company," and Dialogue I, you may have some firm ideas about how to execute the memo. Go ahead and draft it. Assume that you will be attaching a copy of the survey results. You may also attach or include the smoke pollution statistics provided by Rita Benson (see Figure I.1).

**I.2**   Imagine that the president and the vice presidents discuss the issue and decide to proceed with the creation of a smoke-free environment at Bendell. Draft a brief letter from Henry Mandile, Chairman of the Board, announcing the new policy to all employees.

## ■ The Dialogue

RUTH:   We've all read "The Case of the Smoke-Free Company," and we are going to be role playing—pretending to be Barbara, who has to write a rather difficult and tricky memo. I'd like you to consider the problems that Barbara is going to encounter and to explain your strategy for dealing with them. And I'd like us to focus on prewriting problems. In our discussion, let's pay considerable attention to the things Barbara would be worrying about before she actually sat down to write. Would anybody like to open this?

PAUL: Well, there are a number of things that Barbara has to consider, but perhaps the foremost is her ultimate purpose. She has to decide whether this is going to be just a presentation of information or an actual argument in favor of a change that she sincerely wants to occur. And related to that, of course, is the issue of who will be reading this memo.

JEFF: But her own boss told her to be objective. I don't see how an argument fits in with that—a pro or con argument.

RUTH: Jeff, why don't you define objectivity as you see it?

JEFF: Well, it consists of simply presenting the facts without making a judgment.

BOB: Yes, keeping her personal feelings out of it.

JEFF: I don't see that she's been asked to argue for or against the measure.

FRAN: Well, didn't Kent say that Dick, his boss, would expect some guidance on this, some feelings on what he should do with this? Dick would want Kent to do some of the work.

RUTH: Would you like to cite the part in the case, Fran, where he specifically said that?

FRAN: Barbara says, "Stay calm, Kent! You know as well as I do that you're the one to approach Dick with the survey results. We've done our job. Now we'll put the ball in top management's court." And then Kent says, "It's not that simple. Everything depends on *how* I present the situation. Dick will want me to interpret the available data and to predict the probable employee response to a total ban as well as the probable external reactions . . . " And Kent doesn't know where he stands, but he knows it's expected of him to provide more than just plain information.

RUTH: Jeff, are you willing to agree now that Barbara should put in some sort of argument? Would you go along with Fran's feeling that, at least in some limited way, an analysis has to be presented?

JEFF: I think so. Yes, she should.

RUTH: Okay, but for a minute let's pretend that you *were* originally right, Jeff—that Kent didn't say, "I want you to interpret the available data." And that Barbara felt sure that she didn't want to offer any opinion at all. One of the problems I've seen students wrestle with (and one I think Barbara would be wrestling with down the road) is how to keep her own feelings out entirely. By "feelings," I mean those based on an analysis of the data before her rather than feelings she has because her mother once told her that smoking was a terrible thing. If she began to write this memo and just presented that data, I suspect that her tone and, specifically, the way she ordered the material would be a direct giveaway as to where she stands. The point I'd like to make here is that once you have done some analysis I don't think objectivity in the sense of eliminating every shred of your personal opinion is possible.

DON: I think it's possible, Ruth, if she sticks only to numbers and statistics and shows only the objective data without making her own interpretation of it. She could just go as far as saying "Okay, nearly 80 percent of the people here want a smoke-free environment." That would be entirely objective.

FRAN: But Don, I don't think that it's really objective to say that *nearly* 80 percent of the people want a smoke-free environment. You could just as easily say that *less than* 80 percent were in favor of it. As soon as you say "nearly" instead of "less than" you've given an opinion.

PAUL: Yeah, right! Or instead of saying 80 percent, you could say "an overwhelming majority . . ."

BOB: ". . .are passionately in favor of it." Or, in the other direction, . . . "would go along with a smoke-free environment and not object." All of those versions are supported by the 80 percent vote!

FRAN: Using the same figures, Barbara could even stress that more than 20 percent of the employees would be very upset if a smoke-free environment were to be created.

RUTH: And I think that within the limits of honesty the business writer has the right to express an opinion, but it should be firmly backed by a numerical statistic. It can't be backed by "I feel smoking is a crime." It has to be tacked onto "80 percent checked the block that says they would prefer a nonsmoking environment and, therefore, it seems that the majority would go along with this." So, you're almost always interpreting every inch of the way.

PAUL: Really, it's required that you approximate some attempt at interpretation.

RUTH: Okay, if we can accept the fact that "argument" implies *interpretation* and "objectivity" means *based on the facts*, or at least on the data, which may not all be factual—what else should we be concerned about? Paul, you mentioned purpose. So far we agree that part of Barbara's purpose is to interpret the data that she found. What else?

JEFF: I'm sure I read somewhere that the purpose of the memo is to ask Dick LaSalle if he wants to recommend action to management.

RUTH: So, you would say her purpose is to persuade Dick to present the evidence rather than to persuade the Management Committee to take any specific action? Does everybody agree with that?

FRAN: Well, you have to persuade Dick at least to give the Management Committee enough information so that they can make an intelligent decision.

DON: Is Barbara trying to get Dick to bring the issue up for consideration or to actually make a yes-or-no decision on the issue?

JEFF: I don't think she's after his decision. It's just supposed to be shoved along to the Management Committee.

DAVE: I think the purpose of the memo also has to be to smooth Kent's feathers. He's Barbara's boss.

RUTH: Good, now we're getting to the question of audience. Let's try to enumerate some of the audiences for this memo and what might be important to each one of them.

DON: I guess I'm still unclear whether she . . .

RUTH: Dave, would you say just a little bit more about Kent and his feathers before we move on to Don's question?

DAVE: Well, Kent is very antagonistic to the whole project. He resents Rita's being brought in, and he feels that Barbara is not being objective and not doing her job very well. So, since he's going to sign the memo, he can't disagree with it. I feel that his interests need to be served.

RUTH: Don, your turn.

DON: I'm still not clear on whether Barbara is going to be trying to *convince*—you know, to persuade, not just to explain. Is she going to go beyond interpreting the data and really push for action?

RUTH: I guess we have to try to get under Barbara's skin a little, and that doesn't mean each one of you would be the same Barbara. Does she feel it's in her own interest to have this issue presented to the Management Committee? Or is there an element of her not giving a darn whether or not Dick presents it to the committee?

DON: Perhaps she just wants to serve the purpose of the ad hoc committee.

PAUL: That's another audience we haven't mentioned. Is there pressure to represent that group or to bring their cause to light?

RUTH: So you're suggesting she's feeling pressure from the ad hoc committee?

PAUL: I think it's probable.

JEFF: Who's going to get copies of this memo? I'm not clear on that.

DON: Well, we can't decide that either until we determine what Barbara is trying to accomplish. Is it really to get some action that she's personally in favor of or just to present and interpret the data as objectively as possible?

RUTH: Let's list the possible audiences who might get copies. And then, looking at those audiences, let's decide what might make her want to copy them on it, and in what cases it would be a far better strategy for her not to copy them. Also, there may be cases where, no matter what she thinks, she would *have* to copy them.

JEFF: Well, to begin with, there's Henry.

PAUL: He's kind of the godfather. He's probably high enough up that he would have to be copied.

FRAN: Well, if he hadn't already met Rita, he wouldn't have to be copied.

JOHN: And you'd be going over Dick's head, really, to give Henry a copy.

RUTH: Well, chances are both he and Dick already have a fairly good idea of where things stand so far. And that's another question: How much of the memo is formalizing what a lot of people know already?

DAVE: Well, they surveyed the entire company.

BOB: Everybody knows what's going on.

JOHN: Well, then, I don't think that Henry's much of a problem.

FRAN: So he would be copied, then?

JEFF: I think he's receptive to new ideas.

RUTH: So I guess we agree that we'd copy Henry. Who else?

DON: Definitely Rita; we'd have to copy Rita.

PAUL: Well, I don't think we do. Rita's an outside consultant.

DON: But she could give advice on alternatives on how to implement the policy.

PAUL: I would think maybe it would be better to involve her earlier on in writing the memo. To see what her experience in health care has shown her about the most politic way of doing this might be useful, but she doesn't need to be involved after it's in Barbara's hands.

JEFF: Kent doesn't like Rita to begin with.

PAUL: Right. Exactly. Rita's an outsider who's coming in and stirring up a hornet's nest.

FRAN: I think that's a good point because, internally, there's really no need for her to be copied.

PAUL: She does have the aura of being something of a fanatic. This is her business—Pure Air, Inc. She goes into companies and tries to convince them of the usefulness of being smoke-free; so in effect she has a vested interest in this. Also, she has no interest whatsoever in the company itself; so I don't think she should be copied.

BOB: And if Kent knew that she'd been copied, he'd be upset.

FRAN: Of course, it could be a *blind* copy.

RUTH: I was just about to throw that into the discussion. What do you think about the effectiveness of a blind copy? If you, as Barbara, want to see this happen, would you or would you not send Rita a blind copy? What might make you want to send her one, and what might make you feel that it would not be a good idea to do so? We're nearly unanimous that an open copy on the letter to Rita might not be such a good idea. (By the way, does everybody understand that a blind copy allows you to note on your own copy that you are sending someone—

say, Rita—a copy, while at the same time other people who are receiving copies—such as Henry—aren't told that Rita has been sent a copy?)

DAVE: Caring about Rita's business would cause me to send her a blind copy because it would be giving Rita feedback on how her work is going in this company, and it might help her continue her business.

RUTH: Okay, so let's say that if you, as Barbara, like and respect Rita, even though your boss thinks she's the dregs, you might want to do this.

DAVE: If I believed in her work.

RUTH: Oh, not only if you liked and respected Rita, but also if you were a believer in a smoke-free environment and wanted to further the work, then. . . .

FRAN: But if you're taking a middle-of-the-road attitude in the memo, then you *wouldn't* want Rita to know that. Perhaps, though, if you did send her a copy, you could explain the necessity of a toned-down memo in a short cover letter to her. And the cover letter could be friendly and warm.

JOHN: If Rita's perception is that you are her friend, wouldn't she be antagonized when she sees someone she thought was her friend not being strong in her cause?

FRAN: Well, not if she understood that we had to play it carefully. But another possibility just occurred to me: If you don't copy Rita, but you do copy the ad hoc committee, Rita's going to see the memo anyway.

RUTH: Yes, Fran, a copy could very well fall into her hands.

PAUL: Well, again, she's an outside consultant. I don't know if she ever needs to be involved again, or—because she's a controversial figure— if she ought to be involved at all. A phone call to say "This is what we're doing and thanks for your help" would be adequate, rather than sending her a copy of the memo, whether it's blind or not. Even if it is blind, it could leak out that she got one, and someone's feathers might be ruffled.

RUTH: That's a good observation, Paul—that you don't necessarily need to go on record in writing but can try to accomplish the same thing by phone. The strategy in this case might be, if Rita were your friend, to say "We've had to take the middle road, but I think we've done a good job in presenting your case, Rita. We'll be back to you just as soon as we have the answer, and you'll be kept informed." And that might be said warmly on the phone instead of in a cover letter.

I think you've all done a good job in discussing the problem of copying and how to get different kinds of messages across, but there's one question still to be raised. Suppose you had to decide who is your *primary* audience among all these people. Who is the key reader? There might be some differences of opinion on this. Also, *is* there a key reader in this case?

FRAN: I agree with Dave. Barbara has to look to her boss's feelings. If I were Barbara, my key reader would be Kent, because my job might be on the line.

PAUL: And Kent's going to have to sign this memo. Not only is he going to have to approve it, it's going to go out as if he wrote it.

BOB: On the other hand, Dick is the person who can really do the most about getting action on this issue, so shouldn't he be the primary audience if he's the prime mover in this?

PAUL: But if her boss doesn't want it done, Barbara's job may be on the line.

BOB: I don't think Kent can really keep it from moving on up to the higher level.

PAUL: No, he can't, which makes it even more important that he feel as comfortable as he can about it. There has to be an effort to meet his personal needs.

RUTH: Let me step in and try to resolve this, because I think you're both absolutely right.

PAUL: Hey, we can't both be right!

RUTH: I *do* think you're both absolutely right. The textbook definition of *key reader* is "the person who will use the information." And so, by that definition, the key reader is probably Dick. On the other hand, Paul is absolutely right in believing that people may never lay eyes on the memo if it isn't written in a way that's palatable to Kent. So, in this case, you not only have a key reader, but you have a secondary audience that is of utmost importance. Kent is almost as key as the key reader.

DAVE: Key in a different way.

RUTH: In a different way, yes, exactly.

DAVE: And even if Kent wasn't Barbara's direct superior, he is in a position of influence. He has a lot more at stake with this issue than Dick does. As far as we know, Dick may have a strong personal preference, but we don't know what it is. We do know all about Kent's feelings.

RUTH: What *does* Kent have at stake? That's an interesting thought: What's at stake here? The trickiest part of writing this memo is going to be to write something that Kent's going to let out the door.

JOHN: His pride.

RUTH: Tell me a little more about that.

JOHN: Well, he's an upper-level manager. To have someone prevent him from smoking—when that's one of his favorite things to do—would be a kick to his pride. That's taking away his control over his own lifestyle.

RUTH: His own personal environment.

JOHN: Yeah.

RUTH: Okay, yes, anything else that Kent's got at stake here?

TOM: His job might be at stake.

JOHN: His job?

TOM: Yeah, we know Henry's a health nut, and we know that a majority of the staff want a smoke-free environment, so Kent is pretty well surrounded. He wants to voice his preference, but he has to be careful about how he does it.

RUTH: So his situation is tricky, too.

FRAN: It is. And I've thought of something else he should consider. This is such a new issue that maybe it would attract media interest. What if the whole thing kind of backfired? What if one of the employees sued Bendell if the company went through with establishing a smoke-free environment?

PAUL: Or if the policy made it difficult for the company to attract talent when hiring.

FRAN: If anything went wrong, it would go back to Kent, you know. If they wanted to be nasty, they could even blame Kent.

BOB: The company already has an image of being forward-looking.

FRAN: Yeah, but child care and a smoke-free environment are two different things.

RUTH: That's an important point, though, because that company image becomes an objective fact that can perhaps assist Barbara in writing this memo. It presents an argument that doesn't get into "smoking is a sin and crime." And that negative attitude is one of the things she's absolutely got to avoid, or Kent is not going to let this out the door.

JEFF: We also have the city ordinance that was passed. That's also a fact.

FRAN: But that city ordinance had some people ruffled, and to see the smoke-free movement spread to private companies might well get some important people in the community angry.

RUTH: Fran, are you suggesting that we should be *aware* of this, or that we should use it in the memo? I'm not exactly clear about your point.

FRAN: Well, it occurs to me that this whole smoke-free issue is something really new, and it's not just an internal issue at Bendell. It is new and newsworthy, and therefore there's another audience that has to be taken into account.

RUTH: Now I see your point, Fran. That's a very good thought. So we have yet another audience—the media and the general public.

PAUL: Another thing I think we should have mentioned before is that Kent does not enjoy dealing with conflict, and this issue is a can of worms. A memo that's written with an eye toward a gentle implementation of the change—*that* won't have him sitting in the hot seat and might be something he would respond positively to.

RUTH: So there has to be some subtlety in this memo. It can't be blatant. It's going to be a difficult memo to write; I think we're seeing that more and more. Can we go anywhere for help? How about the ad hoc committee? Should we be going back to them to get some advice about how to write this thing?

TOM: I'd say go to the ad hoc committee to get some suggestions about what to say, but be careful to avoid any fanatical-sounding advice from them. Since we know they feel strongly about this, it's important to screen anything you get from them.

JEFF: I disagree. Barbara was chairperson of the committee to begin with. She certainly ought to know what they've been thinking by this time. To add a few more cooks is just going to confuse this whole thing. If I were Barbara, I would sit down and write it myself. She knows enough.

DAVE: Jeff, maybe she is ready to write it, but I think that for reasons of politics she should consult with the ad hoc committee, meet with them, and be careful not to alienate them. It's important that they know she is carrying out their interests. She can even receive feedback from them and then not put it into the memo.

FRAN: So how would they feel included then?

DAVE: Well, by letting them air their feelings to her before she sits down to write. Also by explaining her problem (political and informational) and then brainstorming with then; by getting as many ideas and as many ways of handling it out on the table.

RUTH: I think "brainstorming" is an excellent word here, Dave, because it doesn't imply a commitment to enumerating specific issues. If Barbara held another formal meeting and said "Let's come up with a list of the issues that we're going to address in this memo," she'd be locked in. But your suggestion, I think, may be a good one: to try to unleash the power of the committee's thinking without making any commitments.

DAVE: And that way, they would feel they've been heard.

RUTH: But we seem to have a difference of opinion between Jeff and Tom and Dave. We can see that Jeff would go about this in a different way; and I think that's appropriate because different writers do have different kinds of needs. Some of us are much better alone with our thoughts and our typewriter—or word processor, maybe—and others find that their wheels really get oiled by conversations on the telephone or perhaps another meeting or two. So I think what we're seeing here are two very different kinds of writing processes and, depending on whether Barbara is more like Jeff or Tom, she would decide whether or not to go back to the committee.

TOM: Similarly, as far as showing this to other people, Jeff has great confidence, and I believe legitimately so, in his ability to say things diplomatically. I would be concerned about my own tendency to be aggressive or argumentative, and I would want to show the memo informally to a few very select people who maybe could bring me an objective and different point of view. For instance, I might like to get together with friends and say "This is what I'm trying to achieve with this memo, but I'm also trying to make sure I don't lose my job. What do you think?"

PAUL: Let's not forget that Kent also probably *wants* to be involved. He says, "I want you to write the memo to Dick, and then we'll both sign it," but we should make sure, all along, that Kent's needs and concerns are being addressed. Barbara should say to him, "These are some of the things I'm thinking of talking about. How do you suggest going about it?" And, frankly, if he says, "Write it this way, this way, and this way," she'd better do it!

RUTH: So would you perhaps show Kent a very rough draft, or a list of issues? What would you show Kent, Paul?

PAUL: Well, I'd involve him a number of times—show him a list of issues to be addressed, and discuss the path I intended to take. Then, using his recommendations, I'd write the memo and then show it to him again and say, "Make changes as you see fit."

BOB: There are three important issues: attract potential employees, increase productivity, and do wonders for the company's corporate image. And if the memo stresses those three things, which is why they wanted the day care, I think Kent would sign it.

PAUL: And it should also provide some alternatives: "You and your committee had better come up with some plan that allows smoking somewhere in this place!" Compromise. Set off one of the five floors of the building for smoking, or one corner on every floor.

JEFF: Maybe they could allow smoking only in the day-care center! (laughter)

RUTH: Okay, so it's recruitment, productivity, and corporate image. Those are the three main issues to examine. Any others?

JEFF: Another argument would certainly be saving money, according to those statistics.

DAVE: Higher profits.

BOB: Not to mention the health concern.

RUTH: Which are both very closely tied together, yes. So you have a lot of fairly uncontroversial data that you could rely on. Is there anything else that probably would be difficult for Kent to disagree with?

DAVE: He couldn't disagree with the basic point that the majority of the workers in the company want this. So appeal to his sense of democracy, I guess.

FRAN: But we need to remember that at least 20 percent of the people in this company *don't* want this change.

PAUL: Yeah. And we need to deal with it—to bring that to light, too.

RUTH: There, you hit it, to use the statistic and interpret it. Certainly, you can't argue against the fact that more people want the new policy than don't. But a substantial number of people have real needs that should be addressed. I think we're coming close to closure. We've determined our audience, we've talked about our key reader, we've talked about the purpose of the memo, and now, in the light of all we've understood, we've begun to focus on what content might be appropriate. Can we summarize? Barbara is just about ready to write her memo. Can anyone give us a better idea now of its contents and perhaps the order of those contents?

PAUL: I think it might open with a little bit of the history: why this situation arose, why all of a sudden here is this memo about this obviously controversial issue—because a number of concerned people formed a committee and undertook some research. Then, come up with data: "These are the results of the survey, and attached is Figure 1." To my mind, the main purpose is to give the readers the information, whether or not they want to address it formally.

JEFF: But you've got to put in the benefits somewhere, and also some sort of suggestions.

RUTH: Let's get some other viewpoints. You don't have to follow Paul's plan at all, or you could use some elements of it. How might you organize the memo, Jeff?

JEFF: Essentially the same way, except I would continue with . . . well, the issues we discussed earlier, about morale and higher productivity.

DAVE: I definitely think that those should appear near the beginning of the memo to attract attention and create a positive reaction right away—especially if I hoped to see this get done.

FRAN: Barbara needs to make it clear that the point of this memo is the importance of the situation at this moment for the company, in terms of company politics, but also in terms of those four goals that we mentioned earlier. That's why a decision has to be made.

RUTH: If I think about the way real people in the real world behave, my sense of it is that Barbara will approach this from one of three viewpoints: neutral (which is quite unlikely), as an advocate (even though she will try to be a very factual advocate), or with her eyes firmly on her boss (trying to adjust the memo to get it by him). And her specific viewpoint will determine what she puts into the memo and the order she puts it in.

Now I think if I were Barbara the neutral person, the history of how it all happened (à la Paul) and the importance and the criticality of the situation (à la Fran) would go right up front in my memo. And then, maybe at the bottom, I'd have some pros and cons about the survey results. And again, whether I'd put the cons first or the pros first would depend on how I felt about it all.

And if I were Barbara the advocate, then I think I'd first come in with the survey, showing that 80 percent favor the new policy. Then I would follow by urging that perhaps this is the right time for us to look closely at this policy because it could offer us the a, b, c, and d benefits that we've discussed here. It would be a very different memo from the one Barbara would write if she were neutral. And, especially if she's going to be an advocate, all this thinking she did about her boss and what he could and couldn't tolerate would be extremely useful.

But I would hope that Barbara wouldn't design the memo solely so that Kent doesn't fire her. I'm not saying that a lot of people wouldn't do that, but the position of integrity to me is for her to decide where she really stands and not simply to write whatever she can get out the door.

DAVE: Well, Barbara sounds like a courageous person.

RUTH: Ah! I think we'll end with that.

# BETTER LETTERS AND MEMOS

**7**

*L*etters and memos differ from each other in two ways. First, and most obviously, they differ in format. Second, letters are sent to people both inside and outside an organization, but memos are intended exclusively for internal use: they are sent to fellow employees within departments, divisions, or companies.

At one time, sending a memo generally indicated an attitude of informality, but today memos can be either formal or informal. They run the gamut from personal handwritten notes to rather formal short reports that use the memo format.

For the informal memos, companies frequently supply preprinted memo pads, some of which have the employee's name imprinted (see Figure 7.1). For more formal internal correspondence, many companies sup-

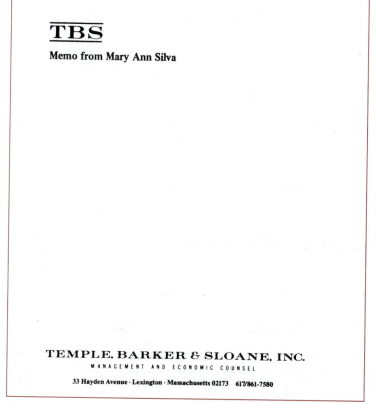

**TBS**

**Memo from Mary Ann Silva**

**TEMPLE, BARKER & SLOANE, INC.**
MANAGEMENT AND ECONOMIC COUNSEL

33 Hayden Avenue · Lexington · Massachusetts 02173   617/861-7580

**Figure 7.1**   A page from a memo pad.

# TBS

# MEMORANDUM

**TO:**                                                   **DATE:**

**FROM:**

**SUBJECT:**

**TEMPLE, BARKER & SLOANE, INC.**
MANAGEMENT AND ECONOMIC COUNSEL

33 Hayden Avenue · Lexington · Massachusetts 02173    617/861-7580

**Figure 7.2**    Example of memo typing paper.

ply memo typing paper that contains a preprinted heading with the key references TO, FROM, SUBJECT (or RE), and DATE (see Figure 7.2). Memo pads and typing paper save employees time by establishing a uniform pattern for these key references. In this way, writers are always reminded to include them, and readers can spot them immediately.

People are more likely to send a letter instead of a memo to someone within their organization when the occasion is rather formal. For example, a personnel director might write a congratulatory letter to an employee who has completed ten years of service (see Figure 7.3); a supervisor might write a letter of condolence to an employee who has suffered a death in her family; a senior officer in the company might send a letter to all employees to communicate an important new policy. As you can see, for internal correspondence, electing to write a letter rather than a memo suggests that something is a bit apart from normal day-to-day business activity.

Aside from keeping in mind that when writing to someone inside the company you will more often than not use the memo format, you can count on facing identical challenges in memo and letter writing. Both are written for roughly five categories of purpose: *to show courtesy, to inform, to*

---

November 1, 198-

**Figure 7.3**
A sample internal letter.

Dear Paul:

On behalf of our president, James Bradshaw, I would like to congratulate you on achieving ten years of exemplary service with I.C.I.

Your dedication and consistency signify the spirit that has helped us to become number three in a market that, as you know, is highly competitive. Because of the efforts of employees of your caliber, we expect to see our company become the number two competitor in the next fiscal year.

Once again, from all of us at I.C.I., thank you for your outstanding contribution, and we look forward to seeing you with us for many more years. I plan to congratulate you personally at the annual Christmas dinner on December 19.

Very sincerely,

*Arnold*

Arnold Archibald
Vice President, Personnel

---

*explain, to convince,* and *to reject.* Both need to be tailored for each occasion and for each reader, as we will see in this chapter and in Chapters 8 and 9.

## ■ What Makes an Effective Letter or Memo?

Primarily, an effective letter or memo accomplishes what the writer intended. As we have emphasized in preceding chapters, all business correspondence is written to carry out a purpose; and most frequently at the heart of that purpose is the need to persuade someone to agree with you, to take action, or often to do both and in that order.

To see this clearly, imagine yourself participating in what is a frequent occurrence at most companies. As chairperson for a particular project, you wrote a memo to remind 12 people in your group that you would all be meeting on Friday at 2:00 p.m. in Conference Room A. After your reminder was delivered, however, you received a phone call telling you that through an oversight Conference Room A was already scheduled for use—you have to use Conference Room B; furthermore, even this room cannot be made available until 3:00 p.m. To remedy the situation, you now send out a follow-up memo announcing these changes. If all 12 people appear in the right room at the right time, your follow-up memo has been effective, but if only two arrive . . . .

Your second memo faces a greater challenge than one might at first assume. It would be a mistake to view its message as purely informative—as merely intended to convey the facts about the new arrangements. The change in time is likely to impinge on people's schedules, and the change in location might even affect their assessment of the meeting's importance. To be effective, therefore, the follow-up memo must be tactful and persuasive as well as clear. It should include a brief explanation of the reason for the change and should stress the importance of the meeting.

As the complexity, importance, or sensitivity of correspondence increases, so does the need for skill on the part of the writer. And the truth is that you will frequently be asked to handle situations that challenge your ability to write effectively. Suppose, for example, that your manager asks you to explore people's opinions about a highly controversial issue. If you send a survey letter to six people and only two respond, your letter has not been sufficiently effective. Or suppose that your supervisor requests that you write a letter to placate an important customer whose shipment has been delayed. If after reading your letter the customer cancels the order, you should be very concerned about the letter's effectiveness. Just as "the proof of the pudding is in the eating," the proof of the writing is in the reading or—more accurately—in what occurs *after* the reading. Even though much effort and many of the right ingredients go into a memo, its ultimate effectiveness is bound to be measured by what it achieves.

Obviously, some letters and memos succeed better than others, and for the sake of your business career, you want to feel confident that yours will produce the desired results. As the thickness of this book attests, there's a great deal to be learned about effective business writing, and unfortunately it cannot be distilled into a formula or even a list of commandments. Since so many of the choices that writers must make are tied to specific situations, even with a good understanding of business writing theory, you will consistently have to exercise your judgment.

A good way to improve your effectiveness as a business writer is to contact the people who *don't* get back to you. It takes a bit of courage to phone them, but you may discover that they never received your letter or memo; more significantly, you may find that they did nothing because they didn't understand that you wanted anything. If you find out precisely what is going on, then you can determine what you need to do to get results.

Even having said all this, we can't overstress the three guidelines that follow. They represent the observations and practice of experienced writers who know what it takes to get results from business correspondence.

1. Business letters and memos should be founded on careful audience analysis.
2. Usually, they should be direct and brief.
3. They should reflect the business organization's normal practices and expectations in regard to format and general appearance.

In making use of these three guidelines, always remember that the first one (the need to analyze your audience) takes precedence over the other two. For example, if your audience is likely to be caught off guard or offended by a suggestion, directness may not be called for; and brevity may not be a virtue if it eliminates data that are important to the reader. Furthermore, individual preferences can sometimes outweigh the company's usual practice in regard to formats. Perhaps your company has a high tolerance for informal handwritten memos, but your boss insists that all memos be typed; if you are tactful and considerate, you will never send your boss a handwritten memo.

Once you have carefully analyzed the needs of your audience, however, the second and third guidelines can be very helpful. A memo that is direct and brief, and also properly formatted, invites reading.

## ■ Brevity and Directness: When and How Much

A theatrical producer, David Belasco, captured the underlying reason why brevity and directness have become accepted norms for business writing. He frequently told ambitious young writers, "If you can't fit your idea on the back of my calling card, you don't have a clear idea." Belasco didn't want to waste time deciphering rough, undefined ideas, and that is precisely the attitude of most busy people. They recognize that sprawling abstractions or fussy details are usually evidence that little effort has been devoted to clear thinking.

In the vast majority of cases, therefore, the most effective business letters and memos proceed as follows:

- They first deliver their main point succinctly.
- They next add the essentials for clarifying that point.
- They conclude with an appropriate closing.

Unless the subject is complex or sensitive, covering these three bases rarely requires more than three paragraphs. And for run-of-the-mill announcements and requests, there is hardly ever justification for surpassing this limit. Long-winded writers run the risk of having their memos rapidly skimmed or set aside for a "better time," which never materializes.

When you write a lengthy memo, therefore, be absolutely certain that all the content is necessary. Next, see that you have trimmed away unnecessary verbiage. (A senior executive we know and respect regularly tells his employees, "Don't send me a long memo unless you absolutely haven't enough time to write a short one!"*) Finally, make sure that you capture your reader's attention immediately, either with an explicit subject line or with a significant opening paragraph (make use of both if possible).

Most frequently, the way to catch your reader's interest at once is to zero in on the main point: be absolutely direct. This strategy can work well for long or short memos. Consider the example in Figure 7.4. As you can see, Martin Weaver clearly spells out his memo's purpose, both in the subject line and in the initial paragraph. The second paragraph quickly supplies the details, and the third lets his reader know what to do after reading the memo.

The request for action in the third paragraph of Martin Weaver's memo, by the way, is extremely important. Too often writers bury such requests in the middle of their memos; their readers absorb the gist of the message, but miss the main point—that they are expected to *do* something. (If you find it strategically awkward to ask for action outright, you might label a section of your memo "Action Plan.")

Figure 7.5 is a memo that clearly states the action that is needed and even goes one step further: the writer, Barney Adams, takes responsibility for the action of those readers who do not respond.

Few things are more frustrating than waiting while you wonder whether your memo arrived or was read. Therefore, you should think

---

*Our friend doesn't know it, but he's echoing a seventeenth-century logician, Blaise Pascal, who said, "I have made this letter longer than usual only because I have not had time to make it shorter."

about whether to give your readers complete responsibility for initiating a needed action or to assume some of the responsibility yourself. When writing the memo in Figure 7.4, for instance, Martin Weaver was very concerned about establishing the meeting time with John Tobin. Martin might have been wiser to take responsibility for the follow-up call. He

---

TO:   John Tobin, Manager of Marketing Research
FROM:  Martin Weaver, Training Coordinator
DATE:  October 14, 198-
SUBJECT:  Responsibilities for the Marketing Research Writing
          Program

For our mutual understanding, I would like to restate the procedures that you and I agreed on yesterday for developing a writing program for your group.

Our arrangement is that I will continue to work on the design of the course until November 1. After that time you and I will meet to refine the details and to decide which two members of your staff will work with me to coordinate the workshops with the group's ongoing activities.

Does this statement match with what you intended? Please call me on Wednesday to confirm that it does and to set a date for our November meeting.

---

TO:   All District Sales Reps
FROM:  Barney Adams
DATE:  February 14, 198-
SUBJ:  Selecting a Site for Jeanne Boyd's Retirement Party

Please vote for the location you prefer for Jeanne's party. The committee has narrowed the choices to the following:

    The Hillside    (in Shady Grove)
    Emerson's       (in Goshen Center)
    Wing Chow's      (in Pittsfield)

Send your vote to me in the Goshen office at mail zone EW120. The deadline for voting is February 28. If I don't hear from you by then, I'll assume you're willing to go along with the majority. Thanks.

---

could have ended his memo this way: "I will call you on Wednesday to confirm . . . ."

Although it's not without risk, you might on occasion consider using Barney Adams's strategy of stating outright that *you* will act if the reader does not. This tactic should only be employed when you know the message is not controversial and you need to act quickly. To use this tactic, you close with a statement similar to this one: "If I don't hear from you by December 12, I will proceed as we've discussed." Often, however, discretion is the better part of valor; before taking the indicated action, you might be wise to make a precautionary phone call.

Returning to the issue of directness—at times stating your point directly in your opening is not the best strategy. As explained in Chapter 4, directness should be avoided when your reader is likely to be antagonistic to or skeptical about your message. Also, you will encounter situations in which the main point of your letter or memo is not the best attention-getter. The letter in Figure 7.6 illustrates such a situation.

---

**Figure 7.6**
A letter in which the main point is preceded by an attention-getting opening.

August 17, 198-

John Harris, Esquire
8 Avenue of the Americas
New York, NY 10009

Dear Mr. Harris:

    Joseph Farmer, from the New York office of Hunter, Weston, and Reeves, suggested that I write to you. He told me that you are extremely knowledgeable about product liability and were a great help to him in preparing his case.
    I would very much appreciate your advice regarding an incident that occurred two weeks ago . . . .

---

Notice that in this letter, using Mr. Farmer's name as a reference takes precedence over the initial statement of the letter's purpose. We can expect that Harris and Farmer are well acquainted and that the appearance of Farmer's name will immediately get the letter read.

You may often decide that you need to lay the groundwork for your message by an immediate attention-grabber. The following opening lines from several letters provide a few more examples of attention-getting beginnings:

> You and I were introduced to each other at the September sales meeting.

> Our company president recently urged us to . . . .

You recently requested that we give more thought to improving our company's image.

In establishing priorities as to when to be direct, use these three guidelines:

1. Normally, begin by getting your reader's attention.
2. If you can capture his or her attention by concisely stating your main point up front, do so.
3. But avoid such directness if it is likely to offend your reader or to turn him or her against you from the start.

## ■ Formatting: Not Just for Appearance's Sake

If at the onset of your career with a company you take the trouble to learn its preferred formats for letters and memos, you will give your documents a head start toward being perceived as effective. Furthermore, through observation or by asking direct questions, you should be able to learn the individual preferences of your superiors.

Don't make the mistake of persuading yourself that formatting is the responsibility of the typist. A good secretary will know a great deal about formatting and, once your preferences are known, will help you to carry them out consistently. But most secretaries automatically use the formats they learned during their training; furthermore, if your written work is going to a company typing pool, the formatting will be hit-or-miss unless you include complete instructions.

Your first decision in selecting a format is whether to use block or indented margins. Although traditionally paragraphs were indented at the left margin at all times, as a direct result of the advent of word processing, the full block format (see Figure 7.7) is much in vogue today. Many companies prefer the full block format because it reduces set-up time for their word-processing operators. When every line of copy begins flush on the left margin, there's no need to enter indentation specifications into the computer. Perhaps another reason the block style is popular today is that it presents a streamlined, modern appearance that gives the reader a feeling of unimpeded movement down through the text. Even so, the indented, or semiblock format (see Figure 7.8), has its adherents in many businesses.

The standard format for memos has a heading that always includes the key references TO, FROM, SUBJECT (or RE), and DATE. If memo typing paper is not available, you should enter these references in the top left corner; the date may be entered under FROM at the left or at the right on a line parallel to the TO reference. The body of a memo may be written

Figure 7.7
The full block for-
mat for letters.

4 Exeter Drive
Holliston, MA 02185
March 1, 198-

Return address

Date line

Inside address

Roberta Sanchez
Allen Corporation
Personnel Department
4142 Owens Avenue
Detroit, MI 54832

Salutation

Dear Ms. Sanchez:

Body

This is the format for a full block letter. Each line and paragraph
begins at the left margin.

To reiterate, each line and paragraph begins flush left.

In closing, let me say again, each line and paragraph begins at the
left margin.

Complimentary close

Sincerely yours,

*R. L. Lord*

R. L. Lord
President

---

Figure 7.8
The semiblock for-
mat for letters.

45 Open Air Drive
Venice, CA 90291
June 12, 198-

Harvey A. Adams
Vice President, Community Relations
Arlen Corporation
101 Judy Drive
Goshen, AL 36035

Dear Mr. Adams:

This indented style is called the semiblock format. The return
address, date, first line of each paragraph, and complimentary close
are all indented.

I expect to implement the following steps by August 14:

o   Hire a new manager to . . . .
o   Transfer two workers from . . . .

Thank you for all of your assistance on these matters.

Sincerely yours,

*Arlene Sims*

Arlene Sims
Director of Personnel

---

### MEMORANDUM

TO:       Sharon A. Bateson         *RLW*        DATE:   Dec. 9, 198-
FROM:     Robert L. Williams
SUBJECT:  Proposed Conference on Patent Research

Ruth Atlee has agreed to serve as moderator:

o   . . . .
o   . . . .

We have received bids from:

o   . . . .
o   . . . .

Your suggestion of using . . . .
The total number of participants . . . .
The four days should thus require . . . .

*Robert L. Williams*

**Figure 7.9**
The bulleted memo
format.

**Heading
(Initial your name)**

**(Or sign your name at
the bottom)**

---

in normal paragraphs, but many memo writers instead use a bulleted format such as the one shown in Figure 7.9. Although you will rarely see
subheadings in ordinary business letters,* they are often used in memos,
especially when the substance and importance warrant more than one
page of copy.

*Subheadings are commonly used, however, in letter proposals (see Chapter 9) and in
other formal or complex letters.

# Elements of Business Letters and Memos

The following elements are standard for all business letters.

- **Return Address.** If you are not using letterhead stationery or if the letterhead does not include all the necessary information, single-space your full mailing address. For full block style, all lines should be flush with the left margin. If you want to include your phone number, place it immediately below the last line of the address; include the area code.

- **Date Line.** Without skipping any lines, type the date immediately below the return address.

  After the return address and date line, skip three to six lines, depending on the length of the letter. The shorter the letter, the more lines you should skip.

- **Inside Address.** Type the name of the addressee on the first line. Under the name, type the full mailing address. If you are including the addressee's title, type it either (1) after the name on the first line, (2) by itself on the second line, or (3) before the division or company name on the second line. Uniformity of line length should be the criterion for placing the title.

  Double-space between the inside address and the salutation.

- **Salutation.** A formal salutation uses "Dear," a complimentary title (Mr., Ms., Dr., etc.), the addressee's surname (Smith, Jones, etc.), and a colon. An informal salutation uses "Dear," the addressee's given name (John, Mary, etc.), and a comma. Today you will also frequently see a hybrid form, an informal salutation followed by a colon; this form suggests some familiarity but underscores the business relationship.

  Your best guide for selecting a salutation is to be as formal as you would be with the person face to face. In other words, if you use each other's given names in person, do so in your letters; but if your acquaintance is purely for business, you might follow the name with a colon. For a friend, you should probably follow the given name with a comma.

  If you don't know your correspondent's name, try to discover it. You might, for instance, call his or her secretary or contact the company's personnel office. If you cannot get the name, or the situation doesn't warrant your spending time on research, "Dear Sir or Madam" is your best recourse.

- **Text.** Single-space your text; but double-space between paragraphs. You may indent from five to eight spaces at the beginning of each paragraph, or you may choose not to indent. If you include bullet points in your text, skip a line before and after each point.

  Double-space between the text and the complimentary close.

- **Complimentary Close.** For the semiblock style, place the first letter of the complimentary close directly in line under the first letter of your return address. For the full block style, everything goes flush left, of course. If your closing has more than one word (for example, "Very truly yours" or "Yours truly"), capitalize only the first word. Place a comma after the closing.

  Triple-space between the complimentary close and the typed signature.

- **Personal Signature.** Sign your full name (in blue or black ink) if your letter is formal. If your salutation is informal or if you wish to indicate that the addressee should use an informal salutation when answering your letter, sign only your given name or nickname.

- **Typed Signature.** If you are using your personal letterhead, a typed signature is not mandatory; nevertheless, it is commonly used. Type your full name, even if you sign only your given name. If you have a title, you may wish it to appear beneath your typed signature if it does not appear in the letterhead. In the semiblock format, the left-hand edge of the typed signature, the complimentary close, the date line, and the inside address should form a straight line.

The elements listed above are the standard components of business letters, and they should be an integral part of your documents. If you commit the above instructions to memory, you will probably never have to worry about them again. In addition to the standard components, there are several optional ones that will always require careful thought because they have strategic implications. These optional elements of letters and memos are the following:

- **Subject Line in Letters.** Although a subject line is required in memos, in letters it is optional. If you use a subject line in a letter, it should be placed two lines below the salutation and two lines above the first line of the text (see Figure 7.10). It should be specific and brief, highlighting the significance of the letter. When you must choose between them, sacrifice brevity to specificity. For example, write "SUBJECT: Change in Sick Leave Policy" rather than "SUBJECT: Sick Leave."

  Subject lines are being used more and more frequently in letters because they are a powerful tool for getting the reader's attention. When you want your reader immediately to know the reason you are writing, you should use a clear, well-focused subject line. You can also use a subject line to refer your reader to a particular file or account. In such a case, you may write "Attention" (instead of "Re" or "Subject") before the key words, for example, "Attention: File #341" or "Attention: Abbott account."

25 Newland Road
Somerset, VA 22972
January 12, 198-

Mr. Hawthorn Allison
Manager of Creative Services
Abco Training Products
100 Laurel Avenue
Regamont, TN 37160

Dear Mr. Allison:

Re:   Replacement of Damaged Filmstrip

On December 1, 1986, I notified you that your shipment of
filmstrip had been badly damaged, and . . . .

It is essential that this matter . . . .

Thank you for your help.

Sincerely yours,

*R. G. Olsen*

R. G. Olsen
Regional Director

Bear in mind, however, that a subject line implies a rather formal
tone and also can add a note of urgency. Therefore, you should not
use a subject line in every letter you write. It would have no place in a
courtesy letter, and it could work against your strategy when you need
to build a carefully reasoned argument before presenting a sensitive
recommendation.

■  **Enclosure Indication.** Select your enclosures carefully to ensure that
they are pertinent and essential. To indicate that there are enclosures,
skip three to eight lines after the typed signature, depending on the
length of the letter. Type "Encl:" at the left-hand margin, followed either by a number to show how many documents are enclosed (for example, "Encl: 3") or by a single-spaced list (in column form) giving a
brief title to each document, as follows:

```
Encl: File Copy 2467E
      File Copy 1967H
      File Copy 5678K
```

- **Copy Indication.** Double-space between the enclosure indication and the copy indication. After typing "cc:" at the left-hand margin, list (in column form, single-spaced) the full names of the people to whom you are sending copies.

  Deciding who will and who will not receive a copy of a letter or memo can be an extremely important part of your strategy. The decision should be the inevitable outgrowth of your purpose and your audience analysis. For instance, suppose you have received no response to several polite requests for information from an always-too-busy employee in another department. By noting on your next equally polite request that you are sending a copy of the memo to that person's boss, you may considerably increase your chance of getting the needed data. On the other hand, if you have the choice, you should avoid copying a memo to someone who might have a reason to want to frustrate your purpose.

- **Distribution List.** When you write a memo that needs to be distributed to many people in your organization, don't try to cram all their names into the heading or into a huge list after the copy indication. Simply attach a page with a list of the people who are to receive the document. After "TO:" in the heading, type "See Distribution List." It is important to observe your company's usual practice in ordering names on a distribution list. Although in most companies the practice is that names be listed alphabetically, in some you are expected to defer to rank—particularly when senior executives are included in the mailing.

## The Eyes Have It!

"You can't judge a book by its cover" warns the old maxim. And it is equally true that you can't judge a business document by its appearance. Still, first impressions do count. An eccentric format, ragged margins, or careless typing can imply that the author gave the document very little time or attention. Even worse, lack of attention to these important details can suggest that the reader is not held in high esteem.

Therefore, whether you do the typing or your secretary does, you should take responsibility for the final document. See that the format is appropriate and correct, look over the distribution list, proofread carefully and make sure that corrections are entered neatly, and double-check that all enclosures are as indicated. Finally, keep in mind that the letters and memos leaving your desk are surrogates for you; they reflect the good judgment and professionalism that you bring to the workplace.

## ■ Summary

Most business letters and memos are written for one or more of the following purposes: to show courtesy, to inform, to explain, to convince, and to reject. Each needs to be tailored to its specific occasion and audience.

Successful writers stress three guidelines for effective business correspondence:

1. Carefully analyze your audience.
2. Be as direct and brief as possible.
3. Exhibit professionalism in the format and appearance of your letters and memos.

Audience analysis, however, always takes precedence, since it reveals how best to implement the other guidelines.

## ■ Discussion Problems

**7.1** Evan Foster is Purchasing Manager for Illinois Grip and Handle, Inc. He will be speaking at the annual convention of the American Purchasers League and wants data from some of his colleagues to help him prepare his remarks. He has spent several hours working on a letter to request the data he needs but is not happy with the results of his effort.

Review the two drafts of Foster's letter shown in Figure 7.11. What do you like or dislike about each? Why?

---

**Figure 7.11**
Two drafts of a letter requesting information.

January 12, 198-                                             Draft A

William O'Donnell
Purchasing Director
Aircraft Supply
34A Main Street
Allendale, Iowa 50505

Dear Bill:

    I'm looking forward to seeing you at the APL convention in February. As you probably already know, I've been asked to deliver the keynote address on the state of purchasing today. Toward that end, I'd like to solicit some vital information from you. How do you view the state of purchasing? Personally, I find it difficult to answer this with any certainty, since our business changes nearly daily. So please answer two questions for me:

1. What practices are common today versus five years ago?

2. What one issue or event has most influenced the way you do business today?

Thanks for your help; obviously I value your opinion and look forward to hearing from you.

Sincerely yours,

*Evan Foster*

Evan Foster

---

January 12, 198-

Draft B

William O'Donnell
Purchasing Director
Aircraft Supply
34A Main Street
Allendale, Iowa 50505

Dear Bill:

As you know, the APL convention is coming up soon and I have been asked to speak about the state of our business. In preparing my remarks I get about as far as "In the changing world of purchasing . . ." and then stop. I'm interested in hearing from you and some other folks about your opinions of the state of the business.

Since I hope to have my speech prepared by the beginning of February, I'd appreciate it if you'd get back to me by the end of January. I realize that's not much time, and I apologize for the short notice. Hearing from you will certainly help me feel more comfortable about giving this speech. Thanks for your ideas.

Very truly yours,

*Evan Foster*

Evan Foster

**7.2**  Describe in some detail four situations in which you would write a memo rather than a letter. Explain the purpose of each memo. Would you use a direct opening in any memo? Would you copy any of the memos to others? Explain.

**7.3**  Describe in some detail two situations in which you would write a letter rather than a memo. Given your audience, how formal or informal would you make each of the letters? What methods would you use to signal the degree of formality?

**7.4**  Assistant Professor Matthew Reilly is in charge of a nuclear physics project requiring very costly atom-smashing equipment. He knows that Mrs. George Blackwill, wealthy widow of the late Professor Blackwill, would be a very likely donor for his project. However, Reilly is required by university regulation to obtain permission to approach prospective donors from the office of Mark Bader, Director of University Development. Reilly is not happy about this regulation, since he knows there is a good chance that permission will be refused. The Office of University Development often prefers to communicate directly with potential contributors after deciding which projects are most in need of financial support.

Nevertheless, Reilly writes a brief memo to Mr. Bader, describing his financial need and his plan to approach Mrs. Blackwill. Reilly wonders how to word his request for action. Should he propose that he wait for a response from the Office of University Development before contacting Mrs. Blackwill, or should he be more aggressive and state that he will proceed with his plan unless he hears otherwise from Bader within ten days? Consider carefully what Bader's reaction might be to the latter approach.

# ■ Writing Tasks

**7.1**  Many United States agencies (such as the IRS, U.S. Army, and Department of the Interior) publish pamphlets on writing. Write a letter either to the U.S. Government Printing Office to obtain a list of booklets on writing or, if you know the title and source of a booklet you want, to a specific agency to order a copy. Use a subject line in this letter.

**7.2**  Write your own version of Evan Foster's letter (see Discussion Problem 7.1) You may use as much or as little of Foster's drafts as you wish.

Draft letters in correct full block format as specified in the following exercises. Provide all necessary details, and make sure that your closing paragraph contains a direct request for action.

**7.3**  Write to the San Francisco Chamber of Commerce, 100 Federal Street, San Francisco, CA 94101, requesting detailed information concerning conference facilities (hotels, conference rooms, transportation, guided tours, special discounts, etc.) for 500 people from an association holding its annual conference. Give enough details about the requirements of the group attending to ensure that you will receive adequate information.

**7.4**  Write to James Benson, Commissioner of Public Safety, 300 State Street, Hartford, CN 06103, complaining of a particularly perilous intersection at the corner of White and Newton Streets. You pass this corner regularly, have witnessed multiple accidents there over the years, and recently were involved in a close call yourself. Describe the intersection in some detail, and suggest appropriate improvements.

Draft letters in correct semiblock format as specified in the following exercises. As in Tasks 7.3 and 7.4, provide the necessary details, and make sure that your request for action is clearly stated. Use a subject line where you believe one would be effective.

**7.5** Write to Ms. Laura Wainwright, Town Clerk, Milltown, Indiana 47145, requesting photocopies of birth and death certificates for three members of the late Thomas Benson family of Milltown. Explain why you need the documents, and enclose a check for $6.00 for her services. Copy your letter to Thomas Benson, Jr. and to Jane Benson Kanter.

**7.6** Write to the manufacturer of a product you saw advertised in a newspaper or magazine. Ask for details about the item that were not included in the ad. Ask at least three specific questions, one of which requires some explanation on your part. Enclose the ad with your letter.

**7.7** Draft Matthew Reilly's memo to Mark Bader (see Discussion Problem 7.4), in which Reilly requests permission to approach Mrs. Blackwill for a donation to his physics project.

**7.8** Draft the memo that Mark Bader sends in response to Reilly's request. If the response is positive, invent some qualifications to Bader's okay. If you decide on a negative answer, make sure Bader explains his reasons in some detail. Consider whether you would send a blind copy to Mrs. Blackwill, and indicate your intention if you choose this strategy.

**7.9** Kiernan Walters, Art Department Director at Acme Advertising, has just hired a new assistant, Beth Brent. He decides to write a memo to the entire staff to introduce Beth by giving a brief description of her background. Kiernan is clever and creative, and he uses his talents in the memo to make sure that Beth receives a warm welcome from the staff. Write the memo and copy it to Beth. Use a distribution list, making up names and titles.

**7.10** Imagine that you're an accountant for a large furniture manufacturer. You find that the monthly report from Factory J-2 is missing some important shipping information. Write a memo to Frank LaCosta, that factory's shipping manager, requesting the required information. Invent the details.

**7.11** Draft Frank LaCosta's response in memo form, giving part of the information requested in the memo of Task 7.10 and explaining why the remaining data are not yet available. Keep in mind that Frank is constantly under pressure to prove his competence to the people in accounting.

# SHOWING COURTESY, INFORMING, AND EXPLAINING

# 8

# ■ Courtesy in the Business Setting

Perhaps the best way to define courtesy is to say that it means doing more than you have to. That definition certainly holds true in business. Although in its simplest and most obvious form courtesy is embodied in a simple *please* or *thank you*, the courtesy that is most gratifying in the workplace comes from an individual's responsiveness to the problems, needs, and achievements of others. The genuinely courteous business person readily offers praise, congratulations, sympathy, or assistance. But even though courtesy springs from natural and spontaneous feelings, expressing those feelings in writing can often require concentrated effort.

Nevertheless, taking time for courtesy can have some very real and practical rewards for business people. Courteous employees rapidly gain support and trust and more easily influence the actions of others. Although the expectations and norms regarding courtesy differ from company to company, there is a growing awareness in American firms that people work better and harder when they feel they are being treated with dignity and respect. A courteous manager, therefore, can expect to find that his or her employees are more cooperative and productive. Similarly, employees discover that their fellow workers respond better to courteous treatment. And, of course, the people at the top are not immune: they too are likely to be impressed and inspired by acts of courtesy. You may wonder if sending a memo to your boss to congratulate him or her on a noteworthy achievement goes beyond what is required; but if your admiration comes across as genuine, it will not be unwelcome, nor will your time have been wasted.

Perhaps it seems a little hardnosed to underscore the utilitarian value of courtesy, but in the rush of a busy day it can be tempting to postpone or completely overlook small, gracious acts that take thought and effort. This temptation is easier to resist if you understand the practical effects of courtesy. A story about a certain vice president of operations makes this point well. Several senior executives are discussing some new theories about how important the quality of the work environment is for maintaining high worker productivity. Questioning the value of praising his subordinates, the vice president argues, "I don't see the point. I mean, after all, do I thank my tires for not being flat?" To which one of his colleagues quickly responds, "You would if that's what you had to do to keep them from going flat!"

Not only does courtesy help get things done, but also it tends to be remembered. Courteous people build bridges between themselves and others; they inspire support and confidence. This fact is perhaps at no time more important than when you are trying to get a job. In Chapter 12 we will demonstrate how to write an effective thank-you letter following an interview. No one is required to write such a letter. But to thank the interviewer for taking time to meet with you and for showing you consideration suggests that you are not only thoughtful but also willing to take the initiative to do a bit more than is required. A thank-you letter might provide the margin of difference between you and the applicant who is your chief competitor for the position.

Last but not least, courtesy can be its own reward; it makes the dispenser feel good. When you are actively supportive, sympathetic, helpful, or gracious, you are in touch with your best self. Consequently, you have every reason to feel confident about your maturity, humanity, and good judgment.

## ■ Courtesy Letters

Your colleague is promoted; several members of another department are exceptionally helpful to your group; an associate has an accident; your boss has a baby. On such occasions, even if you're in the midst of demanding projects, you'll find yourself writing courtesy letters (at least you *should* find yourself writing them). Often, your courtesy letters will be informal notes to people you know well, but on occasion you will need to write a formal letter—perhaps to a senior person in the firm or to someone you scarcely know. Before writing, think carefully about that person's circumstances and about the feeling you wish to convey. Hear yourself "speaking" to your reader.

It is possible to make a courtesy letter serve more than one purpose. This does not imply that you should be disingenuous or insensitive to the letter's primary purpose. But the circumstances of such a letter can provide an opportunity for you to touch on subjects important to you professionally. For instance, after a job interview you have a real reason to say thank you, but you can also make the same letter convey your increased interest in the position. Or a congratulatory letter to someone just promoted can allow you to mention a way that you might assist him or her. The following case describes another occasion providing an opportunity to write a dual-purpose thank-you letter:

**The Case**

You have just completed a major Management Information Systems (MIS) project for your company. One senior manager (your superior by two levels), Sean Gleason, has been particularly helpful. He gave you lists of all the reports coming into his division. He also spent considerable time reviewing each report with you and noting how useful it was to his division. You now wish to express your thanks, and so you write the letter shown in Figure 8.1.

**Figure 8.1**
The Letter

Dear Sean:

Thanks for your help with the Management Information Systems project. Your assistance was invaluable and allowed me to get accurate, timely information. As a direct result of what I learned, I've been able to reduce the number of interdepartmental reports by a third. You'll soon observe that this reduction was achieved by eliminating some reports and consolidating others. I know you will find that the new system will relieve some of your department's workload.

During the coming six months I expect to continue this work. My next goal is to refine the quality of information we produce, as well as to provide everyone with easy access to those reports kept on file in the system. I hope you will keep me informed of your reactions to this work as we progress.

Thanks again for your help.

Sincerely,

[Your Signature]

**Analysis**

We can begin an analysis of this courtesy letter by looking closely at its salutation, which addresses the recipient by his first name. There was a time when no one addressed a superior by his or her first name and, in fact, when few people addressed their peers informally in business correspondence. But with informality becoming much more the rule today, first names are now frequently used even between people who have established only minimal contact—through a telephone conversation, perhaps.

How can you be sure you are addressing your reader appropriately? For internal letters, the correct salutation depends somewhat on company practice. Some firms are fairly informal; others are not. If you are new to your organization, be observant. Until you are certain exactly what is called for, it is best to lean toward formality, even if you would prefer to be informal. This is especially true if you are writing to a superior. When you are writing to someone outside your organization, the question of what salutation to use is even more complex. If you have met the person and first names were used on both sides, it is usually best to continue to do so, especially if the time you spent together was considerable or informal (such as a lunch appointment). If you have never met, ask yourself whether or not you could comfortably walk into that person's office and immediately speak on a first-name basis. (Would you say "John, I've come here to. . ." or "Mr. Green, I've come here to . . ."?)

After the salutation, the letter in Figure 8.1 gets right to the point. Even though a first-name-only salutation is used, the tone is somewhat formal. For instance, think of the difference it would make to the tone if the second sentence read "You were a great help." The more formal language and somewhat longer sentence telegraph the writer's recognition of the reader's status.

Notice how the letter carries out its secondary purpose—to update Sean on the progress of the project. A good deal of the letter's content "promotes" the writer's project and accomplishments. This is a fine strategy as long as

- the thank you doesn't get lost,
- the "marketing" is not excessive,
- the secondary information benefits or at least interests the reader.

The final sentence of this courtesy letter underscores its main message. Whenever supplementary ideas have been added before the closing, this repetition is a good strategy.

As a complimentary close, "Sincerely" has gained a great deal of popularity and is used frequently in formal letters. Not too long ago "Yours truly" or "Sincerely yours" were the preferred formal closings. (Of course, if you go back far enough in time, you will find that "Your obedient servant" and even "Your most humble and obedient servant" were the closings of choice! Today, we have definitely moved toward informality.)

Depending on the occasion, your firm's usual practice, and your own preference, select one of the following closings, listed here in order of *decreasing* formality:

Very truly yours,

Yours truly,

Sincerely yours,

Sincerely,

Cordially (or Best regards),

Yours,

Obviously, the letter in Figure 8.1 would be signed with your first name (although your full name would normally be typed underneath).

Let's look at two other examples of occasions calling for courtesy correspondence. The first is an event on which someone is to be congratulated.

Terry's boss's boss has just been promoted. His promotion will have no immediate effect on her, but she feels a brief personal memo is in order. Her memo is shown in Figure 8.2.

Our final example of courtesy correspondence is a thank-you letter to a helpful co-worker.

During a recent crunch, a clerk from another department helped Margaret out by coming in early each morning and working evenings and weekends. The pressure is starting to subside, and Margaret wants to thank him. She writes the note shown in Figure 8.3.

---

TO:     Rich
FROM:   Terry
DATE:   July 9, 198-

I realize you've waited a long time for this to happen, which I'm sure makes your promotion especially gratifying. Congratulations! I've very much enjoyed working for you, and if there's anything I can do to help, just ask.

*Terry*

**Figure 8.2**
A brief memo of congratulations.

---

Dear Bob,

I really appreciated your coming to our rescue during these past two weeks. I honestly don't know how we would have made it without your help.

I want you to know that I've sent a note to your boss and copies to his boss and to your personnel file. I know you did what you did because you're the kind of person who always pitches in. I hope you realize that I as well as many others in the department greatly appreciated your enormous efforts during this critical time.

Sincerely,

*Margaret*

**Figure 8.3**
A thank-you note to a co-worker.

---

## ■ Letters and Memos to Inform

Business writers find many occasions to write informative letters or memos. For the most part, such documents are easy to compose—short, to the point, and for a specific purpose. For instance, you may find yourself telling customers that their orders have been shipped, announcing a change of date for an event, or introducing a new product. Although clarity and brevity are by-words for such simple letters and memos, you should remember that many informative messages also need to be persuasive. When writing about a dispatched order, you want the customer to perceive your firm as reliable and courteous; when establishing a new date, you want the readers to believe the change was necessary; and, of course, you want potential customers to find a new product appealing.

If a point can be made in two sentences, resist the temptation to fill a page. Typical workday information can normally be conveyed in–house in a one–page memo. On the other hand, don't hesitate to write a longer memo if the subject is complex or if additional data are essential. Being convincing may require you to spend extra time checking to be sure that the information you are sending is complete; however, you should also aim to be as brief as possible. For instance, when telling someone that their merchandise is in the mail, you want to include a careful description of the articles sent and the date the shipment was dispatched. But you certainly don't need to ramble on about the firm's reliability and reputation for promptness. Similarly in introducing a new product, you should carefully describe its features and the benefits a purchaser would receive from it; you might also include information about where and when it will be available. But you should not provide a long history of the trials and tribulations that accompanied this product's development.

## Important Matters

Occasionally you may be asked to draft an especially important letter or memo. Because the document has great significance, you know in advance that it is likely to be read closely and its implications are probably going to be examined with care. For example, a letter to employees informing them about an impending layoff has its purpose to calm people's fears and to rebuild company morale. But if it is poorly planned or badly worded, such a letter will serve only to frighten people. Although the case is extreme, this letter about a layoff is typical of important informative correspondence for two reasons: first, the writer is only slightly (or not at all) familiar with the recipients; and second, the audience is large and diverse. With such letters, the stakes are very high because they present an opportunity for either extraordinary gains or losses. Therefore, if you are given the opportunity to draft such a letter, chances are that your superiors have a good deal of confidence in you, or are at least testing abilities they suspect you possess. In either case, you will want to approach the task with good sense and a great deal of care.

## Sensitive Subjects

When you write a letter to inform people about a sensitive subject, your audience analysis must be more painstaking than under any other circumstances. If you have to make assumptions about how people feel about the subject, try to base them on real research and fact-finding. As part of your preparation, arrange a meeting with the people who have asked you to develop the letter; share their viewpoints, and test a few of your own ideas.

If you are permitted to do so, talk to some of the people who will receive the letter and determine their attitudes and concerns. If the subject of the letter is confidential or proprietary and you cannot ask for opinions from potential readers, check to see whether letters concerning this issue (or a similar issue) were written in the past. You may be able to find file copies of those letters to study and evaluate. You may also be able to discover whether or not they accomplished their purpose and to learn from their example. Even if some or all of these paths are blocked, you should try to visualize the various kinds of people who will be reading the document. Consider people with varied needs and preconceived notions. Hear yourself telling them the information, and imagine their reactions; try out various words and phrases, and project the responses they might elicit. In short, use your "empathy muscles."

When you have done your preliminary research, you will probably have a much clearer idea of how to proceed. But it is also possible that you will have a number of conflicting ideas about the potential content and wording of the letter. You might try to eliminate some of the more sensitive material by distinguishing between what people *have to know* and what they *want to know*. Including only the former will keep your letter brief and factual. Alternatively, you might decide that a careful, up-front explanation of the circumstances should precede the factual material.

As you face these issues, work closely with an experienced supervisor if possible. If you are unsure about the best writing strategy, a good tactic is to prepare two or more drafts and arrange for a preliminary discussion of their strengths and weaknesses. Finally, before you distribute a sensitive letter, *be certain that you have the necessary approval from your superiors*. No stories are sadder than those frequently told about overly ambitious, impatient, or aggressive employees who disseminated information before they received clearance to do so.

To help you with this challenging kind of assignment, we have compiled a list of seven steps to follow when writing a letter or memo to inform:

1. Identify your primary audience (who are the main people you are writing to and what are their principal concerns?).
2. Identify all secondary audiences (other interested parties with some stake in the outcome) and hidden audiences (such as top management, other departments, shareholders, customers, or the media).
3. Do as much preliminary research as possible, including talking to supervisors and to a relevant sample of people (unless the information is confidential).
4. Decide what you must say (essential information), what you don't have to say (optional information), and what you would like to say (words intended for diplomacy, courtesy, etc.).

5. Structure your letter strategically. (Remember that the beginning and end usually have the most impact on the readers.)
6. Experiment with ways of making your message diplomatic; if necessary, review alternative approaches with your supervisor.
7. Get all necessary approvals before releasing the letter for distribution.

In the following case, a letter is written to announce a new appointment. Most of the time, a notice that a new employee has joined the firm is a courteous but routine announcement. In this situation, the new appointee will hold an exceptionally high office, and so the event has unusually important implications for many potential audiences. Clearly, this is a special kind of informative letter.

**The Case**

Slowly but persistently, your company, a major manufacturer of electrical components, has been acquiring companies that are active participants in alternative energy research and development. Two years ago, your firm bought Soletek, Inc., a manufacturer of solar energy systems, in which it has invested heavily. This month Soletek is going to announce that Dr. Emile C. Burdensen from the University of California at Berkeley has accepted the position of Chief Operating Officer. Because of his reputation as a major innovator in the solar industry, Dr. Burdensen's affiliation with Soletek establishes that company's standing in the industry.

You are a marketing communications specialist with the parent company, Consolidated Industries. Matthew Bleiberg, Consolidated's President and Chief Executive Officer, wants stockholders to recognize that the hiring of Burdensen signifies a deep commitment to solar energy. Bleiberg asks your supervisor to draft a letter announcing Burdensen's appointment, which is to be included in this year's annual report over Bleiberg's signature. Your supervisor in turn asks you to make the first pass at composing the letter. You submit the draft in Figure 8.4 for approval.

**Figure 8.4**
The Letter

Dear Fellow Stockholders:

This is an especially significant year because it marks a time when we have all made an important investment in the future of Consolidated Industries. It is with great pride that I welcome Emile C. Burdensen as Chief Operating Officer of our newest subsidiary, Soletek, Inc.

Dr. Burdensen's name has come to symbolize an entire industry. Over the last twenty years, he has been a pioneer in the field of solar energy. This industry, which he has led through its infancy, is now beginning to realize its rich potential. With his leadership, we can expect Soletek not only to take command of major domestic markets but also to become dominant in world markets.

Soletek has shown continuous growth over its ten-year history. Two years ago, at the time Consolidated acquired it, we underwrote a major rebuilding project that allowed the size of its workforce to triple. In return, Soletek has won fourteen key government contracts, the most significant of which is to develop a prototype for one of the world's most sophisticated solar power installations.

I know that we have just begun to witness the rewards of this exceptional acquisition.

Sincerely,


Matthew A. Bleiberg
President and
Chief Executive Officer
Consolidated Industries

---

**Analysis**

Writing this letter is a difficult assignment. For one thing, the task is to announce the appointment of a new chief operating officer, but the letter's main purpose is to persuade stockholders, potential investors, employees, and perhaps even some customers that exciting and potentially profitable things are happening in the company. In addition, there is the difficulty of drafting a letter that is to have someone else's signature and that is directed at an extremely large and undifferentiated audience, whose only common denominator is their stake in the company's profitability.

As you know, when writing for someone else's signature, the first step is to concentrate on what you know about that person's professional attitudes and behavior. You need to try to picture that person reacting to the situation at hand. In this case, it is well known that Bleiberg takes a great deal of pride in the fact that Consolidated keeps its investors and employees well informed. He has frequently asserted in speeches and interviews that each stockholder and employee is involved in the company's destiny and therefore should understand its long-range objectives. Accordingly, the opening paragraph of the letter quickly establishes the perspective he shares with all of his readers (note the use of the first person plural, *we* and *our*).

Although there is no way to identify the individual characteristics of this highly diverse audience, you do know that the annual report is intended for stockholders and potential investors, as well as for employees, customers, and potential customers. Many of these people are likely to regard the letter with only perfunctory interest or to skim through it before deciding whether or not to read it closely. Your goal is to make these readers *want* to read and absorb the letter. The first sentence, therefore, is an attention-grabber that tries to establish a focus of concern to all—the future of the firm.

Once Mr. Bleiberg's important announcement is made, the letter carefully leads up to the rather sensitive information about the company's large investment in its new acquisition. To give it the least emphasis, you located this statement midway through the letter and carefully tied it to facts about the favorable results. The letter ends on an extremely optimistic note. Observe that the complimentary close is not overly formal, underscoring that Bleiberg is writing to people who, even though their faces may not be familiar, at least share his concern for Consolidated's welfare.

## ■ Letters and Memos to Explain

The line between a letter written to inform and one written to explain is a thin one. Certainly there is a good deal of explaining implicit in Matthew Bleiberg's letter to the stockholders. But on some occasions the main reason for writing is to make something easy to understand. You may need to explain the difference between two similar products, help a job candidate understand the responsibilities of a position in your company or delineate the steps that someone from another department has to take to complete a project. Although in all of these cases the reader receives some information, the emphasis on explanation distinguishes these letters and memos from those that are purely informative.

When your intent is to explain, clarity should be your foremost concern. "I know you know what you *think* I said, but do you really understand what I meant?" is a tongue-in-cheek query that training supervisors sometimes use to make the point that communication is far more difficult than we might believe. In preparing an explanation, audience analysis is once again crucial and can make the difference between a letter or memo that misfires and one that accomplishes the author's objectives.

A misconception about what your audience already knows can greatly inhibit your ability to transmit a lucid explanation. If you are trying to explain the difference between two products, for instance, you can make a simple comparison if one product is already familiar to your readers. But if both products are unfamiliar, you will start from a very different vantage point. Similarly, if your task requires explaining a technical process, you need to know whether your readers are familiar with the appropriate technical vocabulary. If they are not, you will have to translate or define the terminology. It is also very important for you to understand why they need the explanation and how they intend to use it.

As you try to appraise your audience, don't overlook their feelings and emotions. When people have closely held attitudes or deeply felt concerns, their preconceptions tend to affect their understanding. As a case in point, consider the following unpunctuated sentence:

Woman without her man is nothing

When asked to supply punctuation, most men are apt to do nothing more than place a period after the last word. But women more frequently produce a version of the sentence similar to this:

Woman—without her, man is nothing.

Readers often see what they prefer to see; therefore, you should strive to be both tactful and clear when offering explanations about controversial or sensitive issues.

Even when the task of explaining seems to be straightforward, the situation may be anxiety-producing for the person on the receiving end. This is particularly true when the recipient is under pressure to perform well and needs the explanation to complete a project or to execute a vital task. The following case depicts such a situation.

**The Case**

You are a junior associate at Information Resource Consultants (IRC), a marketing research firm that conducts surveys for businesses and government agencies. Your supervisor, Chris Nichols, has asked you to prepare a brief memo for new employees explaining how interviewers should introduce themselves to their telephone contacts and what their general demeanor during such interviews should be. Figure 8.5 contains the memo you write for him.

**Figure 8.5**
The Memo

TO:        New Interviewers          DATE: January 14, 198-
FROM:      Chris Nichols
SUBJECT:   Interviewing Skills

The purpose of our surveys is to compile useful information for our clients so that they can tailor their products and services to meet their customers' needs and preferences. Therefore, as an IRC interviewer, you can feel assured that you are performing a very useful service. Nevertheless, some of the people you call may find the timing inconvenient or may be reluctant to speak for other reasons. The following suggestions should help you to achieve good rapport with the people you phone and should get your interviews off to a good start:

o   As soon as the phone is answered, introduce yourself by name and explain the purpose of your call, being certain to stress the objective of IRC surveys (as stated above).

o   Quickly explain the criteria used to establish who is able to participate in the survey.

o   When you have determined that an appropriate person is on the line, explain that all answers are kept anonymous and that the survey will take no more than five minutes.

o   If the person you are speaking with says that this is an inconvenient time for an interview, politely inquire as to what would be a good time to call back.

o   If he or she objects to answering on the basis of a distrust of surveys, listen to the complaint and respond courteously by explaining in further detail the potential benefits of this survey.

o   If the person on the line is still not receptive, end the conversation as courteously as possible—usually by thanking the listener for his or her time.

Should you have any special problems, please feel free to discuss them with me. In general, people are receptive to IRC calls; many recognize our name, know our professional reputation, and are eager to partcipate.

---

**Analysis**

Explaining the interview procedure is the main reason for this memo, but you, the writer, realize that it is also very important to build the interviewers' confidence and to dispel their anxieties. The memo does so in two ways: first, by helping the interviewers feel they are performing a useful, professional task; second, by using clear, explicit language to describe the steps to be taken.

Notice that the memo reflects the writer's understanding of the interviewers' possible misgivings and also a shared sense of pride in the firm's reputation for professionalism. The memo speaks of "our surveys" and "our clients." Also, the interviewers are addressed as "you," helping them feel that the communication is more than just a formal set of instructions. (Consider how different the tone would have been if the directions were phrased like this: "As soon as the phone is answered, the interviewer should introduce himself or herself. . . .") Finally, observe that the memo ends on a note of encouragement and optimism.

As important as it is to understand the readers' feelings with respect to receiving an explanation, it is equally important to understand your own feelings about giving one. If you know how you feel about both the situation and your audience, you will have an easier time finding words that help you establish rapport. For instance, in the above case Chris Nichols holds a higher position than the interviewers. As we noted in Chapter 4, in such situations a writer must strive for a tone that is authoritative but avoids "talking down." Although Nichols wants to be supportive, for the most part he is just explaining a procedure to an audience who is likely to be receptive. There are times, however, when delivering an explanation can be an extremely difficult task that calls for an unusual amount of self-insight, empathy, and tact.

# ■ Explanations versus Apologies

One of the least welcome but crucial business writing tasks you will face is that of having to explain an unpleasant reality. Unfortunately, we know that lost accounts, errors in judgment, tardy shipments, and an endless list of equally unwelcome events crop up as inevitably as bad weather. These situations require remedies and also nearly always require written explanations.

Apologies are sometimes necessary when things go wrong, but there is a great deal of difference between an explanation and an apology. An apology focuses on feelings; an explanation takes feelings into account, but it mainly rests its case on facts or realities. To understand this difference, compare the two memos in Figures 8.6 and 8.7.

---

TO:     Robert DeWitt, Tot-Line Product Manager
FROM:  Rudy Kramer, Manager, Marketing Communications
DATE:   March 5, 198-
RE:     Delay in Tot-Line Brochure

     I'm extremely sorry to tell you that the new marketing brochure for Tot-Line will not be completed by March 15, the deadline we had established. I know that this will greatly disappoint your group, but, as a result of an unanticipated problem, the printer will not be able to meet the schedule. I wish that I had better news for you, Rob. I certainly apologize for this delay.

**Figure 8.6**
A memo of apology.

---

TO:     Robert DeWitt, Tot-Line Product Manager
FROM:  Rudy Kramer, Manager, Marketing Communications
DATE:   March 5, 198-
RE:     New Delivery Date for Tot-Line Brochure

     As you know, we had intended to have the new Tot-Line brochure in your hands by March 15. I regret that we will have to revise the delivery date to April 1.

     I am sure you recall my telling you several weeks ago that the printer informed me that the paper we selected was in short supply and that he would need to substitute a similar stock from another manufacturer. At that time it seemed wise to accept the substitution so that we could meet your mid-March deadline. Yesterday I saw the first proofs of the new brochure, and I was greatly disappointed in the quality of the imprint. All the charts have a rather shadowy,

**Figure 8.7**
A memo of explanation.

grayed-out appearance. The problem, of course, is the paper. The original stock we ordered can be available in two weeks, and I have decided to wait for it.

Rob, I know that this delay is an inconvenience for your group, but I also know that you want a high-quality brochure. I take complete responsibility for the delay, and I promise you that you will be entirely pleased with the brochure we deliver.

cc: Fred Cody

Although the explanation took more time to write than the apology (and also will take longer to read), the extra effort will certainly pay off by increasing Robert DeWitt's understanding of the problem and restoring his confidence in Rudy Kramer. In the second memo, Kramer not only explains the cause of the delay but also takes complete responsibility for both of his decisions; furthermore, he clearly stipulates the new delivery date for the brochure. By his words and actions he conveys his assurance that, although there has been an unfortunate slip-up, he is entirely in control of the situation.

## ■ Summary

Courtesy—doing more than you have to—brings rewards in business as it does in other walks of life. Taking the time to write a letter of thanks for a job interview, a note of congratulation or sympathy to a colleague or client, reveals your best self to others. At times you can appropriately touch on other matters in a courtesy letter. Courtesy is appreciated and remembered.

Informative letters should be clear and brief; frequently, they also need to be persuasive. Those dealing with sensitive issues call for special tact and diplomacy. Identify your primary and secondary audiences; conduct preliminary research; decide on essential versus optional information; structure your writing strategically; experiment with alternative diplomatic approaches; obtain necessary approval from superiors.

Letters of explanation often supply information, of course, but their emphasis is on the process of explaining. Clarity is a foremost concern, as is audience analysis—how much knowledge do your readers already possess? Although apologies are necessary when things go wrong, a letter of explanation will do much more to satisfy the reader. It goes beyond feelings to facts; it tells exactly what has been done to correct the slip-up, and conveys the assurance that matters are under control.

## ■ Discussion Problems

**8.1**  Your favorite uncle, Harry, just wrote to you from California to tell you that he heard that one of his closest college friends, Paul Brigham (whom he had lost track of in the last ten years), apparently is an employee at your company. Harry suggests that you look Paul up. Examining the company roster of employees, you discover with mixed feelings that Paul Brigham is the senior vice president of your division. You have seen his name many times but never connected it with the friend your uncle frequently mentioned.

Will you write to Paul Brigham or contact him by phone? If you write, how formal will your letter be? Will you worry that any overture on your part might be interpreted as seeking favor and therefore tell Harry to make the contact himself? In short, how will you handle this situation?

**8.2**  To understand the difficulties in trying to explain a process, try this experiment. Draw a simple geometric figure somewhat like the one in Figure 8.8. Then write out directions describing how you drew the figure so that someone can duplicate your drawing. Show the directions but *not* your drawing to a classmate or friend, and ask him or her to draw the figure. Then compare the two drawings. If you observe differences, discuss with each other why they occurred.

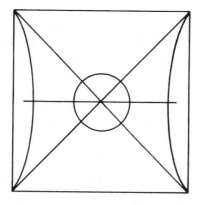

**Figure 8.8**
Sample geometric figure.

**8.3**  We have seen in this chapter that courtesy in business can have practical rewards. Often, a thoughtful letter offering thanks, praise, congratulations, or assistance can contain secondary information that may fulfill a very different purpose. For example, a thank-you note after a job interview might contain some new piece of evidence to prove that you're the ideal candidate for the position. Decide how the courtesy letters described below might serve a dual purpose. What additional information might you include to further the second purpose? How would you artfully combine courtesy with practicality?

- You are a technical writer at a very large high-tech corporation, and a former colleague, Paula Beckwith, has just started her own software consulting firm. You are writing to congratulate her on this promising new venture.
- You've just finished a fascinating 12-week editing course at your local community college. You feel that you've learned a lot in such a short period, and you decide to write an enthusiastic thank-you note to the teacher, who is a senior editor at a major publishing firm.

- As a junior consultant at a busy environmental consulting firm, you've just managed to meet the deadline on your first major client proposal—a 300-page document filled with technical language and complicated charts. You decide to write an informal thank-you memo to the four secretaries who worked overtime all week to get the document out in time. Of course, you send a copy to the head of your department.

- As secretary of the local chapter of NOW (National Organization of Women), you are writing to your congressman, praising him for his role in the passage of the new equal rights legislation in your state.

- As the assistant to the president of Tarrytown Bank, you write a thank-you note to Mr. and Mrs. Jones for the savings account they just opened.

**8.4** After months of planning and deliberation, Kathy DeVoto has decided to leave her job as a social worker at St. Margaret's Hospital to start her own geriatric counseling service. She proposes to use her many years of experience and her network of personal and professional contacts to advise clients about the available health care alternatives for the elderly: Medicare and Medicaid benefits, nursing homes, home health care, day care for the elderly, Meals on Wheels, etc. To introduce her new business, she writes an informative letter to a select list of lawyers, physicians, and members of the clergy in her area in the hope that they will begin to refer clients to her.

Discuss this letter in some detail:

- What should DeVoto's tone or attitude be in addressing her audience?

- How long should the letter be?

- What details should she include in her opening paragraph?

- Suggest additional details or strategies that would strengthen her letter.

- How can she best persuade her readers to refer clients to her?

- What should be included in her closing paragraph?

**8.5** Imagine that you've just been offered a job as a marketing communications specialist at a large insurance company. After careful consideration, you have decided not to accept the position, even though you don't have a concrete alternative yet (you found the literature they gave you extremely tedious, and the people you met inspired equally negative feelings).

In your letter of refusal to the director of marketing communications, you want to be sure to explain your decision firmly and carefully while remaining sensitive to the feelings your words are likely to evoke. What implications do you want to avoid? How can you achieve your primary purpose without damaging the ego of your reader or questioning the excellence of the firm?

**8.6** Are there *ever* occasions when a straight apology—with little or no explanation—is the better alternative? Imagine the details of such an occasion.

# ■ Writing Tasks

**8.1** You have been nominated by your department head to be the department's candidate for the Wainwright Fellowship, which is awarded to ten deserving employees each year. If you are among the ten selected, you will be given the opportunity to complete a year of company-financed study in the discipline of your choice, as well as a guarantee that your current job or a better one will be waiting for you when the year is over. Write to your department head to accept this honor and its potential opportunity.

**8.2**   Traditionally, your company has treated employees and their families to a catered dinner at Christmas time. This year, due to particularly low revenues, the board decided that the party must be for employees only; family members and other guests will not be included. You report to the director of human resources, who must prepare a memo announcing the board's decision. You have been asked to write a first draft; do so.

**8.3**   Your company just furnished and outfitted a new coffee room in your group's area. The facility includes a table, two chairs, a refrigerator, and a cabinet containing Styrofoam cups and plastic spoons, instant hot chocolate, and tea bags. It is also equipped with a sink with hot and cold water, a paper-towel rack, a coffee-making machine (which also supplies boiling water for tea and hot chocolate), and several automatic vending machines that dispense candy, crackers, and other snacks. Coffee, tea, and hot chocolate will be supplied on a pay-as-you-go honor system at a quarter a cup. You have been asked to prepare a memo to circulate to group members that clearly spells out the procedures and responsibilities for using and taking care of this facility. Prepare the memo.

**8.4**   Draft at least two of the dual-purpose courtesy letters described in Discussion Problem 8.3.

**8.5**   Draft Kathy DeVoto's informative letter, described in Discussion Problem 8.4.

**8.6**   Write the sensitive letter of refusal described in Discussion Problem 8.5, in which you turn down a job offer from the Iroquois Mutual Insurance Company. Invent additional details.

Write appropriate letters for the situations described below.

- Write to the manager of the Whitford College bookstore, who ordered 300 copies of your firm's *American Literature Anthology*. This particular text is now out of print, but you have an alternative to suggest.

- Write to a job applicant whom you interviewed for an assistant professorship at Whitford College's History Department. You have decided to hire another candidate.

- Write to the president of the Whitford College Student Council and explain that you cannot fulfill his request that you speak at Whitford's commencement ceremony.

- Write to Whitford's Publications Manager, informing her that the new fall course catalogue being printed by your company will be at least three weeks late. Last-minute course changes and a particularly busy summer workload at your firm are responsible for the delay.

- Write to one of your clients (a young novelist), who invited you, as his editor, to attend the talk he gave at Whitford last Friday. You meant to attend but simply forgot.

# WRITING TO PERSUADE; WRITING TO SAY NO

## 9

# ■ Letters and Memos to Persuade

Since so much of business writing is persuasive, it is especially important to become skillful at writing letters that lead others to accept your ideas or opinions and convince them to follow through with the specific actions you intend.

Perhaps the most overtly persuasive business letters are sales letters, letters written to convince people to buy your company's goods or services. In their simplest and most traditional form, sales letters first catch the prospective customer's attention, then describe the product or service, and quickly show how its special features match the customer's needs. They normally close with an *action statement,* clear directions to the potential customer about how to obtain the product or service. Figure 9.1 is an example of a traditional sales letter.

---

Dear (Name of Prospective Customer):

    With April fast approaching, you undoubtedly are worried about your tax bill for 1986. Would you like to increase this year's deductions substantially over previous years?

    Enclosed is a detailed description of a new, greatly simplified, fool-proof method for cutting the pain out of filing this year's return—a method that could legally save you hundreds of dollars, and perhaps more. Filing Can Almost Be Fun, by George Wilmette, C.P.A., has literally hundreds of tips that will save you hours of time and will reveal many deductions you have overlooked in past years.

    Read the enclosed brochure carefully, and learn how you can examine a copy of this valuable book for fifteen days with no obligation on your part.

                                  Yours truly,

                                  [Signature]

**Figure 9.1**
A traditional sales letter.

**Attention-grabber**

**Description of product or service and statement of needs and benefits**

**Action statement**

---

Chances are that you have received traditional sales letters at home and at work. You may be relieved to know that, unless you have a specific talent for advertising or marketing communications, you will seldom if ever be asked to write this kind of letter.

## Cold-Call Sales Letters

The letter in Figure 9.1 is a *cold-call sales letter,* so named because the writer has not had a chance to "warm up" the relationship with the reader. Writer and reader have never met, and there is no likelihood that they ever will. The recipients of such letters are selected because market research has indicated that their shared characteristics make them a good target group for the marketing of the product or service.

Typically, most large businesses today use professional writers who specialize in direct mail advertising to develop cold-call letters. A letter such as the one in Figure 9.1 will be reproduced many times; most probably it will be a key element of a mass mailing to thousands of recipients.

Unless you work for a small firm or for yourself or your job is directly related to marketing or sales, you will not write many cold-call letters. However, there is one occasion when it is entirely likely that you will write such letters—when you are seeking a job. Job applicants are, of course, selling themselves, and they frequently need to write to people who have not requested them to do so. Job application "sales" letters, both cold-call and personal, will be studied in detail in Chapter 12.

## Personal Sales Letters

Personal sales letters are written to people with whom you are acquainted. You may know them well or only slightly. At the very least, you will have received some first-hand knowledge about them from your supervisors or co-workers. Taking the word "selling" in its broadest sense (to mean persuading someone you know to accept your views and ideas) we can almost guarantee that you will need to write many selling letters and memos in your business career.

Negotiating, persuading, and sometimes even demanding are integral to the daily routine of most business people, and frequently these responsibilities require writing. Such letters and memos run the gamut from the most simple and mundane (such as persuading your boss to reschedule a meeting) to the most complex and important (for example, writing a letter proposal to sell your company's services to an important client). In every case of this kind, you will need to prepare carefully before writing. That preparation normally will include the following steps:

- Decide precisely what you want to accomplish.
- Carefully research and analyze your audience's needs or objectives.
- Try to predict the advantages and disadvantages your reader may perceive concerning your point of view and how he or she might react to them.
- Decide how much and what kind of attention you should give to objections the reader is likely to raise.

- Construct a logical, powerful argument that moves the reader toward "buying" your viewpoint.
- Give careful thought to the tone of your letter or memo.

## Convincing a Reluctant Reader

In Chapter 3 we stressed the importance of allowing your audience's needs to help determine your purpose for writing. We underscore that point here. Nevertheless, we recognize that a needs analysis only increases your anxiety when you are bent on achieving an objective that your reader does not share. When you perceive that your audience is indifferent to your views, you expect that convincing them will not be easy; and, of course, when you discover that your reader almost certainly has strong negative feelings, you may feel extremely insecure or worried. But handling indifferent, skeptical, or hostile audiences requires methods that differ only in *degree*, not in basic technique. Therefore, let's again review the method outlined above, showing how it applies to the task of convincing a reluctant reader.

As with a reader whose needs are in line with your own objectives, the first step is to see where your interests and your reader's are aligned. First, think carefully about your own needs and goals; establish priorities, and consider whether you can offer the reader alternatives or choices. Next, perform as intense an audience analysis as you can, relying on facts first and then on intuitions, when facts are missing. *Try to figure out how you can make the reader feel that the actions you are urging are in his or her best interest.* When you have done everything possible to analyze and understand the reader-writer relationship, very carefully review the data you have on hand. You will need to organize your argument with great care. In overcoming a reader's strong objections, it is especially important to structure an argument that moves the reader step-by-step toward the conclusion that you have in mind. Finally, you must select an appropriate tone.

Although you will seldom have to overcome the objections of a completely hostile audience, on occasion you will be confronted with such a task. And certainly you can expect to deal frequently with people who are indifferent or who have specific misgivings about what you are urging. Let's first take a look at a case in which the writer's opinion and objective are not likely to be welcomed by the reader. Through analysis of this case, we can better understand how to approach such challenging situations.

Jennifer Dugan is a research and development (R&D) specialist in a large manufacturing company whose principal products are highly specialized machines used in the automotive and farm equipment industries. For the ten months since she joined the company, Jennifer has been assigned to

**The Case**

Quality Control, a group that is responsible for the final stages of the testing of new machines. The job has its pros and cons. Because the group is somewhat understaffed, Jennifer has been given a good deal of responsibility, which she has certainly enjoyed. On the other hand, she has always preferred the research end of engineering; she would very much like to work with a team doing primary research on new product ideas.

Three weeks ago, Jennifer was invited to join another group whose focus is innovation; however, Brent Keane, the manager of that group, cautioned her that he will not go ahead with the transfer if her present manager, Harry Grant, does not approve. Knowing that Harry will not want to lose her, Jennifer decides that before speaking with him she will lay the groundwork by sending him a carefully worded memo. In Figure 9.2 Jennifer tries to argue persuasively for Harry to approve the transfer.

---

**Figure 9.2**
The Memo

TO:  Harry Grant, Manager, Quality Control
FROM:  Jennifer Dugan
DATE:  October 14, 198-
RE:  Current and Future Responsibilities

In the past ten months I have participated in six major testing projects—the last two in a supervisory capacity. At my six-month performance review, you gave me a generous evaluation, and I have always found you supportive of my endeavors. As a member of the Quality Control group, I have learned a great deal in a stimulating environment. But despite so many gains, I would still like you to approve my transfer to Product Development. Not only will the transfer mean a great deal for my own professional development, but I believe it will ultimately benefit the Quality Control group.

As you know, I joined the firm with the full intention of seeking an assignment that would allow me to work with product innovations. Because you were extremely persuasive and Quality Control had an evident need, I detoured and joined your group. Nevertheless, I knew that I would eventually again feel the pull of my original intentions. I think that now is the most appropriate time for me to make this change. We are between projects and Stan Denton (who is, as you know, a highly skilled quality control specialist) told me that he feels ready and eager to try his supervisory skills on our next assignment. Stan also informed me that quality control is his main interest and has been for some time.

Brent Keane would like me to go over to Product Development as soon as possible. However, he would allow me to spend one day a week for the next month working with Stan to ensure that he is ready for his new responsibilities.

Since there is a capable replacement for me in Quality Control, and since I will ultimately be seeking this change, I hope you will approve my transfer at this time. Could we have lunch on Thursday to discuss my request and the needed arrangements?

**Analysis**

There's no question about Jennifer's purpose: she knows that she wants the transfer. She also knows her audience well: Harry Grant's first priority is the performance of the Quality Control group. At this time the group is shorthanded, and Harry will be reluctant to part with Jennifer's capable assistance. Because she has shown a great deal of leadership potential, Harry has expectations of her becoming an extremely valuable employee in the future. Jennifer knows all this; she also knows that Harry's plans for her do not match her own professional aspirations.

Jennifer begins her memo by reminding Harry that she has indeed contributed much to the group. Then she quickly states her position: she wants a transfer. Knowing that Harry's primary objective is the welfare of the group, she ends her first paragraph by telling him that the transfer could possibly be in the group's best interest. Harry's attention is now caught, and she has offered him something positive.

In her second paragraph, Jennifer provides two solid reasons why the group could benefit from her transfer. First, she lets him know that, at best, she would only be a temporary member of Quality Control. Second, she focuses on the existence of a good, permanent replacement, who has a genuine commitment to quality control.

Jennifer ends the memo by reiterating the two main points of her argument and setting up an action plan for proceeding.

Jennifer's memo was particularly difficult to write because she faces an audience that would be hard to convince and also because she herself has a very personal, vested interest in the outcome. In writing her memo, she needs to monitor the intensity of her feelings, or at least control the way her emotions filter through her words. Imagine the effect on Harry if she wrote something like this: "Harry, you know I've done a lot of good work for the group, and I told you from the very beginning that I was interested in product development. It would really be very unfair of you to hold me back." Or consider the response that this tone would elicit: "Please try to do this for me, Harry. It really means an awful lot to me to have this transfer."

Trying to "hear" how she would speak to Harry on this rather formal occasion, Jennifer gives the memo a more formal tone than she ordinarily uses in her daily conversations with her boss. Also, she has given some thought to the hidden audiences that may read the memo. She realizes that Harry might show her request to the vice president to whom he reports. Also, she recognizes that it is likely that her memo and Harry's response will be kept in her permanent file, a record of her professional development at the firm, which other superiors may consult when she is up for salary increases or promotions.

Normally, the writing tasks you will face, although challenging, will not have the strong emotional overtones attached to Jennifer Dugan's memo. In the next case, for instance, you are asked to imagine that you need to write a letter to convince a reader who may be reluctant to accept your suggestion. However, the issue here does not have strong personal implications.

**The Case**

Your employer, A. Hollis & Company, a supplier of office furniture and equipment, has never been very active in community affairs. You feel that the company could and should do more to support worthy organizations. You have felt this way for some time, and recent shifts in the economy and cutbacks in federal aid have now prompted you to discuss your feelings with your manager. Not only does your manager agree with you, but she lets you know that several of Hollis's competitors have programs for matching employee contributions to educational institutions. She encourages you to write a letter to M. E. Hoyt, Senior Vice President of Corporate and Employee Communications, summarizing your position. She offers to give the letter to Hoyt personally and to explain to him that she shares your views. She suggests that you keep in mind that Hoyt has resisted similar proposals in the past. You try to do that as you compose the letter shown in Figure 9.3.

**Figure 9.3**
The Letter

Dear Mr. Hoyt:

Hollis & Company has been my employer for more than four years. My current position is Sales Supervisor for Educational Markets.

I came into the company in an entry-level sales position, and the company has given me many opportunities to learn and to achieve. I am grateful for these opportunities, but I am also committed to the college that laid the groundwork for my career here. As a way of recognizing the importance of my education, each time I've been promoted, I've increased my contribution to my school's alumni association.

Today my school is desperately in need of money. Clearly this is not an isolated case; many schools are in grave financial trouble.

I propose that Hollis begin a program to match our employees' contributions to their educational institutions. Such a program not only would benefit the schools but also would be sound business. In addition to the expected tax benefits, a matching program would allow my salespeople to show customers real evidence of the company's support to higher education. This commitment, I believe, could be a significant marketing and public relations tool.

I hope you will lend your support to such a program. I look forward to hearing from you soon.

Sincerely,


[Signature]

**Analysis**

You are enthusiastic about your idea, but you know that your reader is apt to be unreceptive. It seems wise, therefore, not to plunge directly into the sensitive subject. Rather, you decide to open some distance away from the main point. Your work history is relevant here, and it is likely to interest Hoyt. Notice how the letter *leads* Hoyt to the idea of a matching program. Once the recommendation has been made, the argument is strengthened by the suggestion that the program is sound business. This point is followed by an allusion to the public relations and marketing implications of the program—something likely to impress Hoyt.

The closing paragraph of the letter is a rather low-keyed action statement. Depending on your own personality and on your assessment of Hoyt, you might be more assertive and close by telling him that you will call him for a response. If your manager had previously indicated a willingness to cooperate, you might invite Hoyt to meet with both of you to discuss next steps. In either case, when a request or a strong suggestion is the dominant reason for communicating, it is very important to show that you expect a response.

## The Letter Proposal

A *proposal* is an offer in writing to provide specified services or goods at a set cost. It presents the offer and also attempts to induce the customer or client to accept it—and, if there are competing proposals, to prefer your offer over others. Proposals can be very lengthy, formal documents that look much like reports, or they can be short, less formal letters. (In Chapter 14, we will consider longer proposals.)

No matter what their form, proposals are essentially sales presentations. They present accurate, factual information about the goods or services offered and valid reasons why the recipient of the proposal should purchase those goods or services. Typically, a proposal includes objectives, procedures and materials (as applicable), time table, summary of expertise, and costs. These components are not locked into the sequence given here, but objectives will invariably be explained near the beginning of the proposal and costs will be described near the end.

Before writing a proposal, you should make every effort to understand the needs of the recipient. Often you will need to have preliminary conversations with the recipient or with other people. Your research may also entail extensive checking of facts and figures related to earlier projects. You may even need to read reports and memoranda about those projects and to review articles in periodicals and newspapers. (Chapter 14 will offer you specific help with such research techniques.)

In many cases your preliminary research will help you to discover the customer's overriding need or primary concern. Once you are fortunate enough to possess such knowledge, you should make sure that need remains your main focus. Keep in mind that your job as proposal writer is to match the features of your product or service to the customer's needs—to show that you can provide benefits to the customer that outweigh, or at least equal, the required expenditure.

Let's now look at a situation that requires a letter proposal.

---

**The Case**

Merril, Browne & Townsend (MB&T) is a marketing research firm. The firm advises its clients on issues such as company image, customers' perceptions of new and existing products, and advertising strategies. David Paulson, a research associate at MB&T, is the newest member of a six-person team. David assists with analyses of both quantitative and qualitative data and often helps to draft proposals and reports.

MB&T would like to be selected to evaluate the current advertising strategy of Ajax Appliances, a large chain of home appliance stores. The projected market study would use telephone surveys and on-site customer interviews to gather information about how customers perceive the stores and what sort of media campaign might improve or clarify Ajax's image. Since MB&T has successfully completed several other assignments for Ajax, Daniel Merril, President of MB&T, and Helen Peterson, President of Ajax, are well acquainted. Therefore, a detailed, formal proposal is not necessary. David Paulson has instead drafted a letter proposal, addressed to Helen Peterson and signed by Daniel Merril (see Figure 9.4).

---

**Figure 9.4**
The Letter Proposal

Dear Helen:

Last week at your office, you and I reviewed Ajax's current need to reappraise its advertising strategy. You told me that Ajax is now ready to engage in a major media campaign throughout the Northeast but would like some assistance in determining the exact focus and conduct of that campaign. As you know, MB&T successfully conducted a market study for Ajax three years ago, and I am pleased that you have invited us to submit a plan for a similar study at this time.

Below I have outlined the objectives, design, work plan, and costs of the study we propose to do for you.

Objectives
The study will provide answers to the following questions:

o   Does Ajax reach more customers through print, radio, or TV advertising? Which of these media ensures best customer recall of the message?

o   What image does Ajax project in regard to its stores' quality, prices, and service?

Design
The study team will design a survey instrument specifically aimed at acquiring detailed information on the above questions. The questionnaire will be mailed to 500 randomly selected customers (people who have purchased appliances in the past twelve months) and 250 randomly selected noncustomers. In addition, our trained interviewers will spend one day at each of Ajax's seven stores interviewing customers on-site.

Workplan
When we have drafted the survey instrument, we will submit it to Ajax management for review and suggestions. Within one week after we have your approval, we will begin mailing the survey.

Within six weeks, we will provide you with computer output of the data and our preliminary analysis and conclusions. These data will be mailed to you in an interim summary report.

Three weeks later, we will provide you with our complete analysis of the combined results of the survey and the on-site customer interviews. At that time I will personally present our findings to you and your managers at a meeting at your offices.

Staffing
I will personally lead the team assigned to the project. Supporting me will be Thelma Lederle, a senior marketing analyst with over six years of experience in marketing research and a background that includes three years in retailing. We will be assisted by David Paulson, a research associate who joined our firm this year after graduating with high honors as a marketing major from Indiana State's business management program. Our résumés are enclosed with this letter.

<u>Costs</u>
We estimate the following costs for this project:

| | |
|---|---|
| Design of the survey instrument | $4,000.00 |
| Administration and analysis of the survey | 6,500.00 |
| On-site interviewing and data analysis | 4,000.00 |
| Preparation and delivery of the final report | 2,000.00 |
| TOTAL: | $16,500.00 |

The above estimate does not include expenses for travel and other incidental costs (not to exceed $1000.00).

MB&T guarantees that the data you receive will be complete and statistically accurate within a 10 percent variance. Furthermore, we will work closely with you to see that you are entirely satisfied that the final report provides you with a sound basis for planning your advertising strategy in the coming year.

Sincerely,

*Dan Merril*

Daniel Merril
President

---

**Analysis**

As we said, before deciding on the content of a proposal, the writer should identify the recipient's primary concern. Because of preliminary discussions with Helen Peterson, Daniel Merril is aware that Ajax needs to know (1) how to reach the greatest number of potential customers in their upcoming advertising campaign and (2) what to emphasize in that campaign.

David Paulson's draft focuses on those twin needs and offers a carefully planned and clearly described program to secure the vital information:

- First, the proposal carefully reviews why the study is needed; it then states the explicit *objectives* of the study.
- Next, it describes the exact *procedures* that will be used in completing the study and provides a *time table* for those procedures to be carried out.

- The proposal then emphasizes the *expertise* of the people who will complete the study and provides evidence of their abilities.
- Finally, the schedule of *costs* is presented, including a breakdown of the costs for specific segments of the study. In this case, costs are immediately followed by an explicit description of the expected results of the study and Daniel Merril's personal assurance that satisfaction will be provided.

As with any other business correspondence, the tone of a letter proposal should reflect the relationship between the reader and the writer (in this case, the signer), and it should also be appropriate to the particular situation. Here, the first-name salutation and the opening paragraph imply that Merril and Peterson are on an equal footing—both are presidents of their firms. The personal tone in the opening of the letter also suggests that the two are fairly well acquainted. But the occasion for the letter is an important business enterprise for their companies. Therefore, once the presentation begins in earnest, the tone subtly shifts; it becomes noticeably more formal. Also, the subheadings and the careful documentation underscore the serious intent of the letter.

## ■ Letters and Memos to Say No

Decision making and responsibility go hand in hand, and as you gain authority in the workplace you will frequently face the potentially unpleasant task of saying no. Even when you have good reasons, turning people down can make you feel uncomfortable. Like most people, you probably like to be perceived as agreeable and open to new ideas and suggestions, and you prefer to be the bearer of good news rather than bad. The fact remains, however, that from time to time you will have to reject requests, suggestions, and proposals for good reasons. And you will need to do so even though you may see some merit in what is being asked for or even when you have high personal regard for the person making the request. If you are sure of your decision, however, and if you have learned how to say no in ways that are firm yet tactful, you will feel far more secure when writing rejections.

### Turning Down a Request

Let's reconsider the case of Jennifer Dugan, this time from the perspective of her boss, Harry Grant, to whom she has applied for permission to transfer to another group.

Harry is really a pretty nice fellow, and he likes and respects Jennifer. Nevertheless, the fact remains that his group is understaffed and under a **The Case** great deal of pressure. If he grants Jennifer's request, her transfer could cause hardships for others who report to him, and almost certainly the performance of the whole group would be impaired. Since Jennifer has made a formal request, Harry knows he should respond in a written memo. But how should he handle this? What should he say?

Harry is sure of where he stands: he must firmly say no to the request. On the other hand, he doesn't want to demoralize Jennifer, who has been an exceptionally fine worker. He tries very hard to put himself into her shoes. How would he feel if *he* received this refusal?

"I'd definitely feel upset!" he tells himself. "I'd want a really good explanation." Then and there he decides to give Jennifer a thorough, factual explanation, to show her the actual numbers regarding the projected workload for the next six months. "But," he tells himself, "facts alone won't be enough. She may swallow the bad news and stay on peacefully, but she certainly won't feel very good about it. What can I tell her to boost her morale?"

It doesn't take Harry long to realize that what he must do is assure Jennifer that he sees her viewpoint. She *did* tell him at the outset that she is more interested in product innovation than in quality control, and Brent Keane *is* offering her an excellent opportunity. Harry decides that to keep Jennifer's good will, he will not only tell her that he sees merit in her request but will also offer her a reasonable alternative. "If Brent approves," he tells himself, "I'll let her spend one morning each week working over there so that she can learn the ropes, and I'll also promise to reconsider her request in six months. By then we can have Stan Denton up and running to replace her as supervisor.

---

**Analysis**

Let's sum up Harry's techniques for carrying out his purpose of saying no to Jennifer:

- He will be sure from the start that he knows what he wants to do.
- He decides his refusal will be absolutely firm.
- He will show empathy for Jennifer's needs and objectives.
- He will provide a clear, factual account to explain the refusal.
- He will support the merits of her position as far as he can.
- He will suggest a reasonable alternative plan.

---

## Turning Down a Suggestion

---

**The Case**

Let's look back at another case with which we are already familiar—that of the employee at A. Hollis & Company who suggested a program to match employee contributions to educational institutions. The letter making the suggestion, as you may remember, was addressed to M. E. Hoyt, Senior Vice President of Corporate and Employee Communications. This time, rather than seeing yourself as the person making the request, imagine that you are Mr. Hoyt's administrative assistant.

Mr. Hoyt has decided to turn down the suggestion and has assigned you the task of drafting the letter. He suggests that you and he have a 15-minute conference that afternoon to discuss the content of the letter. Obviously, that short conference will be crucial to producing a good letter, so you spend time carefully deciding what points you will explore with him.

In your conference with Hoyt that afternoon, you bring up the following key issues:

- Is Hoyt's decision irrevocable, or might he reconsider the request in the future? That is, what are his underlying reasons for rejecting the suggestion?
- Does he see *any* merit in the plan?
- Are there alternatives he might offer to this employee?
- Are there any steps he would like this employee to take in regard to this matter?
- Are there any steps that Hoyt himself plans to take?
- Would he welcome additional suggestions of this type?

Hoyt answers your questions openly and completely. Feeling confident, you write the letter in Figure 9.5.

**Figure 9.5**
The Letter

Dear (Name of Employee):

Speaking for both the company and myself, I would like to thank you for your forthright letter and interesting suggestion. I am certainly a supporter of my own alma mater and endorse gift matching as an excellent philanthropic effort at some companies. Nevertheless, after giving your proposal some hard thought, I have decided that a gift-matching program would not be appropriate for Hollis & Company. Let me outline my reasons.

Hollis & Company is, as you may know, primarily an employer of local people. Over 60 percent of our employees who hold college degrees attended the main campus or branches of our state university. In recognition of this fact, the company last year provided all of the furnishings for the recently completed business library on the main campus and set up a generous trust fund for the acquisition of books. You can understand, therefore, why I am reluctant to recommend a matching fund for contributions to private educational institutions, even though I entirely agree with you that support of higher education is critical to our marketing effort.

Please do not hesitate to write to me again if you wish to make another innovative suggestion. I congratulate you on your initiative.

Yours truly,

*M. E. Hoyt*

M. E. Hoyt
Sr. Vice President,
Corporate and Employee Communications

## Rejecting Proposals

Since people who submit business proposals know there is a high likelihood that they are competing with others for acceptance, rejecting a proposal is normally a less delicate task than turning down personal requests and suggestions. On the other hand, a proposal can represent a great deal of hard work and be the object of high hopes. Furthermore, a company seeking to sell you its products or services may at some time in the future become a potential customer for your products and services. For both of these reasons, courtesy and tact are mandatory.

When you say no to a proposal, it is especially important to be absolutely clear about where you stand. If you wish to see a revised proposal, say so; but if the rejection is final, don't equivocate. The more indecisive you sound, the greater the chance that you will be contacted again with a new request. Consider how John Cochran might react to the letter shown in Figure 9.6.

**Figure 9.6**
A rejection letter that seems indecisive.

Dear Mr. Cochran:

Thank you for inviting me to the demonstration of your Exec-U-Sec word-processing system. Indeed, we are in the market for a word-processing system, but unfortunately yours is not the one we have ranked highest.

Sincerely yours,

[Signature]

This letter of rejection is reasonably courteous, and it appears to say no. But from Cochran's point of view it presents some legitimate and compelling reasons to try again. First, it tells him that the writer's company is in the market for a product similar to the one he's offering. Furthermore, since he doesn't know why his company's system isn't being considered, he is apt to feel that he might be able to turn the situation around. A much clearer rejection of Cochran's proposal is the one shown in Figure 9.7.

---

Dear Mr. Cochran:

Thank you for inviting me to your demonstration of the Exec-U-Sec word-processing system. After carefully assessing your system, we have determined that Exec-U-Sec—although an excellent system—does not provide the memory capacity or flexibility that we currently need. We are therefore now completing arrangements to purchase a different system.

Yours truly,


[Signature]

**Figure 9.7**
A clearer, firmer version of the rejection letter in Figure 9.6.

---

When there isn't the slimmest chance that you will change your mind, it is tactless to equivocate or vacillate. If you really mean to say no, writing something like "At this time it appears that we should say no" is neither kind nor sensible. On the other hand, do offer whatever hope you can; if you want further contact, say so. As always, try to empathize with the reader and to treat him or her with respect.

Let's look at another case in which a proposal has to be rejected and a tactful letter is needed.

---

As project manager for a program to upgrade the skills of your sales force, you contact Alberta Livingston of Simmons, Ltd., an international consulting firm specializing in sales training and communications skills. Livingston visits your office and spends several hours talking to staff members and examining sales correspondence. Nevertheless, when you receive her firm's proposal two weeks later, you realize that the projected fee is not competitive with the other proposals you have received. You therefore compose the letter shown in Figure 9.8.

**The Case**

**Figure 9.8**
The Letter

Dear Ms. Livingston:

Thank you for your proposal outlining a training program for our outside sales force. I regret to inform you that we have not selected your program. Although your program competently addressed many of our needs, the total cost was not competitive with the other bids we received for equally strong programs.

I encourage you to remain in touch with us. This is not the last time we will be looking for staff-development programs, and we appreciate your interest.

Sincerely yours,

[Your Signature]

---

**Analysis**

In this rejection letter, the writer's strategy is to be *honest* and *direct*. The cost problem is real, so why not say so? If Livingston is unaware that she may be pricing herself out of the market, you might even be doing her a favor by letting her know.

The first sentence of the letter reminds Livingston of the specific proposal, and the second tells her immediately that it was not accepted. The rest of the paragraph explains the reason for the rejection. The closing paragraph invites her to remain in touch.

Perhaps at this point you are thinking that this was not a difficult rejection letter to write. After all, Livingston wrote a good proposal, and the cost problem is a simple, factual reality. Suppose the proposal is completely inappropriate or very badly done? You should still write courteously; but, of course, you should not praise the proposal. Perhaps you could thank the proposal writer for promptness. On the other hand, if you view the whole thing as an unmitigated disaster, you will want to be very brief. You might write something as simple as this: "Thank you for your proposal. Unfortunately, it does not meet our needs as we perceive them at this time."

As we've already stated, never invite the person to contact you again unless you really mean it. A closing paragraph like the one that concludes the letter in Figure 9.8 is appropriate only when the writer is being completely honest.

## Rejecting Applications

Saying no to an applicant probably requires more sensitivity than any other kind of written rejection. In this case, a human being, not a suggestion or idea, is being turned down. If you recollect your own emotions while waiting to hear about college acceptance or a job application, you can understand the strong reaction a negative response can evoke.

What least helps an applicant who is being turned down is an apology or a plea for understanding. A letter such as the one in Figure 9.9 is meant to salve the feelings of the writer rather than the reader.

---

Dear (Name of Applicant):

    On behalf of the Selection Committee, I deeply regret to inform you that we cannot accept you into this year's training program for department supervisors. I am sorry that we are unable to take everyone who applies to the program, but I'm sure you understand that choices need to be made. Please feel free to reapply when the program is offered again next year.

                            Yours truly,

                            [Signature]

**Figure 9.9**
An unhelpful letter rejecting an applicant.

---

Although this letter politely tells the applicant that he or she has not been chosen, it is flagrantly unhelpful. Its recipient has absolutely no idea how the selection was made or why he or she has been rejected. And even though invited to reapply, the letter's reader would hardly wish to do so.

A better letter is one that does not contain an apology for the negative decision. Instead, it offers the unsuccessful applicant some insights into the selection process and some support to counteract the inevitable feelings of disappointment. For example, the letter in Figure 9.10 is an improvement over that in Figure 9.9.

---

Dear (Name of Applicant):

    We have completed our review of the applications of those seeking admittance to this year's training program for department supervisors. We are sorry to tell you that you are not among those selected to participate in the 1986 program.

    Although your background and experience impressed us, we believe that you would find the program's strong emphasis on speaking and writing skills a heavy burden. The company currently offers several excellent, short, in-house training programs for increasing verbal skills. We suggest that these might be helpful to

**Figure 9.10**
An improved version of the letter in Figure 9.9.

you, especially if there is a likelihood that you will reapply for the supervisor's training program next year.

Thank you for your application, and please feel free to contact the Selection Committee for any further help.

Sincerely,


[Signature]

---

In reading this letter, the applicant is likely to find it painful to be told about his or her precise weakness—for a moment it will be an uncomfortable experience. But on reflection, don't you think anyone would rather learn how to improve his or her chances than hear about some committee's "deep regrets"? Of course, there is no "right" way to convey a rejection, but genuinely helpful advice is certainly better than the most abject apology.

## ■ Saying No, Plain and Not So Simple

This chapter has focused on writing refusal letters with complex emotional underpinnings, arising from situations in which the recipient has a heavy stake in the outcome and the writer may have, too. As we all know, however, there is another kind of "no" letter—the plain, homely, everyday variety that all too often appears in our mailboxes, both at home and at work. Most frequently written by people who are unknown to us, these letters carry bad news about the more mundane matters of life. Because these communications serve common and proliferating needs, their components are often entered into computer data bases, from which—in assembly-line fashion—whole letters are synthesized and sent off with messages we would much prefer never to receive: "We're sorry, but your warranty has expired"; "We regret that we cannot extend credit"; "The part you ordered is temporarily out of stock." Many times these bad-news letters are not explicitly "no" statements, yet their overall effect is to cast a dark cloud over our day.

Is it really possible for business writers to make such letters palatable to their recipients? Certainly not! But it *is* possible for a careful and thoughtful writer to avoid deepening the reader's inevitable gloom. In most instances, this means orienting the reader before launching into the bad news, avoiding a haughty "this is our policy" tone, and supplying a clear and reasonably complete explanation.

If you are called upon to write bad-news letters, be assured that everything we have said so far about handling letters of refusal and rejection continues to hold true. Briefly, these principles are as follows: before writing a single word, be perfectly clear in your own mind as to where you stand and why; next, think about the effect your words will have on the reader, and try to envision what your own reaction to them in a similar situation would be; and when you do begin to write, be factual, clear, and courteous.

Even while underscoring that the above advice must take precedence, we recognize that composing these short, impersonal letters is almost inescapably different from preparing other forms of business correspondence. First, the writers of bad-news letters usually have little if any real knowledge about their readers; a detailed audience analysis is virtually impossible to achieve. Second, because such letters deal with situations that commonly recur in the lives of most people, it is possible to make some working assumptions and valid generalizations about what sort of presentation is likely to be most effective. Moreover (and this probably can't be proven) because we all have become habituated to a commonly used presentation of bad news, we tend to find some small comfort in digesting the expected elements of such a message in their anticipated order.

When faced with the need to write a short, impersonal bad-news letter, you can pretty much depend on the following five elements to carry you through the task:

1. A courteous buffer statement
2. Explanation underlying the bad news
3. The decision or action taken
4. Suggestions or directions (with selling overtones, if appropriate)
5. A courteous closing

The order given here and in Figure 9.11 is most typical, but there will be occasions when you will need to vary it. Furthermore, you will always have to exert good judgment concerning how much to develop each component. For instance, when circumstances call for either a matter-of-fact, this-is-the-way-it-is attitude or a very decisive tone, the second and third elements should be interchanged: the decision should precede the explanation. Occasionally, for a stern warning, you may even want to do away with the buffer statement. To understand the use of the separate components and to see the effects of changing their order or degree of development, we'll take a close look at a series of three impersonal bad-news letters.

**Figure 9.11**
How to deliver the
bad-news message.

Letterhead

Date

Name, Title
Company
Street Address
City, State Zip Code

Dear (Name of Reader):

Buffer: Should courteously orient the reader; often expresses appreciation or offers praise. Omit for shock value.

Explanation: Should be factual and as complete as possible. Must be courteous.

Decision: Should be clear and unambiguous. Will precede explanation if writer wishes to be forceful.

Suggestions: May include advice, information, instructions for recipient, and sales pitch if appropriate.

Closing: Should be short and courteous. May include sales pitch if appropriate.


Sincerely yours,


(Signature)


Name
Title


**The Case**

On February 5, Mickey Broderick, a busy customer service representative in a fast-paced catalogue sales office, headed for a word processor and prepared to process a pile of orders, all requiring special correspondence. Each of the first three orders on the stack was dated January 28 by the respective customer; however, Mickey's supervisor had clipped a note to the order form sent by the second customer stating that the order was clearly postmarked February 3. Mickey composed the three letters in Figures 9.12–9.14.

Dear (Name of First Customer):

Your January 28, 198- order has been received, and we sincerely appreciate your taking advantage of our special January white sale.

Because there was such a heavy demand for our high-quality merchandise at these exceptional prices, we quickly sold out of some of the most desirable items, even though we thought we were extremely well prepared for a large response.

Your order will be mailed to you within two weeks. We hope this delay will not seriously inconvenience you.

If for any reason you decide either to cancel or to change your order, please contact a customer service representative by calling our convenient 800 number, or simply check the appropriate box on the enclosed form. Should you decide to substitute any other items included in our January sale, we will, of course, supply them to you at the sale prices.

Again, let me offer our sincere apology for this delay. We are eager to continue to serve you as one of our valued catalogue sales customers.

Sincerely yours,

*Mickey Broderick*

Mickey Broderick
Customer Service Representative

**Figure 9.12**
Letter to
Customer #1

Buffer

Explanation

Decision

Suggestion

Courteous closing

---

Dear (Name of Second Customer):

Your order dated January 28, 198- has been received, and we sincerely appreciate your taking advantage of our special January white sale.

Our January catalogue clearly stated, however, that the sale prices would be available only through January 31, 198-. When you posted your order, the items you requested were no longer available at half price.

Although we cannot process your order at this time, we are holding your merchandise for further instructions. If we have not heard from you in three weeks, we will return your check.

**Figure 9.13**
Letter to
Customer #2

Buffer

Explanation

Decision

You probably recognize that, even without the unusual discounts offered during our January sale, our prices are exceptionally low for first-quality, brand-name linens. We therefore are confident that you will want us to ship your merchandise as soon as possible. To help us process your order, you can use our convenient 800 number to contact a customer service representative. Or, if you prefer, simply return the enclosed form, checking the appropriate box.

Courteous closing

Again, let me assure you that we were pleased to receive your order and we hope that we can continue to serve you.

Sincerely yours,

*Mickey Broderick*

Mickey Broderick
Customer Service Representative

**Figure 9.14**
Letter to
Customer #3

**Buffer**

Dear (Name of Third Customer):

Your January 28, 198- order has been received, and we sincerely appreciate your taking advantage of our special January white sale.

Decision

We regret, however, that we will not be able to process your order at this time.

Explanation

According to our records, you have already charged merchandise to the extent allowed by your credit line. Furthermore, despite several written requests, it appears that you have not sent us the required payments for over three months.

Suggestion

Until recently, you have been a reliable and valued customer. Perhaps there is a good reason why you have allowed your monthly payments to fall so far behind. If you would like to discuss this matter with a customer service representative, we would be pleased to have you call us directly on our convenient 800 number, or you may contact me personally by mail.

Courteous closing

Again, let me assure you that we were pleased to receive your order and we hope that we can continue to serve you.

Sincerely yours,

*Mickey Broderick*

Mickey Broderick
Customer Service Representative

Mickey's three letters were all sent to customers whose orders could not be filled, but for different reasons. The firm itself is to blame for the first customer's problem. The second customer made an unintentional error (or at least what appears to be an oversight). And the third customer's formerly good credit standing has lapsed for some reason.

Mickey decided that the same friendly buffer is appropriate for each of the letters, and that paragraph is retrievable from the word processor's memory bank. Luckily, too, the letters to the second and third customers (Figures 9.13 and 9.14) adapt themselves well to the same closing even though their underlying circumstances are so dissimilar.

Let's consider the buffer paragraph. Its purpose is to set the context and to give the reader a short breather before launching into the real meat of the letter. As Mickey moves from the first to the second and then the third customer, the tone of each letter reflects the firm's diminishing tolerance of the given situation. However, in no case does the letter imply a complete loss of good will. Mickey perceived that even the third customer might ultimately return to the fold as a valued customer. Both the use of the buffer and the patient tone of the letter in Figure 9.14 suggest the firm's willingness to help that customer make amends.

Those cases in which the time for good will has run out call for a letter with real shock value. Then, the buffer paragraph is the first thing to omit. Consider the severe tone the letter in Figure 9.14 would have if the buffer were omitted and the opening line was "We regret that your order cannot be processed at this time." Note, also, that even in the reasonably mild letter that Mickey chose to send to this customer, the decision precedes the explanation—a subtle but effective signal that the decision is not to be taken lightly.

In all three letters, the explanations are clear and factual, and the suggestions anticipate each customer's feelings and needs. For example, Mickey made an effort to see that the first customer will not feel injured by the firm's mistake. The sale prices will be honored even for substitute merchandise; or, if the customer prefers, a refund will be sent. In all three cases, too, the task of responding is made easy. A response form is enclosed, and provisions are made for a free telephone call.

It is also important to note how Mickey handled the "selling" element in each letter. The first customer is already sold; all that is needed is to maintain his or her good will. Rather than including an explicit sales message, Mickey recognized that the generous options offered to this customer implicitly carry a strong sales message. The letter's closing, which compliments the reader as a valued customer, also does a bit of selling. In the case of the third customer, circumstances prevent any real selling; nevertheless, the closing contains a low-keyed sales pitch. It is the second customer who requires the greatest selling effort. Mickey recognized that, rightly or wrongly, this regular customer will probably feel slighted by the decision not to honor the sale prices. This customer needs to be reminded of the real value that the firm consistently provides.

---

In this short series of letters, we've examined bad-news messages that touch on three kinds of problems. These messages are only the tip of the iceberg. Bad-news notices can also tell people, "Your payment has not been received" (collection), "Your account is overdrawn" (credit), "Your warranty is no longer valid" (manufacturer's warranty), or, "Your manuscript does not fit our current needs" (publisher's rejection). And even these do not begin to exhaust the possibilities for bad news.

It's a safe bet that composing bad-news letters provides almost as little pleasure as reading them. But, since bad news is a fact of life, we suggest that you judiciously use the advice we've offered to improve such letters and to make writing them an easier task.

## ■ Summary

The first part of this chapter deals with correspondence whose primary purpose is to persuade. In most large firms, professional advertising and direct-mail specialists write sales letters, especially the cold-call variety. But taking the meaning of "sell" less literally, we can say that almost all employees have occasion to write letters and memos that sell their ideas and opinions.

To persuade a reluctant audience, it is especially important to anticipate his or her objections and concerns. Then structure an argument that moves the reader step-by-step toward your desired conclusion.

A proposal is a written offer to provide specified goods or services at a set cost. Proposals are essentially sales presentations; they typically include objectives, procedures and materials, a timetable, a summary of expertise, and costs. Your task as a proposal writer is to show that your product or service meets the customer's needs.

The balance of the chapter deals with the delicate problem of saying no. Be certain of your decision; be firm; show empathy for the reader; provide a clear explanation; acknowledge merits of the reader's position; where possible, suggest a reasonable alternative.

In rejecting a proposal, be honest and direct, tactful but decisive. When your decision is final, it is neither wise nor courteous to leave room for hope.

Saying no to an applicant requires special sensitivity. Apologies and regrets are of little help. Try, rather, to explain the reasons for rejection in terms that will enable the reader to imporove his or her chances on another occasion.

Routine bad-news letters—about expired warranties, delayed deliveries, etc.—should incorporate a courteous buffer statement, an explanation, the decision or action taken, suggestions or directions, and a polite closing.

# ■ Discussion Problems

**9.1**   Do you like to sell, or is selling repugnant to you? In either case, why is this so? Do you agree that persuading and selling have much in common? Are there ways in which they are different? Explain.

**9.2**   Can you recollect an occasion when you had to say no to someone's request for your help or approval? How did that responsibility make you feel? Did you express those feelings in any way? How?

**9.3**   Your company is badly in need of a graphic artist. You have a talented friend who has received job offers from a number of companies including your own. You would like to persuade her to accept the offer from your company even though you are certain another company has offered her a salary higher than your company is currently able to pay. How might you go about trying to convince her to join your firm? Be as specific as you can.

**9.4**   You are a copy writer for a rather small direct mail advertising agency. You would very much like the company to purchase a word processor for your office. Before formally requesting the word processor, what actions might you take? What possible objections to your request might your superiors make? How would you answer them?

**9.5**   You are preparing a letter proposal offering to design a full line of company stationery and calling cards for a customer whose firm has just changed its name and wishes to change its logo. What kinds of information should you include in the proposal?

**9.6**   The emphasis in a negative communication should be on a *reason* rather than on an *apology*. Why is a reason inevitably more positive, active, and concrete than an apology? How are the following apologetic statements likely to affect a disappointed reader?

■   I certainly wish we could have . . . .

■   We sincerely regret that . . . .

■   Unfortunately, we are unable to . . . .

■   We regret to inform you that we do not currently have in stock . . . .

- It is my unhappy duty to inform you . . . .
- We are very sorry to have to . . . .
- We hope you will understand our embarrassment . . . .
- Regretfully, it is impossible at this point to . . . .

**9.7**   As editor of your university's alumni quarterly, you've advertised for an experienced writer/editor to assist you. Among the more than 100 applications you've received, about 25 applicants have no real qualifications for the job, 65 are reasonably qualified, and 10 are outstanding. After choosing one of these 10 for the position, you are faced with the task of saying no to all the rest. Will you send the same letter to each unsuccessful applicant, or will you design several different negative responses? If you choose the latter alternative, how will your letters vary in content, length, and tone?

**9.8**   Which of the following negative messages require an explanation of some length? Which, on the other hand, can more appropriately be answered with a brief and direct explanation? Give your reasons.

- A note to your boss to say you won't be able to accept the invitation to his wedding
- A memo to an employee indicating that her request for an extra week's vacation cannot be approved
- A letter to John Smith advising him that his recent credit application has not been successful
- A note to your newspaper distributor requesting that all deliveries be discontinued as of June 1
- A letter to Weston Printers indicating that their bid to print your college yearbook has been turned down (the three other bids submitted were all considerably more attractive)
- A note to a local rock band advising them that the prom committee has chosen another group for the upcoming senior prom

**9.9**   As a service representative for an academic publishing company, you have the unpleasant responsibility of turning down teachers' requests for free copies of your firm's textbooks. This is a new policy, made necessary by diminishing profits, and obviously the last thing you want is to alienate potential customers. How can you transform these refusal letters into selling tools? Can you think of a good buffer or some creative sales techniques to offset your negative message and perhaps to sell some books in the process?

**9.10**   Can you suggest specific tactics to present each of the following negative messages in a reasonably positive light? Be careful to avoid insincerity or indecision.

- Product A is no longer in stock.
- Our policy is to refuse credit to unemployed clients.
- There are no openings in our accounting department.

- We cannot grant your request for full reimbursement of travel expenses for attending the conference in Hawaii.
- I cannot accept your invitation to address the university student body on June 6.
- We no longer provide free home delivery.

# ■ Writing Tasks

**9.1** Sidney Harris, a rather unpopular, cantankerous senior vice president of your company, just announced his retirement. As a personnel assistant, you have been given the task of writing a memo to invite all employees to a company buffet dinner and reception for Harris and to request that each department establish a fund for an appropriate gift. Write the memo.

**9.2** After reviewing Harry Grant's thought processes (see pages 183–84), write his memo telling Jennifer Dugan that he cannot agree to her transfer.

**9.3** Prepare an outline of the letter proposal mentioned in Discussion Problem 9.5.

**9.4** Since graduating from college, you have been particularly successful as an entrepreneur. You now own a thriving catering business, and it's becoming too much to handle; you need an assistant. You interview a number of people, among them your long-time friend, Hank McLatchy. Hank is a great guy, but you're afraid he may be a poor risk because he has no real interest in the food business and has always been a bit disorganized. You know this job will require long hours, dedication, and a great deal of meticulous paperwork to keep track of orders and supplies. Write Hank a letter rejecting his application for the job.

**9.5** As manager of your own catering business, you frequently follow leads for prospective customers by sending out letter proposals. Yesterday, you heard that Carol Cavendish, principal of the local high school, will retire this spring. You know that the town will be honoring her at a formal dinner, and you would like to be the caterer. Write a letter proposal to Ed Banks, Chairman of the Board of Education, offering your catering services. The dinner will be for about 200 people. Invent any other facts and figures that you want to include in your proposal.

**9.6** Reread Discussion Problem 9.9 and then draft a letter to Associate Professor Elizabeth Liddell, Department of English, Benson University, Ogden, Utah 84409. Explain your company's new policy regarding free samples, but try to sell her your latest composition textbook as well.

**9.7** Richard Bradley, a millionaire alumnus of your college and an avid birdwatcher, has submitted to the alumni quarterly a highly specialized article on the mating habits of a rare species of wild duck. You, the quarterly's editor, can guess how much this article must mean to old Mr. Bradley, but it is, of course, entirely inappropriate for publication in the alumni magazine. Write a letter to Bradley in which you firmly decline to print his article. Make a special effort to be courteous and helpful.

**9.8**  Lydia Tree, an alumna of your college, teaches eighth grade in Lancaster, Nebraska. She particularly enjoyed a recent article in the alumni quarterly concerning a local Indian community, and she has written to you, the editor, to request 24 reprints for her class. She clearly expects the reprints to be free, but you have no funds to fulfill such requests. Draft a letter offering to send her one copy of the article and granting her permission to have it copied for her students.

**9.9**  Assume you are the business manager of the Mumford Township Adult Education Center. It is your job to keep the center solvent while doing everything in your power to increase enrollment and to develop enthusiasm for adult education in your community. The center's policy is to give full tuition refunds until the beginning of the second week of classes, 50 percent refunds until the beginning of the fourth week, and no refunds after that time. Draft the following letters of refusal, inventing explanations for the refund policy, deciding when and if to make exceptions, and offering an alternative course or a small "consolation prize" in those cases in which you feel this tactic would preserve the good will of a student denied a refund. Make up any necessary details.

- Write to Ralph Stone, who wants a refund after attending three weeks of "Stress Management through Running." He sprained his ankle during class and feels tenser than ever.

- Write to Maggie Johnson, who wants to quit a course called "Eating and Emotions" after six weeks because all that talk about eating caused her to gain 15 pounds.

- Write to Vin Spiglia, who attended one week of "Advanced French Conversation" and wants a refund because "90 percent of the class can't put a sentence together."

- Write to Aurora Gere who wants out of "Basic Drawing" after four weeks because the teacher "insists on using live, *undraped* models!"

- Write to Peter Martin, who, without offering any explanation whatever, rather aggressively demands a refund after five weeks of class.

**9.10**  As the office manager at Wentworth Industries, you've received a memo from a group of eight secretaries. In it they request permission to photocopy all letters and memos instead of having to produce two carbon copies, as required by current company policy. Their main argument is that making carbon copies is enormously time-consuming, since each copy must be corrected separately when a typing error is made. Furthermore, the office now has an impressive new photocopier, and the secretaries feel that the time has come to modernize company policy.

Unfortunately, the President of the firm, Frank Wentworth, is strong-minded and stubbornly conservative. He dislikes all change, especially when initiated "from below." You've tried your best to change his mind (using cost comparisons, etc.), but it's hopeless. Now you must draft a memo informing the secretaries that for the time being carbon copies are here to stay.

How can you soften the blow in order to keep up office morale and maintain your own personal effectiveness as office manager? Obviously, you must state the bad news decisively, but you also want to convey some moral support to the secretarial staff. Try to come up with a creative solution, but remember that Mr. Wentworth will be receiving a (carbon!) copy of your efforts.

# THE CASE OF THE PART-TIME POLITICIAN*

A senior executive has a bad-news message to deliver to a valued employee. In addition, the executive needs to get in touch with the employee's immediate supervisor regarding the matter.

The students in the seminar were asked to pretend that they were the senior executive and to devise an appropriate strategy for handling the communication. Then they were given the task of writing the memo or letter necessary to carry out their strategy.

The dialogue presented here tunes in on discussions of letters written by two students. Paul Ramsay is preoccupied with questions concerning the style and tone of his letter, but his fellow students are even more concerned about the way he has constructed his argument. Jim Stanley, the second student is rightly concerned with the clarity of his letter, and his instructor and classmates point out ways to make it clearer and more coherent.

## ■ The Case

" . . . and so Congressman Bryson has asked me to help coordinate his coming campaign for the Senate. It's a challenging assignment, but I think I'm up to it. And I think those of us in business should participate actively in politics. But, Mr. Sindall, I'll need a six-week leave of absence."

Sitting in the office of Ed Sindall, President and CEO of Sindall Lumber Company, is the company's rising star, Bob Payton, Assistant to the Vice President for Resources. Bob is requesting that he be given a six-week leave of absence to accept an invitation to work as a full-time volun-

*Adapted from an article by Stephen A. Greyser, published in the *Harvard Business Review*, January/February, 1962, by special permission.

teer on the campaign staff of Congressman Arthur F. Bryson, Republican candidate for the United States Senate.

The Sindall Lumber Company is a medium-sized firm with headquarters in the Pacific Northwest. It was founded just over 50 years ago by Ed Sindall's grandfather and was substantially diversified by Ed's father. The firm sells its products all over the West Coast and has timber rights in three states. Employing 1,500 people, it is one of the most important suppliers of doors and window frames in the area. Family owned and controlled, it has been consistently successful at adapting itself to the changing circumstances and needs of the housing industry. Only a small amount of Sindall's business is with the federal government.

Bob Payton is a tall, lean young man with a deep, resonant voice and a warm, friendly smile. Twenty-eight years old and extremely energetic, Bob has worked for Sindall since he graduated from a well-known business school in 1982. With his wife and his two-year old son, Bob lives in a residential suburb of the city where Sindall's headquarters are located. Both Bob and his wife, Carol, are natives of the state.

When asked what he does for Sindall, Bob explained his job as follows: "Believe it or not, I pick up almost anything that comes along. Recently, for example, I devoted all my time to union negotiations, traveling between our cutting operations, this office, and the headquarters of several of our competitors to make sure that our bargaining positions were coordinated. I wasn't doing the actual negotiating with the union myself, but I was responsible for supplying the background material on which our decisions and arguments would be based and for making that material comprehensible to the negotiators. Once that job wound up, I went back to the facts and figures of our resources program. I now survey possible land for exploitation, keep track of our reserves, and make recommendations to the vice president on the timing, location, quantity, and quality of our purchases. I suppose, in short, you could call me a jack-of-all-trades in the fields of resources and industrial relations."

After Bob's request the conversation in Ed Sindall's office continued like this:

SINDALL: Well, Bob, I'm sure you realize that this is an unusual request. In fact, I guess it would establish at least a couple of precedents for the company. But before we go into that, I'd be interested in hearing about how you got involved in this campaign. I know you've been active in our local civic organizations, but I never knew you were especially interested in politics. That's why I was somewhat surprised when

Stu Broderick [Sindall Lumber's Vice President for Resources and Bob Payton's immediate superior] told me about your request to work in Bryson's campaign. When did it all start?

PAYTON: It was late last spring, Mr. Sindall, when I first met Congressman Bryson. You probably remember that there was a luncheon meeting here in town, where a group of local business people gathered to meet with the then-prospective candidate. The purpose of the get-together was to form a paper committee, which would provide some publicity and a skeleton organization to be activated if and when needed. Several of the members who helped organize this skeleton group were friends and former classmates of mine. They knew I was a Republican, and I guess because of my work in other community projects they invited me to join in the effort for Bryson.

In the early stages of the campaign, there wasn't too much need for my services. Bryson's immediate objective at that time was to win the Republican nomination. Because he didn't have any substantial competition in the party primary at the beginning of this month, he won pretty easily. However, after the primary several of my friends called on me to ask for my help. They indicated that the organization needed an able and vigorous campaigner to serve as a full-time advance agent for Bryson's proposed whistle-stop tour of the state. They told me that they thought I was right for the job. And, of course, they asked me if I could possibly arrange a leave of absence from the last week of September to Election Day in November to take on the assignment.

SINDALL: Didn't you think this was a rather big assignment for someone with your limited political experience?

PAYTON: Well, at first I did feel that way. I had some real doubts about my ability to do the job. After all, I know I'm a political neophyte—I have no political experience or acquaintances. But my friends convinced me that this would be no handicap. They told me that basic ability was what counted, that I would find my community-activities experience helpful, and that I would soon enough catch on to the strictly political angles. In addition, they told me that they were having a lot of trouble trying to line up campaign workers who have enough potential ability to do a job for them and the time to do it.

(Ed Sindall believes that the major reason the task of recruiting Republican workers for this particular campaign has been proving difficult is that Congressman Bryson is not generally given much of a chance to win. His

Democratic opponent, Robert L. Johnson, is a former United States Senator who retired voluntarily six years earlier, only to return to active politics when his successor became ill toward the end of his term and announced his plan to withdraw.)

SINDALL: Bob, do you really think Bryson can win?

PAYTON: Well, let's face it, Mr. Sindall, he has an uphill fight on his hands. But personally I believe he has a fair chance of making it. You probably saw the Senate campaign status report in yesterday's *Sunday News*. I brought along a copy of it because I think it's a pretty accurate analysis of the political situation and of the candidates. Here it is. All things considered, Mr. Sindall, I don't think the prospects are overly discouraging. The more I find out about Congressman Bryson, the more I like him. Also I am challenged by this assignment and by the chance to learn something about politics. I really think that business people have an obligation to participate actively in politics, to support the principles and the candidates in which they believe.

SINDALL: What does Stu Broderick say about this? What would your absence mean to the department?

PAYTON: As Stu mentioned to you, I've talked this thing over with him. He says that there will obviously have to be some temporary reassignment of duties, but he doesn't think there would be any serious problems.

SINDALL: I'm sure you're aware that we've never allowed anything like this before here at Sindall Lumber. In fact, it's only been a few years since I reversed my father's policy of not letting executives have time off even for community project work. But let me think about it, Bob, and I'll try to get back to you before the end of the day.

Reflecting on Bob Payton's request, Ed Sindall finds that his first considerations relate to the company's role in various community affairs. The firm has no set policy in this area; rather, as President, Ed examines each situation individually as it arises. However, he does have some general guidelines that he follows in ruling on these specific cases:

- *Sindall Lumber Company executives' participation in community affairs.* When Ed's father was president of the company, no executives were allowed to have time off to work on any community projects, nor were they encouraged to take on nonbusiness, civic responsibilities on their own time. In Ed's opinion, the company's reputation in the cities where it operated suffered drastically as a result of this policy. Believing in the need for good community relations, he urged his managers to join in community endeavors. He suggested that they participate in nonpartisan town politics, serve with the Red Cross or United Fund, become directors of local banks, and so on. Furthermore, Ed had been receptive to requests for a reasonable amount of company time off to pursue such activities.

- *Ed Sindall's own community activities.* Ed himself became very active in the affairs of the city in which the company headquarters are located. For five or six years, he spent 20 percent of his time on a number of projects about which he once said, "They didn't bring in any new orders or increase our bank balance, but as a result of working on them, I got on a first-name basis with people in the major companies in this area. I suppose that, somehow, this work may be useful from a business standpoint in the future. But at any rate it has helped our reputation in the community."

- *Demands on company time.* In recent years, Ed has become increasingly concerned about the amount of his own time that he's been spending on community projects. Consequently he has grown hesitant about releasing any of his top executives for large-scale endeavors. For example, Ed refused to loan any executives to the local United Fund to serve as president or as chairperson of the annual fund drive, although he had encouraged them to serve in any other post in the organization.

- *Ed Sindall's political inclinations and beliefs.* Ed is a strong Republican and had been pleased when any of his managers participated on a part-time, volunteer basis in Republican Party politics. Consequently, when the general superintendent of Sindall Lumber's main manufacturing plant, who was a Republican county chairman, asked for permission to run for mayor, Ed gave his approval with the condition that the executive had to do full justice to his company responsibilities if he were elected.

Because of his firm Republican convictions, Ed honestly does not believe that he would look with approval on a request similar to Payton's from a Democrat. He has said this: "The Republicans are better for business and the economy because the Democrats keep trying to give the store away. Consequently, if someone came to me asking for time off to work for Senator Johnson or to run for office as a Democrat, I would not grant that request. As a staunch Republican, I'm convinced that my party is right and is better for Sindall Lumber

Company. I would be a hypocrite if I used either my own resources or those of the company to help out the opposition."

Although he would not want the company identified in any way with the Democrats, Ed feels that a person's politics, like religion, is a personal affair. If someone wanted to vote Democratic or work for the Democrats, Ed thought he would try to present the arguments on the Republican side, but he honestly believes that he would not hold it against the person when it came to promotion or compensation.

■ *Political favors.* As he has often expressed it, Ed's interest in politics "arises purely from my belief in good government. I have never used political help in securing anything for the Sindall Lumber Company, and I never will."

Ed takes one further information-gathering step as he considers Bob's request. He calls Stu Broderick to check on whether the leave would present serious staffing problems to his department. Broderick indicates that Payton's absence would mean some temporary reassignment of duties and an increased workload for himself and several other people. "However," Broderick concludes, "none of this creates an insuperable obstacle. I guess we could work something out if we had to." Before making a final decision, Ed reviews both his conversation with Bob earlier in the day and his own thoughts on the subject: Payton is asking for a full-time leave of absence for political service; it involves federal instead of local or state office; it is obvious that Payton is becoming more deeply (and, perhaps, more permanently) involved in politics than any of the company's executives has ever been before.

After a good deal more consideration, Ed Sindall decides to refuse Bob Payton's request.

## ■ Discussion Problems

Imagine that you are Ed Sindall.

**II.1**  Would you phone either Bob Payton or Stu Broderick before sending a memo to Bob explaining your answer?

**II.2**  Would you send Stu a copy of the memo you are writing to Bob?

**II.3**  Would you plan to meet with either or both of them after Bob receives the memo? What might be the focus of these discussions?

**II.4**  Can you suggest any other actions you might take regarding this matter?

# ■ Writing Tasks

**II.1**   Write a substantive memo to Bob refusing his request. Since this is an extremely serious matter, you may choose to use a letter rather than a memo format. (You should make this decision carefully.) Keep in mind that this memo or letter to Bob Payton willl establish a policy for handling similar requests. Therefore, a copy of it will be placed in a permanent file.

**II.2**   If you think it would be helpful and appropriate, prepare a brief covering memo to be attached to Stu Broderick's copy of the memo or letter to Bob Payton.

# ■ The Dialogue

PAUL:   I guess I mostly want my letter [see Paul's letter in Figure II.1.] to be firm. This is an absolute no-recourse refusal. On the other hand, the company doesn't want to lose this guy. I've tried to present some strong arguments to Payton, but even if he doesn't buy them I won't change my mind.

RUTH:   Paul, would you call Bob Payton before sending him this letter?

PAUL:   I thought about that a lot. I think I wouldn't. I would want him to have a chance to read my letter carefully and digest my reasons before

**Figure II.1**   Student Paul Ramsay's letter to Bob Payton.

SINDALL LUMBER COMPANY
Box 1000
Boise, Idaho 64002

August 7, 198-

Mr. Robert L. Payton
Assistant to the Vice President
for Resources

Dear Bob:

   Each time I think of the success of the many community projects you have participated in, I'm glad I decided to encourage our executives to become active in local affairs.

In particular, your ability to fulfill most of your community responsibilities outside company time has demonstrated a sense of balance that the rest of us could benefit from. As you know, I've been guilty of overextending myself lately, and I must admit that, if it weren't for people like you minding the store, the company would have suffered.

I've given the whole question of communty involvement a lot of thought since we discussed your request for a leave of absence, and I've decided that your abilities would best be put to use here at Sindall Lumber. Our recent labor negotiations illustrate how problems can develop. We need someone like you on hand who can adapt to situations quickly.

Our primary corporate purpose is to provide inexpensive goods and services. In the housing industry, staying on top of people's changing needs requires day-to-day attention from all of us. When we do our jobs well, the community benefits from more jobs, higher pay, and better products.

I think that granting your leave of absence would establish a precedent that would carry us away from our business objectives. If I allow an executive to work for a political candidate on company time, I have endorsed that candidate just as surely as if I made a contribution to his or her campaign. Such involvement oversteps the bounds of community service and becomes partisanship. I don't think it is fair for me to use the company's resources to impose my political beliefs on others.

Many people might assume that Sindall Lumber Company was benefiting from its political endorsements. The political opposition would be properly outraged that I had set myself up to rule on other people's political beliefs. This resentment would not help the company's image.

In closing, let me pass on Stu Broderick's words of praise for the fine job you are doing. Keep up the good work.

Sincerely,

Edwin Sindall
President

cc: Stu Broderick

having to respond to me. But I would call his boss, Stu, and let him know what the letter contained. After all, Stu may have to face a storm. Also, I'd like *him* to be the one to send me a signal when Bob is ready to be seen. I imagine it could take this guy a day or two to calm down.

RUTH: Your general strategy is pretty clear, Paul, but do you have any specific comments on the letter itself?

PAUL: Yes. I'm not clear in terms of tone—toward the middle and near the end. I want to be strong, but am I lecturing? Look at about the fifth paragraph down.

RUTH: You're worried about the tone?

PAUL: Yes, I may be coming on *too* strong, and especially getting too specific and too particular for what Payton needs to hear.

RUTH: You feel this way now that you've read it to us and are hearing it in retrospect? You're getting uncomfortable?

PAUL: Yes, absolutely.

RUTH: Okay, we can open that up for discussion.

PAUL: The other question I have (and I guess I have it about every letter I write) is whether or not the sentences are too long.

RUTH: Can you pick out one sentence that bothered you when you read the letter aloud?

PAUL: No, but if I read it out loud again, I could. I was having breathing problems reading quite a few of the sentences.

RUTH: You may be right. That's usually a good test. Still, I don't think I found the sentences as troublesome as some of yours have been in the past. You're improving on that, Paul. Fred?

FRED: What you said about the tone, Paul—I didn't find a tone problem in the two places you mentioned, I thought those were rather good. But the fourth paragraph, where you talk about the housing industry staying on top of people's changing needs, and so on, that's a little much. The other two were fine, though. I think you make a good solid case right there for why you can't let him go.

RUTH: Fred's right, I think. "In the housing industry, staying on top of people's changing needs, etc., etc. . . ." is sort of preaching because it's talking about the whole industry. But when he says, "granting your leave of absence would establish a precedent," he's talking directly about Sindall Lumber. And I think that's what we can buy without any embarrassment. Yes, Don.

DON: Well, I had the same problem with it. I thought it was just a little bit patronizing. But in the third paragraph, where he says, " . . . I've decided that your abilities would best be put to use here at Sindall Lumber," I wondered if that wasn't too strong and if you couldn't maybe word that more indirectly.

PAUL: You mean the word "decided" is a little . . .

DON: " . . . *I've decided* that your abilities . . . "

RUTH: How would you change that, Don?

DON: Ummm—"We *need* your abilities here at Sindall's."

PAUL: Hey! Okay. I like it. The "we need" is a different tone entirely.

LARRY: I think that your sentence structure is clear. Like you said, you have a tendency to make your sentences long; but they aren't overpoweringly long. Maybe it's your word choice that's the problem. For instance, in the third paragraph, where you say "illustrate," I would say "show." And in the next paragraph, where you say "inexpensive," I would say "low-cost." And I'd change "requires" to "needs"—except that I see you've said "needs" immediately before.

RUTH: I think that "illustrate" versus "show" example is really good, Larry. The thing is, you've substituted Anglo-Saxon words for Latinate. And the effect is different. Well, anything else to tell Paul?

DAVE: A small thing, but I think the clauses and sentences would read better if they didn't end with prepositions: " . . . projects you have participated *in*" probably could be worded differently. And then in the second paragraph " . . . a sense of balance that the rest of us could benefit from." I guess that's a question of usage there, too.

RUTH: Well, Dave. You *can* certainly end with prepositions. The rule that says you can't is old-fashioned; maybe it never was a rule. Winston Churchill zapped it with his famous example: "This is a mistake up with which I will not put."

DAVE: Well, in the case of "participated in," I just thought that was weaker phraseology than something like "you organized."

RUTH: Okay. I buy the "organized," but I wouldn't want him to write "in which you have participated." I think that sounds stuffy. I'd much prefer "participated in." But your revision is good, Dave.

DAVE: I'm with you, Ruth. I hate those "whichy" combinations, too.

BILL: I'd like to talk about a rather large issue—the way the arguments are used. The main argument here is the importance of company time and how you don't want to lose an important man, or lose his services for a while. Then about halfway through the letter, I think the writer shifts tracks and starts talking about partisanship. It's been a week since I've read the case, but it seems to me that Sindall had *himself* been pretty partisan. Didn't he support a mayor or someone like that for office? And I wonder if maybe it wouldn't have been better to use just one argument rather than to bring in another one with some holes in it.

PAUL: I'll tell you what I was thinking. I assumed from reading the case that Sindall had been partisan, but now he wanted to change; and this letter was being written not only to Payton but in effect to his other managers and the company as a whole. In other words, he knew he might need to refer back to it, so he was recording his decision—not just for Payton but for his own future reference.

BILL: Okay. But I think the structure of the letter is first of all a denial on the basis of "we can't afford to lose his talents." Then we have the issue of partisanship, and then a sort of implied denial on the basis of partisanship. It seems to me that the structure gets kind of . . . well, it goes one way and then another.

RUTH: Fran?

FRAN: I had trouble moving from the fifth paragraph to the sixth. I think the sixth paragraph might just be tacked on. I don't feel there's a very good transition between those two paragraphs. The first sentence of the sixth paragraph—"Many people might assume . . . "—seems to flow directly from the fifth paragraph. But as a separate paragraph, there's something lost.

RUTH: I didn't have trouble with that transition, Fran, but I marked the transitions between the third and fourth and the fourth and fifth as troublesome; so maybe as an overall view, transitions *are* a bit bumpy in this letter. "Our primary corporate purpose is to provide inexpensive goods and services." To me, that was a real leap.

FRAN: If you deleted the fourth paragraph then you would have a good transition from the first to the second, the second to the third, and the third to the fifth.

RUTH: "We need someone like you on hand who can adapt to situations quickly. . . . I think that granting your leave of absence would establish a precedent that would . . . " Well, I'm not sure, Fran.

FRAN: Add "In addition" between those sentences.

RUTH: Yes, I think that would do it, Fran. Okay. Let's look back to the first sentence of the second paragraph now. "In particular, your ability to fulfill most of your community responsibilities outside company time has demonstrated a sense of balance that the rest of us . . . ." It bothered me when I read that because I wondered whether Payton fulfilled the *other* responsibilities. It's a little ambiguous, isn't it?

PAUL: I guess it implies that Payton may not be fulfilling some of his responsibilities.

RUTH: Yes, that's what I mean exactly. That's what hit me. Also, I spotted trouble in the closing. "In closing let me pass on Stu Broderick's words of praise for the fine job you are doing." I'm waiting for those words and they're not there. What *did* Broderick say?

Well, Paul, we've pointed out a number of problems, but with a few changes [see Figure II.2] I think we're all agreed that this is a strong letter that may have the effect you want.

Shall we look at Jim's letter next? [See Figure II.3 for Jim's letter.] Jim, do you want to open the discussion of your letter?

**Figure II.2**   A revised version of Paul Ramsay's letter.

SINDALL LUMBER COMPANY
Box 1000
Boise, Idaho 64002

August 7, 198-

Robert L. Payton
Assistant to the Vice President
for Resources
Sindall Lumber Company

Dear Bob:

Each time I hear of the success of your many community projects, I'm glad I encourage our executives to participate in local affairs.

In particular, your ability to fulfill your community responsibilities without impinging on company time demonstrates an admirable sense of balance. As you know, I've been guilty of overextending myself lately; and I must admit that, if it weren't for people like you minding the store, the company would have suffered.

I've thought a lot about community involvement since we discussed your request for a leave of absence. I've concluded that we need you here at Sindall Lumber. Our recent labor negotiations show how problems can develop. We needed to rely on your experience and skill then; I suspect we will again.

Not only am I concerned about missing your services at the company, but also I believe granting a leave in this specific case might set an unwelcome precedent. If I allow a talented executive to work for a political candidate on company time, I endorse that candidate as surely as if I contribute to his or her campaign fund. Such involvement oversteps the bounds of community service and becomes partisanship. It would be unfair of me to use the company's resources to further my political beliefs.

Also, if Sindall Lumber Company appears to publicly endorse a candidate, many people could assume that we are hoping for political favors. The political opposition would be justifiably enraged, and their resentment could damage the company's image.

Although I must refuse your request, I would not want to close without mentioning that Stu Broderick often comments on the fine job you are doing.

Sincerely,

Edwin Sindall
President

cc: Stu Broderick

**Figure II.3**   Student Jim Stanley's memo to Bob Payton.

To:       Bob Payton
From:     Ed Sindall
Date:     August 7, 198-
Subject:  Your request for a six-week leave of absence

Your enthusiastic support of several community groups has been, to my mind, commendable. In addition to the personal satisfaction you must derive from these activities, your efforts demonstrate that people at Sindall Lumber Company care about the communities in which they work and live. We have been happy to support you in your community activities by giving you some time off.

Your current request is for a much longer leave of absence than we have given in the past and is for political work at the national, rather than the community, level. As such, the decision has been a difficult one for me because I want to establish a policy that is best for the company.

Managers at Sindall Lumber have been encouraged to participate in local politics. I feel that it is in the company's interest to be a positive force in the communities where we operate. Since a Senate campaign is for national office, the local benefit that the company is likely to receive from your participaton is small. On the other hand, the cost of losing you for six weeks is quite high. I find it impossible to establish a policy whereby key managers are allowed long leaves of absence for projects of little direct benefit to the company.

One thing that still concerns me, Bob, is your need to look outside the company for more challenging work. Let's have lunch next week, with Stu, and discuss how you can be more challenged, and move ahead more quickly, in this organization.

cc: Stu Broderick

JIM: My strategy is not quite the same as Paul's. I've previously called Bob and told him that I would have to refuse him and would be soon sending him a detailed memo. Although I agree the memo has to be firm, I want to come across more as a friend and colleague than as a boss. I want Bob to see me in this way, and then maybe he'll call me or come to me after he reads my memo. I hope he does and that he feels conciliatory. I also want Stu Broderick to know that I'm handling Bob carefully. Still, even though I'm trying hard not to make Bob mad, I think my refusal to grant him his request is a little too "implied." I don't know how to change it, but I think the denial is not explicit enough.

Another thing that I don't like is this part: "As such, the decision has been a difficult one for me because I want to establish a policy . . . ." I don't think the transition is good enough there; it's hard to see the logic that connects the difficulty and the necessity of establishing a new policy. It doesn't seem clear enough what Sindall's reasoning is.

RUTH: The "because" is kind of rough. "As such, the decision has been difficult for me *because* I want to establish a policy. It's not clear. Does the "because" also trouble you, Jim?

JIM: Yes—I don't think that whole part is clear enough.

RUTH: Comments?

TOM: Not about that, but I want to say that the most striking thing about this memo is the first sentence of the last paragraph: it's ambiguous. Jim is trying to make Sindall be friendly, but Payton could look at it and interpret that he's been fired! Shocking! He might stop reading there.

RUTH: Well, okay. But at least *we* know from the case that the concern Sindall is expressing there is real. Tom, can you think of a tactful way of suggesting to Payton that maybe he's not being stimulated enough?

TOM: Well, the last sentence suggests that what Sindall is trying to convey to Payton is "Well, gee, maybe we can do something inside the company to make your job more interesting." But the way it comes across is "Hey, why don't you go look elsewhere?"

RUTH: Did it strike everyone that way?

TOM: "Let's have lunch and discuss how you can be more challenged!" [Laughter] Well, one thing I definitely feel is that this guy Payton is teetering on the edge of leaving anyway. And if he's going to stay, he's going to have to be willing to connect himself to the company. There's nothing you want less, I think, than a half-committed executive.

FRED: Jim, you know, what bothered Tom bothers me too. You seem to be saying in this sentence that Payton might have tipped you off—that he's not interested in working at Sindall any more.

JIM: Well, you're right. That's exactly what I want Payton to think. I want him to think that he'd better prove to me that he really wants to work here and wants to get ahead in this company. I want him to work hard. But, if my tone is kind of like beating him up a little, well . . . .

RUTH: He is asking for a six-week leave. He's not asking to spend one day a week—six weeks is a good long time off.

FRAN: That same sentence bothered me, but not in the way that Tom suggested. It seems to me that if I were Payton, I'd be somewhat insulted, because my thinking process in reading this would be, "Well, I go out and do what you, the president, told me to do—get the company involved in community activities. And when I do it to a greater extent, to a more successful extent, than the other executives in your organization, then you come back and take this as an indication that I want to leave." And I would feel that there's some contradiction here. I am following your explicit suggestion to your executives, and then when I take the next logical step (namely, asking for six weeks as opposed to what I've been getting before), you jump on me. I'm sure if I were Payton I'd be insulted.

RUTH: Fran, perhaps Jim could alter the tone there some. For instance, he could write "One thing that concerns me, Bob, is the possibility of your needing more challenging work," or something like that, instead of " . . . your need to look outside the company."

BOB: A small point, but the use of the word "is" kind of weakens certain sentences in the letter—particularly the first sentence in the second paragraph: "Your current request *is* for a much longer leave of absence than we have given in the past and *is* for political work . . . . "

RUTH: Can you improve it, Bob?

BOB: You could write "You have requested a much longer leave of absence than we have given in the past," and then start another sentence for the rest of the thought. "Also, you'll be involved in national politics . . . . "

RUTH: Bob, Jim used the word "current," I'm almost sure, to try to make the transition (a sort of chronological tie). And I think your dropping it damages that transition. On the other hand, in favor of your revision, I'm not sure "current" is a *strong* enough transition. I think you really need a qualifying "however" or something like that to connect the paragraphs.

You all might be interested in knowing that similar problems with connecting ideas turned up on several other papers. The transitions between paragraphs were frequently weak. Maybe the reason is that there was rather a lot of complex information in this case, and you had to do some real organizing to put ideas into unified packets. Most of you succeeded in coming up with good paragraphs, but you made fairly big leaps from paragraph to paragraph.

JIM: One question about that "to my mind" thing. Isn't that the kind of qualification that we've learned is a no-no? And I did the same thing in the third paragraph—I used "*quite* high." But I don't think I want to eliminate them. As a matter of fact, I added those words after I wrote the whole thing, because I didn't think it flowed very well. Now I'm wondering if there's a better way to handle it.

RUTH: It's funny, I didn't have a negative reaction to "quite," although, as you know, I dislike the word. This time I think you *meant* to qualify. Here it is: " . . . the cost of losing you for six weeks is *quite* high." You really don't mean *extremely* high; I don't want to strike out the "quite." On the other hand, the "to my mind"—why do you want to qualify there? You've complimented Payton: "Your enthusiastic support of several community groups has been commendable." Why do you want to qualify that?

PAUL: I thought the phrase "to my mind" kind of personalized it, but if it doesn't . . .

RUTH: It doesn't, to my mind; no.

DAVE: I think the implication of those words is clear: there are some people who don't think community work is such a hot idea. There may be a lot of controversy about this. If I were Bob Payton reading those words, I might get the idea that I should go and ask Sindall, "Hey, wait a minute—are there some people who are giving you a hard time about my request?"

RUTH: Okay, Dave. And I suspect you don't think that's Jim's intent.

DAVE: Right.

PAUL: Where he talks about "communities in which they work and live," I've got a negative reaction to that. You hear it so often now. Every time you hear the word "communities," it's always followed by "in which you work and live." I'd just say "their communities," implying that they work and live there. I'd get rid of the cliché.

TOM: I think there are a few other words that can be trimmed out. In the first sentence, you could say, "Your enthusiastic support of community groups has been . . . . " And in the second sentence: "In addition to the satisfaction you must derive from these activities . . . . "—delete "personal." And in the last sentence: "We have been happy to support your community activities . . . . "—you can delete "you in." Oh, yes—still another word: in the first sentence of the second paragraph delete "much."

RUTH: I'm with you, Tom. There's something beautiful about good clean prose. But it's funny—we all clutter our writing, especially when we're first getting something down. If Jim came back to this letter in a few days, he'd probably delete some of those words himself. And perhaps in a month he'd find a lot more to chop out.

FRAN: I'd like to take up another matter that has to do with style. Look at the last paragraph, the last sentence; there are a lot of commas used. I'd like to discuss them. I'm not saying it's wrong that he's using them. But in a memo that is more or less informal (as opposed to a formal report), I suspect you don't need that many commas. Wouldn't less punctuation be better here?

RUTH: I'll bet Jim again thought he was giving his style a more conversational tone by adding those commas. But actually, you are right, Fran.

The modern practice is to leave out the excess punctuation in informal writing. And as we discussed last week, modern business writing leans toward sounding less formal. Still, it's difficult to achieve just the right tone and rhythm. I can hear Jim thinking aloud: "Let's have lunch//next week//with Stu//and discuss. . . . " There's a kind of trade-off between the audible effect and the rather stuffy overpunctuation. I know what Jim was trying to accomplish, but as the sentence strikes the eye, as opposed to the ear, it's pretty formal. I'd eliminate some of those commas, but I guess ultimately it's the writer's decision.

   Well, thanks, Jim. With a little work your memo will be fine. [See Figure II.4 for a revision of Jim's memo.]

**Figure II.4**   A revised version of Jim Stanley's memo.

To:        Bob Payton
From:      Ed Sindall
Date:      August 7, 198-
Subject:   Your request for a six-week leave

Your enthusiastic support of community groups is commendable. I expect that these activities bring you much personal satisfaction. Your efforts also demonstrate that people at Sindall Lumber Company care about their communities. Because of these benefits, we have been happy in the past to support such activities by allowing time off.

Currently, however, you are not only requesting a longer leave than we've ever allowed, but you also plan to work in national rather than community politics. On both these counts, I must regretfully refuse your request. Although this action is difficult for me, I feel that my decision establishes a policy that is right for the company.

Managers at Sindall Lumber have been encouraged to participate in local politics. As you know, I feel that it is in the company's interest for our employees to be a positive force in the communities where we operate. The benefit that the company is likely to receive from your participating in a U.S. Senate campaign, however, would be small. And the cost of losing you for six weeks, on the other hand, would be high. I'm sure you can see that we cannot establish a policy where key managers are allowed long leaves for projects of little direct benefit to the company.

Still, I recognize that a man of your energy and talents constantly needs real challenges. Why look outside the company? Let's have lunch next week with Stu and review some of the key issues Sindall Lumber is facing this year. Your perspective is important to me, because I expect you'll be moving ahead quickly in our organization.

cc: Stu Broderick

## ■ Letters to Discuss and Revise

Figures II.5–II.10 are additional letters written by the seminar students for "The Case of the Part-Time Politician." Study them, discuss them with your classmates, and revise them as requested by your instructor or for self-help.

Although he submitted the letter in Figure II.5 to fulfill the assignment, one student stated that he would have chosen not to write at all. He explains this strategy this way: "I would want to handle this whole matter face-to-face with Bob Payton. Because I was approached directly by him, I feel that it is only fair to respond in a like manner. Consequently, I would call him into the office (after I have informed Stu Broderick of my decision) and explain what I have decided. In this particular case I feel that sensitivity is required and that a letter would not provide that sensitivity as well as an interview would."

- Do you agree with this student? Explain.
- Does the letter in Figure II.5 reflect the student's reluctance to write?
- Having read the letter, what advice might you offer this student concerning his strategy?

**Figure II.5**

SINDALL LUMBER COMPANY
Box 1000
Boise, Idaho 64002

August 7, 198-

Mr. Robert L. Payton
Assistant to the Vice President for Resources

Dear Bob,

I applaud your interest in politics. The work you propose to do for Congressman Bryson would undoubtedly benefit his efforts for reelection. And as a Republican, I am especially pleased when Sindall executives work for the Republican Party.

My objection is not with your request, per se. Quite the contrary. Like yourself, I feel business people should take an active role in politics, supporting those candidates and causes in which they believe. However, I feel the company's interest must come first.

Because we are small we do not enjoy the management depth of a larger organization. As a result, each of our managers carries a greater range of responsibilities than his or her counterpart in a larger company. In general, the loss of any manager, even for short time periods, hinders operations. Although arrangements can be made in this case to minimize this problem, it is unlikely that similar requests could always be accommodated in the future. Concerned with the precedent that would be set in granting your request and in the interest of fairness to everyone, I am instituting a policy prohibiting time off for employee participation in political affairs.

I share the confidence Congressman Bryson's organization and your friends have in your ability and I hope you will remain active in Republican politics.

Warm regards,

Edwin Sindall

cc: Stuart Broderick

**Figure II.6**

TO:     Bob Payton
FROM:  Edwin Sindall
DATE:   August 7, 198-
RE:     Six-week leave request for political reasons

Your active interest in politics pleases me because concerned citizens, like you, ensure good government. With new government scandals appearing constantly, this country certainly needs honest lawmakers.

Many of these scandals are caused by illegal attempts by corporations to influence government officials. These few unethical corporations have made people suspicious of all business.

Sindall Lumber is involved in a particularly suspect industry, the management of our country's timberlands. This industry is a controversial one and is discussed extensively in Congress. Consequently Sindall must be careful to avoid even the appearance of seeking government favors.

I know that you are not seeking to gain anything for Sindall by working for Congressman Bryson. However, your full-time assistance to Congressman Bryson will appear to be an improper relation between a Congressman and a Sindall employee. It is not possible in this case to separate a businessperson from his business. If you become involved with Bryson on a full-time basis, then it will appear that Sindall is involved in the Congressman's campaign as well.

Your proposed association would leave all of us wide open to all sorts of allegations. Although no money is involved, Sindall would be making payment in kind—the services of one of our ablest employees. I am sorry to refuse your request, but it will be better for everyone in the long run.

I encourage you to continue your part-time affiliation with Congressman Bryson's campaign, and wish Congressman Bryson the best of luck.

**Figure II.7**

TO:      Robert L. Payton
FROM:   Edwin Sindall, President

I certainly share your conviction that Congressman Bryson would make an excellent U.S. senator for this state. His strengths are evident from the campaign status report you lent me. It can be considered an honor to be selected his advance agent.

I also agree that we at Sindall Lumber must actively fulfill our civic responsibilities as members of this community. I therefore modified our long-standing policies to allow our empoloyees to participate in community organizations on a part-time or volunteer basis. As a result, our community relations have greatly improved. However, these external activities have recently been placing increasing demands on our executives' valuable time. Three months ago I even had to restrict our involvement with the local United Fund's annual drive.

Since federal politics is a more sensitive issue, Sindall must be very careful with its public profile. We have never solicited political favors and are not dependent on government business. We consider politics strictly a personal matter and our policy is to remain non-partisan.

Your request for leave of absence would place Sindall in an embarrassing position. Our supporting a Republican with little chance of winning against a Democrat would only jeopardize our relationship with the incumbent. Given the threat from environmental groups, it is vital that the lumber trade have a receptive ear and a powerful voice in the legislature. Therefore, we cannot sponsor your highly visible role in a political organization.

As you know, Bob, my own community activities divert too much of my time and energy from the operations of this company where they really belong. I have decided to resign my seat on the hospital board. I will be happy to nominate you as my successor. Would you be interested?

**Figure II.8**

August 7, 198-

Dear Bob,

Your sense of obligation to participate in politics shows good citizenship. I am also personally happy that your sympathy lies with the Republican Party.

The company recognizes its obligation to contribute to society. Since a few years back, we have been allowing a reasonable amount of time off for community work. Naturally, we are also obliged to continue as a viable company and to be consistent in the treatment of employees. Therefore we require that a person's community work not prevent him from doing full justice to his job at Sindall. Although your job, Bob, is flexible, it would be unfair to grant you a leave of absence but not someone else who is more critical in day-to-day operations. Nor would it be fair to refuse a leave to someone for work in the Democratic Party, a leave that my social conscience would prevent me from granting.

Within these limits, Bob, I strongly encourage you to continue your political work. Democracy depends on your participation.

Very sincerely yours,

Edwin Sindall
President

Figure II.9

SINDALL LUMBER COMPANY
Box 1000
Boise, Idaho 64002

August 7, 198-

Dear Bob,

I have been working on your request since we talked this morning. In the absence of precedent or company policy, I began asking myself what criteria would be used to judge requests like yours. Two fundamental questions came to mind. First, what is the intent of encouraging external community involvement? Second, what should the company be willing to pay to support this involvement?

My intent in reversing my father's policy was twofold. Noninvolvement was hurting Sindall's community reputation. Noninvolvement also restricted the natural extension of our managers' skills and stymied their desire to become integral members of the community. Therefore, to turn these trends around I adopted the policy of supporting external community activity. The important fact is that any request should serve both goals, positive company image and individual development, simultaneously. Although your request undoubtedly furthers your personal development, I think we have to question its impact on our image, especially since you would be dealing with a federal government position.

I approached the question of company support using a cost/benefit analysis. By encouraging responsible activities, the company gains a well-rounded, more satisfied manager. We pay for this improved manager by allowing time off to engage in community programs. But, I believe the boundary on allowed time should be determined by how much extra work our other managers must assume to fill the gap. This time limit is especially important given the small size of our management team. Each member has several functions. My judgment is that any outside involvement shoud cause minimum burden for the other managers and should not transfer any job responsibility to other team members.

Since I wanted to be completely fair regarding workload, I checked with Stu. His willingness to pick up the extra load speaks well of your relationship with him. However, I believe that in granting your request I would be asking too much of the other managers.

The final criterion of a policy must be that it can be administered fairly. I have strong beliefs in the purpose of the Republican Party and personally encourage participation. However, in fairness to the company and to its employees, I have to ask myself "what if a bright, young Democrat came to me requesting time to work for Johnson?" I could not bring myself to say yes. Therefore, as President of Sindall, to be nondiscriminatory, the company policy necessarily must provide equal opportunities for any political belief within reason.

As a staunch Republican, the last thing I want to do is discourage your party involvement. Perhaps you can get your feet wet and still make a meaningful contribution by volunteering to be responsible for the local campaign. I'm sure this type of activity would meet the criteria outlined above, and I would be interested in joining you in the effort in light of your high regard for our candidate.

Sincerely,

Edwin Sindall

cc: Stuart Broderick

**Figure II.10**  Memorandum submitted with the letter in Figure II.9.

TO:        Stuart Broderick
FROM:      Ed Sindall
DATE:      August 7, 198-
SUBJECT:   Payton's Request for a Leave of Absence

    As I stated in the attached letter, I appreciate your attempt to pick up the slack but I really believe it is too much to ask of the other managers. After Bob has had a chance to read the letter, get his reactions. If he believes his personal development cannot be satisfied with less than the six-week leave, then I think the three of us should meet to discuss his career plans.

# WRITING STYLE AND MANAGEMENT STYLE

## 10

When you write, your writing style often says as much about you as about your subject matter. Your words carry your image to your readers and make them see you as a particular kind of person; rightly or wrongly your words imply that you are aggressive, assertive, timid, caring, aloof, pretentious, easy-going, or some other personality type. Day by day these images coalesce and combine with the impressions people receive of you during face-to-face encounters. Together they reflect your own personal style of conducting business—or, if you will, your *management style*.

Your management style reveals a great deal about the way you feel about yourself and the people around you. Capable writers project confidence and appropriately congenial attitudes toward their readers. Talented business writers almost always are able to project a compelling and attractive personality. On the other hand, ineffective writers appear to forget who they really are; they hide every semblance of their best self behind a facade of officiousness, phony objectivity, cloying politeness, or pomposity. Some of these ineffective writers are unaware that their writing style implies an odious personality. Others look at their own creations and shudder; they know something is very wrong, but somehow feel that this kind of writing is the way of the world.

Actually, it is not. And if in truth a great deal of such writing is produced today, it is time we put an end to it.

## ■ What's In (and Out of) Style Today

Good contemporary business writing reflects each writer's own inner world and personal management style. Also, to a large extent, it mirrors the external world. Like the way we dress, the way we write has changed throughout the years. Moreover, writing style continues to be affected by slowly evolving trends and quickly vanishing fads.

Consider for a moment two of the dominant writing styles of preceding centuries. In the eighteenth century (the Age of Reason) writers strove for clarity, and the best of them achieved an unadorned, lucid style. In the nineteenth century, however, the Victorians crammed their homes with knick-knacks and their writing with words. As the novelist Virginia Woolf once commented, ". . . sentences swelled, adjectives multiplied, lyrics became epics, and little trifles that had been essays a column long were now encyclopaedias in ten or twenty volumes." Furthermore, in the Victorian era, the dominant attitude expressed in business correspondence was stiff formality, a style parodied by Charles Dickens, whose awesomely pompous Mr. Micawber told his friend David Copperfield in a famous letter, "I have discharged the pecuniary liability incurred at this establishment," a statement meant to inform David that Micawber had paid his rent. (The preceding sentence—from "Furthermore" to "rent"— could not compete in length with many of its nineteenth-century prototypes!)

Time is valuable today. We don't like to see it wasted, especially in the fast-paced business environment. Clarity and directness command our respect; we try to "tell it like it is." If you look at samples of some of today's best business writing, you see clean, clear sentences with few wasted words. The sentences are reasonably short, move quickly, and carry overtones of the writer's voice and personality.

Notwithstanding these good points, our best business writing is as vulnerable to fads as was that of other centuries; for better or worse, it is colored by the language of technology. Having passed through a time when a large share of business writing reflected our infatuation with space-age jargon, today's writers are now hip-deep in the language of computers. This willingness to learn, use, and discard new words (probably a reflection of a practical, pragmatic approach to life) enriches our language. We enjoy these new options; we are far more interested in finding new ways to carry our precise meaning than in keeping our language "pure."

On the other hand, this "easy come, easy go" attitude toward the words we use is not entirely a virtue. As words such as "trajectory," "countdown," and now "interface," "input," and "output," get used over and over again, their newness stales. Although initially clear and vivid, they grow pale and lifeless. Nevertheless, such words remain in vogue, offering writers a seductive and habit-forming escape from the necessary effort of searching for precise and vigorous language.

*Shoe* by Jeff MacNelly. Reprinted by permission. Tribune Media Services.

If you examine the *worst* examples of today's business writing style, you will find sentences that curl like snail trails and move almost as slowly, a super-abundance of worn-out jargon, and a pompous, impersonal tone that tries to impress rather than to inform. A graphic example of this diction and tone was recently spotlighted by *The Wall Street Journal*: a reporter cast a bemused eye on a Pentagon request that called for specifications for "a wood interdental stimulator," more commonly known as a "toothpick."

## ■ A Parade of Monsters

You may be less than astonished to find this kind of writing in a military contract, but the Pentagon has not cornered the market for pompous, verbose expression. The following excerpts parade forth from the writings of contemporary business people working in a variety of settings:

- **From an Advertising Agency:** In the future, we will make every attempt to advise you of additional costs pertaining to any requested revisions prior to the actual work's being done.
  **Translation:** From now on, before we do revisions, we will tell you how much they will cost.
- **From a Marketing Research Firm:** Based upon our observations, customers will utilize various retail-related products prior to recognizing the potential positive impact of interfacing with wholesalers directly.
  **Translation:** From what we've observed, customers will use retail products until they recognize the advantages of dealing directly with wholesalers.
- **From a High-Tech Manufacturing Company:** The Systems Engineering area has a rather simple and somewhat easy responsibility of accounting for the revenue and costs and expenses associated with the sale of such services to our present customers and others in need of programming and systems-type assistance.
  **Translation:** Systems Engineering is responsible for keeping track of costs and revenues derived from assisting customers with programming and systems design.
- **From an Investment Brokerage Firm:** The firm's standard of service to its clients must be of the caliber to ensure that clients return to the firm each and every time they require service, and knowing that the service received is of the highest standard, we will acquire through the personal recommendations of our clients, other clients.
  **Translation:** By seeing that our clients receive the highest standard of service, we can ensure that they will continually return to us and will recommend our services to others.

- **From a Mail Order Company:** As we are a company that is entirely concerned with our customers' needs and satisfactions, your input regarding the omission of two pages from our spring catalogue was much appreciated. We have utilized it to correct the error in the summer edition.

  **Translation:** Since we are very concerned about your needs, we appreciate your telling us that two pages were omitted from our spring catalogue. The summer edition will not contain this error.

- **From an Insurance Company:** Because of the very high nonutilization factor, the switchboard will be shut down on weekends.

  **Translation:** Because few calls are handled on weekends, the switchboard will be shut down then.

- **From a Department Manager at a Bank:** The department is growing, as is the bank. Therefore, the use of initials on memoranda has outlived any meaningful purpose and will be prohibited as of today in all written correspondence, intradepartmental and interdepartmental. This restriction is necessitated by the fact that we now have so many employees that initials are no longer unique, nor do they register with the receiver any recognition of the sender.

  **Translation:** As of now, we will no longer use initials for names on memos sent inside or outside the department. Because both the bank and this department are growing rapidly, many of our people have identical initials, making it difficult to recognize the author of an initialed memo.

The people who created these monsters honestly believed that they were writing effectively—or at least as business people are supposed to write. They are intelligent people with good working vocabularies. They made very few grammatical errors and are good spellers. Nevertheless, they leave their readers paralyzed with frustration and boredom, victims of an epidemic of stylistic blunders.

Style, as defined in Chapter 2, is determined by *the words we choose* and *the way we arrange them in sentences*. Clearly, the above writers did not use good judgment in choosing their words, and they combined their words into sentences that are disfigured with awkwardness.

## ■ Word Choice: Where Style Begins

English is a language so rich in choice that its abundance creates as many problems as opportunities for writers. As we struggle to express a thought, too many words can rush into our minds; we are faced with so many possibilities for phrasing that our immediate choice may be far from the best. Sometimes we settle for words that convey only a pale and lifeless version of our idea; at other times we carelessly select words that carry inappropriate overtones.

To communicate what we really intend, we need to keep in mind that words have both explicit (denotative) and implicit (connotative) meanings. For example, an "error," a "mistake," a "blunder," and a "goof" all denote something gone wrong, but each word connotes a very different attitude on the part of the writer. Business writers, especially, must be aware that the connotation of words can affect readers deeply. A judicious choice of words sometimes can help get us through a tough situation: a "deficit" can become a "shortfall"; or a drop in profitability a "downturn." On the other hand, insensitive word choices can cause serious problems. Today, for instance, women in the business environment are not referred to as "girls" (at least not by astute men who perceive the barnacles of connotation that now cling to that word).

Sometimes the most obvious problem with a piece of business writing is that the writer simply did *not* choose at all. The translations provided above not only substitute better words and untangle awkward constructions, they also remove a great deal of excess verbiage. They show us clearly that *to have a way with words we must do away with words!*

Busy people with ample vocabularies can be the worst culprits of all, hastily spilling out their words on reams of memo paper, with little attention to word choice or phrasing. Unless these writers become convinced that effective style is crucial to attaining their ends, they refuse to take the time to discipline themselves. Often, like the people who composed the above excerpts, they allow themselves to write sentences that stagger or lumber along, delivering meaning in a damaged, distorted form—if at all.

In a frequently quoted admonition, Mark Twain urged writers to use care in selecting their words. He warned, "The difference between the almost right word and the right word is really a large matter—'tis the difference between the lightning bug and the lightning." How do you find words that spark the lightning? How do you substitute words that have animation, sizzle, and force for those that are inert, limp, and dull? Let's look at some basic techniques for choosing effective words.

## Verbs

First focus on your verbs. The verb has rightly been called the engine that drives the sentence. When verbs are weak or static, we feel that the writer lacks energy or (even worse) conviction. The second important reason why verbs have so much influence on the effectiveness of writing can be boiled down to two brief tenets:

- Strong, active verbs stimulate the reader's interest.
- Strong, active verbs produce images the reader's memory will retain.

To convince yourself of the truth of these two assertions, consider the following statement:

He came into the room.

As you think about this sentence, try to picture the man who entered the room. What sort of person is he?

Chances are that you had to labor to come up with any impression at all. If you conceived an image of this person, it was probably vague and shadowy.

Now consider the following sentences:

He *trudged* into the room.

He *staggered* into the room.

He *dashed* into the room.

In each case, the colorless word "came" has been replaced by a more graphic verb. Each of these verbs communicates an image of a particular person entering the room; when the verb changes, the image also changes. Your image is likely to differ from mine, but each of us is able to see "him."

This exercise demonstrates the power of the verb. Since we find it just about impossible to picture an action without seeing the doer, we are forced to reach into our store of memories for an appropriate image. Even though we are not told what he looks like, we feel that we know. Our senses have been stirred.

Fresh and specific verbs can make us see and can stimulate us to perceive sound, odor, touch, taste, and motion. These sensory images strike chords within our memories; they interest us because they are both vivid and familiar. For the same reasons, long after more abstract ideas have vanished from memory, we are apt to recall the thoughts and ideas that active images communicate. Strong verbs are also far more effective in stimulating the senses than are weak verbs combined with modifiers. For example, "He *came slowly* into the room" is far less effective than "He *trudged* into the room." Similarly, "He *came swiftly* into the room" lacks the power of "He *dashed* into the room."

But how does this theory carry over into actual business correspondence? Are vivid verbs really appropriate in memos, letters, and reports? Of course they are! To prove it to yourself, consider the following pairs of sentences:

The firm made a great deal of rapid progress in terms of profitability and productivity in this fiscal year.

The firm's profitability and productivity climbed rapidly in this fiscal year.

The president gave our words a lot of consideration before responding.

The president digested our words slowly before responding.

In both cases, using more vivid verbs has resulted in a far more readable, memorable, and concise style. It follows that if you want your readers' complete attention and if you expect your words to be retained longer than the first few minutes after they are read, you should devote maximum care to selecting verbs.

Colorless verbs, too many linking verbs, and overuse of the passive voice are faults that greatly detract from your writing style. Although it is possible to get a "gut feeling" for the difference between vigorous writing and limp, plodding prose, you will not really be in control until you master certain rules of style and syntax. Explanations of points of grammar such as the passive voice and linking verbs will therefore be included in the section entitled "Rules for Writers" in Chapter 11. In that chapter, you will also find specific techniques for recognizing and correcting stylistic weaknesses and grammatical blunders.

## Nouns

Second only to verbs in ability to attract and hold a reader's attention are nouns. But the more abstract and unspecific the noun, the less power it generates.

At this moment you are most likely sitting in a chair. The word "chair," however, is not the chair itself. It is an abstraction—an idea that represents the actuality. If you prefer, you can refer to the chair as "a piece of furniture," "an object," or even as "a part of the immediate environment." Each subsequent choice of words, of course, draws you further and further away from the reality of the chair beneath you. A reader will be unlikely to envision a chair if you choose to call it an "object." If you designate it as "part of the environment," the odds against comprehension will be even greater.

As you move from the concrete and specific to a more generalized and abstract idea, you are climbing higher on what semanticists call a "ladder of abstraction" (see Figure 10.1). As a business writer, you should select words as far down on the ladder as you can get while still retaining the meaning you intend. Unless you have a good reason to do otherwise, you should refer to "John Jones" and not to "one or our employees"; and if you are speaking of your company's "employees," you should not refer to them as "persons within the organization."

As we have seen in Chapters 5 and 6, generalizations and abstractions *are* essential to communication. They help us to classify ideas and to structure our thinking. But abstractions do great harm if we allow them to deprive our writing of all that commands a reader's interest. There are appropriate times to write about "salespeople" rather than about "John Jones and Mary Smith," or to refer to "office equipment" rather than to "typewriters, telephones, and copying machines." But far too frequently business writers wallow in abstractions out of sheer carelessness; we fail to take time to push beyond the shadowy generalization to the palpable idea that lies just out of reach.

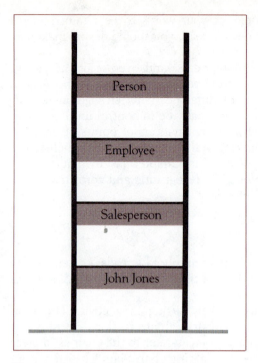

**Figure 10.1** Ladder of abstraction.

For example, consider the following sentence:

In regard to a *case* of this *type,* the company should consider the *situation* in all of its *aspects.*

All of the italicized words are abstractions. They are like windowglass: search them for meaning, and you gaze right through them to a blank nothingness. But the writer of these words, a personnel director, did have an important point on his mind. He wanted to communicate the following warning:

When a capable employee leaves a job immediately after a performance review, the company should attempt to discover the reason.

This second version focuses on the experience that underlies the abstraction and describes it in specific, concrete language. By doing so, it provides us with an idea that we can grapple with and respond to.

## Verb/Noun Construction: "Camouflaged" Verbs

It is easy to fall into the habit of using a colorless verb/noun combination instead of a specific, active verb. Typical examples of this lifeless construction are "give a presentation" for "present," "make a recommendation" for "recommend," and "do an evaluation" for "evaluate." Teach yourself to listen for "tion" words—nouns usually of three or more syllables ending in *-tion*. They weigh down your writing with extra syllables and words. As you can see, in each of the above examples the real verb is embedded in the noun. It is literally camouflaged. By carving away the excess syllables and eliminating the weak verb, you change your style from ponderous and stuffy to crisp and assertive.

In Figures 10.2 and 10.3 are two versions of a fairly routine memo composed by a personnel staff assistant. You will quickly see that the second version is a great deal better than the first; it transmits the same mes-

---

TO:   Third-Floor Employees          DATE: March 15, 198-
FROM: Peter Fargo, Personnel
RE:   Revision of the Lunch Schedule

The following situation concerning the third-floor cafeteria has been brought to our attention. Recent overcrowding during the lunch period seems to indicate that it might be to everyone's advantage to take a revised lunch schedule under consideration.

After examining all relevant factors, we would like to make the following recommendation. As of Monday, April 5, all third-floor employees should make a choice between two separate lunch periods— the first from 11:30 to 12:30 and the second from 12:30 to 1:30. Although it is assumed that this arrangement will involve some slight inconvenience, the ultimate effect will be to correct the current situation. The serving of lunch will thereby be able to be accomplished more quickly and efficiently by the cafeteria staff.

**Figure 10.2**
First version of a fairly routine memo.

---

TO:   Third-Floor Employees          DATE: March 5, 198-
FROM: Peter Fargo, Personnel
RE:   Revised Lunch Schedule

We have learned that recent overcrowding in the third-floor cafeteria has frequently caused long lines and poor service. After carefully considering all of our options, we believe that a revised lunch schedule will solve the problem most effectively.

We therefore request that as of Monday, April 5, all third-floor employees choose between two separate lunch periods—the first from 11:30 to 12:30 and the second from 12:30 to 1:30. Dividing the lunch crowd into two groups will enable the cafeteria staff to serve all of you more quickly and efficiently.

**Figure 10.3**
An improved version of the memo in Figure 10.2.

---

sage in far fewer words and with far more persuasiveness. The improvement results primarily from getting rid of weak verbs, abstract nouns, and verb/noun constructions. Study the changes, and see if you can pinpoint the precise faults that have been remedied.

## ■ Word Order: Style in the Making

Writers who are conscientious but inexperienced often write with a great deal of self-conscious effort. Worrying constantly, they inch ahead word by word. When they have finally reached the end of the piece, they breathe a sigh of relief. They have done their best. They are off the hook.

Before they start to write, experienced writers generally think very hard about their audience and their purpose. They devote time to sketching out the structure of the piece and perhaps to obsessing a bit about their first few sentences. But once over these hurdles, these writers do not fastidiously choose their words like cherries from a tree. Rather, they let them fall upon the page as if their order were predestined. Such writers know well enough that nothing about this first rush of words has any relationship to destiny. Even though it frequently contains much worth retaining, this spontaneous outpouring represents only one of many possibilities for expressing the same thoughts.

Most writers want and need the luxury of shaking the tree and letting the fruit fall as it will. If we free our inner voice, it speaks to us rapidly and distinctly. By recording the words we hear, we quickly give form and substance to our thoughts. Half-formed ideas drifting through a writer's mind are, of course, nearly impossible to evaluate or revise. And frequently they are lost before we even have the opportunity to try. But an idea that has been made tangible and visible can be clarified and refined at will. And writers *must* revise. The more knowledgeable and particular the writer, the more complex or sensitive the purpose, the more time the revision may take, and the better the result is likely to be.

Your "gut" reaction to your first draft can provide some insights, but it will only carry you a short distance. To strengthen your phrasing and sentence structure, you again need to know precisely what you are trying to do and how you are going to do it. As with word choice, revising word order with confidence requires some real knowledge of specific rules and techniques. Although this knowledge permeates even your first drafts, you appreciate it the most when you revise. It helps you to spot weaknesses immediately and to know exactly what remedies to apply.

## ■ Clarity, Conciseness, Vigor

When your words are well chosen and you have used them effectively, your writing style will exhibit *clarity*, *conciseness*, and *vigor*. These three characteristics represent the broad objectives you should set for your business writing style. *Clarity* implies that, with no more than the expected effort, a reader can grasp your meaning. *Conciseness* means that you have no wasted words in your sentences. And *vigor* is the quality in your writing that keeps the reader awake, even when the content of the piece is routine or highly technical.

These objectives take time and effort to attain, but the good news is that they are so closely interrelated that they are often achieved simultaneously. The two versions of the memo written by Peter Fargo, personnel staff assistant (see Figures 10.2 and 10.3), graphically illustrate this relatedness. Clear writing is usually concise, and concise writing is almost always vigorous. Meaning shines through when unneeded verbiage is pruned away. The same techniques that rid a piece of writing of extraneous words also produce a crisper and more persuasive style. As we have stressed, such a writing style produces positive effects immediately: you project an image of yourself as knowledgeable and responsible. Perhaps as much as the substance of your remarks, this image gains you credibility with your readers.

## Clarity

What happens when your writing lacks clarity? First, consider your readers' reactions. Even if they puzzle out your meaning, they are likely to feel annoyed. They may decide that you didn't think them important enough to take the time to make yourself clear. Or worse, they may interpret your unclear writing as a sign that you had so little respect for their intelligence that you felt you could snow them with empty words.

Most importantly, unclear writing rebounds on the writer. It inhibits your ability to think. Each phrase and each sentence that you write is, in part, a response to the one that precedes it. Or, to put it another way, each word you write provides the impetus for the next. Therefore, if your writing is tangled or muddy, your thinking will probably follow suit. (An excellent exploration of this problem is presented in Marvin H. Swift's article, "Clear Writing Means Clear Thinking Means . . . ," included in the readings at the end of this text. In Swift's article, a manager peels away the wordiness in his memo to discover that it says something totally different from what he believed.)

## Conciseness

Clarity and vigor are not easy to measure because they are subjective qualities. We know that something is clear when we understand it; we know it is vigorous when it gives us pleasure or satisfaction to read it. Conciseness, on the other hand, can be measured objectively. If you remove verbiage, you can see the result; you can even prove it by counting the words. For this reason, conciseness often points the way to the other two objectives. (For example, in the article mentioned above, Swift's manager discovers how to make his memo clear and vigorous only after he has made it concise.)

Unfortunately, too many business writers act as though they are being paid by the word. Some of this long-windedness is a throwback to their junior high school days when a strict teacher ordered up a specific number of pages, and students met that requirement no matter how little they had to say. In other cases, wordiness arises from a mistaken belief that business writing ought to sound and look a certain way, that it requires a bit of pomp and circumstance to pass muster. Perhaps more forgivably, some writers are too wordy because they believe that by eliminating words they will also eliminate needed information. This is not true. The conciseness that is appropriate to business writing does not require that you deplete the substance of your documents. (On the contrary, once the heavy-handed verbosity is removed, a one-page memo will often have space for a needed explanation or additional supporting data.)

Consider the following sentence, taken from the first draft of a consultant's report to a client:

> The introduction of new products appears to be inadvisable during the current period of time.

Here is a pared-down version:

> Introducing new products appears inadvisable at this time.

As you can see, no part of the idea is lost in the revised version; it is merely less wordy.

Experienced writers routinely wait for the heat of creativity to cool and then reread their work with a critical eye. Knowing that almost any first draft will contain deadwood, they look for the stylistic weaknesses that breed verbosity, and they eliminate them.

## Vigor

Vigorous writing is difficult to describe. Although in most contexts "vigor" implies forcefulness, all vigorous business writing is not forceful. It can be tactful, matter-of-fact, descriptive, and even technical. It can be formal or informal, and it can deal with matters that are important or routine, complex or simple. Although a more vigorous writing style can often be achieved by editing or conciseness, vigorous writing is not always concise. Vigorous writing is inevitably clear, and yet clarity and vigor are not synonymous.

The common denominator of all vigorous writing is that it invites reading. A subtle force in a spirited vigorous style carries the reader forward. Even when the subject matter may seem difficult or dull, a strong writing style compels the reader's attention.

Strong verbs impart vigor to writing, and so do concrete, specific nouns. As we have discussed above, both of these stimulate the senses and attract our interest. But choosing effective verbs and nouns is only a beginning. To make your writing vigorous, you must work to achieve *rhythm*, *variety*, and *emphasis* in your writing style. Because vigor is so much to be desired and so subtle and complex, we will spend considerable time here analyzing these three elements.

## ■ Rhythm

President John F. Kennedy did not say:

"It is better not to ask what your country can do for you."

Nor did he say:

"You should not ask what your country can do for you."

Rather, he opened his famous statement with these words:

"Ask not what your country can do for you."

The meaning remains constant in all three versions, but the rhythm changes. The powerful, driving rhythm of his actual words provides emphasis and force.

It is interesting to note how rhythm affects the way we hear this statement. It is even more interesting to note that we do *hear* it. Even as we silently read, we react to the sound and beat of the phrasing. We are in some ways like musicians hearing the notes we see on sheets of music. And to some degree we also are affected by the *sound* of the words. Consider the different effect if President Kennedy had said: "Question not what your country can do for you."

Obviously, business writers are neither orators nor poets. Even if we would like to pay scrupulous attention to sound and rhythm, we don't have the time. How then, can we harness (at least to some degree) the potential that both sound and rhythm have for affecting our readers? As we stated in early chapters, letters, memos, and reports *speak* to their readers. At their best, they echo the natural voice of a writer expressing ideas in words especially well chosen for the circumstances and the audience. The first and simplest technique for getting rhythm into your writing is therefore to listen to yourself talking to your reader as you write. Your writing should, of course, eliminate the false starts and stops that come from unsureness. But it should include the pauses that create emphasis, as well as the short, sharp sentences and rhythmic repetitions that call for attention.

The letter shown in Figure 10.4 was sent by Patricia St. Pierre, a young entrepreneur, to potential customers for her new art rental business. To get a feeling for its sound and rhythm, try reading this letter aloud. Read a bit slower than you ordinarily do, and concentrate on what you hear. You will sense the slightly formal but still conversational quality of

**Figure 10.4**
A letter to prospective customers.

ARTRENDS, INC. 54 NEWBURY STREET
BOSTON, MA 02116

March 15, 198-
Customer's Name
Address
City, State, Zip Code

Dear (Name of Customer):

Whether your business is large or small, established or new, you
undoubtedly want your surroundings to show that you know and
value quality. Displaying fine pieces of art in your reception areas
and offices will get this point across subtly—but immediately.

At ARTRENDS, INC., I can assist you in selecting paintings and
sculpture suited to your particular taste and decor. Moreover, I can
guide you in the placement and arrangement of these objects. As
part of this service, I will personally visit your place of business
and suggest how and where pictures or sculpture can achieve effects that will please you.

Acting as a liaison between businesses and highly respected artists
throughout the country, I can secure fine originals for you to rent
or to purchase. If you prefer, I also have access to excellent repro-
ductions and posters representing the finest artists of other centuries. Rental or purchase costs are not as high as you might expect. And they're certainly much lower than you could achieve
without my professional assistance.

Would you like more information? Don't hesitate to call me directly
at any time. In the meantime, I hope you enjoy browsing through
the enclosed brochure. It will introduce you to just a few of the
beautiful art objects available at this time.

Sincerely yours,

*Patricia St. Pierre*

Patricia St. Pierre
General Manager

PSP:sec

the letter. You will hear definite pauses such as the one that comes before the last two words of the first paragraph and the one that follows the question in the last paragraph. You should also be able to tell when the "speaker" is talking rapidly; for example, in the third paragraph, beginning the last sentence with "And" slides the reader quickly from one sentence to another.

Perhaps the most powerful technique of all for putting sound and rhythm to work is *parallel construction*, which uses the repetition of grammatical structure to achieve emphasis and clarity. Consider the opening sentence of Patricia St. Pierre's letter; note the rhythmic repetition of "large or small, established or new." Because the parallel elements can be both seen and heard, they evoke an especially strong reaction:

- The reader hears the rhythm that results from the repetition.
- The reader sees the alignment of similar ideas in similar forms.

## ■ Variety

Rhythm and variety are inextricably related. When you vary the length or pattern of your sentences, you affect their rhythm. And by increasing your consciousness of rhythm, you will automatically vary your sentences, both in length and in pattern.

Sentence length is to a great extent determined by sentence structure. Except for a few one-word oddities like "Help!" or "Go!" any sentence that you write will contain at least one independent clause composed of a subject noun and a predicate verb. For example, "John spoke" and "Sue responded" are both *simple sentences.*

*Compound sentences* contain two independent clauses, for example, "John spoke, and Sue responded." *Complex sentences* are constructed from an independent clause and a dependent clause (one that cannot stand alone), such as "When John spoke, Sue responded." (The first clause obviously does not express a complete thought.) Writers can also create *compound-complex sentences*, for example, "When John spoke, Sue responded, and the rest of us remained silent." This kind of sentence frequently begins with a dependent clause, followed by two independent clauses.

Once you understand this kind of sentence building, you will see clear-cut options for varying your sentences in order to change their rhythm and emphasis. Instead of the compound-complex example, we could write either of the following: "John spoke. Sue responded, and the rest of us remained silent"; or "When John spoke, Sue responded while the rest of us remained silent." (There are, of course, numerous other options.)

When you have learned the trick of elongating sentences by adding clauses, you may feel strongly tempted to add too many. Even if its syntax is impeccable, a complicated compound-complex sentence can sink under its own weight. For business writing, therefore, it is sensible to limit yourself to no more than one dependent clause per sentence.

We already stated that developing an ear for rhythm will inevitably cause you to vary your sentence length. While you are consciously striving for variety, however, you might abide by this rule: whenever you write three short sentences, follow them with a lengthier one; alternatively, whenever you write two long sentences, follow them with at least one short one. To divide a compound sentence into two shorter sentences, don't hesitate to begin the second sentence with "And" or "But." And keep in mind that two related short sentences can be joined by a semicolon to produce a longer one. Experiment with these techniques; practice them frequently. (If you study this paragraph closely, you will see that it contains sentences that exemplify the techniques mentioned.)

Varying your sentence *patterns* has an even greater effect on rhythm than does varying sentence length. The standard sentence pattern, called the *loose pattern* or the *cumulative pattern*, begins with an independent clause and expands it with additional information. Consider the following example: "Profits increased as we increased production, controlled expenditures, and did a far better job of marketing." In this sentence, there is no waiting for the main point; the initial independent clause makes it apparent at the outset. Now consider the following version: "As we increased production, controlled expenditures, and did a far better job of marketing, profits increased." Here the standard order has been reversed, and the sentence builds to a climax; this is the *periodic pattern*. Periodic sentences can be extremely effective in leaving a message resounding in the reader's mind.

## ■ Emphasis

Even if grammar is not your cup of tea, it will be well worth your while to become familiar with the ways you can vary sentence structure and pattern to achieve emphasis. Mastering a few specific techniques can enable you to build sentences that are subtly but powerfully persuasive. You can learn how to stress or to minimize points by positioning them carefully in the sentences you build. For instance, an idea that is inserted in a dependent clause that opens a sentence tends to lose its force. Compare the following three sentences:

> I will not be able to attend your presentation, but I will be certain to review the videotape carefully. (*two independent clauses*)

> I will be certain to review the videotape carefully because I will not be able to attend your presentation. (*an independent clause followed by a dependent clause*)

Because I will not be able to attend your presentation, I will be certain to review the videotape carefully. (*a dependent clause followed by an independent clause*)

Can you sense how the first version presents a rather balanced view, the second stresses the disappointing news, and the third emphasizes the positive side?

You probably observed from our example of the periodic pattern that periodic sentences end with a clash of cymbals: the emphasis is heavily in the last words. Similarly, you saw in the last section how parallel structure enforces meaning by emphasizing similar elements. Finally, regarding emphasis, we can point to the effects you can achieve by varying sentence length. An idea buried in the middle of a long sentence gets very little emphasis; on the other hand, a short sharp statement rivets the reader's attention.

## ■ Style as an Issue: Nonsexist Language

During the last decade, an issue that compounds the perplexities of business writers has surfaced: women, and many men, too, are insisting that today's business documents reflect the fact that business people are both males *and* females. A manager is not always a *he*; neither is an engineer, an accountant, a bank officer, nor even the once sacroscanct CEO. Moreover, a secretary, nurse, or a telephone operator is not always a *she*. As soon as we acknowledge the validity of this observation, we are catapulted into uncharted territories; writing style becomes a matter of manners, politics, and even ethics.

In a world where both men and women are struggling to overcome limiting stereotypes and where more and more women are striving to make their mark in the corporate arena, a writing style that implies questionable attitudes and assumptions about gender is at best insensitive. Moreover, even if it's only to appear "with it," most business people today prefer to avoid sexist implications in their writing. But unless care and good sense are applied, management style and writing style collide so awkwardly on this issue that the result can be a parody of the writer's good intentions.

For those of you who wish to acknowledge the issue while avoiding the awkwardness, we offer the following simple and commonsensical suggestions:*

■ Whenever it is possible to refer to groups rather than individuals, do so. By using the plural you can avoid the sexist perspective of referring

---

*We credit David W. Ewing, *Writing for Results in Business, Governmemt, the Sciences, and the Professions*, 2nd Ed., John Wiley & Sons, Inc., New York (1979) for a number of these sensible suggestions.

to everyone as "he" or "him" and still refrain from repeating "he or she" interminably.

**Sexist**    The customer has every right to his own opinion about what constitutes good service.

**Revised**    Customers have every right to their own opinions about what constitutes good service.

- If your context demands that you use the singular third-person pronoun, "he or she" is less obvious than "he/she" and—unless you must repeat yourself many times—is less unwieldy. Use the turnabout s/he only if you want to make a point. (If you use this structure, you are not incorrect, but you are certainly interjecting a political note!)

- Be consistent in the way you refer to males and females. Don't send out a memo copied to Mr. Brown, Mr. Jones, Mr. Smith, and Lois. If you address a man as Mr., address a woman as Ms.; if you use a man's first name, don't apply pseudo-courtesy to a woman by calling her Mrs. Green.

- When dealing with occupations or positions, avoid terminology that stresses gender. Unless all the people referred to are men, don't say "Our salesmen did an excellent job." Allude to the group as "our salespeople" or "our salesforce." "Chairperson" is acceptable today, and so are a number of similar designations. It is also a simple matter to talk about lawyers, doctors, engineers, police officers, and fire fighters without implying gender. On the other hand, don't deal in the obviously ridiculous: we are still not ready to accept "peoplekind" for "mankind," and almost certainly we never will be.

- Look closely at the *meaning* of any statement that contains sexist overtones, and try to choose a better alternative. For instance, don't insist that your department should "man" a project when it could just as easily "staff" it. Don't speak of "the average man around here" when you really mean "the average employee."

- Finally, show that you acknowledge that women's presence in the business environment is natural and immutable. Don't refer to the secretarial staff as "the office girls" (even "the women" is offensive) or label female professionals as "authoresses," "lady engineers," etc. When men and women are not treated as equals or when the wrong gender is implied, gender is a significant issue in today's business environment. Otherwise, in 99 cases out of 100, allusion to gender is not appropriate in a business discussion.

## ■ Summary

Talented business writers employ a style that projects a compelling and attractive personality—one that exhibits clarity, conciseness, and vigor.

Good style beings with judicious word choice, with an awareness of word connotations. Favor strong, active verbs, specific and concrete nouns, crisp and assertive constructions.

Put sound and rhythm to work; listen to yourself talking to your reader. Employ parallel constructions for clarity and emphasis. Vary the length and pattern of your sentences.

Avoid sexist language and stereotypes. Whenever possible, refer to groups rather than individuals: *they/their* rather than *he/his* or *she/her*. In dealing with occupations use vocabulary—sales representative, police officer—that does not assume one gender or the other. Recognize the place of women in today's business and social world without going to absurd lengths—personkind/peoplekind, etc.—in tinkering with language.

# ■ Discussion Problems

**10.1**   What kinds of writing make you most aware of the personality behind the writing style—fiction, news or feature articles, reviews, business correspondence, or personal correspondence? Are you sometimes conscious of liking or disliking the implied personality? What characteristics give you a favorable or unfavorable impression? Can you think of some examples you encountered recently? In the case of business writing, which personal qualities seem to you most appropriate?

**10.2**   Can you remember having seen or heard a particularly offensive television or radio commercial, one that made you determined *not* to buy the product or services being offered? Describe the commercial, and try to specify exactly what repelled you in the wording or the presentation. Did an implied personality have anything to do with your negative reaction? What personality traits revealed in such advertisements don't work for you?

**10.3**   Imagine that you've been asked by a potential employer to write a five-sentence description of your last job. Draft the description, and then, without referring to what you've written, describe the job to the class or to the student sitting next to you. Tape-record your words if at all possible. Now read your written job description out loud and discuss the following questions with your fellow student(s): Which version is more lively? more detailed? more orderly? more impressive? more personal? After analyzing the differences between the two versions, decide what qualities of each version can be combined to produce the most effective written description.

**10.4**   Can you think of three or more reasons why the use of verbs in the passive voice (for example, the report *was written* by the committee, or the date *has been determined* by factors beyond our control) should be avoided in business writing? What impression is created by passive verbs? Can you describe specific business situations when passive verbs are appropriate?

**10.5**   In this chapter we maintained that concrete detail is more vigorous and ultimately more persuasive than abstract generalization. Try to persuade your classmates or a friend to see a film you recently enjoyed. First, describe the film in broad, abstract terms, trying to generalize about its story line, visual style, and overall effect. Then zero in on a few concrete details from the film (characters, conversations, or settings) that you especially recommend.

Discuss which description is more persuasive—the more general, or the more concrete? Which was easier for you to put into words? What does this suggest about the ease or difficulty of the writing process and the potential effect of written communication on its audience?

**10.6** Select a short passage from a magazine article, novel, or short story. Cross out all the adjectives and adverbs. Is any of the meaning lost? Is *anything* lost? Would it be possible to restore the lost information by strengthening the nouns and verbs in the passage? Try it!

**10.7** Jason DeWinter was given an unpleasant writing task—he had to impart some bad news to his co-workers. Struggling to be tactful, he wrote two versions of the same memo (see Figure 10.5). If you were Jason, which one would you send? Why? If neither pleases you, suggest how you could improve the better of the two to meet your standards.

**Figure 10.5**
Two drafts of the same bad-news memo.

TO:   All Employees                    DATE:   October 1, 198-
FROM:   Jason DeWinter, Personnel Director
RE:   New Policy Regarding Employee Parking

    Because of a very poor quarter, we have had to rethink our benefits program. Increased competition from overseas, higher costs, and a drop in productivity have made a cutback essential.
    Although we hope this step is temporary, the company will no longer supplement employee parking in the D Street parking garage. We suggest that until a turnabout is achieved, car pooling or public transportation might provide an acceptable alternative to using your own vehicle exclusively.

TO:   All Employees                    DATE:   October 1, 198-
FROM:   Jason DeWinter, Personnel Director
RE:   New Policy Regarding Employee Parking

    Increased competition from overseas, high costs, and a drop in productivity have resulted in a very poor quarter. We therefore have had to rethink our benefits program.
    Although the company will no longer be able to supplement employee parking in the D Street garage, we expect this step to be temporary. Car pooling and public transportation might provide acceptable alternatives to using your own vehicle exclusively. Although this cutback is essential, we believe a turnabout will soon be achieved.

**10.8** Imagine that you must write a letter to Terry E. Bradshaw, Vice President of Accounting at an English company that is one of your firm's most valued customers. You do not know whether Bradshaw is a man or a woman. What salutation will you use in your letter? Would you consider postponing writing until you get more information? How would you get the information you need? Assuming timing is important, do you think worrying about the issue is worth the delay?

**10.9** Discrimination because of gender is a real issue today; legal suits have been fought and won by those who have suffered from such discrimination in the workplace. But what constitutes unfair or unequal treatment? Should we really be sensitive to ramifications as subtle as the ways in which we imply gender in our daily interactions and our correspondence? As you discuss this issue with your instructor and fellow students, remember that the mere fact that you *are* discussing it suggests that standards have changed.

# ■ Writing Tasks

**10.1** Write a memo introducing Pat Levy, your new publications assistant, to your colleagues on the staff of Benson College. Use the most impersonal, colorless style you can achieve. Now rewrite the memo, attempting to inject your own personality. What kinds of specific changes did you make? Explain them with reference to points covered in this chapter.

**10.2** Assume that you're responding to a disappointed customer to explain the reason for some unsatisfactory product or service (you supply the details). To demonstrate that writing style reflects personal characteristics, write four brief, realistic responses that suggest the following management styles:

1. assertiveness
2. timidity
3. pomposity
4. genuine concern

**10.3** Draft a memo of eight to ten sentences to your institution's director of campus security, describing a potentially dangerous or disruptive situation in your dormitory and requesting that it be given serious attention. Ask a classmate to edit your finished work for clarity, vigor, and conciseness. Can he or she shorten your memo significantly without altering its meaning? What other suggestions can your colleague make based on the guidelines in this chapter?

**10.4** Review the following excerpts, and revise them for clarity, conciseness, and vigor:

- Such alterations will be effected at this point in time so as to essentially transform all aspects of the manufacturing process from the initial implementation through to the final stages of production.

- It might well be pointed out here that for numerous and varied reasons the output figures for July seem to indicate a considerable decrease in productivity due to a wide range of factors that have been generally overlooked, probably because very often they are too difficult to be ascertained in any given situation.

- On the other hand, on balance, I think I tend to view the situation with increasing, tough, guarded, optimism, as long as current variables seem to indicate a reasonably constant level of input from a considerable majority of the various individuals actively involved at this point.

- Following my conversation with your representative, John Felton, during which he acquainted me with the availability of your new TX-80 line catalogue, I would appreciate very much receiving said catalogue at your earliest convenience.

- Pending your guarantee of delivery within 60 days of the receipt of an order, and assuming that your prices are truly competitive within the Southwest, our order is likely to be placed in the very near future.

- It is urgently requested that all employees make reference to their department code number when in the process of ordering materials for the purpose of expediting day-to-day procedures and functions.

- You may well be aware that we have been undergoing considerable potentially divisive occasions of disagreement involving matters of various levels of seriousness.

**10.5** Choose any full-length page of explanatory writing from this or any other textbook. Imagine that you are the author and that your editor has insisted that you cut the length of the text while retaining as much of the meaning as possible. After studying the style and content carefully, reduce the text to approximately one-half of its original length.

**10.6** You are a research associate in the corporate planning department of a growing software firm. Incorporate the following information into a well-organized memo to the director of marketing. The memo should contain an effective mixture of simple, compound, and complex sentence structures.

- We are in danger of losing the Hydrex account.
- Personal relationships between client representatives and our account executives have been deteriorating.
- As you know, competition for software accounts has never been greater.
- Hydrex is considering opening a new London office. Our firm has considerable European experience.
- The Hydrex account has provided us with over 5 percent of our billing for the past three years.
- We can't easily afford to lose this business.
- Linda Peabody might be able to help us out on this.
- Hydrex will be re-evaluating our work during January.
- I propose that we meet on Wednesday morning at 10 a.m. to further evaluate performance on this account and to discuss emergency strategies.

**10.7** As in Task 10.6, incorporate the following data into a well-organized, vigorous memo. Your role here is that of a research associate for a large manufacturer of toys. Again, you are writing to the director of marketing.

- The Voltrex III toy robot is currently our best seller.
- We should be considering spin-off products during the next six weeks.
- Market research results indicate a strong continuing demand for such robots.
- Dick Henderson suggests that we monitor popular robot cartoons for new product ideas.
- We must constantly keep track of our competitors' new product lines.
- We must determine the price range we should be aiming for.
- Potential copyright complications might have to be considered at this stage.
- Jeff Kelly of Snow, Jackson, and Marley is a copyright specialist.
- I hope we can come up with some concrete suggestions during the next six weeks.
- I look forward to hearing your thoughts on this.

**10.8**   Check the memos you wrote for Tasks 10.6 and 10.7 to see whether you varied your sentence structure in ways that enforce your meaning. Remember that short sentences, parallel structures, and periodic sentences can all be used to achieve emphasis. Revise your memos to achieve better emphasis; include one periodic sentence in each memo.

# MAKING FRIENDS
# WITH THE "RULES"

## 11

*I* n a conversation we can quickly restate or clarify our ideas, but we have very little control over the total effect. An unintended inflection, a word we didn't mean to utter, a spontaneous gesture, or a fleeting expression can demolish a carefully cultivated facade of poise and confidence.

Writing, however, is a different game. It allows almost as much control over the medium as we are ready to accept. As writers, we have the time to choose carefully. If so inclined, we can reconsider, erase, and start again, and we can do so without exposing our mistakes or misfires to our reading audience. But to succeed at writing requires far more than a willingness to try hard. It requires knowledge. Although the best business writing reads as if it happened effortlessly, in almost every case the writer has learned specific techniques to sharpen focus, carve away unneeded words, and keep sentences running smoothly on the rails of meaning.

In this chapter we will refer to these techniques as "rules." It is only fair, however, to note that most are not, strictly speaking, rules. Mainly, they are methods, tested by experience, for improving writing style. They help us to confront English—our sprawling, gargantuan language—and to gain mastery over it.

Accepting on faith that subjects such as economics and accounting are important business disciplines, students dig in and commit themselves to learning the basics. "Making friends" with the rules of style means acknowledging that writing is likewise a key business discipline, and that it too requires bedrock knowledge. Moreover, such knowledge is critical to the success of countless business transactions.

A plant production and operations manager who participated in a series of writing seminars expressed this insight in memorable words to author Ruth Newman. "I never thought of my work as writing or writing as my work," he admitted. "When I recently grasped both these facts, my writing greatly improved. Furthermore, the job of writing has become far more interesting and challenging."

Review the following rules thoroughly. Then, while they are fresh in your mind, go back and reevaluate some current samples of your writing. If you feel insecure about one or more of these rules, take the time to fill the gaps in your knowledge. Study in the old-fashioned "I'm-going-to-be-tested" way: be sure you understand the troublesome rules, and then commit them to memory. Finally, promise yourself to review every draft, first to final, for lapses and to make all needed revisions.

# ■ Rules for Writers

1. **Avoid colorless verbs; learn to recognize camouflaged verbs.**
   Among the most commonly used colorless verbs are the following:

   | | | |
   |---|---|---|
   | to do | to get | to have |
   | to hold | to make | to put |
   | to take | | |

   Colorless verbs often go hand in hand with nouns that contain camouflaged verbs. If you extract the verb that is hidden within the noun, you will achieve greater conciseness, clarity, and vigor. For example, the noun "recommendation" camouflages the verb "recommend"; the noun "implementation" camouflages the verb "implement."

2. **Shun "tion" words.**
   This is a corollary to Rule 1. This rule is easy to remember and provides a reliable method for spotting most camouflaged verbs. Consider the following:

   Weak    We made a recommend*ation* calling for the substitu*tion* of our equipment for theirs.

   Improved    We recommended that they substitute our equipment for theirs.

3. **Beware of vague verbs.**
   This is another corollary to Rule 1. Some verbs are so unspecific that they can be used to convey a multiplicity of meanings. Because these verbs come so quickly to mind, they frequently displace more specific and vivid words. Two such verbs are currently in vogue: "involve" (a traditional favorite) and "impact" (a popular newcomer). "Involve" is currently used to mean "require," "include," "entail," "concern," "imply," "implicate," and "participate." It also is substituted for other specific verbs.

   Weak    The program *involved* hard work.

   Improved    The program *required* hard work.

   Weak    The process *involved* four steps.

   Improved    The process *included* four steps.

   Weak    Many people *were involved in the layoff.*

   Improved    Many people *were laid off.*

   Through overuse, "impact" has lost much of its original punch as a verb. Also, it frequently requires further explanation to communicate the whole story.

| Weak | Introducing a new product *impacted* our profits. |
|---|---|
| Improved | Introducing a new product *increased* our profits. |

4. **Use linking verbs with great care or not at all.**
A linking verb connects the subject of a sentence to a noun or adjective that expresses something about the subject's state or condition. In business writing, the most commonly used (and abused) linking verbs are the following:

| | |
|---|---|
| to appear | to look |
| to be | to seem |
| to become | |

Avoid substituting a linking verb for an action verb.

| Weak | Your estimate *is* in agreement with our calculations. |
|---|---|
| Improved | Your estimate *agrees* with our calculations. |

5. **Be especially cautious about using "waffle" verbs.**
This is a corollary to Rules 3 and 4. Verbs that waffle fail to take a stand. The worst of this group is "to seem," but "to appear," and "to look" can also be culprits. (Remember, however, that if you really mean to equivocate, these are the very words to use.) Notice, too, that waffle verbs often attach themselves to the verb "to be."

| Weak | Their presentation *seemed* to cover all of the important issues. |
|---|---|
| Improved | Their presentation *covered* all of the important issues. |

| Weak | The solution *appeared to be* an accurate reflection of the committee's research. |
|---|---|
| Improved | The solution accurately *reflected* the committee's research. |

6. **Recognize the passive voice, and use passive verbs only when you are sure they are effective.**
In most cases, an active verb will be more natural, direct, complete, and concise than a passive one. (*Note:* Rules 6, 7, and 8 all deal with the passive voice.)

| Active voice | I *wrote* the report. (4 words) |
|---|---|
| Passive voice | The report *was written* by me. (6 words) |

The passive voice can be identified by the presence of the verb "to be" or any of its derivatives, plus the *past participle* (usually ending in *ed* or *en*).

For instance, the passive sentence you have just read can be expressed in the active voice as follows: "You can identify the passive voice by the presence of . . . ."

Notice that in a passive sentence the subject *receives* the action (it is literally passive); in an active sentence the subject *initiates* the action.

Weak     A report should *be written.*

Weak     A report should *be written* by the department head.

The first sentence does not state who should write the report. The second sentence dilutes the intended meaning by stressing the object of the action (the report) rather than the subject (department head). It also uses two more words than this improved version:

Improved     The department head should *write* the report.

7. **Do not use the impersonal passive voice for attribution unless you do not want to be held responsible for a statement.** (The impersonal passive voice combines the passive verb form with the pronoun "it.")

Weak     *It is felt that* the department head should write the report. (But this version is appropriate if you are trying to remain incognito.)

Improved     *I feel that* the department head should write the report. (You may not be absolutely sure.)

Improved     The department head should write the report. (You are absolutely confirmed in your opinion.)

8. **Always use the passive voice when you intend to stress the object being acted upon or when the actor is unknown.**

Correct     *Form B-2* must be completed by all employees.

Correct     *The phone* should be answered promptly.

9. **Watch out for "There" and "It" as openings to sentences.** (Grammarians refer to this fault as "excessive predication.")
Both "there" and "it" are often used in constructions that cloud meaning, weaken emphasis, and result in stilted expression.

Weak     *There* are some companies in Massachusetts that do not carry our product.

Improved     Some companies in Massachusetts do not carry our product.

Weak     *It* is necessary to place that machine in the alcove on the first floor.

Improved     We must place that machine in the alcove on the first floor.

"There" and "It" are, of course, effective when the former stands for a place and the latter stands for a concrete object.

Correct     Japan has taught us much about production; I hope to go *there* soon.

| Correct | John wrote the letter; *it* arrived on Tuesday. |
|---|---|

10. **Whenever possible, substitute more specific words for abstract nouns.**
Some of the most overused abstract nouns are the following:

| | | |
|---|---|---|
| area | field | regard |
| aspect | instance | situation |
| case | manner | thing |
| character | matter | type |
| element | means | way |
| factor | nature | |

Circle the words on this list that you use most frequently, and add any favorites that do not appear here.

11. **Avoid the unnecessary use of "who," "which," or "that."**
These three relative pronouns can often be spotted following unneeded explanatory phrases.

| Weak | Mr. Jones *is a man who* can get the job done. |
|---|---|
| Improved | Mr. Jones can get the job done. (We don't have to be told Mr. Jones is a man!) |
| Weak | Our company *is a company that* is concerned with employee needs. |
| Improved | Our company is concerned with employee needs. (Why repeat "company"?) |

12. **Eliminate sentence openings that wind up for the pitch.**

| Weak | What he means is that prices will fall. |
|---|---|
| Improved | He means that prices will fall. |
| Weak | In Smith's case, he was fired unjustly. |
| Improved | Smith was fired unjustly. |

13. **Avoid wasting words on empty conclusions or generalizations.**

| Weak | In both Smith's and Johnson's reports the information was vital. |
|---|---|
| Improved | Both Smith and Johnson looked at the recent upturn in profits. |

14. **Use conversational words, and take the shortest route to say what you mean.**

| Weak | It is recommended that the aforementioned problem be alleviated. |
|---|---|
| Improved | The problem just discussed should be corrected. |

| | |
|---|---|
| Weak | Following our initial assessment of all of the received data, we will seek to develop optimum solutions for those problems that can be identified. |
| Improved | When we have studied the data, we will try to resolve any problems we find. |

15. **Avoid substituting compound prepositions and conjunctions for simple ones that do the job equally well.**

| *Weak* | *Improved* |
|---|---|
| in the event of | if |
| along the lines of | like |
| for the purpose of | for |
| on the basis of | by |
| for the reason that | since |
| in favor of | for |
| with a view to | to |
| with the result that | so that |
| in order to | to |
| in view of the fact that | since |

16. **Don't clutter your writing with useless qualifiers and intensifiers.**

The most common offenders are "very," "extremely," "some," "quite," "really," and "actually." Consider the following example:

Management was *quite* concerned about the *extremely* critical drop in sales for November.

Does "quite" imply that management was slightly or highly concerned? Are there degrees of "critical"? Almost any adjective or adverb can be needlessly pinned to an already effective word. Beware of creating ludicrous combinations: for example, *unexpected* emergency, *serious* crisis, and *beneficial* improvement.

17. **Avoid vague statements.**

| | |
|---|---|
| Weak | In New Hampshire, where I had the opportunity of interviewing many individuals, I recognized that a person's enthusiasm could be destroyed by the attitude of his or her supervisor. |
| Improved | In New Hampshire, where I interviewed technicians and clerical workers, I saw that overbearing or disinterested supervisors can destroy morale. |

18. **Vary the lengths and structures of your sentences.**

| | |
|---|---|
| Weak | The speaker arrived late. We became impatient. The meeting was delayed 20 minutes. |
| Improved | The speaker arrived late, and we became impatient. The meeting was delayed 20 minutes. |

| | |
|---|---|
| Weak | Equipment costs doubled this year, and production did not improve. Management acted quickly, and they ordered an investigation. |
| Improved | Although equipment costs doubled this year, production did not improve. Acting quickly, management ordered an investigation. |

19. **Avoid sentences that contain too many ideas.**
In business writing, "one dependent clause per sentence" is a good rule of thumb.

| | |
|---|---|
| Weak | In selecting a new location for our plant, we should take advantage of the available public transportation, which would enable our personnel to use their cars less and allow us to build a smaller parking facility. |
| Improved | In selecting a new location for our plant, we should take advantage of available public transportation. Such availability would enable our personnel to use their cars less; it would also allow us to build a smaller parking facility. |

20. **Use semicolons to help achieve variety and clarity.**
The semicolon is used to connect two related sentences, each capable of standing on its own.

| | |
|---|---|
| Short, choppy sentences | We monitored efficiency. Two tests were run. Our new procedure proved best. |
| Improved | To monitor efficiency, we ran two tests; our new procedure proved best. |
| Long, overly complex sentence | Despite company policy, employees are smoking at their workstations, which is strictly unfair because separate smoking areas have been set aside on every floor, and those who wish to smoke should use them. |
| Improved | Despite company policy, employees are smoking at their workstations; this practice is strictly unfair. Separate smoking areas have been set aside on every floor; those who wish to smoke should use them. |

21. **Use parallel structures to highlight relationships and to make effective use of rhythm.**

| | |
|---|---|
| Weak | By improving morale, and with a greater emphasis on cooperation, and by providing incentives, we can increase productivity. |
| Improved | By improving morale, emphasizing cooperation, and providing incentives, we can increase productivity. |

22. **Build periodic sentences to provide strong emphasis and to make effective use of rhythm.**

Parallel structures are often used to build effective periodic sentences.

| | |
|---|---|
| Standard sentence | We will not achieve our goals unless we improve morale, emphasize cooperation, and provide incentives. |
| Periodic sentence | Unless we improve morale, emphasize cooperation, and provide incentives, we will not achieve our goals. |

## ■ Common Grammatical Blunders

Sins against grammar are most reprehensible when they destroy clarity or mangle meaning, but even minor slip-ups can create a distraction or destroy the effect you hope to make. To leave an otherwise good piece of writing flawed with errors in grammar is a bit like dressing up in your finest for an important meeting and arriving with egg on your chin or catsup on your sleeve.

Below we have compiled some of the grammatical errors frequently made by business writers, as well as some advice to help you avoid making them. In no way does this brief section constitute a course in English grammar. It is intended only to guide you past some of the grammatical pitfalls that lie in wait for busy people who often need to compose rapidly.

1. **Keep your modifiers under control.**

Place every modifier as close as possible to the word it modifies.

*Misplaced Modifiers*

| | |
|---|---|
| Wrong | We filled the order *under pressure.* |
| Revised | *Under pressure,* we filled the order. (The original version might have been a bit more correct if the order comprised rubber tires!) |

*Dangling Modifiers*

| | |
|---|---|
| Wrong | *After interviewing several customers,* the product line was dropped. |
| Revised | *After we interviewed several customers,* the product line was dropped. (The product line did not do the interviewing.) |
| Wrong | *Talking to my supervisor,* the phone went dead. |
| Revised | *While I was talking to my supervisor,* the phone went dead. (The phone was not talking to your supervisor.) |

In both these examples of dangling modifiers, reference to the *agent* (the person or thing performing the act) has been omitted. A classic example that communicates a ludicrous image may help you to avoid this blunder. It goes like this: "Walking down the street, the bus went by." Imagine the bus walking on its rear tires!

### Janus Modifiers

**Wrong**    Officers *only* may use this parking lot.

**Revised**    *Only* officers may use this parking lot.

**Wrong**    Working with computers *more and more* intrigues me.

**Revised**    Working with computers intrigues me *more and more*.

The Roman God Janus had two faces—one looking toward the past and one looking toward the future. *Janus modifiers* also look in two directions.

## 2. Pronoun reference should be clear and specific.

### Ambiguous Pronoun Reference

**Wrong**    He placed the slides in the containers although *they* were dusty. (What needs dusting—the slides or the containers?)

**Revised**    Although the containers were dusty, he placed the slides in them.

**Wrong**    Our company guarantees customer satisfaction. *This* means that customers frequently return merchandise. (What does "this" refer to—the guarantee or the satisfaction?)

**Revised**    *This guarantee* means that customers frequently return merchandise.

Follow "this" or "that" with a noun whenever there is any chance of ambiguity.

### Vague Pronoun Reference

**Wrong**    Because our competitors are more interested in price than quality, they often slight *it*. (Do they slight price or quality?)

**Revised**    Our competitors' interest in price often causes them to slight quality.

**Wrong**    The complaints are being investigated. At present *they* think the problem is correctable.

**Revised**    The complaints are being investigated. The *engineering department* thinks the problem is correctable.

**Wrong**    We have not budgeted for overtime, but we have planned for absenteeism, *which* is a major problem.

**Revised**    A major problem is that we have planned for absenteeism but not for overtime.

| | |
|---|---|
| **Wrong** | Personnel staff members are in charge of this year's Christmas party. *It* may result in a slight delay in scheduling interviews. |
| **Improved** | Personnel staff members are in charge of this year's Christmas party. *Their busy calendar* may result in a slight delay in scheduling interviews. |

Beware of allowing "it" to refer to an entire independent clause. Be especially wary if the underlying idea is at all abstract or complex. Vagueness can be eliminated by substituting a specific noun for "it."

3. **Learn to distinguish separable from nonseparable elements of a sentence and to punctuate accordingly.**

| | |
|---|---|
| **Nonseparable** | *Employees who fail to arrive on time* should be notified. |
| **Wrong** | Employees, who fail to arrive on time, should be notified. (All employees do not fail to arrive on time; nor should all be notified.) |

Think of the two commas that surround the separable element as parentheses. If the separable element is eliminated, the sentence should still make sense.

| | |
|---|---|
| **Separable** | Your last report, *which had temporarily been misfiled*, contained the data we had requested. |
| **Wrong** | Your last report which had temporarily been misfiled contained the data we had requested. (Only one report had been misfiled. The interjected idea is parenthetic.) |

4. **Avoid the following punctuation errors.**
   a. *Punctuation of "its" and "it's."*
   The possessive form is "its"; "it's" is a contraction of "it is." "Its" is one of the few English words forming the possessive without an apostrophe (others include "his," "hers," "ours," and "theirs").

   b. *Comma splice (especially common with "however").*
   When two complete sentences are joined by a comma, we call the error a *comma splice*. Business writers are particularly prone to committing this blunder when they use "however" in a compound sentence.

| | |
|---|---|
| **Wrong** | He agreed to my terms, however, I still postponed shipment. |
| **Revised** | He agreed to my terms; however, I still postponed shipment. |

   c. *"And" and "But" sentences.*
   Although at some time in your life you may have been told otherwise, sentences can properly begin with "and" or "but." However, "and" or "but" must not be followed by a comma when they introduce a sentence. The reason to open a sentence with "and" or "but" is to suggest speed; you want the reader to read on rapidly. Therefore, inserting a comma entirely defeats your purpose.

| Wrong | They offered to double their investment. And, we quickly accepted. |
|---|---|
| Revised | They offered to double their investment. *And we* quickly accepted. |

# ■ Spelling Advice

It is probably true that good spellers are born that way. This means that the rest of us probably will need to make a constant effort to avoid the embarrassment caused by spelling errors. The business world allows no room for laziness here; nothing destroys the effect of an otherwise excellent letter more quickly than a glaring spelling error. Since most of your readers will fall into two categories—those who spell well naturally and those who struggle daily to give that impression—they normally won't be able to resist the urge to pounce upon the little weaknesses of less fortunate or less diligent writers. No one who wants to attain a reputation for professionalism can afford to allow others this advantage. Therefore, if you yearn to win your boss's approval and respect but have trouble recalling how many *c*'s and *s*'s are in "occasion" or how many *m*'s in "accommodate," you have only two choices: either expend the time and energy required to kick your sloppy spelling habit, or link up with a trusty colleague or secretary who will regularly ferret out your misspellings before the final draft.

If you opt to tackle spelling on your own, the best suggestion we can offer is perhaps the most obvious: create a handy list of those words you regularly misspell and refer to that list *every* time one of those words is needed in your business communications. There are a number of ways to compile such a list and to make use of it.

First, you might accustom yourself to carrying a small pocket dictionary and recording your pet misspellings inside the back cover in rough alphabetical order. (Clump together the *a* words, *b* words, etc., but don't worry about being more precise.) Most business people regularly carry around items like pocket calculators, calendars, and address books. For a congenitally weak speller, a pocket dictionary can be an enormously valuable addition to this arsenal, whether you are dashing off a note on a sales call, filling in a form while visiting another office, or drafting a report on an airplane. You should update your back-cover list about once each month, using whatever code suits you. You might, for instance, red-line or circle repeated offenders and cross off those words you feel you have conquered.

A more traditional list-keeping method is to monitor and record your own misspellings over a predetermined period (perhaps six weeks or several months, depending on how often you or others spot your mistakes). Then compile a personal trouble-shooting list, giving priority to those that you use most often and have the most difficulty remembering. Settle down to memorize these words—one at a time—mustering grit and determination. Also, force yourself to use them with even greater regularity than usual, always checking for spelling accuracy.

Just to get you started, we've compiled our own list of words that are frequently misspelled in business writing. No doubt many of these words will appear on your own list. Master them, and you will have taken a giant step toward building your spelling confidence.

### Words Frequently Misspelled in a Business Context

| | | |
|---|---|---|
| accommodate | exaggerate | privilege |
| acquire | February | questionnaire |
| affect/effect | formally/formerly | reasonable |
| all right (two words) | height | receipt |
| a lot (two words) | indispensable | recurrence |
| analysis | inquiry | separate |
| attorney | leisure | sincerely |
| auditor | mileage | stationary (immobile) |
| bookkeeping | miscellaneous | stationery (pap_er_) |
| bulletin | noticeable | subtle |
| calendar | occurred | susceptible |
| collateral | omission | transferred |
| committed | parallel | truly |
| committee | permanent | unmistakable |
| consensus | personal/personnel | waive |
| eighth | precedence | wholly |
| eligible | principal (adj: m_ai_n) | |
| embarrass | principle (noun: ru_le_) | |

If you find this bootstrap method of "memorize and practice" repugnant or impossible, you might turn to technology for some help. For instance, if you like our first suggestion of keeping your list close at hand but feel a pocket dictionary is simply too cumbersome to tote around, here's what to do. If your list is a reasonable size and not apt to change markedly over time, compile it, alphabetize it carefully, and then use a photocopy machine to reduce its size. When you have a sufficiently compact list, you can have it laminated in plastic—not a bad idea even if you have to create two or three small plastic cards. Another technological tool that can facilitate your list-compiling is, of course, the word processor. If you have access to a word processor, you can regularly update your list, adding new words, eliminating those you have learned, and keeping everything nicely alphabetized. You can either access a display on a terminal or tack an updated printout to your office wall or bulletin board.

Of course, if you work for a company where word-processing equipment is available, you can probably also take advantage of speller-checker software. Although not infallible, these programs help eliminate many

**"Want me to spell something?"**

From *The Wall Street Journal*. Permission: Cartoon
Features Syndicate.

common spelling errors at the time your document is entered into the
computer. Such a tool could temporarily obviate your need to compile
lists or otherwise attend to your spelling deficiencies. But remember—you
won't be able to carry your computer terminal around with you! Furthermore, bad spelling is not a disease that one recovers from without care and
attention. Relying on a secretary or friend to monitor your spelling will at
least improve *their* spelling; relying on a computer aid will save you time
and help you to save face, but your own spelling problems will remain
constant.

Finally, if you are serious about becoming a better speller, you should
consider investing in a very helpful nontechnological tool, a paperback
spelling guide,* particularly one that emphasizes business vocabulary. Such
guides are readily available in most bookstores. They cover the basic
spelling rules, the catchy ones that rhyme or that work by clever associations (for example, "stationery" contains "er" as in "letter").

## ■ The Rule of All Rules

Business people are in general not a patient crowd. Moreover, they aren't
the most avid readers. You may want to believe that if something is important, it is bound to get read in good time. But even when documents
deal with weighty matters, if they are cloudy or poorly written they frequently get set aside for "later." And unfortunately those same documents

*For example, *A Pocket Guide to Correct Spelling* by Francis Griffith, Barron's Educational
Series, Inc., 1982.

tend to find their way to the bottom of the next day's pile, to surface eventually, too late, or never again.

As we have previously stressed, style must work hand in hand with the larger structural elements of a piece of writing. For your ideas to receive timely and careful attention, style and structure must together communicate that you are competent and personable—a clear thinker whose vitality and humanity are apparent. Writing that projects such a strong, positive image carries the reader forward without confusion or perplexity. In effective business writing, no incoherence, no ambiguity, no awkwardness impedes the forward momentum of the message. All of the pieces, large and small, fit smoothly together and there are no obstacles to comprehension.

Once you have learned how to create a sound structure and have developed some control of the style components covered here and in Chapter 10, your confidence in your ability to communicate will escalate dramatically. At that time you will feel motivated to completely master the "rules" and to become fastidious about grammar and spelling. Don't let that determination fade away, even though this phase of the learning process often requires that you fuss, fume, and once again feel insecure about your writing. (During this interim, you can also expect most writing tasks to take you longer than ever before!)

Ultimately, however, your apprenticeship will be over. You will no longer feel insecure about the effectiveness of your writing style; moreover, you will almost intuitively know how to make it reflect your management style. From then on, although you revise more scrupulously than ever before, you will do so more rapidly and with far greater ease.

Having attained skill and confidence, you will be ready to rely heavily on the rule-of-all-rules: *"If it works, it's good."* The rule-of-all-rules is extremely seductive because it offers writers the greatest opportunity to enjoy their craft. It allows them to experiment, to make unexpected connections, to improve rhythm, and to try new ways of capturing and holding a reader's attention. Nevertheless, inexperienced writers should be exceedingly wary, because this rule has a codicil of overriding importance. The codicil is, "If you break a rule you have never learned, the mistake will be immediately obvious to your reader."

## ■ Summary

To succeed at writing requires knowledge. The "rules" in this chapter are in reality techniques, tested by experience, for improving your writing. Once you have mastered these techniques, learned to avoid the common grammatical blunders that follow, and reviewed the spelling advice, you will be able to write and revise with skill and confidence.

Only then will you be ready to apply the rule-of-all-rules: *"If it works, it's good."*

# ■ Discussion Problems

**11.1**  Do you recollect being asked to memorize material in other college courses? If so, how did you go about accomplishing this task? Would such a method help you to learn the rules of style? What better method(s) can you suggest?

**11.2**  Ask a friend who is taking this course to monitor your writing assignments for the next three weeks to determine whether a particular stylistic weakness is evident in your work. Also ask him or her to note if you repeatedly make any kind of grammatical error. Make a list of these weaknesses or errors, and post them near your desk. Each week, focus on one flaw. Memorize the relevant rule, and think about it every time you write. In a few weeks or in a month, again ask your friend to check samples of your work, focusing only on those weaknesses mentioned on your list. Discuss where your writing shows marked improvement and where you need to apply yourself further.

**11.3**  Discuss the rules for writers listed in this chapter with respect to clarity, conciseness, and vigor. Which rules seem to relate specifically to each attribute? Which ones help you achieve more than one attribute simultaneously?

**11.4**  Working with a small group of fellow students, reexamine the two versions of the letter written by Peter Fargo, in Figures 10.2 and 10.3, and discuss them in terms of the rules for writers. Not only should you now be able to do a much better job at improving word choice, you should also be able to make some knowledgeable statements about sentence structure.

**11.5**  Bring to class a product warranty statement, a contract, or an insurance policy. A number of states have legislated that these documents must be written in clear, understandable English. Does your state have such a law? How do you feel about your example and those submitted by your classmates? If they are unclear, suggest style changes that might improve them. Would such changes also help to make the documents more concise? If so, how would that be of value?

**11.6**  Lawyers have frequently argued that to make style changes in legal documents alters their meaning and endangers legal precedents. Assuming this is true (and it may well be), are you content to struggle to comprehend warranties and other such documents? Can you suggest a solution to this problem? If so, discuss it with your fellow students.

# ■ Writing Tasks

**11.1**  Improve the following sentences. With each revision, include a note that identifies the kinds of flaws you eliminated.

- It is often required that there be strong evidence before management makes an effort to discipline a careless or inefficient employee.

- What we suggest is that a committee be convened to look into the matter of compensation.

- Forgetting that the report needed Mr. Bennett's signature, it was sent out by Federal Express.

- Our division is the division that won the award for exceeding productivity goals by the very highest percentage.

- I will interview the new candidate, however, his references have not yet been checked.

- All of the steps in this process involve a great deal of concentration and careful attention to detail.

- We are sorry that your new memory phone needed the enclosed part. If you have any trouble correcting the situation, please return it to us.

- We are all in favor of making the change for the reason that the system you described has long been outmoded.

- On the basis of last month's earnings, the planning committee made its recommendation to increase bonuses for all eligible employees by 10 percent.

- The customer advised us that the paint was quite streaked, and we offered to return her money if she would mail the sign back to us in its original carton, but she did not follow our instructions, which resulted in our receiving it in severely damaged condition.

- The new model was distributed by our outlet stores to customers in three states.

**11.2**  Substitute a one-word equivalent for each of the following noun/verb constructions.

make a resolution

give an estimate

come to a decision

make a projection

make a recommendation

give an indication

form an opinion

conduct an analysis

perform an evaluation

make an estimate

**11.3**  Compose three standard sentences, and revise them into periodic sentences.

**11.4**  Write three sentences in which the passive voice is used appropriately.

**11.5**  Describe your three most important accomplishments this week in one sentence that contains parallel structure.

**11.6**  The following examples of business writing are grammatically correct, but they are wordy, weak, and imprecise. Rewrite each excerpt, giving special attention to strengthening verbs and eliminating abstractions and unnecessary words.

The purpose of this memorandum is to make you aware of a situation that, it is hoped, can be remedied in the near future. Certain persons within the organization have indicated an unwillingness to make the effort to cut down on energy consumption in the form of heating costs. This has had the result of raising significantly certain aspects of our operations budget for this year. It is therefore urgently requested that office thermostats be kept at the level of 65°F for the duration of the winter period. Your cooperation in this matter would be greatly appreciated.

There are several factors to be considered when making a decision between two alternatives. After making an analysis of existing conditions, one should ascertain which alternative offers the better hope of improving the situation rapidly, efficiently, and cost-effectively. We therefore propose to make the following recommendations concerning the choice to be made between the two proposals under discussion.

As per your inquiry of May 3 concerning additional information, it is my pleasure to inform you that the report of the external auditing group has been reviewed to determine wherein the fund balances of the institution may have been presented incompletely or inaccurately; furthermore, proposed revisions in format, graphics, and textual content have been developed for possible consideration when preparing future reports of this nature and intent.

**11.7**  Select one of the legal documents discussed in Discussion Problem 11.5, and rewrite it in clear, lucid prose.

**11.8**  Select a letter or memo that you've written previously for this course, and underline all the nouns and verbs. Are they as strong and vivid as they might be? Rewrite the piece to incorporate improved nouns and verbs.

**11.9**  Select two memos that you wrote earlier in this course, and rewrite them to reflect what you have learned about the rules of style. (Submit both versions to your instructor.)

**11.10**  Write a bad-news letter to your assistant telling him or her that the company did not approve the raise that he or she requested. Let your assistant know that you recommended the raise be given but that you were overruled by your superior. On the other hand, you were assured that the raise would probably be forthcoming in six months. Keep in mind all that you learned in Chapter 9 about structuring bad-news letters, but also use sentence structure and sentence patterns to help soften the blow—or at least to present the bad news tactfully.

# WRITE TO WORK: THE JOB CAMPAIGN

## 12

## ■ Brainstorming:
# Where Your Search for a Job Begins

F ew of us can contemplate a leap into the job market with serenity. The prospect of "sink or swim" almost always produces uncomfortable internal upheavals—bubblings and brewings of self-esteem and self-doubt. To regulate our confidence, we need to take stock.

Finding the right job is neither harder nor easier than finding the right buyer in a highly competitive market. The job market is just that—a *market*. The trick is to find a fit between the product (your talents and experience) and the needs of the buyer (a potential employer). A successful sales campaign is not, however, achieved without preliminary research.

The first task of your campaign, therefore, is to study yourself while carefully appraising the job market. We'll call this activity *brainstorming*. It may produce a flash of lightning that reveals your potential employer; more likely, the storm will be one of turbulent activity and soul-searching.

## A Time for Questioning

A good way to start brainstorming is to compile lists of questions. First, try to imagine yourself as a close friend quizzing you on your aspirations and your talents. Then, try to picture yourself before a potential employer. What questions might he or she ask? Write them out, and ponder each one carefully.

For starters, try these questions:

- What do I most like to do?
- What do I do best?
- Do I prefer to lead or to follow?
- Do I work best alone or in a group?
- Do I stand up well under pressure?
- Do I like to work with my hands?
- Am I a good listener? speaker? analyst? technician? teacher?
- Am I artistic?
- Do I have any unique skills?

Chances are that as you form your questions they will become increasingly specific, and so will your answers. If this doesn't happen, go back and pry open the more general questions. Force yourself to be very honest and to acknowledge your weaknesses as well as your strengths. This list is, after all, only for your eyes; no one but you need ever see it.

If you are very lucky, the answers to the first two questions above ("What do I most like to do?" and "What do I do best?") will be the same, and you will have begun to define your career choice. Frequently, however, what one does best and what gives the most satisfaction do not entirely coincide. For example, you might be a particularly talented writer, a student who does well in every subject because your term papers are preeminently readable. Your job search tells you that there are many good opportunities for strong writers. But putting pen to paper has always been something of a trial for you. You dislike the loneliness of the writing process and prefer to communicate by talking to people. This assessment, then, calls for hard thinking. What sort of job might combine writing and interpersonal contact, with an emphasis on the latter? How can you make yourself marketable? If the answer isn't obvious, some serious research is in order.

## Preliminary Research

Your best first step may be a prolonged and careful study of the "Help Wanted" sections of your local and regional newspapers, especially the Sunday editions. After a few weeks (or months), you'll have a good feel for current trends in the job market. Meanwhile, you can be tracking down and using other sources of information: a reference librarian should be able to suggest books and pamphlets listing job descriptions (see the last section of this chapter); a career counselor could surely offer some helpful advice; and employed friends could provide invaluable, practical information. Not only will this research help you narrow your field of interest, but it will also get you started in building a *network*, that vital process of making yourself known to key people who can give you specific information about the field of your choice. And most importantly, your research will put you face to face with potential employers. This happy outcome is likely to occur as you become more and more knowledgeable about your field of interest and the specific qualifications you bring to it.

Of course, by the time you have your objective in sight, you will have still more questions to face:

- Do I have sufficient experience relevant to the jobs I am seeking?
- What salary range am I in?
- Should I consider a lower salary if the position is likely to give me valuable experience?

Although absolute answers to these questions are not to be found, you will have gained a great deal of helpful information and insight through your research. For instance, newspaper ads frequently list salary ranges for positions, and prospective employers often quickly communicate this information. (You should not broach the issue of salary yourself, however, until the interview process is well under way.)

As you continue to probe, your questions will become more personal and practical:

- Do I prefer a large corporation that will offer me multiple opportunities for advancement, or is my personality more suited to the family atmosphere of a small firm?
- How long a commute am I willing to face each day?
- Should I consider relocation and, if so, to where?

You may have to weigh your desire to settle into a permanent career slot against your need to acquire short-term experience. Or you may need to mesh your own career goals with those of your mate.

Your lists will help you to juxtapose your talents with your goals, and to match both with the opportunities you uncover. These lists will also help you to decide what additional steps you need to take. For example, you may need to learn an additional computer language or to purchase a car. Remember, the point of brainstorming is to consider *all* possibilities while narrowing your choices. With each successive list, you will eliminate items that don't fit.

## Second-Stage Brainstorming

With little job experience, there's no use kidding yourself—you *are* facing a greater challenge. Whether you are a recent graduate who has just spent the last four or more years toiling for your degree(s), or a woman or man returning to the job market after a hiatus, every step of job hunting will probably take you a longer time. But hang in there! Adjust your sights so that you are looking at the near rather than the distant future. Forget about finding a job; concentrate on defining your goals and getting interviews. And the fact is—that's what you should be doing now, even if you do have solid gold credentials.

If compiling lists of questions about qualifications and goals deflates your ego, concentrate on compiling lists of things you do well. Next, turn to the things you really like to do. Then start thinking about activities you would like to do but are not currently doing. Next list any occupations where your attitudes and hopes might prove to be an advantage. In assessing yourself, be objective, but don't diminish your abilities, preferences, and ambitions. With effort, you will begin to envision one or more career goals that interest you, and for which you may be genuinely qualified.

Finally, when you feel ready, prepare a list of people (relatives, friends, teachers, friends of friends, even persons whose names you've only heard mentioned)—anyone who might listen while you brainstorm your way to a clearer definition of your career objectives. Ask these people for ideas and suggestions. Urge them to refer you to others who might be able to counsel you. Everyone likes to give advice; everyone knows someone else who likes to give advice. Much of the talk that you hear will melt away, but there will remain a fine residue of ideas to ponder. And invariably your "people" list will grow longer.

At some point—and probably much sooner than you expect—the counseling sessions will begin to sound like conferences, and the people you speak with will start to mention "contacts." If you haven't already passed that hurdle, you're about to discover that the entry ticket to offices and opportunities is a résumé.

## ■ Your Résumé: Creating Your Alter Ego

Your résumé is your personal data sheet; it lists all the information that might be relevant to a potential employer. It's been said with much wisdom that your résumé represents you in offices where you've never been; furthermore, if badly done, it represents you in offices where you never will be.

Anyone who has ever sought advice on how to assemble a résumé has probably learned that the quest can be long, tiring, and filled with well-meaning people who contradict one another, and even themselves. Still, with effort and imagination, you can learn how to create an effective résumé.

In Figures 12.1–12.7 are a number of sample résumés, each geared to its writer's specific circumstances. Each writer tried to create a résumé that would conjure up his or her image for a potential employer, an image that would convey education, experience, and skills in the most positive light. You may or may not feel that each has succeeded. Evaluating another's résumé is almost always easier (and less painful) than evaluating your own; you can notice weaknesses or flaws more easily. If you have access to a whole pile of résumés, you can learn a great deal from the process of studying them and jotting down notes about their best and worst features.

As you review the résumés presented here, try to imagine the people who wrote them, and make some judgments as to how effectively they have presented their qualifications. Ask yourself the following questions:

- Do you have a clear picture of the résumé-writer's career focus? If there is a stated objective, do the majority of the details presented appear relevant?
- Are the job descriptions specific enough? complete enough? too specific or too complete?
- Does the applicant come across as *likable* as well as competent? Does your intuition tell you that this person is overly egotistical and convinced of his or her superiority? Or alternatively, is this person too shy and self-effacing for the stated career goals?

WILLIAM O'KEEFE

45 Beech Street
Garden City, NY 11530
(914) 731-0445

Objective:    A challenging, entry-level position in industrial
              sales.

Work Experience:

1979—Present    ARLENE GEE COSMETICS            DUMARE, TX
                Sales Representative: Arranges sales presentations
                and plans marketing strategy as an independent
                representative. In five years I have tripled sales
                volume.

Summer
1983—1984       EAGLE LIGHT EQUIPMENT           ORLANDO, FL
                Sales Assistant: Supported an 80-member sales force
                in researching prospects and answering customers'
                inquiries; responsible for office management and
                special projects; also helped implement a computer-
                based system to control over $550K inventory.

1980—1982       OPEN SKY RESTAURANT             SARASOTA, FL
                Assistant to the Night Manager: Helped schedule
                the workforce, managed the work flow, and ordered
                supplies; served as host, waiter, and bartender.

Education:

1981—1985       FLORIDA STATE UNIVERSITY    TALLAHASSEE, FL
                Received Bachelor of Arts degree in Business
                Administration.

References:     Available on request.

**Figure 12.1**  Résumé of William O'Keefe.

Amy Jordan
Country Way
Franklin, TN 37064
(615) 511-3112

| | |
|---|---|
| Objective | Sales or Marketing Manager in a small electronics company |

Work
Experience

SALES

| 1982–Present | NASHVILLE ELECTRICAL CALIBRATION |
|---|---|
| | NASHVILLE, TN |

- o Built the sales support function from a department of two to a department of twelve

- o Responsible for inside sales in excess of $250K annually

- o Develops sales/customer-service training for entire sales force

- o Manages a $400K budget

MARKETING

| 1980–1982 | BOLT DYNAMICS, INC. | FRANKFORT, KY |
|---|---|---|
| | Assistant Marketing Manager | |

- o Helped to develop marketing strategy for this major electronics firm

- o Supervised staff of two market researchers and two product analysts

1979–1980    TENNESSEE POWER AND ELECTRIC COMPANY
NASHVILLE, TN
Public Relations Assistant

- o Wrote promotional materials and assembled press kits

- o Edited press releases and other media announcements.

| Education June 1985 | Master's of Business Administration STATE UNIVERSITY, Nashville, TN |
|---|---|
| June 1979 | Bachelor of Arts in Romance Languages WELLESLEY COLLEGE, Wellesley, MA |
| Achievements, Honors | President of Marketing Club, Sept. 1984–Present French Scholarship Award, June 1979 |

**Figure 12.2**  Résumé of Amy Jordan.

MARGARET FLINT

150 Grenville Street
Atlanta, GA 30603
(912) 428-2095

PROFESSIONAL
EXPERIENCE

Marketing/Sales
Support

January 1983–
Present

NEWCOMB & BABCOCK, INC., Atlanta, GA—
Have helped to plan and develop a new concept
in the computer and communications industry.
Interact with marketing and sales to define a
target market, develop programs to meet their
needs, and generate sales leads. Position demands
a well-rounded business background, good
communication skills, and a creative and
analytical mind.

Marketing
Assistant

1981–82

MALDEN COMPANY, INC., Atlanta, GA—
Responsible for design and implementation of
marketing programs for both new and existing
products. Acted as liaison between marketing
and internal support groups as well as external
advertising, design, and data collection agencies.
Duties included coordination of packaging design,
market research projects, taste tests, display
centers, and sales kits.

Assistant Bank
Manager

1980–81

FEDERAL RESERVE BANK OF ATLANTA,
Atlanta, GA—Serviced member banks of the
Southeast through careful monitoring of
operating procedures and annual review of
overall financial condition. Work required
detailed attention to figures, financial analysis,
credit investigation, and report preparation.

Salesperson

1978–79

ELIOT'S CLOTHING STORE, Baton Rouge, LA—
Direct customer contact through personalized
selling in small specialty store. Work included
merchandise display, pricing, and movement.

EDUCATION

Bachelor of Science in Business Administration
Southeastern University, Atlanta, GA—January
1983

Associate of Science Degree in Merchandising
and Retailing
Brook College, Baton Rouge, LA—1979

PERSONAL
ACHIEVEMENTS

Standard Oil Scholarship Award recipient.
Dean's list throughout college years. Graduated
from Southeastern University with highest
honors.

**Figure 12.3** Résumé of Margaret Flint.

RICHARD P. MASON

77 Hughes Avenue
Apartment 3
Los Angeles, CA 90053
(213) 836-5532

OBJECTIVE:             A position as management trainee in a
                       large, cosmopolitan hotel

WORK EXPERIENCE:       Hotel Atlantis
                       Los Angeles, CA

1986–Present           CONCIERGE

                       o   Service special needs and requests of
                           hotel guests, with special attention to
                           foreign visitors
                       o   Compose international correspondence
                           regarding reservations and conference
                           facilities
                       o   Host welcoming receptions and special
                           functions
                       o   Perform analysis of international
                           clientele by country of origin to
                           determine dominant needs and
                           preferences

1984–1985              FRONT DESK RECEPTIONIST

                       o   Greeted guests and assigned available
                           rooms
                       o   Handled switchboard for over 100 rooms
                       o   Computed bills and composed and typed
                           routine correspondence

SPECIAL SKILLS:        o   Fluent French, good Spanish and
                           Italian
                       o   Excellent interpersonal abilities
                       o   Strong written and oral communications
                           skills
                       o   Keen sense of organization and attention
                           to detail

EDUCATION:             Cornell University, Ithaca, NY
                       Bachelor of Arts in Psychology, concentration
                       in Business Management, 1984
                       Université de Paris VII, Paris, France, 1983

                       REFERENCES AVAILABLE UPON REQUEST

**Figure 12.4**   Résumé of Richard Mason.

AMOS VAN DEERE
ONE OAK TERRACE
BELTSVILLE, MARYLAND 20705
(301) 621-0151

| | |
|---|---|
| Education | DEPAUW UNIVERSITY          GREENCASTLE, IN |
| | Bachelor of Arts in Economics |
| | June 1984 |

Employers      GREATER INDIANAPOLIS FOOD BANK
Indianapolis, IN (1984–Present)

UNIVERSITY BOOK STORE
DePauw University (1983–1984)

ARNOLD CONSTRUCTION COMPANY
Gaithersburg, MD (1980–1983, Summers)

Work            PROGRAM LEADER—With three other people,
Experience   conceived and runs a project to bring food and care
to destitute people

o   administers shoestring budget
o   manages all financial statements and records
o   negotiates agreements with local businesses
o   serves as a liaison to local municipalities

STORE MANAGER—student manager for off-campus
bookstore

o   controlled inventory
o   managed security
o   interviewed sales people and managed
personnel issues
o   represented the bookstore on the College Board
of Governors
o   trained new staff

LABORER—responsible for two changes in
procedure that reduced costs by approximately
$30,000

**Figure 12.5**   Résumé of Amos van Deere.

```
                          Betty Harris
                          21 Heath Street
                          Newton, MA 02158
                          (617) 244-9997
```

---

**EMPLOYMENT**

```
WEEI Radio, Boston, MA          Promotion Director      (1982–Present)
White Associates, Cambridge, MA  Media Coordinator       (1980–1982)
New Horizons, Framingham, MA     Sales Coordinator       (1977–1980)
Clark and Murray, Ltd., Boston, MA  Manufacturer's Rep   (1976–1977)
Boston YWCA, Boston, MA          Counseling Supervisor   (Summer 1976)
```

**SKILLS AND ACCOMPLISHMENTS**

**PROMOTION**

- o Create, plan, and implement major promotions

- o Participate in implementing revenue-producing radio programming concepts

- o Represent New Horizons, Inc., at trade shows and consumer exhibitions

**ADVERTISING & MEDIA**

- o Researched and assessed advertising needs; targeted markets; planned media campaigns for major retail department stores and discount houses

- o Managed total advertising project for sporting goods manufacturer, including research, demographics, market segmentation, and planning media campaign

**FISCAL & ADMINISTRATIVE RESPONSIBILITY**

- o Evaluated and reported radio station's weekly sales projection figures

- o Directed major expenditures of federal and state funds for Boston YWCA

- o Supervised and administered activities of staff of ten counselors and office workers

**EDUCATION**

M.A.  University of Massachusetts, School of Education (part-time student), Boston, MA; graduated 1982, Summa Cum Laude

B.A.  University of Massachusetts, Amherst, MA; graduated 1976, Magna Cum Laude

**Figure 12.6**   Résumé of Betty Harris.

JAMES M. LOPEZ
14 Post Road
Dallas, Texas 75221
(713) 771-0993

Skills

- o Team building
- o Communicating
- o Interviewing
- o Negotiating
- o Leadership
- o Bilingual

Education

1977–1981    TEXAS CHRISTIAN UNIVERSITY          Fort Worth, Texas
Bachelor of Arts in Psychology

Work
Experience    DEPARTMENT OF SOCIAL SERVICES          Upland, Texas

1983–
Present       Assistant to the Director

- o Acts as spokesperson for department in Director's absence

- o Facilitates and leads large-group discussions to define department goals

- o Designs and delivers training programs to improve negotiating and interviewing skills

- o Ran highly regarded staff development workshop for secretarial and clerical personnel

- o Researched and wrote a proposal that led to funding for a $250,000 project

Publications

- o "Quality Counts," article published in Training Magazine, August 1980

- o "Keep on!" short story published in Dallas Sunday News Magazine, April 12, 1979

References

- o Available upon request

**Figure 12.7**  Résumé of James Lopez.

- Does the writing style suggest an articulate, energetic, wide-awake employee? Is the style too verbose? too bland and colorless?
- What about the résumé's overall appearance? Does it coincide with the writer's stated goals and objectives? For example, is it well organized and accurate (a potential accountant) or attractive and eye-catching (a graphic artist)? In all cases, is it neat and readable?
- Do the format and presentation work well? Do you immediately like the look of the résumé? Is there too much white space? too little? Is it printed on good-quality paper? Is it pretentious and overdone? Does the résumé have a professional aura, or a "homemade" quality that suggests a rush job?

In creating your own résumé, you will need to assemble information that communicates a strong image of your qualifications and that will attract the attention of potential employers, who may have many other applicants to choose from. As you begin to design your résumé, you may wonder how to deemphasize certain problem areas (for example, lack of experience or uncertainty about your career focus). In résumé writing the best measure of effectiveness is the "rule of all rules" stated earlier: "If it works, it's good." We can also add a corollary: "If it works, *you* work!"

## Choosing the Right Résumé Format

Résumés can vary considerably in form and content: your challenge is to custom design the particular résumé that puts your best foot forward.

You might first want to consider the most traditional kind of résumé, one that cites your education and experience in reverse-chronological order. You should probably choose this kind of résumé if you believe that your education and the jobs you have held make you a strong candidate for a particular kind of position. As a rule of thumb, you can predict that this order will be *most* effective for someone who is highly qualified for a particular position and *least* appropriate for someone just starting out or wanting to make a career change.

In preparing a reverse-chronological résumé, you should include your job titles along with the names and general locations of your past employers. It is essential to provide a careful, concise description of the specific responsibilities and activities you performed in each position listed. A crucial point to remember, however, is that even with this standard form of résumé you can opt for significant variations to suit your needs.

First you can decide whether to list your work experience or education first. The logical choice, of course, is whichever presents your strongest qualifications or does the most to support your case. For instance, if you graduated with honors from a top-flight university but have not had much work experience, you will naturally lead off with your education. On the other hand, if you have had several jobs that make you an oustanding candidate for the kind of position you are applying for, you should give precedence to your work experience.

Next you might give some thought to the placement of dates. Because a reverse-chronological résumé is meant to highlight an ongoing accumulation of experience, dates of employment are usually entered in the left margin, where they have prominence. But if you want to play down the fact that most of your jobs have been part-time or that there has been a gap when you were not employed, you can place dates where they are less conspicuous. (Note that in Figures 12.5 and 12.7 Amos van Deere and James Lopez, who both had rather limited experience, chose to list their employers and dates in a separate section at the end of their résumés.) As for special devices for emphasis, such as bullets, underlining, and uppercase letters, use them to bring out what is most significant, but try to keep your résumé uncluttered and attractive; also, be absolutely certain that any highlighting technique is used consistently throughout all sections.

## Emphasizing Your Capabilities

Perhaps the most important variation of the reverse-chronological résumé is a technique that has been made popular by recent books on job hunting. In this alternative, you *generalize* about your skills and achievements. Rather than describing specific jobs, you highlight your special talents, any of which might be valuable in a number of different types of jobs. In other words, you emphasize what you are capable of doing, whether or not you actually have performed such duties in the context of a particular job. To do this, you concentrate on outlining your abilities and skills (inborn or developed on the job) rather than on presenting a strict chronological narrative of your actual accomplishments at specific jobs. (Figures 12.6 and 12.7 are examples of this variation.) Of course, you must list specific work experience *somewhere* in your résumé, even if your have only worked summers, part-time, or as a volunteer. The point to remember is that you have the option of deemphasizing your chronological job history if it is not significant, recent, or relevant to the positions you are seeking.

Emphasizing capabilities rather than experiences also allows you to highlight transferable skills. You can use your natural talents, or skills gained from a less significant job, as evidence to support your entry into a more desirable position or field. For example, James Lopez (see Figure 12.7) tried to show that the skills he developed in a university social service department qualify him for a position in industrial organizational development. This is an indispensable tactic for job applicants coming straight from an academic environment; it is also helpful to people trying to change fields. For instance, a former teacher might find it difficult to convince a marketing manager that his classroom techniques are applicable to selling software packages. But a well-designed résumé that emphasizes transferable skills (for example, strong interpersonal skills) could provide him with a good entry card.

As you can see from our sample résumés, each job applicant tried to feature his or her strongest points. Betty Harris (see Figure 12.6), a strong candidate with an ample work history, chose to spotlight the three discrete areas of expertise she offers to potential employers. After mentioning her numerous employers, she then classified her accomplishments and skills under three relevant headings. Amy Jordan (see Figure 12.2) felt that her job experience was reasonably sufficient; she too used discrete categories of experience ("sales" and "marketing"), but she described her job and her accomplishments under each category. Richard Mason (Figure 12.4) and James Lopez (Figure 12.7) were not so confident: they listed their skills separately, for emphasis, because their on-the-job experience was rather thin. Lopez was especially conscious of his limited work history, so he listed his general skills first, followed by his actual achievements. Only then did he describe the specifics of his first—and only—job. Even so, he designed a reasonably impressive résumé.

## Résumé Writing Style

Note how action verbs and specific details strengthen these excerpts from the résumés in Figures 12.1–12.7:

- "Supported an 80-member sales force"
- "Helped implement a computer-based system to control over $550K inventory"
- "Have built the sales support function from a department of two to a department of twelve"
- "Supervised staff of two market researchers and two product analysts"
- "Interacts with marketing and sales to define a target market, develop programs to meet their needs, and generate sales leads"
- "Duties included coordination of packaging design, market research projects, taste tests, display centers, and sales kits"
- "Service special needs and requests of hotel guests, with special attention to foreign visitors"
- "Negotiated agreements with local businesses"
- "Created, planned, and implemented major promotions"
- "Researched and wrote a proposal that led to funding for a $250,000 project"

The point is to describe your experience as *briefly* and *specifically* as possible. If you are absolutely sure you know them, you might try to use a few of the current buzz words in your field. If used carefully, this tactic can identify you as a professional and make potential employers feel that you are already a "member of the club."

## What About a Job Objective?

No matter how you design your résumé, you should specify a job objective only if your mind is absolutely set on one specific kind of job. A clearly stated, well-focused job objective shows employers that you have a strong sense of who you are and where you are headed. On the other hand, even when you are confident that you know what you want and you have stated your objective clearly, there are some inherent dangers.

For example, if you listed as your job objective "public relations specialist for a nonprofit organization" and you are applying for a position as a development writer at a university, your potential employer might well conclude that fund-raising isn't really what you have in mind. Or, if you have specified your goal as "production engineer with responsibility for manufacturing supervision" and you apply for a job with a computer software development firm, you could lose your chance for an interview, even if your background includes software capabilities.

Also, it is always possible that you've underestimated your potential and could have aimed higher! But don't resort to the copout of devising a vague or catchall objective, such as "a chance to use my programming skills in a high-tech environment" or "an entry-level position in corporate training, technical documentation, or employee communications," or, worse still, "a position demanding creative ability and leadership skills." This kind of bluff only highlights your uncertainty.

Only you can know if a job objective will serve you well. Be cautious. If you decide to include a job objective, a study of the following examples should help you to design one that is appropriately focused:

- To apply my knowledge and experience of client-side marketing to an account service position in an advertising agency
- Sales or Marketing Manager for an electronics company
- Production engineer with responsibility for technical or manufacturing supervision
- Training specialist in a high-tech corporation, with a view toward an eventual management position in human resources

## How Much Detail?

Deciding on the level of detail to include in a résumé often causes headaches. For those with strong credentials, it's hard to omit accomplishments. For those who lack such credentials, it's hard to find data to support general assertions of competence, and the problem becomes how to fill the page. It is *never* advisable to cover a base by stating that you have no relevant experience. Even if you've never worked full time, you should list significant school projects, summer or part-time positions, unpaid internships, volunteer work—anything that demonstrates practical or financial know-how, written and interpersonal skills, a sense of responsibility, and the general willingness to get a job done. Of course, if you do have considerable work experience, your résumé should include part-time or volunteer work only if such experience bears directly on your current job objective.

Perhaps the best advice is to try to put yourself in the place of a potential employer who has the résumé in hand. How much would you need to know *to want to hear more*? Remember that you can expand on important and particularly relevant qualifications in your cover letter. Also, such details can be supplied later in a face-to-face interview. The strong candidate should rein in the impulse to overstuff the résumé. At all costs, don't resort to a "kitchen-sink" approach, dumping in a hodgepodge of detail that has nothing to do with your career goals.

## How Far Back?

How much of your history should you include in your résumé? Again, not an easy decision to make. If you are young, employers expect your résumé to be brief; there's no need to reach back and detail your high school days. But you might make an exception if you have steadily kept on the same career track (for instance, short order cook, maitre d', and now a degree in hotel management).

If you have a gap of five or more years away from your professional career, the same sort of reasoning should prevail: reach back only for those experiences that show continuity with your present objectives. (Recognize, however, that at some point you will need to explain your reason for having left the job scene.)

## What Is "Personal"?

Use good judgment in supplying personal data. You are not obliged to give such information and should include only the facts that will help you attain your present objective. You certainly need not mention height and weight. If you feel you must allude to health, designate yours as "excellent." Even "good" implies a problem. That you enjoy golf or classical music is at best of minor interest. (If asked for, such information can appropriately be revealed during an interview.) But *do* consider mentioning that you are fluent in French or can pilot a plane; and if your job objective implies travel, you might state that you enjoy traveling and are free to do it.

## Salary Data and References?

Do not include salary data in your résumé. It's far better to let an employer raise this question during an interview.

As for references, state only that they are available on request. You don't want your references worn thin by queries about positions in which you have little interest; also, you may want to match certain references with specific inquiries. And if you should later decide to omit someone from your list, you can do so without supplying an explanation or revising your résumé.

## Printed or Not?

Your résumé's appearance will be important to prospective employers; therefore, it should be important to you.

You may be wondering whether to invest in offset printing or simply to utilize a good photocopier. If you are starting on a job search, you may want to try out a preliminary version of your résumé before investing in printing. Chances are that after a few interviews (or none at all) you will want to make some changes. Also, you may want to develop two versions of your résumé for two different career goals, and this doubling can make printing very expensive. If your objective is a high-level position in a corporate environment, printing does add a touch of class. However, there is some question as to whether printing is ever *essential.* The unequivocally essential qualities of a résumé are clarity, correct grammar and spelling, and neatness.

What about colored paper or highly individual designs? Quality white bond paper is all that is required and is usually the best choice. (Some people, however, feel that gray or cream-colored paper helps to attract attention.) For someone seeking a career in design or advertising, a truly innovative presentation may be appropriate. But if you choose this route, be absolutely certain that your ideas are clever and attractive and are executed with the same professional care required for a more traditional résumé.

## ■ Cover Letters: Probing for Opportunities

You've inventoried your experience, skills, and interests. You've put together a darned good résumé and have had copies made. You've even developed a preliminary list of people to contact. You're ready to begin writing letters that probe for opportunities.

In general, you will be sending out three kinds of inquiries: prospecting letters to companies that might have an opening in your field, applications for positions that you know are open, and responses to *blind ads* (those ads that describe a job but do not identify the company). In almost all cases, you'll need to send both your résumé and a cover letter. The résumé gives a panoramic view of your qualifications. The cover letter, on the other hand, helps the recipient to zero in on the specific details of the résumé that are pertinent to the job in question.

The cover letter should be substantive yet reasonably brief. You don't want to say too much, but "I saw your ad and have enclosed my résumé" is definitely not enough. You can picture the scope and tone of a good cover letter if you imagine yourself walking into the addressee's office with your résumé in hand and having only five minutes to present your case. Obviously, you'd be foolish to believe that in that time you could persuade your listener to hire you. Your real goal would be to capture his or her attention and earn the right to a full-scale interview.

Let's look at some of the dos and don'ts of writing successful cover letters:

- *Do* focus on what you can do for the company and not on what they can do for you.

   For example, don't write "I'm looking for a job that will. . . ." Instead, write "With my experience, I can contribute. . . ."
- *Don't* tell employers what they already know about the jobs they offer.

   For example, don't say "A good sales manager needs to have experience in. . . ." Instead, say "While working at Fabco Sales, I developed skills in. . . ."
- *Don't* ask questions with ridiculously obvious answers.

   For example, don't ask "Are you looking for a hardworking and capable engineer?"
- *Do* read the ad or job description carefully (or question your contacts closely) to discover how your qualifications match the stated or implied needs and to determine your strongest suit.

   A good opening for a letter might be "Since you are seeking someone with selling skills and knowledge of computer programming . . ."
- *Do* guide the employer to the data in your résumé that support your claims, but do so unobtrusively. Let the format of the résumé work for you.

   If you have listed your work experience chronologically, you might write "In 1978 at Adcock, Inc., I. . . ." But if you outlined your skills separately, you might write "My experience in technical documentation at Adcock, Inc., increased my knowledge of. . . ."
- *Don't* apologize for deficiencies. If you must allude to a weakness, cast it in a positive light.

   For example, if the job description asks for five years of experience and you've had only two, you might say "While at Adcock, Inc., I had both direct sales experience and the opportunity to plan and carry out a full-scale marketing campaign for a key product." (The résumé dates will reveal the actual number of years on the job.)

- *Don't* be shy about dropping a name as a referral *if and only if* the person is a bona fide acquaintance of the recipient *and* you have received permission to use his or her name in the specific case.

    For example, a good opening might be "Joan Davidson, Vice President of Marketing at your company, suggested that I might be an excellent candidate for. . . ."

- *Do* try to determine the proper person to receive your letter, and be careful to use his or her correct title.

    Because personnel offices do far more screening out than hiring, you need to try to contact the person who has the power to hire. In a large company, this usually means the manager to whom you will report; in a small company, it means the president or a senior officer. (It's better to reach too high than too low. Your application will be routed to the appropriate level.)

- *Do* try to adjust the tone of your letter so that you sound both professional and human.

    For example, avoid stuffy expressions such as "As per your request for information concerning. . . ." ("Since you wanted to know if . . ." has the same meaning but doesn't make you appear stiff or pompous.)

- *Do* ask for an interview, and make it as easy as possible for the employer to grant your request.

    Take the initiative of saying that you will phone the following week,* or indicate that you would like an interview during a specific interval and will call to verify.

- *Do* be certain that every letter you send is scrupulously neat and correct and, of course, that it is not a photocopy.

    Sections of your letter may be reused again and again, but each letter should be carefully tailored. (*Never* send obvious copies with detectable fill-ins.)

Let's review a pair of cover letters written by two of the preceding résumé writers. Try to evaluate how closely the two writers adhere to the above guidelines.

The cover letter that accompanied Margaret Flint's résumé (Figure 12.3) when she applied for the position of junior account executive at a large advertising agency presented a strong case. Margaret was fortunate in that George Banfield, Vice President of Marketing at the Malden Company (where she had previously worked) had told her about the opening at New Age Advertising and had given her a clear idea of the agency's needs. Also, he had referred her to Linda Lerner, who, as an account su-

---

*If you are answering a newspaper ad, call in approximately three weeks.

pervisor, could either directly influence the hiring decision or put Margaret in contact with the people who could. Margaret's letter to Linda is shown in Figure 12.8.

Amy Jordan, whose résumé appears as Figure 12.2, answered a blind ad (company name not given) in the *Chattanooga Times* "Help Wanted" section. The ad read as follows:

> Small electronics company seeks aggressive marketing manager to expand current markets and identify new opportunities for industrial product line. Must have advanced degree in business or electronics and at least 3–5 yrs. experience. Send résumé and salary requirements to Box 119, *Chattanooga Times*.

Amy has a strong background in marketing and sales and can meet all the requirements but the advanced degree. She is still attending night school to complete her MBA. In applying for this position, she enclosed the cover letter shown in Figure 12.9.

---

**Figure 12.8**
Cover letter to accompany the résumé in Figure 12.3.

150 Grenville Street
Atlanta, GA 30603
March 18, 198-

Ms. Linda Lerner
Account Supervisor
New Age Advertising, Inc.
142 Federal Street
Atlanta, GA 30603

Dear Ms. Lerner:

My good friend and mentor, George Banfield, suggested that I contact you about the possibility of a junior account executive position at New Age.

As you can see from the enclosed résumé, I have been active in marketing and sales support at two major firms since 1981. My job responsibilities have increased regularly: after starting as a marketing and advertising coordinator working in market research, package design, display centers, and sales kits, I have progressed to a planning and development position at Newcomb & Babcock that calls for the promotion of their state-of-the-art network communications system. I help define a target market and interview prospective users to determine their potential hardware and software requirements.

At this point in my career, my objective is to apply my sales and marketing experience to an account service position with an advertising firm. I think that my high-tech background would make me a particularly valuable asset to New Age: my basic programming skills and my growing familiarity with state-of-the-art hardware developments have been central to my success at Newcomb & Babcock. I am especially attracted to the idea of working with New Age because of your growing reputation as specialists in high-tech assignments.

In addition to my strong marketing background, I have proven oral and written communications skills and sharp creative instincts. I enjoy above all the challenge of thinking on my feet in situations of direct personal interaction.

I will call you in a week to inquire whether my background and skills might be put to good use at New Age. In the meantime, I can be reached at 428-2095. I would be happy to have the opportunity to discuss my qualifications further with you in person.

Sincerely yours,

*Margaret Flint*

Margaret Flint

Enclosure
cc: George Banfield

---

Country Way
Franklin, TN 37064
October 20, 198-

**Figure 12.9**
Cover letter in response to a blind ad.

Chattanooga Times
Reply Box 119
Chattanooga, TN 37401

Dear Sir or Madam:

I read your ad in the Chattanooga Times with great interest. I believe that I am a highly qualified candidate for the position you described. Not only can I offer a strong marketing background, but I also have relevant experience in sales.

As you can see from the enclosed résumé, while at Bolt Dynamics, Inc., I actively assisted in developing several important marketing campaigns. As Assistant to the Marketing Manager, I had frequent interactions with the marketing research staff and the sales department, often acting as the liaison between them. In my more recent position at Nashville Electrical Calibration, I had complete responsibility for the sales support function and was able to develop a top-notch group.

With almost five years of marketing and sales experience, I feel that I am now ready to assume full responsibility for a marketing department. If you agree that I have the potential to fill your company's present need, I would be pleased to hear from you so as to arrange to meet with you in person.

Yours truly,

Amy Jordan

Amy Jordan

Enclosure

# ■ Negotiating: Tying the Knot

Phone calls because you said you'd call, phone calls to follow up on an unanswered letter . . . interviews . . . thank-you letters . . . more phone calls . . . and sometimes, more interviews.

The letters you write and, if you're lucky, the letters you receive will proliferate—as will phone calls. Therefore, you'll need to keep careful records. A good system is to collect all of your letters, the related ads or job descriptions, and the replies in a looseleaf notebook. Date everything, and keep a record of phone calls, always jotting down a word or two about what was said.

When a potential employer *asks you* to get in touch, picking up the phone is not very hard. When a friend supplies you with a contact, following through is a little harder. But when your promise to phone is a by-product of your own unsolicited prospecting letter, it is very difficult to plunge ahead. Just remember that most busy people welcome reminders: the prospective employer may have half-resolved to call you but simply never found the time. And if you strike rock instead of oil, at least you'll know the true situation.

## The Interview: Before, During, and After

Before an interview, look back at your records. Review the ad or what your contact told you about the person, position, or company. Reread your application letter to review what you wrote. And do everything in your power to learn about the company. Make use of a business reference library. If possible, read the company's annual report. Check out periodical indexes such as the *Business Periodicals Index,* which lists articles about specific industries and companies, and *Predicasts F & S Index,* which also can supply leads to relevant articles. (Both of these indexes are updated quarterly.) As a source of current data about the annual sales, number of employees, names of officers and directors, etc., *Standard & Poor's Register* is also very useful; it is revised yearly. (Of course, it is an excellent idea to check names and titles with a phone call to the company itself; often a receptionist or secretary will happily supply the very information you need.)

If you have been invited to an interview in a distant city, you can usually expect the potential employer to pay for your transportation and lodging. However, you should raise this question in advance or be prepared to pay your own way. If the employer agrees to pay, you will need to submit receipts and an accurate account of your expenses.

You can uncover a great deal of good (and bad) advice about how to behave during job interviews. Here you'll find only three suggestions. First, *listen carefully*. Second, *respond thoughtfully*. And third, *show enthusiasm*.

One additional point: the subject of salary. If possible, let the employer raise this question. If you have definite expectations, state them; otherwise, get the employer to define the salary range. In any case, be certain salary is discussed before you make any commitment.

After any interview or conference, no matter how brief, immediately write a follow-up thank-you letter. If possible, include a brief allusion to a particularly interesting point that was discussed or a memorable feature of your day. For example, you might reiterate your interest in learning about the company's new product line, or compliment the firm on a new piece of equipment seen on your tour of the plant. Referring directly to something the interviewer said can an be especially effective way of demonstrating that you were attentive. In Figures 12.10 and 12.11 are examples of follow-up thank-you letters from the two job applicants whose résumés appeared in Figures 12.2 and 12.3.

---

150 Grenville Street
Atlanta, GA 30603
April 3, 198-

**Figure 12.10**
A thank-you letter sent as a follow-up to a job interview.

Ms. Linda Lerner
New Age Advertising, Inc.
142 Federal Street
Atlanta, GA 30603

Dear Ms. Lerner:

    Thank you very much for taking the time to discuss the Simplon and Technidata accounts with me this morning. I feel now that I have a solid grasp of the responsibilities of a junior account executive at New Age, and I am sure that my background and skills would be a real asset to the firm.

My involvement with computer technology at Newcomb & Babcock has been an ideal preparation for dealing effectively with your growing number of high-tech clients. Although I realize that you plan to interview a number of applicants in the coming weeks, I look forward to hearing from you again before the end of the month. I am impressed with the level of achievement at New Age, and I would welcome the chance to contribute to your future success.

Sincerely yours,

*Margaret Flint*

Margaret Flint

---

**Figure 12.11**
Another follow-up
thank-you letter.

Country Way
Franklin, TN 37064
November 17, 198-

Mr. Robert Townsend
PWC Electronics
72 Industrial Way
Chattanooga, TN 37401

Dear Mr. Townsend:

I wanted you to know how much I enjoyed our interview on Wednesday. Your enthusiasm about the brilliant future of PWC's new PW-10 range was contagious. I came away convinced that heading up the new sales promotion would be an exciting challenge.

As promised, I enclose the sales training manual that I developed at Knoxville Electrical Calibration. I think you'll agree that this is just the sort of manual that could be used in the PW-10 sales campaign.

Thank you again for such a lively and informative interview. I hope to have the opportunity to talk with you again soon.

Yours truly,

*Amy Jordan*

Amy Jordan

Enclosure

# All's Well That Ends Well

One day you'll leave an interview with that heady sense that all went *very* well. And in a few days, or a few weeks, you'll receive an offer. Usually that's cause for celebration, but occasionally it's not.

If you receive a job offer that does not interest you, your reply should be prompt and polite. You will want to be remembered with favor, and the possibility always exists that the firm is a client or customer of your future employer. If you refuse an offer *before* you have a definite commitment elsewhere, simply say that you are pursuing other options. Should you be refusing *after* you have accepted another job, you'll have to decide whether to identify your new position. The advantage of giving your location is that contacts can reach you in the future. Nevertheless, you may properly feel reluctant to give this information. In any case, an extremely courteous reply to a job offer is essential. One other point—if you have established a good relationship with someone in the company, you may wish to precede your refusal letter with a face-to-face or telephoned explanation. An example of a courteous refusal letter is shown in Figure 12.12.

Return Address
City, State, Zip
Date

**Figure 12.12**
A courteous letter refusing a job offer.

Mr. Benson Dunn
Sales Manager
Cardinal Wholesale Jewelers
1000 Front Street
Philadelphia, PA 19106

Dear Mr. Dunn:

After careful consideration, I have decided to refuse your offer of the position of Assistant Buyer. My present plans are to accept a position with a wholesaler on the West Coast, where my family currently resides.

I appreciated the time you and your people took to carefully explain the requirements of the job. Your establishment certainly would be an attractive place to work, and I wish you the best of luck in finding a suitable person for your current opening.

Sincerely,

[Your Signature]

If you need time to consider the offer or to attempt further negotiations regarding salary or responsibilities, ask for it. Whether you telephone or write, recognize that you will need to be exceedingly tactful so as not to jeopardize the offer. Still, this *is* the right time to negotiate and, although playing games is foolhardy, a clear statement of your requirements will usually receive serious considerations.

If and when you are ready to accept an offer, telephone your primary contact at the company. Then, immediately write a formal letter of acceptance to the person who signed the formal job-offer letter. The combined content of the company's letter and your response sets the terms of your employment. Therefore, be certain that the employer has included and you have reiterated all essential points, such as your job title, salary, starting date, and exact location. Also, be sure to let the employer know where you can be reached until you start work. Figure 12.13 shows a typical acceptance letter.

As a final step, you may wish to telephone or to send brief thank-you letters to other persons in the organization who assisted you during the negotiations.

---

**Figure 12.13**
A letter accepting a job.

Return Address
City, State, Zip
Date

Ms. Carol Kingsley
Manager
Sterling Gems, Inc.
237 San Pedro Road
Los Angeles, CA 90053

Dear Ms. Kingsley:

I am very pleased to accept your offer to be an Assistant Buyer at Sterling Gems, Inc., for a starting salary of $16,000. As I told you, your firm was by far my first choice, because of both your exceptional merchandising standards and your established reputation as an outstanding dealer in fine gems.

According to my understanding, my salary will be reviewed in six months. Also, as you explained, the benefits of the position include two weeks' paid vacation and medical and dental health insurance.

I plan to be in Los Angeles on September 3 and, as we discussed, will report to your office at Sterling Gems at 8:30 a.m. on

September 7. Until September 2, you can reach me at my present phone number (804-249-8886).

Again, let me express my wholehearted enthusiasm regarding this excellent offer to join your firm.

Sincerely,

[Your Signature]

# ■ Reference Guides for the Job Hunter

Library research is an invaluable strategy often overlooked by job hunters. University libraries, those libraries specializing in business resources, and also most public libraries have reference sections containing thick directories of every description, listing corporations, professional associations, executive recruiters, personnel managers, and much more. All of these listings are arranged alphabetically, by geographical location, by field, or by product. In addition, the shelves of many libraries are filled with the most current career information guides, which cover every aspect of the job-hunting process: defining job descriptions, identifying potential employers, designing résumés, handling interviews, and all the rest.

The best procedure is to choose a library of some size and then approach the reference librarian. He or she will know immediately the extent and location of that library's career information holdings and will be able to explain how to use the card catalogue to best advantage.

The following listings are certainly not exhaustive, but they do suggest the research potential of many local libraries. Note that career guides can rapidly become outdated, so supplement those listed here with the most recent publications you can find.

## Directories

First ask the reference librarian which directories might contain the information you are seeking. If a librarian is not available, check the title section of the card catalogue under "Directory of . . . ." Or head for one of the following "super-directories," which can lead you to the appropriate directory for your purpose.

### Super-Directories

*Business Information Sources*
By Lorna M. Daniells
University of California Press, Berkeley, CA

*Directory of Business & Financial Services*
By Norma and Grant Cote
Special Library Association, New York, NY

*Directory of Directories*
Gale Research, Detroit, MI

*Encyclopedia of Associations*
Gale Research, Detroit, MI

*Enclyclopedia of Business Information Sources*
Gale Research, Detroit, MI

*Encyclopedia of Information Systems & Services*
Anthony Kruzas Associates, Ann Arbor, MI

*Guide to American Directories*
B. Klein & Co., Rye, NY

*How to Use the Business Library*
By Herbert Webster Johnson
South-West Publishing Company, Cincinnati, OH

*The Standard Periodical Directory*
Oxbridge Publishing Company, Inc., New York, NY

*Standard Rate & Data Business Publications Directory*
Standard Rate & Data Service, Skokie, IL

**General Directories.** The following is just a sampling of the directories
you might find helpful during your job search.

*Angel's National Directory of Personnel Managers*
Trade Academy Press, New York, NY

*Directory of Executive Recruiters*
Consultants News, Fitzwilliam, NH

*Directory of Executive Recruiters*
Manford Ettinger Publisher, Springfield, MO

*National Directory of Employment Service*
Gale Research Company, Detroit, MI

*Poor's Register of Corporations, Directors & Executives*
Standard & Poor's, Subsidiary of McGraw-Hill, New York, NY

*Standard Directory of Advertisers*
National Register Publishing Company, Skokie, IL

*Thomas' Register of American Manufacturers*
Thomas Publishing Company, New York, NY

## Career Information Guides

The following are examples of career guides that have been popular in recent years. Most of these books are regularly updated, so choose the latest

edition whenever possible. Also, check the shelves to locate similar guides that have been published even more recently.

Boll, Carl R. *Executive Jobs Unlimited.* Macmillan Co., New York, NY.

Bolles, Richard N. *What Color Is Your Parachute? A Practical Manual for Job Hunters and Career Planners.* Ten Speed Press, Berkeley, CA.

Boswick, Burdette E. *Résumé Writing: A Comprehensive Guide.* John Wiley & Sons, New York, NY.

Cannastra, Lyn, Tom Raynor, and Sharon Whitney. *A Guide to Career Planning & Job Hunting.* Edison Electric Institute, Washington, DC.

Crystal, John C., and Richard N. Bolles. *Where Do I Go from Here with My Life? The Crystal Life Planning Manual.* Seabury Press, New York, NY.

Erdlen, John D., ed. *Job Hunting Guide: Official Manual of the Employment Management Association.* Herman Publishing Co., Boston, MA.

Ginzberg, Eli, ed. *Jobs for Americans.* Prentice-Hall, Englewood Cliffs, NJ.

Haldane, Bernard. *Job Power Now: The Young People's Guide to Job Finding.* Grosset & Dunlap, New York, NY.

Holland, John L. *Making Career Choices: A Theory of Careers.* Prentice-Hall, Englewood Cliffs, NJ.

Jackson, Tom. *Guerrilla Tactics in the Job Market.* Bantam Books, New York, NY.

Jackson, Tom, and Davidyne Mayleas. *The Hidden Job Market for the 80's.* Quadrangle/New York Times Book Co., New York, NY.

Lederer, Muriel. *The Guide to Career Education.* Quadrangle/New York Times Book Co., New York, NY.

Lembeck, Ruth. *Job Ideas for Today's Woman, for Profit, for Pleasure, for Personal Growth, for Self-Esteem.* Prentice-Hall, Englewood Cliffs, NJ.

Salmon, Richard D. *The Job Hunter's Guide to Eight Great American Cities.* Brattle Publications, Cambridge, MA.

Thompson, Melvin R. *Why Should I Hire You? How to Get the Job You Really Want.* Harcourt Brace Jovanovich, New York, NY.

U.S. Department of Labor. *Occupational Handbook.* Superintendent of Documents, Washington, DC.

U.S. Department of Labor. *Occupational Outlook for College Graduates.* Superintendent of Documents, Washington, DC.

## ■ Summary

Your first step in a job search might be called *brainstorming*—evaluating yourself as you appraise the job market. Write out a list of questions about yourself and answer them honestly. Then research various sources for current employment trends. In the second stage of brainstorming, make a list of people from whom to seek advice and talk with them, one by one.

Next prepare your résumé. Although a résumé must not diverge from the truth, it need not give equal emphasis to each fact. Tailor your résumé to highlight your strong points. Remember that its purpose is to provide a panoramic view of your qualifications, not exhaustive detail.

A cover letter should accompany your résumé to prospective employers. The cover letter zeros in on specific items on your résumé that are pertinent to the job in question.

Keep careful records of employment correspondence, ads, and phone calls. Review your files before an interview. During the interview listen carefully, respond thoughtfully, and show enthusiasm. Immediately after the interview write a follow-up thank-you letter.

The chapter concludes with a list of reference guides for library research.

## ■ Discussion Problems

**12.1**  Study Betty Harris's résumé (Figure 12.6), and decide whether or not she has chosen the format most suited to her education and work experience. If you disagree with her choice, describe an alternative version of her résumé and defend it.

**12.2**  Which of the sample résumés included in this chapter seem most successful to you? Which are less effective? Discuss your preferences, giving specific reasons for them.

**12.3**  Many job applicants exaggerate the extent of their work experience when they compose their résumés. There are many ways to do this; you can probably suggest several after a few minutes of thought. Do you feel this truth stretching is entirely ethical, a little questionable, or completely out of line? What are the obvious disadvantages of such tactics? Would you ever consider "padding" your résumé? Why or why not?

**12.4**  The application letter in Figure 12.14 is very similar to one that appears in a current business communications textbook. Read it carefully, and try to imagine the reaction of Mr. Seidel. Do you think that this letter uses effective "marketing strategy"? Can you suggest improvements?

**12.5**  Michael Hadley is trying to change careers. He's been a high-school math teacher for three years, and during that time he has been taking computer programming courses two evenings a week. Now he wants to use his recently acquired skills to move into a programming job at a large downtown bank.

Figure 12.14
A letter that "markets" the job applicant.

Dear Mr. Seidel:

Are you looking for a first-rate salesman with a knack for persuasion, four years of successful experience, plenty of technical know-how, and a powerful drive to succeed? Look no further. I'm your man.

I've got the education—a B.S. in Sales & Marketing from Holby College. And I've got the experience—two years selling small appliances at Norton's Department Store and another two years selling computer hardware at Fisher Electronics. I can sell, I enjoy selling, and I want to continue selling. What's more, I proved my sales potential by winning the Norton Achievement Award, which I mentioned on the enclosed data sheet.

I want the challenge of the "big time": marketing hardware on a large scale to your clients. And I'm ready to travel to do it. I like your product—the Simplon SDC-20 processor is the best in its category—and I want to have a hand in making it Number One.

Once you've had a chance to study my résumé, why not call me at 824-8654 between 6 and 8 P.M. and let me know when we can meet to discuss my new career at Simplon?

Sincerely,

*Steven Walpole*

Steven Walpole

---

Should he mention his teaching experience in the cover letter he encloses with his résumé? If so, how much detail should he include and what attitude should he express toward this work experience? What should he emphasize in the early part of his letter; that is, what is the most important information he wants to get across?

**12.6**  Mary MacWilliams is very interested in a position as an assistant to the president at a well-known business college in Massachusetts. The advertisement for the position requests that candidates send their résumés to James Millbank, Executive Assistant to the President. Mary is excited because she knows that Millbank is a close friend of one of her best friends, Pat Loudon, who is now an attorney living in New York City. In fact, Mary, Pat, and James all went to the same college in New York and share many of the same friends and acquaintances, although Mary has never met James.

There is no doubt that James will receive many qualified applications for the position. Mary feels that her qualifications are excellent, and she really wants the job. She wonders how to handle the situation as diplomatically as possible.

Should she contact Pat? And if so, by phone or by letter? What should she ask Pat to do? Should she mention her friendship with Pat or their shared affiliation with the New York college in her cover letter to James? If so, *where* in the letter should she place this information? Give good reasons for each of your recommendations.

**12.7**　Figure 12.15 is a shortened version of a cover letter sent to us by the incredulous personnel manager who had received it. We've changed only the name and address of the firm. We couldn't resist including it here for your comments.

**Figure 12.15**
A remarkable cover letter.

June 19, 198-
Personnel Manager
Anonymous Business Systems
730 Central Street
Chicago, IL 60610

Dear Sir:

Intrigued with the learning factor as impliedly suggested by your firm's advertised position in human resource management, I submit my credentials for consideration of placement.

My employment search has been focused upon the identification of strong growth opportunities. While conveying the possession of technical skills and portraying the worth of work and human relations experiences, I have tried to secure a fit between an organization's need for such proffered expertise and my desire for professional advancement. I do not believe that the two need be mutually exclusive.

With the cause-effect relationship, as spawned by the economic environment, serving to delineate the tremendous number of qualified people, the concept of meeting this fit has become a critical task. With an appreciation for the tenor of this situation, I would like to introduce certain off-résumé attributes. A most inclusive characteristic is a factor of resiliency. Encompassing the mere obvious quality of undiminished attack in the face of adversity, this trait is descriptive on many personal levels. It revolves around the idea of substantial and proper preparation to allay most contingencies; it infers sustained effort in all circumstances.

I take pride in my ability to complete projects which have been cast aside as holding few apparent directions for resolution. With a keen appetite for new challenge, I work well under time constraints.

In regard to salary and job location preference, I admit that I have firm expectations of the former, and a reserved softness with the latter. A salary must represent the value of my educational background and must present a viable saving/earning ratio. Potential worth is so hard to quantify in a reliable fashion; present worth is numerically sound as one establishes assumptions of continuity.

Through personal interview, I would hope to distinguish these and other qualities as being compelling reason for my employment with your firm. I recognize the magnitude of your review process and I offer my gratitude for your time and effort in this matter.

I shall initiate a follow-up inquiry into the status of this review within fifteen days.

Sincerely,


Enc.

---

**12.8** Evaluate Scott Brady's résumé (see Figure 12.16) for content, style, overall appearance, and presentation. Then draft a better version. You may add details if you choose, but don't significantly expand Scott's job experience.

---

Scott Brady, CPA
1112 Michigan Avenue
Santa Monica, CA 90406
(213) 575-7162

**Figure 12.16**
Résumé of Scott Brady.

Education  University of Missouri
          B.A. in Accounting, 1982


ExperienceLettner and Lowe                          Kansas City, MO
          Certified Public Accountants


STAFF ACCOUNTANT: Responsible for certified audits in two medium-sized retail operations. Presently working closely with a nonprofit client in serious financial difficulty, helping to prepare documents for banks, creditors, and lawyers. Assisting in the design of an inventory control system to help client manage remaining resources.


Reliance House                                      New Cordova, CA


VOLUNTEER: Helped this halfway house design a budgeting system to control costs and to account for income and expenses. Prepared appropriate documents for various social service agencies and filed assorted certified documents.


References available on request

**Case for Discussion.**\* John Martin, a graduate student, received an invitation to meet with a potential employer in another city. John found that he had a real interest in the firm and the position. When he returned home, he decided to write his host, Jerome Anderson, a letter that would reinforce the good impression that he believed he had made during the visit. Much to his surprise, John received a very downbeat reply in which Anderson expressed some obvious reservations about John's candidacy. Although the job opportunity was not entirely lost, it certainly was slipping away.

John Martin planned to go to Washington to discuss the situation with Mr. Anderson. He thought it would be useful first to study the letter he had sent to Anderson to see if he could uncover what might have led to Anderson's response.

Read John Martin's letter (Figure 12.17) and the response from Jerome Anderson (Figure 12.18). Then discuss the following questions with your classmates:

- Why do you believe Anderson has developed reservations about John Martin's appropriateness for the position? Support your answer by referring to specific passages in John's letter.
- What issues do you believe that Anderson will raise in his conversation with John during their meeting in Washington, D.C.? If you were John, what kinds of responses might you try to make to those issues? What preparation, if any, would you make for the meeting?

\*Copyright © 1969 by the President and Fellows of Harvard College. This case was prepared as the basis for class discussion rather than to illustrate either effective or ineffective handling of an administrative situation. Reprinted by permission of the Harvard Business School.

---

**Figure 12.17**
John Martin's
thank-you letter.

Dear Mr. Anderson:

I was anxious to let you know how very pleased I was with the day we spent together and with your generous offer. It was a very good trip for me, and I wish to thank you again.

From our discussion I can visualize the position you offered as having tremendous potential for my own personal development. The opportunities with Marshall Industries, and as your assistant, appear to be very significant. I want to assure you that I consider this one of my top two offers, and I will be giving this my utmost consideration during the next month. I have already thought of several questions and I am sure that many more will come up in the next few weeks.

I am most interested in the growth opportunites for Marshall—how strong is the company's and your own commitment to grow, and what do you consider the goals for the next five to ten years? Where will the emphasis on growth be focused—earnings, stock price, sales, etc.? What are the real strengths and weaknesses of the company that could affect the attainment of the goals? What is the distinctive characteristic of Marshall that will help it in the future? How many employees does the whole company have, and what are the backgrounds of the men who head each of the subsidiaries? These are the primary questions that I have now, and I feel that the answers will help me in making my decision.

My wife reminded me to ask you about two other things—holiday and vacation schedules, and medical and insurance coverage. I consider these minor points, and they will in no way affect my decision, but they would be helpful to know.

I will anxiously await your consideration and cooperation.

You told me to inform you of the additional costs I incurred on my trip; these came to $28.00 and included cab fares in New York and New Orleans plus two breakfasts. Thank you for having me down.

Very truly yours,

*John Martin*

John Martin

---

Dear Mr. Martin:

I have your letter of January 30, 1969. Frankly, it raises a substantial question in my mind as to whether the job we have here is the right one for you. I know this is an important matter to each of us and I would suggest that we should discuss it again.

I plan to be in Washington, D.C., February 25 through 27 and could arrange some free time in the late afternoon and evening of the 27th.

Would you like to join me in Washington one of these days?

Yours very truly,

*Jerome L. Anderson*

Jerome L. Anderson

**Figure 12.18**
Jerome Anderson's response.

---

# ■ Writing Tasks

**12.1**   Perform a close appraisal of your own skills, qualifications, and career preferences by preparing the kinds of lists discussed in this chapter.* First, list all of the things you believe you do best; next, all jobs, extracurricular and volunteer

*Unlike other writing tasks, this one will not be evaluated by your instructor.

activities; and then all of the activities you most enjoy. Finally, list your career preferences, trying to specify at least two or more options. Under each option, list the data from your other three lists that support the appropriateness of that career choice. Also include any reasons why the choice could be inappropriate.

**12.2**   After reviewing the following list of facts about a person who is interested in applying for the job described in the ad in Figure 12.19, decide whether a standard reverse-chronological résumé is appropriate. If not, how would you choose to present this candidate's education and experience? Justify your choice in 150–200 words.

- Graduated with honors from Shady Grove High School, South Elm, Illinois, in June 1981, and received a Bachelor of Arts Degree in Economics, with a concentration in economics and statistics, from Michigan State University in June 1985.

- Employed in the summers of 1982 and 1983 at ASA Manufacturing, Inc., as an accounts payable clerk. Reconciled accounts, negotiated with vendors, designed new daily-receipts form. Worked part-time in 1984 for H & R Block, Inc., as a tax preparer. Completed training program, and prepared over 50 tax returns.

- Volunteered in community outreach program to help poor and or illiterate people with state and federal tax returns. Chaired Student Government Subcommittee in junior year at Michigan State; planned and monitored annual budget; made monthly financial presentation. Wrote a seminar thesis on "Audit Practices in the Retail Industry."

- Single, sports enthusiast, active in Young Republicans, excellent health (except for eyeglasses to correct astigmatism).

**Figure 12.19**   Help-wanted ad for Writing Tasks 12.2 and 12.3.

---

### Budgets and Financial Analysis

We are a multiplant manufacturing division of a billion-dollar corporation located in a highly desirable, low-tax area less than one hour from Chicago.

Current and projected geometric business growth patterns create an immediate need for an individual with a business or accounting degree.

Reporting to the Manager of Budgets and Financial Analysis, you will be responsible for developing financial plans as well as operational and financial analysis and audit.

We offer an excellent starting salary and a complete benefits program, but, most importantly, we offer the opportunity to become a contributing member of an aggressive, growth-oriented team.

To pursue this opportunity, please forward your résumé to

M. K. Arnold
Management Recruiter
Bates and Hollings, Inc.
1312 Lake Shore Drive
Billings, IL 61022

---

**12.3**  Prepare a résumé based on information selected from the list of facts in Writing Task 12.2. Keep in mind that the résumé is to be used in applying for the job described in the ad in Figure 12.19.

**12.4**  You are a marketing major who will graduate with a B.S. degree this spring. During your four years of college, you have achieved high grades. You have managed a student-run travel agency this year. During your last two summer vacations, you worked as a salesperson in a clothing store. You were president of your class in your junior year and this year's chairperson of the United Way fund drive.

Write a letter to apply for the position advertised in Figure 12.20. You may make up additional data if you wish.

**Figure 12.20**  Help-wanted ad for Writing Task 12.4.

---

### Marketing Specialists

We are a growing, innovative company that is looking for marketing specialists to work with our product development teams.

The ideal candidate will have marketing or sales experience, good people skills, and a degree in business or economics (marketing majors preferred).

Send résumé to

Mr. Frank Bartlett
Personnel Director
Wesley Products Company
Toledo, OH 43601

---

**12.5**  Using either a newspaper ad or a job description from your school placement office, compose a cover letter to accompany your résumé in applying for the position advertised. If you have not yet prepared a résumé, refer to the self-appraising lists you prepared in Task 12.1.

**12.6**  Using the same ad or job description as in Task 12.5, assume that your friend, Anne Ingersoll, worked for the firm in question the preceding summer. Having seen the ad (or job description) and knowing that the requirements listed were in line with your qualifications, she suggested that you apply. She advised you to write directly to Diana Sanchez, Director of Personnel, to whom she reported during her summer job. Diana and Anne enjoy many common interests and have continued to socialize with each other. Write a cover letter to Diana Sanchez.

**12.7**  Read the advertisement in Figure 12.21 carefully, and then draft a cover letter to accompany your résumé in applying for the position. Assume that your work experience consists of two relevant internships plus part-time or summer work that is only indirectly relevant to the position described.

**Figure 12.21**    Help-wanted ad for Writing Task 12.7.

---

## PROPOSAL SPECIALIST

Jones & Smith, Inc., a leading environmental consulting firm, is currently seeking a career-oriented individual for our Business Development Department. This individual will participate in the preparation of proposals and standard materials for business development use. Additional responsibilities include writing, editing, proofreading, and overseeing the production of proposals.

This position requires 1–2 years of related work experience and a bachelor's degree in marketing, communications, or a related technical area.

Jones & Smith, Inc., offers a salary commensurate with experience and a comprehensive benefits package. To apply for this position, forward your résumé to Doris Spenser. Please include a daytime phone number and your current salary.

JONES & SMITH, INC.
50 Pleasant Street
Tulsa, OK 74101

---

**12.8**    Imagine that you've had an interesting interview for the job you applied for Writing Task 12.6. Write a thank-you letter to Diana Sanchez, your primary contact at the company. Refer to Figures 12.10 and 12.11 for ideas.

**12.9**    After a long and frustrating search, Lennie Wilson was offered two jobs in the same week. He did some hard thinking for a few days and, as a result, decided to accept a position as a market researcher at Denton Technologies, Inc., instead of a position as a case writer at Southwest Business College.

Draft Lennie's firm but courteous refusal letter to Dr. Bob O'Conner at Southwest Business College in Tucson, Arizona (see Figure 12.12) and a formal letter of acceptance to Leslie Penski at Denton Technologies in the same city (see Figure 12.13).

**12.10**    Write a note to Doris Spenser at Jones & Smith, Inc. (see Task 12.7) thanking her for the lively interview you had with her this morning concerning the position of proposal specialist.

**Case and Writing Task.**    Read the Colby and Smith case* which follows. Assume that *you* are the candidate for a position at Colby and Smith. Define the firm's specific business and the position offered according to your own career interests and expectations.

As part of the job campaign described in the case, correspondence is required on the following dates: April 18, May 3, May 22, June 5, and June 7. For this assignment, you are required to complete the correspondence for June 5 and 7 and to write one additional letter (four letters in all). You may, however, want to

---

*This case was prepared by Ruth G. Newman as the basis for class discussion rather than to illustrate either effective or ineffective handling of an administrative situation. Copyright © 1976 by the President and Fellows of Harvard College.

try your hand at the entire series of letters. (If you write the other letters, you will receive more feedback from your instructor and perhaps from your classmates.)

As you compose your letters, feel free to invent circumstances that might have taken place—for instance, conversations that occurred during an interview, lunch, or phone call.

If you have prepared your résumé, enclose a copy with this assignment. It may provide your instructor and fellow students with some insights into the content of your letters.

### Colby and Smith

On the first of March the placement office at your college posts a notice that Colby and Smith, one of the outstanding _____ firms in the country, wants someone with your background and qualifications to join their operations next September. Since you are very much interested in the position, you immediately send a formal letter of application, your résumé, and a request for an interview when the firm's recruiter visits your campus.

The interviews are held on April 15. Mr. Bradford Brown, Director of Personnel for Colby and Smith, conducts the meetings with candidates. You are favorably impressed with Brown and the job opportunity he describes. At the end of the interview he suggests that you think over all that has been discussed and that, if you are still interested in the position, you write to him as soon as possible. The next day, talking with two other candidates, you learn that neither had been asked to write a letter to the company. You therefore feel that you made a favorable impression on Mr. Brown.

On April 18 you write a letter to Mr. Brown, thanking him for the interview and telling him that your interest in the position has increased since your conversation.

On May 1 you receive an answer from the firm—an invitation to meet with Brown and two vice presidents at the New York offices. The firm will take care of your expenses. On May 3 you accept the invitation in a brief letter.

On May 20 you meet with Mr. Brown, Mr. O'Hara, and Ms. Greenberg at the New York offices. Following the interview, they invite you to lunch. You find all three friendly and stimulating. They are thorough and candid in replies to your questions. You leave no doubt in their minds that you are genuinely interested in the position; in fact, it will be your first choice. Before you leave, Brown tells you that a decision will be made by June 15.

On May 22 you write a brief note to Brown, O'Hara, and Greenberg thanking them for their courtesy during your visit.

On June 5 you receive an offer from Carter, Wheeling, and Deeling for a position similar to the one at Colby and Smith. They have requested an answer from you within the week. Since you prefer the position at Colby and Smith, you immediately send Mr. Brown a certified letter explaining that you must make an immediate decision and requesting an early decision from them.

On June 7 you receive a call from Brown. They offer you the position you desire for an excellent salary. You immediately write a formal letter of acceptance and confirm the starting date and arrangements. You also immediately call Carter, Wheeling, and Deeling to let them know you are refusing their offer; then you compose a short, polite letter of refusal to follow up on the phone conversation.

# III

# APPLYING FOR A JOB

As you saw in Chapter 12, campaigning for a job can be both strenuous and challenging. It is also undoubtedly one of the most crucial communications enterprises of anyone's life.

Once you have taken time for a probing self-analysis and performed a careful survey of the job market, you are faced with the task of preparing a persuasive written presentation of your qualifications. In many cases, you need to tailor that presentation to match the requirements of a specific job opportunity. In this dialogue, the seminar students appraise one of their classmate's efforts to do just that. As a response to the Copymax ad (shown in Figure III.1), Gene Terry's letter (see Figure III.2) has real potential; but it also has many flaws that, despite Gene's strong qualifications, could prevent him from making the impression he wants. In a related problem, his résumé (Figure III.3) is also noticeably off base.

As Gene listens to his fellow students' attempts to understand and interpret specific passages of the letter and relate them to his qualifications, he discovers that his letter is frequently unclear and ineffectual. His initial reaction is a bit defensive, but as the group good-humoredly hammers away, his discomfort changes to gratitude and relief. His confidence in his ability to attract Copymax's notice is greatly increased.

As you read this dialogue, try to empathize with Gene's concerns and to share his new insights. *

---

*Gene Terry's résumé and letter and the subsequent discussion have been adapted slightly to reflect the orientation of undergraduate rather than graduate students. The discussion still accurately depicts the primary concerns of the seminar students and their evaluation of Gene's approach.

**Figure III.1**  Ad describing a position with Copymax Corporation.

## SALES

## Sales Representative

A sales rep is required to be a business analyst as well as a consultant, a generalist who functions as a specialist. You will be interacting with a large corporation vice president as well as a secretary of a three-man enterprise. You will be handling a rapidly expanding product line that includes copiers, duplicators, facsimile equipment, and computer technology.

Requirements include adeptness in interpersonal transactions, leadership, and desire to achieve.

Opportunities exist in over 90 branch offices throughout the United States.

Contact:   Mr. Ronald G. Marx
            Director of College Recruitment
            Copymax Corporation
            130 Lake Michigan Drive
            Chicago, IL 60607

**Figure III.2**  Gene Terry's application letter.

February 18, 1985
8 Brown Street
South Benton, OH 44654

Ronald G. Marx
Director of College Recruitment
Copymax Corporation
130 Lake Michigan Drive
Chicago, IL 60607

Dear Mr. Marx:

When I receive my degree in business administration this June, I believe that my demonstrated leadership capabilities and strong desire to achieve will qualify me to be a sales representative for Copymax Corporation.

A high level of motivation and ability is apparent from my academic record. At college I achieved high honors in all four years. In addition, I was named the outstanding business student in my junior year.

I also have work experience that is relevant to a career, beginning in sales, with Copymax. You will note from my enclosed résumé that I served as staff assistant to a marketing manager. In this position I analyzed the market and developed marketing strategies for the group's most important product line. The fact that even after my internship ended I continued to work on related projects as a consultant bears out the value of my efforts to this company.

I would like to discuss my career opportunities at Copymax when you visit our campus.

Sincerely,

*Gene N. Terry*

Gene N. Terry

Enclosed: Résumé

**Figure III.3**  Gene Terry's résumé.

GENE TERRY

8 Brown Street                                   6 feet 2 inches
South Benton, OH 44654                           190 pounds
Phone: 000-000-0000                              excellent health

OREGON STATE UNIVERSITY AT EUGENE

Education       Bachelor of Arts with honors June 1985 from
1982–1985       Oregon State University at Eugene. Majored in
                Business Administration emphasizing Finance.
                Earned 'A' grades in all but one class. I
                completed over three years of coursework in
                less than two years while working part-time.
                Also:

Outstanding Student Award, 1984. School of Business Administration and Economics. "In recognition of outstanding undergraduate performance and leadership contributions to the School and the University."

President of the Finance Association, 1983. While president for one semester, I organized a program that resulted in a tripling of membership.

Student Representative to the Faculty of the Department of Finance, 1984–1985.

| | |
|---|---|
| **Business Experience** | CLEVELAND PNEUMATIC TOOL COMPANY CLEVELAND, OHIO |
| **Internship Sept. 1984– Jan. 1985** | Employed as Staff Assistant to the Marketing Manager for Automotive Tools. Concerned with analysis of the market and development of marketing strategies for the group's most important product line. I designed, conducted and used the results of extensive market research. My recommendations dealt with production, distribution, pricing and communications policies. I have continued to act as a consultant on related projects during this academic year. |
| **Summers 1983, 1984** | Assistant Manager and Automotive Mechanic at Gold Tree Oil Service. Class 'A' license with State of Oregon. Sales ability demonstrated by doubling firm's nongas volume. |
| | Other part-time and summer jobs beginning at the age of fourteen. |
| **Community Service** | Leader of Children's Church for six- and seven-year-olds. Eugene Christian Center, 1982–1984. |
| **Personal Background** | Born in the Midwest but grew up mostly in Oregon. Interests include attending the theatre, swimming, and playing basketball. |
| **References** | Provided on request. |

## ■ Writing Task

You are beginning your job search. Choose a position you would like to apply for, and write a letter of application. With the letter, submit a copy of your résumé. If possible, also include a description of the position (a newspaper ad or an announcement from your college placement office).

## ■ The Dialogue

GENE: [before reading his application letter to the group] The job is for a sales representative with Copymax. I couldn't make much headway with the ad; I'm not sure what it all means—"a business analyst as well as a consultant, a generalist who functions as a specialist"! I guess you don't have to write too well if you want this job!

DAVE: Careful, Gene. Better watch it anyhow. They may need *you* to do a lot of their editing!

•     •     •

GENE: [after reading his letter to the group] I have a bias toward very short letters . . . probably because I type them myself. Still, I'd appreciate comments about the letter in reference to my résumé. And if you want to comment on what other information should be included, that's fine with me.

BILL: As far as adding things goes, I think you should add the name of the marketing manager you worked for at Copymax so that they can talk to him if they want.

GENE: I wasn't *at* Copymax. It was a different company.

BILL: He wasn't your manager at Copymax? You mean it? I really misread that sentence—first sentence, third paragraph.

CHUCK: I had the same impression—that you'd worked at Copymax.

FRED: I think that "beginning in sales" part creates a problem. You can bet this letter will be passed on by this guy Marx to people in sales. And they're going to be awfully concerned about getting someone who is already making noises about going into some other field! You sound like you may want to learn what's going on in sales and then go on to something better.

GENE: The normal career path at Copymax, I think, is from sales to sales management and then to marketing management. It seemed to me that I was implying that logical progression.

FRED: Well, I'm not sure. I'd be careful. It made me feel you were using sales only as an entry point.

GENE: How would you clarify that?

CHUCK: I'd just omit the whole sentence.

FRED: Or at least the phrase "beginning in sales."

RUTH: That sentence bothered me a lot, too. I changed it to "My work experience is relevant to a career at Copymax." But that's obviously very weak. Perhaps Chuck's solution is best. Omit it. I have a motto—did I ever tell you about it? "When in doubt, leave it out!"

TOM: Hey, I can't wait any longer. I just have to ask a question about that ad. "You will be interacting with a large corporation vice president. . . ." Just how large *is* this vice president? [laughter]

Well, getting back to Gene's letter: in the first paragraph, it's a little ambiguous there, too. "When I receive my degree in Business Administration this June, I believe . . . ." That suggested to me that this belief won't occur until after he receives the degree. And then it reads "my demonstrated leadership capabilities," etc., etc. I've come to suspect a string of adjectives; I especially don't like to see them together. Someone (I think Voltaire) said that the adjective is the enemy of the verb. The more adjectives you put in, the weaker the verb you pick, and the weaker your sentence, too. So, I would try to simplify and use one adjective at the most.

GENE: Which ones would you cut?

TOM: How about this: "I believe I've demonstrated leadership capabilities"?

RUTH: That's fine, Tom. You've even given him an active verb. I also found that ambiguity in the first paragraph. In my review of Gene's letter, I wrote "Don't you already have such capabilities?" So my version, I think, would be something like this: "When I receive my degree in business administration this June, I will be looking for a challenging position in marketing." And then take off with your sentence, Tom, the one you just gave us.

FRAN: This is a kind of different focus, but when *I* first read this letter, I skipped that part about "my demonstrated leadership capabilities and strong desire." I was trying to figure out where you were *going* in this letter, so my eyes sort of skipped to "sales representative for Copymax Corporation." Maybe that's what an employer would do. I was looking for your purpose, and I missed the whole line. To me it seems that it would be more effective to *demonstrate* your leadership and your desire for achievement in the letter, as you do with your achievement in school and the internship experience in the third paragraph.

RUTH: That seems like a sound strategy, Fran. Now I think we need to pull some of our comments together. Gene, perhaps you should leave out the cake-icing and say, more informally, "When I graduate next June, I'll want a challenging position in sales, such as the one you are offering."

FRAN: Right. Less description before you make the letter's purpose clear.

DAVE: Another suggestion for that opening paragraph. I think you might seriously think of rewording it to say ". . . my desire to achieve would make me an *effective* Copymax sales representative." Qualifying to be a sales rep isn't nearly as important as saying he can be an effective one. I would also switch "my academic record" and "high level of motivation." In other words, start out that second paragraph with "My academic record demonstrates a high level of motivation and ability," as opposed to "is apparent," which uses "is"—one of those lifeless linking verbs. The three sentences beginning with "You will note from my enclosed résumé. . ." I think, could effectively be reduced to this: "As staff assistant to the marketing manager of Cleveland Pneumatic Tool Company, I analyzed the market and developed selling strategies for the most important product line." I don't like "You will note from my enclosed résumé" and all that jazz. You don't need it. By making a statement—just a straight assertion about your internship—you send the reader of the letter right back to the résumé.

GENE: Let me hear that third paragraph again—your version, Dave.

DAVE: "I also have work experience that is relevant to a career with Copymax. As staff assistant to the marketing manager of Cleveland Pneumatic Tool Company, I analyzed the market and developed selling strategies . . ." I'd replace "marketing strategies" with "*selling*" strategies." It's a fair switch, and it's a selling job you're after. ". . . developed selling strategies for the most important product line." You've reduced it to what is now two sentences; you've eliminated a whole bunch of words, and it's a much more direct statement. In fact, having eliminated those words, you might add a sentence, you know, "The resulting report was presented to and approved by the board of directors."

RUTH: Did you get that last sentence, Gene?

GENE: Yeah. And I really liked it.!

RUTH: Bob, you've been looking like there's something on your mind.

BOB: I've been concerned about that same section—". . . staff assistant to a marketing manager." I'd like to see you refer to Cleveland Pneumatic in that paragraph; that should be there. And then take out "In this position"; that's just not needed. Also, "I analyzed the market"—that could go, too, because if you developed marketing strategies, you've obviously "analyzed the market." It's rather a nothing phrase.

GENE: Well, you've really pared it down, Bob. And it was probably already a little short.

BOB: Yes, the problem of shortness. I was going to get on to that. Look at your résumé. *That's* written like a letter. Maybe it would be a better strategy if you could put more of the information into the letter instead of the résumé. Turn it—tailor it to each job. Make it more tailor-made in every case, pointing out how the position you had relates to their requirements. By keeping it all in the résumé, you have boxed yourself into having a standard thing for all jobs you apply for.

GENE: You'd cut a lot of stuff out of the résumé?

BOB: Right. And I'd keep the résumé factual, much shorter and yet clearer.

RUTH: See, Gene, by saying less in the résumé, but making sure, as Bob says, that the hard facts are there, you leave yourself good material that you can lift from your experience and put into the letter. There you can specifically zero in on those experiences that apply to the Copymax position.

GENE: Okay. That makes sense, but I honestly still don't know what I'd cut from the résumé.

BOB: Well, first I would make it neutral, third person—no I's. Use phrases rather than sentences. And inject fewer comments. For example, save all the stuff about what your recommendations dealt with for the letter. In the résumé, all you need to do is document your internship position in 1984 and 1985 and mention that you developed strategies for the top product line.

RUTH: Good. But then Gene should be sure to repeat the name of the company in the letter, and probably the internship date, too. That way Marx has an easy cross-reference.

GENE: Must the résumé and the letter be mutually exclusive? Can't I have the same commentary in both?

RUTH: No and yes. They are not mutually exclusive: they will overlap. But in the résumé you only highlight your experience, locate and define it. In the letter you comment on it and explain its relevance.

BOB: Sort of the reverse of the way you have it now, Gene. In the letter, you should be picking out those few things that you think will sell you to this company.

FRAN: I agree to all that. And I'd like to emphasize that you'll be helping the résumé just as much as the letter. I found that résumé awfully difficult to read. The truth is that all that copy made me want to skip the whole ordeal. And you certainly don't want an employer to feel that way, Gene.

CHUCK: Right on. And the guy who gets to go through résumés may have a stack of them. You sure want him to read yours; *and* when he does, you want the things you feel are most outstanding about yourself to jump right out at him.

GENE: I surrender. I'm going to revise my tactics. I'd like to show you all my new résumé when I have it done. (See Figures III.4 and III.5 for revisions of Gene's résumé and cover letter to Copymax.)

RUTH: You've all been pretty sharp, and I think you've helped Gene in a very real way. We might keep on with this, but we have a pile of letters to go through, so we'd better move on.

**Figure III.4**  Possible revision of Gene Terry's letter.

February 18, 1985
8 Brown Street
South Benton, OH 44654

Ronald G. Marx
Director of College Recruitment
Copymax Corporation
130 Lake Michigan Drive
Chicago, IL 60607

Dear Mr. Marx:

When I receive my degree in business administration this June, I will be looking for a challenging position in marketing. I believe you will find that I am well qualified to be a sales representative for Copymax Corporation.

My academic record demonstrates a high level of motivation and ability. During my junior year at Oregon State University, I was named the outstanding business student in the school. In all four years, I achieved high honors.

My work experience is also relevant to the position you offer. As staff assistant to a marketing manager at Cleveland Pneumatic Tool in 1984/1985, I analyzed the market and developed selling strategies for the most important product line. My work dealt with distribution, pricing, and communication policies. Since concluding my internship there, I have continued to act as a consultant to that company.

I believe that my education and marketing experience will make me
an effective sales rep for Copymax. I hope we can meet to discuss
career opportunities when you visit this campus.

Sincerely yours,

*Gene N. Terry*

Gene N. Terry

Enclosure: Résumé

**Figure III.5**  Revised résumé of Gene Terry.

GENE TERRY
8 Brown Street
South Benton, OHIO 44654
000-000-0000

| | |
|---|---|
| Education<br>1982–1985 | OREGON STATE UNIVERSITY AT EUGENE<br><br>o   Bachelor of Arts in Business<br>    Administration, June 1985<br>o   Emphasis in Finance<br>o   Completed three-year program in less than<br>    two years<br>o   Outstanding Student Award, School of<br>    Business Administration and Economics,<br>    1984<br>o   President of Finance Association<br>o   Student Representative to Faculty<br>    Department of Finance |
| Business Experience | CLEVELAND PNEUMATIC TOOL COMPANY,<br>CLEVELAND, OHIO |
| Internship<br>Sept. 1984–Jan. 1985 | <u>Staff Assistant to Marketing Manager</u><br><br>o   Analyzed the market and developed<br>    marketing strategies for the company's<br>    most important product line<br>o   Designed and conducted extensive<br>    marketing research<br>o   Currently employed as a consultant |

| | |
|---|---|
| Summers<br>1983, 1984 | GOLDEN TREE OIL SERVICE, PORTLAND,<br>OREGON |
| | <u>Assistant Manager and Automotive Mechanic</u> |
| | o     Doubled firm's sales of nongas products<br>o     Supervised four drivers |
| Community Service<br>1982–1984 | Christian Center, Eugene, Oregon<br><u>Leader of Children's Church</u> |
| References | Available on request |

# ■ Letters and Résumés to Discuss and Revise

In Figures III.6–III.11, you will find two advertisements and two letters of response and their accompanying résumés. Again, the letters and résumés were adapted from writings actually prepared by students in the business seminar. The two letters vary in content and approach; both of the résumés are in reverse-chronological format because the school's placement office mandated this format for their campus recruitment program.

You can learn a lot by studying the ads, comparing the letters with their respective résumés, and determining how each might be strengthened. You might also consider whether a different résumé format might be more effective for either of these students.

We strongly recommend, however, that you not stop there. The time has come to discuss your own résumé and cover letters with your instructor and fellow students. If you have not yet bitten the bullet, refer back to your self-appraisal (See Writing Task 12.1) and prepare your résumé. If you have not yet completed Writing Task 12.5, do so now (prepare a strong cover letter to send with your résumé in applying for a specific job, either one described in an ad or one posted at your school's placement office). If you have already done this writing task, revise your letter now in any way that might strengthen it.

Your instructor will help you to compile and distribute copies of the résumés and letters to study, evaluate, and discuss in an open forum with your classmates.

**Figure III.6** Ad for a planning analyst.

## ENTRY-LEVEL CHALLENGE: PLANNING ANALYST

Our overseas operation is seeking an entry-level planning analyst to support our senior analysts in improving corporate systems. Willingness to travel and learn about Western European market practices a must.

Although this position is at the entry level, it has outstanding growth potential. If you have education, experience, and maturity, we'd like to hear from you!

Send résumé and salary requirements to

Mr. Abraham Schwartz
Personnel Director
Samson Corporation
417 W. 33 Street
New York, NY 10037

**Figure III.7** Letter responding to the ad in Figure III.6.

Brown Hall D9
Rutgers University
New Brunswick, NJ 08903
September 30, 1986

Mr. Abraham Schwartz
Personnel Director
Samson Corporation, Inc.
417 West 33rd Street
New York, NY 10037

Dear Mr. Schwartz:

The combination of my business education, personal background, and previous business experience makes me an ideal candidate for the job of planning analyst in your new European division.

During my four years of university study, I have pursued a business curriculum evenly divided among the major functional specialties. Within each subject, however, I have taken all available courses relating to international business. I would therefore bring to Samson an understanding of business broad enough to cover all the concerns of a planner, yet specific enough to illuminate the special problems of your Europoean operation.

My personal experience and circumstances also fit your needs. I spent four summers in Europe living with an Austrian family. I speak two European languages. I would be happy to renew my acquaintance with Europe whenever you required me to travel from home base in New York.

Business study and familiarity with Europe would not by themselves make me an effective member of your planning staff. But my knowledge has been refined by the experience I gained during my college internship in helping to set up the controller's department of Delta Medical Systems. Hammering out a travel expense reimbursement system acceptable to both the controller and the sales manager taught me a great deal about the art of negotiation.

Mr. Schwartz, I hope that you will call me at (555)555-5555 or write to the above address to arrange an interview at your office in New York. If you need any information about me besides the data on the enclosed resume, you may contact Professor Wasserman here at Rutgers, or Mr. Robert Holmes, Controller of DMS in Maryland. Both of them will confirm my credentials as an excellent prospect for your new division.

Sincerely,

*Darryl Gates*

Darryl Gates

**Figure III.8** Résumé of Darryl Gates.

DARRYL GATES

Home Address:

Brown Hall D9
Rutgers Univresity
New Brunswick, NJ, 08903
Phone: 555-555-5555

14 Atlanta Drive
Huntington, New York 11743
Phone: 666-666-6666

Single          6 feet 1 inch          170 pounds          Excellent Health

Education
1982–1985

RUTGERS UNIVERSITY
NEW BRUNSWICK, NEW JERSEY

Received B.S. degree magna cum laude in
Business Administration in June, 1985. Prizes
in English and German. Research assistant to
professor of business policy. Announcer on
university-based commercial radio station.

Business Experience

DELTA INC.
NEW YORK, NEW YORK

Internship Jan.–June
1985

Compensation Assistant. Responsible for
research and analysis relating to corporate
wage and salary policies for exempt and
nonexempt personnel in the Pharmaceutical,
Central Research, and Quality Control
Divisions.

Part-time Positions
1984–1985

College Relations Coordinator (September
1984–July 1985). Responsible for arranging
campus visits and preparing correspondence.
Assisted College Relations Manager, setting
corporate recruiting schedules and negotiating
outside preparation of recruitment materials.

```
Summers              CONTEMPORARY FURNITURE, INC.
1982, 1983           SPRINGWOOD, NEW YORK

                     Employed as retail salesman of residential
                     furniture in a small manufacturer's company-
                     owned showroom.

Personal Background  Fluent in German and Italian. Interests
                     include water sports, travel, languages, music,
                     and reading.

References            References available upon request.
```

**Figure III.9**   Ad for a product manager's assistant.

## PRODUCT MANAGER'S ASSISTANT

United Products is seeking a successful self-starter to contribute to the development and production of a highly diverse product line.

You must possess excellent communications skills and be able to function effectively in a multi-discipline environment which includes contact with both customers and technical individuals. Business degree required and some related experience a plus.

We offer excellent salary and benefits including profit sharing, stock purchase plan, stock bonus plan, medical and dental insurance.

Please send résumé, including salary history, to

> Ms. Lisa Brown
> Personnel Director
> United Products
> 52 Main Street
> Boston, MA 02101

**Figure III.10** Letter responding to the ad in Figure III.9.

17 Winkler Road
Baltimore, Maryland 21203
September 30, 1986

Ms. Lisa Brown
Personnel Director
United Products
52 Main Street
Boston, MA 02101

Dear Ms. Brown:

Combine my bachelor's degree in marketing at the University of Maryland and my three years' experience in the Navy, and you have the qualities you seek: knowledge, leadership, and maturity.

With the professional marketing and analytic skills I have acquired at Maryland, I am equipped to make an immediate contribution to United Products' marketing efforts. Course work in consumer behavior, advertising, and marketing management has given me an excellent understanding of what it takes to coordinate a successful marketing program. I don't assume to know all there is to know; however, I am eager to learn the complexities of United Products' business. I believe I have what it takes!

My military service provided experience that I could directly apply at United Products. As a Navy lieutenant (junior grade), I supervised a communications center manned by 40 enlisted men. I had to effectively coordinate the efforts of others and maximize utilization of available resources. When our manning level was cut in half, I had to supervise a complete overhaul of operating procedures and the installation of labor-saving equipment. I also had to insure that each individual was thoroughly trained and motivated. This last point taught me the importance of developing interpersonal skills, which I feel is one of my strongest assets. A product manager's assistant must efficiently utilize the people assets available to him.

This experience also helped develop my skills in budgeting and control, and in communication and administration. I helped to write reports and develop oral presentations for the admiral, the chief of staff and other high ranking officers. These skills will be invaluable in assisting the product manager, who must sell himself and his ideas to top management.

Would you write me a brief note to let me know when we could discuss your needs and my qualifications. I would be more than glad to supply you with additional information or letters of reference.

Sincerely yours,

*Donald Wu*

Donald Wu

**Figure III.11**   Résumé of Donald Wu.

DONALD WU

7 Winkler Road
Baltimore, Maryland 21203
Phone: 123-456-789

| | |
|---|---|
| Education<br>1982–1986 | UNIVERSITY OF MARYLAND<br>BALTIMORE, MARYLAND<br><br>Received Bachelor of Science degree with honors in Business Administration in June 1986. Distinguished Senior Award College of Business and Economics. President, Beta Gamma Sigma Honor Society. Phi Kappa Phi Honor Society. Residence Hall Treasurer and Intramural Sports Chairman. |
| Military Experience<br>1978–1981 | UNITED STATES NAVY (Lieutenant, Junior Grade)<br><br>Served as Assistant Staff Communications Officer on the staff of Commander Naval Air Force, United States Atlantic Fleet |

(COMNAVAIRLANT) in Norfolk, Virginia. Responsible for supervising operations of the staff communications center. Custodian of classified communications security material. Held Top Secret clearance.

| | |
|---|---|
| Student Employment 1982–1986 | MARYLAND TRUST COMPANY BALTIMORE, MARYLAND<br><br>Worked summers and part-time during college as a teller to support education. |
| Personal Background | Raised in Baltimore, Maryland. Interests include golf, jogging, sailing, and cabinetmaking. Married. Excellent health. |
| References | Personal references available upon request. |

# THE POLITICS OF REPORT WRITING: ROLES AND RESPONSIBILITIES

## 13

"And so we'll need a full report on . . . ."

These words often intimidate people who routinely write excellent letters and memos without undue concern. The very word "report" seems to carry a weight of significance and to conjure up a heavy document that reflects countless hours of wearisome labor and intensive research.

But the truth is that, although by their very nature most reports tend to be longer than memos, their preparation is often a normal and routine part of a business person's responsibilities. Just like memos, some reports are extremely important and complex, requiring exceptional time and energy; others are routine, straightforward, and less demanding. In fact, in most ways, writing a good report—even a very long one—is a process very similar to writing a good letter or memo. *Purpose, audience, scope, structure, tone,* and *style* remain your primary concerns. In preparing a report, however, a new component often takes on paramount importance: you need to consider *role definition* and its implications. Each person involved in planning, developing, and producing a report must have a clear understanding of his or her roles and responsibilities.

Important reports do tend to be labor-intensive and time-consuming. Often they require careful research, deal with complex issues, serve multiple purposes, or are aimed at a large number of different audiences with varied needs. At times, a number of these factors are at play simultaneously. Therefore, it is highly likely that in developing such a report you will need to work in close cooperation with other people. These may be persons of higher or lower rank than you; they may be from within your organization, from the community at large, or from other business organizations. You may find yourself receiving or giving instructions, responding to requests or making them yourself. Moreover, you may find that you are working with other people sequentially (individually or a few at a time) or participating in highly interactive group sessions. In these encounters, you may exchange information, plan how to proceed, designate roles and responsibilities, or help to review and assess the progress being made.

## ■ Role Definition: Key Questions

From the start of your involvement in the process of putting together a report, it is extremely important that you know what is expected of you. The main reason that report writing creates tension and even rancor in some organizations is that both report writers and their superiors have not initially given role definition the time and attention it deserves. Bent on quickly moving the project forward, they tend to overlook political realities within the organization. Specifically, they fail to provide clear, definite answers to the following sensitive questions:

- Who is empowered to establish the report's main purpose (or purposes) and to determine which issues have highest priority?
- Who will identify the key reader(s) and signify the existence or importance of other audiences?
- Who will define the scope of the report and specify the amount of data required to support key arguments or recommendations?
- Who will be the chief arbiter(s) in matters concerning the actual writing of the document, such as format, structure, tone, and style?
- Who will be responsible for the accuracy of the data?
- Who will review the document to eliminate typos and errors in grammar or spelling?
- Who has the authority and responsibility to review and approve the final draft?

## ■ Collaborative Reports: When You Are the Project Manager

Sorting out the key roles and responsibilities in developing a report is not difficult if you are the project manager and you and your immediate supervisor are the only people who need to collaborate. If you have questions, a short conference usually provides the answers. Generally, your supervisor assigns you the task, specifies the report's purpose, and helps you to identify the key readers. You then collect and sort the data, write a first draft, give it to your supervisor for review, make needed corrections and revisions, and send the document on its way. In some cases you can rely on clerical support for typing and producing copies for circulation; if word-processing technology is at your disposal, however, you may be expected to handle typing and production on your own.

As you can see, none of this is very different from the process of developing an important memo. For this reason, in a busy season, you may be tempted to run with the whole process yourself. Sometimes taking such initiative is a good idea—it can mark you as a person who can independently assume responsibility. But be cautious! If you suspect you need orientation, ask for it. If you preempt authority without justification, or if you misjudge the nature of your responsibilities, the mistake may turn out to be serious.

For instance, suppose you have the task of writing monthly reports on your department's expenditures on personal computing. At first glance, this assignment appears fairly routine: you just need to collect the relevant numbers and present them in understandable form. But, as you have learned, purpose and audience are the critical underpinnings of decisions about what to say, how much to say, and the sequence of points. Do you *really* understand the underlying purpose of this monthly report? Or is it your responsibility to establish the focus each month?

The truth is that over the course of time this routine report has served a number of very different purposes, none of which you would be aware of without conferring with your supervisor.

When personal computers (PCs) were an innovation in the company, your manager wanted the monthly computing expense report to document that the benefits of using PCs in your department exceeded the costs. Six months later, however, she started to have misgivings: she wondered whether the staff was abusing the privilege of purchasing software on an as-needed basis. At that time she asked you to focus your report on software purchases, documenting "who made them and why." More recently, her boss, a senior vice president, has been leaning on her to cut the department's expenditures to the bone. For your next report, your manager has suggested that you compare the department's computing costs during the last two months with those of other departments to prove that your department has been operating well within established parameters.

From this case, you can see how failing to manage roles and responsibilities can impede the process of report writing. Although the task seemed routine, the purpose of each report was not. Had you not conferred with your manager before preparing the first draft of each report, you probably would have been forced to duplicate your effort. Even worse, had you not given her the drafts for review, you might have seriously misjudged her purpose. If any of the reports had proved damaging to her objectives, she probably would not have taken it kindly!

# ■ Collaborative Reports: When You Are Asked to Contribute

A likely alternative to the situation we just examined is that you will be given a portion of the responsibility for developing or improving someone else's report. Often, an entry-level employee is asked to oversee the *research*, *editing*, or overall *production* of a more senior person's report. Let's consider the roles, responsibilities, and probable interactions attached to these three important assignments.

# Research

If you are asked to undertake the research for a report, the proper place to begin is to arrange a meeting with the person (or persons) ultimately responsible for seeing that the report achieves its intended purpose. In most cases this means the person who will actually write the report; occasionally, it means the report writer's manager or supervisor. (In the latter case, you should confer with both individuals if possible.) If the report is important, try to arrange for at least two such meetings: one to establish the scope of your initial research, and a follow-up meeting when you have accumulated a good deal of data and wish to discover whether your findings suggest new areas to be investigated. At the first meeting, it is also extremely important to establish the time frame for delivering the data and to select the preferred format.

# Editing

Editing another person's work—especially someone higher ranking than yourself—requires a clear understanding of the limits of your responsibility.

When *copyediting*, you are expected only to eliminate mistakes in grammar, syntax, and spelling, and, of course, to see that there are no typing errors. If your firm has a standard report format or a style manual, you may also be expected to see that these established conventions are observed throughout the document.

*Editing to improve style and tone* carries a much higher level of responsibility than simple copyediting does. As you might imagine, this job demands as much tact as editing skill. Perhaps nothing is more frustrating than spending many hours improving a document and then having an angry writer entirely reject your approach. To prevent such unfortunate confrontations, you should first clearly establish that you have the authority to make significant alterations in style. If you are assigned to a group project, make sure that the word "edit" is explicitly defined. If you are working with an individual report writer, expectations on both sides should be spelled out. Often this clarification entails a conference.

When your mission includes editing for style and tone, you should initially try to learn as much as possible about the intended audience and the writer's relationship to that audience. Also, when making your changes,* do so tactfully. Don't play the old-fashioned, stern English teacher by writing terse complaints in the margins. "Awk" "??" and "!" have no place in an editor's lexicon of comments. A good tactic is to bracket the words

---

*You may want to review Chapter 10 to refresh your knowledge of what constitutes effective modern business style.

*Shoe* by Jeff MacNelly. Reprinted by permission. Tribune Media Services.

or phrases that need changing and write your revisions immediately above them.

If you feel the document calls for considerable revision, your best strategy may be to edit a portion of the manuscript and then check to see whether the writer feels comfortable with your changes. When the report writer sees how much you have strengthened a part of the report, he or she often accepts further changes with enthusiasm—or at least with equanimity.

The process of polishing the report varies according to the writer's inclinations and the project's time and budgetary constraints. Some report writers prefer not to see the manuscript until the editor is ready for a final review; others, because the editor's changes inspire them to make additional improvements, want frequent reviews. But remember—in business time means money. The time you and the writer devote to this project should be equivalent to its importance and value. For many projects the budgetary constraints are set at the outset; you will have to work within the established limits.

*Analytical editing* is the most challenging editing of all. The analytical editor must analyze the strengths and weaknesses of the document and do everything in his or her power to improve it. An analytical editor is expected either to make or to recommend major structural changes as well as alterations in style and tone. Obviously, such strenuous editing requires a thorough understanding of the report's content and close familiarity with its purpose and intended audience. Good analytical editors, however, know the limits of their authority. Although they identify places where logic calls for additional data or suggest new ways to organize the information on hand, they do not add, delete, or change data without explicit instructions to do so.

The first responsibility in serving as an analytical editor is to understand the project and its objectives. This entails close communication with the writer or writers. At your initial conference, you should also make sure that you know precisely what your contribution is to be. Are you expected to make major revisions yourself? Or are you merely supposed to evaluate the report and suggest how it can be strengthened?

To begin your actual appraisal of the document, read the executive summary carefully and scan all of the report's subheads. Do you have a clear idea of the overriding purpose, the major issues, where the writers stand? Now, go back and read the entire report. In this initial reading, you probably should not attempt to make style changes or to copyedit. Your primary goal is to judge whether or not the report has a clear purpose and to see if the arguments carry the reader forward logically and smoothly. Headings, introductory paaragraphs, topic sentences, and paragraph structure should be used to mark off unified sections and to link related ideas coherently. In reviewing for structure, you may want to test the logic and coherence by creating a traditional outline of the main and supporting points.* At any juncture in outlining, if you are unable to distinguish major points from supporting information or are surprised at the order established for either major or minor points, you have discovered a place where revision is called for. Often, such a problem can be so serious that major structural changes are required within the section or within the whole report.

If you decide major revisions are needed, you will probably want to hold a conference with the writer(s) before setting to work. If, because of time constraints (or for other good reasons), a conference does not seem feasible, be sure to retain a copy of the original document in case a writer or a superior disallows your changes. Use good judgment about whether to attach the original version to your revised copy. (If you have been requested to do so, obviously you have no choice.) Some writers can see an editor's improvements more readily by comparing both versions; other writers cannot view a revision objectively with their own creation in hand. The first time you play an analytical role for a specific writer, you may guess wrong about this matter; but you will then have all the clues you'll need to handle a follow-up assignment more tactfully!

## Using an Editor's Services

At times in your career, your responsibilities may call for you to use the services of an editor or an editing department to further your own

---

*At this time you may want to review Chapter 5, "Patterns of Relationship," and Chapter 6, "Prewriting: the Process of Creating Structure." (See especially "The Tried-and-True Outline," pp. 105–07.)

projects. Be certain that you are clear about which of the three levels of editing you require. In addition, if you want more than copyediting, be sure that you provide the editor with a clear understanding of your expectations and sufficient time to do the work well. Moreover, whenever you are working with an analytical editor, you must provide that person with a thorough orientation, and expect to have additional interactions along the way.

## Supervising Production

The third possible way that you can contribute to the creation of a report is to manage all the aspects of production. When the author or authors of a major report are at a high level in the organization, a more junior associate is frequently assigned the task of overseeing all steps in report production. Perhaps the best way to understand the requirements of this role is to consider an example. Let's look further at the situation described above, in which computing costs have become an issue in your firm.

Let's say that your manager's problem of rationalizing computing costs is endemic to the whole company. At high corporate levels, management has called for a complete audit of the firm's current use of information technology, with projections for the future. Your manager's boss, a senior vice president, is given the task of overseeing the audit and writing the report. He expects your manager to assist him in data gathering and analysis. She expects you to assist her by overseeing all production aspects of the report.

Although the responsibilities of a production supervisor change with each set of circumstances, many duties are standard. The following list suggests the tasks you might attend to in the next six weeks while overseeing production of the major report described above:

- You will contact the secretary of every department's senior operations manager to set up a schedule of meetings between these managers, your supervisor, and her boss.
- You will write a memo to the managers, explaining that the objective of these meetings is to collect data on past, present, and future use of computing in the company. The memo will list the issues that they will need to consider and it will go out under the name of your manager's boss. Both your manager and her boss will interact with you to help you develop the memo's content, and both will approve your final version.
- You will meet with your company's information officer, who has access to a great deal of information in several on-line data bases. Working closely with him, you will gather and organize all available data on

ways in which your company's three major competitors have been using information technology during the past year. (As part of this process, you will see that the information officer is provided with the list of key issues and that he understands all their implications.)

- You will set up an editing schedule for the report, communicate the importance of this project to the editor assigned to it, and explain the kind of editing that will be needed. At each repetition during the review process, you will tactfully work at getting the editor's full cooperation in meeting a rather tight schedule.
- You will phone six major hardware and software vendors to request that they send you copies of all of their marketing brochures and other materials describing their latest technology, as well as any nonproprietary information about products currently being developed.
- You will inform members of the graphics department that their assistance will be needed. You will schedule time to work with them in developing the five major charts that will be an important part of the report.
- You will assist your manager in developing roughs of these exhibits.
- You will work closely with the supervisor of word processing to coordinate the typing with the editing schedule and to ensure that none of the numerous versions of early drafts are backlogged by other projects in this hectic and busy area.
- You will work with the people in the mailroom to see that the report is delivered to all of the recipients on time and with the correct attachments. (There will be two different versions of the letter of transmittal; also, one special version of the report with a highly technical appendix is to go to the information officer and two high-level technicians in the information systems department.)

As you can see from the above interactions, even if you don't write one word of a report, your contribution can still be of major importance.

## ■ Collaborative Reports: Vertical and Horizontal Interactions

In the preceding situation, although many people will have contributed to the project, the full and final responsibility for the report will clearly rest with the senior vice president who is your manager's boss. Also, the majority of interactions are *vertical*—either upward or downward between people at varied levels within the organization. Each of these people (with the possible exception of the production supervisor) has clear-cut tasks to perform, and these tasks are integral to their job descriptions and to their usual everyday responsibilities (See Figure 13.1.)

**Report Writing**
**A Typical Vertical Process*.**

- Senior executive specifies the objectives of a report to manager
- Manager assigns project to writer and briefs him or her
- Writer performs research

  Interviews with persons inside or outside the organization

  Library research

  Electronic data base research

- Writer submits preliminary outline or draft to manager for review and suggestions

  Document is returned to writer with comments

  Manager and writer meet to discuss document

- Writer composes the second draft
- Editor receives document with specific instructions about the kind of editing required (if editor is assigned)
- Writer and editor discuss objectives, audience, etc. (if analytical editor is assigned)
- Writer incorporates the editor's suggestions and sends the third draft to manager for review
- Manager returns the document with suggestions
- Writer creates the final draft
- Writer and copyeditor proof the final draft (if copyeditor is assigned)
- Manager approves the final document and sends it to senior executive

*Any of the major steps could require one or more repetitions.

**Figure 13.1**

Frequently, however, when a complex report is to be written, the personal interactions are *horizontal*, and people's roles are not explicitly clear at the outset. It is not at all uncommon for people who are more or less peers to collaborate, each holding responsibility for a particular segment of a document. (See Figure 13.2.)

Sometimes this division of responsibility occurs simply because the project is too massive for one person to carry out alone. Or it may be that

**Report Writing**
**A Typical Horizontal Process***

- Senior executive specifies objectives of a report to group of managers
- Managers meet to define roles and responsibilities

  Manager A, Manager B, Manager C will collect the data and be responsible for data accuracy

  Manager B will write the first draft

  Manager A and Manager C will review the draft

  Manager B will be responsible for production of report (Manager B will assign the role of production supervisor to a junior-level employee in his department)

- Manager B receives the data and requests a meeting with Manager A and Manager C to get consensus on interpretation of the data
- Manager B writes the first draft (Production supervisor handles all the interim interactions with the editor and the word processing center)
- Managers A and C review the draft and send along comments and suggestions
- Manager B writes the final draft, and sends the finished report to the senior executive and copies to Managers A and C

*Any of the major steps could require one or more repetitions.

Figure 13.2

each person has a different but equally vital kind of expertise or perspective. Less desirably (but often unavoidably), group reports may evolve because a number of influential people with different vested interests all insist on being heard.

Report writing that depends on horizontal interactions must be carefully and tactfully managed. If the contributors do not share a clear understanding of the report's purpose, the result can be a chaotic collection of unrelated data. Or, if there is no agreement about what constitutes a good format or appropriate style, then each contributor is likely to write as he or she pleases, creating either a horrendous task for an editor or a monstrosity for the reader.

When collaboration is horizontal, the first step is to define everyone's responsibilities at the outset. Each member of the team must know exactly what he or she is to contribute and, most particularly, what parts of the process he or she has authority over. Role definition may be accomplished by a formal directive from above in which the senior person requesting the report explicitly assigns all responsibilities. Frequently, however, the team members are expected to define and allocate roles by consensus during a preliminary meeting.* In this case, they must also quickly resolve the following issues:

- How will the division and allocation of the key responsibilities (see the list of key questions at the beginning of this chapter) be accomplished?
- If some of these responsibilities are to be shared by all parties, how can the review process be carried out efficiently (to avoid a log jam when other commitments demand a team member's attention, or when individuals are locked into opposing viewpoints)?
- Will each member of the team contribute data to the one person selected as the report writer, or will each member write a segment according to agreed-on standards?

In most cases, a person at a higher level will select someone to chair a preliminary planning meeting. At that time the group will resolve these three critical process issues together.

Designing a smoothly operating process can be a thorny task, but it is the essential first step if a collaborative report is to succeed in its objectives and be delivered on schedule. It usually takes a bit of political savvy and dedication to create an effective working team. But people who frequently interact on the job do know a great deal about one another's character traits, abilities, and expertise. They generally recognize who is a capable leader, who never fails to meet a deadline, who can be counted on to ferret out hidden data, etc. Moreover, if everyone's primary objective is to see the project succeed, roles and responsibilities can be allocated quickly and effectively.

## ■ Summary

Like writing a good letter or memo, writing a good report requires careful attention to purpose, audience, scope, structure, tone, and style. But here a new element—role definition—often assumes great importance. Each person involved in the process must have a clear understanding of his or her roles and responsibilities.

*See Chapter 19, "Meetings and More Meetings."

When you are project manager for a report, confer with your supervisor if you have any doubt concerning purpose and audience.

As an entry-level employee you may be assigned to oversee only the research, editing, or production of a senior person's report. In handling research or editing, meet first with the report writer (or with his or her manager or supervisor) to establish schedules, scope, and type of editing required. The third instance, managing the production of a report, demands strict control of timetables and coordination among several individuals and departments.

In a vertical project, roles are usually defined from top to bottom in terms of everyday job responsibilities. In horizontal interactions, on the other hand, several employees at the same level participate in preparing the report. In such cases it is vital to establish specific roles and responsibilities from the outset.

# ■ Discussion Problems

**13.1**   What are some of the hidden "political" issues involved in producing a report? In terms of the political problems you might encounter, explain why the following four reports might be difficult to write or produce. What process do you think would be best for gathering data, writing, editing, and producing each of them?

- A performance review of the five secretaries in your department
- An analysis of the market potential for three proposed new products
- An overview of the pros and cons of establishing a Paris office of your advertising firm
- A projection of enrollment goals for your college during the next ten years

**13.2**   Imagine that your boss has asked you to manage the production of a report on space requirements for the three departments inhabiting the ground floor of your building. Of course, you will require input from members of each of these departments. In addition, you will have to ascertain whether or not recommendations are in order and, if so, who will participate in that decision-making process.

Suggest the steps you might take in organizing the production of this report. Who are the key contributors likely to be? Who will write the first draft? Who will review the draft for revision? Who will be responsible for the accuracy of the information included? Who will determine the style, tone, and purpose of the final document?

**13.3**   As an executive assistant to the president of a large electronics company, it is your responsibility to prepare the first draft of the president's semiannual report to the board of trustees. To do this, you study each of the vice presidents' reports to the president to determine which details will be included in this report.

In the course of analyzing the vice presidents' reports, you discover that there is a conflict between the budget figures projected by two of the vice presidents. How will you resolve the discrepancy in order to produce a consistent first draft?

**13.4**  As an assistant product manager at the S/J Company, your assignment is to compare sales figures for ten of the company's most representative products over the past three years. After gathering the appropriate data, it seems obvious to you that two of these products should be discontinued because of a significant and steady decline in their sales.

You want your report to be impressive, since you are hoping for a promotion during the coming year. Your inclination is to conclude your report with a recommendation to discontinue the products in question. But you realize that the company president has personally pushed those two products for years. You're really not sure whether your recommendation would be well received. It's possible that a straightforward, factual account of sales records—without any attempt on your part to interpret these figures—would be less risky. What will you do?

**13.5**  Your boss is a senior partner in a management consulting firm, and he has just produced a draft of an article for a prominent business journal. He has asked you to read over his work to check for any obvious spelling or grammar errors and to give him your general impression of the piece. You know that he has worked hard on this draft and is well pleased with it.

You proceed to correct the punctuation and the few typos. Your overall impression of the article is positive, but you find that your boss has an odd habit of describing complex business and competitive situations with barnyard images and metaphors. He frequently talks about going "whole hog" and "not chickening out." This language seems completely out of place to you, but you are reluctant to suggest changing it because he has not really given you the authority to change his style. On the other hand, you feel strongly that these constant allusions to livestock are inappropriate and should be edited out. What will you do?

**13.6**  As head of the publications department at your university, you are responsible for writing the copy for the institution's annual report. To do this, you study the reports of each of the vice presidents and then condense the material into a cohesive text that covers all aspects of the university's progress during the past year.

Your problem is that two of the vice presidents have failed to submit their reports on time, even though you had carefully informed them of your tight schedule almost two months ago. You have already notified their secretaries that the delay is causing a serious problem: at this rate the annual report will never be ready for review at the fall meeting of the trustees. If it isn't ready on time, your job is on the line. What steps will you take next to ensure that you meet your deadline?

**13.7**  You work as an editor in your state's auditor's office. You've been editing audit reports for over five years, and your editorial expertise is highly valued in the department.

Recently, a promising young auditor was hired. This is the third time you have been assigned to edit his work, and once again you find that you have to rewrite the report almost completely if it is to be at all comprehensible. You've already had two conferences with the auditor, during which you explained in detail what sorts of changes were necessary. On both occasions you were sure he understood your points, but now the third report is as bad as the first. You have serious doubts that this man can cope with the job. How will you handle this sensitive situation?

**13.8** You're approaching the end of your first year on the sales force of the AAA Company, and the deadline for the fourth quarterly report on your activities is drawing near. This report is actually a joint effort: each of the department's five salespeople contributes his or her own section.

The difficulty is that in the past three quarterly reports your section was noticeably shorter than the other four. It's clear to you that the main reason for this is that your colleagues tend to pad their reports with accounts of activities that they have not actually carried out. There are obviously several courses of action available to you as you get ready to prepare your contribution to this quarterly report. What are they? Which will you elect to follow? Why?

## ■ Writing Tasks

**13.1** Choose one of the following topics, and organize a team of four or five classmates who will each research and write one section of the report. This means that you will have to meet beforehand to determine how the tasks will be shared, from the planning stage to the finished product. Be sure to write down the game plan so that each participant is sure to accomplish his or her contribution in time to meet the final deadline.

- Major business mergers of the past decade
- Technological advances during the 1920s (or any other decade)
- The growth of the textile industry in the South
- The effect of automatic teller machines on the banking industry .
- A comparison of compact microwave ovens currently on the market
- The projected effect of declining population growth on college enrollments in the next decade
- The correlation between college internships and full-time employment after graduation
- A comparison of automobile export figures for the United States, Japan, Germany, France, and Italy

**13.2** Prepare an account of the process your team used to complete your report for Writing Task 13.1. Again, you and your classmates may assign the necessary tasks as you see fit.

**13.3** Ask a friend for a copy of an uncorrected term paper in a subject you know something about. Photocopy the paper so that you have two clean copies. Copyedit the first copy (that is, correct only spelling, punctuation, grammar, and typing errors). Then play the role of an analytical editor with the second copy. (Study the paper carefully and make any changes you think will improve the style, tone, clarity, and overall effectiveness of the work.) If possible, sit down with your friend afterwards and explain the reasons for your changes. If there are any disagreements about which version is better, try to determine the best possible solution.

**13.4** Interview someone whose job requires frequent report writing. Focus on the political complexities he or she has encountered. You might ask about the kinds of situations described in this chapter, but encourage the interviewee to discuss any problems that come to mind. Write a brief report covering both the difficulties and the solutions described by your subject. Include your opinions about how he or she resolved these problems. If you can, suggest better procedures.

# REPORT WRITING I
# PROCESS & PRODUCT
# THE PROPOSAL

## 14

**W**hile reading the preceding chapter, you may have paused to ask yourself whether it really is worth spending so much time and effort to generate reports. In fact, in our computerized world, where we frequently hear talk of the coming "paperless" workplace, the odds strongly favor that such a thought did cross your mind. Has the long report—or, for that matter, even the short one—become a dinosaur?

All evidence indicates that the answer is no.

Today's information technology gives us access to more information than ever before, and businesses are responding by finding new ways to apply it. But the raw facts and figures must be packaged so that businesses can analyze, use, and communicate them. A clear, well-written proposal or report continues to be the best vehicle for making information of some length or complexity accessible to a number of people. It also provides them with a permanent document to study and to keep on record. Many reports have very long life spans, lying dormant in a file for months or even years and then springing back to life as a touchstone for measuring progress or evaluating new directions.

Not only the need for efficient access to today's abundant information but also the typical interactions that take place in a business environment mandate that we write proposals and reports. These documents are the primary means by which plans are communicated, ideas shared, problems analyzed, and many transactions initiated and completed.

The process by which information is gathered and analyzed and turned into a report is not a phenomenon special to the business environment. Rather, it reflects the normal way that all thoughtful human beings approach problems and initiate actions. When we suspect that something could or should be improved, we try to define the problem, analyze it, and discover a solution. At various milestones, we may need to seek additional information to help us proceed. On many occasions, although we have uncovered a good solution, we may need to work hard to persuade others to accept it. In difficult cases, we may even have to step back and produce evidence that there really is a problem.

Let's say you are troubled because you are spending too much money each month heating your condominium. After speaking to several heating companies, you conclude that the problem is an old and inefficient heating system in the building. To get the condo association to act, you first need to establish that others in the building think heating costs are a serious problem. This probably will mean calling your neighbors or polling them in some other way. You may also need to produce some proof in the form of heating cost comparisons to show them that a better, more modern system will greatly cut costs. You may have to be extremely persuasive to convince a few of your neighbors that a new system should be purchased.

In this case, if you decided to write a report to circulate to your neighbors, the impulse to do so would have been commonsensical, stemming from your desire to do what is needed to persuade your neighbors to take the appropriate action. And, not surprisingly, the actual process by which you *wrote* the report also rests on a common-sense approach—even though the steps entailed are rigorous. Listed below, these steps should look familiar to you because they are also integral to creating memos and letters:

1. Understand your purpose well.
2. Understand your role and responsibilities in developing the document.
3. Correctly identify the needs and expectations of all important audiences.
4. Clearly define the problem or issue to be examined (you may need to research for additional data).
5. Collect all data that are important and relevant to the problem or issue defined.
6. Analyze and interpret the data honestly, logically, and completely.
7. Present your findings clearly and persuasively.
8. Ensure that the final document is carefully and correctly produced and is delivered to its intended readers on time.

A proposal or report is the visible result of decisions a writer has made about both process and product. The *process* will include all of the above steps. The *product* will demonstrate that those steps have been taken. In this chapter and the next, you will be given basic information about how to gather information, order it, and present it in an effective format. Perhaps most importantly, through a detailed case study, you will share the experience of a group of people engaged in the process of developing a series of reports. You will be able to observe their interactions closely and to identify with the report writer's perspective. As the case evolves, you can pause at intervals to consider the options the writer faces and to evaluate his choices. You will also have the opportunity to study the products of his effort: the proposal and reports that are the backbone of a program to accomplish an important business objective.

# ■ The Sta-Brite Corporation: Case History(1)

Sta-Brite is a large corporation with offices and plants throughout the Northwest. Its revenues exceed a billion dollars annually, and its employees number over 15,000. The company's product lines include a multitude of household cleaning products and related items. Recognized for over 20 years as preeminent in its markets, the company has always taken special pride in maintaining excellent relationships with its employees, customers, and the communities in which it operates. In Boston, where it maintains its corporate headquarters, it has been especially active in community affairs.

The company operates a large, subsidized cafeteria in the building that houses its headquarters. In establishing the cafeteria six years ago, Sta-Brite's management vigorously published their belief that the cafeteria should not support a "class system." Rather, employees from all levels should use the facility "to mingle and share news, ideas, and concerns about the company and to exchange views about their professional and personal lives."

Approximately a year ago, at about ten minutes before noon, a man and a woman were seated at a table normally meant for five people. Since the cafeteria was still relatively empty, they had plenty of space to spread out the sheaf of papers they were studying while munching their sandwiches. The woman was Kim Matsushita, Sta-Brite's Director of Personnel. The man was her new assistant, Scott Stanton, whose title was Personnel Specialist. The papers they were studying were computer printouts of employee absenteeism and tardiness during the last two quarters.

"Scott, look here," Kim said as she pointed to the figures for the past month. "They are still trending upward at a steady pace. And I am beginning to think I know why. It struck me this weekend while I was reading the lead story in Sunday's *Parade Magazine*. Do you by chance remember what that story was about?"

"I'm not sure I do, Kim."

"Well, I've just left a copy of the article on your desk, Scott. But, listen to this." She reached under the computer printout material for a page of handwritten notes. "I've brought along the notes I took. Let me share a few of the statistics with you." Kim proceeded to read, "Fifty-two percent of women in the United States now work outside the home. Forty-nine percent are mothers with preschool-age children, and 60 percent of all American families have two working parents." She paused meaningfully. "Now, can you guess where I'm coming from? Scott, the average age of our employees at Sta-Brite is 30.6 years, and in the past five years the number of women employees here has increased over 25 percent."

"So you are thinking that our absenteeism rate has to do with the needs of working parents. Right?"

"Absolutely!"

Scott was about to respond, but at that moment he noticed two people with food trays approaching their table. The room was rapidly filling, so Kim and Scott quickly scooped up their papers and invited the newcomers to join them. The new arrivals were Pauline Atticus, Sta-Brite's Health and Safety Officer, and Jed MacDonald, Vice President of Human Resources, to whom Kim reported. They had been planning to lunch to-

*On the Fastrack* by Bill Holbrook. Reprinted with special permission of King Features Syndicate, Inc.

gether to discuss a proposed addendum the company's maternity-leave policy, which would grant paternity leave to new fathers under certain well-defined circumstances. As they sat down, Kim introduced Scott to Jed.

"Jed, I don't believe you've met my new assistant, Scott Stanton. He's only been with us three weeks. Scott, Jed and I are due to meet on Friday to go over these absenteeism statistics, and I think he's someone who'll also be intrigued by my recent line of thought." After the formalities of the introduction were taken care of, Kim continued, "Jed, Pauline, I'm beginning to believe that what we are facing is much more than an increased absenteeism rate. I think we are beginning to contend with what may be the major human resource problem for the eighties—the need that working parents have for child care. I can't document it, but I think that our high absenteeism is just the tip of the iceberg. I suspect that it has companywide ramifications, affecting recruitment, morale, and even productivity."

Pauline leaned forward in her chair. "Funny you should bring this up just today, Kim. I spent my morning talking to the heads of several nursery schools in the suburbs to see if I can't find space for two company kids. You see, Barbara Howe, who just joined us to manage the Information Systems area, and Ted Bond, our Comptroller, whose wife was hospitalizd last week, both had to bring their toddlers in to work yesterday. Several of their co-workers lodged complaints with me—not just because of the distraction but because the kids seemed to need more supervision than their parents could provide. Even on an emergency basis, I think we'd better not have small children wandering around our offices!"

Jed slowly stirred his strawberry yogurt. Kim, who knew him well, recognized that his prolonged silence signaled interest. She turned to him. "Jed, don't you think the time has come for us to consider offering our employees some real assistance in handling their child-care problems?"

"Well, I'll tell you, Kim," he responded. "You may be right. We may be facing a really significant issue here . . . or, on the other hand, this could all be just a tempest in a teapot. I'll tell you what. Let's postpone our Friday meeting until the following week and then meet for two hours. I'd like you to get me a memo or a short report by next Wednesday. Try to get a handle on the problem, and define it for me. Let's get an estimate of its scope and see if we can expect it to increase or go away in the next few months. I'll review your findings, and then I'll get back to you with my opinion when we have our meeting."

Immediately after lunch, Kim gave Scott his first really important assignment: "I'd like you to do a bit of research and take a stab at drafting a short report defining the child care problem as it exists today."

## Process: Defining the Problem

Scott's first step was to read the article that Kim had left on his desk. Entitled "Who's Raising Our Children?" it presented a short but sharp overview of the problem nationally. It provided Scott with some solid statistics and the names of experts and organizations that were looking at the day-care problem.

Scott immediately broke open two stacks of index cards. On one of the 3 × 5 cards, he recorded the bibliographical information concerning the *Parade Magazine* article; and on the 5 × 7 cards, he recorded statistical information, the names of people and organizations, and a number of well-worded quotes (See Figure 14.1).

Based on what he had read, Scott then wrote the following problem statement:

> "Finding quality day care in America is becoming an increasingly urgent problem today."

But as he considered his words, he realized that he was in no way ready to develop a draft for Kim. Although he had some good data on the scarcity of day care and the difficulties this problem caused for parents, he had virtually no information on the direct effects on Sta-Brite or on other businesses.

Since this was to be only a brief preliminary report, Scott recognized that he was not expected to conduct hours of intensive research. Moreover, his tight deadline would in no way allow such an in-depth effort. On the other hand, he also knew that he would have to dig a bit further.

His first step was to head for the periodical library at a nearby university. To locate periodicals that contained significant articles about his topic, he checked the following indexes:*

*Readers' Guide to Periodical Literature*
*New York Times Index*
*Wall Street Journal Index*

*See the annotated listing of directories and other reference sources at the end of this chapter.

①                                 Article

_Wall Street Journal,_ August 15, 1985

"Companies Becoming Part of the Family," Wendy Paulson, pp. 1, 5.

---

Quote:                                     Statistics

"The number of companies with child care programs has grown from 400 nationally in 1983 to roughly 2000 today."

Source: Dr. Janet Elson, a professor at the University of Wisconsin.

Ref: Bibliography Card # 1.

**Figure 14.1**

Examples of a 3 × 5 card used for recording bibliographical information about an article and a 5 × 7 card used for recording a significant quotation from the article. Using 5 × 7 cards for data provides you with more space. Some researchers prefer to use 3 × 5 cards for both bibliographic items and data, employing two colors of cards to distinguish between the two types of entries. You should include a cross-reference on all data cards. One way of doing this is shown in Figure 14.1. Another method that you can use if you have only a few data cards for each bibliographical one is to mark the data cards 1-A, 1-B, 1-C, etc.

As he surveyed the indexes, he carefully recorded on index cards the bibliographical information (periodical name, issue, article, author, and page). Although he knew he only had time to read about a dozen articles, he catalogued all those with relevant titles that had been published in the last two years. From the more than 20 titles, he selected 10 to read.

Scott was especially fortunate in that Sta-Brite employed an information specialist at their corporate headquarters. He had been warned that using this service carelessly could incur significant expense for his department, so he carefully prepared a list of key words that he hoped would develop some on-line leads. As a result of his library research, key words came readily to his mind. He listed "working parents" and "corporate day care" as the phrases that might locate useful articles.

Marla Johnson, the information specialist, let him know that she would be accessing *Newsearch*, an on-line data base that provides indexes to leading newspapers throughout the country, and *ABI* (Abstracted Business Information), which provides 10–15 sentence abstracts of articles from business periodicals. In 24 hours, Marla had the printouts of two interesting abstracts on Scott's desk.

By the time Scott had finished his reading and had sorted through the data, he could confidently make and document a considerable number of statements about the child-care problem, among them the following:

- Day care was receiving national attention in the media and was even becoming a recurrent topic in the business press.
- Day-care expenses averaged at least 10 percent of the gross income for working families, making it the fourth largest expenditure (after housing, food, and taxes).
- The problem was growing (by 1990, an estimated 10.5 million American children would have mothers in the workforce).
- Both state and federal governments were beginning to take notice of the day-care problem, and in Massachusetts, a major study commissioned by the governor was due to be published in the next month.
- At least 2000 U.S. companies were exploring options for day-care programs (including Taylor Corporation, Sta-Brite's major competitor).
- Among the options currently being examined by major companies were on-site facilities, referral services, paid day care as an employee benefit, paternity leave for new fathers, extended maternity leave, liberal flextime programs, and work-at-home options.
- At a large high-tech company in the Boston area, where paid day care was recently offered as a benefit, management stated that the policy had been an enormous plus in their effort to recruit high-level professionals.

Looking at the data he had collected, Scott still felt uncertain about just how to proceed. Although he knew he was to draft a short report to "define the child-care problem," in reality the scope of that problem was so broad that he could not possibly cover it in only a few pages. Moreover, the subject intrigued him so much that he began to feel he would really like the opportunity to develop a full-scale report. He decided to meet with Kim to share his feelings.

**Commentary.** If you consider the process of defining the child-care problem at Sta-Brite as it has evolved so far, you will note that the following has occurred:

- An employee (Kim) observed a problem and had some preliminary ideas about its cause.
- A higher-level employee (Jed) became interested in both the problem and its solution and commissioned some of the manager's or supervisor's time for continuing the investigation.
- A junior-level employee (Scott) was asked to collect additional data and to draft a report.

Although frequently the interest in exploring a particular problem arises at the highest level, this sequence of events is a common one in many businesses. In the early years of your business career, you almost certainly will find yourself handling an assignment similar to Scott's.

Up to this point, Scott has done a good job. To review his approach, let's enumerate the steps he has taken:

- He quickly familiarized himself with the basic components of the problem as his supervisor saw it (by reading the article Kim gave him).
- He attempted to develop a written problem statement.
- He conducted a data search within the limits appropriate to his assignment.
    He conducted library research and recorded data concerning additional sources of information (individuals and organizations), statistics, quotations, and bibliography.
    He used an internal resource to assist him in data collection, keeping in mind budgetary constraints.

Now, however, he is at somewhat of an impasse and rightly has turned to his supervisor for advice.

## Process: Establishing Purpose

Kim is pleased with the work that Scott has done so far, and she agrees that they need to do a bit more thinking about what they are up to. But Jed definitely asked for a "report," and they must respond to his request. Kim suggested that they consider the following alternatives:

- They could ask Jed for authority to conduct full-scale research and for time to write an in-depth report.
- They could submit a short preliminary report on Friday defining the problem and recommending that a full-scale study be undertaken.

"And you know, Scott," she said, "I'm inclined to believe that we should follow the latter course. You see, although your data definitely and clearly show that day care is a national problem, there is only a hint so far of what this problem really means to Sta-Brite. You've touched on the fact that it has implications for recruitment and that one of our competitors is definitely considering day care as a strategic advantage, but isn't there a lot more we should be thinking about? You've done some excellent groundwork, but now we need to sit down together and brainstorm about how we can explicitly spell out the dimensions of the problem here at Sta-Brite."

"Kim, shouldn't we also be thinking about what programs to initiate to contend with the day-care situation?"

"Well, I think trying to do that now would put you right back into the same box you were just in. How could we document recommendations for specific actions in this short, preliminary report? And more importantly, we don't yet have enough data to support our recommendations. What you and I need to do is to establish what kinds of information we need to uncover if Jed okays a major study and how we intend to go about getting that data."

"Are you suggesting that this preliminary report be a sort of proposal to sell Jed on the need to budget a major study?"

Kim smiled. "Right. That's exactly what I mean. And I think we definitely can and should persuade him to let us go ahead. Let's document this proposal carefully. You'll want to spell out a detailed work plan, and I'll help you to refine your estimate of costs and time. You should also give some thought to whom we will need to assist us in getting this research accomplished. Oh, yes. One other thing, Scott. Jed is expecting a fairly short document, so don't overload it with extraneous material. And let's use a memo format. I think we'll do better to not be overly formal at this point."

**Commentary.** With Kim's help, Scott has been forced to rethink the purpose of the document he is to draft. Rather than focusing on what he will put into it, he is now concentrating on what he hopes it will accomplish. On the other hand, Kim has also urged him not to lose sight of two other important matters. Since he will actually be writing a proposal, he needs to plan for the elements that Jed will expect to see in such a document (work plan, costs, time, and staffing). And, since he will be writing to accomplish a specific task, he must, of course, focus the proposal accordingly.

# Product: Draft of the Proposal

Scott was grateful to have been handed such an interesting project so early in his career at Sta-Brite. His first step was to secure the budgeting data and to run the numbers on internal staffing costs. Next, he called two major consulting firms to obtain estimates of the costs of designing and implementing a program to survey employee needs and attitudes in regard to child care.

As he prepared to draft his proposal, he reviewed all of the data he had assembled. He felt more than a little pleased with his effort and surprised at how much of an expert he was becoming on the issue of corporate-sponsored child care. He hoped he could give Kim a proposal that would clearly demonstrate the extent of his newfound knowledge.

But despite his wish to impress his boss, Scott put the brakes on his initial impulse to find a way to display all the data he had collected. Remembering Kim's admonition to focus, he forced himself to try to write a clear position statement. His first thought was to make use of the problem statement he had written a few days ago:

> "Finding quality day care in America is becoming an increasingly urgent problem today."

However, just as he had once dismissed this statement because it did not focus on Sta-Brite's needs, he now put it aside because it did not reflect the real purpose of his proposal. "And what is the real purpose?" he asked himself. The answer was obvious: "To persuade Jed to allocate funds for the needed research."

A few more attempts produced the following revised position statement:

> "Sta-Brite needs to perform careful research to learn about employees' current needs for child-care assistance."

With this statement in front of him, he next put himself through a strenuous analyst's couch* brainstorming session. In about an hour, he had developed a list of the questions he believed needed to be answered before Sta-Brite could begin to implement an effective program. He had also found a logical structure to contain those questions. Although none of his questions directly alluded to his previous research, he was confident that they would reflect his growing expertise.

After taking a minute to quickly review what he had learned in business school about the typical components of a proposal, he began to write. It took him the remainder of the afternoon and most of the following day to develop the draft that follows.

---

*Refer to Chapter 6 for a review of the analyst's couch method of organizing material.

# Product: Draft of the Proposal

MEMORANDUM

TO: Jed MacDonald
FROM: Kim Matsushita, Scott Stanton
RE: Proposed Study of Child-Care Needs at Sta-Brite
DATE: November 12, 1986
CC: Pauline Atticus

---

## BACKGROUND AND POSITION

During the last two years (and especially in the past six months), Sta-Brite has experienced markedly increased absenteeism and turnover, particularly among two groups: women at all levels and upper-level salaried employees. Recent reports in the media as well as occurrences within Sta-Brite suggest that a primary cause of these problems is the lack of child-care assistance for working parents.

At this date, we have gathered a good deal of information that enforces this belief. Some of this information is statistical, from media and government sources, and some of it is anecdotal, from the records of Sta-Brite's Personnel Department and its Safety Officer. We have also discovered that 2000 companies throughout the United States, including the Taylor Corporation, are now exploring and adopting a number of workable options for providing child care for their employees. We feel certain that Sta-Brite should also be considering these options; nonetheless, we are not yet prepared to recommend a specific plan or program. The primary need at this time is for information about our own employees' behaviors and preferences.

We therefore recommend that time and resources be allocated to a major three-pronged study with the following objectives:

o   A statistical profile of working parents at Sta-Brite
o   A statistical survey of absenteeism, tardiness, and turnover during the last three years
o   A broad-based survey and in-depth study of employee attitudes, needs, and preferences concerning child-care benefits for working parents

DISCUSSION OF OBJECTIVES

A full-scale program for child care might entail funding and operating a day-care center, and offering specific benefits such as referral services, more generous maternity leave and paternity leave, an increased tolerance for job sharing, and wider applications of flexible work hours. We have selected the above three objectives because, without the critical information they represent, there is no way to predict which of these options, if any, are needed and appropriate at Sta-Brite.

The research we have proposed should provide us with answers to the following questions:

Statistical Profile of Working Parents

o   How many parents of school-age or preschool children are currently employed at Sta-Brite?

o   What are the ages of the children? (Is there a greater need for preschool or for after-school day care? Are both needed?)

o   How many Sta-Brite parents are employed in clerical and other nonexempt positions? How many are among the ranks of exempt employees, officers, and managers?

<u>Statistical Survey of Absenteeism, Tardiness, Turnover</u>

o   How prevalent are these problems among Sta-Brite's employees?

o   Are they more prevalent among certain groups (such as females, males, managers and officers, specific age groups, married or single, exempt or nonexempt employees)?

o   To what precise degree have these problems been increasing over the past three years? over the past six months?

<u>Broad-Based Survey And In-Depth Study Of Attitudes</u>

o   Are a large number of employees in favor of the company increasing its commitment to assisting working parents?

o   What forms of assistance are favored? By whom? Why?

o   Would employees who do not have child-care needs favor or resent the allocation of resources to day care? Would some options be more acceptable than others?

<u>SCOPE OF THE STUDY</u>

To respond to these questions, we propose a three months' intensive study to include the following two elements:

o   A statistical analysis of Sta-Brite's employment history since January 1985 to determine patterns of absenteeism, tardiness, and attrition.

o   A survey of all employees to determine the number who desire assistance with child care, the specific characteristics of these employees (age, age of children, years with Sta-Brite, rank, and responsibilities), and their perceived needs; in addition, the survey should provide data on the attitudes of employees who do not seek such assistance.

## WORK PLAN AND STAFFING

To accomplish the proposed objectives, we suggest that the Personnel Department be allocated sufficient time to collect and study existing data on employment history (approximately 21 days of person-time). Kim Matsushita will supervise the data collection; she will be assisted by Scott Stanton.

We also recommend that the services of an outside expert be secured to prepare a suitable survey and to analyze the results; in addition, we suggest that the consultant provide a proposal for exploring in-depth attitudes; for example, by employee interviews and focus groups. To select an appropriate consultant, Sta-Brite should seek proposals from three leading data research firms. Kim Matsushita, Scott Stanton, and Pauline Atticus will review the proposals and recommend the leading contender. The choice of consultant will be approved by Jed MacDonald.

## BUDGET REQUIREMENTS

We currently estimate that internal staffing cost will equal $35,000 and that the cost of securing an outside consultant will range from $35,000 to $50,000. In short, the total costs should approximate a maximum of $85,000 (see attached cost breakdown).

SUMMARY STATEMENT

    Sta-Brite has always taken pride in maintaining excellent employee relations. We believe that the proposed study not only will produce real gains in our understanding of current staffing problems but also will assure Sta-Brite's employees that we remain committed to providing them with an excellent work environment and a more-than-competitive benefit program.

Attachment: Cost Breakdown

**Commentary.** As the Sta-Brite case has evolved, we have seen a growing interest in investigating the problems faced by working parents. If Scott's proposal succeeds, that interest will become a full-fledged commitment to allocate major resources to studying child-care needs. And there is a high likelihood that it will succeed because, even at first glance, we can see that Scott has argued well. But to comment more knowledgeably on his proposal, we should first consider business proposals in general. It is important to understand why they are written, how some differ from others, and what options proposal writers have in selecting and organizing their materials.

# ■ Rationale for Writing Proposals

A business proposal is just what it sounds like—an offer or expression of intention. Generally, it identifies a need and then lays out a specific plan responding to that need. The proposal supplies evidence that the need actually exists and explains the resulting plan in detail.

In daily life, we usually make proposals (whether to friends, family, or future mates) in person or by phone. But, for two important reasons, business proposals are almost always made in writing. First, recipients need to have a document to study and to discuss. Second, on acceptance, the terms of the proposal stand as a firm commitment concerning the services or product to be delivered. In the case of a proposal to a customer or client, this commitment may have the strong legal implications of a contract. When (as in the case of Scott's proposal) the document describes work to be done within one's own company, the commitment has career implications. If the writer (in this case, both Kim and Scott) does not deliver what has been promised, on time and within budget, the firm may very well view the failure as a breach of responsibility.

In companies that frequently sell their products or services to other large corporations or to the federal government and its agencies, preparing formal proposals is a frequent and important task. Moreover, since writing such proposals is usually exacting and difficult, it is often a collaborative effort. At such times, entry-level employees are frequently drawn into the loop to assist the project team.

Formal proposals, especially those intended for the federal government, generally require very specific and extensive information, which sometimes must be made to fit, willy-nilly, into an ironclad format prescribed by the prospective buyer. Historically, therefore, preparing these documents has been less than a pleasure, even for highly skilled writers.

On the other hand, many companies today are taking a strong interest in good writing and are insisting that it be one of the standards met by proposals. And good writing is also getting better press in government circles. Since the Carter administration, the federal government has proclaimed its interest in clear writing. Although writing proposals for the federal government and the military still presents many formidable obstacles, good writers are finding opportunities to put their skills to work. Moreover, evidence indicates that it is becoming worth their while to do so.

Proposals are often submitted to the government and to research foundations to generate funding for particular projects. Also, universities and medical centers regularly prepare proposals for grants to support education and research. Depending on where they are headed, these proposals may or may not need to conform to a specific format. In any case, it is important that they present a case that will persuade the audience for whom they are intended.

## ■ Standard Formats: Their Uses and Abuses

Many companies have their own proposal and report formats. Such formats can be both a convenience and an aid. They can help to ensure that a given document is coherent and complete. Furthermore, if used properly, a standard format can help you in the following specific ways:

- To structure information into manageable units
- To group concepts in ways that logically enforce the chief arguments of the presentation
- To provide readers with a road map to orient themselves or locate specific pieces of information
- To act as a checklist for determining whether you have included every component that can be employed to achieve your purpose.

Don't forget, however, that the writer "owns" the format, and not the other way around. Use good judgment about when and how to use a standard format. To get internal projects approved or to request funds or resources, you will normally tailor the company's standard format to your needs. You may want to combine sections or even eliminate a subsection that has no applicability. However, give careful consideration to the conventions your company prefers. For instance, if the standard format asks you to state the purpose of the proposal at the outset, you should do so under almost all circumstances.

If at all possible, you should check to see whether your intended audience has any special formatting requirements; you may discover strong preferences within certain departments. In addition, for some external proposals, guidelines on formatting should be obtained as part of your preliminary research. As we have already stated, the federal government has strict requirements for many kinds of proposals; and in many cases, universities, individual government agencies, companies, and high-ranking decision makers also have strong preferences.

# ■ Components of Formal Proposals

Before looking back at Scott's draft, let's review all of the components of a formal proposal. Although it is important to understand each component and to know how it might be used, keep in mind that only a long, very formal document is likely to include every element listed here. Also, the order given here is usually the most serviceable, but it is not set in cement. If a stronger, more logical case can be built by changing the order, you should certainly do so.

## Transmittal Letter or Memo*

The transmittal letter explains who is submitting the proposal and why. If the proposal is a response to a request from the recipient (business jargon calls this a "Request for Proposal," or "RFP"), then this fact is clearly stated early in the letter, usually in the opening sentence.

If the formal proposal is an internal document, the transmittal "letter" will normally be a memo. The tone of this memo should reflect the relationship of the proposal writer to the recipient. Even a formal transmittal letter for an external audience should be straightforward, courteous, and human, with absolutely no hint of pomposity.

The following elements should usually be included in the transmittal letter or memo:

- A *brief* description of the problem or issues discussed
- Special features or benefits offered in the proposal
- Special circumstances, concerns, or problems about the process of developing the proposal or about its contents
- Reference to the work that needs to be done, either in the short term or in the long term.
- Acknowledgment of assistance by others (this can be especially important if the contributors are in the recipient's company or department)
- A list of all persons who will receive the proposal (usually arranged alphabetically; on occasion, according to rank)

When the document is meant for a large group of people, the transmittal letter or memo is often omitted and, instead, a preface is included. Although the format differs, the preface includes the very same elements that you would place in the letter or memo. (The distribution list is placed at its conclusion.)

## Cover and/or Title Page

For formal proposals, a neat, attractive cover with an inside title page** suggests attention to quality; a cover also protects the contents from being soiled or damaged. Although never ostentatious, a good cover should be

*See Chapter 15, p. 403, for an example of a transmittal memo.
**See Chapter 15, p. 404, for an example of a cover page.

composed of high-quality material and attractive typography. A typed cover page may be used alone for less formal proposals. Normally, the title page or typed cover page contains the following elements:

- Title of the document (brief, descriptive, and as specific as possible)
- The name of the company or individual for whom the proposal has been prepared
- The authors' names; their titles are optional
- The date of submission
- The company logo (optional)

## Submittal Letter

Even though a formal proposal is accompanied by a transmittal letter, a submittal letter may also be bound into it. The submittal letter is always impersonal and precise, clearly stating who has authorized the submission of the proposal and what is expected to be accomplished. A transmittal letter may contain *any* relevant information, but the submittal letter should not discuss anything that is not in the proposal itself. If a submittal letter is used, it is separated from the body of the proposal by a single sheet of white paper.

## Executive Summary

A proposal represents an offer to do work and a report evidences work that is under way or completed; if either one is long or complex, a concise executive summary* is in order. In both cases, a preliminary summary helps readers decide whether to read the document in its entirety, to focus on one or more sections, or to pass it along to a more appropriate audience. Also, even those readers who intend to study the entire document closely are grateful for the orientation provided by a clear executive summary. Obviously, an executive summary is not meant exclusively for executives but for all prospective readers with heavy workloads and tight schedules.

For proposals, the executive summary includes some or all of the following components:

Purpose: The service or product being offered

Background: The pertinent history or facts surrounding the specific need or problem the proposal addresses

Objectives: Criteria to be met or goals to be attained

Conclusions: The outcome (based on verifiable data) substantiating the main claims made for the product or service (for example, "As you have seen by comparing our product with those of ABC Company and ZED Company, our Model X-100 is $350 cheaper per machine, operates with fewer bells and whistles, and produces 10 additional widgets per minute.")

*See Chapter 15, pp. 407–08, for an example of an executive summary.

| Position Statement: | The chief inference drawn from the sum of the major conclusions (for example, "You should purchase our Model X-100.") |
| --- | --- |
| Recommendations: | Suggestions that focus on a follow-on service that might be performed or a related product that might be purchased in the future |

## Body of the Proposal

All of the elements capsulized in the executive summary are expanded in the body. The position statement and all of the major conclusions are carefully supported. In addition, the body of a proposal normally includes sections that describe how the service or product offered will be supplied:

| Work Plan and Deliverables: | The explicit plan for meeting the commitment, including a clear description of what the customer or client will receive and when. Deliverables may be a preliminary service, an interim report, a prototype product, or a group of products delivered sequentially over time (for example, "We will be able to deliver a Model X-100 for you to examine and approve on April 1, 1987. Ten more machines will be available for delivery within one week after we have your full order."). |
| --- | --- |
| Staffing: | The people responsible for meeting the commitment, their rank, experience, and other qualifications. (In some cases, staffing is important enough to warrant a complete section of its own; for example, in a consulting firm's proposal to perform a full-scale review of a company's products or services.) |
| Costs: | A clear and precise breakdown of the costs of the project. (For an external proposal, this may also include a schedule for payment.) |
| Summary Statement: | A brief, sharp recapitualization of the position statement and major conclusions. (The summary statement might follow the recommendations, or it might precede or follow the cost breakdown. Although optional, it is the writer's last opportunity to really *sell* the proposal.) |

**Commentary on Scott's Proposal.** Scott took into account what he knew about the components of a formal proposal, but he did not forget

Kim's advice to avoid undue formality. As she directed, he used a memo format and employed a number of the traditional elements very thoughtfully—molding them into a rigorous argument to persuade Jed to allocate the needed resources. He combined the background section and position statement into a brief introduction. The objectives to be pursued by the study have become the backbone of the entire document. By spelling out the study's objectives in his second-level subheadings, Scott made it likely that Jed would see and absorb the main elements of the proposal even before taking the time to read it thoroughly.

Scott also carefully tailored the tone and style of his proposal. Wanting to sound confident and assertive, he was not afraid to state his findings and recommendations clearly. But he was sure to preface them with words like "suggest" and "recommend" to underscore that he is *proposing* and not insisting. Although for the most part he used conversational language, he chose to refer to Kim, Pauline, and himself by their full names. This tactic provided a bit more formality than he originally intended, but he decided it was called for in a report on a matter of companywide interest. Given the report's importance, Scott guessed that Jed would almost certainly circulate it; at the very least, he would keep it on file for later consideration.

Scott's draft represents many hours of thought and hard work. In addition, it called for considerable resourcefulness and innovation in organizing the material and in uncovering information and using it effectively.

From his preliminary research, Scott selected the three main facts that would carry weight with Jed at this point: first, that many U.S. companies already support corporate-sponsored child-care programs; second, that a major competitor is currently adopting such a program; and third, that a number of good day-care options are available. From his college course in marketing, Scott retained and applied some basic knowledge about how to measure opinion. Finally, he used a combination of common sense and creativity to design a sound plan for securing the needed data.

Kim was very favorably impressed. She suggested that Scott attach a detailed breakdown of his cost estimates and send the proposal off to Jed as soon as possible.

# ■ Business Research Sources: An Annotated List

The following list is not inclusive, but it will certainly carry you a long way in researching any business topic.*

*Much of this reference information is presented by courtesy of Larry Prusak, Director, Information Resource Center, Temple, Barker & Sloane Inc., Lexington, MA.

# Business Directories

There are so many directories available to researchers that at least one thick reference volume exists just to list them all—*Directory of Directories* (Gale Publishing Company, Detroit, MI).

When you need to know about a particular corporation, a business directory is often the place to begin. (Your next step might be a phone call to the company.) All directories reflect space and budget limitations and should be used in conjunction with one another. Often, for no apparent reason, a company will show up in one volume and not in another. (This seems especially true for private companies, banks, holding companies, and service institutions.)

Another important point for the researcher to keep in mind is that the annual sales figures given in many of these directories are, by necessity, likely to be more than a year old. Because of this, these numbers are best used as guides or approximations. *Moody's Manuals*, updated weekly, are an obvious exception to this rule.

- *Million Dollar Directory*, 3 volumes, Dun & Bradstreet, 99 Church Street, New York, NY 10007
  This annual work is probably the most used general business reference source. Over 115,000 establishments are listed in these three volumes. Volume 1 has 43,000 companies whose net worth is over $1,670,000. Volume 2 has 36,000 companies whose net worth ranges from $847,000 to $1,670,000, and Volume 3 lists 36,000 businesses whose net worth ranges from $500,000 to $847,000.
- The *Million Dollar Directory* concentrates on industrial, wholesale, and retail businesses and offers less comprehensive coverage of service or financial institutions. However, it remains a very useful source as long as the precautions mentioned above are kept in mind.
- *Standard & Poor's Register*, 3 volumes, Standard & Poor's Corporation, 25 Broadway, New York, NY 10275.
  Published annually in three volumes, this set is somewhat different from the *Million Dollar Directory*. The first volume, *Corporations*, lists alphabetically the full entries for over 40,000 companies.
  The second volume, *Directors and Executives*, lists approximately 70,000 individuals serving as officers or directors of the corporations listed in Volume 1. For most individuals, there is included a short biographical statement listing date of birth, education, employment history, and professional affiliations.
  The third volume, *Index*, lists all the companies in the set by four-digit SIC codes, by states and principal cities within states, and by "Ultimate Parent," a useful classification showing corporate relationships (that is, subsidiaries, divisions, etc.).

- *Moody's Manuals,* Moody's Investory Service, 99 Church Street, New York, NY 10007.

  *Moody's Manuals* are technically not directories; they offer more information than most directories and make judgments in their various ratings. However, since they are often used in the same ways as the other volumes listed here, we include them.

  Moody's publishes six manuals: *Banking and Finance, Industrial, International,* OTC (Over the Counter), *Public Utilities,* and *Transportation.* Taken together, these manuals provide information on over 20,000 public or regulated companies. There is a comprehensive paperback index covering all the manuals, as well as indexes in each volume. All manuals are updated either weekly or twice a week, so very recent information (on sales and earnings, for example) is available.

  An entry in a *Moody's Manual* is often the best short introduction you can get to a company. For larger corporations, it can frequently serve as a substitute for an annual report.

- *Ward's Directory of 55,000 Largest U.S. Corporations,* Brown Ward Publications, Petaluma, CA 94953.

  This unique book is a very good one-volume source for any type of business or marketing research. The data are also available on computer tapes from the publisher.

- *Thomas' Register,* 17 volumes, Thomas Publishing Company, One Penn Plaza, New York, NY 10001.

  This 17-volume set lists companies that are not found in any other directory. It specializes in providing data on manufacturers and industrial services, and these establishments are often private and quite small.

- *U.S. Industrial Directory,* 4 volumes, Cahivers Publications, 999 Summer Street, P.O. Box 3809. Stanford, CA 94305.

  This four-volume work lists over 500,000 industrial suppliers under approximately 25,000 subject headings. The fourth volume contains listings of free catalogs and promotional material from over 5,000 firms.

- *The Top 1500 Private Companies, and the Second 1500 Companies,* Economic Information Systems, 310 Madison Avenue, New York, NY 10017.

  The annual directory lists the top 1500 private companies ranked by sales. Each entry also includes number of employees, number of plants, the company's lines of business (broadly defined), and sales figures broken down into manufacturing and nonmanufacturing sections. The volume also lists the 1500 companies in alphabetical and geographical sequences.

- *The Fortune Double 500 Directory,* Fortune Directories, P.O. Box 8001, Trenton, NJ 08650.

This small volume is a reprint of the various *Fortune* directories published during the preceding year. Listings include the 1000 largest industrial corporations, the 50 largest diversified service companies, the 50 largest commercial banking companies, the 50 largest life insurance companies, the 50 largest diversified financial companies, the 50 largest retailing companies, the 50 largest transportation companies, and the 50 largest utilities.

- *Directory of Corporate Affiliations*, National Register Publishing Company, 5201 Old Orchard Road, Skokie, IL 60077.

  This valuable reference work enables a researcher to find the "family" relationship of a company. It contains information on over 35,000 divisions, subsidiaries, etc., and data on over 4000 parent companies. Given the complexity of modern corporate life, this book is necessary for understanding the full stature and functions of a large company.

- *Directory of Industry Data Sources*, 3 volumes, Ballinger Publishing Company, 54 Church Street, Cambridge, MA 02138.

  This three-volume work is divided into five parts. The first part lists general reference sources for business information, with bibliographic data and costs. The second part identifies specific sources for 65 separate industries. The categories used to arrange each of these sections are the following: market research reports, investment banking reports, industry statistical reports, forecasts, directories and yearbooks, and special issues and journal articles. The third part of the work lists all the publishers alphabetically and by type (for example, newsletter, conference report). The fourth part is a subject index in which all the citations from the second part are arranged by SIC codes and also alphabetically by subject. The final part of the set is a comprehensive title index.

- *Reference Book for Corporate Management*, Dun & Bradstreet, 99 Church Street, New York, NY 10007.

  This volume lists all the officers and directors of more than 3000 firms, including most major U.S. corporations. A short biographical statement is included for all of the officers, giving date of birth, education, and employment history.

## Book Guides

- *Books in Print* and *Subject Guide to Books in Print*. Published annually. These two references list available books (those currently in print) for about 3600 U.S. publishers. *Books in Print* provides author, title, date of publication, edition, price, and publisher. *Subject Guide to Books in Print* lists all books by the subject headings assigned by the Library of Congress; it also lists them by author, with title and other bibliographic data.

- *Cumulative Book Index*, 1928–Present.
  This extensive index provides a worldwide listing of all books published in English by author, title, and subject, arranged in a dictionary sequence. The main entry, containing the most extensive information, is under author. This index provides author, title, edition, series, pagination, price, publisher, date, and Library of Congress card number.

## Major References on Public Companies

- *Annual Reports/10-K Forms*
  Filed annually with the Securities Exchange Commission (SEC), 10-K forms provide financial snapshots of all public companies in the United States. Annual reports are prepared for stockholders and include information about a company's mission, image, and outlook.
- *Standard & Poor's Reports*
  Issued quarterly in a loose-leaf format, these reports provide an excellent quick look at any public company, including financial data for the previous ten years and important company news.

## A Major Reference Book

- *Guide to Reference Books*, Eugene P. Sheehy, ed., 9th edition, Chicago: American Library Association, 1976.
  This book is especially useful when one is approaching a new subject or a new field of study. Sheehy's guide lists all the available literature by subject. Supplements are issued biennially.

## Periodical Indexes

- *Index to U.S. Government Periodicals*
  This index provides access to over 139 periodicals by author and by subject; it is computer-generated.
- *New York Times Index*
  This index is organized by subject with reference to date, page, and column for each article. It contains brief synopses of articles and is thoroughly cross-referenced. By providing dates of events, etc., it can also help you to locate articles in other newspapers. It is compiled quarterly and annually.
- *Predicasts F & S Index*
  This index of articles on U.S. companies, industries, and events (mergers, products, statistics) is published quarterly and will help you track down recent articles.
- *Predicasts Europe and International Index*
  This index is a valuable tool for finding articles on international companies, industries, and events; it is published quarterly.

- *Public Affairs Information Service Bulletin (PAIS).*
  A particularly useful index to government, economics, sociology, etc., this bulletin provides selective indexing of over 1000 periodicals. Besides periodicals, it covers books, documents, and reports.
- *Readers' Guide to Periodical Literature*
  This guide covers over 100 U.S. commercial periodicals on a multitude of topics. It is published every two weeks and gathered into cumulative volumes quarterly and yearly. It includes both a subject and an author index.
- *Wall Street Journal Index*
  This is an invaluable aid for researching current events, trends, or new products or ideas. It is updated monthly and cumulated yearly.
- *Special Issues Index,* Greenwood Press, 88 Post Road West, Westport, CT 06881.
  One of the most important sources of business information are professional, trade, and industry journals. There are thousands of these publications, and many of them have special issues or yearbooks in which they periodically publish such material as yearly statistics, forecasts, or directories. The *Special Issues Index* lists over 1300 journals that have special issues.

## Atlases and Statistical Guides

A good-quality atlas generally contains much more than maps. Statistical guides are extremely useful for researching economic, industrial, and social questions. Two of the most helpful for business research are described here.

- *Commercial Atlas and Marketing Guide*
  This guide contains both maps and statistics on trade, manufacturing, business, and transportation.
- *Statistical Abstract of the United States*
  Produced annually by the United States Bureau of the Census, this guide provides data on social, political, and economic structure and behavior in the United States.

## On-Line Data Bases

Many libraries and individuals can access a great variety of information in on-line data bases. Using a computer terminal and a telephone, a researcher can plug into a network of data bases offering data on virtually any subject. Here is how it works.

An institution (library, corporation, etc.) or individual applies for an identification or "log-on" number from an information vendor or provider. These companies (Dialog Information Services, Dun & Bradstreet, Mead Data Central, etc.) either produce their own data bases or buy the computerized tapes from another company or government agency.

Once you have your "log-on" number, you can go on-line and execute a search to acquire information. Data base information usually comes in one of three formats: (1) bibliographical, in which you receive either citations or abstracts of articles or books about the subjects you are interested in; (2) numerical, in which you receive a numerical series, or some form of quantitative data; or (3) full-text, a format in which you get the complete text of an article from a magazine or report.

When you have identified the subject you are interested in, and the data base that will best satisfy your needs, you can retrieve the material. If you have a video display terminal, you will be able to read the information on its screen. If you also have access to a printer, you will be able to print the information and keep a record for future use.

Your reference librarian can assist you, but the following are three of the more popular data bases offering business information:

*Disclosure* offers lengthy abstracts of annual reports and extensive financial data on all public companies in the United States.

*Newsearch* provides thorough indexing of articles in *The New York Times* and *Wall Street Journal*, among other newspapers.

*ABI (Abstracted Business Information)* gives abstracts (usually 10–15 sentences long) of articles from over 300 business periodicals.

Fees for using on-line data bases are determined by the number of minutes a file is used and the number of citations received (usually by air-mail delivery or off-line printing). Currently, there are over 14 million citations, starting from 1970, available for searching. An average search can cost anywhere from $20 to $50; an experienced operator who preplans the search terms and strategy can reduce costs. These services are now offered by many major colleges, universities, and information centers through service bureaus or libraries, with some libraries paying part or all of the costs.

Also, with the right software and some inexpensive auxiliary hardware, you can conduct research at an available PC. Although each of the on-line data base services has its own language, a number of PC programs enable you to select the appropriate data base and define your search. Then, when you feel well prepared, you can communicate with the mainframe. It is also possible to move information onto your own disk, enabling data to be stored for later use. This system obviously gives the user much more autonomy; it also cuts the cost of the search by conserving time spent on-line.

# ■ Summary

A business proposal is a written offer or expression of intention. It usually identifies a need and presents a plan to respond to that need. Formal proposals, especially those intended for the federal government, generally require very specific information and extensive detail presented in a rigidly prescribed format.

Any proposal may include some or all of the following elements: transmittal letter or memo, cover and/or title page, submittal letter, and executive summary. The body of the proposal expands upon the executive summary; it also normally covers workplan and deliverables, staffing, costs, and a summary statement.

The chapter concludes with an annotated list of business research sources.

# ■ Discussion Problems

**14.1**   What is the basic distinction between a report and a proposal? Can you think of situations in which the two might overlap?

**14.2**   Can you think of an occasion—whether at work or in your private life—when it was necessary to collect information in order to suggest a solution to a problem? What was the problem, and how did you find the data required to solve it? Did you need to persuade others of the wisdom of your solution? If so, how did you do so?

**14.3**   How would you research the data required in each of the following situations?

■   Your boss will be introducing Lee Iacocca at a large fund-raising dinner in your community, and you have been assigned the task of writing the introduction.

■   Your firm proposes to buy a parcel of land currently used as a park in a nearby suburb. The problem is to discover whether there are any legal or zoning restrictions tied to this property.

■   Your company regularly ships air-mail orders to Mexico and South America, and lately almost 10 percent fail to arrive at their destinations. It's your job to suggest a solution.

■   You want to learn what towns in your state might be good places to buy investment property.

■   You want to find out who heads up the marketing area at General Electric.

■   You are a woman about to start your own business. You would like to learn more about the current trend in the United States of women starting entrepreneurial ventures.

■   You would like to know more about the current popularity of "cents-off" coupons for selling groceries and other retail products, especially about new ways they are being used in direct marketing.

- You are interested in studying the history and current status of the management at Apple Computer.
- You would like to locate a few good books and articles about multinational corporations.

**14.4** Discuss the differences between internal and external proposals. Enumerate a number of situations that might call for an internal proposal. Describe at least three situations in which an external proposal would be needed.

**14.5** Have you had the experience—while holding either a job or an internship—of proposing a change in policy or procedure? Did you submit a written proposal? Describe its content and format. If you did not prepare a written proposal, explain how you handled the situation. In either case, how successful were you?

**14.6** Have you used an electronic data base either at a library or within a business environment? If you have had such an opportunity, describe the situation and task. Were the results satisfactory? Explain.

**14.7** Think of some service you are able to perform (such as typing, painting, bookkeeping, child care, editing), and decide whether an oral or written bid would be most appropriate for a given circumstance when you might perform that service for a company or individual. What factors determine the necessity of a written bid or proposal? Even when an offer is made orally, what details should be covered before the service is performed? Why?

**14.8** Your college or university undoubtedly depends on government funds for a whole range of special programs. Choose one of these programs, find out as much about its operation as you can, and then try to reconstruct what elements might have gone into the original proposal that sought funding for that program. In fact, a cooperative administrator might show you an actual proposal or even let you bring one to class. The development office is a likely source for such a document, but many other college departments submit proposals as well.

**14.9** Refer to the Sta-Brite case, and imagine that Jed MacDonald, Vice President of Human Resouces and Kim's boss, is not at all enthusiastic about the idea of day care at Sta-Brite. Although Kim and Scott are convinced they are right to pursue the matter further, they will have to find some means of persuading Jed to let them proceed. What would you recommend? What steps could they take to overcome Jed's objections—or possibly to work around them? Should they involve other people? pursue further research? work directly with employee groups? Obviously they have to be sure not to alienate Jed in the process.

**14.10** Imagine that you recently submitted a carefully researched proposal to your immediate superior concerning a better method of filing back-orders. Since you and several of your colleagues on the sales force have often been inconvenienced by the old system, you have a real stake in improving the situation. But three weeks have passed, and you've still received no response to your proposal. What will you do?

**14.11** Bill Haddock is Assistant Director of the Office of Career Planning and Placement at Chadwick College, an undergraduate college specializing in business education. Barbara Mello of the development office just informed Bill that funds might be available from the Lattell Foundation for a creative program that incorporates experiential learning.

Bill has been trying for over a year to expand Chadwick College's internship program to include students with majors other than accounting. The accounting internship program has been in existence for almost ten years and is highly successful. Currently the placement office is unable to fill the corporate demand for accounting interns. Bill is convinced that students in fields such as marketing, management, and human resources would benefit greatly from the practical experience of a semester-long internship, and he has no doubt that he and his staff could find at least 30 such supervised positions among the corporate contacts already established through the accounting internship program.

Bill intends to submit a proposal to the Lattell Foundation, with Barbara's help. What specific information might he need concerning the foundation's requirements? What sort of data concerning Chadwick College and its existing accounting internship program would strengthen his proposal? In what format might such data best be presented? Can you think of relevant budget considerations? What questions need to be asked before a concrete budget can take shape? What kind of material could be attached as appendixes to make the proposal more effective?

## ■ Writing Tasks

**14.1**   Your position as office manager of a management consulting firm requires that you discover the cheapest airline rates for regular business travel between Boston and Washington, D.C. The consultants from your firm will be traveling on weekdays, staying from one to three days, and almost always renting a car at the airport to travel the 45 miles to the client's headquarters.

After collecting sufficient data to make a well-informed recommendation, draft an informal proposal in memo form to your vice president, specifying the criteria you used in coming to your decision.

**14.2**   After studying Discussion Problem 14.11, draft Bill's proposal to the Lattell Foundation. Assume that you will be asking for an award of $67,500 to cover two years' support of 30 internships during the fall semester and another 30 during the spring semester. Chadwick College will match each dollar contributed by Lattell as well as provide 10 percent of the total grant in administrative expenses. Individual student awards will be calculated on the basis of a $5 per hour wage rate, as follows:

$$\$5/\text{hour} \times 15 \text{ hours/week} \times 15 \text{ weeks} = \$1125$$

Be sure to specify the need for the grant and the purpose it will serve, to stress the ability of the college to administer the grant money effectively, and to include any other background information you think will strengthen your case. At the beginning of the proposal, include an executive summary, a table of contents, and a list of appendixes.

**14.3**   Norma Belson is the director of public relations for a rapidly growing software firm that is run with an iron hand by its founder and president, Harry Dinin.

Although the firm produces numerous brochures and newsletters for external marketing purposes, as yet there is no internal newsletter to improve communications among the firm's ever growing staff. Norma recently proposed such a newsletter to Harry for the third time in the past 18 months, and this time Harry seemed to be weakening. He promised to consider the idea seriously if Norma could prove that all the vice presidents and senior administrators think the newsletter would be useful.

Norma wasted no time in preparing an appropriate questionnaire and within two weeks collected the following results:

A total of 46 questionnaires were returned, for an 85 percent response rate. Ninety-nine percent of the respondents favor such a newsletter.

Below are the results of the question: "Do you feel that there is a need for an internal employee newsletter?

| | Total | VPs (5) | Division Heads (8) | Department Heads (9) | Associate/ Assistant Heads (21) | Others (3) |
|---|---|---|---|---|---|---|
| Strongly agree (72%) | 33 | 3 | 4 | 6 | 18 | 2 |
| Somewhat agree (20%) | 9 | 2 | 3 | 3 | 1 | 0 |
| Agree (6%) | 3 | 0 | 1 | 0 | 2 | 0 |
| Somewhat disagree (2%) | 1 | 0 | 0 | 0 | 0 | 1 |
| Strongly disagree (0%) | 0 | 0 | 0 | 0 | 0 | 0 |

In addition, Norma decided to solicit senior administrators' personal reactions to the newsletter idea. She collected the following comments:

"I applaud the idea."

"Such a companywide document is long overdue."

"The only drawback is that by the time some information reaches print, it is out of date."

"I strongly support your efforts."

"Good idea."

"Not only is a newsletter a good idea, it is really a necessity."

"Badly needed."

"I have not had a problem receiving timely communication."

"I have for a long time felt that such an internal newsletter would be a great idea."

"Would be interested."

"Think it's a great idea if it eliminates duplication."

"Publicizing staff activities is important."

"Let's give it a try."

"A newsletter isued at least once a month is needed."

"We need one badly."

"Great idea."

"Do one."

"A good idea."

"Great idea."

"Reducing printed notices would be great."

"Sounds like a great idea."

"Greatly needed to further communication between professional and support staff."

"I believe there is a definite need for such a newsletter."

"All other companies in which I have worked have had such an in-house organ."

Norma knows from experience that the cost of such a newsletter would vary according to the quality of the printing and graphics, the frequency of publication, and the number of pages. Her estimates vary from $4500 to $24,000, and she feels sure that her present staff could handle the reporting and writing, at least for a monthly publication.

Write a relatively informal proposal from Norma to Harry using as much data as you think necessary to be persuasive. Be sure to explain why you think such a newsletter is essential, what purpose it would achieve, and the particular recommendations you would make regarding its size and quality. But leave the final decision up to Harry. In fact, if possible, make it all sound as though it's his idea!

**14.4**  As an administrative assistant to John Wheeler, Chief Operating Officer of a large mill in New England, you've been asked to give some thought to recommending social functions for the mill employees during the coming year. The traditional Christmas dinner dance has been pretty unexciting in recent years, the turkey distribution at Thanksgiving is almost taken for granted, and the Fourth of July picnic is no longer drawing a sizeable turnout.

First decide what means of "research" would be most effective in this case. (For example, whose opinions would you solicit? How would you manage to discover at lease a sampling of opinions?) Then draft a brief memo to John in which you make some tentative recommendations. Don't hesitate to be creative, but remember that many of the employees are old-fashioned in their tastes and habits.

**14.5**  Margo Shaver is the assistant manager of Campus Catering Company and is responsible for submitting a bid to the President of the College to cater a formal dinner for the board of trustees and their spouses in the president's house. Her proposal must cover the costs of food and beverages; waitress service; rental of linens, glasses, and silverware; and floral decorations. Using the format of a memo, draft a proposal to the president including the following details:

- Time: Thursday, November 21, cocktails at 6:30 p.m., dinner at 7:30 p.m.
- Prime rib dinner for 76 guests at $18.50 per person
- Open bar: top brands at cost; beer and wine
- Mixed hors d'oeuvres:

    Shrimp bowl at $2.00 per person

    Scallops in bacon at $1.50 per person

    Swedish meatballs at $1.00 per person

    Mixed imported cheese tray at $.50 per person

- 4 waitresses at $6.00 per hour, minimum 6 hours
- Rental of linens, glasses, and silverware at $3.00 per person
- Floral centerpiece (roses) at each of 10 tables of 8 people, $15 each
- Large floral centerpieces for bar and hors d'oeuvres table, $25 each

Since this is the first time that the president has considered using the services of Campus Catering, you should include an introduction that convinces him that you can do the job with elegance and flair. The format of the proposal should be highly professional. Add any details that you feel would make the best case for choosing your bid.

**14.6**  Crawford Company is looking for a writing consultant who can conduct a program to train a group of about 50 mid-level managers to be more effective letter and memo writers. They have invited bids of no more than $10,000 to cover the following:

- Three two-day workshops will be held one month apart in Des Moines starting in the spring
- Each workshop should include no more than 20 students
- Expenditures for hotels, food, and travel must be estimated carefully and included as part of the bid
- The workshops should be based on an initial needs analysis performed by the consultant and based on an evaluation of a sampling of the company's documents

Draft a proposal to run the workshops. Include an overall description of your program and a breakdown of your expenses. The proposal should be in the form of a letter to Mr. Donald Sargent, Director of Human Resources.

**14.7**  A shoe company has chosen your advertising agency to introduce their new line of sports shoes. They have specified a budget of $1.5 million to cover account service, media service, and creative development. Assume that each of these services will consume approximately one-third of your budget.

- Account supervisors will be billed at the rate of $100/hour, account managers at $80/hour, and account coordinators at $50/hour. The account service department will act as a liaison between the agency and the client, will coordinate all work within the agency, work directly with third-party vendors, and supervise all billing.

- The media director's billing rate is $100/hour, and the media planner will be billed at $80/hour. The media department is responsible for determining which publications would be the most effective vehicles for the client's advertisements.
- The head of the creative department is billed at $100/hour, copywriters and art directors are billed at $80/hour. The creative department produces the concepts for the ads and executes their production.

Devise a believable proposal for an advertising campaign consisting of full-color ads in two or three well-known magazines with wide circulations. Include a transmittal letter to Pat O'Rourke, Director of Marketing Communications, Sporting Life Shoe Company.

**14.8** You are a project coordinator at United Philanthropies, a private social service agency that offers education and counseling to low-income individuals and families in East Hartford, Connecticut. As part of your responsibilities, you research and write proposals to obtain grants to fund the agency's projects. Currently, you are faced with the task of writing a proposal to the Department of Health and Human Services in Washington, D.C., to seek funding for a neighborhood food co-op. The following parameters have been set for the project.

- The co-op will be located in a neighborhood inhabited chiefly by elderly persons and single-parent families.
- The site for the co-op will be the basement of the First Presbyterian Church, which the church will make available for $50 per month.
- The co-op will sell only food and absolute necessities.
- The co-op will be managed by a director and run by volunteers, who will earn membership by service.
- The director will be paid $18,000 per year.
- Overhead costs are estimated at $30 per month for electricity and $42 per month for the phone. Heat will be donated by the church.
- In addition, you have projected that the following items need to be purchased as part of the initial investment:
  Refrigerator          $700
  Shelving and counters $325
  Cash register         $200
- You also recognize that the co-op will need to be publicized through ads in local papers and through flyers circulated in the neighborhood. You have estimated advertising costs at $150.

One of the goals you have set for the co-op is to provide low-cost food and necessities for people who currently must take two buses to shop for food. In addition, you plan to have the co-op's director run a community workshop on nutrition.

Write a formal proposal to the Department of Health and Human Services (which has no formatting restrictions, but you need to cover all important bases). Include a transmittal letter addressed to Chester Harrison, Assistant Secretary of Health and Human Services.

**14.9**   At Caton Mills, Inc., a large manufacturing company on the West Coast, senior management is facing an urgent request from the vice president of marketing. Currently, the marketing division urgently needs additional computer resources to carry out analyses of customers and competitors and to improve market projections. Traditionally, the information management department has managed all such needs, providing run time on their large mainframe computer. At this time, however, the vice president of marketing is insisting that his people must have their own personal computers. To resolve this problem, senior management has called on Bolton, Mansfield, Inc. (BMI), a management consulting firm specializing in problems relating to information management.

Ellen Levinson, a senior associate at BMI, has been given the West Coast manufacturer's request for proposal (RFP). She has decided to propose that her firm conduct a complete audit of the marketing department's needs and of the comany's current information management policies and procedures. The purpose of this study will be to determine whether to give the marketing department its own personal computers or to insist they continue to operate through the central information management function. In her proposal she will offer to research the following questions:

- Is the company's corporate culture mostly centralized or decentralized? (In other words, do the division vice presidents run their areas autonomously, without needing approval from senior management?)

- To what degree is marketing integrated with other divisions in the company? For instance, are marketing decisions closely coordinated with those of research and development or of manufacturing?

- Is the marketing division engaged in facilitating a major change in business strategy that might require special computer capabilities? For instance, is the company trying to break into a new market or introduce a major new product?

- What computing resources do the company and the marketing division currently have? How would introducing personal computers into marketing affect the overall management of other existing resources? Specifically, how would the information management department be affected?

To find the answers to these questions, BMI will design and administer a survey, conduct focus groups,* and interview key company personnel. The entire project would take three months. It would be conducted by a team of three consultants and would cost $40,000 plus expenses for travel, clerical work, etc.

As Ellen Levinson, write the proposal to Henry Greenspan, Chief Executive Officer of Caton Mills, Inc.

---

*Focus groups are discussion groups brought together to share their opinions about a product, service, or issue. As the discussion proceeds, it is either observed or videotaped for subsequent evaluation.

# REPORT WRITING II
# PROCESS & PRODUCT
# THE REPORT

## 15

R eaders normally expect to find certain components present in a report, and this expectation should not be taken lightly. But whether they are for memos, letters, proposals, or reports, standard formats have always been a reflection of preference and convention rather than of rule. One cannot argue that a given format is "right"—only that it is useful. And a format's usefulness depends entirely on how well it assists the writer in achieving the objectives for which the document is intended.

## ■ Categories: Are They Helpful?

If one *could* know precisely what steps to take (in their precise order) and what elements to include (in their precise order), the task of writing a report would obviously be greatly simplified. Attempts have therefore been made to stipulate preparation steps and components of various kinds of reports. Among the more frequently mentioned categories of reports are proposals, research reports, feasibility reports, progress reports, periodic reports, information reports, problem-solving reports, analytical reports, and long and short reports.

No one would deny that it is helpful to know as much as possible concerning how and where to get specific kinds of data and how and where to insert information effectively. But as Scott's efforts in the first part of the Sta-Brite case demonstrate, it is very difficult to slip either the preparation process or the report itself into a mold. Scott's preliminary research mainly showed him that he would need to do additional research of a much wider scope. Moreover, although he originally expected to write a research report, he soon discovered that he had to prepare a proposal.

But Scott's proposal really was, in fact, partially a research report. Similarly, since many research reports are aimed at problem solving or analysis, they need to contain proposals. Information reports are supposedly nonjudgmental, but judgment enters into decisions about what data to include and the way information is to be organized (and, consequently, about what gets the most emphasis or coverage). Progress reports can monitor progress on a one-time basis or they can be issued periodically; in most cases, they look at the feasibility of next steps. And certainly all of the above mentioned categories include both long and short reports. Lengthy studies are produced not to satisfy formatting requirements but because their subjects are important and require in-depth analysis and discussion.

As soon as you try to pigeonhole a specific report, you are likely to discover that it will not fit very well. Frequently, you need elements that properly belong to a different category, or your purpose mandates that you shuffle the prescribed order.

Perhaps the primary problem with classification systems is that they force writers to focus on what a particular report *is* and not on what it *does*. In other words, such systems obscure the fact that a report operates as part of an ongoing business transaction and that its effectiveness must be measured in the context of that enterprise. Business reports are not meant to be dusty collections of data, no matter how scrupulously researched. Although the information they contain is expected to be as accurate and complete as possible (and integrity should be a given) their main reason for existing is to *accomplish* something.

## ■ What Does Help?

Since classification systems are neither reliable nor especially helpful, what can you depend on to help you to develop successful reports?

The two best aids are not derived from any external source, nor can they be given to you as a packaged format or a set of rules. Both originate within your own thought processes: they are *objectivity* and *consistency*.

### Objectivity

When used to describe thought or behavior, the word "objectivity" has several opposing meanings. And this opposition has provided a perennial headache for business writers who strive to be objective. The definitions from one dictionary spotlight the problem.*

One definition of objectivity maintains that it is "existing independent of mind," and a second similarly asserts that it is "emphasizing or expressing the nature of reality as it is apart from personal reflections or feelings." But the same dictionary states that objectivity also means "of or relating to an object, action or feeling" and "expressing or involving the use of facts without distortion by personal feelings or prejudices." The first two definitions do not apply to business writing; the second two definitely do. Let's see why this is so.

Objectivity in business writing most certainly does not imply the total absence of thinking and feeling. Reports are not intended to be neatly packed containers of facts untouched by human thoughts or beliefs. The writer's presence is always felt in a good report; it is evidenced by the style and tone and also by the amount and kind of data presented. We also sense the writer's mind at work selecting the most powerful arguments and

*Definitions are from *Webster's Ninth New Collegiate Dictionary*, Merriam-Webster Inc. Springfield MA, ©1983.

sequencing them to highlight relationships and to establish priorities. In respect to feelings, the distinction is a bit finer. There are times when, like scientists, business people must stand back and report observations without any reference to feelings or opinions. But in most of your business transactions you will be called on to interpret what you have seen or experienced. Your personal insights will be needed and valued. Tact and restraint are requisite, but frequently it will be both appropriate and useful for your business writing to reflect feelings of confidence, misgiving, surprise, enthusiasm, approval, etc.

For example, if you were asked to examine three plans for improving customer relations, you would not respond by stating that one is "idiotic," one is "terrible," and one is "fabulous." But you might properly say that you believe the first "won't work," the second is "impractical," and the third has "a high potential for success." You would support these judgments with factual evidence, but you certainly would not want to avoid making them. If you omitted your evaluation and only described the features of each plan, your contribution would be minimal. It is true that some assignments emphasize detailed data collection and others stress thoughtful interpretation. But even in the former case, your superiors and readers will expect you to *think*.

Also keep in mind that phrases such as "It has been observed that . . . ." or "It is recommended that . . . ." do not make your writing objective—they only make it pretentious. You can maintain an appropriately formal tone by writing "The data demonstrate that . . . ." When informality is appropriate, you can write "I recommend that . . . ."

Real objectivity in report writing is, as you can see, derived from a chain reaction between hard work and integrity. A good report is built on a strenuous effort to gather facts and on clear-headed integrity in interpreting them. The pattern of behavior should look something like this: work ⇆ integrity ⇆ interpretation ⇆ work ⇆ integrity ⇆ interpretation. Most importantly, true objectivity rests on an inner attitude that mandates playing fair with your reader and a style that speaks calmly and with sweet reason. It avoids declamatory language or haranguing. It neither threatens nor cajoles. But it is definitely not afraid to stand its ground and make its meaning clear.

## Consistency

The dictionary gives us one definition of "consistency" that aptly describes the preferred personal qualities of a business writer, and a second definition that describes the preferred qualities in a report. The first definition is "firmness of constitution or character; persistency"; the second is "harmony of parts of features to one another or a whole."

In other words, consistency suggests a writer intent on uncovering meaning. Such a writer performs needed research and then repeatedly draws together two or more facts to produce a finding, two or more findings to discover an inference, and two or more inferences to form a conclusion. And those conclusions are then drawn together to yield significant assertions and recommendations. As David W. Ewing has suggested, organizing a report "is more like making a movie than taking a photograph."* The writer is in control of the medium, actively organizing and arranging facts and ideas so that the arguments move in a discernible direction. And the end product of this effort is a report that implicitly or explicitly demonstrates the significance of the data it contains (see Figure 15.1).

The thinking process that produces a consistent report is always reflected in the unity and coherence** of the report's organization. The separate components of the report (transmittal letter, executive summary, background, approach, etc.) should form a harmonious whole. Subsections and paragraphs should be clearly marked entities, and, like the larger elements, they should work together to carry the reader forward. (See Figures 15.2 and 15.3.)

To guide the reader, a systematic network of headings should highlight the thought process. Figure 15.4 illustrates two systems for headings. (These systems are not absolute. You firm may have one that differs from both of those shown. Whatever system you use, use it consistently throughout the document.) Enumeration (*First*, we . . . . *Second*, we . . . .) should be used appropriately to link ideas and provide momentum. In addition, connections should be made visible though the use of repetition,† synonyms, and directional words ("therefore," "however," "moreover," "also," "next," etc.). Finally, parallel structure should be employed to highlight relationships and to emphasize key points (see Figure 15.5).

Scott Stanton was really very lucky. His first assignment at Sta-Brite was challenging and interesting; it was therefore not especially difficult for him to approach it with true objectivity and to follow through with consistency. It would, however, be naive to suggest that this is always the case. At many times in your business career, you will find yourself collecting and sorting facts and figures and writing reports about dry or very routine matters. At such times, you will be wise to pause and try to place what you are doing in the larger context of the business goals it supports.

---

*David W. Ewing, *Writing for Results in Business, Government, Science and the Professions*, 2nd Edition, John Wiley and Sons, 1979.
**See "Patterns of Relationship," Chapter 5.
†Don't be afraid to repeat a word to link ideas. Students often doggedly avoid repetition because they fear they will bore their readers. Not so! A friend of ours insists that writers who will never repeat a word belong to "The Elongated-Yellow-Fruit School of Writing"; that is, they are people who will never say "banana" twice! (In this brief note, we used the word "repeat" twice and "repetition" once.)

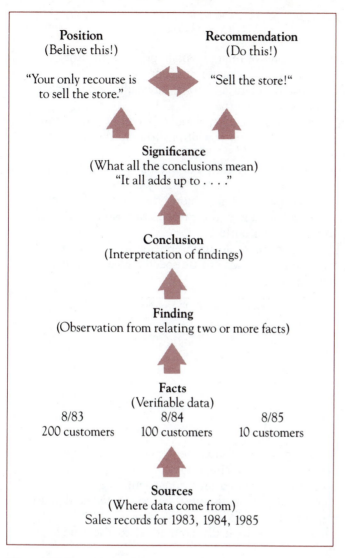

Position
(Believe this!)

Recommendation
(Do this!)

"Your only recourse is
to sell the store."

"Sell the store!"

Significance
(What all the conclusions mean)
"It all adds up to . . . ."

Conclusion
(Interpretation of findings)

Finding
(Observation from relating two or more facts)

Facts
(Verifiable data)

8/83
200 customers

8/84
100 customers

8/85
10 customers

Sources
(Where data come from)
Sales records for 1983, 1984, 1985

**Figure 15.1**
"Sell the Store!"—Building Consistency into a Report

Although you will be expected to observe your firm's established conventions for reporting data, if you do so with a clear understanding of the larger implications of your task, the project is much more likely to benefit from your contribution. Moreover, you will probably find that you have enhanced your business knowledge and gained skill as a report writer.

> ## The Subsection
>
> - A subsection is a group of related paragraphs that together explain, support, or expand a major concept.
> - A subsection must be identified by a subheading that briefly and aptly forecasts its concerns.
> - Paragraphs within a subsection should be unified and connected to each other by clear transitions to help the reader see the progress of ideas.
> - A subsection should be logically connected to the subsection that precedes it.
> - Too many subsections (usually more than three first-level headings to a page) fragment the presentation and create the impression of reading an outline.
> - Too few subsections create an uninteresting-looking text and make it difficult for the reader to tie specific ideas together or to locate them later on.

**Figure 15.2**

> ## The Paragraph
>
> - A paragraph is a group of related sentences that together explain, support, or expand a single idea.
> - A paragraph must be founded on a topic sentence.
> - The sentences in a paragraph must be connected and must demonstrate a progress of ideas—a direction.
> - A paragraph should be logically connected to the paragraph that precedes it.
> - A paragraph must make the reader aware of its function in the total report, of why it has been included.
> - In modern business practice, paragraphs are reasonbly short, at least two on each typewritten page.
> - On the other hand, paragraph units should be logical; too many short paragraphs can make relationships difficult to discern.

**Figure 15.3**

I.

FIRST-LEVEL HEADINGS

(centered and all caps)

<u>Second-Level Headings</u>

(centered, underlined, caps and lower case*)

<u>Third-Level Headings</u>

(left-hand margin, underlined, caps and lower case*)

<u>Fourth-Level Headings</u>

(at paragraph indentation, underlined, caps and lower case*)

<u>Fifth-level headings</u> <u>may be integrated into the text as the opening
sentence of a group of related paragraphs.</u>

II.

<u>FIRST-LEVEL HEADINGS</u>

(left-hand margin, underlined, all caps)

<u>Second-Level Headings</u>

(left-hand margin, underlined, caps and lower case*)

<u>Third-Level Headings</u>

(at paragraph indentation, underlined, caps and lower case*)

<u>Fourth-level headings</u>. (at paragraph indentation followed by period
and the first complete sentence of the text of the paragraph; initial caps only)

<u>Fifth-level headings</u> are indicated by underlining the key words that
open a paragraph.

*When using caps and lower case, do not capitalize articles, conjunctions, or preposi-
tions.

**Figure 15.4** Two systems for headings

**Parallel Structure**

Parallel structure employs the repetition of similar grammatical forms to increase coherence and to emphasize key points. It relies on both sight and sound to foster comprehension:

- The reader hears the rhythm that results from repetition.
- The reader sees the alignment of similar ideas in similar forms.

The above two sentences have parallel structure. Because they are parallel, their rhythm is better, their relationship is clearer, and their tone is more forceful.

**Figure 15.5**

## The Sta-Brite Corporation: Case History (2)

Two weeks after their informal luncheon meeting, Kim Matsushita met with her boss, Jed MacDonald, to discuss progress in the personnel area. The plan was that Kim and Jed would have their regular Friday morning meeting and then Scott would join them for a briefing on where things stood in regard to the child-care proprosal. As Scott entered Jed's office at 10:30, both Kim and Jed were looking a bit perplexed. Jed spoke first.

"Scott, Kim tells me that most of the work that went into that proposal was yours. You've done a good job in defining what we need to know and how we ought to get it. I've talked to the folks upstairs, in corporate, and everyone seems to agree that this is an area that needs to be looked into right away. The problem is that Kim just hasn't the time to take on full responsibility for something of this size for at least another two weeks. I'm inclined to let you run with it for a while on your own, but we're both concerned that's too much to dump into the lap of a brand-new employee. How do you feel about it, Scott?"

"Jed, I'm not sure I know what you mean by 'full responsibility.' But I do know this project interests me greatly."

Jed continued, "Well, what I mean, Scott, is that you will need to do the spade work of turning up a good consultant and seeing that the facts we need start to get collected. When it comes time to analyzing the stuff you and the consultant turn up, Kim will be there to supervise—and I'll certainly want to get my hand in. But I'd at least like to see you get this thing rolling on your own, if you feel you can handle it."

Scott didn't hesitate. "I'd like to do it. The fact is that *because* I'm new, this is a great project. I'm sure to learn more about Sta-Brite's employees than I would in months under less demanding circumstances."

The argument was persuasive. Scott's project was launched with the following admonition from Kim: "Great, but keep me posted in writing. I'd like a written run-down on the consultants as soon as you have our three candidates."

## Process: Conducting Research

Scott's first objective was to locate an appropriate consultant to assist with the research. First by telephone, and later through personal visits to their offices, Scott interviewed representatives of two Boston-area consulting firms. In addition, he conferred with the two co-owners of a Chicago-based firm, who had agreed to visit Boston at no initial charge. In all three cases, he asked to examine available literature describing the firm's history and services and to speak with one or more organizations for whom the firm had previously done a survey. When he had gathered all of this data together, Scott proceeded to analyze the results. All three of the consulting organizations offered some advantages and some disadvantages. Scott needed to communicate these to Kim, but he knew that she would also expect him to recommend the firm that would best suit Sta-Brite's current needs.

He spent a full hour reviewing and organizing the data he had collected. Then, after careful thought, a Snickers bar, a trip to the coffee machine, more careful thought, a quick look at his new copy of *Business Week*, a telephone call, and yet more careful thought, he settled down and drafted the short report shown on pages 390–95.

# Product: Scott's Interim Report

MEMORANDUM

TO:   Kim Matsushita
FROM:   Scott Stanton
RE:   Consultant for Child-Care Research
DATE:   September 2, 198-

Two weeks ago you and Jed commissioned me to find and evaluate candidates to assist us in gathering data concerning Sta-Brite's child-care needs. At this time, I have received the attached proposals from three leading consulting firms and have met with members of their staffs. This report includes my findings and my preliminary conclusion as to which of the three could serve us best.

SELECTION CRITERIA

To evaluate the three firms, I felt we needed to establish some clear criteria to measure their appropriateness for this project. Since, as you can see from the attached proposals, all three have named fees that fall within a $200 variance, price does not appear to be an important issue here. The most significant criteria, I believe, are the following:

o   Experience in conducting similar kinds of research
o   The services each proposes to deliver
o   The compatibility of each firm's style with Sta-Brite's corporate environment

Below I have described each candidate in reference to these three criteria.

## DATA RESEARCH ASSOCIATES (DRA)

DRA is a ten-year-old firm located in Cambridge, Massachusetts. It has an exceptionally fine reputation for collecting economic data. Although the firm established its reputation by doing macroeconomic research, in the last two years it has begun to focus on the problems of businesses in major industries. As part of this work, DRA's consulting staff has done a considerable amount of marketing research for their clients. Although some projects have focused on assessing attitudes concerning specific new products and services, none has dealt with internal human relations problems.

DRA proposes to perform an in-depth study of what other firms in the country are doing in regard to the child-care issue. In addition, they will design a survey instrument that Sta-Brite can use for gathering data on our employees' attitudes and needs. They will not administer the survey, but they will provide us with a full-scope written analysis of the results.

John Hanks, a principal of the firm, told me that he and his team would be responsible for the project. All of their résumés are included with DRA's proposal. As you can see, although John has over 30 years of consulting experience, he has never worked on a human relations problem. The group's résumés are also impressive, but they all seem to be economists and marketing experts.

## INFORMATION EXPERTS, INC. (IEI)

IEI is a relatively new firm, but it has an outstanding reputation in market research. Located in Burlington, Massachusetts, the company works closely with high-technology firms in the greater Boston area. The firm has designed and administered many surveys of employee attitudes toward computer technology, especially in regard to how technology impinges on job performance. IEI proposes to help us prepare and administer the survey instrument. They will also provide us with a detailed written analysis of the results. In addition, they are willing to conduct two full days of interviews of personnel here at our corporate headquarters.

John Robertson, IEI's Senior Vice President, met with me here and told me that he would personally direct the project and handle all of the interviews. Although he's known as somewhat of a whiz kid in the consulting industry and has a very impressive list of credentials, my impression of him was not positive. He kept insisting that he ought to be talking to my superiors and continually addressed me as "son." Perhaps I shouldn't place so much weight on my personal discomfort, but since he would be working closely with Sta-Brite's personnel at all levels, I'm questioning whether his evidently weak interpersonal skills might not impede the interview process.

## KIDD ASSOCIATES

Located in Chicago, Kidd Associates, a six-year-old firm, was recommended to me by Pauline Atticus, who used their services last year when we did a pilot study of stress among first-line supervisors at our Illinois facility. Although not particularly well known in Boston, Kidd Associates has begun to establish a fine reputation in the Midwest.

Kidd Associates will provide the same services as IEI; but, in addition, they propose to oversee a series of six focus groups—either here at Sta-Brite's headquarters or, if we are willing to incur travel expenses, at their offices, where they have a specially equipped one-way viewing room with hidden video equipment. Using this facility would allow us to closely monitor interactions of employees with varying viewpoints.

Marvin and Molly Kidd, who jointly oversee their firm, have worked with a number of major companies to resolve human resources issues. Jasper Night, Vice President of Human Resources at First Bank of Chicago, told me that Kidd Associates performed an excellent study there on employee attitudes about current retirement benefits, and he substantiated his comments in a detailed letter (attached). The Kidds are both personally interested in the subject of child-care programs. (They already knew a great deal about the forthcoming study commissioned by the governor of Massachusetts.)

## CONCLUSIONS

In regard to the experience each firm can bring to our project, Kidd Associates is our best choice. Although DRA is clearly an older and better recognized firm, their success has been in gathering a different kind of information than we currently require. IEI has the advantages of having done attitudinal studies and of knowing the Boston environment, but they appear to be wed to the high-tech industry and its problems; moreover, as I've said, I'm not confident that Robertson has the appropriate skills for this project. Kidd Associates, as we know, has done many studies on human relations problems—including one that was successfully accomplished for Sta-Brite.

Concerning the services each could deliver, DRA's offer to report on the plans of other firms seems to me to parallel work that we could do on our own. I already have a pretty good start on collecting this information, and I feel confident that with the capabilities offered by Marla Johnson's office, I can complete the job. Clearly, we would do better to pay for someone to help us administer the survey of our own employees. Both IEI and Kidd will do this for us, but Kidd will also conduct focus groups—a feature that would unquestionably be very valuable. Putting people together who have opposing viewpoints will help us to evaluate the real strength of their feelings and attitudes.

Finally, I think there's no question but that we'll benefit from Kidd Associates' previous success in working within Sta-Brite's environment, as well as from their enthusiasm for the current study.

RECOMMENDATION

Unless you and Jed can find some overriding reason to select one of the first two candidates, I believe we should accept Kidd Associates' proposal. I therefore suggest that I invite Marvin and Molly Kidd to visit our offices next week to meet with Jed, Pauline, you, and me to discuss their proposal in further detail and to initiate their part of the study.

Attachments

1. Proposal: Data Research Associates
2. Proposal: Information Experts, Inc.
3. Proposal: Kidd Associates
4. Brochure: DRA
5. Résumé: John Robertson, IEI
6. Letter from Jasper Night, Vice President of Human Resources, First Bank of Chicago
7. Internal memo from Pauline Atticus re Kidd Associates
8. Brochure: Kidd Associates

**Commentary on Scott's Interim Report.** Scott had been under pressure to gather his data and select a consultant in fairly short order. He therefore had to design the scope of his research carefully. It had been established that he would investigate only three candidates in depth, but he did have to decide which three. Marla Johnson had provided him with a list of possible candidates, and he had reviewed it with Kim and Pauline. He selected three front-runners, who could each bring very different qualifications and skills to the project.

But having chosen his three top candidates, Scott still had to set further boundaries in regard to the scope of his research. What criteria should he use to measure suitability for this job? Although cost was certainly the most obvious criterion, he knew that it could not be the sole factor in his decision. And, as it turned out, the slight difference in the fees proposed made price important only in reference to the services each offered to perform. He decided on his other two criteria—*experience* and *style*—while reviewing the literature each firm had sent for him to examine.

In actually writing his report, Scott also faced several important decisions. First, he needed to decide whether to announce his recommendation at the outset or to argue to the point. Second, he had to decide how much detail to include in the body of his report and how much to rely on the attachments. Finally, he needed to feel confident that he had written in a tone and style that were appropriate to the occasion and reflected his working relationship with Kim.

Scott opted for witholding his recommendation until he had developed his arguments. He felt that, given Kidd Associates' relative newness to the field of consulting and also the firm's location in the Midwest, he should forestall Kim's initial surprise and possible objection to his choice. Moreover, it was Kim who had first mentioned IEI, and he suspected she might favor it slightly.

To build a persuasive case for Kidd Associates, Scott decided that he would stay within the parameters of his three criteria, but he would also be careful to supply sufficient data concerning each. He did not, for instance, merely state that Kidd Associates would do more; he specifically documented what each firm would do. Nor did he just assert that the other firms lacked appropriate experience; rather, he supported that viewpoint by specifying the particular focus of each. Most important of all, he presented his arguments with consistency and genuine objectivity. Scott not only carefully researched and ordered his data but also analyzed the information thoughtfully and honestly.

He also gave a great deal of thought to selecting the data to present. Although he did not want to omit important details, Scott also tried not to clutter the report with facts that did not bear directly on the case he was making. But to be entirely certain that he was not unfairly stacking the deck, he included as attachments all of the literature he had received; and, at the end of the report, he called attention to each item.

Perhaps the most difficult decision Scott faced in writing this report was how to handle the unpleasant go-around with John Robertson, IEI's rather brash and condescending young Senior VP. On the one hand, considering that Kim might know Robertson personally, Scott had been tempted not to mention that painful interlude; on the other hand, he also felt a strong urge to highlight the fact that "the guy was a bona fide turkey."

The course he chose was to provide Kim with a factual account of what had occurred and to interpret those facts in the light of what they could mean to the project. In doing so, he couched his feelings in language that was both tactful and appropriate to the occasion. (A week later at lunch, Kim laughingly asked Scott to say a bit more about that encounter. And he did!)

## ■ The Sta-Brite Corporation: Case History (3)

Kim forwarded Scott's report to Jed with a cover memo stating that she agreed with the recommendation. Within the week a meeting was held with Marvin and Molly Kidd to make sure that all concerned understood their responsibilities and to establish time parameters for each part of the study. Jed, Kim, Pauline, Scott, and two specialists from Sta-Brite's data-processing department attended the round-table discussion in the third-floor conference room. Jed chaired the meeting and kept the proceedings informal.

Ten minutes into the meeting, Molly Kidd addressed the group: "I think that we'd be wise to see this research as a three-stage process. The first two stages—gathering the data on attrition and tardiness and designing the survey instrument—can occur simultaneously. I'd like to complete a preliminary analysis of all these data before we conduct the interviews and focus groups. In that way, I believe, we will be able to do a better job of selecting people to participate."

After some discussion, in which it was agreed that the interview process should begin in approximately six weeks, Jed suggested the following assignment of roles and responsibilities. Kim would oversee the collection of the data from Sta-Brite personnel records and would be responsible for its accuracy. She would be fully supported by the two people from data processing. She and Jed would jointly analyze these data, and Kim would write an interim report. Their findings would then be sent to the Kidds for further analysis and interpretation. Kidd Associates would deliver their final analysis at an informal presentation in Boston.

While Kim was assembling her report, Scott would stand ready to assist her; but his primary responsibility at that time would be to work closely with the Kidds to see that they had access to any information they might need, and to facilitate the distribution and collection of the survey form. In addition, he would be responsible for a preliminary review of Kim's interim report, also making sure that he would be able to respond to any questions that Marvin or Molly might raise concerning the data supplied.

When all the data were collected (Kim's research completed, the survey results analyzed, and the interviews and focus groups completed), the Kidds would provide a formal presentation of the data as well as their analysis and recommendations. It would be followed by an open discussion of their findings, with an eye to making a formal recommendation to Sta-Brite's Management Committee.

Scott felt a sense of mingled pain and pleasure when Jed turned to him near the end of the meeting and announced, "And by that time, Scott, I'm going to assume that you will be our resident expert on this matter. I'll want you to flesh out that research you did for us earlier—you know, the stuff you had on national trends and what other corporations are doing—and then use all that we've got to draft the final report for the Management Committee. Kim and I will review it carefully, but I'm confident that you can give us a draft that will need very little attention from us. And actually, we won't have much time to fine-tune it. I'd like to have our recommendations in the hands of the committee within ten days of our final meeting with Molly and Marvin."

## Process: Preparing a Schedule

Contemplating his heavy responsibilities over the next several weeks, Scott recognized that he would need to budget his time carefully. Since he knew that he would have to be extremely flexible in his ability to respond to the Kidds' requests for assistance, it seemed imperative to maintain control of the time needed to carry out his two critically important tasks: reviewing Kim's report and drafting the final report.

His first step was to phone Kim and request that she instruct him as to what kind of editorial assistance she would require—copyediting, style editing, or an in-depth analytical review. He was relieved to hear that, although she would welcome any suggestions he might want to make, she primarily wanted him to proof the statistical data carefully and to see that there were no punctuation, grammar, or spelling errors in the report. This part of his assignment, he felt, could probably be handled in a single day. But preparing the final report draft was another matter.

Scott first listed all of the components of the task, and then, to the best of his ability, allocated the time he anticipated he would need to complete each one. He next blocked out these time periods on his calendar—recognizing, of course, that when the Kidds required his assistance, he would have to juggle his time slots. His list of components and time estimates was as follows:

| | |
|---|---|
| Library and on-line research | 2 days |
| Reviewing Kim's report | 1 day |
| Kidd Associates' presentation and meeting | 1 day |
| Prewriting (sorting and organizing all available information) | 2 days |
| First draft | 3 days |
| Word-processing assistance and chart production | 2 days |
| Revisions | $\frac{1}{2}$ day |
| Word processing of revised copy | $\frac{1}{2}$ day |
| Proofing | $\frac{1}{4}$ day |

Scott saw that, even without factoring in the time he would need to spend with the Kidds, he had allocated over two work-weeks for carrying out these responsibilities. And since Jed said that he wanted to deliver the final report to the Management Committee within ten days of Kidd Associates' presentation, if Scott included time for Jed and Kim to review his draft there would not be a moment to spare.

**Commentary.** Scott's report is meant for top management at his company. Therefore, on a spectrum of least formal to most formal, it stands with those reports that require a very high degree of formality. The only reports that might require even more formality are those intended for high-level external audiences. The primary distinction, as with proposals, is that external reports are covered by a transmittal *letter* rather than a transmittal memo; also, in some cases a submittal letter is bound into the report.

Before examining major sections of the draft that Scott presented for approval, we will (as we did in Chapter 14) review the standard components of a formal report.

**Transmittal Letter or Memo:** See Chapter 14, page 362.

**Cover and/or Title Page:** See Chapter 14, pages 362–63.

**Submittal Letter:** See Chapter 14, page 363.

**Table of Contents:** If the report is long, page numbers should be provided for major and secondary headings.

**List of Figures:** If there are numerous charts or graphs, or even a few critical ones, a list of figures should be provided.

**Glossary:** Where many technical terms or acronyms are used in the text, a glossary should be provided.

**Executive Summary:** As a rule of thumb, the longer the report, the more complex the data, and the more senior the audience—the more essential the executive summary. Unlike the abstract that often precedes an academic paper or formal research report, the executive summary is not a general description of the content. Rather, it distills the major points, enabling readers to decide whether to read the report carefully, to scan it, or to pass it on. If the chief conclusions or recommendations are highly sensitive or controversial, the executive summary may omit them and focus instead on the purpose or problem and the objectives. The chief arguments can then be built inductively (data or findings first) into the body of the report.

In a formal report, the executive summary will include some or all of the following components:

| | |
|---|---|
| **Purpose or Position Statement:** | The overriding reason why the report is being written, or the chief inference drawn from the sum of the major conclusions |
| **Background:** | Information needed for comprehending the purpose of the report and its specific objectives |
| **Scope:** | The set limits concerning what the report will examine |
| **Objectives:** | Specific beliefs the report intends to convey, or actions it intends to bring about |
| **Conclusions:** | The chief inferences drawn from the key findings |
| **Recommendations:** | Steps that should be taken in the short or long term. |

**Body of the Report:** As in a proposal, all of the elements capsulized in the executive summary are expanded in the body. The order of these elements will depend on the readers' needs and the writer's strategy. For instance, at times background will need to be provided before the purpose can be explained; at other times the first item discussed should be the purpose. Similarly, sometimes the major conclusions need to be examined in detail before the main purpose of the report can be understood. It is also possible for two elements to be appropriately combined into a single section. Frequently, for instance, the report's background and objectives are handled in one section. Another common technique is to combine the scope and objectives.

**References:** References are usually given for quoted materials and major sources of information. Documenting systems vary from company to company (and from college to college). If no system is recommended, use an accepted guide such as *The Chicago Manual of Style.* Supply references to give credit to sources and to enable readers to return to the source materials for further study. Try to be truly helpful, not to impress readers with your hard work. Don't clutter business documents with notes on multiple sources containing identical material. (Note that on page 4 Scott referred only to the primary source, the report published by the Department of Health and Human Services, rather than to the many periodicals containing the same data. On the other hand, at the end of the report, he listed the chief articles as secondary references for those readers who might care to review them.)

**Appendixes:** Include as appendixes documents containing significant supporting data or information relevant only to secondary audiences.

Figure 15.6 outlines the components and structure of a typical formal report. Although this illustration should help you to envision how the pieces fit together, it should not be used as a matrix for all your formal reports. You will deepen your understanding of how and when to use these components by giving careful thought to how Scott incorporated them into his draft of the child-care report.

## Product: Scott's Formal Report

The actual report, including the Appendixes, was over 25 pages in length. Figures 15.7 through 15.12 show portions selected to highlight the overall writing strategy and treatment of the formal elements.*

---

*Although the excerpts on pages 406–19 have been numbered to show standard practice, some page numbers differ—because of omissions—from those in Scott's Table of Contents on page 405.

**Components of a typical formal report.**

- *Transmittal Letter* (not bound)
- *Cover*
- *Table of Contents*
- *List of Figures*
- *Executive Summary*
    Purpose
    Scope
    Background and Objectives
    Conclusions
- *Body of Report*
    Position Statement
    Conclusion A
        Finding 1
            Factual Support
        Finding 2
            Factual Support
    Conclusion B
        Finding 1
            Factual Support
        Finding 2
            Factual Support
        Finding 3
            Factual  Support
    Recommendation A
    Recommendation B
- *References*
- *Appendixes*

**Figure 15.6**

TO:   The Management Committee, Sta-Brite Corporation
FROM: Jed MacDonald, Vice President, Human Resources
DATE: October 4, 198-
CC:   K. L. Matsushita, P. T. Atticus, S. E. Stanton; Marvin H. Kidd
      and Molly P. Kidd, Consultants

The accompanying report represents approximately three months of intensive research geared toward understanding and responding to one of the major causes of attrition, absenteeism, and tardiness at Sta-Brite. The problem examined concerns the increasing pressures on working parents who hope to provide a safe and caring environment for their children during the normal workday. Not only does this problem inhibit productivity, but also, as the study has shown, companies responsive to this need are excelling in recruiting qualified workers and managers.

This report presents an overview of the problem nationally and an in-depth examination of its effects on Sta-Brite. In addition, it contains specific recommendations for building a strong child-care program at Sta-Brite.

I invite the committee to give immediate attention to this pressing matter. As an initial step, I suggest that we set a time for the consultants and research team to meet with committee members to discuss these findings in further detail and to establish exact time parameters for carrying out the recommendations of this report.

**Figure 15.7** Scott's Transmittal Memo.

A CHILD-CARE PROGRAM AT
STA-BRITE CORPORATION


Submitted to
THE STA-BRITE MANAGEMENT COMMITTEE


Prepared by
Jed MacDonald, Vice President of Human Resources
Kim L. Matsushita, Director of Personnel
Scott E. Stanton, Personnel Specialist


October 4, 198-

**Figure 15.8**  Cover Page of Scott's report.

TABLE OF CONTENTS

**Figure 15.9**   Table of Contents of Scott's report.

LIST OF FIGURES

**Figure 15.10**  List of Figures from Scott's report.

## EXECUTIVE SUMMARY

This study establishes that Sta-Brite should take affirmative steps to meet the child-care needs of our employees, and most specifically that the company should build and operate a prototype day-care center at our Boston headquarters.

### BACKGROUND

In recent years the nation has seen dramatic shifts in the composition of the workforce. Most evident are the facts that 52 percent of all American women now work outside the home and that 60 percent of all two-parent homes depend on two paychecks. During these recent years, Sta-Brite has experienced increasing absenteeism, tardiness, and attrition. Therefore, we conducted an in-depth study to see if there is a direct relationship between these problems and the increasing needs and anxieties faced by working parents.

### SCOPE AND OBJECTIVES

The study focused on our Boston headquarters and our Chicago facility. Working with outside experts for the past three months, we surveyed employees and conducted a series of interviews and focus groups to evaluate relevant needs and attitudes. Comparing the results of this research to existing personnel data, we hoped to learn the extent of our problems at Sta-Brite and to set appropriate goals for remedying them.

### CONCLUSIONS

The data indicate that a relationship does exist between increased absenteeism, tardiness, and attrition and the problems of Sta-Brite's working parents. The study suggests that these problems

**Figure 15.11**   Executive Summary from Scott's report.

bear directly on employee morale and productivity. There is evidence that a strong child-care program might greatly benefit our recruitment program. Finally, the study establishes that a substantial number of Sta-Brite employees would support our opening some portion of a company day-care facility to the community at large.

RECOMMENDATIONS

The report recommends that the following actions be approved by the Management Committee:

o Sta-Brite should build and operate a prototype day-care and drop-off center at its Boston headquarters.

o Paternity leave should be added to Sta-Brite's current employee benefits package—to be awarded on an as-needed basis.

o Sick time should be granted to parents with seriously ill children.

o The Personnel Department should evaluate all existing benefits bearing on the needs of working parents and provide a detailed report on how these benefits might be strengthened.

**Figure 15.11** Continued

## PURPOSE OF THE STUDY

The overriding purpose of this study was to determine whether Sta-Brite Corporation would benefit from embarking on a program to assist working parents in providing care for their children during the workday, and to examine what specific programs and policies, if any, would be most effective now and in the future.

## BACKGROUND

Demographic trends within the nation's workforce are affecting the majority of U. S. corporations and in the past two years have had evident repercussions at Sta-Brite. Specifically, these trends are the increasing number of women in the workforce, the increasing number of single parents, the emergence of dual-career families, and the scarcity and high cost of quality private day care.

Among the most striking facts about these demographic trends are the following:

o   Fifty-two percent of American women now work outside the home, and 49 percent of these women have preschool children.[1]

o   Over two-thirds of American women of child-bearing age now participate in the workforce—a marked increase since ten years ago. (Appendix A provides an analysis of women in the workforce by age, industry, and job level.)

o   Sixty percent of all two-parent homes in the United States receive two paychecks.

o   The number of single-parent families has increased 80 percent during the past ten years.

[1]The data presented here were drawn from Day Care In America, United States Department of Health and Human Services, March 198-, pp. 8–25.

**Figure 15.12**   Portions of the body of Scott's report.

Among those facts bearing on the availability of day-care assistance, the following are most notable:

o   Ten percent of the gross income of American working families goes to day care, making it the fourth largest expenditure (after housing, food, and taxes).

o   In 1965, 11 percent of American three- and four-year-olds were in nursery school (approximately 886,000 children). In 1983, 36 percent of the three- and four-year-old group were enrolled in nursery schools (over 2.5 million children).

o   The U.S. birth rate, which peaked in the 1950s and then began to decline, is once again steadily increasing.

o   By 1990, an estimated 10.5 million American children will have mothers in the workforce.

o   For every available day-care slot at present, there are 6.2 children.

With these facts in mind, we need not wonder that Sta-Brite's employees, when surveyed, overwhelmingly indicated that they are having difficulty finding appropriate day-care facilities for their children. Moreover, since the average age of all Sta-Brite employees is 30.6 years, and since 59 percent of the female employees (who represent 65.1 percent of our workforce) are of child-bearing age, we can see that this problem is companywide and is becoming more critical with each passing month.

## SCOPE AND OBJECTIVES

The study entailed two primary areas of investigation and a third that surfaced as part of the ongoing research. The first two areas included a study of Sta-Brite's personnel records during the past two years (on recruitment, attrition, and absenteeism) and a study of employee attitudes and behavior conducted at our Boston headquarters and our Chicago facility. The third area represented preliminary research into the question of how the issue of day care intersects with Sta-Brite's commitment to good citizenship in the communities in which we operate.

The four specific objectives of the study were the following:

I. To learn how escalating child-care needs are affecting Sta-Brite employees and to determine whether there is a direct relationship between these needs and Sta-Brite's increasing rates of <u>absenteeism</u>, <u>tardiness</u>, and <u>attrition</u>.

II. To learn whether increased child-care benefits would significantly aid us in our <u>recruitment efforts</u>—both at managerial levels and in employee ranks.

III. To examine what child-care <u>options</u> are available and currently offered by other corporations, especially by our competitors; in addition, to determine which of these options, if any, are appropriate for Sta-Brite.

IV. To examine the proposition that Sta-Brite might enhance its image as a corporate citizen by opening an on-site day-care center that would allow <u>enrollment of children from neighboring communities</u>.

APPROACH AND METHODOLOGY

Our approach in this study was both quantitative and qualitative. Using two years of personnel data, we attempted to identify trends in absenteeism and attrition according to employees' age, sex, and level. We also compared Sta-Brite's rates with those of companies with on-site day-care facilities. In addition, we . . . .

*Relying heavily on information in Kim's interim report, Scott presents a detailed description of how the personnel research was accomplished.*

In evaluating employee attitudes and needs, we also depended on quantitative data. Through a carefully administered survey, we were able to quantify . . . .

*Here Scott abstracts information from hard copies of the transparencies used in Kidd Associates' formal presentation. He also refers readers to Appendix B, a complete copy of the survey instrument.*

Qualitative data were secured by interviewing Sta-Brite employees both at Boston headquarters and in Chicago . . . .

*A description of how interviewees were selected and the interview methodology follows.*

Focus groups were also used to test . . . .

*Focus group methodology is explained here.*

Concerning the effects of child-care needs on our employees, the data clearly show a direct negative effect on productivity through increased absenteeism and tardiness, as well as through lowered morale. In addition, the evidence indicates that some valuable employees (at managerial and at worker levels) have left the firm, usually permanently, to resolve the conflicting needs of parenting and employment.

I. ABSENTEEISM, TARDINESS, AND ATTRITION

Personnel records indicate that in the last two fiscal years absenteeism has increased at a rate of 3.8 percent per quarter and that tardiness has increased at the rate of 4.7 percent (see Figure 1). If we compare these trends to rates of absenteeism and tardiness ten years ago, we find . . . . (See Figure 2.)

Sta-Brite's Personnel Department maintains a detailed file of counseling, disciplinary, and exit interviews. These records indicate . . . .

A detailed discussion of these findings follows.

When surveyed, over three-quarters of our Boston and Chicago employees indicated that they knew of an employee who had been absent or tardy in order to care for a child's needs; 35 percent indicated that they personally had been absent or tardy for a similar reason. . . .

A detailed discussion of the survey results pertaining to absenteeism and tardiness follows.

Interviews and focus groups elicited many relevant comments concerning this issue: . . .

A compilation of comments and observations follows.

In regard to attrition, the numbers are not as powerful. As a firm with an exceptional reputation for generous benefits and fair treatment of our employees, we have not yet suffered from an increasing number of departures of qualified employees. Nevertheless, since it costs us approximately $5000 to find and train a qualified manager or first-level supervisor, the loss of even a few such valuable employees is significant.

Exit interviews over the last two years have revealed that at-trition due to child-care problems has already occurred. These inter-views also showed that . . . .

What follows next is a discussion of findings from exit interviews.


We therefore conclude that both absenteeism and tardiness have increased as a direct result of child-care needs. Attrition may also . . . .

## II. RECRUITMENT EFFORTS

The discussion of data, findings, and conclusions concerning recruitment follows.


## III. OPTIONS APPROPRIATE FOR STA-BRITE

Among the various options open to Sta-Brite in establishing a program to assist working parents are the following:

o   Building and operating a child-care center (either alone or with a consortium of nearby companies) for preschool children only, or for preschool children with a drop-off center for children aged 5–8

o   Establishing a fund to start a day-care center and reserving a percentage of places for Sta-Brite employees' children

o   Setting up a referral center to counsel parents on the availabil-ity of child-care facilities

o   Offering financial aid to reimburse employees for child-care costs o   Establishing paternity leave as a benefit

o   Increasing existing benefits, including sick-time allowance for parents of ill children and expanded flextime and work-at-home programs

Both the anticipated improvement in productivity and recruitment and the strong preferences on the part of Sta-Brite's employees indicate that we should give serious consideration to building and operating on-site child-care centers. Such facilities should also serve as referral centers and as drop-off centers for after-school care of children in grades one through three. Moreover, we should investigate granting paternity leave on an as-needed basis. And we should also take any necessary steps to strengthen our existing benefits program to meet these needs.

These conclusions are supported by the attitudes and preferences expressed by Sta-Brite's employees on the survey reproduced in this report (Appendix B). As the results of the survey show, over one-third of our employees in Boston and Chicago maintain that they would use a day-care facility, and an equally high percentage favor the other options listed. Figure 3 provides a breakdown of the results of Questionnaire A, the section of the survey that examines these attitudes.

A detailed discussion of the results of the survey as illustrated in Figure 3 follows. This section of the report also examines programs currently offered by competitors.

FIGURE 3

Results of Questionnaire A:

EMPLOYEE ATTITUDES REGARDING DAY-CARE PROGRAMS

(88.6% of Employees in Boston and Chicago Responding)

| Attitude | Exempt | Nonexempt | Men | Women |
|---|---|---|---|---|
| (1) Would favor a corporate day-care facility | 45.3% | 41.2% | 36.5% | 48.9% |
| (2) Would use a corporate day-care facility | 38.6 | 30.8 | 23.9 | 36.7 |
| (3) Would favor internal child-care referral service | 45.2 | 29.6 | 25.4 | 35.7 |
| (4) Would favor increased use of flextime | 50.9 | 40.3 | 35.2 | 43.7 |
| (5) Would favor longer maternity leave | 28.6 | 33.6 | 21.6 | 35.8 |
| (6) Would favor paternity leave | 30.6 | 23.7 | 26.1 | 29.9 |
| (7) Would favor sick time for parent of ill child | 40.8 | 38.9 | 22.8 | 40.7 |
| (8) Would favor after-school drop-off facility | 39.7 | 40.6 | 27.9 | 35.7 |

## IV. ENROLLMENT OF COMMUNITY CHILDREN

This section presents a discussion of this issue, based on Sta-Brite's record of community involvement and on the current study of employee attitudes.

### SUMMARY OF CONCLUSIONS AND RECOMMENDATIONS

Based on the evidence we have examined, we conclude that Sta-Brite is feeling the stress of social change and must respond quickly and effectively. The great influx of women with children into the workforce and the appearance of the dual-income family have saddled our employees with a heavy burden. Our mounting rates of absenteeism and tardiness are a direct outgrowth of these conflicts. Even where the symptoms of stress are silent, interviews and focus groups have shown that valuable employees have been forced to compromise between their parenting responsibilities and their jobs. In some cases, as exit interviews reveal, a point is reached where a highly trained specialist or professional chooses to leave the company permanently.

Although we have abundant data to support our conclusion that child-care problems have had a negative effect on employee morale and productivity, we cannot as easily support our belief that a strong child-care program would substantially improve our recruitment efforts. On the other hand, companies that offer such benefits are enthusiastic about their positive effect on recruitment; moreover, the list of such companies includes one of our strongest competitors. At the very least, such a program would uphold our excellent corporate image and make us even more attractive to potential employees. As the research presented here has established, our current employees are extremely proud of Sta-Brite's posture as a good corporate citizen and are even in favor of including community children in our day-care program.

Our overall recommendation, therefore, is that Sta-Brite take immediate positive actions to assist working parents at all our facilities. We recognize that these steps must be taken in an orderly and timely way and therefore recommend the following two-phase program:

Corporatewide Benefits Program

Sta-Brite's Personnel Department should immediately begin to evaluate our current benefits program carefully to see how it can be improved or expanded to better meet the needs of working parents. Our preliminary evaluation suggests that offering paternity leave as needed should be the first benefit added. In addition, we recommend that sick time be granted to employees with seriously ill children.

A Prototype Day-Care Center in 198-

As soon as our current benefits program has been evaluated, Sta-Brite should begin to plan a day-care center to be operable at our Boston headquarters by the second quarter of 198–. This center should provide day care for preschool children and serve as an after-school drop-off center for children in grades one through three. In addition, the center's professional staff should provide a full range of information concerning alternative child-care options in the greater Boston area. Within two years after the Boston center is operating, a similar facility should be established at our Chicago location.

We further believe that Sta-Brite should allocate a portion of the available places in the day-care center to non—Sta-Brite children in the Cambridge-Boston area, and should work closely with both communities to maximize the center's services.

PRIMARY REFERENCES

Kidd, Marvin H., and Molly P. Kidd. "Day Care at Sta-Brite Corporation." A presentation delivered at Sta-Brite Corporation, Boston,
MA, July 15, 198-.

Day Care in America. Washington, D.C.: United States Department of
Health and Human Services, January 198-.

SECONDARY REFERENCES

Badger, John, and Mary B. Canton. Latchkey Children in America.
New York: McGraw-Hill Book Company, 198—.

Belasco, Allen D. "Fluid Work Hours Yield Dividends." The Boston
Globe, March 6, 198-, pp. 10–12, 14.

Grisby, Ellen. "Child Care: Employers Can Help." 9 to 5 News, April
1, 198-, pp. 3–5.

Michaels, Olivia. "Who's Raising Our Children?" Parade Magazine,
February 28, 198-, pp. 2–4.

Van Buren, Dennis K. "Corporate Kinder Care." The Wall Street
Journal, March 10, 198-, pp. 1, 22.

Weisman, Dale S. "Companies That Care." Management Review. New
York: American Management Association, April 198-, pp. 6–8.

**Commentary.** The formal report you just examined culminates a series of business transactions that occurred over a three-month period. It should not be construed as a *final* report; rather, it represents a major milestone in an ongoing process. Each initiative that carried Sta-Brite further toward an effective child-care program was derived from a previous effort. And each employed a written document of substance to move the enterprise forward and to capture and preserve what had already been accomplished.

If you carefully consider what you have read in Chapters 14 and 15, you will perceive that the processes and products of report writing are nearly inseparable; moreover, they are continuous. Information almost always is a catalyst producing a need for more information. For instance, Kim's study of previous reports on absenteeism and tardiness stimulated her concerns about working parents. Similarly, if Scott's formal report succeeds in its purpose, he and his colleagues will soon be reporting their findings concerning the company's existing benefits program.

It is also important to recognize that a major report is likely to create a widening circle of need for additional reports throughout the company. Scott's formal report can be expected to have such repercussions. Accounting will probably be asked to do a funding report. Human Resources may need to reevaluate Sta-Brite's entire employee benefits program, including the health and disability insurance currently available. Manufacturing may want to analyze the new program's expected impact on productivity. And Marketing and Public Relations may decide to propose ways to maximize the program's positive effect on Sta-Brite's image.

## ■ Summary

Although attempts have been made to classify various types of business reports, it is more useful to focus on what a report *does*. The two keys to developing a successful report are objectivity and consistency.

Objectivity derives from a chain reaction between hard work and integrity. It rests on an inner attitude that mandates playing fair with your reader, and a style that speaks calmly and with reason. It neither threatens nor cajoles, but it is definitely not afraid to stand its ground and make its meaning clear.

Consistency suggests a writer intent on uncovering meaning, one who organizes facts and ideas to move in a discernible and logical direction. The thinking process that produces a consistent report is reflected in the unity and coherence of its organization. A systematic network of subheadings guides the reader; signpost words, enumeration, prudent repetition, and parallel structure serve to highlight relationships and emphasize key points. All components of the report unite to form a harmonious whole.

# ■ Discussion Problems

**15.1**   Imagine that you've been assigned the task of reporting on the division of office space on the second floor of your company's headquarters. What are some of the factors that would determine the length of your report, the kinds of details it should include, and your ability to exert objectivity. If you weren't sure about any of these factors, how would you resolve your uncertainty?

**15.2**   Suppose that it is your job to report on the quarterly progress of your department and that this quarter the news is very mixed. How will you structure your report? Will you include all the news, both good and bad? Could you leave the bad news out altogether? Are there any other alternatives?

**15.3**   Your co-worker and good friend Charlie Mason is being considered for a higher-ranking position in the marketing department. The marketing manager has asked you to write a confidential objective appraisal of Charlie's performance and ability. What sort of information will you include in your report? Give examples where possible, and explain your response.

**15.4**   You have been asked to select a restaurant in which to hold a dinner party celebrating your company's fifteenth anniversary. The choice is between Maison Pierre, an elegant French restaurant, and House of Chang, a favorite Chinese eating place frequented by the company's CEO. In this context, give specific examples of sources, data, findings, conclusions, and recommendations.

**15.5**   Select three well-written, effective paragraphs from Chapters 13, 14, and 15. Explain and defend your choices.

**15.6**   Underline all the linking words and phrases and instances of parallel structure you see in Scott Stanton's interim report (pages 390–95). Are connections and transitions handled effectively in this report? If there are places where you could strengthen connections or make smoother transitions, point them out and provide appropriate revisions.

**15.7**   Choose a long news or feature article from a newspaper or magazine (one that has no divisional subheadings), and suggest useful subheadings.

**15.8**   Imagine that you are reporting the results of a market survey that was done to determine which Tuesday-evening television programs are watched regularly by families throughout the country. There are obviously several ways to subdivide your report. Which would be the most effective?

**15.9**   Think of a job you've held, and suggest how you would have structured a quarterly report to your immediate superior in which you listed all of your activities and accomplishments for a three-month period.

**15.10**   You've been asked to report on the feasibility of your company's switching to a four-day work week during the summer. This would require working longer hours from Monday to Thursday, and the whole staff would be affected by the change. You know that your boss has been one of the most enthusiastic supporters of this new idea, but your research clearly shows that the economic consequences to the company of a four-day week would be decidedly negative. How will you handle the situation? What are some relevant factors to be considered?

**15.11**  Choose one of the following situations calling for a report, and suggest probable subsections or divisions for structuring the final document. Indicate which divisions are major and which subordinate. Use your imagination to supply logical details, and try to sketch an outline of the report you would write.

- An office manager must evaluate the performance of two department secretaries.

- A production manager must evaluate three particular production-line systems that have been proposed to improve a particular production-line activity.

- A market analyst must report on strategies for improving the market share of a certain supermarket chain.

- An internal auditor must report on current telephone expenditures and provide recommendations for cost cutting.

- Management of a national fast-food franchise has asked a particular restaurant to report back on how it can increase its profit margin.

- A college president must summarize institutional activities during the past quarter for the board of trustees.

- A magazine publisher wants a report on the profile of that magazine's readership.

- An investment analyst reports to a client on the pros and cons of investing in a new shopping mall complex.

**15.12**  What are some of the major objectives of the transmittal letter that accompanies a formal report? How long would you expect such a letter to be under ordinary circumstances? What situations might require a longer transmittal letter? How do you decide which explanations belong in the letter and which in the report itself?

**15.13**  Referring to Scott's formal report, compare the transmittal memo (Figure 15.7), executive summary (Figure 15.11), and the body of the report (Figure 15.12). Discuss any differences you note in content, structure, or tone. Would you have treated any part differently?

**15.14**  Study Figure 15.1 for a few minutes, and then discuss the relationship of facts, findings, and conclusions. Give some examples of each. Why might it sometimes be necessary to report findings without conclusions or conclusions without recommendations? Would you ever present conclusions without describing your findings? Explain your answers, and give examples where possible.

# ■ Writing Tasks

**15.1**  As the assistant to the president of Southern Business College, you've been asked to draft a report analyzing the composition of the institution's board of trustees. After researching the backgrounds of the 34 board members, you compile the profile shown in Figure 15.13.

Write up the report, incorporating recommendations to the Trustee Nominating Committee regarding potential new appointments to the board. Include a brief executive summary at the beginning of your report.

| | Number | Percentage |
|---|---|---|
| Active trustees | | |
| (i.e., nonemeritus, nonhonorary) | 34 | |
| Average age of trustees | 57.64 years | |
| Still working | 24 | 70.6% |
| Retired | 10 | 29.4 |
| Alumni | 22 | 64.7 |
| Nonalumni | 12 | 35.3 |
| Female trustees | 5 | 14.7 |
| Male trustees | 29 | 85.3 |
| Minority trustees | 1 | 2.9 |
| Holders of two-year associate's degree only | 19 | 55.9 |
| Holders of graduate degrees | 4 | 11.7 |
| Educated at institutions other than | | |
| or in addition to SBC | 13 | 38.2 |
| Located out of state | 12 | 35.3 |

**Figure 15.13** Profile of the trustees of Southern Business College.

**15.2** Beverly Evans is Affirmative Action Coordinator for the Kincaid Corporation. The board of trustees recently requested a five-year report on the progress of Kincaid's affirmative action program. Beverly compiled the data shown in Figure 15.14. (The numbers are percentages.)

Draft Beverly's report, keeping in mind that your goal is to be able to report progress, even though there are obviously several areas that still need improvement.

**15.3** As the assistant to the vice president for academic affairs at Eastern Ivy College, it is your job to research data to determine which personal computer next year's business majors will be required to purchase. The initial criteria out-

| Job Title | White Males 1982 | White Males 1987 | White Females 1982 | White Females 1987 | Black Males & Females 1982 | Black Males & Females 1987 | Spanish Males & Females 1982 | Spanish Males & Females 1987 | Other Minorities 1982 | Other Minorities 1987 |
|---|---|---|---|---|---|---|---|---|---|---|
| Managers and professionals | 90 | 80.5 | 1.5 | 8 | 7.5 | 8 | 0 | 1 | 1 | 2 |
| Technical staff | 100 | 79.3 | 0 | 3 | 0 | 7 | 0 | 5.7 | 0 | 5 |
| Salespeople | 93 | 71 | 4 | 14 | 1.6 | 9.9 | 0.4 | 1 | 3 | 4.1 |
| Clerical | 53 | 30 | 36 | 40 | 9 | 12.6 | 0.1 | 9.2 | 1.9 | 8.2 |
| Skilled trades | 100 | 86.8 | 0 | 0.5 | 0 | 12.2 | 0 | 0 | 0 | 0.5 |
| Laborers | 98 | 53 | 0 | 5.2 | 1 | 30.6 | 0 | 8.8 | 1 | 2.5 |
| All categories | 89 | 66.8 | 6.9 | 10.4 | 3.2 | 11.6 | 0.1 | 4.4 | 1.2 | 3.7 |

**Figure 15.14** Data on Kincaid Corporation's affirmative action program.

lined by the Ad Hoc Computer Committee are that the personal computer should cost less than $1600, be extremely user-friendly, and be able to produce graphics and spreadsheets. The committee also expressed a high interest in some of the new portable machines. In addition, the committee suggested that students should purchase desk-top printers—although this is not to be mandatory.

Identify a personal computer that meets the minimum requirements, collect as much relevant data about the machine as you can, and write a recommendation to your boss, Dr. Michelle Chan. You can assume that you have also studied a number of other PCs and that you have selected this model over the others. If you are also able to recommend a printer, do so.

**15.4** Analyze the chart and graphs that appear in Figure 15.15. Write a brief report in letter form. Summarize the information contained in the figure and recommend a course of action to your clients, Mr. and Mrs. Ralph Simione, 345 Cliff Road, Newtown, Oklahoma. Assume that the Simiones financed their current home four years ago at 15 percent for $100,000 over 30 years. It is now September of the year graphed in Figure 15.15(c), and they have asked your advice concerning refinancing at this time.

**15.5** As a market analyst for a U.S. automobile manufacturer, your job is to make sure that your firm's new cars have the best possible chance of attracting the maximum number of buyers. The top management of your company is currently planning a new line of four-cylinder subcompacts, and you have been asked to research the probable impact of foreign imports on this new line. Use the resources of your library, starting with the *Readers' Guide to Periodical Literature*, to try to determine how the Voluntary Restraint Program on Imports is likely to affect the subcompact market during the next few years. Then draft a report recommending several major guidelines to follow in planning the details of the firm's new subcompact.

**15.6** You are employed by a consumer interest group, and your boss, Eileen Caitlin, has asked you to research the pros and cons of plastic versus paper grocery bags. You should cover such topics as efficiency, safety, durability, ecology, convenience, and cost to the retailer (you may assume the retailer will pass such costs on to the consumer). Establish a position protecting consumer interests. Draft a report to be sent by Eileen to other members of the group. This report is to be preliminary to a study they will be releasing to the media soon.

**15.7** You work for a large U.S. pharmaceutical firm that is currently considering building a plant in Puerto Rico. Research the probable tax advantages to your firm, but be careful to consider the potential impact of proposed changes in tax laws that will affect Puerto Rican investments. Once you have come to some preliminary conclusions, draft a report to Mark DiCarlo, Vice President of Foreign Operations, in which you defend your position for or against the new plant.

**15.8** As office manager in a busy law firm, it is your responsibility to recommend the most economic long-distance telephone service. After researching at least three major services, draft a report that compares them by cost, quality, and range of services, availability of credit-card options, and coverage of geographical areas. Assume that employees of the firm will be calling most parts of the United States frequently; Canada, Europe, and the Middle East fairly regularly; and other

## (a) Refinancing savings

| Original rate | Current monthly payment | Monthly savings at 13% | Annual savings at 13% |
|---|---|---|---|
| **$60,000, 30-year mortgage** | | | |
| 15.0% | 759 | 95 | 1,138 |
| 15.5 | 783 | 119 | 1,426 |
| 16.0 | 807 | 143 | 1,714 |
| 16.5 | 832 | 167 | 2,009 |
| 17.0 | 856 | 191 | 2,296 |
| 17.5 | 880 | 216 | 2,592 |
| **$120,000, 30-year mortgage** | | | |
| 15.0% | 1,518 | 190 | 2,275 |
| 15.5 | 1,566 | 238 | 2,851 |
| 16.0 | 1,614 | 286 | 3,427 |
| 16.5 | 1,663 | 335 | 4,018 |
| 17.0 | 1,711 | 383 | 4,594 |
| 17.5 | 1,750 | 432 | 5,184 |

## (b) Home refinance payback period

The lower the new mortgage rate, the less time needed to recoup the costs of refinancing. Figures are in months

Interest rate reduction

## (c) Home mortgage closing rates

**Figure 15.15**  Simione home refinancing.

foreign countries only occasionally. In addition, all the firm's lawyers must be able to call long-distance from their homes and from elsewhere at the firm's expense.

Your report should be in memo form and should contain tabulations of information arranged in an effective format.

1. Please identify the category that best describes yourself:
   ____ Faculty                              ____ Staff

2. In what town or city does your trip to campus originate?
   _____

3. Where do you work on campus? _____
                                        (name of building)

4. Please check off those times when you are on campus during a typical week of the fall
   semester:

   |            | Sun. | Mon. | Tues. | Wed. | Thurs. | Fri. | Sat. |
   |------------|------|------|-------|------|--------|------|------|
   | Morning    | ____ | ____ | ____  | ____ | ____   | ____ | ____ |
   | Afternoon  | ____ | ____ | ____  | ____ | ____   | ____ | ____ |
   | Evening    | ____ | ____ | ____  | ____ | ____   | ____ | ____ |

5. Do you own a car? Yes ____      No ____

6. If yes, do you generally drive to work? Yes ____      No ____

7. How did you arrive at work on Monday, October 7, 1985?

   ____ Drove own car
   ____ Passenger in car that parked on campus
   ____ Dropped off in car that did not park
   ____ Rode a bicycle
   ____ Took a bus
   ____ Took a taxi
   ____ Walked
   ____ Other (please specify) _____

If you drove (see question 7), please answer the following questions:

8. How many riders including yourself were in the car?
   One ____ Two ____ Three ____ Four ____ Five ____ Six or more ____

9. What time did you arrive on campus at the beginning of your day?
   _____ a.m.      _____ p.m.

10. Which entrance did you use to access the campus?
    ____ Main Street      ____ North Street      ____ West Road

11. What time did you leave campus at the end of your day?
    _____ a.m.      _____ p.m.

12. Which exit did you use to leave the campus?
    ____ Main Street      ____ North Street      ____ West Road

13. Did you move your car at any time during the day? ____ Yes      ____ No

14. Did you have difficulty finding a parking space? ____ Yes      ____ No

Comments:

**Figure 15.16**   Survey of parking at Southern University.

**15.9** Imagine that you are a planning analyst for Southern University in Austin, Texas, and your assignment is to submit a preliminary report on the results of the parking survey reproduced in Figure 15.16. The university is beginning to have a shortage of parking, and the administration is trying to determine how much additional parking might be necessary and where such parking might best be located.

Assume that the survey was distributed to 300 faculty and staff and you have received 250 responses. You should make up the responses yourself and include just enough statistical information in your report to be able to make some preliminary suggestions about additional parking.

**15.10** You work for a market research firm. A venture capital group has asked you to gather data on Videotext. They know that Videotext is a product that disseminates information using some sort of screen and that it has been highly successful in Europe, especially in England. On the other hand, it does not appear to be catching on in the U.S. market. Your client wants you to find out all you can about the product and to learn if it has any possibilities for growth in the United States. Use the resources of your library to research Videotext. You will not need to access an on-line data base, but if such help is available, use it. Write a short report recommending whether or not your client should pursue its interest in investing in Videotext.

**15.11** You are employed by a well-known chain of franchised stores specializing in expensive ladies' lingerie. As a product planning specialist, your responsibility is to oversee research into potential new product lines. Your manager has become interested in the question of whether the merchandise line might be broadened to include medium-priced items. He has therefore asked that you do some research on the Playtex line. He seems to believe that Playtex is no longer in business, and he'd like to know what happened to their customer base. Using the resources of your college or city library, provide him with a report on the current status of Playtex.

**15.12** In the fall of 1985, Pantry Pride (a conglomerate) decided to attempt to acquire Revlon. You are a strategic planning specialist for Da-Glo Cosmetics, Inc. Your manager has asked you to assist in researching this event for its strategy implications. Using the resources of your reference library (including on-line data bases, if available), find out as much as you can about this acquisition. Write a short report for your manager that explains what happened in 1985. Was Pantry Pride successful? Remember that the purpose of your report is to establish some guidelines for Da-Glo, where rumors have been heard that Acme Industries, also a conglomerate, may be looking for a cosmetic company to acquire.

**15.13** In 1985, R. J. Reynolds acquired Nabisco, and Phillip Morris acquired General Foods. You and a fellow student are account executives for a public relations firm. The two of you have been assigned as a team to provide public relations counsel to the Give-Smokers-A-Fair-Deal Committee, a group of lobbyists sponsored by the major tobacco companies. Your client has asked you to research and write a report on the reasoning underlying these acquisitions. The purpose is to determine whether acquiring these companies was sound strategy for the tobacco companies.

# GRAPHIC AIDS FOR REPORTS AND PRESENTATIONS

## 16

here is a good reason why so many successful business reports and presentations include graphic displays to reinforce the verbal message. Research psychologists assure us that we generally remember 20 percent of what we hear, but 50 percent of what we hear *and* see. In fact, only 10 percent of all learning occurs by listening; 80 percent occurs by seeing.

Equally important, most business information is by definition quantifiable. For example, sales figures, employment data, construction specifications, results of customer surveys, and records of expenses all are communicated more effectively by tables, charts, or graphs than by words alone. This means that when a report or presentation relies completely on a verbal description of numerical data, it probably needs more work. Even though you manage to communicate your information accurately and grammatically, if you're dealing with complex numerical data chances are that your readers or your listening audience will run out of patience long before you explain your last set of figures.

Compare the following prose description of one company's pretax profit over a five-year period to the simple line graph in Figure 16.1 which conveys the same information:

> Five years ago, in 1982, our actual pretax profit amounted to $1,802,659, measurably lower than the budgeted figure of $2,280,000 for that year. In 1983, however, the actual pretax profit of $5,826,079 was almost twice the conservative budget estimate of $3,300,000. This trend continued into 1984, when the actual profit was $5,692,523 again significantly higher than the $3,700,000 that had been budgeted. The year 1985 brought the highest discrepancy between actual and estimated profits: the budgeted figure remained at $3,700,000 while actual profits reached a surprising $7,908,710 (fully $4,200,000 above projections). But 1986 brought a disheartening reversal: although we budgeted a $6,500,000 pretax profit, the actual figure turned out to be a disappointing $5,835,009.

The implication is clear: if you want your readers or your audience to understand and retain as much of your report as possible, supplement your words with graphic displays. This is particularly true in cases where your message focuses on any of the following:

- A complex or technical product or process
- The analysis of relationships among parts to each other and to the whole

- Comparisons or contrasts of performance, size, amount, or duration
- Past achievements or future goals occurring over a specified time span

Since so many business reports, written or oral, contain one or more of the above kinds of information, you are bound to need a basic knowledge of graphic techniques.

# ■ Graphics for Written Reports

## Location and Numbering of Graphics

Locating graphic aids in the right place in your report makes them even more effective. If you have ever tried to read a lengthy report in which all charts and graphs were gathered in an appendix, then you already know how much placement matters. The goal is to make it easy on your readers. Therefore, unless a display seriously interrupts the narrative, insert it right after the place in the text that mentions the material in question. Such placement is almost always possible unless the illustration is very large or when a *series* of charts or graphs is necessary. Introduce a graphic aid with a simple statement like "Sales lagged behind production during 1985, as illustrated in Figure 3." Don't put the burden of proof on your exhibit by writing, for instance, "Figure 3 demonstrates that sales lagged behind production in 1985." Even worse, don't write something like "Figure 3 compares sales to production in 1985," which forces your readers to puzzle out your meaning.

Larger displays should appear on a separate page placed immediately after the page on which the material is first discussed. A graphic aid that is very complex might take more than a full page. One obvious solution is to produce an oversized page that is carefully folded so that the reader can open it easily.

Although you may choose to differentiate among tables, graphs, and illustrations (maps, diagrams, etc.), note that the current trend is to label all tables, charts, graphs, diagrams, and photographs with the word "Figure" followed by an Arabic numeral (1,2,3, etc.). If an appendix includes further illustrations those displays can be labeled Figures A, B, C, etc., to distinguish them from the ones placed in the main text.

## Title Captions

Every graphic aid you produce should have a clear, succinct caption. If at all possible, it should let your readers know precisely why the graphic is there. Don't force your readers to go back to the text in order to decipher the meaning of a display. It generally is not sufficient for the caption merely to indicate what the chart is *about*; even though the text has done so adequately, the caption should explain the display's significance. For

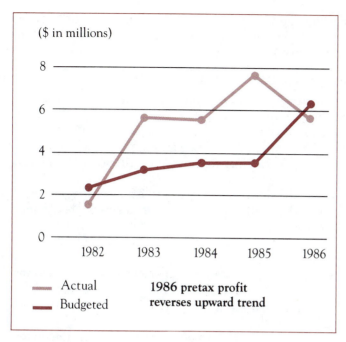

($ in millions)

Actual
Budgeted

**1986 pretax profit
reverses upward trend**

**Figure 16.1**
Graph of a company's pretax profit for 1982-1986 showing
how upward trend in actual profit ended in 1985.

example, a caption such as "Pretax profit (budgeted versus actual)" would
provide very limited help to a reader encountering Figure 16.1.

One good way of ensuring that a caption is on target is to remember
the five questions that journalists try to answer in the lead of each article:
who, what, when, where, and why. For instance, the caption of a chart
that compares average salaries of computer engineers employed by the Lattell Corporation during 1985 in their Boston and San Francisco offices
might be determined like this:

Who:   Lattell Corporation
What:   Average salaries of computer engineers
When:   1985
Where:   Boston and San Francisco
Why:   For comparison

The resulting caption would read "Average 1985 Salaries for Lattell Computer Engineers in Boston Exceeded Those in San Francisco."

As for placement of captions, a simple rule is to place all titles above the displays. Of course, the captions may appear below instead. The point is to choose one alternative and be consistent.

## Footnotes and Acknowledgments

If certain figures in your display require special explanation, use an asterisk or superscript number to indicate the presence of a footnote. Place the footnote immediately below the illustration, not at the bottom of the page. For example, if one of your numbers is an estimate, because the exact figure was unavailable at the time you were preparing your report, that fact should be mentioned in a footnote.

Another detail that should be footnoted is the source of your data if that source is someone other than you or your staff (for example, "*Source:* U.S. Bureau of the Census.").

## Using Tables

A table is simply the orderly presentation of data in rows and columns. But perhaps you have noticed that some tables are considerably more orderly than others. It takes some real thought to determine how the rows and columns should be labeled.

You should start by asking yourself what message you want to convey. If the data suggest no identifiable trend or pattern, you might need to rethink your table. Adding more data might help, but sometimes the solution calls for simplifying the table by including less data. Or you might want to consider combining your information with other related facts to arrive at a more interesting and relevant comparison.

Figure 16.2 is a standard table showing the usual components of a clearly ordered illustration. Keep in mind that Figure 16.2 is just one example of an acceptable format. There is room for variation here, as long as row and column labels are explicit and meaningful. Sometimes a caption head may be unnecessary; the word "Totals" is often indented or omitted altogether; if necessary, line titles can exceed one line, in which case the additional lines are often indented.

The secret of producing effective tables is to understand the significance of your data. In nine cases out of ten, your goal will be to convince your audience to accept a finding or to take some recommended action as suggested by the logic of your numbers. If your table lacks logic or if it suggests no particular course of action, you should consider starting over.

Worse than a "no message" table is one that distorts the available data to create a false message or to provide meaning where none exists. Unfortunately, since the misuse of business data is not always inadvertent, both as a reader and as a writer you should recognize that faulty labels, distorted graphs, or hidden data can produce misleading comparisons and false con-

| Line identification | Caption head | | |
| | Subcaption | Subcaption | Subcaption |
| Line title | XXXXX | XXXXX | XXXXX |
| Line title | XXXXX | XXXXX | XXXXX |
| Line title | XXXXX | XXXXX | XXXXX |
| Line title | XXXXX | XXXXX | XXXXX |
| Totals | XXXXXXX | XXXXXXX | XXXXXXX |
| Footnotes | | | |
| Source: | | | |

**Figure 16.2**   One standard table format.

clusions. For example, in a productivity study of two plants, the employee count at Plant A comprises full-time, part-time, and temporary workers, while that at Plant B comprises only full-time permanent workers. A chart with these numbers could not be used to justify a finding that Plant A is underproductive.

## Charts and Graphs

Tables are invaluable condensations of information that require no great degree of expertise to assemble. However, for more complex data, charts and graphs are often the better alternative. Especially when you need to emphasize relationships or make comparisons, graphic displays speak a language that the eye can interpret with great speed and precision. The key concept to understand here is that the type of chart or graph you choose should depend on the kind of relationships you want to illustrate.

**Pie Charts.** If you want to portray the size or importance of various parts relative to the whole, a pie chart is probably your best choice, especially if there are only a small number of segments to deal with. No matter how often this standard type of chart is used, it never seems to lose its effectiveness. Apparently, everyone is ready, willing and able to visualize component parts as larger or smaller portions of a whole pie.

The one sticky decision concerning the pie chart is where to place your labels. When the portions are large enough—and there are not too many of them—it's best to put the labels right on the pie. But for thinner

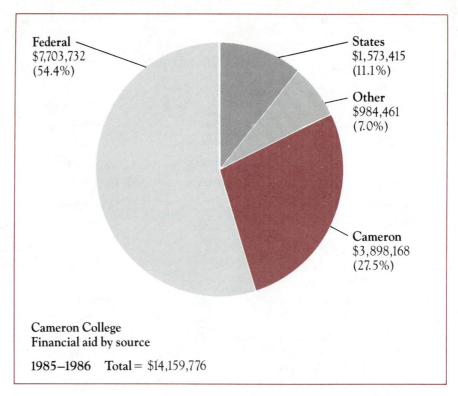

**Figure 16.3**
An example of a pie chart.

slices you will probably need to position your labels outside the circle and use lines or arrows to indicate which label applies to which segment. Another common technique is to separate and enlarge the segment you're highlighting, leaving the rest of the pie somewhat in the background.

Just remember that your total pie must always equal 100 percent and that each segment should be labeled by name (what item does it represent?) and by percentage (what portion of the entire 100 percent does this section represent?), and by dollar amounts, if relevant. And if you are producing your pie chart by computer, the convention is to cover each slice with a different pattern, such as cross-hatching, vertical or diagonal lines, or a dot pattern (see Figure 16.3).

**Bar Charts.** Bar charts are more versatile than pie charts. Like pie charts, they can be used to portray the parts of a whole, but bar charts are particularly effective in showing the components of *several* wholes simultaneously. As you can see in Figure 16.4, if you are indicating the different

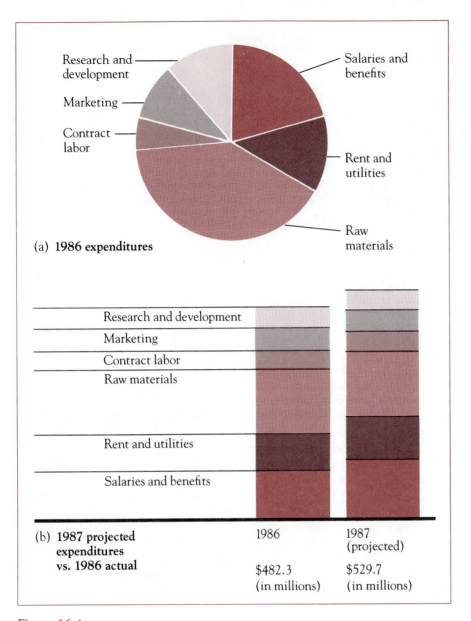

(a) **1986 expenditures**

Research and development

Marketing

Contract labor

Raw materials

Rent and utilities

Salaries and benefits

(b) **1987 projected expenditures vs. 1986 actual**

1986

$482.3 (in millions)

1987 (projected)

$529.7 (in millions)

**Figure 16.4**
(a) A pie chart is used to identify the components of a company's total expenditures for one year. (b) A bar chart works better for comparing expenditures during two years.

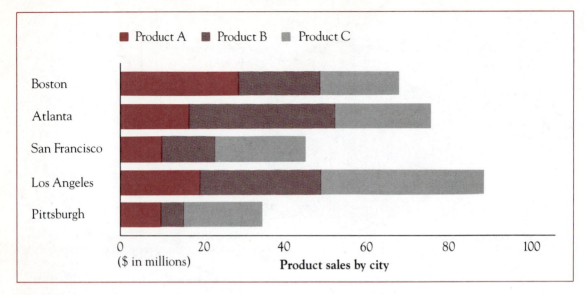

**Figure 16.5**
A horizontal bar chart showing sales in dollars of a company's three major products.

components of a company's total expenditures for one fiscal year, you will probably do best with a pie chart. But if your point is to compare total expenditures during 1985 with those projected for 1987, a bar chart (sometimes called a column chart) is the better choice. It is easier for the eye to compare two segmented bars than to compare two segmented circles.

Another obvious time to use bar charts is when your point is to compare the sizes or quantities of two or more items to each other but not to the whole. The amounts can be expressed in absolute numbers, in percentages, or just in relative lengths. Also, the bars can be drawn horizontally (as shown in Figure 16.5) or vertically.

But the greatest advantage of the bar chart is that it allows you to express variations over time. In this way you can emphasize trends and patterns of change by indicating how an element fluctuates in quantity over a given time period. For example, the following information about a company's sales over the past five years can easily be transformed into a meaningful bar chart (see Figure 16.6).

| Year | Sales (in thousands) |
|------|----------------------|
| 1982 | $ 5,480 |
| 1983 | 7,610 |
| 1984 | 7,250 |
| 1985 | 9,160 |
| 1986 | 10,510 |

**Figure 16.6**
A bar chart that reveals overall increase in a company's sales during a five-year period.

**Line Graphs.** Another way to illustrate variations over time (for example, in expenditures, sales, inventory, or personnel) is the line graph. You might prefer to use a line graph (sometimes called a "curve" graph) when there are many time periods to be plotted or when the variability of your separate elements is not particularly notable. A line graph is generally easier to draw than a bar chart (an important consideration when you don't have a computer or a graphics department at your disposal), and it is also more compact when you have a lot of data to plot. Finally, a line graph emphasizes the flow or shape of a change over time rather than the differences between separate items. If your main goal is to illustrate general trends rather than the rate of change from one point in time to another, then a line graph is very likely your best alternative.

In line graphs one axis usually indicates amounts or quantities of a given element, and the other axis represents progressive time periods. Figure 16.7 shows how the sales figures from 1982 to 1986 (depicted in a bar chart in Figure 16.6) are plotted as a line graph. The sales data can obviously be illustrated by bars or a line. You would probably choose the bar chart in this case if your point was to emphasize the large jump in sales be-

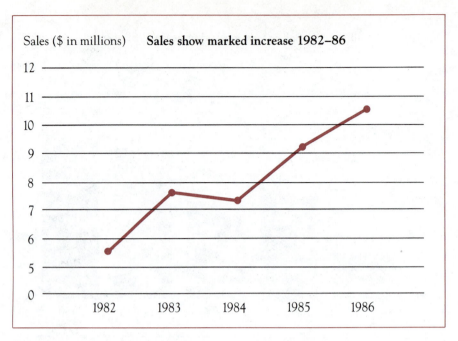

Sales ($ in millions)    **Sales show marked increase 1982–86**

1982  1983  1984  1985  1986

**Figure 16.7**
A line graph of the same sales data charted in Figure 16.6.

tween 1982 and 1983 and again between 1985 and 1986. If, on the other hand, you wanted only to indicate the general upward trend in sales growth, the line graph would better serve your purpose.

Line graphs work best to show the continuity of data over time. Regular price changes, weekly sales figures, and any kind of employee numbers can all be plotted effectively using curves.

A few basic rules must be followed to ensure that a line graph doesn't distort the reality of the numbers. First, draw a horizontal axis and join it on the left at a right angle to a vertical axis. Usually the horizontal axis indicates time, and the vertical axis shows values, as in Figure 16.8. Plot on graph paper or on a standard grid, so you will easily be able to place a point at the appropriate value for each of your time periods. After all your points are in place, simply connect them with straight lines to indicate actual figures or with dotted lines for projected figures (see Figure 16.9).

When labeling your axes, make sure that the proportions of your grid will result in a realistic presentation of your information. If, for example, the space separating the years on the horizontal axis is too narrow, the fluctuations in your data will appear to be extreme. Similarly, if you leave half an inch between each year or between each numerical label on your

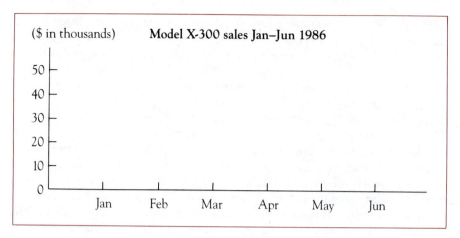

**Figure 16.8**
A format for a line graph to show sales during a six-month period.

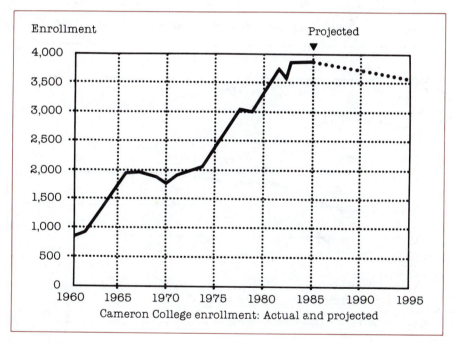

**Figure 16.9**
A line graph of enrollment at a college showing the use of a dotted segment of the curve to indicate projected figures.

vertical axis, then you can't just skip a year or two or jump from 5 to 8 with only a half inch between. This would distort your curve and mislead your audience about the nature of the trend of variation being illustrated.

More complicated line graphs often use lines of different types (solid, dashed, dotted, etc.) to compare more than one set of data on the same chart. In this case, be sure to limit yourself to no more than five or six different lines, and label each type clearly. (See Figure 16.10).

In a variation of the standard line graph, areas between lines are shaded to create the impression of a solid mass broken into component parts. Of course, you can only prepare this kind of graph if none of the lines cross each other. Imagine, for example, that your purpose is to compare the sales records of three different products over the past seven years, with an emphasis on the differences among those figures. You might begin by plotting the curve for each of the three products on the same set of axes. Then, by coloring or cross-hatching the areas between the curves, you can highlight the variations, as though three solid masses were being superimposed. Figure 16.11 exemplifies this useful technique.

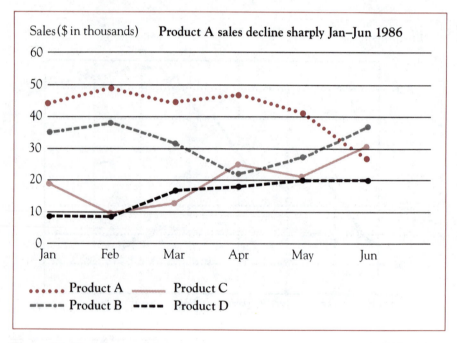

**Figure 16.10**
A composite line graph on which sales of four different products are plotted using four different types of lines.

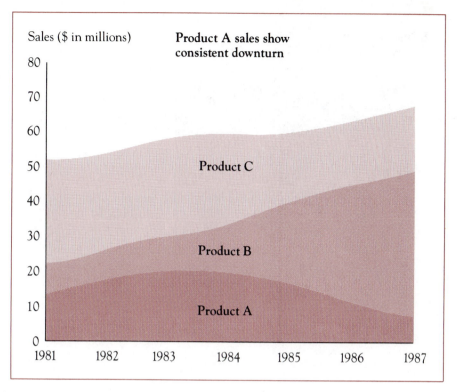

**Figure 16.11**
Shading of areas between curves used to highlight differences between sales figures.

If a line graph is computer-generated, as is Figure 16.9, the curve will probably be more accurate in reflecting the variations *between* the indicated time periods. This is possible because the computer can process more data (for example, daily as well as monthly variations). Also, the computer system's printer can provide a variety of shadings and cross-hatchings.

**Bubble Charts.** In today's corporations bubble charts are frequently used to compare the performances of competitors in an industry or of divisions within a company over a specified period of time. Among the performance indicators that might be shown in a bubble chart are market share, profitability, or productivity. The chart provides a visual comparison of how the competitors or divisions are performing. The respective sizes of the bubble indicate the size or strength of each competitor or division.

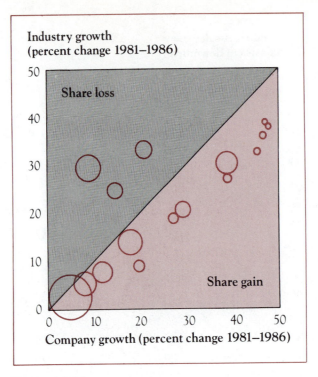

**Figure 16.12**
A bubble chart showing share gain and loss of a company's divisions.

The bubble chart shown in Figure 16.12 compares the share gain and loss of divisions within a company over a five-year period.

**Flow Charts.** Step-by-step directions, systems, and complicated processes are best depicted in flow charts. In a flow chart, boxes or simple shapes that suggest the units in question are connected by lines or arrows to show how they interact. Often these basic shapes contain key words and may be numbered to show the direction of the flow. Figure 16.13, for example, depicts the entire process by which an advertisement is created.

**Organizational Charts.** A flow chart that illustrates the interactions among or the reporting system of members of an organization is called an organizational chart. In this case, labeled boxes, connecting lines, and arrows are used to indicate who reports to whom, who shares authority with

**Creating an advertisement**

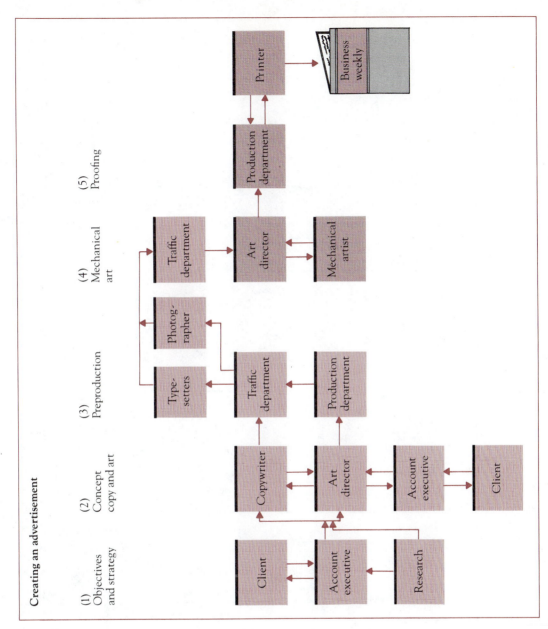

**Figure 16.13**  A flow chart illustrating the process of creating an ad.

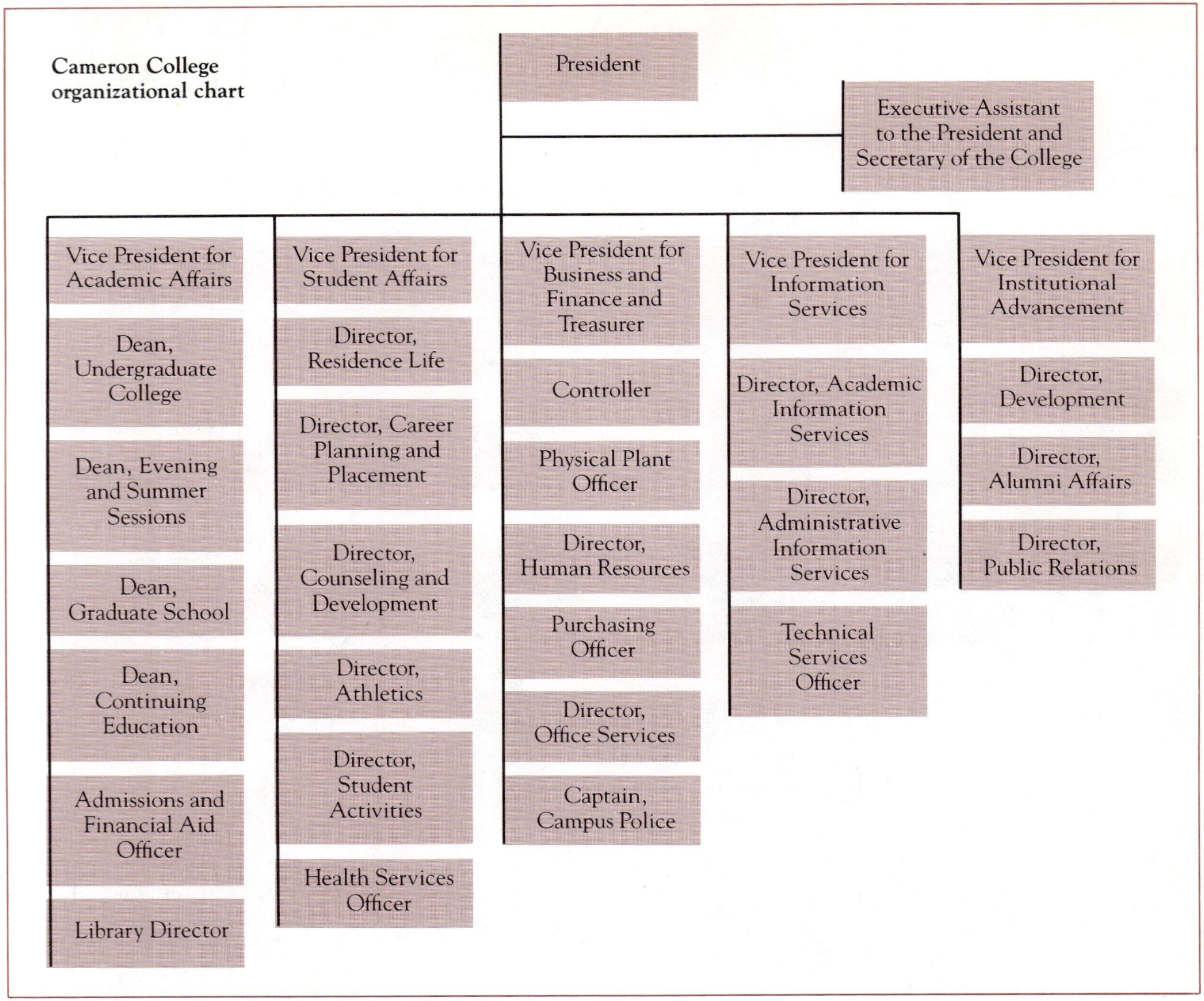

**Cameron College organizational chart**

**President**

**Executive Assistant to the President and Secretary of the College**

**Vice President for Academic Affairs**
- Dean, Undergraduate College
- Dean, Evening and Summer Sessions
- Dean, Graduate School
- Dean, Continuing Education
- Admissions and Financial Aid Officer
- Library Director

**Vice President for Student Affairs**
- Director, Residence Life
- Director, Career Planning and Placement
- Director, Counseling and Development
- Director, Athletics
- Director, Student Activities
- Health Services Officer

**Vice President for Business and Finance and Treasurer**
- Controller
- Physical Plant Officer
- Director, Human Resources
- Purchasing Officer
- Director, Office Services
- Captain, Campus Police

**Vice President for Information Services**
- Director, Academic Information Services
- Director, Administrative Information Services
- Technical Services Officer

**Vice President for Institutional Advancement**
- Director, Development
- Director, Alumni Affairs
- Director, Public Relations

**Figure 16.14** Organizational chart of the administration of a large college.

whom, and who has responsibility for what. Organizational charts can be vertical (reading from top to bottom), horizontal (reading from left to right), or even circular (showing organizational power emanating from the center). Sometimes, solid lines are used between boxes to indicate direct connections, and dotted lines to indicate indirect relationships.

For example, the organizational chart in Figure 16.14 illustrates the administrative framework of a large urban college. The president, with the help of an executive assistant, manages the activities of five vice presidents. Each of the vice presidents is in turn responsible for various college departments. Presumably, all of these departments have their own organizational structures, so this chart could be very much more complex. But by focusing on the managerial roles of the vice presidents, the chart is clear enough to be quickly understood. If the person presenting this chart wanted to introduce more details, he or she might create separate charts for each of the vice presidents and use progressive disclosure to display them. Frequently, employees need to understand complex reporting systems, and the organizational chart serves that purpose with surprising effectiveness.

**Pictograms.** A type of graph that is becoming more and more popular, especially in newspapers and magazines, is the pictogram. If you have artistic talent, computer graphics software, or graphic assistance available to you, you may want to impress your readers by sometimes employing pictograms. Essentially, a pictogram is a graph that uses simple pictures to represent numerical relationships. The picture should suggest the nature of the item being described. The most obvious examples are pictures of coins to illustrate financial figures or basic human shapes to represent numbers of people. Of course, there's plenty of room to use imagination here, as a glance at any major news magazine will demonstrate. But for the average report writer, the most basic pictograms will probably suffice. Without access to computer graphics, only a professional artist should experiment beyond the level of Figure 16.15, which uses a standard human symbol most effectively.

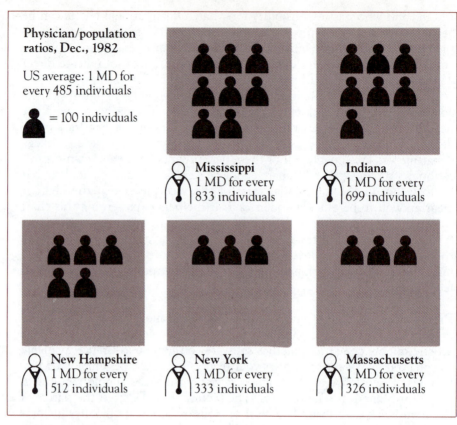

**Physician/population ratios, Dec., 1982**

US average: 1 MD for every 485 individuals

= 100 individuals

**Mississippi**
1 MD for every 833 individuals

**Indiana**
1 MD for every 699 individuals

**New Hampshire**
1 MD for every 512 individuals

**New York**
1 MD for every 333 individuals

**Massachusetts**
1 MD for every 326 individuals

**Figure 16.15**   A simple pictogram.

## ■ Graphics for Oral Presentations

Tables, charts, and graphs are suitable for both written and oral reports only if they are unquestionably clear and simple. Depending on the sophistication of your audience, you may sometimes be able to include rather complicated graphics in a written report. However, complex visuals are never effective in an oral presentation no matter how brilliant your listeners are.

Clarity is important to graphics found in written reports, but it is absolutely essential to graphics used in oral presentations. Visuals must be digested quickly during a spoken presentation; there is no time for the audience to decipher the significance of an ornate or exceedingly intricate chart. Even if the graphic aid has been carefully created, an audience can quickly lose interest while the speaker explains its intricacies. And even when you have produced clear, concise visuals, you will have to determine exactly when and how often to use them for maximum effectiveness.

## Which Medium to Choose?

The media most frequently used to present visual aids during business presentations include the following:

Chalkboard (traditional blackboard, sometimes portable)

Flipchart (a large pad on an easel, with brightly colored markers)

Overhead projector and screen (uses transparencies, sometimes called viewgraphs or foils)

Slide projector and screen

For a large audience, you almost certainly will want to use either transparencies or slides. The larger the room, the more formal the occasion, and the more ample your budget—the more likely it is that you will choose a slide presentation. Slides give a presentation a more finished and professional look, and they can be seen clearly even by people sitting in the rear of a very large room. Transparencies usually have a more homemade appearance; moreover, they lose their effectiveness and grow "thin" when the image needs to be greatly enlarged for viewing in a large room. However, slides do have some drawbacks. Unless your company has its own facilities for making slides, they can be time-consuming and costly to prepare. You will need to give your slide vendor plenty of lead time; and you must be willing to accept the reality that any last-minute changes are likely to be extremely expensive. Another possible drawback is that a slide presentation requires that you darken the room, hindering your ability to project your personality and your management style effectively.

When you are preparing a major presentation for a large audience, some of the important decisions will be made for you by your superiors. You will have to learn to live with this fact of life. The presence of the audience represents a large expenditure, in both time and money. Like yourself, the people who have come to hear you are paid for their time; moreover, travel and hotel accommodations are often necessary to bring key people to the presentation. When you are asked to choose the graphic medium yourself, you should, therefore, carefully evaluate the available options.

## How Many Visuals Are Too Many?

Visuals help to make ideas and concepts memorable. In addition, they clarify difficult or complex material, emphasize important points, and add considerable interest and variety to a presentation. Many speakers, however, diminish the power of their visuals by using too many of them. The trick is to use a visual only when you are sure you need emphasis or clarification.

How many visuals are the right number for a particular presentation? Some textbooks on speaking advise you to use about one visual every three minutes; others admonish you to use no more than ten in any presentation. Our advice is to be guided by the presentation itself, by the occasion, by the graphic medium, and by your own personal style of presenting. If you don't allow your graphics to serve as cue cards but do concentrate on getting your message across to your audience, you will probably do a good job of deciding where to insert visuals. As you plan your presentation, think first about how you might use visuals to highlight your transitions. Next, look for ideas you want to emphasize and that definitely can be transmitted more clearly or dynamically in graphic form.

Slide presentations usually contain a greater number of visuals than other kinds of presentations. This practice may simply be based on custom, but more likely it has developed because in the darkened room the speaker has low visibility. The slides *are* the presentation.

No matter what medium you use, remember that complex ideas usually need to be presented in component parts. Use one or more additional visuals rather than cramming in too many words or mystifying people with an overly intricate graph or chart. Also, as with graphics for written reports, make every effort to provide meaningful, concise captions.

## What Kind of Display?

**Word Visuals.** To emphasize important facts or a series of points, word visuals are often effective. But be careful here. A picture may be worth a thousand words, but a thousand words are definitely not a picture! If you

---

### Major weaknesses in the current organization

- Stocks and bonds' present management structure has several weaknesses
- No single recognized head of firm
- No clear authority and
  - Assignments of responsibility vague in many areas
  - Little general understanding of what individuals should be doing
- Insufficient top-management attention paid to problems of running growing—and complex—firm
- In short, the organization is all screwed up and nobody gives a hoot
- If you've gotten this far, you can't possibly be paying attention to what I'm saying

---

**Figure 16.16**

An example of a wordy visual (with a punch line!). Adapted from *Making the Most of Your Presentation: Communication Versus Recitation*, Gene Zelazny, McKinsey & Company, Inc. 1972.

flash a wordy visual onto the screen, your audience will inevitably fasten their eyes—and their complete attention—onto the words. Since they can read much faster than you can talk, they will tune you out, perhaps expecting to catch your remaining words about the concept after they have finished reading. (In the case of Figure 16.16, used by a sly speaker who wanted to make this very point, the audience was in for a surprise!)

If you're going to use word visuals to transmit important facts or points, a good rule is to present no more than 25 words at a time, ideally with a limit of 5 words to a line, as in the following:

DESIGNING READABLE

WORD VISUALS


o    LIMIT THE NUMBER OF

WORDS YOU INCLUDE

TO 25


o    MAKE SURE THE WORDS

CONTRAST ADEQUATELY

WITH THE BACKGROUND


It is possible to create slides or transparencies that are readable but that don't effectively communicate the point. Sometimes words alone are not enough. For example, in Figure 16.17 the depiction of the service ter-

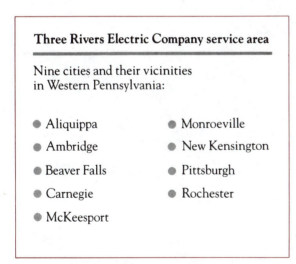

**Three Rivers Electric Company service area**

Nine cities and their vicinities
in Western Pennsylvania:

- Aliquippa
- Ambridge
- Beaver Falls
- Carnegie
- McKeesport

- Monroeville
- New Kensington
- Pittsburgh
- Rochester

**Figure 16.17**
A word visual that is less than inspired.

ritory of Three Rivers Electric Company is easy enough to read but it's neither helpful nor memorable. However, the same information presented on a map of western Pennsylvania (see Figure 16.18) makes the extent of the service territory immediately apparent.

As for type size, the most obvious guideline is that any word displayed or projected before an audience should be legible to those sitting in the last row. If possible, check this out beforehand by sitting back there yourself. Otherwise, a good estimate is that letters should be 1 inch high for each 25 feet between the display and the last row of the audience.

**Charts and Graphs for Oral Presentations.** The pie charts, bar graphs, and line graphs discussed earlier in this chapter are suitable for oral presentations as well as for written reports. They are simple and straightforward enough to be grasped almost immediately by an attentive audience. But flow charts and organizational charts (see Figures 16.13 and 16.14) are probably too complicated for a single slide or transparency.

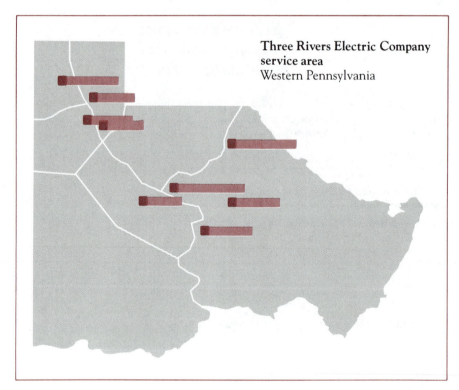

**Figure 16.18**
A more effective graphic presentation of the information in figure 16.17

Does this mean that more complicated visuals can never be presented "live" to an audience? Not really. In some cases, there are effective ways to break down complex graphics into several components.

**Progressive Disclosure.** Let's use as an example the flow chart depicted in Figure 16.13. In this chart the entire process of producing an advertisement is broken down into a series of related steps. We have already implied that understanding this whole process would require more time and effort than most audiences are able to muster. Although a reader can take the time to study a diagram by relating its various components, an audience can only digest so much in one bite. Just as with a wordy slide, the audience may begin to ignore the speaker while trying to decipher the entire complex process.

Progressive disclosure is one solution to this problem. In this useful technique, the whole visual is gradually revealed one section at a time. For example, Figure 16.13 could easily be divided, as shown in Figure 16.19. The speaker could then describe only that portion of the process illustrated by each individual slide or transparency. Then, when all the stages have been covered, the speaker might display the entire process.

Progressive disclosure obviously necessitates employing a greater number of visuals, but where clarity demands that concepts be simplified, this abundance of visuals is more than justified.

A very simple kind of progressive disclosure can be employed to preview and review the major segments of a presentation. Using this technique, the speaker reveals all of the main segments in a visual that is shown during the introduction of the talk. Later, as each main segment is discussed, it is highlighted. Although the highlighted segment draws the audience's attention, the other segments are remembered as guides to the progress of the talk. In concluding or summarizing, the speaker can once again show the complete visual. Figure 16.20 shows how progressive disclosure can be used to preview and review the major sections of a talk on how to create a presentation.

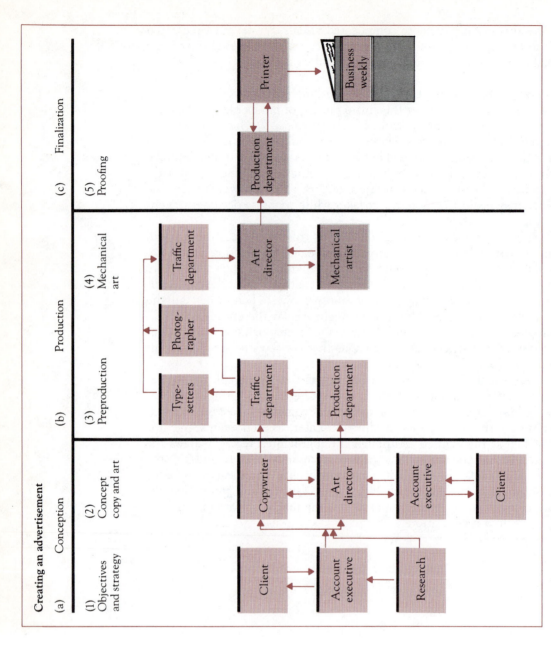

**Figure 16.19** Progressive disclosure of the flow chart in Figure 16.13 breaks down the process of creating an advertisement into three stages: (a) conception, (b) production, and (c) finalization.

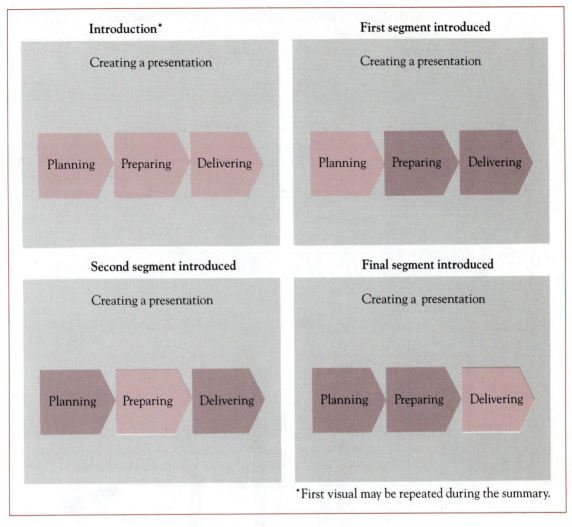

**Figure 16.20**
Using progressive disclosure to preview and review the major sections of a talk.

**Overlay Transparencies.** Another good technique for simplifying complex charts during presentations is to lay one simple transparency over another, explaining each one individually, until you have covered the whole picture. This works well for flow charts and especially well for line or bar charts that contrast two sets of figures. You might superimpose current sales on projected sales or New York production rates on Minneapolis ones; the possibilities are endless. When your audience has digested one set of data, overlay the contrasting set of data to emphasize the significant differences.

Figure 16.21 shows two overlaid transparencies, with one illustrating 1985 sales figures for the MAF Container Corporation and the other showing the projected figures for 1986.

There are two even simpler methods of displaying data in parts when you use transparencies. One is a form of the progressive disclosure described above. It entails covering most of a complex diagram with a blank piece of paper. When you are ready to discuss the next part, you simply move the blank paper to disclose the relevant section of the visual aid. You can do this three or four times, until the whole diagram is revealed.

Alternatively, you might use an oil crayon to add information to a

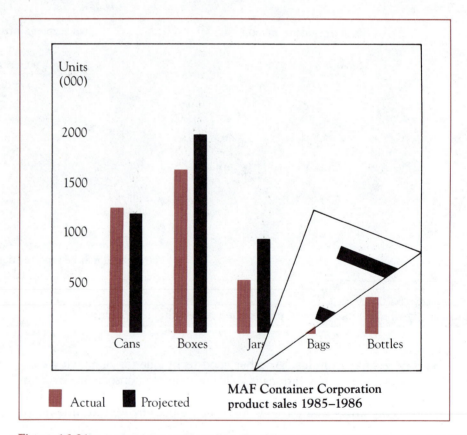

**Figure 16.21**
Overlay transparencies effectively highlight the differences between two sets of comparable data.

transparency as you talk. This can be risky—especially if your hands shake when you're nervous—but if the chart or diagram is simple enough to begin with, you should be able to add further details without producing an indecipherable mess.

Learning to use graphics effectively takes practice and attention. How much you will be able to achieve will depend somewhat on the resources at your disposal and budgetary and time constraints. Nevertheless, a stick figure drawn on a flipchart or a simple word visual can often serve you well. Do your best. If a graphic aid makes your message clear or more emphatic, you can count it a success.

## ■ Summary

The judicious use of graphic displays to reinforce your words will help the audience better understand and retain your message. Visuals are particularly useful if you are focusing on a complex product or process, on relationships of parts to each other and to the whole, on comparisons and contrasts, or on past performances and projected goals.

In written reports, unless graphic aids greatly interrupt the flow of the narration, they are most effective when placed near the point in the text that treats the material displayed. Use clear captions and appropriate acknowledgments. Tables are suitable for presenting relatively simple data. More complex information is usually best displayed via one of the several types of charts and graphs.

Oral presentations are also enhanced by tables, charts, and graphs— but only if these are clear and simple. Visuals can be displayed by means of chalkboard, flipchart, overhead projector, or slide projector. The medium selected should take into account the audience and occasion. Word graphics should include no more than 25 words. Complex visuals can be presented via progressive disclosure or by overlay transparencies.

## ■ Discussion Problems

**16.1** Which specific kind of graphic aid would you use for portraying each of the following sets of data in a written report? State your reasons. Suggest more than one alternative if you feel each could be appropriate. Explain how your choices might be changed if the graphic aids were to be used in an oral presentation.

- A comparison of the final exam grades of juniors and seniors
- How the city or town where you reside spent its annual budget last year
- Your city's or town's yearly expenditures compared to those of another city or town of comparable size during the same year
- How to operate a particular machine

- Attendance at your school's graduation ceremonies over the past ten years
- Percentage of graduates of the class of 1986 employed within six months of graduation, classified by major field of study
- Breakdown of the senior class by state of residence
- The process of applying for a job through your college's placement office

**16.2** Explain why and how visuals for oral presentations differ from the graphics found in textbooks, periodicals, or written reports. Photocopy three charts or graphs from another textbook (or other source), and discuss how you might modify each of them for use in an oral presentation.

**16.3** Describe the table, chart, or graph you would devise to illustrate the following information in a formal written report:

- Your firm's research-and-development fund as a percentage of the total budget
- The number of advertising dollars spent in relation to sales for three separate products over the past five years
- A comparison of the personnel budget at the New Jersey plant versus that at the Tennessee facility
- Changes in the price of Product A over a 20-year period
- Changes in the price of Product A as compared to the prices of Products B and C over a five-year period
- Comparison of the number of hospitals to the population in San Francisco, in Detroit, and in Atlanta
- Price of pork versus the price of beef and lamb in Miami, in New York, and in Seattle
- The decline in acreage of evergreens in the state of Washington over the past 20 years
- The electronic configuration of Model 230T versus that of Model 530T
- A comparison of the number of color televisions per household in France, in Italy, in Germany, and in Spain

**16.4** Find a faculty or staff member at your college who regularly uses a computer, and interview him or her about the use of computer graphics. If he or she already uses computer graphics, find out how and why, and ask for copies of some samples. (You might submit your findings as an oral presentation—with visuals—to your class.)

If the faculty or staff member you interview *doesn't* use computer graphics, determine the reason. If computer graphics software were available, would he or she use it?

**16.5** Discuss the advantages and disadvantages of using a flipchart, viewgraphs, or slides for each of the following presentations. Would you consider using a combination of these at a given presentation? Explain.

- A monthly departmental budget review given by a department's manager to the staff

- A presentation by a senior officer of a firm to the board of directors to outline long-term growth objectives
- A presentation by a junior member of a firm to the chief financial officer to explain a cost overrun (an excess over the projected budget)
- A presentation by a sales manager to sales representatives to explain a new computer application that assigns sales prospects to specific reps
- A presentation by a senior security sales analyst at a large brokerage house to a group of trainees to explain the workings of the commodities market
- A presentation by an assistant personnel director to a group of newly hired clerical workers to explain the company's emphasis on training and development
- A presentation by the same assistant personnel director to three new senior executives for the same purpose as above.

**16.6** Can you think of a business presentation that would be more effective without visual displays? Why?

**16.7** Suggest some types of visuals not mentioned in this chapter that might be used to good advantage in oral presentations. Give specific examples of situations in which these techniques could be used. Focus on the subject matter, the size of the audience, and the formality of the occasion.

# ■ Graphics Tasks

**16.1** Choose four currently popular films, and ask at least 20 people to name the ones they've already seen. Devise an effective chart to indicate the results of your poll.

**16.2** Choose two current films, and ask at least 20 people to rate each of them on a scale from 1 (hated it) to 5 (crazy about it). Chart the results.

**16.3** Photocopy two charts or graphs from a periodical or another textbook. Create simpler versions of those graphs for use during an oral presentation. (Your instructor will want to see both the originals and your simplified versions.)

**16.4** Prepare an appropriate chart or graph to illustrate the following sales figures for five of a company's products during the first and second quarters of last year. Indicate both domestic and foreign sales.

| | First Quarter | | Second Quarter | |
| Product | Net Sales (in millions) | Foreign (percent) | Net Sales (in millions) | Foreign (percent) |
| --- | --- | --- | --- | --- |
| A | $127.2 | 12% | $135.5 | 8% |
| B | 223.8 | 16 | 272.2 | 12 |
| C | 93.6 | 6 | 110.5 | 10 |
| D | 157.8 | 22 | 155.3 | 20 |
| E | 102.5 | 8 | 132.8 | 14 |

**16.5**  Chart the following data on the percentage of work hours lost through absenteeism in three firms during a six-month period.

|           | J & J Assoc. | Swanson & Dodge | Benson & Benson |
|-----------|--------------|-----------------|-----------------|
| January   | 16%          | 7%              | 12%             |
| February  | 19           | 11              | 12              |
| March     | 18           | 9               | 14              |
| April     | 12           | 6               | 9               |
| May       | 14           | 6               | 8               |
| June      | 18           | 10              | 10              |

**16.6**  Prepare a clear, simple graphic display to illustrate each of the following sets of data.

■  The expenditure of each dollar of income of Mr. and Mrs. Robert Jones.

| Rent            | $.32 |
|-----------------|------|
| Utilities       | .10  |
| Food            | .16  |
| Clothing        | .09  |
| Household items | .14  |
| Entertainment   | .08  |
| Transportation  | .11  |

■  The joint income of Mr. and Mrs. Jones over the past six years and projected income for next year:

| 1983             | $46,000 |
|------------------|---------|
| 1984             | 51,500  |
| 1985             | 38,000  |
| 1986             | 40,500  |
| 1987             | 61,200  |
| 1988 (projected) | 69,100  |

■  A breakdown of Mr. Smith's leisure activities compared to Mrs. Smith's leisure activities

| Mr. Smith      |     | Mrs. Smith               |     |
|----------------|-----|--------------------------|-----|
| Watching TV    | 70% | Watching TV              | 45% |
| Reading        | 12  | Reading                  | 22  |
| Golfing        | 9   | Talking on the telephone | 10  |
| Playing cards  | 6   | Sewing                   | 14  |
| Going to movies| 3   | Visiting the health club | 6   |
|                |     | Going to movies          | 3   |

**16.7**  Choose some process that you know well. Illustrate the steps and the interactions between them by means of a flow chart. Is your chart too complicated for use in an oral presentation? If so, break it down into component sections suitable for slides or a flipchart.

**16.8**  Prepare two simple line graphs or bar charts that are suitable for overlay transparencies. When the charts are presented together, they should highlight some striking comparison. Make sure that when one is placed over the other, the resulting display is clear. This means that any doubling of lines or numbers should be avoided. (It would probably be helpful to draw this assignment on tracing paper.)

**16.9**  Make a chart or graph of each of the following items of information using the most effective and creative technique you can think of.

- The number of school holidays in September, in October, in November, and in December, counting weekends

- The square footage of each room in your house or apartment or the number of beds in at least four dormitory buildings on your campus

- The amount of time you listened to the radio (or watched TV) during each 24-hours throughout a specific three-day period, specifying which hours you were listening or watching.

- The color of each shirt, each pair of slacks, and each pair of shoes currently in your closet

- The balance in your checking account versus the balance in your savings account over a four-month period

# OHIO RUBBER CORPORATION*

Eric Cole is Ohio Rubber Corporation's new district manager for the state of Virginia. In the first week in his new position, he has to deal with two very sticky customer problems.

The first concerns an irate stockholder who wrote to the company's president to complain about the poor performance of the tires on his family and business vehicles. Compounding the complexity of this problem is information that he received from the previous district manager concerning a surprising phone conversation with the dealer who sold the tires.

The second problem stems from a letter passed down from Ohio Rubber's chairman. In this case, a disgruntled faculty member from a local college is threatening to go to Ralph Nader's consumer-protection organization with complaints about the quality and safety of his Ohio Rubber tires.

In this dialogue, the seminar students review three letters written by their classmate Jeff DeSalvo. Jeff, by his own admission, tends to write rather long and wordy sentences. The students offer their advice here, and then the conversation turns to issues related to strategy and tone. Chief among them are how much apology is warranted when a customer's complaint is justified, and how much selling is appropriate in a conciliatory letter.

## ■ The Case

Eric Cole, the 26-year-old district manager for Virginia of the Ohio Rubber Corporation, assumed his new position effective July 1, 198-. The pro-

*This case is adapted from one prepared by Professors Ganas K. Rakes of Ohio University and Thomas L. Wheelen of the University of South Florida as the basis for class discussion. Copyright ©1971 by Ganas K. Rakes and Thomas L. Wheelen. Distributed by the Intercollegiate Case Clearing House, Soldiers Field, Boston, MA 02163. All rights reserved to the contributors. Printed in the U.S.A.

motion made him the youngest such manager in the company and was a substantial advancement from his former job as a traveling representative. He replaced Fred Andrews, who retired after 38 years with the company and 9 years as the district manager for Virginia.

Ohio Rubber Corporation manufactures a full line of tires, belts, and hoses for the automotive "after" market. As district manager, Eric is responsible for the distribution and marketing of the company's products through 64 franchise dealers, and sales of private-branded merchandise to six independent chains. Specifically, the district manager forecasts sales, processes and follows up orders, maintains company contacts with dealers, supervises local advertising campaigns, seeks new outlets, and attempts to improve the image of the company in the area.

Eric's first action as district manager was to review the materials left by his predecessor in the in-box. Of the eight or ten items, two appeared to require more than routine attention. Both were from dissatisfied customers. These letters and additional relevant correspondence are reproduced in Figures IV.1 through IV.7.

Quickly reviewing the company policy manuals, Eric underlined the following policies:

The Ohio Rubber Corporation, because of our relatively small size in an industry dominated by giant firms, must provide superior customer service.

Repeat sales are the backbone of our company; employees and dealers are expected to treat each customer request and complaint with courtesy and consideration.

Our new warehouse and distribution system is designed to provide our dealers with the most rapid and efficient service in the industry. This competitive advantage is to be the cornerstone of our promotional and advertising strategy.

Executives of Ohio Rubber are expected to set the leadership standards in customer relations. Their examples are intended to inspire our dealers.

The 12-, 24-, 36-, and the new 40-month guarantees for our tires are among the best in the industry. Public awareness of the quality of our products and our willingness to back that quality with the guarantee should be promoted at every opportunity.

**Figure IV.1**  Letter of complaint from James Adams.

## Adams Floral Company
### NORTH MAIN STREET
### FALLS TOWN, VA 44309

June 15, 198-

John T. French, President
Ohio Rubber Corporation
248 River Drive
Akron, OH 44309

Dear Mr. French:

I am writing both as a dissatisfied customer and as a stock-holder of Ohio Rubber Corporation. Your products have been the only tires, etc., used on my two family cars and on the three delivery vans owned by my business.

The apparent recent deterioration in the quality of your tires distresses me. Two sets of the premium grade Ohio Pride (36-month guarantee) have averaged less than 8,000 miles per set, and a third set is almost worn out. These particular tires were on my wife's car. One of the delivery vans is also getting very poor mileage (Ohio Load Carriers).

Our local dealer, Amos Winn of Winn Tire and Rubber Company, replaced the first two sets of automobile tires. He now tells me that your factory representative has refused to do anything about the third set.

I have checked the alignment of the car, balanced all the tires before mounting, and had the car itself checked thoroughly by the local dealer. The problems are clearly with the tires.

I am concerned not only for the safety of my family because of defective tires, but also about my investment (300 shares) in a company whose products are of such apparent poor quality.

Yours truly,

*James F. Adams*

James F. Adams

**Figure IV.2** Cover memo attached to letter in Figure IV.1.

## OHIO RUBBER CORPORATION
## INTEROFFICE MEMORANDUM

Date: June 18, 198-
From: John T. French, President
To: Harold James, Vice President, Eastern Region
Subject: Adams Complaint

Please initiate immediate action on the attached letter (from a valued stockholder and customer). See that he is personally contacted and the circumstances surrounding the incident investigated. Such attitudes toward our product and company by a reputable business person can only injure our image and reduce sales.

**Figure IV.3** Second cover memo attached to letter in Figure IV.1.

## OHIO RUBBER CORPORATION
## INTEROFFICE MEMORANDUM

Date: June 20, 198-
From: Harold James, Vice President, Eastern Region
To: Fred Andrews, District Manager, Virginia
Subject: Adams Complaint

Please attend to this problem. See Mr. Adams personally, and satisfy his complaints. I shall expect a full report on your results.

MEMO

From the desk of Fred Andrews

June 24, 198__

Per telephone call to Amos Winn of Winn Tire and Rubber.

Adams has a teen-age son who is racing the family car — also one of the delivery vans while working on Saturdays — An only child — parents would not believe the kid could do anything wrong —

**Figure IV.5**   Letter of complaint from Julius Smith.

EASTERN UNIVERSITY
Georgetown, VA 23856

June 19, 198-

Thomas T. Williams, III, Chairman
Ohio Rubber Corporation
248 River Drive
Akron, OH 44309

Dear Mr. Williams:

I am sorry to bother you, but it seems you are the only one who can solve my problem. My problem is that I have an 8:85-15 deluxe whitewall tire that has a major defect—there is a 4″ split where the tread attached to the side. How long it has been like this I don't know, but no one was injured. I brought the tire to George-town Tire & Appliance Co., Inc.—your local dealer and where I bought it. They said they would give me an adjustment price on the replacement, but did not have one in stock (May 15). Problem—five weeks later and they still don't have one and my wife is driving with only four tires and this split one as a spare. I am about to go to Western University on July 15 for a 2-week seminar, Business-Society. This should make a good incident. The dealer has tried, so no complaints in this area. I called your offices in Richmond, and they said they would try to locate one.

To say I am upset over the delay would be an understatement. First to buy a defective tire that could have shed its tread, especially when you have purchased the best to put on your wife's car. Now I cannot get a replacement. You would think I bought a tire from some foreign manufacturer with no back-up system in this country.

It has done one thing for me: I am now in the process of de-veloping several projects for my classes dealing with tires. I might be able to add to Mr. Nader's tire research.

I would appreciate your assistance in this matter. I am sorry to bother you, but it seems only you can solve my problem.

Sincerely yours,

*Julius P. Smith*

Julius P. Smith

**Figure IV.6**   Cover memo attached to letter in Figure IV.5.

OHIO RUBBER CORPORATION
INTEROFFICE MEMORANDUM

Date:   June 21, 198-
From:   T. T. Williams, III
To:   Customer Relations
Subject:   Smith Complaint

    Do something about this guy. All we need is more unfavorable publicity.

**Figure IV.7**   Second cover memo attached to letter in Figure IV.5.

OHIO RUBBER CORPORATION
INTEROFFICE MEMORANDUM

Date:   June 22, 198-
From:   Customer Relations
To:   District Manager, Virginia
Subject:   Smith Complaint and Williams Memo

    See Smith personally. Get him off our back. Please advise this office of your efforts and results. Mr. Williams is very interested.

# ■ Discussion Problems

Imagine that you are Eric Cole.

**IV.1** What would be your primary objectives in handling the Winn/Adams problem? Why?

**IV.2** Explain your strategy for carrying out those objectives. For example, would you phone Winn or Adams before writing to them? Would you meet with either in person? If so, when and why? Would you contact either John French or Harold James? If so, when, how, and why?

**IV.3** Explain your primary objectives and strategy for handling the Smith complaint.

# ■ Writing Tasks

**IV.1** Assume that you have decided to send letters to both Winn and Adams, and write them.

**IV.2** Assume that you have decided to respond to Smith in writing. Write that letter.

# ■ Optional Writing Tasks

**IV.1** Write a letter to Harold James. Assume that he has been alerted to the Smith problem as well as to the Winn/Adams situation. Explain to him how you have handled both problems, and recommend any future steps you feel are indicated.

**IV.2** Assume that Harold James, Vice President of the Eastern Region, has asked Eric Cole to write a formal report on the current state of customer relations. (He will be forwarding the report to President John T. French.) Using data from the Winn/Adams and Smith correspondence, write a report that not only covers the status quo but also recommends steps for the future. Be sure to include a transmittal letter with your report.

# ■ The Dialogue

RUTH: Shall we start with Jeff's paper? Jeff, how about reviewing your approach to the Adams problem.

JEFF: Overall, I decided it would probably be best for Eric Cole, the new district manager, to go out and see these people personally. First of all, because he's just started his job and he's got orders to do so. I don't think he's in any position to start second-guessing his superiors. And secondly, he's going to have to develop a feel for the whole state now, not just for his own territory; he'll probably have to be up in these towns and he might as well go up there now and get to know some of the problems of the customers.

To start with, I assumed that Amos Winn is reliable. I guess the clincher here for me is that there's one set of tires on one car continually wearing, which gives a lot of credibility to what Winn is saying about Adams's kid. I also assumed that Winn is not the kind of guy who's going to be forever pushing his customer troubles onto you. This letter came to the company without any kick from Winn; he didn't put Adams up to it. I've outlined my approach to Adams in the letter to Winn, so I'll read that first.

[Jeff reads aloud the letter he wrote to Amos Winn (see Figure IV.8).]

**Figure IV.8**  Student Jeff DeSalvo's letter to Amos Winn.

OHIO RUBBER CORPORATION
Virginia District
139 East 2nd Street
Richmond, VA 23232

July 1, 198-

Mr. Amos Winn
Winn Tire and Rubber Company
South Main Street
Falls Town, VA 24600

Dear Amos,

Thanks for your hospitality to Fred Andrews and me during my orientation visit last week. Your shop and your employees are impressive to see, and Fred has told me that your sales and service record is equally top-notch. Please call on me whenever you need assistance from the company—I'll certainly try to be as helpful as Fred was.

One problem which I hope to clear up in a few days is Mr. Adams's complaint. As you see in the enclosed copy of the letter I wrote him, I have asked him to meet with me so that we can look over the tires together. I hope that before we meet he will look at the Shell booklet and figure out that his tires are worn, not defective; but if he does not, I will just have to make the point myself. You were right, Amos, to replace the tires the first and even the second time. But I'm sure you'll agree that we only lower our reputation for quality by constantly accepting the blame for customers' abuse of our products.

A word about the Shell booklet. The dealers in my old territory used to order them by the stack—they're cheap (25¢ per hundred copies) and they contain a lot of information on tires written in simple language. You know, I'm sure, that many customer complaints originate from simple ignorance of tire construction and care. I think you'll find that giving a copy of this booklet to each customer will just about eliminate this problem.

Amos, I'll call you the day before I come up to Falls Town and let you know when I'll be meeting with Mr. Adams and when I'll be stopping by your store. If you still have them, please put the old Adams tires out where we can get at them—I may need to convince Mr. Adams that none of his tires were faulty. And I'll try to come up with a couple dozen of the Shell booklets for you.

Hope you have a good Fourth.

Regards,

Eric Cole

RUTH: Jeff, while you were reading the letter to us, did you find anything right off the top that you would like to change?

JEFF: Just off the top, I noticed some style problems. Take that third paragraph, I . . . well, I've never seen tires written in anything—"tires written in simple language"—that phrase is out of place. And there are two "simples" close together: the second one isn't necessary. I'm not quite sure that I need the "constantly" in the last sentence of the second paragraph; I'd like to cut it out. That's about it.

RUTH: How about that phrase, "tires written in simple language"? How would you improve it?

JEFF: Well, I could say "a lot of tire information written in simple language."

RUTH: Anybody else now? Let's stay with style. Jeff has a problem with long sentences—rambling sentences that are often too wordy; you might tackle this problem before we get into some other things. Yes, John?

JOHN: Second paragraph. "I hope that before we meet he will look at the Shell booklet and figure out that his tires are worn, not defective; but if he does not . . . ." I would strike out "but if he does not" and just say "otherwise." "Otherwise, I will just have to make the point myself."

CHUCK: Also, in the second sentence of the second paragraph, you could simplify by saying "As you see in the enclosed letter . . . ." You are being *too* specific by saying "copy of the letter I wrote him."

BOB: I'm not comfortable with the number of pronouns in that second sentence, second paragraph: ". . . I wrote *him*. I've asked *him* to meet with *me* so that *we* . . . ." So many pronouns. And the same thing happens again in the last paragraph, where you use *I* six times—it just seems so repetitive.

RUTH: Yes, it does, Bob. Those pronouns really pop out. I think they emphasize the overcomplexity of many of Jeff's sentences.

JOHN: Wouldn't a large number of I's always be inappropriate—necessarily?

RUTH: No, I don't think so John. You don't want to sound egotistical or self-centered; but most of the time the first person is assertive and personable. No, those I's, like the other pronouns, stick out because Jeff's sentences go on and on, sort of turning and bending: "As *you* can see in the enclosed copy of the letter *I* wrote *him* . . . ." "*I* have asked *him* to meet with *me*, so that *we* . . . ." You really notice those pronouns popping out all over the page. Anybody else on style issues?

PAUL: First sentence, second paragraph: I think I'd say, "I hope to clear up Mr. Adams's complaint in a few days." Because I think that Amos Winn probably knows that it's a *problem*, and that you *will* clear it up as soon as you can.

RUTH: I was going to suggest that change, too, Paul, but I backed off. I began to think Jeff was trying for a transition between the first two paragraphs. At the end of the first paragraph he says "Please call on me whenever you need *assistance*," and then he begins the next with "One problem . . . ." I see I'm reading you right, Jeff. Still, I agree with Paul, that sentence needs some work.

ROB: In the second sentence of the first paragraph, Jeff, you could knock out some words by saying "Your shop and employees are impressive," and leave out the "to see" and the second "your."

DON: You could make the verb active, too. "Your shop and employees impressed me."

RUTH: "Impressed me!" Yes! And not only does that make the verb active instead of passive, the compliment is far more believable if he really saw Winn's place. That praise bothered me: "Your shop and your employees are impressive." Sounds a little bit like ersatz whipped cream. The second part *is* good: "Fred has told me that your sales and service record is equally top-notch." That's real . . . if Fred told him, Fred told him. Incorporating what Don just said, the active "impressed me" is definitely more convincing.

JEFF: I agree. Sure. Also, I've been wondering . . . couldn't I have left out the last word in the first paragraph, the "was"?

RUTH: Yes. Omit it. There's nothing inherently wrong grammatically ending with a verb—that's not the problem. But "was" is a weak word; it doesn't leave *any* impression. Fred had a good record, probably got on well with Amos. Leave his name in Amos's ear; end with "Fred."

DAVE: Could I chop out another word or two? That long second sentence in the second paragraph. "Together" is redundant. "I've asked him to meet with me so that we can look over the tires." Sufficient.

ROB: This is just a question. The first sentence of the third paragraph, is that really a sentence?

RUTH: Well, it's a fragment, Rob. And an acceptable one, I think. An unacceptable fragment is one that makes the reader complain—"hey! what am I reading?"

FRAN: But I *did* have trouble with Jeff's sentence, Ruth. And I'm also wondering if there couldn't be a better transition, something like: "The Shell booklet I mentioned was popular with dealers in my old territory."

RUTH: Well, Fran, maybe your transition *is* clearer. Still, by the look on Jeff's face, he's not happy with the sentence. Let's say you were Jeff's editor; on this point he might want to argue with you, and I think you might just decide to back down. There are times, I think, when the writer should have the last word—given that he or she has carefully considered the editor's suggestion.

ROB: I think he should keep his fragment, Fran. And in Jeff's case, I have to admit, after all those long sentences, I jumped with glee when I saw a short one!

LARRY: I wonder about the use of dashes. In the third paragraph, the dash just prior to "they're cheap" and then again in the last paragraph just before "I may need to convince." Would it be appropriate to use periods? To *end* each sentence and then begin the new one?

RUTH: Well, periods would be correct and appropriate. Jeff also could have chosen semicolons. But if he's trying to sound informal, kind of breezy, the dash works well. Still, too many dashes would make his style seem affected and mannered.

LARRY: I guess what I'm concerned about is that those dashes make his long sentences seem even longer. In Jeff's case, I don't think they *do* make his style breezy.

RUTH: You know, I believe you are right, Larry. Which just goes to prove that punctuation can have some pretty subtle effects. Here, it's the visual impression we get that affects us the most.

PAUL: Sticking with the idea of cutting down Jeff's sentences, in the third paragraph: "I think you'll find that giving a copy of this booklet . . . ." I'd strike "I think you'll find that . . ." and just start with "Giving a copy of this booklet to each customer will just about eliminate this problem."

RUTH: Yes. Fewer words, and it sound more assertive—like he really believes in the booklet. Anybody else?

Well then, I had a few more questions of my own. Notice the first sentence of the second paragraph. Several of you mentioned it; it's one of those "whichy" sentences. "One problem *which* I hope to clear up in a few days . . . ." Strike the "which." "One problem I hope to clear up . . . ." And even the "hope" bothered me. It's like the "I think you'll find" that John just mentioned. The tone is a bit wishy-washy. Either you're going to try to clear it up or you're not. You want to convince this guy, so why not go for "One problem I *plan* to clear up" or maybe even "One problem I plan to tackle immediately." See how your word choice conveys your attitude and changes the tone?

And another question about word choice. This one has to do with connotation. It's probably just me, but the word "cheap" bothers me. "Cheap" always makes me think "shoddy"; I usually want to substitute "inexpensive," but then the other side of my head complains because I like Anglo-Saxon words. That side argues, "Leave *cheap* alone!" Well, it's something to chew on. I'm not sure myself.

FRAN: I share your sentiments about "cheap," but in a case like this—when you're referring to something like a brochure—the only cheapness you can assign to it is maybe the paper is flimsy. So I think the word is okay here.

RUTH: Good distinction, Fran. That helps.

LARRY: A couple of general things, Jeff. It seems to me that the Shell booklet thing comes out of the blue. If I were Amos Winn and hadn't used the booklet before, I'd wonder what the Shell booklet was.

JEFF: Except I've just mentioned "the enclosed letter." I tend to think he would look at the letter right then.

LARRY: Okay. Could be. But maybe you should enclose the booklet for Amos, too. Not just mention it in the letter to Adams.

BOB: I agree with the idea of enclosing the booklet, Larry. After all, Jeff, he might *not* flip over to your letter to Adams at that precise moment.

LARRY: One other thing that bothered me. It's the way the letter talks to Winn. I wondered about the tone of the third sentence in the third paragraph: "You know, I'm sure, that many customer complaints . . . ." If I were Amos, I might feel that was a little condescending. Maybe you ought to say something like this: "Since many customer complaints originate from simple ignorance or from ignorance of tire construction, I think you'll find that . . . ."

RUTH: Um-hum. That sneaky little note of condescension can sometimes slide in without our meaning it to. And nine times out of ten the reader will hear it and react negatively.

FRAN: Ruth, we've been focusing pretty much on issues of style and tone. I'd like to hear a few comments on Jeff's strategy in dealing with Winn. You know, he's adopted a kind of folksy tone—even used a comma in his salutation. But he's actually taking a pretty tough stand. He's no way going to replace those tires for either the customer or Winn.

DAVE: I thought about that too, Fran. And all that emphasis on the Shell booklet seems to be shoving the responsibility for such complaints back onto Winn. Between the lines, I'm reading "Get your customers better informed!"

PAUL: You know, I think Jeff could get away with this strategy a lot more easily if he let Amos know right up front that so far he's done exactly the right thing. I'd move the last sentence in the second paragraph up toward the beginning of the letter. Once Amos is reassured, I think he'll be able to swallow the bit about the Shell booklet.

JEFF: Well, Paul, I really do mean to be nice to Amos—and genuinely friendly. I'm not sure how I would handle future situations; I guess on an individual basis. But I don't mean to be sticking him with the total responsibility for this problem. I still think I'd see that he gets those booklets, but maybe I'd soft-pedal their importance a bit.

RUTH: Well, we probably could keep talking about Jeff's strategy in regard to Winn [a revision of Jeff's letter to Winn is shown in Figure IV.9], but let's move on to his letter to Adams. That will tell us a bit more about it, anyhow.

[Jeff reads aloud his letter to James Adams (see Figure IV.10).]

BOB: There's a sort of double-reverse twist in the last sentence of the second paragraph.

**Figure IV.9** Possible revision of Jeff DeSalvo's letter to Winn.

OHIO RUBBER CORPORATION
Virginia District
139 East 2nd Street
Richmond, VA 23232

July 1, 198-

Mr. Amos Winn
Winn Tire and Rubber Company
South Main Street
Falls Town, VA 24600

Dear Amos:

Thanks for your hospitality to Fred Andrews and me during my orientation visit last week. Your shop and your employees impressed me greatly. Fred has told me that your record of sales and service is equally top-notch. Please call on me whenever you need assistance from the company; I'll certainly try to be as helpful as Fred.

You were right to replace James Adams's tires the first and even the second time. But, as I'm sure you agree, we only damage our reputation for quality by accepting blame for a customer's abuse of our products.

The problem you are currently having should be resolved in a few days. As the enclosed letter to Mr. Adams indicates, I plan to meet with him so that we can look over his tires. I have also sent him a copy of the enclosed Shell booklet. I hope that after he looks at it he'll realize that his tires are worn, not defective. Otherwise, I will make the point myself.

A word about the Shell booklet: written in simple language, it contains a lot of information on tires. Many complaints originate from ignorance of tire construction and care. Therefore, giving this booklet to each customer will just about eliminate this problem. The dealers in my old territory kept a good stock of these booklets on hand. At 25¢ per hundred, they are very cheap.

Amos, I'll call you the day before I come up to Falls Town to let you know when I'll be meeting with Mr. Adams and stopping by your store. If you still have his tires, please put them where we can get at them. I may need them to convince him that they were not faulty. And I'll bring along a few dozen of the Shell booklets for you.

Hope you have a good Fourth.

Regards,

Eric Cole

**Figure IV.10**   Student Jeff DeSalvo's letter to James Adams.

OHIO RUBBER CORPORATION
Virginia District
139 East 2nd Street
Richmond, Virginia 23232

July 1, 198-

Mr. James F. Adams
Adams Floral Company
North Main Street
Falls Town, Virginia 24600

Dear Mr. Adams:

Your concern for the quality of our products has impressed our president, Mr. French. He knows—as do all Ohio Rubber employees and dealers—that the continued loyalty of customers and investors like yourself is the foundation of our company's success.

Your question about your Ohio Prides will get careful attention. I will be in Falls Town all day next Friday and on the following Wednesday morning; may I meet with you on one of those days to inspect the worn tires? As you may read in the booklet sent along with this letter, Shell Oil Company's "Guide to Car Care #11—Tires and Brakes," the wear marks caused by abuse of a tire are easy to recognize. Their absence on your tires will be sufficient evidence not only to replace your tires but also to investigate our manufacturing processes.

Please call my office at 992-7316 to set the time and place for our meeting. Both Mr. French and I hope that you will do so, so that together we may help our company retain its reputation as the highest-quality tire manufacturer in America.

Sincerely,

Eric Cole
District Manager, Virginia

cc: Mr. Amos Winn

RUTH: That's exactly what bothered me. Explain what you mean, Bob.

BOB: Well, the preceding sentence says ". . . the wear marks caused by abuse of a tire are easy to recognize." Then he goes on "Their *absence* on your tires will be sufficient evidence not only to replace your tires but also . . . ." Well, I had to stop and think—*fakes left, goes right!*

RUTH: That's far more succinct and original than my marginal note, Bob. I first tried to improve the clarity with a directional word. I wrote "The absence of *such* marks will be . . . ." I was hoping that "such" would point back to marks, but when I hit the "not only . . . but also," I yelled *help!* When a sentence gets that difficult, the best remedy normally is to rethink and rewrite the whole thing. The problem here is that Jeff probably wanted to say "Their presence on your tires would prove . . ." but decided that would sound too aggressive.

JEFF: Ruth, you and Bob are both right. I wanted Adams to think a bit, but not to get him mad. Clearly, though, that sentence really doesn't work very well.

DAVE: I think the last paragraph . . . well, if I were writing a letter to somebody and trying to ameliorate their concerns, and they were upset, asking *them* to call my office to set the time and place would strike me as . . . . Well, as the customer, I'd feel the ball's in Ohio Rubber's court. If I'm an angry customer, I'll be d—d if I'll call their office—*I want a tire.* If I were Cole, I think I'd be inclined to say "My secretary" or even better "I will be in touch with you" or "I will call"—even if I had my secretary do it. I don't like people throwing their secretaries at me.

And there's something else wrong. The argument is tangled: ". . . and I hope that you will do so, so that together we may help our company retain its reputation as the highest-quality tire manufacturer in America.". . . Hmmm. I don't know. The problem I have with that argument is that I would like to see some evidence of the fact that they *are* high-quality tire manufacturers as opposed to a company anxious to act quickly on customer complaints. Because you've really got two separate issues here: tire quality and service. You are trying to convince Adams, and the guy's obviously intelligent. He must know that companies have *some* defective items: some tires get out and they don't work—it's that simple. So maybe you're hitting him with the wrong issue, Jeff. It's the *service* that's under the gun here.

JEFF: Dave, the origin of my sentence is his own, where he's talking about his major concern. The whole argument he hung his complaint on was this: I'm upset because I bought shares in this company and bought their tires, and I believed it *was* the best tire company in America, and now I have evidence to the contrary!

RUTH: Dave, Jeff is reframing the words of the original letter here, and a number of you did do that. Usually that is a good device: not to literally quote the customer's letter, but to be able to convey the sense that you've read it closely—so closely that you're echoing the writer's thought. I think you all can see why that's often a pretty good tactic.

DAVE: Okay. I see what Jeff is doing now. But I still have a problem. It's not necessarily high-quality *manufacturing* that Adams's complaint deals with; it's the issue of prompt response to customer complaints. I think it's important to let him know you understand this.

RUTH: You've made a solid point, Dave. It really isn't just tire quality Adams is upset about.

DAVE: I think it's more specifically how well the company treats its customers. That issue is tied to both tire quality and the distribution system. And maybe service, too.

JOHN: Dave, I think you've zeroed in on the hardest part of dealing with this complaint—defining what it's all about. I agree with you completely. But I'd like to mention a smaller point that I think is also important.

Last sentence, first paragraph: ". . . customers and investors like yourself . . . ." I wouldn't say "yourself"; I'd say "you." I think it's correct, and it sounds less pretentious, too. And I would turn that sentence right around. Jeff's got the emphasis on "foundation of our company's success." I would say "He knows, as do all Ohio Rubber dealers and employees, that the foundation of our company's success is the continued loyalty of customers and investors like you." End on the "you" principle rather than on the benefit to the company.

JEFF: Hey, I like that, John!

JOHN: And also, down in that last paragraph: "Both Mr. French and I hope that you will do so . . ." Do what? Call, or agree to a meeting? You can't really tell what the "so" refers to.

RUTH: The reference is a little blurred, John. But another thing about that sentence—well, it's one of Jeff's special brand of long sentences: "Both Mr. French and I hope that you will do so, so . . . ." Happily the two so's fell on separate lines; but, Jeff, think of the visual impact if they were both on one line!

Well, we got considerable mileage out of that short letter, and you've touched on some pretty significant strategy issues: empathizing with the reader's state of mind, defining the problem at hand, and employing the "you" principle. Good work. [See Figure IV.11 for a revision of Jeff's letter to Adams.]

**Figure IV.11**   Possible revision of Jeff DeSalvo's letter to Adams.

OHIO RUBBER CORPORATION
Virginia District
139 East 2nd Street
Richmond, VA 23232

July 1, 198-

Mr. James F. Adams
Adams Floral Company
North Main Street
Falls Town, VA 24600

Dear Mr. Adams:

Your concern for the quality of our products and service has impressed Mr. French. Like all of Ohio Rubber Corporation's employes and dealers, he knows that our company's success is founded on the continued loyalty of customers and investors like you.

Your question about your Ohio Prides will receive my personal attention. I'll be in Falls Town all day next Friday and on the following Wednesday morning. Could you arrange to meet with me on one of those days to inspect the worn tires? If we do not find any evidence that the tires have been abused, we will replace your tires and recheck our manufacturing processes. As you can read in the enclosed Shell booklet, wear marks caused by abuse are easily recognized.

I will call your office early next week to set the time and place for our meeting. I am sure that together we will quickly resolve your problem. Both Mr. French and I want you to again feel confident that Ohio Rubber Corporation truly deserves its reputation as the highest-quality tire manufacturer in America.

Sincerely,


Eric Cole
District Manager, Virginia

cc:    John T. French, President
       Harold James, Vice President
       Mr. Amos Winn

RUTH: Shall we move on to Jeff's letter to Smith? [See Figure IV.12.]
JEFF: In Smith's case I feel the company has really fouled up and has to make amends. We need to get Smith his tire quickly and turn him from his dreams of vengeance. Even if my letter gets no reply, I'd call Smith and make a telephone pitch for a personal meeting. At that meeting, I would, of course, give him the material he needs to make Ohio Rubber look like a hero for his upcoming seminar.
PAUL: I think you're right, Jeff. Better see this guy—for a lot of reasons, and one of them is that T. T. Williams is clearly on your tail. In fact,

**Figure IV.12** Student Jeff DeSalvo's letter to Julius Smith.

OHIO RUBBER CORPORATION
Virginia District
139 East 2nd Street
Richmond, VA 23232

July 2, 198-

Professor Julius P. Smith
Eastern University
Georgetown, VA 24200

Dear Professor Smith:

Your new Ohio Pride Deluxe whitewall tire will arrive at Georgetown Tire & Appliance Company this coming Friday. When you put it in your wife's car, she will again have the security of driving with a full set of the best-built and safest tires on the road.

You may have heard or seen one of our recent advertisements in which we announce the installation of what will be the most responsive inventory system in the tire industry. We have spent over a million dollars on this system, in part because we hope it will increase our sales; but more important, we have made this investment because we also want to satisfy an ethical obligation. As Mr. T. T. Williams III said in his annual letter to our stockholders, "If we sell a customer fine tires, we are as responsible as if we had sold a shoddy product in the first place." We are the only company in our industry which explicitly recognizes this duty.

If you are interested in learning more about the development of this sense of responsibility at Ohio Rubber—perhaps for use as a case in your seminar at Western—please call me at 992-7316. I will be happy to give you some articles on the subject, and to share with you some "inside views" on the role of ethics in our decisions.

Sincerely yours,

Eric Cole
District Manager, Virginia

cc: Customer Relations

I wouldn't wait to see what results my letter gets. I'd call the guy first and tell him that both your letter *and* the tire are on their way!

BOB: I agree with that, Paul. And in that regard, there are a couple of things in Jeff's letter that bother me. And maybe they all boil down to one main comment. Here he's got a really irate customer to deal with, and he's doing a lot of hard selling of the company.

RUTH: I think you'd better be more specific, Bob.

BOB: Well, just look at the second sentence in the first paragraph. Just that little word "again." ". . . she will *again* have the security of driving with a full set of the best-built and safest tires on the road." This guy Smith is feeling pretty sure that she *never* had it! Don't you at least want to apologize before giving him the sales pitch?

JEFF: I see what you mean about the "again," and I think I buy it. But I'm not sure I want to apologize. We spent some time in class a few weeks back talking about how important it is to give explanations rather than apologies, and I'm definitely a convert.

LARRY: That was on my mind, too, when I wrote my own letter to Smith. And I decided I'd better go ahead and apologize anyway. The important thing here is that we've really messed up. Not only did we sell this guy a bad tire, but we can't seem to get the new one out to him. I mean, isn't this a case where plain good manners demands an "I'm sorry"?

FRAN: Sure. Why not? But I don't see any harm in pushing the improved inventory system a bit. I think Jeff's idea is pretty good. The only problem is that he hasn't made it all very convincing. If I were an angry customer, I'd hardly want to hear a dissertation by T. T. Williams.

JEFF: Well, *Smith* dragged Williams into this. He's the guy Smith sent his letter to.

FRED: Jeff, how about using Williams more like you used French in your letter to Adams? I mean, let Smith know that Williams took the time to handle this personally. And for that reason (and maybe to cover your own flank) I'd certainly copy this letter to Williams as well as to customer relations. Oh yes, by the way, I also thought that you should have copied the Adams letter to French and to the guy who is your boss, the VP who sent you French's memo.

RUTH: Let's try to sort out a few of the issues you've all been circling. As I see it, you are feeling that Jeff's letter is a little too hard-sell, and that he might have done more to admit the company's at fault here. Also, Fred raised the issue of hidden audiences. And I certainly think that this case gives us a prime example of that.

JEFF: Ruth, I'm beginning to feel, myself, that my letter might have been a little more . . . I don't know exactly what . . . let's say, warmer. I can see that I did kind of hurry into the sales pitch. I think if I had to do it again I would apologize first. And I'd try to use that apology as a transition into informing him about the inventory system. Maybe I'd say something like "We're awfully sorry, but we've taken major steps to correct this situation, and we hope it will never occur again."

ROB: Jeff, that brings me to a word in your letter that really bugs me.

JEFF: Only *one* word? I'm definitely improving!

ROB: Seriously, look at the second sentence in the second paragraph. You've used the word "hope" again there, just as you did in the letter to Adams and a minute ago in your revision. I wouldn't say "we *hope* it's going to increase sales," and I certainly wouldn't tell him "we *hope* this situation won't occur again." Even if we have a little doubt, I think the letter should firmly state that it will not happen again.

JOHN: A slightly different matter, but maybe it's a little related, Jeff. I respect your telling Smith that the company wants "to satisfy an ethical obligation." But I think you ought to translate that into something more solid, like "We know we are obliged to see that our customers stay satisfied throughout the life of the tires they buy from us."

RUTH: Jeff, maybe both Rob and John are telling you to be a bit more confident and talk to Smith in your own voice, rather than in an "annual report–T. T. Williams" style.

ROB: You know, Ruth, we've given this letter a pretty thorough going-over. But I think we also need to emphasize its strong points. As Fran said, stressing the new inventory system is a darned good idea. And so is pointing out that this company takes its ethics seriously.

DAVE: Right. And I also think Jeff is smart to try to interest Smith in the reading materials. We don't know whether Smith teaches 500 students or 10, or whether the Nader thing is a bluff or they're really buddies. But I think that it can't hurt a bit to try to cement relationships with the people at the university.

RUTH: I think you and Rob are right, Dave. Jeff's approach, as most of us agree, is innovative and for the most part sound. But, Jeff, you do need to improve the letter itself. Still, from what you've been telling us, I'm sure you now have a very good idea of what changes are in order. [See Figure IV.13 for a possible revision of Jeff's letter to Smith.]

**Figure IV.13**  Possible revision of Jeff DeSalvo's letter to Smith.

OHIO RUBBER CORPORATION
Virginia District
139 East 2nd Street
Richmond, VA 23232

July 2, 198-

Professor Julius P. Smith
Eastern University
Georgetown, VA 24200

Dear Professor Smith:

Your new Ohio Pride Deluxe whitewall tire will arrive at
Georgetown Tire & Appliance Company on Friday, July 8. We are
truly sorry for this delay and any inconvenience to you and your
wife. Please feel confident that she is now driving with a full set of
the best-built and safest tires on the road.

This unfortunate delay in resolving your problem was caused
by our being in the process of installing our new inventory system.
You may have heard or seen one of our recent advertisements describing what is now the most responsive inventory system in the
tire industry. We believe this million-dollar system will not only increase our sales but also ensure that our customers receive prompt
and correct service during the life of their tires and when replacement is required.

Mr. T. T. Williams III personally saw that your letter received
immediate attention. As he has stated in this year's annual report,
Ohio Rubber Corporation has a real sense of responsibility to our
customers. We are the only company in the industry that has explicitly acknowledged accountability for our customers' continuing
to ride on safe, high-performing tires.

If you are interested in learning the history of Ohio Rubber's
unique sense of responsibility—perhaps for use as a case study in
your seminar at Western—please call me at 992-7316. I will be
happy to give you some current articles and to share some inside
views on the importance of ethics in the way we operate.

Sincerely yours,

Eric Cole
District Manager, Virginia

cc:   T. T. Williams III
      Customer Relations

# ■ Additional Letters To Discuss And Revise

The three sets of letters in Figures IV.14–IV.22 were written by three different students in response to the Ohio Rubber Corporation case. Study the letters carefully. Consider the strategies they represent and how well those strategies are executed. Are the arguments clearly and concisely stated? Are they convincing? Is the tone of each letter appropriate?

Discuss the letters with your classmates, and revise them as requested by your instructor or for self-help.

**Figure IV.14** One student's letter to Amos Winn.

OHIO RUBBER CORPORATION
Anywhere, VA 00000

July 1, 198-

Amos Winn
Winn Tire and Rubber Company
South Main Street
Falls Town, VA 24600

Dear Amos,

James Adams's son evidently does not realize that Ohio tires are not designed for drag-racing. His son also is not aware that we cannot continue supplying him with tires to destroy.

The only way to put an end to this situation is to tell Mr. Adams why his tires do not last very long.

First, you can soften the blow to Mr. Adams by replacing this last set of tires. Then, we will tell Mr. Adams about his son's ambitions as a drag-racer. I say "we" because Akron has taken an active interest in this situation. As a result, they want me personally to attend to this claim. This is an exceptional case because Adams is a stockholder and customer.

However, dealers and adjusters will handle their own customer complaints in the future.

Charlie Davis, our quality specialist, will accompany me to show Mr. Adams the signs of tire abuse on his tires. He will also answer any questions that you have about our product line.

Please set up an appointment for Mr. Adams next week. I have sent him a letter and he should be calling you soon. I will phone you in a few days to find out the time and date.

In the meantime, keep up the good work with the Summer Tire Clearance—your volume is terrific.

Yours truly,

Eric Cole
District Manager

**Figure IV.15** One student's letter to James Adams.

OHIO RUBBER CORPORATION
Anywhere, VA 00000

July 1, 198-

James F. Adams
Adams Floral Company
Falls Town, VA 24600

Dear Mr. Adams,

I have just instructed Amos Winn to replace the worn set of tires on your wife's car. If you call Winn Tire, they will make an appointment for this work right away.

Our president, Mr. French, and all of us share your concern over your recent experiences with Ohio Rubber products. Consequently, Charlie Davis, our quality-control specialist, and I will be on hand when Winn Tire replaces your tires. At this time, we will try to find the cause of your difficulties.

While you are at Winn Tire, I hope that you will take a look at the great tire bargains during his summer clearance.

Yours truly,

Eric Cole
District Manager

**Figure IV.16** One student's letter to Julius Smith.

OHIO RUBBER CORPORATION
Anywhere, VA 00000

July 1, 198-

Professor Julius P. Smith
Eastern University
Georgetown, VA 24200

Dear Professor Smith,

Your replacement tire is on its way to Georgetown Tire & Appliance. Now you can attend the seminar in Chicago knowing that your wife is driving with five good tires.

A human error, made while entering information into our inventory-control computer, caused this delay. I am concerned about this temporary failure in our system and am taking steps to ensure its reliability. Right now, our systems design staff is developing methods to catch these unavoidable human errors more quickly.

As an educator interested in the tire industry, I invite you to visit our district offices. Tire distribution is a complex process, and Ohio Rubber has one of the industry's most sophisticated automated distribution systems. Also, we have an extensive collection of literature on the tire industry, which could help you to develop class projects.

I will check with you next week about your replacement tire and also to arrange a date for you to visit our offices, if you are interested.

Yours truly,

Eric Cole
District Manager

**Figure IV.17**   Second student's letter to Amos Winn.

OHIO RUBBER CORPORATION
139 East 2nd Street
Richmond, VA 23232

July 1, 198-

Amos Winn
Winn Tire and Rubber Company
South Main Street
Falls Town, VA 24600

Dear Mr. Winn:

Peter Barnes, our factory representative, has probably mentioned that I am Ohio Rubber's new district manager for this area. Fred Andrews has just retired.

Fred left the problem of your customer, Mr. James Adams, for me. Since Mr. Adams is a valued stockholder as well as a customer of Ohio Rubber, we would particularly like to keep his good will. Rather than replacing his worn-down tires with other Ohio Rubber tires (which would just delay a confrontation), I have asked him to accept tires from another manufacturer as replacements. I suggested that this alternative solution will show whether his problem lies with manufacture or manner of driving.

Would you please provide him with a set of comparably priced tires from another manufacturer? We will pay you for them and bill him ourselves after he has had time to see if they wear at the same rate as our tires have been wearing.

He also has the option of replacement with Ohio Rubber tires. If he takes that option, please give him the tires, and let me know. We will not give him that option again, when there is reason to believe his son is racing the car.

Although at this time it would probably be better if you do not mention to Mr. Adams that you (or your employees) have seen his son racing the family car, I would appreciate hearing if that problem continues over the next several months.

I plan to visit individual dealers in the district from time to time to identify ways we can serve you better. I look forward to meeting you soon.

Sincerely yours,

Eric Cole
District Manager

**Figure IV.18**  Second student's letter to James Adams.

OHIO RUBBER CORPORATION
139 East 2nd Street
Richmond, VA 23232

July 1, 198-

Mr. James F. Adams
Adams Floral Company
North Main Street
Falls Town, VA 24600

Dear Mr. Adams:

A new set of four premium-grade Ohio Pride tires is available for you at Winn Tire and Rubber Company. Ohio Rubber Corporation wants to treat you fairly.

We share your concern not just for fairness but also for the durability and reliability of our tires. That is why we continue as always to check the quality of our tires 15 separate times during production. Few tire manufacturers are as careful as we are; none are more so.

As you know, the service life of tires is also affected by factors that only the tire user controls. For example, fast starting and stopping while driving, such as teenagers may be inclined to do, wears tires down extraordinarily quickly. The condition of a car, which due to your efforts is not a problem here, also affects tire life.

With this complexity of factors, I suggest an alternative solution to your tire-durability problem. We will replace the worn tires on your family car with comparably priced tires of another manufacturer. We will not bill you for six months. Unusual tire wear apparent at that time will suggest that the problem lies in the manner of driving, not in the manufacture. No unusual wear (assuming, of course, no change in family driving habits) will suggest faulty manufacture. In the latter case, just write what has happened on the bill and send it back. You pay us only if you think it fair.

Because you both use Ohio Rubber tires and own stock in our company, I am happy to make these special arrangements for you. May I notify Mr. Winn of your cooperation in this plan?

Sincerely,

Eric Cole
District Manager

**Figure IV.19**   Second student's letter to Julius Smith.

OHIO RUBBER CORPORATION
139 East 2nd Street
Richmond, VA 23232

September 16, 198-

Mr. Julius P. Smith
Eastern University
Georgetown, VA 24200

Dear Mr. Smith:

Your replacement 8:85-15 deluxe whitewall tire is now ready for you at Georgetown Tire & Appliance Co. You are right to be concerned about tire quality and availability.

We share your concerns. The distribution system of the Ohio Rubber Corporation is among the best in the industry. The production system contains 15 separate quality checks during the production process. But breakdowns do occur, and in order to maintain high-quality service, we depend on people like you to report breakdowns to us.

We will respond. As the newly appointed district manager of this company for Virginia, I have instituted a procedure which ensures that this distribution breakdown will not recur. Furthermore, as soon as you return the defective tire, our engineering laboratory will investigate the cause of its splitting. It will act appropriately to prevent a recurrence of that problem.

The Ohio Rubber Corporation looks forward to serving our customers ever more reliably and efficiently.

Sincerely yours,

Eric Cole
District Manager

**Figure IV.20**  Third student's letter to Amos Winn.

OHIO RUBBER CORPORATION
139 East 2nd Street, Richmond, VA 23232
"The Best Products with the Best Service"

September 23, 198-

Mr. A. Winn
Winn Tire and Rubber Company
South Main Street
Falls Town, VA 24600

Dear Amos,

As Fred Andrews's successor, I have just inherited the pending complaint of Mr. Adams (see enclosures). I have today written to Mr. Adams and offered to replace all eight tires without charge. You will, of course, be reimbursed for your costs.

As a stockholder, Mr. Adams must receive special treatment, and you should personally deal with him. Try to convince him that his wife's car and the van are driven harder than normal. The pattern of wear is obviously not caused by tire defects. Point out to him that racing causes such wear.

Clearly, our regular tires were not made for such hard treatment and no guarantee should be offered with the replacement tires. I have suggested that Mr. Adams purchase sets of triple-belted racers with full credit for the regular tires. I hope you can persuade him that this would be the best solution.

I will be in Falls Town next week and will look forward to meeting you then, Mr. Winn. In the meantime, let me know if I can help with the Adams case.

Sincerely,

Eric Cole
District Manager

Enclosures

**Figure IV.21**  Third student's letter to James Adams.

OHIO RUBBER CORPORATION
139 East 2nd Street, Richmond, VA 23232
"The Best Products with the Best Service"

September 23, 198-

Mr. James F. Adams
Adams Floral Company
North Main Street
Falls Town, VA 24600

Dear Mr. Adams:

I have today instructed your local dealer, Winn Tire and Rubber Company, to replace, at our expense, four new Ohio Pride and four new Ohio Load Carrier tires. Naturally, we are concerned when one of our staunchest customers is dissatisfied, and we are happy to do this for you.

We are at a loss to explain your bad luck with our tires. We take pride in our improved quality as shown by declining numbers of tires returned under warranty, which amount to one-tenth of one percent of sales. We found that 70 percent of the tires returned were not defective when installed. They had been subjected to unusually severe conditions, which contributed to their premature wearing. The common symptom is when all four tires wear out together. Rough roads, young drivers' racing and fast starts were the predominant causes.

Your experience would indicate a similar pattern. Your wife's car has worn out three sets of tires, yet yours are fine; the same with the van's. It appears to me that the two vulnerable vehicles are being driven harder than regular tires were designed for. I would suggest that you discuss with Mr. Winn whether our triple-belted racers would be more suitable. Of course, we would allow you full credit for the regular tires.

As I have recently taken over from Mr. Andrews, I am anxious to explore my district. I will be in Falls Town next week and will personally make sure that you are satisfied. I would also like to meet our valued clients, like yourself. Let me know if it would be convenient to have lunch together.

Yours sincerely,

Eric Cole
District Manager, Virginia

cc: A. Winn

**Figure IV.22**   Third student's letter to Julius Smith.

OHIO RUBBER CORPORATION
139 East 2nd Street, Richmond, VA 23232
"The Best Products with the Best Service"

September 23, 198-

Mr. Julius P. Smith
Eastern University
Georgetown, VA 24200

Dear Mr. Smith:

    I am happy to report that Georgetown Tire & Appliance now has the requested tire in stock and will hold it for you. Your dealer will be glad to replace and install your new tire free of charge.

    Our Richmond office had trouble locating the tire in stock due to the disruption caused by the recent Rubber Workers' strike. Fortunately, a new batch of 8:85-15s has just been produced. We airfreighted your tire from Akron to Georgetown to minimize your inconvenience.

    As the recently appointed district manager for Virginia, I am anxious to familiarize myself with my region and will therefore be visiting Georgetown next week. Would you let me know if you are free for lunch? I notice that your field is business and society. I am particularly interested in this topic with respect to the rubber industry and look forward to discussing it with you.

Yours sincerely,

Eric Cole
District Manager,
Virginia Region

cc: Georgetown Tire & Appliance Co.

bcc: Customer Relations

# PLANNING AND PREPARING AN ORAL PRESENTATION

## 17

# ■ Presentations versus Speeches

A lthough both rely on the spoken word, a presentation and a speech are not the same. Their difference lies in the different set of expectations and priorities that the speaker and the audience bring to the occasion. Even though speeches are given in a business setting, they are incidental to ongoing business activities. But the oral presentation is a dominant form of business communication. Moreover, a good presentation is often the determining factor in the success of a business transaction. The following two short cases illustrate the basic differences between the two media.

Naomi Askew is what is often referred to as a "nontraditional" student. **Case #1**
Three years ago, she and her grandson Paul developed a software program
that allowed homemakers to enter data about their home and lifestyle into
a personal computer and receive a detailed audit of the safety and security
of their living quarters. An outgrowth of a project for Paul's high-school
computer science class, the product was leased to a local software firm,
and—to Naomi's and Paul's astonishment—it took off. Although the software firm offered to employ Naomi, she decided instead to enroll in her
local community college as a marketing major, while Paul worked for a degree in computer science at the University of Vermont. After their graduations, they intend to start their own software company.

Naomi has just been invited to address the attendees at the Marketing
Club's annual student-faculty dinner. She has been informed that she will
be the first of two before-dinner speakers and has been asked to present a
20-minute talk on marketing for the entrepreneur.

Dev Gupta, a recent college graduate with a bachelor's degree in econom- **Case #2**
ics, is employed as a market-research specialist at a large New York City
import-export firm. Since almost his first week on the job, Dev has been
assigned to a team of researchers whose focus is the regulatory environment for shippers of merchandise to Asian markets. Dev's project is to report on shipments to and from countries bordering on the Persian Gulf
and the Arabian Sea. Dev has developed a detailed written report for his
team members, and he intends to distribute that report next Monday at
their weekly review session. At that time, he will also present an oral
summary of his findings and respond to his fellow team members' inquiries. A discussion will follow in which the team will try to establish

some preliminary recommendations for the firm's management. Dev knows that he will be expected to lead that discussion.

**Analysis**

Naomi's assignment is to prepare a speech, but Dev needs to prepare an oral report. Naomi knows that for approximately 20 minutes she will need to be entertaining and informative. Dev knows that he must prepare a presentation that summarizes a great deal of data, highlights his key findings, provokes an orderly and productive discussion, and helps his team establish a consensus concerning their recommendations.

Naomi's audience expects to be stimulated and entertained. Although they have no urgent need for the information she will impart, they are at least mildly interested in her topic. If you asked them to communicate their priorities concerning what she should accomplish, they probably would say that they hoped she wouldn't bore them with too many facts and figures and that she would keep within her time parameters and not cause dinner to be delayed.

Dev's audience expects to be informed and perhaps persuaded. The team members know that Dev has to present a good many facts and figures, and they hope that he will organize the data so that they can isolate the main issues and draw some sound conclusions. Although they expect to be stimulated by Dev's presentation, they neither need nor want to be entertained. Time is of the essence because the deadline for the management presentation is near. Nevertheless, they are willing to give Dev sufficient time to communicate his findings and to help them arrive at a consensus. If you asked the team members for their priorities, they would probably say that they hoped Dev would be well organized, accurate, and persuasive.

Naomi's invitation to speak is a special event—both for her audience and for herself. Dev, on the other hand, is performing a task that is a critical part of his job. Although its exact requirements will differ according to the circumstances, Dev's task is integral to many business transactions; Naomi's is not.

## ■ Planning an Oral Presentation

Just as a good written report requires prewriting, an effective oral report requires planning. The planning process necessitates thinking, research, and legwork, in proportions that vary with each presentation. Inevitably, however, to succeed as a presenter, you must carry out the following steps:

- Determine your purpose.
- Consider the size of your audience and the occasion.
- Assess your own strengths and weaknesses.
- Arrange for an appropriate setting.

- Select an effective graphic medium.
- Analyze your audience in depth.

## Purpose: Front and Center Again

To lack a clear purpose may be even more debilitating for a speaker than for a writer.

Readers who have lost the thread can at least go back, review, and try to put the pieces together. A disoriented listening audience, however, must suffer relentless and increasing confusion. A baffled reader can at least temporarily push the offending document aside, but few listeners have the temerity to push back their chairs and walk away from a poor presentation. Their only recourse is to squirm, glare at the speaker, cough, yawn, or try unobtrusively to nap. For better or worse, once a presentation is under way, speaker and audience are temporarily bonded and somewhat at one another's mercy.

Many a presentation has been doomed because the presenter mistakenly assumed that the task of addressing an audience on a particular topic is in itself a purpose. Such speakers hopefully gather their data together and prepare a few notecards; they then persuade themselves that when the moment comes, all will be well. Generally, however, the outcome is dismal. The presentation is disjointed and unfocused; or (even worse) the speaker freezes with fear when the moment of truth arrives.

Your goals for a presentation may be large or small, major or minor, but you should try to define them clearly before you take any further steps. For instance, if you are asked to describe a new product, decide whether you believe it should be adopted or sent back to the drawing board. Or, more typically, if your task is to report on your department's progress this month, ask yourself if there is one accomplishment that deserves major attention or a problem that you should bring to light. Because all speakers have facts or ideas to communicate, most presentations are at least subtly persuasive. But often the goal is merely to persuade the audience to consider some new insights, not to get them to act in a specific way. Such presentations aim to deepen or expand the perspectives of the audience; their main purpose is to help people clearly understand alternatives and to inspire active discussion. Just as frequently, however, a speaker will try to build a strong argument for a specific proposal and to achieve consensus among those present.

## Assessing Your Audience

Employees are paid for their time. Even one hour of one person's time for attending a presentation represents serious money; multiply that person by 10 or 20, and the costs skyrocket. Moreover, those attending have their own projects and tasks pulling at the corners of their minds. These people need to feel that the report they are listening to will help them carry out their responsibilities in some real way, or that the speaker's purpose has overriding importance—at least for the duration of the talk.

Just like a written report, an oral report has a message to deliver, and that message must build a bridge between the speaker and the audience. You must not only know your own purpose, but must also do your best to analyze your listeners' needs and expectations. As you learned in earlier chapters, your audience analysis can and should influence the structure, style, and tone of a piece of writing. Similarly, when you are planning a presentation, an audience analysis will help you to build an effective structure and establish an appropriate tone. In addition, it will help you to select (or at least to modify) the setting for your presentation and to choose the best graphic medium.

In assessing your audience, ask the following questions:

- Is the audience large or small?
- Is it composed of your colleagues or of strangers?
- Is the group homogenous or mixed?
    Are they peers in rank?
    Are they equally informed about the topic?
    Do they share similar attitudes or concerns?
- Are those attending in tune with your purpose, somewhat doubting, or hostile?

Now, let's consider these questions carefully and learn how to respond in each situation.

**When the Audience Is Large.** When addressing a large audience, you will instinctively attach some formality to the occasion; and chances are, your audience will too. There's an expectation on your part that people will give you their complete attention; and they expect you to be well prepared. To earn their attentiveness, you must make it evident that you have given thought to every detail of your presentation—not only to the components of the talk itself but also to the graphics, the room arrangements, and the equipment you use.

When invited to present to a large group, you normally will be responsible for seeing that the room is suitable. If you need to reserve an auditorium or a large conference room, do so well in advance; if a room is assigned to you, inspect it before the audience arrives. Check to see that the thermostat is set appropriately (people who are freezing squirm; people who are suffocating sleep!), and make sure that your graphics are visible from all seats and your voice can be heard throughout the room.

Since a large auditorium places a speaker in the traditional "lecturer" role (the listeners are forced into the role of passive receivers of information), such a situation mandates that you work especially hard to project warmth and humanity. This is especially true if you want to encourage active participation. Getting a large audience to contribute to a presentation is no easy task for an inexperienced speaker. Usually, the best tactic is to let it be known at the outset that you will welcome questions and discussion at the conclusion of your talk.

Delivering a formal presentation to a large audience is a special event, not often experienced by employees at the entry level. It is not unlikely, however, for a junior member of a staff to be asked to work on a team to develop such a presentation for a senior person in the organization. If you are asked to work with such a group, don't be surprised to discover that people much more experienced than you are feeling anxious (at least just below the surface) about this task. Therefore, if you remain calm and have developed good organizing and writing skills, you may find that you are in a position to gain many points for yourself and your career.

**When the Audience Is Small.** Even early in your career, presenting to a small group may become a fairly regular event. As we mentioned above, you might be responsible for delivering an oral progress report to your group or department on a monthly or weekly basis. Or you might be asked to present data concerning a particular project to your immediate co-workers or to a group of managers. In some job capacities, you may need to explain a process or to unravel the meaning of technical data for a nontechnical audience. You might be asked to communicate the pros and cons of a special purchase for your department; or you might want to take the initiative for recommending a new procedure or policy. The list of such possibilities is almost endless. Many of these presentations will be so interactive and informal that you could equate them with informal meetings. Nevertheless, you are *presenting* when you are called on to orient those attending or to brief them on a specific topic. At these times, you will want to be poised, natural, and persuasive.

Perhaps it's only fair to admit that addressing an audience is easier for some people than for others. For the lucky individual who seldom if ever feels self-conscious before an audience, the challenge itself seems to breed assurance and control. But for the rest of us, it's a different matter. We need to be considerate of ourselves. It is obviously important to think of your audience's comfort and needs; it is less obvious but equally important to think of your own!

If picturing yourself speaking to a group causes you anxiety, don't dwell on your misgivings. Instead, force yourself to imagine that you are presenting to the same group of people and *doing everything right*. In your mind's eye, see yourself in top form: confident, articulate, moving the presentation along at just the right pace. Now analyze that vision. Did you imagine yourself moving briskly about the room? Were your notes spread out before you on a table? Were you using graphic displays? Picturing yourself succeeding not only boosts your morale but also helps you to assess your special needs as a presenter. Did you sense that graphics would help you to explain your points, or would juggling transparencies interrupt your delivery? Should you instead use a flipchart and record ideas from the group? You do have options. Use common sense, and remember that this is your show: *you* are in control.

Many small-group presentations are really round-tables or workshops, crosses between a presentation and a meeting. As the speaker, you supply the impetus for a discussion and keep a firm rein on its direction. On such occasions, you often have the option of standing in front of the room or sitting as part of the group around a table. Again, consider your own delivery style and preferences.

Perhaps you will be told in advance that a high-ranking person will be present, someone you must address frequently. Consider where you might like to seat that person: at your right? Directly in front of you? Or perhaps you will have to address strangers, visitors whom you have never met before. In that case, you may want to prepare name cards (sometimes called "tent cards" because of their shape) to put at each person's place.

Your objective might be a free-wheeling, highly interactive session with your own co-workers. For such an occasion, name cards would, of course, be both unnecessary and inadvisable. Do take the time to arrange the chairs, however; although you should allow everyone to settle where they choose, you certainly don't want to contend with a group that is scattered around a too-large conference room.

Does it surprise you to learn that lugging chairs or moving tables can be a critical part of your responsibility in preparing a presentation? The point is that the more you do to create a setting where your own chemistry and that of your listeners combine to produce purposeful interactions, the easier the rest of your task will be.

As we said in Chapter 16, slides add a great deal of formality to an occasion, probably too much for a typical small-group presentation. Transparencies are less formal than slides, but definitely more formal than a flipchart or a chalkboard. On the other hand, both slides and transparencies provide the important advantage of showing your audience that you have spent considerable time and effort preparing your presentation. Although informality and spontaneity are very desirable in a small-group setting, demonstrating your preparedness can also weigh heavily. An accomplished speaker can keep the tone of a presentation lively and its process interactive, even while using an overhead projector and transparencies. (If you use viewgraphs, one way to temper their formal effect is to use a marker to write directly on them during the course of your talk.)

With all these considerations, how can you determine which medium to select? In a small-group presentation, if you want to impress your audience a bit and feel more secure with a virtually preordained order, then transparencies are probably the way to go. But if you seek continuous interaction with your listeners and expect to act more as a leader than as a presenter, a chalkboard or flipchart will serve you better. With either of the latter, you can rapidly record key words as you speak or jot down the most important points made by your listeners. In fact, you can even invite a colleague to step forward and rough out a suggestion or plan for the group to consider.

As you might imagine, the more fluid approach requires you to think on your feet. Therefore, the time you save by not preparing transparencies should be spent studying your material and building your knowledge of related issues. To help keep things under control, some speakers arm themselves with both a flipchart and a chalkboard—the flipchart for displaying exhibits prepared in advance and the chalkboard for recording comments from the audience.

## In-Depth Audience Analysis: An Approach to Structure

Generally, when you are called on to give a presentation, the size of your audience is already determined. The demands of the occasion or the wishes of your superiors (or both) determine who will attend. It's a little like being the host at a party for which you didn't have much say about the guest list. You simply do what you can to see to everyone's comfort and needs, including your own.

But you can find out a good deal about the "guests" before they arrive! Sometimes you will be faced with a group of colleagues whose desires and expectations are obvious. On other occasions you will have to dig deeper, first gathering information about those attending and then analyzing it with sensitivity and common sense. This analysis is crucial because it will provide preliminary guidelines for structuring your presentation.

To understand how this audience analysis works, let's consider three short cases:

---

You are assisting your boss, the manager of information systems, to explain a new computer application to a group of senior executives. They know very little about computers and are very set in their ways. You suspect they doubt the usefulness of the application.

**Case #1**

You decide to begin your presentation with a careful analysis of several of these executives' current needs. Using virtually no technical language, you will explain how the new application will answer those needs. You will conclude with a brief cost/benefits analysis. At no point will you explain the details of the technology.

---

You are a training specialist for a large automobile manufacturer. Assigned to work with a group of engineers, you have been given the responsibilities of developing a course on general business concepts and of gaining the engineers' commitment to undergo this training. Your boss has told you that most of the engineers will be pretty hostile to the idea; they would

**Case #2**

much prefer to spend their time learning about new technology. You call a meeting of the group so that they can hear you out.

You introduce your presentation with three examples that show in detail how some costly research programs came to be approved at three different firms. In each instance, approval depended on the engineering department's interacting with executives from marketing, finance, and production. You then explain that your course will simplify and explain basic concepts about these functions. You conclude with a strong recommendation that the engineers take the course during the next quarter.

Case #3

You are an assistant account executive at a large advertising agency. You are part of a four-member team that services an extremely important client, a Fortune 500 computer manufacturer. Your group has been working together for six weeks to prepare a major presentation to introduce a new logo for the company and to explain the related advertising campaign. Your supervisor has asked you to "pull things together" for the group as a preliminary step in preparing for the client presentation.

Your job is to provide a thorough review and to inspire discussion. Therefore, you don't try to sell the logo; rather, you point out both its pros and cons, listing them in separate columns on the chalkboard. You then switch on the overhead projector and present a transparency that shows the projected chronology for introducing the logo. As you discuss this time line, you review the tactics corresponding to each date. Then, again heading for the chalkboard, you ask your colleagues to suggest possible objections that the client might raise about the plan.

Analysis

If you look back at these three cases, you will recognize how an astute assessment of the audience influenced the structure of each presentation.

In the first case, if you opened the presentation with a description of the exciting new technology that supports the new application, you would confuse and bore the executives. Similarly, in the second case, opening with a gung-ho statement about the importance of business education, or even with a description of the merits of the particular course you designed, would guarantee that none of the engineers would enroll. In the third case, if you merely listed the good points of the logo, you probably would not provoke a good discussion. Although your audience already knows the plan, the time line provides a basis for their reviewing it and also for envisioning any possible snags.

Now, to review all of the steps in planning a presentation, let's reconsider the case involving Dev Gupta (see page 495). Dev's task, as you may recall, is to report on how the current regulatory environment impinges on shipping in the area of the Persian Gulf and the Arabian Sea. His purpose is to help the members of his team agree on a set of recommendations to be presented later to the firm's management. His audience is a group of ten people with whom he works almost daily, but they represent a rather difficult problem. He knows that three of his listeners are in favor of emphasizing the volatile situation in that area of the world, but the rest of them are far more impressed with the burgeoning opportunities. Dev knows that he must give a balanced and factual report and that he also must try to bring his listeners to a consensus.

He decides to structure his presentation so that the key issues are clearly delineated at the outset. Because he knows that some people will initially disagree with his findings, however, he decides to present each recommendation only after he has carefully analyzed the relevant issue.

To keep the meeting interactive, Dev opts for a workshop format. Although a podium is available, he decides not to use it, and he arranges the chairs in an informal semicircle. Since this is a preliminary presentation, to keep it fluid he decides to use some large maps and a marker rather than to prepare slides or viewgraphs. He also plans to make use of the large chalkboard directly behind him.

## ■ Preparing an Oral Presentation

Once you have given careful thought to your purpose and to your audience, have chosen the medium for your graphics, and have taken steps to reserve a suitable room, you will be confronted with the task of actually preparing the presentation. If you have done your research and gathered your data, creating a coherent structure will be your foremost concern.

It will certainly not surprise you to hear that presentations have a beginning (the introduction), a middle (the message), and a conclusion (closing remarks). But what may strike you as a new thought is that in *preparing* a presentation, the last should be first. That is, you should begin by deciding on your conclusion—what you want your audience to take away with them. If you had only three minutes to speak, what would you say? (Write the answer to this question down, just as you learned to do when preparing a position statement for a written document.)

Be certain that you express your position from your audience's perspective. "Our current telephone system has caused us all many problems and therefore needs to be improved" is not a bad opening. "Because our current telephone system is inadequate, you have all missed many important client calls" is even better. Also, be certain that you will leave your audience with a clear sense of the actions they should take. The talk that began with the statement about the inadequacy of the phone system might conclude with "And there are, as we have seen, three key steps we must take to remedy the telephone situation. First, we must . . . ."

After you have condensed the main thrust of your presentation into a strong concluding statement, it is time to step back and go to work on your message. You will need to develop a clear, coherent structure for the body of your presentation. The prewriting techniques you learned in Chapter 6 can help you here. For instance, using the analyst's couch method, you can sort your data and identify your primary issues. Or for a short, informal presentation, you can do a bit of "free-wheeling" to organize your ideas.

## The Storyboard

The most helpful means for structuring a presentation is commonly referred to as a *storyboard*, and closely resembles the "deck of cards" method for prewriting described in Chapter 6. To create a storyboard, you tape your cards on a convenient wall so that they reflect the point-by-point progression of your presentation. Very early in your preparation, you should "talk through" your storyboard, noticing where transitions are awkward, where facts are missing, or where the order seems illogical. It's easy at this time to change the order of your cards or to fill in the gaps.

You can greatly increase the usefulness of the storyboard by including sketches of your graphics, also laid out in the order in which they will appear. In fact, for presentations that depend heavily on slides or viewgraphs, the very best way to get ready is first to rough out your visuals and then to decide on the specific points you will make about each one. You can jot down these points on the bottom of each sketch, or you can follow each graphic with a series of "clue" cards (see Figure 17.1). (Use the second method if you expect to make a number of changes in the order of the individual points or if you feel you need to work with fairly copious notes.) In both cases, the verbal clues are, of course, only a working tool. In their present form, these words and phrases will rarely appear in your finished graphic displays.

## Review and Preview

Most listeners will not interrupt a speaker for clarification; nor should they, unless the occasion is extremely informal or everyone in the room is obviously totally confused. On the other hand, as we all know, it's easy for a listener's mind to wander. And even an instant's distraction can cause a vital point to slip by. A cardinal rule, therefore, is that oral presentations must be simpler than written reports.

No matter how tempted you may be to cover a broad sweep of topics, don't. Instead, *simplify!* Decide on the major message you hope to get across and the key ideas that will support that message. Then present this material in short, manageable chunks.

For instance, if you are attempting to persuade your boss and several department heads that your company really needs an internal newsletter, don't begin with a list of ten reasons why the newsletter is a good idea, and then go on to defend each. Instead, list the three main benefits to be derived from a newsletter, or perhaps the three major problems it would

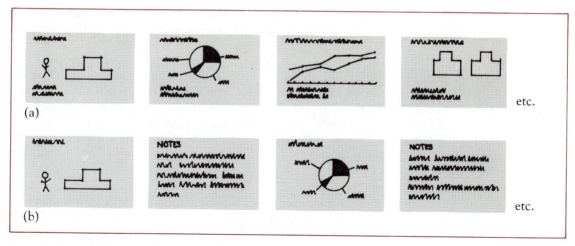

(a)

(b)

etc.

etc.

**Figure 17.1** Making a storyboard: (a) Method #1: Notes written on graphics cards; (b) Method #2: Separate cards for notes.

solve. Then focus on each, one at a time. Your listeners wouldn't be able to remember reason number three by the time you reached number ten!

Writers insert subheads to help readers find their way back to a particular point, and speakers provide an even more overt form of assistance—they use the *review-preview technique*. At each critical juncture, the speaker reviews the main points covered and previews those to come.

For example, suppose you are arguing the case for flextime, a system whereby employees all work an eight-hour day but start their day at different hours. Two-thirds of the way through your talk, you might build in a transition similar to this one:

*So you have seen that* flextime will not in any way reduce productivity and that it will definitely improve morale. *Now I will show you* some statistics demonstrating that flextime will also give this firm a real edge in hiring superior employees.

You have now told your audience precisely where they are and where they will be going.

As part of the review-preview technique, make an effort to use some of the transitional devices that improve coherence in a written document:

*Enumerate* ("There are three essential points. First . . .").

*Repeat* key words ("Applications are our concern here; not technology, but *applications!*")

*Rephrase* important points ("We're always expressing our concern about communicating well. We continually talk and talk about doing a better job of sharing ideas and viewpoints.")

*Use directional words and phrases* ("Moreover, this problem is increasing." "Let me point out that we are beginning to make progress." "Look back at last year's numbers.")

*Emphasize* ("Our third and most important objective is quality.").

As you build your presentation, keep reminding yourself that you have a destination in mind and are steadily leading your listeners toward it. You will need to establish the direction at the outset and continually point to familiar landmarks along the way. You may even need to exhort them to go all the way with you.

## Openings and Introductions.

The opening and introduction of a presentation are usually not one and the same. Both, however, are extremely important.

The *opening* is primarily meant to capture the listeners' attention. These first remarks are sometimes referred to as the "grabber" because their purpose is to grab an audience's interest. Some excellent grabbers include the following:

- A direct statement of the audience's chief concern (frequently, this is the very best opening).
- A key finding of your study (although a noncontroversial finding is less chancy, a bit of controversy can sometimes work well).
- A relevant anecdote or quotation (but be sure it *is* relevant).

What about humor? It is risky. Unless you are very experienced at story-telling and are certain that the story is entirely appropriate *and funny*, you are skating on thin ice. An old saying has it: "A pretty good joke is like a pretty good egg. There just ain't no such thing!"

The *introduction* of a presentation provides an agenda or a road map for the listeners. In a sense, it is the preview of previews. In most cases, it will provide a position statement and enumerate the primary issues that you plan to examine in support of that position. Each of those issues will probably represent a major section of your talk.

As you can see, the introduction of a talk resembles an executive summary. And the same constraints ordinarily apply. If you feel your audience (or even one key person) will be hostile to your position, then introduce only the issues you will explore, holding your conclusions until later. If even that much of a give-away is likely to get the pot boiling, then you may have to introduce your first issue only, reviewing and previewing all along the way.

## Closings

A good *closing* usually consists of a rapid summary of the chief issues and a call for commitment or action. On most occasions, these will be followed by an invitation for discussion or a request for questions.

Whether or not you allow time for a discussion period, be certain that *you* (not a member of the audience) end the presentation. You want to be the person whose words are heard last and remembered longest.

## ■ Summary

The oral presentation is a major form of business communication. Proper planning requires that you determine purpose, occasion and the size of audience. You should also evaluate your own strengths and weaknesses, choose an appropriate setting and effective graphics, and analyze the makeup of the audience.

A large audience tends to occasion formality; therefore, you will need to work especially hard at projecting warmth and humanity. Check the physical conditions of the auditorium or conference room beforehand. To encourage audience participation, announce at the outset that questions and/or discussion will be welcomed at the conclusion of your talk.

You may frequently be called upon to present to a small group. Although informality rules, you will want to be well prepared—poised, natural, and persuasive.

In structuring an oral presentation, begin by deciding exactly what overall message or conclusions you want the audience to take away with them. Express your position from the perspective of the audience. Then step back and go to work on your message, developing a clear, coherent structure. The storyboard, incorporating brief notes on separate cards, is an extremely helpful method for structuring your presentation.

Simplify your message. Employ the review-preview technique as you would use subheads to highlight structure in a written report. A good opening arouses interest and provides a roadmap for the audience. An effective closing usually consists of a rapid summary of key issues and a call for commitment or action.

## ■ Discussion Problems

**17.1**  In attempting to gain and hold their audiences' attention, writers and speakers share some of the same tools of the trade. For instance, both rely on word choice to create vivid and memorable images in their audiences' minds. What other tools do writers and speakers share? Whose task do you feel is most difficult? Why?

**17.2**  Dev Gupta's task is to prepare both a written and an oral report. He decides to distribute his written report after (rather than before) his oral presentation. Would you do the same in his circumstances? Are there times when it would be better to distribute written materials in advance of a presentation? How far in advance? Explain your answers.

**17.3**  Evaluate your own strengths and weaknesses as a speaker. Do you think you would perform better on a formal or informal occasion? Why? Would you prefer to address a large or a small audience? Why? Have you any ideas about how you might minimize your perceived weaknesses as a speaker?

**17.4**   Imagine that you are to give a presentation to a group of 20 students and faculty members, including the dean of students, or someone else of equal status. Your focus is the need to strengthen the career-placement services offered by your school. You can elect to hold this presentation in the school theater or the faculty dining room, or you can select some other appropriate setting at your school. Where would you hold it? Why? Would you use graphics as part of your presentation? If so, what kind? Why?

**17.5**   You and your partner have recently started a promising new entrepreneurial venture. You have a business degree, and your partner is a skilled designer. Together you have created and are marketing a new line of children's clothing and related items. Although you work out of your basement, the line is doing very well. New orders are coming in steadily. Through the recommendation of a mutual friend, you and your partner have been invited to attend the monthly meeting of your town's Retail Merchants' Association to describe your new line and to discuss ways of marketing it. The managers of two of the town's largest department stores are likely to attend, and you've been told that several prominent bankers may be present. Also likely to attend are the owners of several of the boutiques and specialty shops that might be potential customers for your products.

Discuss what topics you might cover in such a presentation. In what order would you discuss them? Would you use visuals? If so, what kind? What might be a good way to open your presentation? How much of your allotted time (15 minutes) would you use for questions and answers? If none, explain why.

**17.6**   Jane Steinman works for Downtown Concepts, a large realty company that is currently developing several new condominium complexes on Boston's waterfront. Tony Olario, Jane's boss, just informed her of a somewhat surprising turn of events. The firm has decided to merge with the Columbine Company, a large developer of luxury condominiums in exurban areas, with holdings extending as far as the New Hampshire border. In two weeks, Tony is to give a presentation to open a get-acquainted session to be hosted by the management of Downtown Concepts. Tony has asked Jane to suggest an appropriate topic and the general outline of his talk. He mentioned that he would appreciate any and all suggestions she might make about the arrangements and the content and focus of his presentation. What do you think should be Jane's primary concerns? Why? What should she do to resolve them? Can you suggest a likely topic for Tony's talk? How might you check to see whether it is on target?

## ■ Presentation Tasks

**17.1**   If you completed the research on computer graphics (Discussion Problem 16.4), prepare a storyboard for a presentation on your findings. The audience for the presentation will be your instructor and fellow students.

**17.2**   Prepare a short script (3–5 pages) for a presentation (topic of your choosing), in which you use all of the following techniques:

- preview-review
- enumeration
- repetition of key words
- directional words and phrases

**17.3**  Prepare an outline for a presentation (topic of your choosing), and convert that outline to a storyboard on 5 × 7 index cards. Submit both the outline and the storyboard cards to your instructor.

**17.4**  You have been asked to give a presentation to eight new employees of your firm as part of their orientation program. Write out three examples of a good "grabber" to open a presentation on one of the following topics:

- The importance of having a mentor in the early stages of a career
- The importance to a woman of having a male mentor in the early stages of her career
- Mentor relationships: they aren't always what they're cracked up to be!

**17.5**  You are an assistant sales manager for the largest auto-leasing firm in your town. Your current assignment is to prepare a sales presentation to be given by your boss, the sales manager, to the town council, the mayor, and the chief of police. The presentation is intended to convince this audience to replace out-of-commission police cars with leased cars so as to gradually build up an entire fleet of leased cars. Prepare a series of cards the sales manager can use as speaker's notes. Indicate where you would use visuals and what kinds you would choose.

**17.6**  Write an appropriate "grabber," or introductory statement, for the following talks and presentations:

- The presentation to the Retail Merchants' Association (Discussion Problem 17.5)
- A talk by a vice president to department managers to let them all know that they will be receiving their own personal computers in the next week and will be expected to be quickly "up to speed" in using them effectively
- Jane Steinman's talk for Tony Olario (Discussion Problem 17.6)
- The presentation to Laurel Laboratories (Writing Task 17.7, below)
- A talk by a department store manager to sales supervisors before the Christmas rush
- A talk to the Finance Club at a large university by a bank president attempting to interest graduating seniors in careers in banking

**17.7**  You are a junior consultant at an environmental risk-assessment consulting firm. Your company assists manufacturers in assessing potential hazards related to their products and procedures—especially in regard to violations of state or federal safety requirements. Your company has been invited to make a preliminary presentation to Laurel Laboratories, a multimillion-dollar pharmaceutical company, on the potential value of its services to that firm. Your boss, a senior consultant and vice president, has asked you to outline a 30-minute slide presentation to be delivered in approximately three weeks at this fairly formal gathering of Laurel Laboratories big-wigs. The presentation is to be based chiefly on past media coverage of suits against pharmaceutical companies over products that inflicted injury on members of the public. Do some research in periodicals in your school's library to gather anecdotal material and cases to use in this presentation. Create a storyboard for the presentation, clearly showing where you would use slides and indicating their general design and content.

# DELIVERING
# AN ORAL
# PRESENTATION

## 18

*T*he wise presenter arrives early and checks to see that all is in order. If you have asked for specific equipment, such as a lectern, flipchart, or chalkboard, it is sensible to see that the equipment is there and is placed appropriately. If you are to use slides or viewgraphs, recheck their order and see that the slides are inserted right-side-up in the carousel. If you are to use a microphone, you should say a few words into it to be certain that it is working properly and that you are speaking into it correctly. Similarly, you'll want to check the light in the projector. Also, locate and adjust the room thermostat, and decide how to separate smokers from nonsmokers. In short, once again, you need to keep in mind that this is your show; do everything you can to guarantee that you and your audience can convene comfortably and without interruption.

## ■ The "Panic-and-Emptiness" Syndrome

According to opinion polls, the fear of giving a presentation is extremely widespread. Look closely and you will often see the hands of an experienced presenter trembling. Moreover, the fatigue that strikes most people after delivering a presentation is acknowledged almost universally. Whether facing an audience of strangers or colleagues, a speaker is prone to feel a momentary sense of panic and emptiness. The individuals in the audience suddenly become a collective identity empowered to sit in judgment of the presenter's knowledge and skill.

If you are the one in the spotlight, you should neither dismiss such feelings nor allow them to demolish you. Something needs to be accomplished or addressed, and you have been given both the opportunity and the responsibility to carry it off. If you have planned and prepared well, you are almost certain to succeed. The whoosh of adrenalin that surges through you as you stand before your listeners signals that your body's chemistry is gearing up so you can deliver your best effort: your alertness to sights, sounds, and your own mental processes has increased. Your ability to project conviction and enthusiasm is tuned to its highest pitch.

If you are particularly prone to the "panic-and-emptiness" syndrome, take comfort in knowing that the more frequently you are called upon to present, the less disturbed you will be by initial anxiety. First, the memory of past successes will be with you. Second, you will probably have learned to perform a calming ritual.

The first step in such a ritual is to force yourself to view your audience as separate individuals. ("See, there's Max in the corner trying to borrow some paper from Harry. And Joanne is looking around the room as usual to see if her boss, Marilyn, has arrived.") If it's a small enough group (and if you are at entry level, it probably will be), you can greet people and converse with them naturally. If the group is large or composed of strangers, you should calmly wait until everyone is seated and then take your place. Before saying a single word, remain quiet for a few seconds and scan the audience; look directly at one or two people. (Those few seconds of silence will seem much longer to you than to anyone else in the room!)

At the outset of your presentation, you should be certain that everyone understands the ground rules. Are hard copies (photocopies) of the visuals or other materials to be distributed later? Do you want questions to be held until the very end of the presentation? Is there an out-of-town guest who needs to be introduced or welcomed? Seeing to these things will help you feel in control of your destiny; in addition, it will prevent distractions from preoccupying your listeners as you speak.

One final suggestion and perhaps the most important of all: *memorize your opening words.* No matter how you plan to handle the rest of your presentation, write out your opening remarks and commit them to memory. The sound of your own voice firmly pronouncing the words that you have learned and practiced will launch you into the rest of the presentation with a feeling of greatly increased confidence.

## ■ Memory-Jogger: Script, Outline, or Notes

Perhaps in the planning stage, and certainly in the preparation stage of your presentation, you will be faced with the question of what kind of memory aid to provide for yourself. In fact, at that time, this issue may seem to be of overriding importance. If you seek advice from experienced presenters, you will probably receive a variety of opinions, from "Don't take any chances—use a script!" to "If you want to succeed, just go ahead and talk. Forget about fiddling around with notes and that kind of stuff."

Such disparate advice is inevitable because there are no absolutes. Each combination of speaker, occasion, and audience will favor a different option. As usual, selecting the one that's right for you requires abundant common sense and good judgment.

The least desirable option for most presenters is reading directly from a script. An officer of a firm may on occasion read a report to his or her managers. Similarly, a specialist in a scientific or technical field may deliver a paper to an association or academic society. But these occasions are few and far between. As we have already explained, business presentations ordinarily are not speeches. Most business people expect presenters to know their subjects well and to communicate by talking naturally. A prepared script usually signals insecurity on the speaker's part.

On the other hand, writing out a script *as part of your preparation* is a very helpful technique. If the occasion is going to be important or you will be talking nonstop for a stretch of ten minutes or more, it's a good idea to practice your delivery by tape-recording the script as you read it aloud. Listening to the tape will help you in two ways: first, you will get some good insights into how you will sound to your listeners; second, each time you play the tape, your words and ideas will become more deeply ingrained in your memory. But don't try to memorize your entire talk! The object is merely to learn some key words and phrases and to become so familiar with the concepts that you can articulate them almost spontaneously.

What about using notes? There are a number of pros and cons; in the end, you must decide what will work best for you and your audience.

To do without notes or an outline takes some courage, but as long as you prepare well, know your material, and rehearse thoroughly, it's by far the better choice. Thomas Leech, whose company specializes in coaching executives to give effective presentations, says that using notes and visuals together is much like "trying to serve two masters."* Juggling notes while trying to flip pages on a chart or change viewgraphs is awkward and burdensome.

But there are some good, inconspicuous techniques for jogging your memory. For instance, you can lightly print a few key words at eye level in the margin of your flipchart, or even draw a very simple sketch of the next exhibit. When using viewgraphs, you can write key words directly on their cardboard frames. Slides present a problem in this respect, but with practice you can learn to anticipate the order you have set. Even if you do have a memory lapse, you can usually recover if you calmly examine the image on the screen (your audience will be doing the same thing!). But, of course, don't *read* the words on the slide to your audience.

If your material is extremely technical or complex, however, you may decide that some form of notes is essential. In this case, be sure to record your cues in a telegraphic style. For example, don't write: "Flextime is an excellent way to improve employee morale." Write something like this: "Builds employee morale." Most people like to write their notes on cards, and even an outline can be transferred to cards. (Some speakers, however, prefer to keep an annotated version of the hard copy in front of them.) Cards allow mobility; you won't need a lectern and can move about with one or more cards in your hand. Moreover, you avoid turning pages or noisily rattling papers. Do be certain to number your cards boldly, and also see that the cues are typed or printed in dark, legible letters.

*"It's show time!" *Communicator's Journal,* March/April, 1984.

# ■ Body Language and Voice

Roger Ailes, a former White House advisor and consultant to many business executives, warns, "There are three things an audience won't forgive you for. One—not being prepared. Two—not being enthusiastic about what you have to say. Three—not being interesting."* So far, most of the advice you've been given here has had to do with preparedness: up-front preparation as you put together the pieces of your presentation, and on-the-spot preparation as you ready the room, the equipment, and yourself. But even if you are meticulously prepared, your presentation will fall flat if you commit Ailes's second and third sins.

If your material is tailored to your audience and you know your subject well, your presentation is likely to be interesting. But enthusiasm is another matter. You may be tempted to believe that you will project enthusiasm automatically if you are sincerely interested in your topic. Not so. Nor is it true that you are doomed to deliver a hopelessly dull presentation if you find your topic less than compelling. Although it is certainly a great help to have a high degree of interest in your subject and a genuine commitment to your objectives, you still need to know how to project enthusiasm through the skillful use of body language and voice techniques. And even when a presentation focuses on a run-of-the-mill, all-in-a-day's work subject, you can use the same skills to invigorate it. By doing so, you may find that you have "psyched yourself up" to a higher level of enthusiasm.

## Body Language

In the next few days, whenever you catch yourself talking animatedly, try to mentally step back from the conversation and note your bearing and gestures. You will probably be able to maintain this objectivity for only a few seconds because as soon as you start to *think* about body language, it changes. But even the momentary effort will help you to observe how integral and natural body language is to your ability to communicate. (Observing someone else's gestures is also helpful, but objectifying your own behavior provides more vivid insight.)

Nonverbal behavior is natural and constant. Even when you are virtually motionless, your posture and facial expressions send clear signals. These signals can enforce verbal meaning or even transmit a more potent message than the spoken words. In general, audiences will believe what they see even more readily than what they hear. A white-knuckled presenter gripping the lectern immediately telegraphs his anxiety, even if his words are assertive and confident. A speaker swaying like a metronome can hypnotize her listeners into boredom, even while she discusses an issue of vital concern.

*"Okay, Ailes, Fix Me!" *Communicator's Journal,* November/December, 1983.

What can you do to help yourself avoid such damaging behavior? If you tend to freeze or to grow stiff and inert in front of an audience, the following practice routines (done during a time when you are *not* presenting) may assist you.

**Practice Routine 1.** First, recollect that people normally use four kinds of gestures. We enumerate ("Not one but *two!*" with two fingers held up). We describe ("About this high and that wide," with hands measuring the space). We point ("Look at the high peak on the left side of the chart," indicating where it is). And we emphasize ("We *won't* let that happen!" thumping the table with a closed fist).

Now think about your presentation carefully. When might you like to use each type of gesture?

Do a dry run, using grossly exaggerated gestures at appropriate points. You can try this odd routine alone in your room or, even better, with a trusted friend as your audience. Your main objective is to have fun—ham it up! If you can't loosen up while rehearsing your presentation, switch to a less threatening topic. Perhaps you can talk for five minutes about your morning wake-up routine, or describe the way you make a bed or prepare a particular gourmet dish. Once you are into the swing of things, you can go back to practicing the presentation.

As your confidence grows, try to think less and less about gestures or body language. On the day of your actual presentation, *don't think about gestures at all.* Just make absolutely certain that your hands are entirely free: don't thrust them into your pockets or grip the lectern or table. With any luck at all, your newly learned behavior will spontaneously take over, and you will punctuate your talk with natural and suitable gestures.

**Practice Routine 2.** Instead of freezing in place, your problem may be a compulsion to sway, to fidget, or to keep moving in other ways. Some presenters find that their anxiety produces a rush of energy that simply must be expressed in movement. The following routine is a good way to learn to overcome this common problem. Again, you can practice it alone in your room or with a group of friends who are willing to help.

Begin talking, giving your presentation or speaking on some other topic. After saying a few lines, walk to a chair or table. Standing before it, count out loud very slowly from one to five. Then move on to a new location. Continue your talk, repeating the counting exercise at intervals. After some practice, you should be able to stroll purposefully to any spot in the room, stand still (without counting), and earnestly address any chosen piece of furniture. (Of course, if you do have a few willing friends, you may find them to be a more responsive audience.)

Addressing your listeners from different vantage points allows you to move naturally. In addition, if you are using transparencies or slides, you can occasionally walk toward the screen and point to a specific place on the image. In an informal setting, you can take a few steps toward someone in the room, establish eye contact, and directly address a few remarks to him or her. Of course, don't always choose the same person, and be sure to move on to a new position after a few minutes. If you don't overdo it, most people welcome this kind of attention—they feel the speaker is really interested in communicating with them personally.

Since we've mentioned eye contact, we should say a few more words about it. Eye contact cannot be established by sweeping your gaze back and forth across the room. In fact, that is a kind of visual swaying or pacing. Select a friendly face, and stay with it for the length of a complete thought or for two or three sentences.

One last point about nonverbal behavior: Don't hide behind a podium! Typically, the most interesting item in a presentation is the speaker. Your personal presence, beyond anything else, has the greatest effect on your audience. Let people get to know you!

## Word Choice and Voice

The words you use and the way you use them also have a strong influence on the quality of your presentation.

Virtually everything we said about word choice with respect to writing style holds true for speaking.* In fact, since spoken words vanish the moment they are expressed, speakers may have an even more urgent need than writers to use langauge that is energetic and memorable. As you have learned, such language is composed of image-provoking, active verbs and specific, concrete nouns. Speakers should also be as sensitive as writers are to the connotations of words: one carelessly chosen word can instantly send a wave of concern washing over every person in the room. (Compare, for instance, the following three statements about a late project: "This delay is *disturbing*." "This delay is *unacceptable*." "This delay is *disastrous*.")

While tone in writing is real but subtle, it is the very stuff of which a talk is made. The speaker's attitude is conveyed in body language, facial expression, choice of words, and—probably most of all—voice signals: loudness, speed and rhythm, and intonation.

*Loudness* is the most obvious of the voice signals. When we raise our voices, we usually mean to intensify the feeling behind our words—to become more forceful. On the other hand, a sudden lowering of the voice can also be an effective attention-getter. If you choose to write out a script as part of your preparation, you can use the following technique:

---

*At this point, you may wish to review the material in Chapters 10 and 11, especially that which deals with word choice and vigor.

- <u>Underline</u> words where voice should rise.

- Draw a line above words where voice should drop.

*Speed and rhythm* in speech closely parallel variety and rhythm in writing. If you drone on at an overly slow pace with few real pauses, you will undoubtedly put your listeners to sleep; if you race ahead full speed, you will begin to sputter for lack of breath, and your listeners will grow weary from trying to keep up with you.

As a speaker, the pause is one of your most effective tools. Pausing not only allows you to breathe, it also provides you with a chance to gather your thoughts. Moreover, the pause is the "punctuation mark" of oral delivery. A short pause is tantamount to a comma; a long, pronounced pause resembles a period; a sudden full stop is as much an attention-getter as an exclamation point. To indicate pauses on a script, you can leave two open lines (//) for each short pause and fill in the lines (■) for each longer or full pause. Keep in mind that what may seem like a long pause to you might be almost imperceptible to your audience. Many inexperienced speakers fear silence; consciously or unconsciously, they attempt to fill the void. The conscious reaction is to race ahead at breakneck speed; the unconscious one is to give way to verbal tics—the "uhh's" or "right?'s" or "you know's" that can recur like an irritating refrain.

*Intonation,* the third way speakers can convey the emotion underlying their words, depends primarily on pitch. As we speak, our voices move from sound to sound with an almost continuous rise and fall of pitch. This change of pitch can occur within a single word or from word to word. To see how we ordinarily inflect individual words, try saying "yes" first as a sentence, next with eagerness, and then with anger or sarcasm. Listen to yourself to see how the pitch of your voice moves up and down with each change of feeling. Intonation from word to word can be clearly heard by varying the meaning of a simple phrase. For instance, you might try saying "you did" first as a question, then expressing anger, excitement, etc.

No one expects an Academy Award performance from a business presenter. On the other hand, speakers who drone on without intonation are quickly pegged as dull and ineffectual. If you suffer from this problem, we suggest once again that, either alone in your room or with a sympathetic friend, you cast aside your inhibitions and *perform.* Punch up your prepared speech with greatly exaggerated intonations. Or, as we recommended for developing expressive gestures, substitute some less threatening material for your presentation. Read aloud a dramatic newspaper story, or if you have a literary bent, work with a poem or a play. The main thing is to pour energy and enthusiasm into your reading. (Your real presentation will, of course, be somewhat toned down.) With practice, you will find that you have learned to make your voice work for you, and you will also discover that your whole outlook on presenting has vastly improved.

# ■ Fielding Questions

Questions from the audience are desirable because they prove that people are listening to and caring about what you have been saying. On the other hand, frequent questions can interrupt the flow of the presentation, trip you up, or allow antagonists to vent their spleen. If you hope to be effective, however, you really don't have the option of deciding whether or not to take questions from the audience. You can only decide when to answer them and how many to answer.

Let the audience know the ground rules at the outset of your presentation. Announce that you will take questions at specific junctures or only at the conclusion of your talk. In the latter case, set a time limit for the question period so that you can conclude firmly at an appropriate point. You should allow questions to be asked *during* your presentation only when the following conditions apply:

■ The occasion is informal.
■ The group is small.
■ Your subject matter is not especially controversial.
■ You are sure you can continue to maintain control.

At an interactive, meeting-like presentation, you certainly want to resolve misunderstandings and clarify points along the way—unless by doing so you risk losing control of the situation. And if the subject matter is highly controversial and feelings are running high, there is real danger of losing control.

What can you do about answering difficult questions? First, you should recognize that they come in five varieties: challenging, complex, irrelevant, personal, and hostile.

*Challenging questions* should be treated with respect. You may even want to compliment the questioner! If to answer the question you need a few minutes to think, create those minutes by restating the question, carefully paraphrasing it. (This tactic will also give your listeners a second chance to digest the question.) On the other hand, if you really don't know the answer, you may want to turn it over to another member of the audience with an honest rejoinder: "Harry, I'm afraid I don't have that information, but Lew is indicating that he has those facts." Or you can promise to deliver the answer at a later date: "Harry, I'll have those numbers for you early tomorrow."

Extremely *complex questions* can also be handled by paraphrasing. As you restate the question, segment it into manageable pieces that can be examined one at a time.

Obviously *irrelevant questions* can be redirected with a paraphrase: "Dana, you're asking whether we plan to hire a new person to manage this product; as I have stressed, the main question is whether we should even continue to offer it at all."

When it comes to fielding *personal questions*, remember, if you can keep your cool, the audience will almost invariably side with you and against your antagonist. Don't answer the personal question: either quietly state that this is not the right forum for that question, or pause for a moment, let the silence sink in, and then go on without responding.

*Hostile questions*, on the other hand, must be answered, but don't hurry. In many cases, hands will shoot up around the room, and a recognized ally will come to your aid. If you are on your own (or prefer to be), give a scrupulously fair paraphrase of the question, eliminating all inflammatory language, and then "march in your troops." Such a question-answer dialogue might go something like this:

HOSTILE HARRY: "You're a #!?*! fool if you think that my department will stand for another budget cut in this fiscal year." [Silence during which Friendly Frank catches your eye.]

FRIENDLY FRANK: "Come on, Harry! You know that my department also took a cut in the last quarter."

HOSTILE HARRY: "And what good did it do you guys? Or anyone else here for that matter? Profits are down again."

YOU: "Harry, you are obviously concerned because you feel your department will be stressed by another budget cut. But, as I demonstrated a few minutes ago, we are now clearly out of the woods but not yet home free. By pulling in our belts just one more time, we can free up the funds we need to introduce the Star-20 Widget a full six months ahead of all competing models. We've got to make this effort."

When you have given a strong, positive response to a question, hostile or otherwise, and you note that the period allotted for questions is nearly over, end on that high point. Once again, it's important to remind yourself that *you* are in control!

## ■ Summary

Arrive early and check to see that the room's physical conditions are suitable and equipment in order. Learn to perform a calming ritual before you begin to speak.

At the outset of your talk make certain that everyone understands your ground rules—when questions will be entertained, materials distributed, etc. Be sure to memorize your opening words.

Decide for yourself which type of memory aid works best for you. Generally, brief notes on numbered cards are preferable. Project enthusiasm through body language—gesture, movement, eye contact—and good vocal techniques—varying volume, speed and rhythm, and intonation.

Treat challenging questions with respect. Create time to formulate a response by restating the question in your own words. If you don't have an answer, you may either request help from another member of the audience or promise to deliver the answer later. Handle complex questions by separating them into manageable pieces. Paraphrase irrelevant questions and redirect them to the topic under discussion. Do not respond to unfriendly personal questions; state quietly that this is not the place for such a question, or simply remain silent for a few seconds and then proceed to the next question. An openly hostile question may find you an ally in the audience. If you prefer to answer it yourself, use paraphrase to separate the factual from emotional content, and then turn the question to your own advantage. Always try to end on a high point.

## ■ Discussion Problems

**18.1**   *With the sound turned completely off*, watch 30 minutes of a movie on television (preferably vintage 1950 or earlier). Ask a friend to watch the same movie with the sound on in another locale. Later, tell your friend as much as you can about the movie. Describe the characters, interpret the actions, and forecast the plot developments. (You can jot down notes while watching if this helps you to recollect what you saw.) Compare your observations and interpretations with your friend's. Which of you observed more details? How close did you come to understanding the situation? Interpret your experience in terms of what it implies about body language and gestures.

**18.2**   A similar exercise to that in Discussion Problem 18.1 can be done with the whole class participating. Your instructor will show the group segments of a silent film tape in five-minute increments. You will then be asked to explain and interpret the characters and actions. After showing several segments, your instructor will show them again with the sound turned on. The class will then discuss the experience, comparing their impressions and interpretations of the film without sound to those of the version with sound.

**18.3**   This is another group exercise. Its purpose is to help you learn to establish eye contact. Give a five-minute presentation on any topic of your choice. Before you begin to speak, however, every person in the room raises his or her hand. As you speak, establish eye contact with one person after another and maintain it long enough for each person to count slowly to three (silently, of course). As soon as a person with whom you have eye contact reaches "three," he or she will lower his or her hand. When you have finished your talk, note how many hands are still raised. These are the people with whom you did not establish sufficient eye contact. Also note whether they are clustered in any one part of the room. (Speakers often tend to neglect one part of their audience and favor another!)

**18.4**   Below are excerpts from two famous speeches. First, mark each for pause and emphasis. Next, have two or three people read their versions aloud. Discuss how these interpretations differ in emphasis and meaning. Can these differences be entirely explained by the way each speaker handles pause and emphasis? Are there other factors that contribute to the differences? Explain.

From "I Will Be Heard" by William Lloyd Garrison

I am aware that many object to the severity of my language; but is there not cause for severity? I will be as harsh as Truth and as uncompromising as Justice. On this subject I do not wish to think, or speak, or write with moderation. No! No! Tell a man whose house is on fire to give a moderate alarm; tell him to moderately rescue his wife from the hands of the ravisher; tell the mother to gradually extricate her babe from the fire into which it has fallen—but urge me not to use moderation in a cause like the present. I am in earnest—I will not equivocate—I will not excuse—I will not retreat a single inch—and I will be heard.

From "Farewell Address at Springfield" by Abraham Lincoln

My Friends: No one not in my position can appreciate the sadness I feel at this parting. To this people I owe all that I am. Here I have lived more than a quarter of a century; here my children were born, and here one of them lies buried. I know not how soon I shall see you again. A duty devolves upon me which is, perhaps, greater than that which has devolved upon any other man since the days of Washington. He never could have succeeded except for the aid of Divine Providence, upon which he at all times relied. I feel that I cannot succeed without the same Divine Aid which sustained him, and in the same Almighty Being I place my reliance for support; and I hope you, my friends, will all pray that I may receive that Divine Assistance, without which I cannot succeed, but with which success is certain. Again I bid you all an affectionate farewell.

# ■ Presentation Tasks

The following topics are suitable for short presentations (five to ten minutes). Your instructor may allow more or less time, depending on how many presentations need to be heard.

**18.1**   Select a controversial topic (it need not be a business issue). Prepare a presentation with three visuals, arguing for a specific position. Establish your position at the outset, and indicate the main issues you will be discussing. You may invent data to support your talk. (A good place to look for a topic is in *Business Week, Newsweek, Time,* or the *Wall Street Journal,* but you don't need to do any serious research or data gathering.)

**18.2**   Give a talk on the importance (or lack of importance) of a business degree to someone pursuing a business career. Or, if you prefer, argue for or against the importance of liberal arts subjects to someone preparing for a business career.

**18.3**   Argue for or against the importance of working in the field for several years before deciding whether or not to pursue an advanced business degree.

**18.4**   Argue for or against the proposition that it is better to be an entrepreneur than to work for a large corporation.

**18.5**   Explain how to read the financial pages of the *Wall Street Journal* or another major newspaper. Create three or more visuals for this talk.

**18.6**  Report on which parts of the country now offer recent college graduates best opportunities for business careers. You may design this as a fairly objective presentation or argue vigorously for one or more locales. Use visuals if they seem appropriate.

**18.7**  Argue for or against the proposition that in our global economy the time is rapidly approaching when business people will need to speak more than one language fluently.

## A Case Problem: Highland Federal Bank and Trust

Ron Pruitt faces a difficult assignment.

Ron is Assistant Manager of Management Information Systems (MIS) at Highland Federal Bank and Trust, a medium-sized financial institution located in Rolling Meadows, Illinois, a town about 50 miles west of Chicago. Serving the community for nearly 100 years, the bank has a long tradition of offering quality service and maintaining enduring customer relationships. But time has caught up with Highland Federal!

During the past six months, Highland Federal's two chief competitors have installed automated teller machines (ATMs) in their facilities. And almost from day one, the officers of Highland Federal have been vigorously debating whether to follow suit and install ATMs at their main branch and possibly at other branches as well.

The consensus in the MIS department is that an ATM system would be manageable, cost effective, and controllable. Ron's boss, Joanne Quinn, Highland Federal's Chief Information Officer, is much in favor of rapidly moving ahead with the new system. And Ron agrees. In fact, for the last month he's felt a bit guilty because he opened a small account at one of the competing banks in order to have 24-hour access to his money.

But not all departments at the bank are proponents of an ATM system. Although there are some strong allies in the marketing department, their vociferous support is counterbalanced by equally vocal opposition from the internal audit department. Arnold Sharma, the senior Vice President who organized that department nearly 30 years ago, consistently maintains that ATMs are a fad: "They're *toys!* Some banks will adopt them; some won't. People may want to try them, yes. But ultimately people will select an institution whose reputation they trust, one where they receive honest, personal, attentive service."

This afternoon Joanne informed Ron that in three weeks she must give an oral report to the bank officers to explain the MIS department's position in the ATM controversy. She asked Ron to pull together a preliminary speech of the presentation and to suggest appropriate visual aids. He is to give her these materials by the end of the week.

Ron began his effort by putting together a fact sheet that summarizes (in no special order) most of the issues and available data concerning the possible adoption of ATMs by Highland Federal. To identify the issues, he used an "analyst's couch" session (see Chapter 6). For the hard data, he relied heavily on a report from the Illinois Banker's Association (IBA). Ron's fact sheet is shown in Figure 18.1.

Figure 18.1
Ron Pruitt's fact
sheet.

Issues to Consider

1. Are these machines reliable?
2. What kind of customers really use these things?
3. Anticipated payback period of initial investment in ATMs?
4. Are costs of installation a real issue?
5. Internal resistance—how serious?
6. Will customers accept ATMs?
7. Staff training costs—money? time?

Hard Data from IBA

1. For Illinois banks installing ATMs, the increase in new savings and checking accounts averaged 22 percent at inner-city locations and 14 percent at suburban locations. Though the net value of these accounts has not yet been clearly determined, evidence shows that many are smaller accounts ($100–$200), opened solely for the purpose of providing customers with access to 24-hour banking.

2. In the state of Illinois, nearly 600 banks have installed ATMs in either one or several locations during the past year. The data indicate that 35 percent of these institutions are moderately happy with the system, 14 percent are unhappy and are thinking of either pulling the system altogether or switching to a different system, and the remaining 51 percent are very satisfied with the system.

3. The MINIMUM cost of installing such a system is estimated at $0.5 million (includes actual equipment costs, the computer, installation, service, maintenance, and building modifications). To install a first-rate system, Highland Federal could easily be looking at a $5–$10 million investment.

4. According to IBA, banks can anticipate a payback period of 3 to 8 years, depending on the number of units installed and the intensity of the marketing effort.

Other Stuff to Consider (Maybe)

1. From article in American Banking, downtime seems to be a real problem: AB reports that the average system is out of commission at least two days per month. AB also indicates that there haven't been many really serious problems. Most have been correctable errors on small accounts (EXCEPT at Long Island Savings and Grand Rapids Mutual Trust!).

2. Sharma is fairminded. Even if he is an old fogey, he'll give this a fair shake. But he'll have to be convinced.

3. Reliance Equipment's vendor, Edna Vincent, says they'll provide a three-day on-site training program for the staff at no charge, and will remain on call for six months.

4. Joel Saxon, the comptroller at Security Savings and Loan, says that their aggressive advertising program for their ATM network has netted them nearly a 50% increase in weekly new-account business.

---

Ron knows that the presentation does not have to touch on every possible issue and does not have to include every bit of data he has collected. But he must produce a strong, cohesive argument for bringing ATMs to Highland Federal.

## Case Assignments

**C.1**  Create an outline of the presentation draft that Ron must prepare for Joanne.

**C.2**  With your outline as a guide, prepare a storyboard on 5 × 7 cards. (You may use either of the two methods shown in Figure 17.1.)

**C.3**  Write out a two- or three-page script for the opening remarks of the talk. Be sure that you include a good "grabber."

**C.4**  Annotate your script to show increasing or decreasing forcefulness and long or short pauses.

**C.5**  Using your annotations, read your script aloud to your fellow students. Identify any changes you would then make in the script, and explain why you would make them.

**C.6**  Create five good visuals for Joanne to use in her talk. At least two of these must be charts based on Ron's hard data.

**C.7**  Working in a small group (three to five people) prepare a presentation to deliver to the "officers" (your fellow students and your instructor). You may invent additional facts if you need them or expand on the data given. Each person on the team is to deliver a part of the presentation. Depending on the size of your team, your presentation should be from 10 to 15 minutes in length, but no longer.

If video equipment is available, your presentation will be videotaped. Depending on your instructor's preference, you will then either review your individual performance in a private conference with your instructor, or the teams will each see and discuss their own presentations at a convenient time after class.

**C.8**  As you listen to each presentation, take note of its strengths and weaknesses—apart from the speakers' personal speaking skills. Write a short critique of each presentation's structure, coherence, graphics, word choice, and tone.

**C.9**  Select a member of your class to be Arnold Sharma. At the end of each presentation, he or she is to ask some hostile and difficult questions. Other members of the class should try to frame less hostile but equally pressing questions. All questions should be directed at a specific member of the presenting team. Each presenter will practice fielding questions. At a specified time, a team member should end the question period on a strong, positive note.

# MEETINGS
# AND MORE
# MEETINGS

## 19

*A*lthough some meetings are chiefly settings for presentations, many others are not. Meetings often have very different objectives from presentations and require very different kinds of preparation. Moreover, although people tend to approach most presentations optimistically, they frequently have a very different feeling about meetings.

In this vein, Hollywood producer David Brown once complained, "In the entertainment business today, people are unable to return their phone calls. Why? They are in a meeting. . . . American business would be much better off if meetings were confined to 30 minutes at 7:30 in the morning."* And Brown's feelings are not unique. Many business people either dislike meetings wholeheartedly or at the very least have a love/hate relationship with them. Meetings are one of the chief ways that work gets done; on the other hand, poorly planned or badly run meetings are one of the chief obstacles to getting work done.

Almost inevitably, a time will come in your business career when you will be asked to chair a meeting; even more certain is the fact that you will be attending meetings at regular intervals. Now is the time, therefore, to consider how to make these opportunities productive for yourself and your colleagues.

## ■ Planning a Meeting**

Business meeetings range from large, carefully planned assemblies that convene representatives of many companies to informal conferences between two or three people. Regularly held meetings include management's annual and semiannual planning meetings, weekly departmental meetings, project staff meetings, and meetings between supervisors and subordinates; and this list is by no means inclusive. But whether two or two hundred people are present, business meetings invariably have one of three kinds of objectives: information exchange, problem solving, or some combination of the two.

When you decide to convene a meeting or are asked to chair one, your first thought should concern not what you want to happen *at* the

---

*Forbes, January 16, 1984.

**Although many good sources were consulted when preparing this material, a particularly helpful one was "A Note on How to Run a Meeting," James Ware, 1977, the President and Fellows of Harvard College, distributed by the Intercollegiate Case Clearing House.

meeting but what you want to happen *after* it is over. You might begin your preparation by sitting down and penning a memo to yourself, starting with "The purpose of this meeting is to see that. . . ." This statement might, for instance, end in one of the following ways:

1. . . . everyone in the company understands our new profit-sharing plan.
2. . . . everyone in the department understands our productivity goals for this quarter.
3. . . . we can come up with a way to simplify our current inventory procedures.
4. . . . Harry, Jane, and Mac have a better understanding of each other's responsibility in regard to this client.
5. . . . Joe commits himself to taking steps to upgrade his writing skills.

The first two items emphasize information exchange and the last three problem solving, but elements of both goals are present in 2, 3, and 4.

Once you have determined the desired outcome for the meeting, you will be able to select the participants, build the *agenda*, establish the *time*, and decide on a *location*.

## Selecting the Participants

You should invite people who either can contribute to a meeting or have a stake in its outcome. If the purpose of the meeting is to share information, do your own part in collecting needed data and see that all those attending know what specific contributions are expected of them. If the information you need from other people is considerable or complex, you should give them plenty of time to prepare. You can even suggest an appropriate medium for sharing their data with the group. You might let them know that you are putting together a hand-out. For example, you could suggest that Charlie's estimates be included in the package or that Ellen let you make copies of her diagram of the current organizational structure.

When selecting participants, you should not think solely about their potential contributions but also about their concerns and attitudes. If this is a problem-solving session and the problem is sensitive or controversial, you will have to be especially careful. Try to limit the participants to a manageable number—certainly no more than ten people. You may even want to do a bit of preliminary attitude exploration, arranging one-on-one conferences with specific participants to get a sense of where they stand or how they will react to a specific proposal.

## Preparing an Agenda

Even if a meeting is simply for information exchange, a well-planned agenda can guarantee a better outcome and make your job as chairperson much easier. The purpose of an agenda is to ensure that the meeting is focused on the appropriate issues or topics, that they are sensibly ordered, and that an appropriate amount of time is alloted to each.

As chairperson, you normally will have the responsibility of preparing the agenda. To do so will require one part diligence and three parts insight and common sense.

Once you have determined the meeting's main purpose and know who will be coming, you have two alternatives. If your objectives are well defined and you want to limit the number of topics, you generally can compose the agenda without seeking any further information or advice. But if it's important to you to first learn what's on people's minds, you should initially send out a brief memo stating the purpose of the meeting and asking participants to suggest their own agenda items.

If there are just a few participants and the meeting is to be informal, you can solicit agenda items by phone. If you make your requests by phone, however, be very certain that everyone clearly understands the meeting's focus; too often people hear what they prefer. You don't want to encounter any "hidden" agendas. Picture the scene at a meeting if George and Henry stubbornly maintain that they have come to establish the timing for a new product's introduction, when your own purpose is to get a consensus as to whether it should be released at all!

In building an agenda, try to sequence the items so that they follow one another logically. Obviously, if the purpose of your meeting is to decide whether a product should be released and, if so, to come up with a preliminary timetable, the agenda will reflect that order. Also, before any issue is to be debated, be sure the necessary information exchange can take place. Build in sufficient time to be able to gather the data yourself or to call an appropriate person to do so.

As you might imagine, it is often difficult to predict just how much time will be needed to cover a particular item. Your best tactic, therefore, is to plan for things to take a bit longer than you expect. Almost no one objects to a meeting's ending early, but few people are willing or able to stay beyond the scheduled time. Moreover, attempting to cram too many items onto an agenda may be a sure way to see that nothing at all gets covered adequately.

Unless the meeting is called on very short notice and is extremely informal, you should see that a typed copy of the final agenda is distributed to each participant a day or two in advance (see Figure 19.1). You also might want to attach relevant background information so that people can be well prepared.

## Picking the Place and Time

Where and when you hold a meeting can also affect its success.

As with a presentation, the setting strongly influences the tone of a meeting. This is true for both group meetings and one-on-one confer-

**Figure 19.1**
A typical agenda
for a weekly meet-
ing.

MARKETING STRATEGY GROUP MEETING

Thursday, September 8, 198-
9:00 a.m.–10:00 a.m.

AGENDA

| | | |
|---|---|---|
| 9:00–9:15 | Direct-mail campaign for spring conference (status report) | Pat P. |
| 9:15–9:20 | New design for company business cards | Art C. |
| 9:20–9:50 | Product-introduction strategies | Gerry M., Pat P., Art C. |
| 9:50–10:00 | Action plans and summary | Gerry M. |

ences. A neutral conference room creates a very different atmosphere for a departmental meeting than does the boss's office. For that matter, even with a two-person conference, whether it is held in the office of the superior or of the subordinate may affect how it will be conducted.

Another consideration in regard to selecting a meeting place is the number of interruptions that can be tolerated. If a group meets in a room with a phone, the chairperson needs to establish some ground rules about how phone calls should be handled. (The best plan is to prohibit phone calls except for extreme emergencies and, if a call does slip through, to ask the recipient to arrange quickly to take it elsewhere.) For an especially important company meeting, an off-site meeting place such as a hotel, restaurant, or conference center is usually best.

The timing of a meeting should also take into account the need to avoid interruptions. There is, however, no perfect time to hold a meeting. In the morning, when interruptions are most likely, people are fresh and energetic. Although they may be tired later in the day, they will be less likely to be thinking about the numerous other matters that have claims on them. One good piece of advice is that if you don't want a meeting to drag on, schedule it to end precisely at noon, when people are ready to head out to lunch. Another tip is to be certain to provide a break if the meeting is to extend past 90 minutes. The participants will be grateful for a chance to stretch and to get some refreshment, and you will be too.

Common sense, empathy, and intuition go a long way in helping a chairperson select an appropriate setting and time for a meeting. But, unfortunately, an influence that is often stronger than all of these is *necessity*. In most cases, you will find yourself making the best of what is available. And, as when scheduling a presentation, you will be wise to reserve your accommodations well in advance.

# ■ Chairing a Meeting

When you are present only as a participant, the extent of your contribution to a meeting is fairly clear-cut. Arrive on time and be well prepared. Be attentive and give others their due. Don't be a clam or a shrinking violet: if you have something relevant and worthwhile to say, say it. Don't interrupt other speakers discourteously; but if you need to be assertive to get past someone's blocking action, do so with calm authority. When you are asked direct questions, give direct answers.

Fulfilling the role of a participant merely demands a combination of common sense and good manners. But, for the chairperson, the responsibilities are heavier. Not only does chairing require careful preparation, as we have described above, it also calls for some strong interpersonal skills.

As chairperson, you must make it clear right away that this is a meeting and not a presentation; that is, it is neither your presentation nor anyone else's! The chairperson's job is to control the discussion without dominating it. If this may sound rather difficult, just remember that the traditional authority of the chairperson goes with the role and carries a good bit of clout. With confidence and a measure of diplomacy, even a novice can normally manage well.

Consider the group as being in your charge: you are their leader, their guide, and even their protector. You will need to assist the weak, draw out the silent, and actively encourage the exchange of ideas. To do all this well, you will have to be very observant and a good listener. Although you don't want irrelevant issues to creep into the discussion and distract people from the task at hand, you should recognize that new ideas often appear in unexpected guises. What at first looks like a caterpillar may become a butterfly if allowed to bask in the light of open discussion. The line between control and tyranny is delicate. Your job is to steer a careful path. If you make it clear that you won't indulge in or tolerate idea-killing, others will usually follow your lead.

The agenda will assist you in maintaining control. With this list in plain sight, everyone present can see what topics still need to be covered and the time allotted for each. Most people will be displeased if the agenda is treated too casually, yet they generally will assent to an important expansion or a truly relevant digression. To track time, you will either have to keep an eye on the clock or ask someone else to be time-keeper. In either case, remember that a quick glance at your watch may be just the thing to keep things moving, or to send a signal to an overly garrulous participant.

# ■ Action Items and Controversies

As a meeting progresses, whenever someone promises to carry out a specific task, the commitment should be recorded. These commitments are often referred to as *action items*. If someone is taking minutes, he or she should carefully record the action items; otherwise, the chairperson should accept this responsibility. (You might record action items on the chalkboard and later copy them for distribution.) In an information-exchanging meeting, the only action items may be specific promises to complete further research or to gather more data. But in a problem-solving meeting, much more is required. It is commonly expected that such meetings will at least identify preliminary actions leading to a full solution. If such a solution is laid out, the chairperson should call for steps to implement it as soon as possible.

As chairperson, it is extremely important for you to make sure that opposing ideas are aired. If a partisan viewpoint is ignored or a proponent is bullied into silence, then the controversy is apt to surface again—either later at the same meeting or in weeks to come. In the latter case, it may ultimately bring about the downfall of the entire project.

But even when the discussion is knowledgeable, thorough, and open, differing objectives, competing departmental needs, and just plain differences of opinion do not necessarily fade away. When tension is high and feelings concerning an issue are running strong, you can usually exert more control by calling on specific people to speak rather than by allowing spontaneous dialogues to erupt. You can also paraphrase or comment on inflammatory statements in language that summarizes the factual content but omits the emotional overtones.

For example, Sam says, "This !#*!! project has been costing us megabucks, and I think it's time we dropped it!" The chairperson's paraphrase is "Sam has registered a strong objection to the project on the grounds of its high cost." A similar technique is to record only the core of the remark on the flipchart or chalkboard. For Sam's remark, the chairperson might write "Objection: high cost."

Although providing the opportunity for discussion is essential, there comes a time during every meeting when discussion must give way to proposals for action. Calling for an open vote works best when the issue is *not* extremely controversial. This conclusion may at first surprise you, but think about it. In an open vote, people are forced to take a yes-or-no stand; there are no allowable gray areas. Yet some people may want other attendees to know and acknowledge that they still have genuine reservations.

A better method to deal with controversy is to call for a *consensus.* Since consensus implies *consent* and not total agreement, people can retain their separate viewpoints while consenting to support a policy or action for the good of the organization. In business, many forward-moving actions are initiated through consensus that would have been stopped in their tracks if a yea-or-nay vote had been mandated. A skillful chairperson calls for a consensus when all of the participants' viewpoints have been heard. When the decision is reached, the chairperson may emphasize that it is a thoughtful and positive response that takes into account all opposing views.

At the conclusion of any meeting, controversial or not, the chairperson summarizes what has been accomplished and reviews the scheduled action plans. (It frequently is a good idea to do this again in a follow-up memo.) Often, the first step in the action plan is to schedule the next meeting!

## ■ Summary

Meetings large and small are a fact of business life. All meetings are convened for information exchange, problem solving, or a combination of the two.

In planning a meeting, first determine its desired outcome. Then select the participants, build the agenda, establish the timing, and decide on a location.

The various agenda items should follow one another logically. Always allow time for extra discussion; no one objects when a meeting ends earlier than scheduled, but the opposite is not true. Distribute a copy of the agenda to participants a few days before the meeting, including relevant background information if necessary.

The surroundings strongly influence the tone of a meeting. Strive to avoid interruptions. Allow time for a break if the meeting exceeds 90 minutes. Reserve your meeting room at the earliest possible time.

Chairing a meeting calls for a solid interpersonal skills; your job is to control the discussion without dominating it. Steer a careful path between control and tyranny. Keep track of time.

When someone volunteers or is asked to carry out a specific task, the fact should be recorded. Such commitments are often called "action items" and are subsequently confirmed in writing.

Softpedal inflammatory remarks by paraphrasing them without the emotional content. When all viewpoints on a controversial issue have been heard, call for a consensus. Summarize the accomplishments of the meeting at its close.

# ■ Discussion Problems

**19.1**   Have you attended a meeting in the last two months? Can you recollect whether it was an information-exchange or problem-solving meeting? Describe the meeting, and explain your answer.

**19.2**   In the first section of this chapter, a meeting whose purpose is to see that everyone understands a new set of productivity goals is labeled as both an information-exchanging and a problem-solving meeting. Do you agree? Explain.

**19.3**   Have you ever chaired a meeting? If so, describe the preparations—if any—that you made before the meeting. With hindsight, would you have handled the meeting differently? Explain.

**19.4**   If possible, attend a meeting at your school or in your local community within the next two weeks. Be prepared to report on how the leader exerted control (or failed to) and how agreements were reached. Also, make any other observations you feel are important.

**19.5**   Discuss the fine line between an interactive presentation and a meeting. From the perspective of planning and preparing, how are they different?

**19.6**   Compare the kinds of problems a presenter encounters in maintaining audience control to those problems a chairperson encounters at meetings. How do control techniques differ in these cases? Are there some that work in both cases?

# ■ Meeting Tasks

**19.1**   Look again at the Highland Federal Bank and Trust case at the end of Chapter 18 (pages 522–25). Assume Joanne Quinn has called a meeting of the MIS department at the end of the week to brief them on the stance she will be taking at the upcoming officers' meeting. She has asked Ron Pruitt to chair the departmental meeting and to prepare the agenda. Although the briefing will be the main focus of the meeting, they will also discuss a proposal by Mike Dorrity, a systems analyst, to investigate setting up an electronic mail system with the branch offices. The meeting will last one hour. Prepare the agenda.

**19.2**   With five classmates, role-play a meeting in which you discuss a requirement that undergraduate business majors must pass a computer literacy test before graduation. The group is to select a chairperson and someone to write summary minutes when the meeting has concluded. The minutes are to be distributed to the entire class for discussion and evaluation at a later date.

**19.3**   Chair a 15-minute meeting whose primary purpose is to arrive at a consensus concerning a controversial issue of your choice. Take responsibility for selecting participants and for distributing any necessary data either before or during the meeting. While the experience is fresh, you and the other participants should write short reports detailing the problems and successes that were encountered.

**19.4**   Plan, prepare for, and chair a meeting of ten or more fellow students in which the main purpose is to plan an event for your school. This event can, of course, be imaginary. On the other hand, if you have the opportunity to plan a real event, do so.

**19.5** Assume that your school has a student-operated travel concession. Each year in September, small groups of interested students propose plans for profitably managing the agency for the next 12 months. A committee composed of the current concession managers, the dean of students, and three faculty members considers the submitted proposals and selects the group with the best plan to manage the concession. (Since managing the travel concession allows students to earn a substantial amount for working only part-time hours, the competition is always keen.)

Chair a mock meeting that has the explicit purpose of coming up with sound but innovative preliminary suggestions to include in a proposal to operate the travel concession. Select four fellow students to participate in the meeting, asking one to be timekeeper and one to keep a record of what goes on. Role-play this meeting while the rest of your class and your instructor serve as observers.

- *Participants:* When the meeting has ended, discuss how effectively the chairperson led the group. Which of the chair's skills need to be strengthened? Also, comment on the interactions of participants. How could they have been more effective?

- *Chair:* Comment specifically on your own performance. Did you have difficulty maintaining control? Why or why not? Did you observe examples of idea-killing? Specify. Were any of the participants especially helpful in keeping things moving forward? Explain.

**19.6** Redo the role-play described in Task 19.5 with a new chairperson and new participants. Discuss the results according to the above procedures. Presumably this group will have benefited from the previous discussion. What specific improvements were obvious? Did new kinds of problems surface? Explain.

**19.7** With other members of your class, discuss the strengths and weaknesses of the role-plays performed in Tasks 19.5 and 19.6.

**19.8** Charles Warden is the president of the student council at Closedoor College, a small college in northern New England that is known for its excellent liberal arts program but that has a declining enrollment. Charles and other members of the council have decided the problem could very well be Closedoor's reputation for ignoring students' needs and interests with respect to practical course content. In fact, two incidents attracted the attention of the media, with one appearing as a feature story in the *Boston Globe*. The first and most infamous incident was the faculty's absolute refusal to introduce courses in computer theory and technology; the second was the school's failure to grant tenure to an exceedingly popular economics professor whose published works had appeared solely in the business media (rather than in scholarly journals).

As Charles, call and chair a 30-minute open meeting of all interested students to recommend new avenues for the students to use in communicating this problem to the faculty. The outcome of this meeting should be three or more proposals for Charles to bring to the joint meeting of the student council and the academic deans, which is to take place in one month. (The participants at the student planning meeting will be all of your classmates.)

At the close of the meeting, the class should perform a self-evaluation of their meeting skills. (Your instructor will also provide a detailed evaluation.)

# SELECTED READINGS

# I. Getting Started

Whether speaking or writing is your objective, getting started is usually the worst part of the ordeal. The following two short and humorous articles deliver a comforting and helpful message: procrastination and nervousness are not at all uncommon among writers and speakers.

# The Watcher at the Gates

## GAIL GODWIN

I first realized I was not the only writer who had a restraining critic who lived inside me and sapped the juice from green inspirations when I was leafing through Freud's "Interpretation of Dreams" a few years ago. Ironically, it was my "inner critic" who had sent me to Freud. I was writing a novel, and my heroine was in the middle of a dream, and then I lost faith in my own invention and rushed to "an authority" to check whether she could have such a dream. In the chapter on dream interpretation, I came upon the following passage that has helped me free myself, in some measure, from my critic and has led to many pleasant and interesting exchanges with other writers.

Freud quotes Schiller, who is writing a letter to a friend. The friend complains of his lack of creative power. Schiller replies with an allegory. He says it is not good if the intellect examines too closely the ideas pouring in at the gates. "In isolation, an idea may be quite insignificant, and venturesome in the extreme, but it may acquire importance from an idea which follows it. . . . In the case of a creative mind, it seems to me, the intellect has withdrawn its watchers from the gates, and the ideas rush in pell-mell, and only then does it review and inspect the multitude. You are ashamed or afraid of the momentary and passing madness which is found in all real creators, the longer or shorter duration of which distinguishes the thinking artist from the dreamer

. . . you reject too soon and discriminate too severely."

So that's what I had: a Watcher at the Gates. I decided to get to know him better. I discussed him with other writers, who told me some of the quirks and habits of their Watchers, each of whom was as individual as his host, and all of whom seemed passionately dedicated to one goal: rejecting too soon and discriminating too severely.

It is amazing the lengths a Watcher will go to to keep you from pursuing the flow of your imagination. Watchers are notorious pencil sharpeners, ribbon changers, plant waterers, home repairers and abhorrers of messy rooms or messy pages. They are compulsive looker-uppers. They are superstitious scaredy-cats. They cultivate self-important eccentricities they think are suitable for "writers." And they'd rather die (and kill your inspiration with them) than risk making a fool of themselves.

My Watcher has a wasteful penchant for 20-pound bond paper above and below the carbon of the first draft. "What's the good of writing out a whole page," he whispers begrudgingly, "if you just have to write it over again later? Get it perfect the first time!" My Watcher adores stopping in the middle of a morning's work to drive down to the library to check on the name of a flower or a World War II battle or a line of metaphysical poetry. "You can't possibly go on till you've got this right!" he admonishes. I go and get the car keys.

Other Watchers have informed their writers that:

"Whenever you get a really good sentence you should stop in the middle of it and go on tomorrow. Otherwise you might run dry."

"Don't try and continue with your book till your dental appointment is over. When you're worried about your teeth, you can't think about art."

Another Watcher makes his owner pin his finished pages to a clothesline and read them through binoculars "to see how they look from a distance." Countless other Watchers demand "bribes" for taking the day off: lethal doses of caffeine, alcoholic doses of Scotch or vodka or wine.

There are various ways to outsmart, pacify or coexist with your Watcher. Here are some I have tried, or my writer-friends have tried, with success:

Look for situations when he's likely to be off-guard. Write too fast for him in an unexpected place, at an unexpected time. (Virginia Woolf captured the "diamonds in the dustheap" by writing at a "rapid haphazard gallop" in her diary.) Write when very tired. Write in purple ink on the back of a Master Charge statement. Write whatever comes into your mind while the kettle is boiling and make the steam whistle your deadline. (Deadlines are a great way to outdistance the Watcher.)

Disguise what you are writing. If your Watcher refuses to let you get on with your story or novel, write a "letter" instead, telling your "correspondent" what you are going to write in your story or next chapter. Dash off a "review" of your own unfinished opus. It will stand up like a bully to your Watcher the next time he throws obstacles in your path. If you write yourself a good one.

Get to know your Watcher. He's yours. Do a drawing of him (or her). Pin it to the wall of your study and turn it gently to the wall when necessary. Let your Watcher feel needed. Watchers are excellent critics after inspiration has been captured; they are dependable, sharp-eyed readers of things already set down. Keep your Watcher in shape and he'll have less time to keep you from shaping. If he's really ruining your whole working day sit down, as Jung did with his personal demons, and write him a letter. On a very bad day I once wrote my Watcher a letter. "Dear Watcher," I wrote, "What is it you're so afraid I'll do?" Then I held his pen for him, and he replied instantly with a candor that has kept me from truly despising him.

"Fail," he wrote back.

---

# Speechless

## TERRY MAROTTA

They want me to make a few remarks at the start of tonight's meeting? No problem, I say.

I bring along an index card scribbled over with key phrases, and, when the moment arrives, I mount the stage.

The hall is packed. I sit among the other speakers, hands folded, smiling genially and remembering not to sprawl in my chair.

But as the meeting is being called to order, strange things start happening to my body.

My legs go rubbery, for one thing. Unaccountably, my knees begin knocking like castanets. I grasp the lectern firmly with both hands to prevent fainting, and resist the temptation to drape myself over it like one of those melting watches in a painting by Dali. I'm sure it wouldn't do to speak from a sitting position on the floor *behind* the thing, but still—it's an appealing notion.

Finally, I anchor myself up there somehow. But as I look out at that chocolate-box assortment of faces,—bam, I'm struck with cottonmouth. The oral cavity, normally well-juiced and flapping, goes dry as a cave in the desert. And my tongue? My tongue thickens and lolls goonily inside it.

I lick my lips frantically—squeeze those saliva glands and pray for the smallest squirt of fluid.

Nothing doing, though. Forget the juice is the message from my mouth. And a mouth, it turns out, is like a garbage disposal: it won't work right without the water on. My words swirl around like coffee grounds in there, going nowhere, or fly out like cornflakes, in disorderly sequence.

On top of that, those firm and rounded tones with which I normally command speech have deserted me. The ones with which we all admonish the newsboy, or summon the waiter—where are they now when I need them?

I open my lips and a twittering squeak comes out. I sound like a gerbil family caught in the spin cycle.

Adrenalin is what they call it, of course; the cause of all this anxiety. Adrenalin, a rush of energy nature equips us with to protect us in perilous situations. It brings on a readiness to fight or flee, the anthropologists tell us, depending on what the circumstances seem to warrant.

A dubious theory, if you ask me. A lot of good I'd be for either fighting *or* fleeing, in this jelly-like state. Picture yourself, coming at your enemy squeaking and gibbering. Or attempting to flee him on legs made of Playdough, all the while yodeling dryly.

No wonder Richard Nixon sweated so in front of the cameras. No wonder his beard grew visibly and sinisterly before its unblinking eye. No wonder Jimmy Carter couldn't begin a speech at all without giving that small pursed-lip, goody-goody smile that the world found so infuriating.

These people were *nervous*; they were experiencing stage fright.

When I was in the fifth grade, I was chosen to recite a poem in an auditorium filled with recess-minded 11-year-olds. Waiting nervously in the wings for my turn, I smoothed and resmoothed my skirt, tucked in and retucked the edges of my blouse. I yanked at my knee socks and pulled up on my half-slip.

When I finished all that smoothing and pulling, I walked out onto the stage to a burst of applause—with my skirt tucked into my underpants.

There's a lesson here. Nervousness, it seems, is an emotion we can all do without. The heck with that candy-box assortment of staring faces. People are rather like chocolates, when you think about it: not everybody can be a fudge cream. Some are licorice-macaroon nougats.

I tell myself this as I gaze out glazy-eyed at my audience. The members are no better than I am, after all.

Except they can talk the right way—and their legs still work.

*Terry Marotta is a free-lance writer from Winchester, Massachusetts.*

---

# II. Style: Sunny-Side Up

These five short articles are painless remedies for overblown style and "business-ese." Moreover, if you are entirely in tune with William Safire's "Fumblerules," you have probably sufficiently mastered the rules of grammar and style.

---

# The Fumblerules of Grammar

## WILLIAM SAFIRE

Not long ago, I advertised for perverse rules of grammar, along the lines of "Remember to never split an infinitive" and "The passive voice should never be used." The notion of making a mistake while laying down rules ("Thimk," "We Never Make Misteaks") is highly unoriginal, and it turns out that English teachers have been circulating lists of fumblerules for years.

As owner of the world's largest collection, and with thanks to scores of readers, let me pass along a bunch of these never-say-neverisms:

- Avoid run-on sentences they are hard to read.
- Don't use no double negatives.

- Use the semicolon properly, always use it where it is appropriate; and never where it isn't.
- Reserve the apostrophe for it's proper use and omit it when its not needed.
- Do not put statements in the negative form.
- Verbs has to agree with their subjects.
- No sentence. fragments.[1]
- Proofread carefully to see if you any words out.
- Avoid commas, that are not necessary.
- If you reread your work, you will find on rereading that a great deal of repetition can be avoided by rereading and editing.
- A writer must not shift your point of view.
- Eschew dialect, irregardless.
- And don't start a sentence with a conjunction.[2]
- Don't overuse exclamation marks!!!
- Place pronouns as close as possible, especially in long sentences, as of 10 or more words, to their antecedents.
- Hyphenate between sy-llables and avoid un-necessary hyphens.

[1] If intentional, often acceptable. RGN

[2] No longer frowned upon in most contexts. RGN

- Write all adverbial forms correct.
- Don't use contractions in formal writing.
- Writing carefully, dangling participles must be avoided.
- It is incumbent on us to avoid archaisms.
- If any word is improper at the end of a sentence, a linking verb is.
- Steer clear of incorrect forms of verbs that have snuck in the language.
- Take the bull by the hand and avoid mixed metaphors.
- Avoid trendy locutions that sound flaky.
- Never, ever use repetitive redundancies.
- Everyone should be careful to use a singular pronoun with singular nouns in their writing.
- If I've told you once, I've told you a thousand times, resist hyperbole.
- Also, avoid awkward or affected alliteration.
- Don't string too many prepositional phrases together unless you are walking through the valley of the shadow of death.
- Always pick on the correct idiom.
- "Avoid overuse of 'quotation "marks."'"
- The adverb always follows the verb.
- Last but not least, avoid cliches like the plague; seek viable alternatives.

# Little Red Riding Hood Revisited

RUSSELL BAKER

In an effort to make the classics accessible to contemporary readers, I am translating them into the modern American language. Here is the translation of "Little Red Riding Hood":

Once upon a point in time, a small person named Little Red Riding Hood initiated plans for the preparation, delivery and transportation of foodstuffs to her grandmother, a senior citizen residing at a place of residence in a forest of indeterminate dimension.

In the process of implementing this program, her incursion into the forest was in mid-transportation process when it attained interface with an alleged perpetrator. This individual, a wolf, made inquiry as to the whereabouts of Little Red Riding Hood's goal as well as inferring that he was desirous of ascertaining the contents of Little Red Riding Hood's foodstuffs basket, and all that.

"It would be inappropriate to lie to me," the wolf said, displaying his huge jaw capability. Sensing that he was a mass of repressed hostility intertwined with acute alienation, she indicated.

"I see you indicating," the wolf said, "but what I don't see is whatever it is you're indicating at, you dig?"

Little Red Riding Hood indicated more fully, making one thing perfectly clear—to wit, that it was to her grandmother's residence and with a consignment of foodstuffs that her mission consisted of taking her to and with.

At this point in time the wolf moderated his rhetoric and proceeded to grandmother's residence. The elderly person was then subjected to the disadvantages of total consumption and transferred to residence in the perpetrator's stomach.

"That will raise the old woman's consciousness," the wolf said to himself. He was not a bad wolf, but only a victim of an oppressive society, a society that not only denied wolves' rights, but actually boasted of its capacity for keeping the wolf from the door. An interior malaise made itself manifest inside the wolf.

"Is that the national malaise I sense within my digestive tract?" wondered the wolf. "Or is it the old person seeking to retaliate for her consumption by telling wolf jokes to my duodenum?" It was time to make a judgment. The time was now, the hour had struck, the body lupine cried out for decision. The wolf was up to the challenge. He took two stomach powders right away and got into bed.

The wolf had adopted the abdominal-distress recovery posture when Little Red Riding Hood achieved his presence.

"Grandmother," she said, "your ocular implements are of an extraordinary order of magnitude."

"The purpose of this enlarged viewing capability," said the wolf, "is to enable your image to register a more precise impression upon my sight systems."

"In reference to your ears," said Little Red Riding Hood, "it is noted with the deepest respect that far from being underprivileged, their elongation and enlargement appear to qualify you for unparalleled distinction."

"I hear you loud and clear, kid," said the wolf, "but what about these new choppers?"

"If it is not inappropriate," said Little Red Riding Hood, "it might be observed that with your new miracle masticating products you may even be able to chew taffy again."

This observation was followed by the adoption of an aggressive posture on the part of the wolf and the assertion that it was also possible for him, due to the high efficiency ratio of his jaw, to consume little persons, plus, as he stated, his firm determination to do so at once without delay and with all due process and propriety, notwithstanding the fact that the ingestion of one entire grandmother had already provided twice his daily recommended cholesterol intake.

There ensued flight by Little Red Riding Hood accompanied by pursuit in respect to the wolf and a subsequent intervention on the part of a third party, heretofore unnoted in the record.

Due to the firmness of the intervention, the wolf's stomach underwent ax-assisted aperture with the result that Red Riding Hood's grandmother was enabled to be removed with only minor discomfort.

The wolf's indigestion was immediately alleviated with such effectiveness that he signed a contract with the intervening third party to perform with grandmother in a television commercial demonstrating the swiftness of this dramatic relief for stomach discontent.

"I'm going to be on television," cried grandmother.

And they all joined her happily in crying, "What a phenomena!"

---

# A Sinister Disease Invades the Business World

## DAVID W. EWING

The other day I read what I estimate conservatively to be the 15,000th manuscript that has come across my desk in several decades at the *Harvard Business Review*. Like so many of its predecessors, the manuscript was full of jargon and, in organization if not in thought, as fiendishly complicated as a road map of Boston. Yet its writer was an educated manager who held an important position in a profitable corporation.

Why, I asked myself for the 15,000th time, don't these intelligent, well-paid business people write better?

In my early years as an editor, and under the influence of Freud, I held to a whimsical theory about the causes of poor writing in business and the professions. My theory was that writing style, like so many other forms of behavior, was a manifestation of mysterious currents deep in the writer's subconscious. It pleased me greatly to believe that these dark currents might show themselves in no other way, perhaps not even to the psychoanalyst—only to the discerning editor or writing instructor. Just as Rorschach tests, handwriting analysis and the stars could reveal deeply hidden traits and tendencies, I reasoned, the manner and quality of a writer's presentation should give away some of his or her best-guarded secrets.

Thus, a tendency to hide or disguise the subject of a verb (as in a sentence beginning "Indoctrination was given the new employees" instead of "We trained the new employees") should be evidence of chronic furtiveness or unwillingness to accept responsibility, probably induced by faulty toilet training. A predilection to long, serpentine sentences that never come to a point should be an indicator of sexual frustration or, worse still, impotence.

In time, as my enchantment with Freud diminished, and especially as I realized that my own writing might reveal occult traits, I turned to other possible explanations. One day I had to read a tortuous manuscript from an executive of a pharmaceutical company, the same firm, I realized with an aching head, that bottled aspirin and other pills in a maddening manner. To take the top off the bottle, one must turn a difficult-to-discern arrow on the cap to a point where it is exactly opposite an equally hard-to-see arrow on the neck of the bottle. It is then possible, if one has a strong thumb, to pry off the top and get to the analgesic. Whenever I arose in the middle of the night with an urgent need for the contents of the bottle, it seemed that it might be easier to break it open—to slash, as it were, the Gordian knot—than solve the riddle of the matching arrows.

It occurred to me, as I sat with that manuscript and thought in hand, that I was on the trail of a significant explanation. Was it a latent mischievous trait suppressed by the business mind that produced so much bad writing? The same prankishness that produced the hard-to-open bottle was, I realized, at work in many other companies. I thought of the paint thinner in the basement at home. The can couldn't be opened until one carried it upstairs to a bright light, put on a pair of strong reading glasses, and deciphered the words punched in metal at the top: "Press Down Firmly and Turn to Right" or "Push Down, Twist and Lift." I recalled the addressing machine at the church that greatly tempts the minister's secretaries to use the Lord's name in vain; the specially coated address cards must be typed before insertion in the machine but they won't go through the typewriter without slipping out of position and having to be retyped. I thought of a professorial friend who spent two years of evenings and weekends writing a textbook only to find that the back of its elegant jacket advertised other books being sold by the publisher, including one in competition with his own volume.

I saw, as if before a burning bush instead of an office desk, that the dense articles, letters and memoranda that business people write are not a symptom of ineptitude or derangement but an extension of the same impish impulse that creates make-you-go-bananas products and instructions.

After further thought, I came upon an alternative theory: In this era of advanced government regulation, business officials spend so much time pondering and sifting through federal and state regulations that they have contracted Government Writers Disease, a galloping gobbledygook virus that paralyzes meaning.

One of the 20th century's greatest judges, the late Learned Hand, once commented on the wording of corporate tax regulations. The words, he said, "dance before my eyes in a meaningless procession: cross-reference to cross-reference, exception upon exception—couched in abstract terms that offer no handle to seize upon." Before me is one contemporary example, a section of a government directive on oil company pricing procedures. The first sentence, all 138 jargon words of it, is as tortuous to understand as the Chinese military code. It brings to mind Alexander Pope's couplet: *Words are like leaves; and where they most abound/Much fruit of sense beneath is rarely found."*

During a recent conversation with a highly placed government official, I learned how sinister Government Writers Disease has become. I mentioned a nasty rumor going around that government agencies soon would require business people to write in the style of the agency directives and regulations they must comply with. "Can this be?" I asked. "Actually," he answered, "we have had such a directive in force for years. The reason nobody knows it is that nobody can understand it."

*David W. Ewing is the former managing editor of the* Harvard Business Review *and a member of the Harvard Business School faculty.*

# A Bureaucrat's Guide to Chocolate Chip Cookies

## SUSAN E. RUSS

For those government employees and bureaucrats who have problems with standard recipes, here's one that should make the grade—a classic version of the chocolate-chip cookie translated for easy reading.

## Total Lead Time: 35 minutes.
## Inputs:

1 cup packed brown sugar
$1/2$ cup granulated sugar
$1/2$ cup softened butter
$1/2$ cup shortening
2 eggs
$1^1/2$ teaspoons vanilla
$2^1/2$ cups all-purpose flour
1 teaspoon baking soda
$1/2$ teaspoon salt
12-ounce package semi-sweet chocolate
   pieces
1 cup chopped walnuts or pecans

## Guidance:

After procurement actions, decontainerize inputs. Perform measurement tasks on a case-by-case basis. In a mixing type bowl, impact heavily on brown sugar, granulated sugar, softened butter and shortening. Coordinate the interface of eggs and vanilla, avoiding an overrun scenario to the best of your skills and abilities.

At this point in time, leverage flour, baking soda and salt into a bowl and aggregate. Equalize with prior mixture and develop intense and continuous liaison among inputs until well-coordinated. Associate key chocolate and nut subsystems and execute stirring operations.

Within this time frame, take action to prepare the heating environment for throughput by manually setting the oven baking unit by hand to a temperature of 375 degrees Fahrenheit (190 degrees Celsius). Drop mixture in an ongoing fashion from a teaspoon implement onto a ungreased cookie sheet at intervals sufficient enough apart to permit total and permanent separation of throughputs to the maximum extent practicable under operating conditions.

Position cookie sheet in a bake situation and surveil for 8 to 10 minutes or until cooking action terminates. Initiate coordination of outputs within the cooling rack function. Containerize, wrap in red tape and disseminate to authorized staff personnel on a timely and expeditious basis.

## Output:

Six dozen official government chocolate-chip cookie units.

# The Gobbledegook

EUGENE McCARTHY AND
JAMES KILPATRICK

Of all the creatures catalogued in this Bestiary, none is more familiar, none more widely distributed in North America, than the Gobbledegook.

This lamentable beast has some of the characteristics of the common garden toad: He sits there, stolidly blinking, warts and all. He has some of the characteristics of the polecat and the inky squid, whose properties are to spread a foul diffusion. He has the gaudy tail of a peacock, the impenetrable hide of the armadillo, the windy inflatability of the blowfish.

It is commonly thought that the Gobbledegook resides only at seats of government, chiefly at the seat of national government, but this is not true. The Gobbledegook is equally at home in academic groves and in corporate mazes. He is often observed on military reservations, in doctors' offices, and in judicial chambers. He feeds on polysyllables, dangling participles and ambivalent antecedents. He sleeps in subordinate clauses.

The Gobbledegook is composed mostly of fatty tissues and pale yellow blubber. The creature is practically boneless. Owing to cloudy vision, once he has launched into a sentence, he cannot see his way clear to the end. In the foggy world of the Gobbledegook, a janitor becomes a material waste disposal engineer and a school bus in Texas a motorized attendance module. Here meaningful events impact; when they do not impact, they interact; sometimes they interface horizontally in structural implementation.

For all its clumsiness, the Gobbledegook is amazingly adept at avoiding capture. President Carter pursued his quarry through 10,000 pages of the Federal Register and emerged with no more than a couple of tail feathers plucked on the trail. The beast can survive for months on a jar of library paste; when startled by an angry editor, the Gobbledegook fakes a retreat, spouting syntactical effluvium as it goes, but once the editor's back is turned, the beast appears anew. It cannot be killed; it cannot even be gravely wounded. It dwells in thickets, in swamps, in heavy brush, in polluted waters, in the miasmic mists of intentional obfuscation.

# III. Strategy

Good business communication demands sensitivity to others and their needs. The following two articles emphasize that a writer's underlying assumptions must be based on careful audience analysis. They also explore how authorship, timing, and tone directly affect the chances that a critical piece of writing will attain its objectives.

# Clear Writing Means Clear Thinking Means...

MARVIN H. SWIFT

## Foreword

*Very few people have the ability to write effortlessly and perfectly; most of us must sweat over the process of revision, drafting, and redrafting until we get it right. Equally, very few people think accurately enough so that mere transcriptions of "what they have in mind" can serve as intelligent communications. Here the author points out that we tend to revise our words and refine out thoughts simultaneously; the improvements we make in our thinking and the improvements we make in our style reinforce each other, and they cannot be divorced. His analysis of the way in which a manager reworks and rethinks a memo of mi-*

*nor importance points up a constant management challenge of major importance—the clear and accurate expression of a well-focused message.*

If you are a manager, you constantly face the problem of putting words on paper. If you are like most managers, this is not the sort of problem you enjoy. It is hard to do, and time consuming; and the task is doubly difficult when, as is usually the case, your words must be designed to change the behavior of others in the organization.

But the chore is there and must be done. How? Let's take a specific case.

Let's suppose that everyone at X Corporation, from the janitor on up to the chairman of the board, is using the office copiers for personal matters; income tax forms, church programs, children's term papers, and God knows what else are being duplicated by the gross. This minor piracy costs the company a pretty penny, both directly and in employee time, and the general manager—let's call him Sam Edwards—decides the time has come to lower the boom.

Sam lets fly by dictating the following memo to his secretary:

To:      All Employees
From:    Samuel Edwards, General Manager
Subject: Abuse of Copiers

It has recently been brought to my attention that many of the people who are employed by this company have taken advantage of their positions by availing themselves of the copiers. More specifically, these machines are being used for other than company business.

Obviously, such practice is contrary to company policy and must cease and desist immediately. I wish therefore to inform all concerned — those who have abused policy or will be abusing it — that their behavior cannot and will not be tolerated. Accordingly, anyone in the future who is unable to control himself will have his employment terminated.

If there are any questions about company policy, please feel free to contact this office.

Now the memo is on his desk for his signature. He looks it over; and the more he looks, the worse it reads. In fact, it's lousy. So he revises it three times, until it finally is in the form that follows:

To:      All Employees
From:    Samuel Edwards, General Manager
Subject: Use of Copiers

We are revamping our policy on the use of copiers for personal matters. In the past we have not encouraged personnel to use them for such purposes because of the costs involved. But we also recognize, perhaps belatedly, that we can solve the problem if each of us pays for what he takes.

We are therefore putting these copiers on a pay-as-you-go basis. The details are simple enough. . . .

*Samuel Edwards*

This time Sam thinks the memo looks good, and it is good. Not only is the writing much improved, but the problem should now be solved. He therefore signs the memo, turns it over to his secretary for distribution, and goes back to other things.

## From verbiage to intent

I can only speculate on what occurs in a writer's mind as he moves from a poor draft to a good revision, but it is clear that Sam went through several specific steps, mentally as well as physically, before he had created his end product:

- He eliminated wordiness.
- He modulated the tone of the memo.
- He revised the policy it stated.

Let's retrace his thinking through each of these processes.

### Eliminating wordiness

Sam's basic message is that employees are not to use the copiers for their own affairs at company expense. As he looks over his first draft, however, it seems so long that this simple message has become diffused. With the idea of trimming the memo down, he takes another look at his first paragraph:

It has recently been brought to my attention that many of the people who are employed by this company have taken advantage of their positions by availing themselves of the copiers. More specifically, these machines are being used for other than company business.

He edits it like this:

*Item:* "recently"
*Comment to himself:* Of course; else why write about the problem? So delete the word.
*Item:* "It has been brought to my attention"
*Comment:* Naturally. Delete it.
*Item:* "the people who are employed by this company"
*Comment:* Assumed. Why not just "employees"?
*Item:* "by availing themselves" and "for other than company business"
*Comment:* Since the second sentence repeats the first, why not coalesce?

And he comes up with this:

Employees have been using the copiers for personal matters.

He proceeds to the second paragraph. More confident of himself, he moves in broader swoops, so that the deletion process looks like this:

Obviously, such practice is contrary to company policy and ~~must cease and desist immediately. I~~ ~~wish therefore to inform all concerned — those~~ ~~who have abused policy or will be abusing it — that~~ ~~their behavior cannot and will not be tolerated. Ac-~~ ~~cordingly, anyone in the future who is unable to~~ ~~control himself will have his employment termi-~~ ~~nated.~~ will result in dismissal.

The final paragraph, apart from "company policy" and "feel free," looks all right, so the total memo now reads as follows:

To: All Employees
From: Samuel Edwards, General Manager
Subject: Abuse of Copiers

Employees have been using the copiers for personal matters. Obviously, such practice is contrary to company policy and will result in dismissal.

If there are any questions, please contact this office.

Sam now examines his efforts by putting these questions to himself:

*Question:* Is the memo free of deadwood?
*Answer:* Very much so. In fact, it's good, tight prose.
*Question:* Is the policy stated?
*Answer:* Yes—sharp and clear.
*Question:* Will the memo achieve its intended purpose?
*Answer:* Yes. But it sounds foolish.
*Question:* Why?
*Answer:* The wording is too harsh; I'm not going to fire anybody over this.
*Question:* How should I tone the thing down?

To answer this last question, Sam takes another look at the memo.

**Correcting the Tone**

What strikes his eye as he looks it over? Perhaps these three words:

- Abuse . . .
- Obviously . . .
- . . . dismissal . . .

The first one is easy enough to correct: he substitutes "use" for "abuse." But "obviously" poses a problem and calls for reflection. If the policy is obvious, why are the copiers being used? Is it that people are outrightly dishonest? Probably not. But that implies the policy isn't obvious; and whose fault is this? Who neglected to clarify policy? And why "dismissal" for something never publicized?

These questions impel him to revise the memo once again:

To: All Employees
From: Samuel Edwards, General Manager
Subject: Use of Copiers

Copiers are not to be used for personal matters. If there are any questions, please contact this office.

## Revising the Policy Itself

The memo now seems courteous enough—at least it is not discourteous—but it is just a blank, perhaps overly simple, statement of policy. Has he really thought through the policy itself?

Reflecting on this, Sam realizes that some people will continue to use the copiers for personal business anyhow. If he seriously intends to enforce the basic policy (first sentence), he will have to police the equipment, and that raises the question of costs all over again.

Also, the memo states that he will maintain an open-door policy (second sentence)—and surely there will be some, probably a good many, who will stroll in and offer to pay for what they use. His secretary has enough to do without keeping track of affairs of that kind.

Finally, the first and second sentences are at odds with each other. The first says that personal copying is out, and the second implies that it can be arranged.

The facts of organizational life thus force Sam to clarify in his own mind exactly what his position on the use of copiers is going to be. As he sees the problem now, what he really wants to do is put the copiers on a pay-as-you-go basis. After making that decision, he begins anew:

To:       All Employees
From:     Samuel Edwards, General Manager
Subject:  Use of copiers

We are revamping our policy on the use of copiers. . . .

This is the draft that goes into distribution and now allows him to turn his attention to other problems.

## The Chicken or the Egg?

What are we to make of all this? It seems a rather lengthy and tedious report of what, after all, is a routine writing task created by a problem of minor importance. In making this kind of analysis, have I simply labored the obvious?

To answer this question, let's drop back to the original draft. If you read it over, you will see that Sam began with this kind of thinking:

- "The employees are taking advantage of the company."
- "I'm a nice guy, but now I'm going to play Dutch uncle."
- ∴ "I'll write them a memo that tells them to shape up or ship out."

In his final version, however, his thinking is quite different:

- "Actually, the employees are pretty mature, responsible people. They're capable of understanding a problem."
- "Company policy itself has never been crystallized. In fact, this is the first memo on the subject."
- "I don't want to overdo this thing—any employee can make an error in judgment."
- ∴ "I'll set a reasonable policy and write a memo that explains how it ought to operate."

Sam obviously gained a lot of ground between the first draft and the final version, and this implies two things. First, if a manager is to write effectively, he needs to isolate and define, as fully as possible, all the critical variables in the writing process and scrutinize what he writes for its clarity, simplicity, tone, and the rest. Second, after he has clarified his thoughts on paper, he may find that what he has written is not what has to be said. In this sense, writing is feedback and a way for the manager to discover himself. What are his real attitudes toward that amorphous, undifferentiated gray mass of employees "out there"? Writing is a way of finding out. By objectifying his thoughts in the medium of language, he gets a chance to see what is going on in his mind.

In other words, *if the manager writes well, he will think well.* Equally, the more clearly he has thought out his message before he starts to dictate, the more likely he is to get it right on paper the first time round. In other words, *if he thinks well, he will write well.* Hence we have a chicken-and-the-egg situation: writing and thinking go hand in hand; and when one is good, the other is likely to be good.

### Revision Sharpens Thinking

More particularly, rewriting is the key to improved thinking. It demands a real openmindedness and objectivity. It demands a willingness to cull verbiage so that ideas stand out clearly. And it demands a willingness to meet logical contradictions head on and trace them to the premises that have created them. In short, it forces a writer to get up his courage and expose his thinking process to his own intelligence.

Obviously, revising is hard work. It demands that you put yourself through the wringer, intellectually and emotionally, to squeeze out the best you can offer. Is it worth the effort? Yes, it is—if you believe you have a responsibility to think and communicate effectively.

# Case of the Questionable Communiqués

## RUTH G. NEWMAN

*Written communications play an important role— sometimes a decisive role—in many management problems. Just as the ineffective letter, memorandum, or report may hamper company operations and add to costs, an effective communication may improve performance and profitability. But what determines the worth of a report or letter? Not simply factual content, though obviously that is important. As the following case shows, tone, timing, authorship, style, and emphasis are potent. The general manager of a textile mill finds that, although the company is beginning to show a profit, he must let workers know they cannot expect a wage increase. He decides to write the employees a tactful and informative letter. He finds, however, that opinions about the letter and its contents differ. Read the case, consider the proposals, and decide what you would do if you were the general manager. Then compare your views with those of HBR's three guest commentators.*

On a warm June day, Ralph Hampton, hoping to catch a breeze, stood near the window of his office at Cooper Fabrics, Inc. Gazing across the grassy fields to the neat frame houses that marked the east border of Parville, he smiled to himself. "With a little luck," he thought, "and if things keep going well, we should have the whole plant air-conditioned by this time next year."

Hampton had reason to feel satisfied. He had been with Cooper Fabrics four years as its general manager. He had seen the company pass through difficult times, but in January Cooper had finally begun to show a profit. Hampton mused, "I think

we're out of the woods now, but we're certainly going to have to convince the workers to wait a little longer for that pay raise."

The Parville, New Hampshire plant had been built in 1840 and had been operated over the years by a long succession of owners. Each, for one reason or another, had been forced out of business. Throughout this long period, the appearance of the plant had changed very little, and one generation of workers followed another with little, if any, management turnover.

In the past fourteen years, the plant had been owned by four different companies. For three years, it had been held by a manufacturer of upholstery fabrics. For the next five years, the Haber Company, a large textile combine, operated the plant to turn out a somewhat different product line; Haber had operated the plant profitably in only one year. The next owner was a company that specialized in the liquidation of plants and companies. Finally, Cooper Fabrics, an operating subsidiary of Atlas Corporation, a large conglomerate, took over the plant in order to manufacture automotive and specialty household fabrics.

It was Ralph Hampton who had seen the possibilities in the product lines abandoned by former owners. A calm, slow-speaking man in his mid-forties, Hampton had previously been employed as an assistant manager of a Massachusetts textile concern. When Hampton took over the management of Cooper Fabrics in 1971, he selected the most suitable machinery from Cooper's two Rhode Island plants, had this equipment moved to Parville, and disposed of excess facilities and equipment. In the process of consolidating the company's operations at one location, he created a yarn and fiber processing department— an operation that the previous owners of the

Parville plant had subcontracted to other manufacturers.

During Hampton's first two years, Cooper Fabrics operated at a loss. Sales were at low levels, and operations were hindered by the necessary renovations and reorganizations. The lack of income and the cost of changes and additions in the plant exerted a severe financial strain. Hampton hoped that next year's operations would be profitable enough to ease the burden.

However, sales were difficult to obtain, the textile industry was depressed, and, more significantly, potential customers were skeptical about dealing with Cooper Fabrics. It was well known in the trade that the company had recently been in the process of liquidation. Fabric buyers did not wish to deal with a company which they feared might soon be in difficulties again.

But Hampton clung to his belief that by persistently providing dependable service and high-quality products, Cooper Fabrics could dispel such doubts. Under his supervision, sales volume greatly increased during the third year and maintenance and machinery replacement costs were held to the minimum. Although the company was still operating at a loss, employment rose to more than 300 workers, and the organization began to reestablish its reputation in its trade circle. In the first month of 1974, Hampton's fourth year, the books finally recorded a small profit.

Also at the beginning of the year, William Rauls joined Cooper Fabrics as company controller. Rauls had been graduated from a leading business school five years previously and had held several positions in a large textile company before coming to Cooper. In May, his responsibility as controller was extended to include the personnel department.

In Hampton's view, Cooper's prospects looked bright (see *Exhibit I*). And he believed that more and more favorable results could be anticipated if the company continued to lower its costs and to improve the quality of its products. In June, employment had leveled off at approximately 340 workers, but actual output was still increasing. The general manager realized, however, that he could not expect to reduce actual

**Exhibit I**
Income statement—24 weeks ending June 19, 1974

| | | |
|---|---:|---:|
| Net Sales | | $1,631,000 |
| Cost of sales | | 1,451,000 |
| Gross profit | | $ 180,000 |
| Selling expense | $58,000 | |
| General & administrative expense | 42,000 | 100,000 |
| Operating profit | | 80,000 |
| Other charges | | 12,000 |
| Net profit | | $ 68,000 |

unit costs more than just slightly below their present level. The plant was operating 24 hours a day, five days a week, with the second and third shifts somewhat smaller than the first.

## Workers and Working Conditions

At this time 55% of Cooper's employees were men and 45% were women. Most of the jobs in the plant could be handled by members of either sex, and there were no wage differentials based on sex. Of the women, 75% were married. Whenever possible, the company tried to employ two or more workers from the same family. It was not unusual, therefore, for a husband and his wife to be working different shifts so that one of them could always be at home with the children.

The plant was surrounded by old but well-kept frame houses, once owned by the factory for rental to employees. At one time, company-owned homes were customary in the textile industry. Almost all textile mills had now divested themselves of such property, and Cooper Fabrics was no exception. Some of the workers did live in the immediate vicinity of the plant, but others commuted from surrounding towns. A substantial number traveled to Parville from neighboring areas of Vermont, over distances of 25 to 35 miles. (The textile industry was so depressed in the adjoining parts of Vermont that workers there were often forced to travel considerable distances to find work.)

The turnover of employees at the Cooper Fabrics plant was low, according to John Rider, personnel manager under William Rauls. Rider had told Hampton that the month of June was fairly typical—fourteen separations, and only five that were voluntary. Rider said that three or four of the people who had voluntarily left lived far from the plant. And, he pointed out, a large part of the remaining turnover represented relatively new employees; some of these were still in the process of finding the type of work that suited them, while others did not perform satisfactorily in their jobs. Rider emphasized that, although their employment usually was not continuous because of work stoppages, more than half the workers had been with the company for ten years or more.

Recently Rider had told Hampton, "Look Ralph, I know that it's sometimes difficult to fill in when we lose a highly skilled worker, but I still can say that the labor market around here is loose." He added, "For example, I almost never have a hard time replacing people who are absent for short periods." Rider believed that, in a large measure, the general availability of labor was due to the recession. Two of the four local textile mills had gone out of business since 1970.

Hourly wage rates at Cooper Fabrics ranged from $2.25 for battery hands (floor men) to $3.25 for weavers and $3.75 for fixers (setup and repair men). In addition to the hourly rate, weavers and fixers were paid an incentive bonus. All basic wages in the plant were subject to a cost-of-living differential which was reviewed every three months. For every eight tenths of a point change in the Consumers' Price Index, wages were raised or lowered $0.02 per hour.

Hampton believed working conditions in the factory were superior to those of many mills in the area. The one-story plant was designed so that all areas were uncluttered and easily accessible. The work areas were clean, well lighted, and reasonably well ventilated. Moreover, as noted, Hampton hoped to see air conditioning installed soon. Noise in the weave room made conversation difficult, but Hampton assumed the workers understood that this was a characteristic of textile plants.

*Union and employee relations:* When the plant reopened in 1970 as Cooper Fabrics, Ralph Hampton had the option of ignoring the Textile Workers Union, which formerly held jurisdiction over the plant's workers. He preferred to establish a stable union relationship from the start. Before reopening the plant, he renewed contact with the local office in Concord, New Hampshire, and secured the union's approval to rehire former workers according to management's convenience rather than according to seniority. Ultimately, 95% of the employees who had previously worked at the plant were reemployed.

Hampton could point out that union sentiment at Cooper Fabrics was rather weak—as it was throughout the southern New Hampshire area. The plant's union shop required 100% membership, but the general manager knew that only 15 to 20 members customarily showed up at the monthly union meeting.

Looking back, Hampton believed that relations with the union had always been amicable. Before the textile recession, the labor supply had been extremely tight, and the union had succeeded in winning a 5% across-the-board wage increase. When the recession became severe, a general industry movement for lower wages ensued and Cooper Fabric's wages fell back to their former level. Recently a two-year contract had been negotiated with the union.

The Haber Corporation, former owner of the Parville plant, had sponsored and emphasized athletic leagues and similar activities for the employees. Under the present management, group activities were limited to a Christmas party and an outing (see *Exhibit II*). One of the employees who had worked under both managements had commented on this de-emphasis to William Rauls: "Look, Mr. Rauls, there sure is a big difference in the amount of activities we've got now—you can't miss that. But I don't think there's any less loyalty to the company because of it."

Communications to the employees during the past four years had been generally routine. Notices of vacations, holidays, and union meetings were posted on bulletin boards in the shop whenever the need for them arose. Infrequently, a notice of an infraction of the rules also ap-

## Exhibit II
Announcement of "Coming Events," dated June 9, 1974

Our Annual Clambake will be help at the Central Recreation Grounds in Parville on Saturday, August 7, 1974. A fine sports program is being planned for the afternoon with prizes for all winners. There will be a charge of 50 cents for all employees of Cooper Fabrics. Guest tickets may be purchased at $2.75—children 5–12 years of age, $1.75. Detailed information will be given later, but save this date for a Grand and Glorious time.

### Committee In Charge

Jim Parker
Martha Kucak
Martin Heinickie
Marjorie Constega
Louis Congores
Pauline McMahan
Henry Boudreau
Joseph Neff
Bill Rider

peared (see *Exhibit III*). Management had recently subscribed to a bulletin board service which supplied the company with a monthly poster on the subject of safety or waste. John Rider reported that sometimes a particular poster created considerable interest at the plant.

Since Hampton had been general manager, two letters had been written to the employees. The first was a notice of production cutbacks, which was posted on the plant bulletin boards in 1971, Cooper's second year of operation (*Exhibit IV*). The second was a letter Hampton sent the following year, first to the union and later to the employees who received it just before their annual vacation. This letter asked the employees to accept a decrease in wages. It touched upon steps the company already had taken to curtail expenses. "You all know," Hampton stated, "that for reasons of economy we have had to cut out the cafeteria. We are giving up our company station wagon and are going to have a truck which will double for both. We are selling whatever ma-

chinery we will not use. In general, we are doing everything possible to cut our overhead and administrative expenses to the bone." Even so, the letter indicated, the company's economies amounted to only about half of its losses.

## Exhibit III
Notice dated May 10, 1974

As we find that certain of our employees are not adhering to the plant regulation applying to "starting" and "stopping" times, we are bringing the following to your attention:

Employees are expected to be at their work or machine, ready to commence, when the starting horn blows for their shift—and to remain until the closing horn has blown at the end of their shift.

Cooper Fabrics, Incorporated.

## Exhibit IV
Announcement of production cutbacks, dated April 15, 1971

Notice to Employees
Cooper Fabrics, Incorporated
Parville, New Hampshire

Unfortunately, due to present industrywide market conditions, it is necessary that for a temporary period we reduce our basic work week in some departments to a 32-hour schedule. This reduction will affect many of our employees; although in order to balance production or satisfy particular consumer demands, a portion of the mill will be operated on a full-time basis.

Please be assured that the management of your company has put off this decision to curtail operations as long as possible with the hope that business conditions would improve. We sincerely hope that this change of schedule will only be for a brief period, and want our employees to feel that we are doing everything possible to speed the return to normal operating conditions.

Cooper Fabrics, Incorporated

R. Hampton
General Manager

Although Hampton presented a fairly bleak picture, the outlook described in his 1972 letter was not completely gloomy. He pointed out that the company was making great strides.

"I believe that we are now producing as good a product as was ever made in this mill. We are gaining back the good reputation that our mill used to have for quality and in the process we are getting new customers—and good ones. . . . What we offer in return for your accepting a temporary reduction in pay is that we are building job security and establishing a permanent business here in Parville."

Finally, the 1972 letter promised that any cut accepted by the union would apply in the same percentage to management and the sales force. Hampton's reasoning was that "we are all in this together and are all interested in making a go of this mill."

The 1972 letter was read to and voted on by the 25 workers who appeared at the next union meeting. (The following week, copies were distributed throughout the plant.) Unfortunately, the union president had misunderstood the letter's intent. He thought that the Cooper management was asking the employees to take a $0.60 rather than a 6% decrease in wages. This mistake generated considerable resentment among the workers at the lower end of the wage scale. Ralph Hampton did not learn about the misunderstanding until some time later. Although the company's proposal was voted down at the union meeting, an industrywide reduction was put into effect at the following contract negotiation. No letters were sent the following year. After their annual vacation, several workers stopped John Rider in the hallway to mention that they felt neglected by the omission.

"You know, they do like us to keep in touch," Rider later told Hampton.

Although the union contract called for only one week's vacation, the level of production during Cooper Fabric's first three years was such that each employee was given two weeks off. Each received a flat percentage of his yearly wages as vacation pay. No more money was allowed for two weeks off than for one, but the percentage given varied depending upon the length of service in the company.

Earlier in the current year, however, Hampton had announced that vacation time would be reduced to the one-week period stipulated in the contract. Customers had been advising him that they could no longer purchase two week's supply of fabrics in advance to keep their operation supplied while the plant was closed for vacation. Hampton felt confident that the employees would be satisfied with a one-week vacation, since the result would be more take-home pay for them. But some employees were disgruntled; they said they considered this change to be a reduction in their vacation period.

*Conference in June:* As he pondered both the recent success of Cooper Fabrics and his concerns about the employees' possible expectation of a raise, Ralph Hampton decided he needed to talk with William Rauls. He reached for his phone, and by three o'clock the two men were discussing the situation together in Hampton's office.

Hampton explained to the controller that, in spite of the difficult times that Cooper Fabrics had recently seen, it was almost impossible to convince employees that the company had been losing money. "Our policy has been not to make our financial statements available to the public. And the workers believe that we couldn't continue to operate if Cooper was not making a profit."

Rauls agreed that this was true.

"Another problem that seems to be related to this," Hampton continued, "is our need to persuade the workers that we're not wasting money when we replace outmoded equipment with more efficient machinery. Lots of the old-timers around here—our most experienced people, too—have worked on one machine all their lives; they've never even seen a different model. In their opinion, the machines they've been using are still perfectly good.

"Bill, you know well enough," Hampton continued, "that I believe that the way to create good employee relations is to treat my people fairly and give them cause to feel secure. I have always maintained that we need to give unswerving attention to the task of building a profitable operation. First and foremost, I'm convinced that equitable treatment and job security are what our employees value most. As a matter of fact, several of our workers recently went into civil service—and I know of a couple of men who have joined the fire and police departments here in Parville. It's a pretty good guess that these people sacrificed the higher take-home pay they get from us for jobs that give them better security. We don't want to lose any more people for such reasons in the future."

Rauls agreed wholeheartedly with Hampton's thesis that security and justice were basic in the employee's system of values. "You're absolutely right, Ralph. But building that kind of trust in the company is certainly a slow process."

"I know my way is slow," Hampton responded. "However, if I have learned anything from my previous experience with employees and customers alike, I've learned that actions speak louder than words."

"That's true, Ralph. But still, don't you think we can handle communications to our people so that they *will* listen and, what's more important, understand and want to help us achieve our goals?"

"You know, Bill, your thinking interests me," the general manager replied emphatically. "I wonder whether we should experiment to see if we can find an answer to your question. Do you think we might try this: we could draft a letter explaining that we're now making a profit. That has been on my mind ever since we learned that things are going a little better this year. We would have to be sure, though, to point out that this won't allow us to raise wages. The people in the plant will know that our company situation has improved and they'll wonder why an increase isn't forthcoming."

Hampton further suggested that they might plan to send the letter so that the employees would receive it just as they began their vacation. In this way, management's best wishes for a pleasant holiday might be included. Hampton said he would draft a letter. He also asked Rauls to draft a version of the letter, and suggested further that Rauls should ask John Rider, the personnel man-

ager, to do the same. "The three of us can get together in a week," Hampton declared with enthusiasm. "We'll compare notes and decide what sort of letter would be of most value at this time."

*The three letters:* One week later the three men met in Hampton's office, each with a copy of the letter he had drafted. Hampton laid them side by side on a table so that the men could read and compare them. The letters are shown in *Exhibit V.*

*Now imagine that you are in Ralph Hampton's position. Would you select one of the letters for distribution to employees? If so, which one—and why? Or would you compose a different letter? Would you make any other changes in the plan Hampton seems to have in mind?*

*Having formed your own opinions, compare them with the reactions of Ms. Newman and the commentators in the next section.*

---

**Exhibit V**
**The three letters**

A. General manager's version

July 2, 1974

To All Employees
Cooper Fabrics, Inc.
Parville, New Hampshire

As general manager of this mill, I am happy to report that as of the 24-week period ending the nineteenth of last month, this mill has finally turned in a profit. This shows, I feel, that our constant attention to keeping overhead low and the quality of our products high is a policy which will, in the end, pay off in the form of a profitable and permanent business here in Parville. What this means to you employees is that with each passing day, your jobs become more secure, and you become safer than ever from layoffs and slowdowns.

Your cooperation in this effort has been, of course, essential to its success. By accepting wage cuts and the necessary curtailment of activities and fringe benefits (such as a shorter vacation), you have done more than your share in making this mill a going concern. The owners of the mill must now be surer than ever that our people here are determined to keep the business in the black. Our customers are again coming to depend on our product and service, and our reputation is growing daily.

I would like to add, however, that in order to continue this favorable trend we must not allow, insofar as it is possible, any of our costs to increase. Among these expenses are employees' wages; I am sure that you can understand the necessity of holding the line on all costs, so that the present trend toward greater profitability can continue. What you are buying with a refusal to ask for more compensation is greater job security. I am sure that we can all agree that having stable employment and reasonable freedom from fears of a layoff is far better than a few cents an hour increase in remuneration.

I know that the owners of this mill are at least as pleased as the rest of us to see this business producing a return for the first time; I want you all to feel that this has been the final payoff in a long, and sometimes discouraging, team effort. Rest assured, however, that this need not be the last time we get into the black. If we can all work together, and hold the line on overhead, and keep providing the kind of dependable service and quality products which we are slowly becoming again known for, we can turn in a profit every quarter.

In closing, I want to extend to you on behalf of the whole management and administrative team here, all best wishes for a pleasant and restful vacation.

Sincerely,

R. Hampton
General Manager

B. Controller's version

July 2, 1974

To All Employees
Cooper Fabrics, Inc.
Parville, New Hampshire

Dear Employees:

As you probably know, our mill here in Parville is owned by the Atlas Corporation, which also has interests in a number of other industries. We have not been one of their better investment bets, to say the least. In fact, I'm afraid that till now, we've been just about their worst—in plain language, they've had to put about $10,000 per month into our operation for the last four years, just to keep us going. They've been losing money on our mill for a number of years; but they've always felt, as we have, that we have a good crew here, and that we'd eventually start making money.

It is my pleasure to report to you that, as a result of the continued efforts of management and workers alike, we have turned in a small profit the first half of this year. We're in a difficult and very competitive business—we've had to decrease our vacation time, and modernize our equipment, just to keep our customers happy—but we've managed to show both the owners and our customers that we can turn out the best product in the business, and make a profit besides. You can be proud of this achievement, because it is due to your efforts as much as anyone else's. We on the management team can take only part of the credit: we direct and organize your work—but you are the ones who turn out our fine product.

And turn it out at a profit, as I said. But our competition from the South is tough, and the business is a very difficult one to prosper in. And the owners of the mill, though they realize they didn't have to put money into the business these past 24 weeks to keep it going, also realize that this could be just a "flash in the pan." From their point of view, they've started to make money, but they have a long way to go before they get back all the money they've put into the business over the last four years. They have to be shown that our recent profit is not just a fluke.

If we all work together as we have this first half of the year, I'm sure we can keep on turning in profits. This means, of course, that expenses have to be held where they are: management salaries and employee wages must both stay at the same level, and all frills must be kept to a minimum. Once we show the owners that we can and will turn in profits month after month, then they will be more likely to want to reward us all with increased salaries and wages, as an incentive to keep up our good work. But we all have to pitch in first and prove to them that we can do it.

We'll get much more than eventually higher wages out of continued hard work now, however: we'll be building our reputation and prestige in the business, and insuring that we'll all have jobs here for many years to come.

I want to thank you all once again for the fine work you've done; we've finally put this mill on a profitable basis, and we'll keep it there, with your help. Have a pleasant vacation, and I hope to see you all at the Clambake.

Very truly yours,

Bill Rauls
Controller

---

## C. Personnel manager's version

July 2, 1974

Notice to Employees
Cooper Fabrics, Inc.
Parville, New Hampshire

I would like to take this opportunity to inform all employees that there has been a change in the financial status of the Cooper Fabrics company—the company has, for the first time in four years of operations, shown a profit on its financial statements. This is a source of considerable pleasure to us in management, and so we would like to communicate it to you.

We know you will understand that, even though we are now turning out a small profit, this is no reason to expect any increases in pay for any of us. The company has lost considerable amounts in the last four years, and the parent company is in no mood to see this continue. We will all be safeguarding our jobs if we keep our noses to the grindstones and keep working at the same level of pay as previously. We are all confronted with whether we want increased salary, or no salary at all. In the sense that if we do go for greater salary now, and then begin losing money again later on as we have been, the parent firm may simply decide to liquidate this mill. The old "bird in hand" story applies here too.

We have to, in short, keep overhead low and productivity high; this is the way to keep a high profit margin. Increasing pay now might be totally premature; it would cut into a very thin profit margin that is only now showing strength. We have two parties we have to satisfy. We have the owners, who want a good profit on their investment, and we have the customers, who want good, steady service and a high quality product. We have had to update our equipment to keep turning out a good product, and we've had to cut vacations, because our customers can't stock two weeks' goods anymore. We've been satisfying the customers for some time, and now we have started with the owners, with this profit. This is only a start, however. In order to win their confidence, the profit margin must continue, and also get better. Your union has been understanding of this, and they know also that security of employment is very important in these days when layoff is constantly a possibility.

As manager of personnel, I can tell you that there are plenty of textile workers looking for work who would gladly take these jobs at present pay. Additionally, our working conditions here in Parville are the best in the area. The way to build job security now for us is to recognize the needs of the owners to have a reasonable profit on their investment.

We wish you the best of vacation holidays, and we will see you when you get back.

Sincerely,

J. Rider
Manager of Personnel

---

## Hampton's Plan Analyzed

All three of the commentators have serious misgivings about Ralph Hampton's plan to send his employees one of the three letters, or for that matter *any* letter in the immediate present.

Marvin H. Swift, associate professor of communication at the General Motors Institute, puts the problem into perspective and explains his view:

> "Communication has to do with a meeting of minds, with a sharing of values—with getting others in the organization to accept a point of view and behave accordingly. In the present case, we have a general manager who wants 340 employees to accept his explanation that they are not yet entitled to increased compensation. So he and two associates have drafted what each considers to be a frank, informative, and courteous letter that will be received and acted upon in that same spirit.

> "But I don't think that will happen with any of these letters because of a difference in perception. What our management people think they are saying and what the employees think is being said will not be the same. In the employees' eyes, these letters will reduce to just about this:

> 'To: All employees
> This plant is starting to make some money, but

you're not going to get any of it. Have a nice vacation.
Ralph Hampton
General Manager'"

To John S. Fielden, dean of the College of Commerce and Business Administration at the University of Alabama, Ralph Hampton's plan brings to mind a homily:

"Once upon a time a kindergarten teacher had her charges playing with dried navy beans. Suddenly an insane thought rushed through her mind. 'For heaven's sake, children! Don't put beans up your nose!' Whereupon half the children started stuffing beans up their noses, wondering why they hadn't thought of the fun themselves." Mr. Fielden warns that writing to the workers to say, 'Things are going well. We are now making a profit. But don't think about a raise' is nothing more than saying 'Don't put beans up your nose!'" He obviously doubts that the workers are beginning to wonder about a raise, as Ralph Hampton imagines.

Robert Ackerman, vice president of Finance and Administration at Preco Corporation, supports this doubt:

"Mr. Hampton has concluded that his employees are primarily interested in job security rather than high wages, or for that matter, working conditions. More appropriately one might say he *wishes* this were the case; he has founded his justification for delaying a pay increase almost entirely on the argument that greater job security would result from higher Parville profits. He also appears to hope that a letter from management will put the matter of a wage increase to rest. The letter's purpose is not to open negotiations; it is intended to nip employee pay expectations in the bud. Little thought has been given to the potential responses."

*Content and style considerations:* Even though the three commentators agree that now is not the time to send the employees an explanatory letter, they have chosen to look closely at the three letters on Hampton's desk and to offer their opinions about the content and language.

Both Mr. Fielden and Mr. Ackerman are concerned about what they deem a crucial omission in all three letters:

Mr. Fielden asserts, "Every one of the letters omits an extremely positive point about wages, i.e. '. . . for every eight tenths of a point change in the Consumer Price Index, wages were raised or lowered $0.02 per hour.' Inflationary forces would have continued to push up the C.P.I. so that workers have been receiving wage increases as stipulated in the bargaining agreement."

And Mr. Ackerman stresses, "Cooper Fabrics is evidently approaching the end of the first year of a two-year labor contract. If the contract provides for a wage adjustment after the first year, Mr. Hampton's letter implies that the company would like to set that portion of the agreement aside. Moreover, the letter is silent on management's intentions as far as the cost-of-living adjustment is concerned. With double-digit inflation in 1974, a 12% increase in the C.P.I. would add $0.30 an hour or about 9% to the wage rates. Surely the employees must be concerned about this important issue."

Looking closely at what *is* included in the letters, Mr. Ackerman points out that "the drafts submitted by Bill Rauls and John Rider, rather than squarely facing the wage problem, raise new issues. Rauls attributes management's request for wage constraint to the parent company, to the customers, and to the competition. By implying that the parent company distributes pay increases, he makes it appear that local management does not really have much influence over a critical area of employee relations.

"Even if this were the case," Mr. Ackerman insists, "Mr. Hampton should be loathe to give such an impression—lest he compromise his ability to guide employment practices in the future." Moreover, Mr. Ackerman declares that even worse than Ralph Hampton's delegation of his responsibility to the parent company is John Rider's heavy handed warning: "Mr. Rider threatens employees with the loss of their jobs and alludes to other textile workers who could be hired at existing wage rates. His letter will certainly not engender the loyalty sought by Mr. Hampton; it may even provoke a backlash."

Marvin H. Swift also winces at Rider's threat. He says, "Of the three letters, the personnel manager's is the most negative: 'I can tell you that there are plenty of textile workers looking for work who would gladly take [your] jobs at present pay.' This translates to: 'If you don't like it here, you should get out.'" And Mr. Swift adds, "Indeed they would if they could; but they are presently locked into their jobs and can't."

*Tone of the letters:* Not only *what* one says but the *way* one says it is critically important in persuasive communication. In a letter, choice of words conveys one's attitude as surely as tone of voice suggests one's underlying feelings in a spoken encounter. Therefore, Mr. Fielden has devoted particular attention to examining each writer's choice of words. He finds that in all three of the letters the tone is at best ineffective, at worst tactless and damaging:

> "Hampton's letter creates the impression of 'I am the big boss.' Four of the five paragraphs begin with a reference to 'I': 'As general manager of this mill I am . . .'; 'I would like to add . . .'; 'I know . . .'; and 'In closing I want . . . .' Even the references to '*you*' in his letter seem patronizing—'*You* employees'; 'I am sure that *you* can understand'; and 'I want to extend to *you* on behalf of the whole management and administration team here'—a classic case of little you and big me. Furthermore, readers are prone to resent statements such as 'I am sure you can understand the necessity of holding a line on all costs,' because what the writer is doing is airily assuming the problem away. His readers may very well neither understand nor agree. Undoubtedly, the general manager anticipates such doubts. To most readers the truth will be hard to miss: Hampton is not at all 'sure.'
> 
> "Rauls's letter reflects clearly the value orientation of management and particularly that of a hard-nosed controller. The letter is full of facts, but they are *management* facts—not necessarily those that will interest and reassure the worker. The letter is tough and boasts of using 'plain language.' But while it is honest, it may merely scare employees rather than motivate them to work harder. It does not emphasize the positive; it emphasizes only what needs to be accomplished. It says, 'Put your shoulder to the wheel and keep pushing like hell, but don't ask for a rag to wipe off your sweat because it costs money!' At least that is the way his words will be heard by the worker-reader."

Mr. Fielden, like the other two commentators, is offended by Rider's unmistakable threats. He points to the remark about other workers who would gladly take the employees' jobs at present salary and he mentions such statements as: "'increased salary or no salary at all'; 'the parent company simply decide to liquidate this mill.'" To Mr. Fielden, not only is Rider's letter flagrantly tactless in tone, but also its closing conveys a sense of dishonest evasiveness. "'Remember our working conditions are the best in the area'—begs a bitter question: From a look at the benefits and pay offered by Cooper Fabrics, this must be a depressed area indeed. For if Cooper's benefits and pay are the best, I would hate to see the worst.'"

*Potential union problems:* To both Mr. Fielden and Mr. Ackerman a crucial issue in the case is who should sign the letter and to whom it should really be addressed. Their concern centers around Cooper's relations with its union. Mr. Fielden states:

> "The management of Cooper Fabrics has a long history of smooth and amicable relations with its union. For management now to communicate unilaterally with employees is sharply questionable. Caught by surprise, the union might be sorely tempted to impugn the motives of management and regard the letter as a sneak punch." Mr. Fielden strongly recommends that "the general manager, controller, and manager of personnel discuss the situation with union representatives and suggest a jointly held series of meetings with employees (near the end of their respective shifts) to explain the circumstances, highlight their benefits, point out the C.P.I. and the salary increases they have received, and answer any and all questions.
> 
> "They should make every possible effort not to embarrass the union, to minimize an outbreak of 'we/they' thinking, and to further as much as possible the notion that *we* are all winning this thing together. Obviously, management's strategy should be to get the union to urge workers to temper their salary demands. If the union buys the notion, then it should be up to the union to choose how to communicate its acceptance. Only after a meeting of minds with the union should the issue be faced of whether a letter need be written and, if so, who should sign it."

Mr. Ackerman does not concur with Mr. Fielden's view that relationships between Cooper and its union have been entirely amicable. Perhaps remembering the resentment caused by the misunderstanding of Hampton's 1972 letter, Mr. Ackerman warns:

> "The general manager has had trouble communicating with the union officers and eliciting concessions from them in the past. Insofar as labor-contract amendments are involved, he could certainly antagonize union leadership by, in effect, ignoring them now. Sending his letter to all employees will probably make it more difficult to obtain union acceptance this time as well, especially if the union draws its chief support from those most interested in wages."

In essence, however, whether they feel that Cooper Fabrics' union relations are friendly or strained, Mr. Fielden and Mr. Ackerman both strongly believe that now is not the time to ignore the feelings of union leadership. Mr. Ackerman proposes the following course of action:

> "My recommendation to Mr. Hampton is that he delay sending a general letter until he has talked with key employees, especially those in the union leadership. He should make the point to them that, although the mill's performance has improved, the heavy investments required to maintain the mill and the difficult competitive climate in the industry force him to hold the line on wage and salary increases. He should provide an indication—not a promise—of when a wage adjustment can be made; he should certainly make sure that any unresolved questions such as the cost-of-living adjustment are fully aired."

Given that the three commentators essentially agree that the proposed letters unnecessarily raise provocative issues, ignore some genuine concerns of the employees, are ineffectively expressed, are probably aimed at the wrong audience, and are premature in timing, each might echo Mr. Swift's firm conclusion:

> "I don't see how these letters will accomplish anything constructive. Therefore, my recommendation for dealing with this particular communication problem at Parville is that they be torn up."

But Mr. Swift then goes on to ask a salient and probing question: "Why is it that three key members of management—presumably competent in many ways—have such little insight into their own communication efforts?"

## Hampton's Shortcomings

I share Mr. Swift's response—his belief that Cooper Fabrics has shown a precarious insensitivity to employee needs; and that, as the man in charge, Ralph Hampton must shoulder the blame. As Mr. Swift points out, "It is easy to show that the general manager has many desirable managerial traits: he is innovative, patient, considerate, confident, and decisive. Yet he has shortcomings, which can be discerned by closely considering some of his actions:

- Recalling laid-off employees 'in an order determined by management's convenience rather than by seniority.'
- Letting the employees pick up the tab for the company picnic.
- Communicating with them only infrequently and routinely. And he does not provide for their communicating with him, i.e., no feedback.
- Forgetting that his 1974 letter repeats the austerity-and-forbearance theme of his 1972 letter.
- Condoning, or actually writing, the notice on starting and stopping times.
- Installing new equipment and not preparing 'the old-timers' for the change in work habits."

Mr. Swift concludes, "As articulate as Hampton is, his actions show that he has isolated himself from his employees."

*No panacea, but at least a start:* Mutually beneficial communication involves two-way perception. Mr. Hampton has too easily accepted John Rider's estimate that turnover is "low." When we consider that 14 workers per month have left Cooper and realize this means that 168 workers—or half the work force—are leaving each year, we have reason to wonder why. And so should Ralph Hampton. When we hear that union sentiment at the plant is weak, that relations with the union have always been amicable—*but* that a misunderstanding with the union had generated resentment only two years ago, we perceive the need to reexamine the rapport between management and union officials. And so should Ralph Hampton.

It may be that Cooper's employees really do value job security more than higher pay. And it also may be true that the union is either disinterested or eager to cooperate and make concessions to help the plant gain stability. But Ralph Hampton and his administrative staff have a great deal more to learn about these matters before they can launch an effective program of communication. To quote Mr. Swift:

"Granted that improving communication is not a panacea for solving profitability problems, yet or-ganizations are, first of all, organizations of human beings. As such, they—managers and managed alike—are more likely to work together when they are encouraged to express themselves. Good two-way communication at Parville might well make the difference between marginal and productive operations."

*Ms. Newman taught from 1973 to 1979 in Written and Oral Communication at the Harvard Business School. The case of Cooper Fabrics, Inc., originally was prepared by Thomas C. Raymond, professor of business administration at the Harvard Business School. A version of the case that included the three sample letters was prepared especially for the WOC course. The company and names are disguised.*

# IV. Good Advice on Process and Product

Focusing on both the creative process and the end product, each of the articles in this section offers good advice and substantial help for writing more effectively.

# Keys to Good Writing

## PAUL S. SWENSSON

I agreed to try to tell how to turn out a beautiful piece of vivid writing and how to report with mirror-like simplicity. And now the deadline crumples my mind.

Why do I fear putting down the first line?

Can't I make up my mind what to say?

And why can't I see you, the reader, any better than yesterday when I could not tell the color of your eyes or hear the sound of your words on paper as you sit at your typewriter and I at mine.

I know why. I do not want to admit that when it comes to writing, we are very much alike. For your sake, don't be like me. Because I procrastinate. I find detours on the eight-foot journey from the door to my desk. I am greedy and impulsive, grasping clusters of words when one would do. My mind is impatient, darting like a polliwog in a pond, to other attractions. I cater to my habits, both good and bad. I am insecure. I sicken when my writing is criticized. I crave encouragement and curse the postman when acceptance letters do not arrive by return mail. I suspect that my writing ills are chronic. But I live for praise from my peers and for those rare moments when one word, or phrase, or short sentence breaks out of my mind to sing gloriously.

If you accept parts of that fat paragraph as plausible images of your work habits, then we have nailed down the most troublesome problems that editors have with reporters and writers. You and I are so wrapped up in our hopes, or fears, or subject matter, that we don't, won't and can't identify the person(s) for whom we write.

If you see a blob of faces as you look up from your typewriter, stop writing. Focus on one reader. Write directly to that person. Some young writers tell me they write for just one person—their editor. That's the wrong reader.

Tons of research have been printed and a mint has been spent to identify audiences. We know much about demographics of our readers and every bit helps. But we rarely discover how we turn off readers, one by one. Readership research explores the one-to-one relationship. One writer. One reader. If you, the writer, see your reader clearly, you are one-third of the way toward serving and satisfying that reader.

It matters not greatly whether you have picked a bright or dull reader, a lazy one or one in a hurry, a young one or an old one, a him or a her; but it must be a real person. Your editor may suggest that you change the reader just as you change subject matter. But you need a reader, one for whom you are a servant.

John Steinbeck said it well when he sat down to write "East of Eden" for his two small sons. "Perhaps by speaking directly to them, I shall speak directly to other people." Later he said: "One can go off into fanciness if one writes to a huge, nebulous group."

What can a writer expect of a reader? What do I expect from this conversation with you?

I want you to be curious and skeptical, but not cynical.

I hope that our eyes will meet and that your head will nod in approval a few times. I expect to see your dissent with a frown and negative shake of the head. I hope that between nods, shakes and frowns, you will give me your attention to the end of this piece.

Two things I must do for you. I must write clearly, so that you are not confused. I must share something of value with you, lest you turn the page and leave without a farewell.

The late Gideon Seymour made a habit of substituting a Greek-rooted word for every Latin word in his first draft of editorials for the *Minneapolis Star*. The Greek words he wanted had powers of persuasion; the Latin words were good, but limited to precision. He wanted to persuade; therefore he swapped syllables until he found the combination that would work for him. You can swap words, too, and you need not be a Latin or Greek student to do it well. But it helps.

Walter Kerr marshaled words of sight and sound to describe a dance in "No, No, Nannette": "The boy's shoes are cleated beneath those diamond-patterned socks, and as the fast-tap begins, the stage floor flinches. It is jackhammer time . . ." Even the "diamond-patterned socks" suggest speed and the image of motion.

Listen to the sound of words from Hemingway's "The Sun Also Rises":

"They had hitched the mules to the dead bull and then the whips cracked, the men ran, and the mules, straining forward, their legs pushing, broke into a gallop, and the bull, one horn up, his head on its side, swept a swath smoothly across the sand and out the red gate."

Look at that sentence. Count the verbs, abverbs, and adverbial phrases which bring together the facts of place and thing and set them in rapid motion.

Between the inertness of the dead bull (he is merely hitched) and the smooth speed with which the body sweeps across the sand and out of sight are verbs of sweat and effort: crack, run, strain, break. Precisely at "broke" the sentence stops straining and moves into the smooth glide to its close.

Look at the s's and the th's of swath and smoothly. These are not inadvertent. They ease the path of the bull's departure and are marks of Hemingway's skill in using the sound of words.

Norman Cousins, the editor and publisher, hunts for persons who use words well in writing about the arts, or politics, or science, or about some remote corner of human experience. Cousins says of this kind of writer:

"Whoever and wherever he is, he likes the clink and purr of words against each other. He likes the crackle of ideas well expressed. He delights, as some men do in thoroughbred horses and racing hulls, in prose that runs sleek and true to its destination."

James Kilpatrick, the columnist, adds this caution: "With a little rearranging you can keep the rhythm going. But do not do this always; you may sound like Hiawatha."

Choosing the right word is a game anyone can play. A Washington sports announcer, having delivered Chris Hamburger to the Redskins training field one week after emergency appendectomy, said Hamburger would not play for two weeks lest "he reinjure" his stomach muscles. The announcer was wrong twice with one word. Hamburger had never injured his stomach muscles. Therefore he could not reinjure that which had not been hurt, unless the surgeon's scalpel counts as injury.

Jerry Lewis, according to Hub Keavy, an Associated Press writer, reads papers for material in his night club acts. "What," he asked a member of the audience, "is a woman's 'yet'?" After a pause Jerry says, "I don't know either, but here's what I read in the paper: 'The prowler shot the woman and the bullet is in her yet.'"

Let's detour around the right word to let strong words beat sense into our erratic habits. A plaque in the Milwaukee Press Club says: "The ability to express ideas is as important as the ability to have ideas." That's where the strong words come in.

Weather stories depend on the selection of words with muscles. Paul Montgomery wrote in the *New York Times*:

> "Punishing winds and driving snow lashed the Northeast yesterday, producing heavy snow accumulations inland and perilous conditions along the coast."

The lead could be faulted for vagueness about the storm, but it uses powerful words to indentify the impact on people. If you wish, underline *punishing* and *driving*, *heavy* and *perilous*. These are words, not meteorological vocabulary.

You may be tempted to remind me that much of your writing deals with technical matters. You feel committed to dullness because of the subject matter. If you really think along those lines, you are digging a grave for your writing. Dullness can be overcome. Here is a method, in the form of a quiz, that works for me.

Below is a list of five kinds of news stories. Rank them in the order you think will get the most reader attention. Put in the No. 1 slot the most interesting type of story. Then list the others down to No. 5 in descending interest.

| Things | 1. |
| Ideas | 2. |
| People | 3. |
| Projects | 4. |
| Problems | 5. |

Researchers confirm that readers are interested above all in what happens to other people. People-oriented stories earn the No. 1 rank. Second are things which are triggered by man or nature. Third are the project stories where something useful is supposed to happen. Fourth, problems. Fifth, ideas which usually require an extra effort to appreciate or understand.

If you are assigned to write about a problem, research it for its human qualities and write it in terms of a real person with a real problem. Do not generalize.

Never write about the Irish problem, the Arab problem, the Israeli problem, the Black problem, the Indian problem, or the Ms. problem. Turn it the other way around; then write.

Alliteration can be used to step up the impact of strong words. A *Time* magazine writer described how the Thad-Jones musicians "blow, beat or belt their way into a piece." Shakespeare played with the impact of words in "Midsummer Night's Dream" when Puck recites:

> "I'll lead you about a round, Through bog, through bush, through brake, through brier; Sometime a horse I'll be, sometime a hound, A hog, a headless bear, sometime a fire, And neigh, and bark, and grunt, and roar, and burn, Like horse, hound, hog, bear, fire, at every turn."

Whether you accept the tip from Shakespeare or *Time*, the words you use in common writing can be put in two piles—the strong words and the soft or weak words.

Below, beat and belt from *Time,* when spoken aloud, are expelled from the throat, they bounce off the roof of the mouth, they sail between parted teeth, and get their final shape from the lips. Puck used strong words 21 times in the passage above.

Soft words also are shaped in the throat; they float up with little effort and out with lips barely parted. Often they are not heard at all. But they provide mood.

Some words shout, others sigh. Make them work for you.

Somehow I missed the real reason for reading Chaucer in school days. He was the greatest among English poets for the use of language as an effective instrument of action. Rexroth says Chaucer used language to get results. He steers readers to 15 lines in the "Prologue" where Chaucer defines mercantile capitalism with the skill and understanding of a Marx, and with considerably fewer words.

When shaping a sentence or rewriting a paragraph, scrutinize the hardness or the softness of the essential words. Add or subtract the decibels or sound as needed. Read the passage aloud, or at least whisper. This is one way to put muscle into your writing.

Newspaper writing, the kind I happen to know best, is edging tentatively toward the broad horizons of the essay and away from the narrow scope of the five W's.

Ken Ringle tried it this way in the *Washington Post:*

> "You can see it best from somewhere atop the Continental Divide: the chilling skyscape of winter coming; the gray quilted snowclouds of late November and early December."

Except for proper nouns, he uses no word longer than two syllables to show what he wants us to see. He goes on:

> "They pour through the passes (usually from the west) on a silent, cutting wind and funnel out through the lonely Rocky Mountain ridges onto the barren landscape of a waiting America."

With simple words he sends your fingers to button the collar against wind and cold. Now for the third paragraph, 26 words long, in which Ringle provides title, theme and outline for his piece:

> "Winter is being born, and with it what Melville called the 'dampy drizzly November in my soul'; an annual late autumn crisis of life and doubt."

I had not realized until recently how far and fast some writers are running in their search for a different kind of lead paragraph. A few of the entries in the 1976 Virginia Press Women's contest were deep into the seventh paragraph before striking the chord on which they would build a melody of words. I suggested then (and now) that three paragraphs ought to be the outer limit because readers (we can't escape them) are lazy. They must be lured with the opening words, such as Ringle's "You can see it best . . ."

But before your next words hop to their perches on the typewriter carriage, please check your clothesline. This piece of rope, on which you hang your literary wash, is also known as the outline. I prefer to call it clothesline because I can look at what I have hung on the line and I can see if all the (verbal) socks are up and matched. I can also see the empty place saved for the shirt of an idea that somehow isn't there.

Jacques Barzun in "Simple and Direct" nails down the importance of logic to writing, if one is to say exactly what one wants to say. "Language is not algebra . . . the symbols do not stay put, nor can they be carried from place to place with an assurance that their value will not change. If language were like algebra, there could be no poetry or other fiction, no diplomacy or intimate correspondence, no persuasion or religious literature."

As soon as your lead or theme is set, the next goal must be the last paragraph. That's where you want to take the reader. The last part may take many forms, but most often it affirms the lead. The writer has not done his/her job well until the reader says: "I'm glad I read all of this. Now I understand what I had not grasped before."

Or even better, the reader may be moved (as you wanted him/her to move) to do something positive on a course of action. Or the reader may give silent thanks to the author of the good words. Grace before and after a meal of words is not a silly thought.

Only the better writers make a habit of starting and finishing each paragraph with an interlocking stitch, the thread which ties ideas together at the same moment it ties the idea to the reader.

You can trust your editor in the role of word surgeon who ties syllables with surgical knots so the thoughts cannot slip away. That's part of the shared labor between writer and editor. But sometimes the editor can only point out passages where passages are not passages. In the margin or in a cover note words appear: "It doesn't hang together."

The reason may be found in one of several traps. It could be departure from the outline or the natural arrangement of the subject matter. Or it could be fouled in the beginnings or endings of difficult sentences or paragraphs. Or it could be in the selection of words, or the omission or insertion of direct quotations. Barzun, like others, avoids dogmatic prescriptions to achieve "linking" in one's writing so that "clusters of untrimmed thought" are connected in the best order. He recommends watching how good writers do it, then learning from them.

How does a person turn out "a beautiful piece of vivid writing," or report with "mirror-like simplicity"? Much can be learned about the correct or acceptable use of English. Strunk and White's "The Elements of Style" is still the best for many of us. Why be grammatical? Simply to insure a safe journey of words from one mind to another. Why fight jargon? For the same reason that environmentalists battle pollution.

Fine writers are born, not made. But every writer, regardless of the gift that is his or hers, must learn to use simple words, must battle adjectives and adverbs, must discover the right word and must realize how well words work in short combinations.

Every writer must find in solitude the rhythms which swing thought into speech . . . and learn without being taught the movement and countermovement of the words to move the action down the page to the story's end. But for every fine plan and procedure there are worms and waste—physical, mental, emotional and spiritual—the aches and agues a writer is susceptible to.

At 75, Carl Sandburg said "If God gives me five more years," he (Sandburg) might become a writer.

John Steinbeck in a letter to his editor wrote: "Sometimes I have felt that I held fire in my hands and spread a page with shining—(but) I have never lost the weight of clumsiness, of ignorance, of aching inability."

If you ache enough, you may be well down (or up) the road to becoming a writer.

# Six Guidelines for Fast, Functional Writing

## HERBERT POPPER

Some types of improvement in the quality of one's writing can only be achieved at the expense of quantity—for instance, by spending more time on the editing of drafts. However, regardless of whether you use longhand or some form of dicta-tion, there are several areas where quantity and quality go hand in hand, and where it can actually take less time to produce an effective piece of communication than an ineffective one. The six guidelines that follow take aim at that area.

Because writing problems vary in kind and degree from person to person, you may find that some of these suggestions either don't apply to you or appear self-evident. However, "fast, functional" writing skills are so important to most engineers and technical managers that even if you only find one or two of the suggestions really useful, this should more than repay you for your reading time.

## 1. Know What Your Audience Expects

A vice-president of operations was making his annual tour of the company's outlying facilities. At one plant, he chatted with the assistant manager about the upcoming labor negotiations with the local union.

"I wish you'd send me a fairly detailed report of those negotiations," asked the vice-president. Flattered by this request, the assistant plant manager resolved to do an outstanding job of reporting. By the time negotiations were over, he had more than 50 pages of handwritten notes, which he decided to amplify with background information on some of the points the union or the management team had raised.

It took him two weeks after the close of negotiations to organize this material into a rough handwritten draft. Because of a secretarial bottleneck, it took him two more weeks to get this draft typed and edited, and then another two weeks to get the massive document typed up in final form. Nevertheless, as he signed the letter of transmittal in which he apologized for imperfections in the typing and commented on the shortage of good secretarial help, he felt rather proud of himself: The report read like a courtroom drama, and had a great degree of polish.

Unfortunately, before the report could even reach headquarters, the vice-president had made an acid phone call to the plant manager. Apparently, what the vice-president had really wanted was brief, day-by-day reports that he could review while negotiations were still in progress, and that he could pass on to another plant that started negotiations a week later. When he finally got the assistant plant managers's monumental opus, a lot of the information was old hat, the key points having been already passed along by the plant manager in a lengthy, long-distance phone call just before the close of negotiations.

Next year, the plant manager decided to handle the job of reporting himself; at the close of each day's session, he dictated his notes into a recorder—his secretary would type them up on the next day, so that he could ink in some comments and send them out as soon as he finished that day's negotiating. Since he didn't use a draft, his daily reports were not particularly polished; the inked-in comments and corrections looked rather informal—and yet these reports were acclaimed by the vice-president.

Moral of the story: Make sure you know what the audience wants. Don't be afraid to ask. There are times when speed, rather than quality or quantity, may be of the essence. In the example above, which is based on an actual situation, the assistant plant manager could have saved himself hours of toil by finding out what sort of details the vice-president did or did not want to know about, and whether quick dictation without a draft was acceptable.

Failure to find out or to really understand the audience's expectations is perhaps the single biggest timewaster in technical writing. An example of such inefficiency involves the engineer who uses exactly the same writing approach regardless of whether his report is primarily intended for the departmental archives, his immediate supervisor, or a financial executive on the appropriations committee.

If the report is just intended for a supervisor, for instance, there is nothing wrong with using technical jargon, and for keeping background information very brief. But if the report is to go to a financial executive—particularly one who lacks any sort of technical background—the engineer must avoid technical jargon, and explain some things that he would not need to explain to his boss, while leaving out technical details. In such a report, it is particularly important to make the first page or two tell the bulk of the story, in terms that are meaningful to the administrator.

If you are writing a dual-function report—say, one intended for both a financial executive and your boss—by all means get squared away with the latter on how the two approaches can be reconciled (e.g., by eventually giving your boss additional sections or informal notes that are omitted from the administrator's copy, by coming up with a preliminary version of the first two pages that you and your boss can review jointly before finalization, etc.).

When writing for publication, rather than for internal use, finding out the audience's expectations can be an equally great timesaver. Many magazines have booklets that discuss their "expectations" in regard to such things as writng style, quality of drawings, compatibility with readers' interests[1]—and are further prepared to conserve the author's time by reviewing outlines in some detail so as to minimize the need for revision of the final manuscript.

## 2.  Mobilize Your Subconscious

Legend has it that on the day the opera "The Magic Flute" was scheduled to get its first performance, someone reminded Mozart that there still wasn't any overture, whereupon the composer calmly sat down and dashed off the magnificent overture just in time to give the score to the orchestra before the curtain went up. Actually, I think if this legend is true, the chances are that Mozart must have "precomposed" the overture in his mind days before he set it down on paper, so that leaving the actual writing until just before the deadline may not have been as risky as it seemed to others at the time.

Unfortunately, many of us tend to display a Mozart-like confidence in being able to meet a last-minute deadline regardless of whether we have done any precomposing or not.

If you have a writing project with a far-off deadline, and you don't feel like starting the actual writing right away, then don't. But I would still suggest that you draw up a rough outline as soon as you can, see how much information you already have available and how much more you will have to dig out, decide when you should start this digging out so that the information will be available at the proper time, and discuss the outline for the project with your boss or with a colleague. That way, you will not only get a feel for the emphasis needed (as discussed in the previous section), but you will be giving your subconscious mind a chance to come up with ideas while the project is incubating.

To come up with useful ideas, your subconscious should have some sort of framework—that way, perhaps some of the framework will be filled in for you while you shave in the morning. But if you wait till the last minute, even to prepare an outline or think about an approach, all your subconscious can do is to provide you with a feeling of anxiety.

Another constructive use for the prewriting period is to do some preselling. People hate shocks—which is what may happen when your recommendations based on a full year's work are coldly dropped on your department head's desk. It is fairer to him, and kinder to you and your writing time, to use the "let's let him in on part of the secret" technique. So, give your boss some inkling of what your report is going to recommend. Don't try to do a complete job of selling, but do give him a chance to get some exposure to your ideas. From his initial comments, you may also be able to obtain pointers on how to best link your ideas to his, and to the current objectives of the department. This can save a great deal of writing time in the long run, and will often let you get the constructive involvement of the reader much sooner than if you use the "This may come as a shock, but . . ." approach.

## 3.  Build Up and Exploit Your Momentum

"I sit down with a fountain pen and paper and the story pours out. However lousy a section is, I let it go. I write on to the end. Then the subconscious mind has done what it can . . . The rest is simple effort . . . going over a chapter time and time again until, though you know it isn't right, it is the best you can do." That's how W. Somerset Maugham said he got his thoughts down on paper. If you have trouble getting started and building up momentum on writing project, then the Maugham approach of putting down your thoughts in any old undisciplined way and eventually going back to polish them up, has a lot to recommend it. Note that this is also the basic approach to combating writer's block that Auren Uris suggested in his "How to Be a Great Dictator" section.

What do you do if you still don't succeed in unplugging your thoughts, regardless of whether you are using pen, pencil, stenographer or dictating machine? Here are a few additional pointers.

■   Go over your outline (or Report Highlights Sheet, as suggested in an earlier section) and pretend a good friend asked you to explain each point to him. If he were to ask questions such as "Why don't we just stick with the old process?" or "How does this gimmick work?", the chances are you wouldn't be at a loss for words—you would just say it like it is. So, pretend your friend is asking you questions that correspond to your outline, and write it like it is.

- Pretend that this is an examinaton, and that you have five minutes to get something down on paper for each thought on your outline— i.e., that if after five minutes you have nothing down on paper on the first point, you have nothing that you can be graded on, and you would thus get zero. (A couple of years ago, I took an aptitude test in which I was given a cast of two or three characters and had to shape them into a plot for a short story within ten minutes; then stop and shape another cast of characters into a new plot; then do this a few more times. Not considering myself a really fast writer, I was amazed at how much I could get down in ten minutes when the pressure was on, and when I knew I would be graded on content rather than style. It occurred to me that if I could pretend that I was in a similar situation when starting on a writing job, it would get me going—and it works!)

- Pick the best time to get started on a tough writing project. For most people, this may be the very beginning of the day, before things have come up to distract them. Others work best right after lunch. Still others find that the best time to unlock their thoughts is after dinner at home, and that once they get started that way, they can continue the project at work without much difficulty. If you haven't already done so, try to find a time pattern in the daily periods during which you feel sharpest and loosest; then exploit these periods to get started on tough projects.

Of course, getting started does not necessarily mean writing a brilliant beginning; it means getting started on the "meat" of the project. Very often a meaty fact-filled beginning is the most brilliant one anyway. But if you do feel the urge to think up something particularly striking or original, you may be better off doing this after most of the project is down on paper, rather than letting it be an initial stumbling block.

Once you have built up your momentum, how do you keep it?

First of all, try not to stop. Let someone take your phone messages. If you see a chance to finish the project by working late, do so. Resist the temptation to take a break until you start slowing down. (Personally, I find that sipping coffee or puffing on a cigar while doing difficult writing is preferable to running the risk of getting sidetracked by taking an unnecessary break.) Putting it into industrial engineering terminology, make sure you have a long enough production run to justify the setup time.

If you can't finish the project by working late, then it is usually better to leave it in the middle of a paragraph than to try and finish the particular section or thought. Finishing the thought the next day will be relatively easy, and this will serve to prime the pump for the next thought. I used to make the mistake of staying up until whatever hour was necessary to get a major section finished, only to find that it would take me all the next morning to stop resting on my laurels and to uncork my thoughts for the next section. Conversely, when I don't try so hard to come to a logical stopping place, I can usually continue the section without any difficulty the next morning and then launch right into the next section. (I can't take full credit for this approach; someone named Hemingway recommended it in a book called "A Movable Feast.")

## 4. Watch out for Time-Wasting Verbosity

Not everybody has the uncoiling problems dealt with in the previous section. In fact, some people who can uncoil most of the time at the drop of a pencil encounter the opposite type of problem: How to avoid the verbosity that wastes their own time as well as that of the reader, so that they can make the most of their fluency as writers.

The first section in the 1966 "Efficient, Effective Writing" report[2] gave good advice on ways of recognizing and avoiding destructive verbosity. Although that section was aimed at making writing more informative, most of the suggestions can also lead to faster writing. For instance, the writer can usually save time by cutting down on passive verbs, abstract nouns, and prepositional phrases. (Obviously, it would have taken me longer to write the previous sentence had I said "Time can be saved by the writer if proper consideration is given to a reduction in the use of passive verbs, etc.")

Here are a few additional suggestions:

- Don't be legalistic in a nonlegal piece of writing. Lawyers have to be extremely careful to cover every possible contingency—hence they may feel justified in using strings of words that may differ only very slightly in meaning (e.g., null, void, of no legal force, etc.). But engineers are seldom justified in coming up with a phrase like "The *development, establishment,* and *implementation* of process-control *philosophies* and *policies* must take place at an *early* or *incipient* stage in a project." There just isn't enough difference between the italicized words to warrant using more than one of each; if you say "philosophies," 99 out of 100 readers will assume that this includes "policies."

- Don't waste time on excess hedging. For instance, when you say "Based on bench-scale experiments run at ten different temperatures, 300 F. produces the best yield," you have clearly indicated on what you base your conclusion, and there is no need to add hedge phrases such as " . . . 300 F. may tend to produce the best yields, assuming that these bench-scale results are freely applicable to commercial conditions . . ." Putting it another way, readers generally realize that almost any technical, business or philosophical statement that can be made is subject to limitations and qualifications; if you insist on pointing out limitations that are either obvious or unimportant, you are wasting time (and probably producing dull writing). Particularly wasteful and deadly is the "triple hedge"—e.g., " . . . may, under some circumstances, tend to . . ."

- Use more tables, illustrations and in-text list-

ings to cut down on verbosity. Earlier in this report, Johnson pointed out how a "1, 2, 3" approach to the Report Highlights page can avoid the verbose generalities that sometimes go into report abstracts; the same sort of item-by-item approach can result in tighter writing of all kinds, including the body of the report. (At the risk of appearing to disregard my own "hedging" caveat, I should point out that itemization can be carried to dull extremes, particularly once the triple sub-indentation stage is reached. But if you haven't been doing much itemizing, the technique can save you a lot of words in reducing generalities to specifics.)

- Consider leaving out some details altogether. Resist the temptation to tell the reader everything you know about the subject—just tell him what you think he needs to know. The latter is quite different from just telling him what you think he would like to hear— or from using a dual standard whereby you exclude all unfavorable details while including all those that are favorable. The memo or report that burdens the reader with every conceivable detail has not only taken the writer much more time than necessary, but suggests that the writer was unsure of himself because he left it to the reader to decide which of the details were significant. (If you are afraid that a short report won't adequately reflect the work that went into a particular study, you can always indicate the *type* of additional data that can be supplied on request.)

Of course, the classic example of detail elimination involves the man who got a letter from his landlord asking if he intended to vacate his apartment. The answer consisted of "Dear Sir: I remain, Yours Truly, Henry Smith."

Unfortunately, it's not always that easy to combine succinctness with politeness in handling one's correspondence, particularly when one is dictating it. Things that can waste the dictator's (and the reader's) time include:

- Marathon sentences. An occasional long sentence can supply useful variety, and may be needed in order to relate ideas to each other, but strings of runaway sentences impede efficient communicaton.

- Ditto for marathon paragraphs.
- Shotgun or overkill attacks on the topic, whereby the dictator, not being sure he has said what he really wanted to say, goes on to re-attack the topic in several other, equally roundabout, ways.
- Tendencies to throw in cliches and meaningless phrases just to keep the dictation process going. It is less wasteful to keep your secretary waiting for a minute while you find the right phrase than to dictate a phrase that adds nothing.

## 5. Save Time via the "Example" Technique

Most of us find the going slow when we write on an abstract, philosophic level for any length of time. True, the amount of such writing can be minimized by translating abstract concepts into dollars and cents, but this cannot always be done. For instance, if you are trying to change the attitudes of foremen towards some community or labor-relations problem, neither payout time nor discounted cash flow is going to be of much help to you. But this does not mean that your communications with the foremen must be entirely on an abstract philosophic level.

Good philosophy is hard to write. There are all sorts of pitfalls: failure to define terms, or to relate them to the reader's frame of mind, failure to avoid either oversimplification or obtuseness, etc. But fortunately, you can write about an abstract topic—e.g., a desired change in attitude—without staying on the abstract level for very long. The idea here is to translate the abstract into the specific by using analogies, miniature case histories (either actual or hypothetical), projections of what might happen if the status quo were maintained, etc.

Of course, this "example" technique is not limited to communications that deal with corporate philosophy but should also be used when generalities and abstract concepts crop up in technical writing. Here, a one-sentence "for instance" can often take the place of a much longer explanation; a liberal sprinkling of such sentences can keep the discussion on the ground, and can result in a easier-to-write yet more-informative communication than one in which all abstract technical concepts are explained or promoted in only theoretical terms.

## 6. Know Thyself, and Thy Writing

The difficulty in many articles dealing with improving your writing is their generality; they presuppose that all writers have the same problems. This report has tried to be more specific—for instance, by showing how *less* discipline can be a timesaver for the engineer who has trouble uncoiling, whereas *more* discipline can be an eventual timesaver for someone whose problem is verbosity or poor organization rather than lack of writing fluency.

Where do you fall within these two extremes? Should your prime emphasis be on boosting your writing output or on boosting its quality? If you have difficulty answering that question, you can get help quite readily.

For example, the 1966 "Efficient, Effective Writing" report[2] supplied some simple tests whereby you can evaluate the informative quality of your writing. If your score is low, perhaps your prime goal should be to make your writing more informative. At the beginning, this may reduce your page output because you will be spending more time on editing and rewriting. However, if you try to learn from your editing, you will find that output will eventually increase along with quality. This means spending a few minutes reviewing an edited draft to see what type of corrections are prevalent, and to think about ways of minimizing the need for these types of corrections in subsequent writing.

Discuss your writing with your boss. Some bosses are reluctant to initiate such a discussion because they have found that it takes almost as much tact to constructively criticize a subordinate's writing as it would to constructively criticize his wife or family. But if you initiate such a discussion (I mean about your writing, not your wife), the chances are that overly defensive postures can be avoided, and that you and your boss will both gain a better insight into problem areas.

Ask your boss whether he thinks you are

spending too much or too little time on writing. For instance, based on samples, would he settle for draftless dictation on some reports in order to give you more time for engineering?

If one of your writing problems is that interruptions are always breaking your train of thought, ask your boss about ways of getting more privacy, or about occasionally working at home to make headway on difficult writing chores.

In order to discuss other aspects of your writing, you may want to go over a sort of writing-inventory checklist, such as the one published in the *Harvard Business Review* article. "What Do You Mean I Can't Write?"[3] This can be a good starting point in getting your supervisor's views on such matters as whether you sometimes present too many opinions and not enough supporting data (or vice versa), whether you tend to under- or overestimate his familiarity with your work, etc.

A concluding thought: The engineer who progresses in his company tends to do more writing every year. Eventually, he may also have to supervise the writing of subordinates; many of their reports and memos will go out over his signature and will reflect on the caliber of the work done under his supervision. Thus the engineer who becomes adept at fast, functional writing is in an enviable position—he can save a significant and increasing amount of time, establish his credentials as an efficient communicator, and eventually help his subordinates solve their own communication problems. We hope that the suggestions in various sections of this report will help point the way, and will let you apply the "work smarter, not harder" principle to your communicating.

*Acknowledgment*

Some of the ideas in this final section stem from various members of *Chemical Engineering's* editorial staff, and also from Manny Meyers of Picatinny Arsenal, and Peter J. Rankin of Basford Inc.

*References*

1. See, for instance, "How to Write for *Chemical Engineering,*" a booklet available from *Chemical Engineering,* 330 W. 42 St., New York City.
2. Johnson, Thomas P., "How Well Do You Inform?," *Chem. Eng.,* Mar. 14, 1966 (Reprint No. 295).
3. Fielden, J., *Harvard Bus. Rev.,* May-June 1964, p. 147.

# Imagination Helps Communication

## THE ROYAL BANK OF CANADA

The Basic Skill in every profession and in most businesses is the ability to organize and express ideas in writing and in speaking.

No matter how clever an engineer may be technically, or an executive managerially, or a research man creatively, he does not show his worth unless he communicates his ideas to others in an influential way.

Language is the most momentous product of the human mind. Between the clearest animal call of love or warning or anger, and man's most trivial word, there lies a whole day of creation— or, as we would say it today, a whole chapter of evolution.

A business man is not called upon to present the elegance of a wit, a novelist or a poet. He must express himself accurately, clearly and briefly, but he need not denude his language of beauty and appeal.

The purpose of the writer is to communicate effectively. He needs a feeling for writing the right thing in the right way at the right time: not a bare-bones recital of facts, unless in a specification or legal document, but a composition of words which will convey his meaning and his sentiment.

This requires use of imagination, which is the cornerstone of human endeavour. John Masefield, the Poet Laureate, wrote: "Man's body is faulty, his mind untrustworthy, but his imagination has made him remarkable."

Writing imaginatively cannot be taught. It can be studied in examples—the writings of Defoe, Shakespeare, La Fontaine and Jules Verne show what can be done, but not how to do it. In this, writing is on a par with art and the product of an artisan's hands. The painter can no more convey the secret of his imaginative handling of colour than the plumber can teach that little extra touch he gives a wiped joint. All three, writer, artist, artisan, have secrets springing from within. After learning the principles, they go on to produce their works inspired by the dignity of accomplishment due to their gifts.

Look at the drama built into small events by choice of words and use of imagination: Defoe gave us Crusoe recoiling from the footprint in the sand; Homer gave us Achilles shouting over against the Trojans and Ulysses bending the great bow; and Bunyan gave us Christian running from the tempter with his fingers in his ears. None of these was an epic event, but by their mastery of putting imagination into their communication these writers painted scenes which stirred us in the reading and linger in our memories.

A good piece of writing, whether it be a novel or a business letter does three things: it communicates a thought, it conveys a feeling, and it gives the reader some benefit.

## The Writer's Tools

What are the writer's tools? A wide range of language, for variety and to avoid the commonplace; active verbs, to keep the action moving; similes, which make words paint a thousand pictures; metaphor and parable, to make meanings clear; and rhythm, which contributes to smooth, easy reading.

To these tools, the writer adds imagination, always being careful to bring it within the scope of facts. Art in writing must not be used as an escape from reality.

This sort of writing is not so simple a thing as fluency, which soap-box orators have in abundance. It is not so simple a thing as grammatical exactitude, which can be hammered into boys and girls by a teacher.

But when it is properly done, imaginative writing is very powerful. Look at Cyrano de Bergerac in the drama by Edmond Rostand. The hero was valiant and romantic, but very sensitive regarding the size of his nose. This sensitivity prevented his making his court to the beautiful Roxane, but he wrote ardent letters to her for a handsome and stupid friend. The power of the written word won Roxane's love for his friend by proxy.

Good writing needs to be appropriate to the occasion, the purpose, the reader and the writer. It must not be too pompous for its load, or hesitant about what it seeks to do, or beneath the intelligence of the reader, or too arrogant for the writer's position.

Writing is only serviceable and good with reference to the object for which it is written. You say: "That is a beautiful dress"; but let the dress slide from the model's shoulders and lie in a heap on the floor, and what is it? A heap of material. Its virtue resides in its fittingness to its purpose.

What is written imaginatively in the daily work of office and industry will get desired results. If the writer looks further, what is written with imagination will live on when this Atomic Age is ancient history. Why? Because imagination is the one common link between human minds in all ages.

Imagination in writing finds expression through the use of accurate and illuminating equivalents for thoughts. You may show your imagination by dealing with something unfamiliar; by calling to attention a commonplace fact that is generally overlooked; by bringing into view familiar things in new relationship; or by drawing together relevant thoughts in a nosegay tied with your own ribbon.

An imaginative writer can look out upon the sprawling incoherence of a factory or a city or a nation or a problem and give it intelligible statement.

## Something About Style

The style in which you write is the living embodiment of your thought, and not merely its dress.

When you put words together you convey not only your purpose in writing but your character and mood, both of which are important to your reader's understanding.

Let the occasion dictate the manner of your writing. Sometimes a manly rough line, with a great deal of meaning in it, may be needed, while a different set of circumstances demands the lubrication of sweet words. A blinding light is not always the best illumination: the delicate colours in moss-covered rock are enhanced by overcast, misty air.

Knowledge of techniques does not give the writer this discrimination. Technique is always a means and not an end. If we allow rules to govern our writing we become tongue-tied by authority. As Rembrandt remarked to someone who was looking closely into one of his paintings, seeking the technique, "pictures are intended to be looked at, not smelled."

We do not find ourselves tripping over technique in the inspired paragraphs of great literary works. Think of the forcefulness, the meaning, the simplicity of expression, in Lincoln's Gettysburg address, in Churchill's "fall of France" radio broadcast. Then contrast the great golden phrases of political campaigners, rising from nothing and leading to nothing: words on words, dexterously arranged, bearing the semblance of argument, but leaving nothing memorable, no image, no exaltation.

At the other end of the scale are those who write speeches and letters stodgily. Too many people who are nice people at heart become another sort when they pick up a pen or a dictaphone. They tighten up. They become unnatural. They curdle into impersonality and choose starchy sentences. Their product is like a page printed with very old and worn-out type. In the vivid prose which marked some seventeenth century writers, James Howell wrote: "Their letters may be said to be like bodies without sinews, they have neither art nor arteries in them."

A letter in which something significant is attempted—a sale, a correction, a changing of opinion, the making of a friend—cannot be written in a neutral and bloodless state of mind.

In letter writing, imagination must supply personal contact. When you call in your stenographer to write a letter you are entering into a personal relationship with the reader. He is no longer a statistic in a mass market. He and you are human beings talking things over.

Most business communications have lucidity rather than emotion as their aim, but none except those which are frankly and openly mere catalogues can afford to exclude humanity. There should be some in-between space in your letters, some small-talk between the important ideas, some irrelevancies which temper the austerity of business.

## The Reader's Interest

No matter what your letter is about, the reader will want to know: "How does this affect me?"

It is a literary vice not to seek out the reader's interest. You may tell him what you want in impeccable language and forceful manner, but you fall short of success unless you pay attention to what he wants or can be made to desire. Your ideas must enter, influence and stick in the mind of the recipient.

As a writer, you may protest that some of the failure in communication may be blamed on the receiver, but it is your responsibility as sender to determine in advance, to the best of your ability, all potential causes of failure and to tune your transmission for the best reception.

Granted, something must be expected of the reader. Every writer is entitled to demand a certain amount of knowledge in those for whom he writes, and a certain degree of dexterity in using the implements of thought. Readers who demand immediate intelligibility in all they read cannot hope to go far beyond the limitations of comic strip language.

However, the writer is bound to eliminate every possible obstacle. He must not grow away from people. He must anticipate their questions.

Let the salesman stand at a bargain counter and listen to what goes on in the minds of prospective customers. He will see women who spend ten minutes examining socks advertised at 35 cents a pair—do they stretch? are they washable? will they stay soft? are they tough enough to wear long? Those women are not up on the plateau of bulk sales, but down where a nickel counts.

That is the imagination of preparation. Then comes the imagination of expression. The most important demand of customers is for friendliness in those who seek to do business with them. A man may pride himself upon being an efficient, logical person, unswayed by sentiment in business matters, but at some stage in his every business deal there is a spark of emotional appeal and response.

You need to study your audience and then write what you want them to understand in the form that is most likely to appeal to them. Any other course is like the childish custom of writing a letter to Santa Claus and burning it up the chimney.

## Give Imagination Wings

If you do not wish your letters to be read yawningly, write them wide awake. When a good idea strikes you for a letter, ride that idea on the dead run: don't wait to ponder, criticize and correct. You can be critical after your imaginative spell subsides.

The search for the exact word should never so usurp the writer's attention that the larger movements of thought on which the letter's argument depends are made to falter and so lose their fire. The first draft of a piece of writing should be done at white heat. The smoothing and polishing may follow later.

Some degree of novelty must be one of the materials in every instrument which works upon the mind.

By "novelty" it is not meant that the letter should be artificial. Great art consists in writing in an interested and straightforward way.

A good writer is not always original. You cannot hope to reproduce in your own words how Keats felt as he listened to the nightingale singing. It is far better to copy his ode. Mr. Churchill could not help it, even if he did not desire it, when his "blood, toil, tears and sweat" echoed Garibaldi, or when his first speech as Prime Minister, declaring it to be his policy "to make war," echoed Clemenceau's "Je fais la guerre." Shakespeare took his plots wherever he could find them, from older plays, English chronicles and Plutarch's *Lives*. His originality consisted in the skill with which he made a story over and covered the skeleton with the living flesh of his language.

If a man has vision and sympathy—ingredients of imagination—and adds sincerity, he will be able to beautify the familiar and illumine the dingy and sordid. Montaigne, one of the world's great essayists, said: "I gather the flowers by the wayside, by the brooks and in the meadows, and only the string with which I bind them together is my own."

Variety in expression is as necessary to a piece of written matter as it is to an attractive bouquet. Monotony in a letter is like a paralyzing frost.

The Greeks knew this: they set off the loveliness of roses and violets by planting them side by side with leeks and onions. Some fastidious or critical people may complain of unevenness in your writing because it is not sustained at a peak. But there is no one more tiresome than the man who is writing always at the top of his voice.

## Use Words Honestly

The effort to bring up the highlights must not bind us to our obligation to be moderate. To be dynamic and forceful we don't need to give the impression of breathlessness. Strong words lose their force if used often. Don't say "the roof is falling in" when you mean that a crack in the ceiling needs patching. If you habitually term a dull party "a disaster" what have you left that is vivid enough to cover your feelings about an earthquake?

From the moment that a writer loses his reverence for words as accurate expressions of his thoughts he becomes second-rate. Even experienced writers testify to their constant search for the right word.

Follow the spirit of what you are saying in the way you write it. Sometimes you will use little, jolting, one-syllable words; in another composition your meaning and feeling may be conveyed better in cascading syllables like Milton's, or in earthy words that fit the urgency of the occasion.

There is no better way to learn the feeling of words than through reading poetry. The use of synonyms so necessary in poetry gives us a grasp of language and readiness in its use. Exercise your imagination by looking up wide choices of words meaning the same thing, in varying shades of strength and attractiveness. A handy book to have on your desk is A *Dictionary of English Synonyms* by Richard Soule (Little, Brown, and Company, Boston).

Be careful to use qualifying words only where they contribute something to the sense you wish to convey. An excessive use of qualifiers vitiates the force of what you write.

Correct modification is an essential of perceptive accuracy, but every modification means a deflection in the reader's flow of understanding.

To test this, take some magazine which professes to popularize news events, and strike out every adjective and adverb which seems dispensable: note how much more authoritative and less tinted by opinion the items appear.

The business man should test business reports and letters by asking "What omission of fact or skimping of research or expression of prejudice does this adjective cover up?"

## Pictures in Words

Our writing creates pictures in the reader's mind. We use metaphors to sharpen and extend the reader's understanding of our ideas by presenting him with images drawn from the world of sensory experience: "She has roses in her cheeks; he has the heart of a lion." If we say that a brook is laughing in the sunlight, an idea of laughter intervenes to symbolize the spontaneous, vivid activity of the brook.

In 240 words of a single soliloquy of *Hamlet*, Shakespeare gives us these imaginative phrases, now part of our everyday language: to be or not to be, the law's delay, the insolence of office, the undiscover'd country from whose bourne no traveller returns, the slings and arrows of outrageous fortune, 'tis a consummation devoutly to be wish'd, there's the rub, shuffled off this mortal coil, conscience doth make cowards of us all.

Metaphors are not confined to poetic writing: they occur in science and business writing, too: the flow of electricity, the stream of consciousness, the thinking machine, getting at the root of the problem, falling into error, indulging in mental gymnastics.

Local colour is an element in imaginative writing. Your highlights and your expressive phrases do not have to come from classics. A good writer, even on the most prosaic of topics, will mix his own mind with his subject. True imagination, no matter how strange may be the regions into which it lifts its head, has its roots in human experience. What arises in your writing from what you have been through will be more vivid than what you glean from the writings and experience of others.

## Background for Imagination

If the imagination is to yield any product useful to the writer, it must have received material from the external world. Images do not spring out of a desert.

The writer will train his mind to roam, to seek food, to experience events. He will read widely, observing words at work in a multitude of combinations.

A library has evocative power. Merely to sit within view of good books draws out the goodness in one. A library has driving power, too: it challenges us to convey meanings and feelings as these writers did.

The books in an executive's office should not consist solely of directories, almanacs, *Canada Year Book*, and the like. In literature are recorded all the thoughts, feelings, passion, and dreams that have passed through the human mind, and these can play their part in the efficiency of the letter writer today. Even on the battlefield, Napoleon had in his tent more than three hundred volumes ranging through science, art, history, poetry, travels, romance and philosophy.

To do all that has been suggested takes times. It requires preparation, practice and participation: preparation through reading and study, practice through revising and rewriting, and participation through putting something of yourself into every letter.

We must get out of the vicious system whereby we spend a forenoon verifying the price to be quoted to a customer, while refusing to spend two minutes in reconstructing a clumsy sentence in the letter we write him. To be slovenly and feeble is not only discourteous to the persons we address but bad business, because it leaves the door open for misunderstanding.

If you are going to describe an event or a product, do not be content with black marks on white paper: at least stipple in the background and use some colour in the foreground.

It is necessary, too, to be in earnest. Many people dream away their lives, talking of the writing they mean to do, and in the end they fall asleep, still babbling of the green fields of literature.

If you make only average grades in your letters when you could with a little effort top the class, you are bound to be disappointed with yourself. The writing of letters, business or personal or professional, is no mean ministry. It deserves the best that can be given it, and when it is rightly done it absorbs the mind wholly.

Why not be one of the knowledgeable elite instead of one of the conforming average?

They are probably best who, having a subject on which they wish to express themselves, sit down to write about it in a loving way. As Cyrano de Bergerac described his genius: "I have but to lay my soul beside my paper and copy!"

# You Are What You Write: Model Memos for All Occasions

DIANNA BOOHER

"The further away your job is from manual work, the larger the organization of which you are a part, the more important it will be that you know how to convey your thoughts in writing and speaking," wrote Peter Drucker in *People and Performance*. Fairly or not, many readers evaluate executives by the memos leaving their desks. Colleagues, clients, and the business community label a service or product by them. Subordinates judge fairness and ability by them. Garmmar and spelling are important, certainly, but just as important—and harder to perfect—are brevity, clarity, and the tone of the message. The best directive does not simply direct; it also explains. A complaint will be more effective if it carries a feeling of conciliation and confidence.

The examples presented here illustrate how to write—and how not to write—memos for various occasions. Remember, memos are more than a forum for opinions; they are a way of dealing with people.

## Directives

### Weak Models

Subject: Copy Machine Use

The largest collating copier located on the second floor has been installed for use by Materials and Services personnel only. It's the responsibility of everyone in the building to show common courtesy in scheduling large copying tasks so as not to prohibit day-to-day operations in all sections.

Subject: Protocol for Phone Calls

Once more I must remind you that there are some members in the field who violate protocol and make phone calls to various staff members in Boston, asking for particular business and personal favors. This must stop once and for all!

In the past I have requested from you an explanation of each week's long-distance calls to both Boston and Los Angeles. Some of you have complied; some have ignored the directive. Only emergency calls should be made to Boston and Los Angeles; all other favors or requests should come through my office.

I will be monitoring this situation carefully.

*Don'ts*

- Don't bury your directive in implications. In the first example, what exactly is the directive? That no one in the building other than Materials and Services personnel may use the second-floor copier for any reason—emergency or otherwise? That Materials and Services people should not tie up the copier for long periods of time? That people in other departments should be more courteous in scheduling large tasks so as not to force others to go to the second-floor machine? That large tasks should be done before or after peak hours? Remember that even though your intention may be to soften the directive, your reader may not infer what you intend.
- Don't be arbitrary. When possible, give reasons. Why is the phone-call protocol necessary?
- Don't fail to give all details necessary to take the action, or inaction, as the case may be. For instance, how should readers of the second memo distinguish between emergency and "regular calls?" What are the guidelines?
- Don't use such "fight" words as "ignored," "failed to," "refused," even "must" at times. Such words emphasize a negative and hostile attitude.
- Don't resort to sarcasm.

**Good Model**

Subject: Air-Conditioning Filter Screens

Since our discussion three weeks ago, nothing has been done to correct the problem of the air-conditioning filter screens. Please install them immediately and confirm to me in writing when they are in place.

Apparently you disagree with my opinion that the cost of the manpower involved in testing for the exact problem is prohibitive. Nevertheless, whether the screens do or do not solve our problem, this ounce of prevention should be our first step.

If you have any problem in the installation process, please let me know so that we can work them out immediately.

*Dos*

- State the clear, firm directive up front. If necessary, ask the subordinate to verify compliance.
- Give reasons for your directives when you can. Giving reasons does not suggest weakness or the need for justification of your decisions. Instead, reasons help the reader to determine whether to approach you again if the situation or circumstances change, thus allowing correction. People cooperate better with a "why" even when they don't agree.
- Give all details and guidelines to accomplish the directive. Include times, dates, costs, preparation, procedures, and expected follow-up. Missing details provide an escape hatch for reluctant followers.
- Acknowledge that the reader may not agree with your evaluation of the situation, but be firm about your directive nonetheless.
- Include courtesy words even when you have authority to command.

## Complaints

### Weak Model

Subject: Computerized Purchasing System

Your Mr. Tom Brown and Fred Smith visited me this week and wanted to know where I wanted two data-processing consoles installed. I had no idea what they were talking about, and yet they told me you had advised that we were to receive this equipment in March. I told them to forget about installation until I had been informed of what all this is about and what your intentions are.

On January 6 I sent a memo to your Mr. Ted Jones to confirm a meeting with him. Enclosed with the memo were our comments on the data printout form he was proposing. We received absolutely no response from him, nor have we had subsequent discussions of how our needs could be programmed.

Then on February 16, when we questioned the purpose of your requisition 1224-55 for contract programming services, we phoned your office again. We were assured that this invoice had nothing to do with our project but rather was for work done for the Indonesian group.

Frankly, John, I'm upset over this development. You have not kept me informed on progress nor advised me of your intentions.

Obviously, we do not plan to proceed with anything until we know what is involved, what is required, and why it is required. Frankly, we don't believe that computer programmers should decide what the user should have. I had assumed from out initial discussions that the development of a purchasing-system program would be a mutual task between us—not a unilateral decision from your end. Obviously, I was wrong.

*Don'ts*

- Don't start with once-upon-a-time detail. The reader here cannot be sure of the exact nature of the complaint until the fourth paragraph above.
- Don't omit detail about the *real* problem. The reader must have enough explanation to follow the developments and correct the situation. In this case, the reader still does not know where his programmers and the memo writer differ about computer needs: Is the actual program design inefficient for the purchasing department, or is the writer simply angry that he didn't have the proper input and notification? The person handling the complaint from this point must read between the lines or pull the past memos and meeting minutes from the files to see which is the case.
- Don't fail to suggest how the problem can be remedied. In this case, the reader has no clearly outlined steps to follow to mend damage to the relationship or to the project.
- Don't use a self-righteous or aggressive tone. Note the "fight" words in this model: "Your Mr. Tom Brown and Fred Smith" and "your Mr. Ted Jones" (patronizing); "I had no idea what they were talking about" (exaggeration—of course he had some idea); "forget about installation" (hint of patronizing dismissal); "your intentions" (sounds as if they are underhanded); "I'm upset.. . . You have not kept me informed.. . ." (personal attack); "Frankly, we don't believe that computer programmers should decide what the user should have" (assumes that this is the reader's intention); "Obviously, I was wrong" (sarcastic, self-righteous statement).

### Good Model

Subject: Passing the Buck, er, Boxes

Help, I've got a problem. Would you lend a hand to a department and damsel in distress? We need the counter and cabinet space in the copier room, which is now filled to overflowing with boxes of computer paper.

Our only consolation is that Data Processing is using computer paper like Carter's Little Liver Pills. Ah, and even that provides only temporary relief before the little blue delivery truck unloads more boxes on our turf.

I spoke with John Ikeman about moving these boxes, who spoke with Fred Little, who spoke with Harold Smith, who at last mention had spoken with everybody except the pope. All to no avail. According to all supervisors, their own storage space is occupied by things from outer space—or at least from someone else's department.

Any help you can provide to get other departments to remove their paper and supplies from our copier room (even trapdoors may be a possibility) will be appreciated. Otherwise, the next time the little blue delivery truck pulls up, I may have to leave in a little white van.

*Dos*

- Let the reader know immediately what your exact complaint is.
- Suggest, even if you can't command, the action you want your reader to take to resolve the problem. Leaving correction to your reader's discretion increases the likelihood that the complaint will not be handled quickly and appropriately. If you have no suggestions, say so.
- Give enough detail so that the person stepping in to remedy the situation knows or recalls what has happened in the past. But be brief; avoid throwing in irrelevant details about how much trouble the situation has caused you—unless such detail is pertinent to correcting the problem or creates urgency. Always give names or dates involved and copies of past correspondence for the reader's convenience in following and verifying what you say. By informing the reader of your previous action, you eliminate repetition of those nonsolutions.
- Use a conciliatory tone. First, that means not assuming that the harm or mistake has been intentional. Don't take away all your reader's possible "excuses" for the situation; allow him to save face. (There's no harm in his saving face as long as the problem gets corrected.) Second, use "I messages" to minimize attack on the other person: "*I* do not feel that *my* staff and *I* are up-to-date on the project or that *we've* had sufficient input about our specific needs." Not: "*You* have not kept us up-to-date on the project and *you* have not allowed us sufficient input about our specific needs." Also, play down a self-righteous tone by passive-voice rather than active-voice constructons: "A problem has

developed." Not: "You have created a problem."

- Show confidence that the complaint will be handled appropriately.
- End on a business-as-usual note.
- Use humor when you can to attract attention to the problem and make the corrective action less arduous. Make sure, however, that you know your audience, so that your humor is not offensive and does not make light of a situation that others consider no laughing matter.

## Pointing Out Another's Errors

### Weak Model

Subject: Handling Incentive Payments

One more time, everybody. Although some of you have been handling incentive computations for years, I still find persistent errors. For the last time, I do hope we can get this straight!

You are to send *three* (not one, not two) copies of the incentive computation forms. After I review and approve the forms, I will send one to the sales rep and one to Beaumont, and then keep one for my files. Each of you has a copy machine; please use it.

When you do your computations on the sales split, be sure to compute your figures accurately— I have found several errors here again.

Please, if you have further questions about this record-keeping system, call me before you send the forms, I would appreciate your assistance in doing this correctly.

*Don'ts*

- Don't patronize. Even the insertion of courtesy words such as "please" and "appreciate" fails to compensate for sarcasm. Watch unusual punctuation marks and underlined words to avoid "screaming" in print. Also, avoid showing your "tolerance" in overlooking or correcting another's error.
- Don't assume that the error is intentional or due to carelessness. Consider the possibility that your instructions have been unclear or

that circumstances prevented compliance or perfection. At the very least, consider that the reader may not have been aware of the importance of accuracy. Assume some of the responsibility for the error yourself.

- Don't focus on the error to the exclusion of how the matter should be corrected. Your memo should not begin a game of "gotcha."
- Don't exaggerate results of the error. If the reader thinks you have overplayed the subject, he'll compensate by playing down its importance.

## Good Models

Subject: Handling Incentive Payments

There are still some problems in routing incentive forms and computing payments. Let me repeat the procedure for handling such forms:

Send three copies of the incentive-computation forms to me. After I review and approve the forms, I'll send one to the sales rep and one to Beaumont and then keep one for my files.

Please make a special effort to recheck all computations before they leave your office. We do not have the manpower to do this double-checking here. When checks go out incorrectly and must be returned and reprocessed, the cost goes up considerably, not to mention the inconvenience of the delayed payment.

If you have any questions at all about this record-keeping system and routing, or about computing unusual splits, please call me before sending the forms. I appreciate your help in handling these correctly.

Subject: Leasehold Improvements—Account 468

Thanks for your memo on the Cedarpoint account; I do understand your reasoning behind expending the costs for remodeling the headquarters office.

In my opinion, however, these expenditures should be accounted for as leasehold improvements. Here's my reasoning:

1. The improvement's useful life exceeds one year.
2. Generally accepted practice is to capitalize

and depreciate these improvements over the remaining term of the lease.

I'd like to give this further thought and talk to Ed Weese before I ask you to make definite changes. If I'm wrong, I assure you, it won't be the first time.

*Dos*

- Begin on a neutral note. Then "creep up" on the error if you can. Notice that in the cash-forecast memo, the writer simply offers a better method to accomplish the task rather than pointing out the deficiency per se. Passive-voice constructions can be useful here: "In the future, spare parts should be sent by air freight." (You do not say that the sender has made a mistake this time.) At other times, you can walk around a direct assault with a "there are problems" approach, as in the revised incentive-payment model.
- Focus on what you have done or what the reader should do to correct the problem, rather than trying to assign blame.
- Emphasize the importance of accuracy.
- Suggest precautions against future problems.
- Show diffidence and humility.

## Admitting Your Own Errors

### Weak Model

Subject: Boyton Contracts

I deeply regret my error in mailing the Boyton contracts to Mr. Jorgensen's old address. It's our policy always to verify new and existing addresses by phone before we mail any such documents. I don't know how we could have overlooked this client's address.

Certainly, I can understand why Mr. Jorgensen was so upset when he phoned you yesterday about the delay. If he had called here, I would have been glad to assure him that the error was completely mine. Please let me assure you that this kind of error does not happen often, because I realize the importance of a timely signature.

The returned contracts went out today by Express Mail; I do hope this mistake has not jeopardized the negotiations in any way. My sincerest apologies; this won't happen again.

*Don'ts*

- Don't "bleed" all over the memo. Briefly explain how the error happened and then focus on the correction.
- Don't be dramatic. Remember that all errors are not created equal. Overblown apologies and explanations sound insincere.
- Don't promise that the error will never occur again. Rather, state what actions you have taken to correct the problem and to make its recurrence less likely.

### Good Model

Subject: Incorrect Number on Pumping Order

Yes, my scheduler did indeed make an error on the attached pumping order; he used the custody index number rather than the transfer code.

I have cautioned him about confusing the numbers on future orders and have asked him to check his hard copy of all orders after they have been entered into the computer.

Since we've had trouble before, I should have given closer supervision here. Please let me know if you uncover still other such errors; I'll follow them up immediately.

*Dos*

- State the error *and* correction immediately.
- Evaluate the seriousness of your mistake; explain and apologize accordingly.
- When the situation has political undertones to your disadvantage, play down the error with a matter-of-fact tone. After all, everybody makes mistakes. On the other hand, a poor-me approach can work sometimes—that is, exaggerate the seriousness of the error and be profuse in your apology so that your reader must console you that things aren't that bad. However, "bleed" only when you know the

politics involved and the probable reaction of your reader to your play for sympathy.

- Take responsibility for errors that come from your office; don't pass the buck to subordinates even though they may have made the error. After all, you are the supervisor.
- Report and correct the error immediately. Delay usually compounds the problem.

## Policy Statements

### Weak Model

Subject: Policy on Sick Days

Let me remind you that falsifying company records with regard to absence or sickness is a Class "A" Offense. The penalty for such an offense is immediate discharge without prior warning.

In order for you to be paid for sick days, a doctor's excuse must be presented to your immediate supervisor. If your illness is not severe enough to require a doctor's visit, then you may elect to take a vacation day—provided you are entitled to a vacation exceeding one week. If you are not eligible for vacation time longer than one week, you will not be paid for the absence due to sickness without a doctor's excuse.

*Don'ts*

- Don't state the policy in a negative format and tone. The first paragraph in this memo is a threat rather than a statement of benefit, which sick-pay policy really is. To give this information in a positive manner, begin the memo, "To be eligible for sick pay, you must present a . . ."; then, as a matter of further information, add a reminder about falsification of records.

### Good Model

Subject: Change in Eligibility Requirements for Employee Stock-Purchase Plan

At the November board meeting, the directors of Forbas Manufacturing approved a change in the eligibilty requirements for participation in the Employee Stock-Purchase Plan. Effective with the fiscal quarter beginning January 1, 1985, all employees who have completed *one* year of service with the company (prior policy called for two years of service) will be eligible to join the plan.

The Employee Stock-Purchase Plan is an effective savings plan in which 1,200 Forbas Manufacturing employees are now enrolled. In fact, during the past fiscal year, enrollment has increased by 46 percent.

New enrollments for each quarter must be received by the 10th day of the new quarter. Should you have questions about "jumping on the bandwagon," or if you want to get an enrollment form, contact Liz Smith (ext. 282).

*Dos*

- Summarize the policy up front.
- Use the subject line to distinguish between a new or revised policy and an already established one. Without such a subject-line clue, the reader often skips reading the memo, thinking that he is already informed about the stated policy.
- Mention the reasoning behind the policy or change in policy—unless it is obvious.
- As much as possible, make policy sound like guidelines and benefits rather than restrictions and penalties.
- Give clear instructions for following the policy.

## To Cut, Watch, Or Justify Expenses

### Weak Model

Subject: Mailing and Printing Costs

I have just come from the supply room; boxes and boxes of *Bylines* and thousands and thousands of financial statements are stacked around the room. Why? Obviously, you are printing too many copies of each, and that, in turn, creates a huge mailing cost in shipping excessive copies to all the branches.

Wayne, this is a function of your department. What have you done to develop a savings in mailing? What kind of controls do you have for not ordering hundreds of thousands of dollars

of extra printing? Something has to be done immediately.

As I review the operations of various offices across the country, I find over and over that those managers who control the checkbook and watch expenses make profits. Rarely do the big spenders pay attention to reviewing costs and rarely do they make a profit in difficult times.

I'm sending a copy of this memo to all who I think are involved in this plethora of printing and mailing, hoping you can get together with them to work out something to alleviate this problem.

*Don'ts*

- Don't base your request to cut or watch expenses on personal observation alone. You need facts to back up what you say; otherwise, the reader will probably argue that you have latched onto the "exceptional." If you don't want to gather the facts yourself, then ask the responsible person (perhaps your reader) to do so. Without authoritative data, the issue remains vague.
- Don't sound abrasive. In a "problem" statement, calling someone by name in direct address ("Wayne, this is a function of your department") makes the issue a personal attack. Including yourself in a we-need-to-cut-or-watch-expenses statement makes a much more palatable suggestion. Also, watch implications. The above model implies that Wayne is one of the "big spenders" who rarely make a profit.
- Don't reprimand by way of a cutting-expenses memo sent to more than one reader. In pointing out someone's weakness, communicate individually, not with a distribution list.

### Good Model

Subject: Reducing Mailing and Printing Costs

Wayne, what can we do to reduce our mailing and printing costs? Down in the supply room, I noticed boxes and boxes of *Bylines* and last month's financial statements; I assume that these were leftover copies.

I'd like you to do some kind of study of our

actual printing and mailing costs and then see what we might do to control these expenditures. Here are some suggestions for your consideration:

1. Manual audit of mail-outs from each branch;
2. Combining financial statements and *Bylines* into one publication;
3. Cheaper mailing rates;
4. Survey of distribution problems.

We need to control the checkbook and watch pennies to make profits in these difficult times. Your suggestions for printing and mailing controls will insure that we do that. Thanks for your help; I'll look forward to your conclusions.

*Dos*

- State your concern immediately. Even in a persuasive memo, your reader still needs to know to what conclusion you intend to lead him. Without knowing the "bottom-line" message, he feels manipulated. Another inherent danger in building your case before making your request is that your reader may examine your evidence and arrive at an altogether different conclusion. By giving your statement of "wants" first, you can guide the reader's thinking toward your own conclusion.
- Include a *why*. Readers need motivation for both belt-tightening and spending.
- Translate vague costs to specific, understandable dollars when possible. Could you survey others for their opinions? Talk to experts from inside and outside the company? Do a literature search? Keep a log of the situation? Identify exact causes and calculate real savings or expenses?
- When ordering a "cut," offer alternatives. Suggest ways to accomplish the same activities with fewer dollars. Pinpoint your priorities for spending.
- When justifying expenses, anticipate alternative solutions and address them. What limitations do these other options have?
- Assume your part in the situation, making your reader feel that thrift is a team effort.
- Describe the financial climate accurately. You don't want to sound so ominous that you create panic among the employees and have them scrambling for jobs elsewhere. Neither do you want to start a game of "Wolf, Wolf."

## Reprimands

### Weak Model

Subject: Interfering with Assigned Work

Would you please tell me what emergency at Bloomington's was so urgent that you pulled one of our men (Jack Donne) to be a "gofer" without getting his supervisor's approval?

*Don'ts*

- Don't hide a reprimand behind a trapping question. If the reader has committed an offense, say so. If you mean only to verify what you have been told or have assumed, ask for verification outright.
- Don't leave to the reader's discretion how you want the action, behavior, attitude, or situation corrected.

### Good Models

Subject: Supervisory Approval on Change in Assigned Work

In the future, please be sure to get a supervisor's approval before changing anyone's job assignment.

Yesterday, Jack Donne was sent without his supervisor's approval to Bloomington's on what I consider a routine, rather than emergency, errand. Such a situation undercuts authority and may create serious problems with the abandoned project assignment.

Subject: Sick-Leave Restriction

This is to notify you that effective January 1, 1985, you must submit medical certification to support all absences due to illness. This restriction will remain in effect for at least six months and until further notice from me.

If your substantiated absences, medical or otherwise, exceed three days during the next six months, we will be forced to terminate your employment.

You are being placed under this restriction because an analysis of your attendance record shows that some of your absences may have been unjustified. Your records show that you missed work on three Mondays and four Fridays during the last quarter: October 3, 14, 17, 24; November 4, 18; and December 2.

*Dos*

- Focus on the offense. Communicate clearly and specifically what behavior, attitude, or decision is in error and how you expect it to be corrected.
- Document your complaints and past reprimands.
- Impress upon the reader the importance for corrective action and get him to "buy into" complying with your request or company policy.
- When possible and not already obvious, explain why the behavior, situation, or decision needs correction or why the policy or rule has been established. A *why* generally improves cooperation.
- On second or later reprimands, warn the reader of your next action if the problem is not corrected.
- Try to minimize resentment by focusing on behavior and results or consequences rather than motives or intentions.
- Match your tone to the seriousness and frequency of the offense, getting firmer after a first warning: "I note that there's a problem in that you . . ." to, "This is the second warning about . . ." to, "I must warn you that any repetition of this situation will be cause for immediate dismissal."

## Rumors

### Weak Model

Subject: Percaarisus Permentol

After hearing several conversations at the convention last week, I became increasingly aware that some of you are trying to kill this product line before it ever catches hold. A negative attitude on your part will kill the promotion quicker than a defective product will.

This is an excellent product line, and we intend to get sales off dead center. Concentrated effort will mean some additional time in zeroing in on primary markets; but once you qualify your leads, you will begin to pick up additional customers and enjoy substantial commissions. If you need help in qualifying specific leads, contact Frank Bohon.

I want these rumors about product test results to cease, and I expect to see sales of this line on your next reports.

*Don'ts*

- Don't feel that you must trace the origin of a rumor or place blame for its spreading.
- Don't use an accusatory, watchdog tone when you intend to mend rumor damage; such a tone tends to cast a shadow on the truth or at least fuel further speculation.

### Good Model

Subject: Percaarisus Permentol—Marketing Efforts

At the convention last week I heard some of you express concern over the marketability of our Percaarisus Permentol line. Let me clear up some misunderstandings: Our continued, concentrated research over the past 18 months shows this line, without a doubt, to be effective in treating the symptoms for which it was developed.

But I will acknowledge the difficulty you may have in selling such an innovative approach to treatment. To this end, let me remind you that we have test kits for you to offer the customer so that he can gather and examine results for himself. Please order and deliver these test kits; without them, you will have trouble in selling this product until more publicity has been done.

Concentrated effort will mean additional time zeroing in on primary markets; but once you qualify your leads, you will begin to pick up additional customers and enjoy substantial commissions. If you need help in qualifying specific leads, contact Frank Bohon.

Because a negative attitude always diminishes your selling success, I hope that this will clear up any concerns you may have had about test results. I look forward to seeing sales of this new line on your next reports.

*Dos*

- State the rumor and the "correction" up front.
- Acknowledge tidbits of truth, from which almost all rumors have their origin. Such acknowledgment adds credibility to your explanations, corrections, or denials. In this memo, note that the writer acknowledges difficulty selling an innovative, unpublicized breakthrough that some may still consider unproven.
- If the rumor is damaging, emphasize the importance of "keeping the record straight."
- Be tactful about wording; no one liks to be considered a gossip or rumormonger. Notice the substitution of the word "concerns" for "rumors" in the example.
- End with a positive, business-as-usual closing.

## Thank Yous

### Good Models

Subject: Thank You for June 14 Conference

Ms. Henley, thank you for giving me so much of your time last Monday afternoon and for your welcome advice on my career advancement.

I did follow up on both of your suggestions. Bob Holloway has asked me to come to work on his new project; I'll be assuming those new responsibilities after the first of the month. Also, I notified Training of my interest in the upcoming computer course, and due to a last-minute cancellation, I am enrolled to attend next week.

Please know how much I appreciate your interest in my studies and career advancement.

Subject: Florida Hospitality

Harvey, just a note to say thank you for your hospitality while I was soaking up the sunny Southern atmosphere and doing my homework in learning to fine-tune a MOG system. Do tell your wife thanks for giving up her evening alone with you and joining us for Tuesday night's "fiesta."

Please let me repay the favor when you're out our way next fall; I know of a skeet-shooting range you would enjoy. If you let me know a day or two in advance, I'll make the arrangements.

Thanks again.

*Dos*

- State your "thank you" immediately as the primary reason for writing.
- Be specific in detailing the "whys" of your thankfulness. In other words, let the reader know that you understand and appreciate the efforts he put forth in your behalf.
- Mention the good results of the reader's information, advice, or project. What benefits did you or someone else derive? Omit any disastrous results that would detract from the thanks.
- Name names; thank individuals, not groups.

*Dianna Booher is president of Booher Writing Consultants in Houston. Her article is adapted from* Send Me a Memo, *by Dianna Booher;* © 1983 by *Dianna Booher, reprinted by permission of Facts on File Inc., New York.*

# V.  Speaking and Listening Skills

Whether participating in a telephone conference or giving a presentation, you will find that it is important to use your voice effectively. Listening skills are also critical to interacting well with others, especially if you are called on to supervise other employees.

# What You Don't Say: Nonverbal Telephone Tactics

## CAROL A. GOSSELINK AND SUZANNE J. McKINLEY

Sue Benson gathered some notes into her briefcase and told her secretary she'd be having lunch with a potential client at The Cordon Bleu.

After her pleasant telephone conversation with businessman John Kingsley, Sue was looking forward to explaining how her agency could promote his new enterprise. Listening to Kingsley's dynamic, resonant voice, Sue had conjured up mental images of a young, attractive, athletic entrepreneur. Thus, on entering the restaurant, she paused only briefly before heading toward a tall blond wearing a sporty cashmere sweater, tweed jacket and beige corduroy slacks.

When a short, stout redhead in a well-tailored navy suit stepped into her path and introduced himself as John Kingsley, Sue concealed her surprise with professional composure.

Inwardly, however, she resolved never to make assumptions about appearances based on telephone conversations.

Even though the voice is an "influential factor" in nonverbal communication, Sue was correct in recognizing the relative inaccuracy of predicting physical appearances based on "blind" nonverbal cues.

But if telephone contact does not reveal whether you're talking to a stunning Venus or a stocky brunette, studies show that most people can accurately gauge several characteristics based solely on this nonverbal information, including a person's general age, level of education or sophistication, regional or ethnic background, and mood.

One trait commonly detectable on vocal cues is the speaker's gender. As with all nonverbal cues, however, the obvious is not always as it seems.

One experienced telephone interviewer recalls, "I had conducted an entire interview believing my deep-voiced respondent was a man until I asked 'his' wife's occupation.

"'That's me, baby,' was the gruff reply."

Limitations of judgment based solely on telephone conversations should not obscure the importance of Alexander Bell's invention as a tool for projecting positive images.

John Kingsley, the young entrepreneur who was successful despite a less-than-Olympic physical appearance, obviously knew how to use the telephone to his advantage, projecting attractiveness, energy and enthusiasm. And his success on the telephone was based less on what he said than on how he said it.

For those who stay up all night perfecting wording of a speech, the following data may be a startling reversal of what one might expect:

A study examining message conveyance revealed that 55 percent of the meaning of communication is conveyed through visual channels, while 38 percent is conveyed through tone, inflection, energy level and pacing of the voice.

The actual words convey a mere 7 percent of the meaning. One need only recall the last time he or she was put to sleep by the monotone, lifeless delivery of an otherwise brilliant expert to find meaning in the percentages.

A dynamic speaker who employs varied pitch, good pacing, and a pleasant resonance can captivate and inspire an audience with a very ordinary speech.

How, then, does one go about achieving the favorable telephone impression that John Kingsley demonstrated?

A good place to start is with pitch. Voice teacher and speech consultant Dorothy Darnoff says, "The body is sound sensitive." High-pitched voices are irritating, while deeper voices are easy to listen to for longer periods. Darnoff suggests that relaxation of the vocal cords is a key to developing the deeper, richer pitch that will appeal to a listener.

On the phone, speed of delivery influences the receptivity of the listener.

Since the listener must interpret meaning based on words and vocal cues without seeing you, the rate of delivery becomes increasingly important. Fast talking—associated with glib salespersons and con-artists—contradicts the image of a reliable, personable individual.

At the other end of the spectrum, slow talkers frequently are perceived as dull, unintelligent, unsure or even deceptive—do they need to stall in order to make up lines as they go along?

Darnoff recommends you pace your speech at about 170 words per minute, a rate that allows the listener to keep up with what you are saying without being bored or unsure of your authenticity.

The enthusiasm, variation, intensity and energy level conveyed by the voice also are major components of telephone image management. At the end of a long day, callers can detect boredom or exhaustion in your voice even if you are not aware of it.

The caller may get a negative impression of being treated coolly and impersonally. An upright posture and a smile on your face—unseen by the caller—helps you project the right kind of attitude.

Following are some guidelines for improving your nonverbal telephone skills:

- Treat the call as a face-to-face conversation. Mentally picture the person to whom you are speaking so your voice expresses the stage presence and vitality you naturally display during a personal encounter.
- Sit up straight to give your diaphragm room to fully support your voice.
- Leave a good first—and last—impression. A "smiling voice" conveys an alert interest in the person on the other end of the line.
- Remember to pace your speaking rate and pronounce words clearly.
- Vary your tone, emphasis, pitch and inflection. A monotone or tired delivery is the kiss of death to a telephone conversation.
- Above all, *listen* attentively to the other person. In making the appropriate response, you tell callers you are concerned enough to value what they are saying and are eager to respond.

Psychiatrist Leonard Zunin maintains that the first four minutes of contact are the most influential part of any human interaction. Within this brief period, impressions are formed which will determine whether a relationship will be developed or terminated.

Given the significance of this initial impression, it becomes imperative for that first contact, so often conveyed over the telephone, to be a favorable one.

Don't take nonverbal telephone techniques for granted.

# A Strong Voice Is a Valuable Managerial Asset

## RALPH PROODIAN

Most executives are hampered by speech that doesn't match their professional stature. Some sound immature because of too high a pitch, others lull their listeners with a monotone, and still others sound tough and unreasonable because of a throaty or harsh voice.

Clearly, speech faults won't prevent your success in business. Many chairmen of leading corporations are dull public speakers and monotonous conversationalists. Others have made it to the top in spite of barely audible voices with a mix of foreign and regional accents.

But since most executives spend a good part of their time talking with others—usually, according to a recent article in the *Harvard Business Review*, 75% to 90% of their working day—a strong voice can be a valuable managerial asset. Conversely, poor speech can take its toll. Many suffer a lack of confidence and shrink from necessary exposure, or feel inadequate to express themselves to their staff and the public. Some executives who take great pains with their clothing nevertheless make weak first impressions as a result of their speech.

Improving your speech isn't difficult. It requires far less than learning to be a good golf, tennis or squash player. Since you already know how to speak, improvement is basically a brushing up. You will be amazed, for example, how much the quality of your voice will improve if you simply remember to say the final sounds in words—for example, the *n* in "man," "position" and "mountain." The first step in improving your speech is to do well what you already can do.

If your problem is an unexpressive monotone, you must deal with meaning. The statement "There is an *adequate supply of oil*" contains three important words and four insignificant ones. (Which words would you put in a cable-gram?) Note that the unimportant words take almost 50% of the space and carry none of the meaning. Try saying *thrzn* for the first three words and say *of* quickly. The listener will pay much more attention to what you are trying to convey. And by deliberately focusing on the meaning of what you're saying, you'll become more expressive instinctively.

Notice, also, that while words are separated on the page for easy recognition, the ear doesn't need that help. Try reading aloud a short paragraph by separating each word with a silent space. It's not only tiring to say, but boring to hear. In clear speech, words are linked into a continuous blur of sounds. Try saying the last sound of each word within a phrase as if it were the first sound of the following word. If you plunge into doing this all the time, you will gain natural fluency.

If your worry is high pitch, breathiness, throaty quality, hoarseness, or a weak or nasal voice, then your problem is most likely strain on the vocal cords. Your vocal cords are probably either pressed together too tightly or stretched too much, with the result that the vibrations they make as air passes through them are distorted.

The first remedy for vocal strain is to learn how to exhale properly. You should be using your whole body when you speak. Athletes don't hit home runs or tennis serves with their arms only; they also drill on follow-through and timing. Rarely does a baby develop laryngitis from crying loudly. Its arms and legs are waving about, and its torso is pumping away when it cries. Nature knows what it's doing.

There are two ways to pump air out of the lungs. The more common—and wrong—way is to press downward on the lungs with the breastbone, an action which causes the shoulders and neck, where the larynx is housed, to tense. By contrast, trained speakers and singers pull in the abdominal wall, causing the diaphragm, an involuntary muscle located under the lungs, to press upward. This leaves the larynx alone, so that tensions don't build. Learn to exhale this way—you may need to straighten up your posture a bit—

and you will have a stronger, sonorous voice which is free of distortions.

The second remedy for vocal strain is to make your consonants more precise, particularly ones you can sustain, like m, n, z, v and l. (Other consonants, such as b, d, f, g, k, p and t, are not sustained.) For example, try giving a bit extra time to the *v* in *love*, the *l* in *oil*, and the *z* in *booze*. You will project your voice without strain because you are focusing your speaking in the forward part of the mouth where most consonants are made—away from the larynx. Your pitch will drop because the stretch in your vocal cords will diminish; your voice will expand because the cords will vibrate more fully, and your quality will improve.

In addition, you will never again be told you are speaking too fast or that you cannot be understood. Conversely, if you wish to moderate a New York City or Western twang or a Southern drawl, focusing on final consonants helps you cut down on the length of your vowels. The consonants, especially the final ones, define the borders of words and give them identity.

If you don't want to fade when you speak, or give the wrong impression just when you need support, make your voice and speech more responsive. People are more influenced by your sound than even they are aware. Besides, if you learn to enjoy speaking, you will enjoy the greater part of your business.

*Mr. Proodian is professor of speech at Brooklyn College.*

# Active Listening

CARL B. ROGERS AND
RICHARD E. FARSON

## The Meaning of Active Listening

One basic responsibility of the supervisor or executive is the development, adjustment, and integration of individual employees. He tries to develop employee potential, delegate responsibility, and achieve cooperation. To do so, he must have, among other abilities, the ability to listen intelligently and carefully to those with whom he works.

There are, however, many kinds of listening skills. The lawyer, for example, when questioning a witness, listens for contradictions, irrelevancies, errors, and weaknesses. But this is not the kind of listening skill we are concerned with. The lawyer usually is not listening in order to help the witness adjust or cooperate or produce. On the other hand, we will be concerned with listening skills which *will help* employees gain a clearer understanding of their situations, take responsibility, and cooperate with each other.

### Two Examples

The kind of listening we have in mind is called "active listening." It is called "active" because the listener has a very definite responsibility. He does not passively absorb the words which are spoken to him. He actively tries to grasp the facts and the feelings in what he hears, and he tries, by his listening, to help the speaker work out his own problems.

To get a fuller picture of what is meant by active listening, let us consider two different approaches to the same work problem.

*Example No. 1*

FOREMAN: Hey, Al, I don't get this production order. We can't handle this run today. What do they think we are?

SUPERVISOR: But that's the order. So get it out as soon as you can. We're under terrific pressure this week.

FOREMAN: Don't they know we're behind schedule already because of that press breakdown?

SUPERVISOR: Look, Kelly, I don't decide what goes on upstairs. I just have to see that the work gets out, and that's what I'm gonna do.

FOREMAN: The guys aren't gonna like this.

SUPERVISOR: That's something you'll have to work out with them, not me.

*Example No. 2*

FOREMAN: Hey, Ross, I don't get this production order. We can't handle this run today. What do they think we are?

SUPERVISOR: Sounds like you're pretty sore about it, Kelly.

FOREMAN: I sure am. We were just about getting back to schedule after that press breakdown. Now this comes along.

SUPERVISOR: As if you didn't have enough work to do, huh?

FOREMAN: Yeah. I don't know how I'm gonna tell the guys about this.

SUPERVISOR: Hate to face 'em with it now, is that it?

FOREMAN: I really do. They're under a real strain today. Seems like everything we do around here is rush, rush.

SUPERVISOR: I guess you feel like it's unfair to load anything more on them.

FOREMAN: Well, yeah. I know there must be plenty of pressure on everybody up the line, but—well, if that's the way it is—guess I'd better get the word to 'em.

There are obviously many differences between these two examples. The main one, however, is that Ross, the supervisor in the second example, is using the active-listening approach. He is listening and responding in a way that makes it clear that he appreciates both the meaning and the feeling behind what Kelly is saying.

Active listening does not necessarily mean long sessions spent listening to grievances, personal or otherwise. It is simply a way of approaching those problems which arise out of the usual day-to-day events of any job.

To be effective, active listening must be firmly grounded in the basic attitudes of the user. We cannot employ it as a technique if our fundamental attitudes are in conflict with its basic concepts. If we try, our behavior will be empty and sterile, and our associates will be quick to recognize this. Until we can demonstrate a spirit which genuinely respects the potential worth of the individual, which considers his sights and trusts his capacity for self-direction, we cannot begin to be effective listeners.

## What We Achieve by Listening

Active listening is an important way to bring about changes in people. Despite the popular notion that listening is a passive approach, clinical and research evidence clearly shows that sensitive listening is a most effective agent for individual personality change and group development. Listening brings about changes in people's attitudes toward themselves and others; it also brings about changes in their basic values and personal philosophy. People who have been listened to in this new and special way become more emotionally mature, more open to their experiences, less defensive, more democratic, and less authoritarian.

When people are listened to sensitively, they tend to listen to themselves with more care and to make clear exactly what they are feeling and thinking. Group members tend to listen more to each other, to become less argumentative, more ready to incorporate other points of view. Because listening reduces the threat of having one's ideas criticized, the person is better able to see them for what they are and is more likely to feel that his contributions are worthwhile.

Not the least important result of listening is the change that takes place within the listener himself. Besides providing more information than any other activity, listening builds deep, positive relationships and tends to alter constructively the attitudes of the listener. Listening is a growth experience.

These, then, are some of the worthwhile results we can expect from active listening. But how do we go about this kind of listening? How do we become active listeners?

## How to Listen

Active listening aims to bring about changes in people. To achieve this end, it relies upon definite techniques—things to do and things to avoid doing. Before discussing these techniques, however, we should first understand why they are effective. To do so, we must understand how the individual personality develops.

## The Growth of the Individual

Through all of our lives, from early childhood on, we have learned to think of ourselves in certain very definite ways. We have built up pictures of ourselves. Sometimes these self-pictures are pretty realistic, but at other times they are not. For example, an overage, overweight lady may fancy herself a youthful, ravishing siren, or an awkward teen-ager regard himself a star athlete.

All of us have experiences which fit the way we need to think about ourselves. These we accept. But it is much harder to accept experiences which don't fit. And sometimes, if it is very important for us to hang on to this self-picture, we don't accept or admit these experiences at all.

These self-pictures are not necessarily attractive. A man, for example, may regard himself as incompetent and worthless. He may feel that he is doing his job poorly in spite of favorable appraisals by the company. As long as he has these feelings about himself, he must deny any experiences which would seem not to fit this self-picture—in this case any that might indicate to him that he is competent. It is so necessary for him to maintain this self-picture that he is threatened by anything which would tend to change it. Thus, when the company raises his salary, it may seem to him only additional proof that he is a fraud. He must hold onto this self-picture, because, bad or good, it's the only thing he has by which he can identify himself.

This is why direct attempts to change this individual or change his self-picture are particularly threatening. He is forced to defend himself or to completely deny the experience. This denial of experience and defense of the self-picture tend to bring on rigidity of behavior and create difficulties in personal adjustment.

The active-listening approach, on the other hand, does not present a threat to the individual's self-picture. He does not have to defend it. He is able to explore it, see it for what it is, and make his own decision about how realistic it is. And he is then in a position to change.

If I want to help a man reduce his defensiveness and become more adaptive, I must try to remove the threat of myself as his potential changer. As long as the atmosphere is threatening, there can be no effective communication. So I must create a climate which is neither critical, evaluative, nor moralizing. It must be an atmosphere of equality and freedom, permissiveness and understanding, acceptance and warmth. It is in this climate and this climate only that the individual feels safe enough to incorporate new experiences and new values into his concept of himself. Let's see how active listening helps to create this climate.

## What to Avoid

When we encounter a person with a problem our usual response is to try to change his way of looking at things—to get him to see his situation the way we see it or would like him to see it. We plead, reason, scold, encourage, insult, prod—anything to bring about a change in the desired direction, that is, in the direction we want him to travel. What we seldom realize, however, is that, under these circumstances, we are usually responding to *our own* needs to see the world in certain ways. It is always difficult for us to tolerate and understand actions which are different from the ways in which *we* believe *we* should act. If, however, we can free ourselves from the need to influence and direct others in our own paths, we enable ourselves to listen with understanding and thereby employ the most potent available agent of change.

One problem the listener faces is that of responding to demands for decisions, judgments, and evaluations. He is constantly called upon to agree or disagree with someone or something. Yet, as he well knows, the question or challenge frequently is a masked expression of feelings or needs which the speaker is far more anxious to communicate than he is to have the surface questions answered. Because he cannot speak these feelings openly, the speaker must disguise them to himself and to others in an acceptable form. To illustrate, let us examine some typical questions and the types of answers that might best elicit the feelings beneath them.

| _Employee's Question_ | _Listener's Answer_ |
|---|---|
| Just whose responsibility is the toolroom? | Do you feel that someone is challenging your authority in there? |
| Don't you think younger able people should be promoted before senior but less able ones? | It seems to you they should, I take it. |
| What does the super expect us to do about those broken-down machines? | You're pretty disgusted with those machines, aren't you? |
| Don't you think I've improved over the last review period? | Sounds as if you feel like you've really picked up over these last few months. |

These responses recognize the questions but leave the way open for the employee to say what is really bothering him. They allow the listener to participate in the problem or situation without shouldering all responsibility for decision making or actions. This is a process of thinking _with_ people instead of _for_ or _about_ them.

Passing judgment, whether critical or favorable, makes free expression difficult. Similarly, advice and information are almost always seen as efforts to change a person and thus serve as barriers to his self-expression and the development of a creative relationship. Moreover, advice is seldom taken, and information hardly ever utilized. The eager young trainee probably will not become patient just because he is advised that "the road to success in business is a long, difficult one, and you must be patient." And it is no more helpful for him to learn that "only one out of a hundred trainees reaches a top management position." Interestingly, it is a difficult lesson to learn that positive _evaluations_ are sometimes as blocking as negative ones. It is almost as destructive to the freedom of a relationship to tell a person that he is good or capable or right, as to tell him otherwise. To evaluate him positively may make it more difficult for him to tell of the faults that distress him or the ways in which he believes he is not competent.

Encouragement also may be seen as an attempt to motivate the speaker in certain directions or hold him off, rather than as support. "I'm sure everything will work out O.K." is not a helpful response to the person who is deeply discouraged about a problem.

In other words, most of the techniques and devices common to human relationships are found to be of little use in establishing the type of relationship we are seeking here.

## What to Do

Just what does active listening entail, then? Basically, it requires that we get inside the speaker, that we grasp, _from his point of view_, just what it is he is communicating to us. More than that, we must convey to the speaker that we are seeing things from his point of view. To listen actively, then, means that there are several things we must do.

**Listen for Total Meaning.** Any message a person tries to get across usually has two components: the _content_ of the message and the _feeling_ or attitude underlying this content. Both are important; both give the message _meaning_. It is this total meaning of the message that we try to understand. For example, a machinist comes to his foreman and says, "I've finished that lathe setup." This message has obvious content and perhaps calls upon the foreman for another work assignment. Suppose, on the other hand, that he says, "Well, I'm finally finished with that damned lathe setup." The content is the same, but the total meaning of the message has changed—and changed in an important way for both the foreman and the worker. Here sensitive listening can facilitate the relationship. Suppose the foreman were to respond by simply giving another work assignment. Would the employee feel that he had gotten his total message across? Would he feel free to talk to his foreman? Will he feel better about his job, more anxious to do good work on the next assignment?

Now, on the other hand, suppose the foreman were to respond with, "Glad to have it over with, huh?" or "Had a pretty rough time of it?" or "Guess you don't feel like doing anything like that again," or anything else that tells the worker

CARL B. RODGERS AND RICHARD E. FARSON

that he heard and understands. It doesn't necessarily mean that the next work assignment need be changed or that he must spend an hour listening to the worker complain about the setup problems he encountered. He may do a number of things differently in the light of the new information he has from the worker—but not necessarily. It's just that extra sensitivity on the part of the foreman which can transform an average working climate into a good one.

**Respond to Feelings.** In some instances, the content is far less important than the feeling which underlies it. To catch the full flavor or meaning of the message, one must respond particularly to the feeling component. If, for instance, our machinist had said, "I'd like to melt this lathe down and make paper clips out of it," responding to content would be obviously absurd. But to respond to his disgust or anger in trying to work with his lathe recognizes the meaning of this message. There are various shadings of these components in the meaning of any message. Each time, the listener must try to remain sensitive to the total meaning the message has to the speaker. What is he trying to tell me? What does this mean to him? How does he see this situation?

**Note All Cues.** Not all communication is verbal. The speaker's words alone don't tell us everything he is communicating. And hence, truly sensitive listening requires that we become aware of several kinds of communication besides verbal. The way in which a speaker hesitates in his speech can tell us much about his feelings. So, too, can the inflection of his voice. He may stress certain points loudly and clearly and may mumble others. We should also note such things as the person's facial expressions, body posture, hand movements, eye movements, and breathing. All of these help to convey his total message.

## What We Communicate by Listening

The first reaction of most people when they consider listening as a possible method for dealing with human beings is that listening cannot be sufficient in itself. Because it is passive, they feel, listening does not communicate anything to the speaker. Actually, nothing could be farther from the truth.

By consistently listening to a speaker, you are conveying the idea that: "I'm interested in you as a person, and I think that what you feel is important. I respect your thoughts, and even if I don't agree with them, I know that they are valid for you. I feel sure that you have a contribution to make. I'm not trying to change you or evaluate you. I just want to understand you. I think you're worth listening to, and I want you to know that I'm the kind of a person you can talk to."

The subtle but more important aspect of this is that it is the *demonstration* of the message that works. While it is most difficult to convince someone that you respect him by *telling* him so, you are much more likely to get this message across by really *behaving* that way—by actually *having* and *demonstrating* respect for this person. Listening does this most effectively.

Like other behavior, listening behavior is contagious. This has implications for all communication problems, whether between two people or within a large organization. To ensure good communication between associates up and down the line, one must first take the responsibility for setting a pattern of listening. Just as one learns that anger is usually met with anger, argument with argument, and deception with deception, one can learn that listening can be met with listening. Every person who feels responsibility in a situation can set the tone of the interaction, and the important lesson in this is that any behavior exhibited by one person will eventually be responded to with similar behavior in the other person.

It is far more difficult to stimulate constructive behavior in another person but far more profitable. Listening is one of these constructive behaviors, but if one's attitude is to "wait out" the speaker rather than really listen to him, it will fail. The one who consistently listens with understanding, however, is the one who eventually is most likely to be listened to. If you really want to be heard and understood by another, you can develop him as a potential listener, ready for new ideas, provided you can first develop yourself in these ways and sincerely listen with understanding and respect.

## Testing for Understanding

Because understanding another person is actually far more difficult than it at first seems, it is important to test constantly your ability to see the world in the way the speaker sees it. You can do this by reflecting in your own words what the speaker seems to mean by his words and actions. His response to this will tell you whether or not he feels understood. A good rule of thumb is to assume that you never really understand until you can communicate this understanding to the other's satisfaction.

Here is an experiment to test your skill in listening. The next time you become involved in a lively or controversial discussion with another person, stop for a moment and suggest that you adopt this ground rule for continued discussion: Before either participant in the discussion can make a point or express an opinion of his own, he must first restate aloud the previous point or position of the other person. This restatement must be in his own words (merely parroting the words of another does not prove that one has understood but only that he has heard the words). The restatement must be accurate enough to satisfy the speaker before the listener can be allowed to speak for himself.

This is something you could try in your own discussion group. Have someone express himself on some topic of emotional concern to the group. Then, before another member expresses his own feelings and thought, he must rephrase the *meaning* expressed by the previous speaker to that individual's satisfaction. Note the changes in the emotional climate and in the quality of the discussion when you try this.

# Problems in Active Listening

Active listening is not an easy skill to acquire. It demands practice. Perhaps more important, it may require changes in our own basic attitudes. These changes come slowly and sometimes with considerable difficulty. Let us look at some of the major problems in active listening and what can be done to overcome them.

## The Personal Risk

To be effective at all in active listening, one must have a sincere interest in the speaker. We all live in glass houses as far as our attitudes are concerned. They always show through. And if we are only making a pretense of interest in the speaker, he will quickly pick this up, either consciously or unconsciously. And once he does, he will no longer express himself freely.

Active listening carries a strong element of personal risk. If we manage to accomplish what we are describing here—to sense deeply the feeling of another person, to understand the meaning his experiences have for him, to see the world as he sees it—we risk being changed ourselves. For example, if we permit ourselves to listen our way into the psychological life of a labor leader or agitator—to get the meaning which life has for him—we risk coming to see the world as he sees it. It is threatening to give up, even momentarily, what we believe and start thinking in someone else's terms. It takes a great deal of inner security and courage to be able to risk one's self in understanding another.

For the supervisor, the courage to take another's point of view generally means that he must see *himself* through another's eyes—he must be able to see himself as others see him. To do this may sometimes be unpleasant, but it is far more *difficult* than unpleasant. We are so accustomed to viewing ourselves in certain ways—to seeing and hearing only what we want to see and hear—that it is extremely difficult for a person to free himself from his needs to see things these ways.

Developing an attitude of sincere interest in the speaker is thus no easy task. It can be developed only by being willing to risk seeing the world from the speaker's point of view. If we have a number of such experiences, however, they will shape an attitude which will allow us to be truly genuine in our interest in the speaker.

## Hostile Expressions

The listener will often hear negative, hostile expressions directed at himself. Such expressions are always hard to listen to. No one likes to hear hostile words. And it is not easy to get to the

CARL B. RODGERS AND RICHARD E. FARSON

point where one is strong enough to permit these attacks without finding it necessary to defend oneself or retaliate.

Because we all fear that people will crumble under the attack of genuine negative feelings, we tend to perpetuate an attitude of pseudo peace. It is as if we cannot tolerate conflict at all for fear of the damage it could do to us, to the situation, to the others involved. But of course the real damage is done to all these by the denial and suppression of negative feelings.

### Out-of-Place Expressions

There is also the problem of out-of-place expressions—expressions dealing with behavior which is not usually acceptable in our society. In the extreme forms that present themselves before psychotherapists, expressions of sexual perversity or homicidal fantasies are often found blocking to the listener because of their obvious threatening quality. At less extreme levels, we all find unnatural or inappropriate behavior difficult to handle. That is, anything from an off-color story told in mixed company to a man weeping is likely to produce a problem situation.

In any face-to-face situation, we will find instances of this type which will momentarily, if not permanently, block any communication. In business and industry, any expressions of weakness or incompetency will generally be regarded as unacceptable and therefore will block good two-way communication. For example, it is difficult to listen to a supervisor tell of his feelings of failure in being able to "take charge" of a situation in his department, because *all* administrators are supposed to be able to "take charge."

### Accepting Positive Feelings

It is both interesting and perplexing to note that negative or hostile feelings or expressions are much easier to deal with in any face-to-face relationship than are truly and deeply positive feelings. This is especially true for the businessman, because the culture expects him to be independent, bold, clever, and aggressive and manifest no feelings of warmth, gentleness, and intimacy. He therefore comes to regard these feelings as soft and inappropriate. But no matter how they are

regarded, they remain a human need. The denial of these feelings in himself and his associates does not get the executive out of the problem of dealing with them. They simply become veiled and confused. If recognized, they would work for the total effort; unrecognized, they work against it.

### Emotional Danger Signals

The listener's own emotions are sometimes a barrier to active listening. When emotions are at their height, which is when listening is most necessary, it is most difficult to set aside one's own concerns and be understanding. Our emotions are often our own worst enemies when we try to become listeners. The more involved and invested we are in a particular situation or problem, the less we are likely to be willing or able to listen to the feelings and attitudes of others. That is, the more we find it necessary to respond to our own needs, the less we are able to respond to the needs of another. Let us look at some of the main danger signals that warn us that our emotions may be interfering with our listening.

**Defensiveness.** The points about which one is most vocal and dogmatic, the points which one is most anxious to impose on others—these are always the points one is trying to talk oneself into believing. So one danger signal becomes apparent when you find yourself stressing a point or trying to convince another. It is at these times that you are likely to be less secure and consequently less able to listen.

**Resentment of Opposition.** It is always easier to listen to an idea which is similar to one of your own than to an opposing view. Sometimes, in order to clear the air, it is helpful to pause for a moment when you feel your ideas and position being challenged, reflect on the situation, and express your concern to the speaker.

**Clash of Personalities.** Here again, our experience has consistently shown us that the genuine expression of feelings on the part of the listener will be more helpful in developing a sound relationship than the suppression of them. This is so whether the feelings be resentment, hostility, threat, or admiration. A basically honest relationship, whatever the nature of it, is the most productive of all. The other party becomes secure when he learns that the listener can express his feelings honestly and openly to him. We should keep this in mind when we begin to fear a clash of personalities in the listening relationship. Otherwise, fear of our own emotions will choke off full expression of feelings.

### Listening to Ourselves

To listen to oneself is a prerequisite for listening to others. And it is often an effective means of dealing with the problems we have outlined above. When we are most aroused, excited, and demanding, we are least able to understand our own feelings and attitudes. Yet, in dealing with the problems of others, it becomes most important to be sure of one's own position, values, and needs.

The ability to recognize and understand the meaning which a particular episode has for you, with all the feelings which it stimulates in you, and the ability to express this meaning when you find it getting in the way of active listening will clear the air and enable you once again to be free to listen. That is, if some person or situation touches off feelings within you which tend to block your attempts to listen with understanding, begin listening to yourself. It is much more helpful in developing effective relationships to avoid suppressing these feelings. Speak them out as clearly as you can, and try to enlist the other person as a listener to your feelings. A person's listening ability is limited by his ability to listen to himself.

## Active Listening and Company Goals

How can listening improve production?
We're in business, and it's a rugged, competitive affair. How are we going to find time to counsel our employees?
We have to concern ourselves with organizational problems first.
We can't afford to spend all day listening when there's a job to be done.

What's morale got to do with production?
Sometimes we have to sacrifice an individual for the good of the rest of the people in the company.

Those of us who are trying to advance the listening approach in industry hear these comments frequently. And because they are so honest and legitimate, they pose a real problem. Unfortunately, the answers are not so clear-cut as the questions.

### Individual Importance

One answer is based on an assumption that is central to the listening approach. That assumption is: The kind of behavior which helps the individual will eventually be the best thing that could be done for the group. Or saying it another way: The things that are best for the individual are the best for the company. This is a conviction of ours, based on our experience in psychology and education. The research evidence from industry is only beginning to come in. We find that putting the group first, at the expense of the individual, besides being an uncomfortable individual experience, does *not* unify the group. In fact, it tends to make the group less a group. The members become anxious and suspicious.

We are not at all sure in just what ways the group does benefit from a concern demonstrated for an individual, but we have several strong leads. One is that the group feels more secure when an individual is being listened to and provided for with concern and sensitivity. And we assume that a secure group will ultimately be a better group. When each individual feels that he need not fear exposing himself to the group, he is likely to contribute more freely and spontaneously. When the leader of a group responds to the individual, puts the individual first, the other members of the group will follow suit, and the group will come to act as a unit in recognizing and responding to the needs of a particular member. This positive, constructive action seems to be a much more satisfying experience for a group than the experience of dispensing with a member.

CARL B. RODGERS AND RICHARD E. FARSON

## Listening and Production

Whether listening or any other activity designed to better human relations in an industry actually raises production—whether morale has a definite relationship to production—is not known for sure. There are some who frankly hold that there is no relationship to be expected between morale and production—that production often depends upon the social misfit, the eccentric, or the isolate. And there are some who simply choose to work in a climate of cooperation and harmony, in a high-morale group, quite aside from the question of increased production.

A report from the Survey Research Center[1] at the University of Michigan on research conducted at the Prudential Life Insurance Company lists seven findings relating to production and morale. First-line supervisors in high-production work groups were found to differ from those in low-production work groups in that they:

1. Are under less close supervision from their own supervisors.
2. Place less direct emphasis upon production as the goal.
3. Encourage employee participation in the making of decisions.
4. Are more employee-centered.
5. Spend more of their time in supervision and less in straight production work.
6. Have a greater feeling of confidence in their supervisory roles.
7. Feel that they know where they stand with the company.

After mentioning that other dimensions of morale, such as identification with the company, intrinsic job satisfaction, and satisfaction with job status, were not found significantly related to productivity, the report goes on to suggest the following psychological interpretation:

> People are more effectively motivated when they are given some degree of freedom in the way in which they do their work than when every action is prescribed in advance. They do better when some degree of decision making about their jobs is possible than when all decisions are made for them. They respond more adequately when

they are treated as personalities than as cogs in a machine. In short, if the ego motivations of self-determination, of self-expression, of a sense of personal worth can be tapped, the individual can be more effectively energized. The use of external sanctions or pressuring for production may work to some degree, but not to the extent that the more internalized motives do. When the individual comes to identify himself with his job and with the work of his group, human resources are much more fully utilized in the production process.

The Survey Research Center has also conducted studies among workers in other industries. In discussing the results of these studies, Robert L. Kahn writes:

> In the studies of clerical workers, railroad workers, and workers in heavy industry, the supervisors with the better production records gave a larger proportion of their time to supervisory functions, especially to the interpersonal aspects of their jobs. The supervisors of the lower-producing sections were more likely to spend their time in tasks which the men themselves were performing, or in the paperwork aspects of their jobs.[2]

## Maximum Creativeness

There may never be enough research evidence to satisfy everyone on this question. But speaking from a business point of view, in terms of the problem of developing resources for production, the maximum creativeness and productive effort of the human beings in the organization are the richest untapped source of power still existing. The difference between the maximum productive capacity of people and that output which industry is now realizing is immense. We simply suggest that this maximum capacity might be closer to realization if we sought to release the motivation that already exists within people rather than try to stimulate them externally.

This releasing of the individual is made possible, first of all, by sensitive listening, with respect and understanding. Listening is a beginning toward making the individual feel himself worthy of making contributions, and this could result in a very dynamic and productive organization. Competitive business is never too rugged or too busy to take time to procure the most efficient technological advances or to develop rich raw material resources. But these in comparison to the resources that are already within the people in the plant are paltry. This is industry's major procurement problem.

G.L. Clements, president of Jewel Tea Co., Inc., in talking about the collaborative approach in management, says:

> We feel that this type of approach recognizes that there is a secret ballot going on at all times among the people in any business. They vote for or against their supervisors. A favorable vote for the supervisor shows up in the cooperation, teamwork, understanding, and production of the group. To win this secret ballot, each supervisor must share the problems of his group and work for them.[3]

The decision to spend time listening to his employees is a decision each supervisor or executive has to make for himself. Executives seldom have much to do with products or processes. They have to deal with people who must in turn deal with people who will deal with products or processes. The higher one goes up the line, the more one will be concerned with human relations problems, simply because people are all one has to work with. The minute we take a man from his bench and make him a foreman, he is removed from the basic production of goods and now must begin relating to individuals instead of nuts and bolts. People are different from things, and our foreman is called upon for a different line of skills completely. His new tasks call upon him to be a special kind of person. The development of himself as a listener is a first step in becoming this special person.

[1]"Productivity, Supervision, and Employee Morale." *Human Relations*, Series I. Report 1, Survey Research Center, University of Michigan, Ann Arbor, Mich.

[2]Robert L. Kahn, "The Human Factors Underlying Industrial Productivity," *Michigan Business Review*, November, 1952.

[3]G. L. Clements, "Time for 'Democracy in Action' at the Executive Level," address given before the AMA Personnel Conference, Feb. 28, 1951.

# VI. Two Topics for Today: Office Automation and International Communications

Two new fields of knowledge have become vitally important to the business communicator.

Office automation presents a wide sweep of new options for both written and oral communication. As the new technology becomes more and more prevalent, it is important to assess its potential for increasing your own effectiveness at your job.

International communications is rapidly becoming the focus of attention both in corporations and on college campuses. Since the United States is actively competing in the global marketplace, we must make a strenuous effort to develop greater sensitivity to the behavior norms of other cultures.

## Today, Tomorrow, and Always: Office Automation

### JONATHAN NEWMAN

PC, TC, WP, OA, DB, APL, SNA, SDLC, HDLC, IBM, mini, micro, mainframe. What do they all mean? For the most part, only the information management specialist cares, because this is the language of the people responsible for providing office automation (OA) services. The users of OA services need not be fluent in this language; nor are they compelled to comprehend its many complex implications.

In most business offices today, carbon paper is as much a relic of the past as are quill pens. When we need to duplicate material, we know that the copying machine will deliver our copy in less than ten seconds. Typically, we are indifferent to the technology that makes this minor miracle possible. We require only access to the machine and a working knowledge of how to make it operate. Similarly, users of OA technology (and this has begun to mean a very large percentage of business people) need only know what automation tools are available to make their work easier or better and how to use those tools efficiently.

In the fall of 1985, the *Wall Street Journal* reported that sales of personal computers for the office will approach 20 million units before 1987. This is indeed a striking phenomenon, but office automation is not at all an invention of our time or society. At one point in history, the fountain pen was deemed a technological watershed; at another, the typewriter. Later electric and electronic typewriters were considered equally impressive innovations.

What *is* new today is that OA tools no longer chiefly serve secretarial and clerical needs. Today, senior executives, middle managers, and people with a wide variety of management and operational responsibilities depend heavily on the personal computer and other office automation products. These products have come to play a critical role in documentation, administration, and especially in communication. They are used daily to record, transfer, and help analyze the information that is essential to carrying out a wide variety of responsibilities.

If you work for a large corporation, you will

probably find an abundance of OA products in use. Large corporations are buying and using OA equipment at an impressive pace—so much so that some of the technology described in this article is apt to be overtaken by new products before you have completed this academic year. And even if you work for a small company, there is a high probability that you will be exposed to some form of office automation—probably either word-processing equipment or an updated telephone system.

The industry within which your business operates will also influence the amount and sophistication of the OA tools that will be made available. In general, service industries such as banking and insurance, where administration of many people and servicing of multiple accounts are essential, rely most heavily on office automation equipment. On the other hand, industries as diverse as airlines and pharmaceutical houses have made these tools central to the way they operate, and manufacturing companies are in no way exempt from their use.

## Word Processing and Its Ramifications ("But Can He Type?")

Using a word processor or word-processing software at its most basic level is a simple typing skill. One strikes the keys and instead of the text going onto paper, it is stored in a form that is usable by the computer—typically on a disk or diskette. In the past, because typing was perceived as purely a secretarial duty, managers (and particularly males) were reluctant to approach a keyboard. But today the situation has changed markedly. In a recent office automation advertising supplement, *BusinessWeek* reported that middle managers who formerly insisted "I can't type—where's the typist?" are now pleading "I can type—when can I get my PC?" In addition, many older executives who feel intimidated by the familiarity that recent college graduates have with their PCs are signing up for hands-on training sessions.

Although the predominant use of computing at executive levels is information retrieval and analysis, managers and other professionals increasingly use word processing to create memoranda, letters, and reports. Word processing greatly facilitates collaborative writing. A common scenario is for an executive to create a draft at his or her workstation and then ask an assistant to provide formatting and copyediting. Another common process is for an entry-level employee to create a first draft at the word processor and later incorporate the revisions or additions supplied by a supervisor.

Many of today's larger organizations have established word-processing centers that operate as a separate function serving either one department or an entire company. Typists at these centers often work hand-in-glove with computer graphics experts (see the next section) and a team of editors. Typically, copy for finished typing is drafted by a writer working at the terminal at his or her workstation and is then transmitted to the center. When several iterations are needed, the output from the center can be accessesd via the terminal. The writer can proofread at the terminal and request hard copies as needed. Or, writers can dictate their documents to a transcriber at the center (see the section "Dictation Equipment and Electronic Mail") or else send hard-copy drafts for production.

There are many advantages to word processing, but the following are perhaps the most evident:

- Mistakes are quickly corrected without retyping the entire document.
- Whole sections can be rearranged, deleted, or added.
- Writers can experiment by trying several versions before selecting the best.
- Changing formatting parameters is greatly simplified, and uniform formatting standards can be maintained.
- Sections of a document can be stored and retrieved for insertion into other documents.

In addition to these traditional benefits, newer software provides capabilities that facilitate correct spelling. Spelling verifiers automatically search for misspelled words and greatly reduce the time needed for proofreading. Some of the more modern spelling verifiers also suggest corrected versions; their are, however, no spelling verifiers that provide a perfect alternative to proofreading. (For example, none could find the incorrect spelling of "there" in the previous sentence!)

Even more sophisticated software finds grammatical errors and highlights weaknesses in style. Products such as "Writer's Workbench" suggest ways to vary sentences, decrease wordiness, and eliminate an overabundance of passives. To help writers increase their word power, interactive thesauruses are also now available. By pressing a single key, the writer receives a list of synonyms and alternative expressions. If you keep in mind that these programs do not deal with subtleties or differentiate among audiences, situations, and writers' personalities, they can all be helpful tools. Software has even been customized in some cases to achieve specific writing objectives. For instance, Malcolm Baldridge, Secretary of Commerce and a devotee of clear writing, has had the department's word-processing equipment programmed to type XXXXXXXX whenever a writer indulges in heavy-handed jargon!

Perhaps the most sophisticated software extant today is known as "artificial intelligence" or "expert systems." These programs mirror the logical processes of the way we analyze and resolve problems. To what degree expert systems will affect the way writers organize information and build logical arguments is a question worth contemplating. It's probably safe to say, however, that these systems are likely to be tested before very long.

## Computer Graphics

Graphics software has already begun to change the look of many business reports, allowing writers to produce high-quality graphs, charts, and even pictures without the assistance of an art department. In addition, many of these products allow users to immediately integrate the graphics with the word-processing output, providing the maximum benefit from both kinds of technology. Today there are three main categories of graphics software available.

"Business graphics" software produces a variety of graphs and charts from numerical data. Almost all business graphics packages allow you to modify different attributes of the graph so that you can present your data as clearly as possible. Not only can you select the kind of graph you want (bar, pie, line, etc.), but you can also choose colors and other features. Some business graphics products include statistical routines that allow users to graph common statistical functions, such as the mean or standard deviation. Commonly, the software allows data to be input either from the keyboard or from an existing file created from another package.

A second category of software product allows you to create not just a chart, but a detailed picture. Often called a "paint" or "draw" package, it is frequently used in conjunction with a piece of hardware called a "mouse." The mouse is a small, hand-held device that allows the "artist" to move the cursor quickly from one place to another on the screen. Like writing, "painting" at a computer terminal allows a great deal of experimentation: the image can instantly be altered, with no need to start over. In addition, the computer allows a very high degree of technical accuracy: lines are straight, squares perfectly square, and circles are really circles.

Now found in an increasing number of offices, "publishing systems" are a third kind of graphics software package. These products provide even more formatting capabilities than either word processors or standard graphics programs. Publishing systems allow you to change type styles, vary type size, place textual material in columns, and increase or decrease the size of pictures and graphs. Perhaps their most impressive feature is that they usually allow the screen to display an exact replica of the final page. Until recently, because they were prohibitively expensive, these systems were used primarily by publishing departments and technical writers. Costs have begun to drop dramatically, however. More and more, such systems are becoming available for use by those who produce reports and other more-or-less routine company documents.

## Dictation Equipment and Electronic Mail

Traditional procedures for creating and sending memos and letters have been greatly altered by new technology.

Dictation equipment has long been available. But not since shorthand was introduced in the early 1900s has the process of dictating a letter undergone such major changes as today. Moreover, even greater innovations are just around the corner.

Today's managers can dictate both content and precise formatting instructions and then turn the document over to a word-processing specialist to be readied for any needed revision. As we have seen, part of the production process can include checking for spelling and grammar errors on the initial draft. Dictation is normally accomplished today by the author speaking into a hand-held tape recorder; however, an increasing number of large companies have sophisticated dictation centers that can be accessed through their intra-office phone systems.

Although not yet available commercially, prototype systems have been developed that will allow authors to generate their documents on a word processor simply by speaking into a microphone. These experimental systems are able to understand thousands of words; and when they are up and working, they will provide automated dictation systems that will have a profound effect on the way business documents are composed. Managers who "talk" their memos will probably become more aware of the way their writing *sounds*. In addition, they may routinely expect that their initial drafts will require a great deal of polishing.

In many modern offices paperwork has been greatly reduced by the use of electronic mail. Using an electronic mail system, a writer composes a memo at his or her terminal. The user decides to whom the message is to be sent, including both the primary recipient and those persons who are to be "copied." In many cases, a computerized directory is available to help the user locate recipients; there might be, for instance, a list of coded initials or numbers for each person on the system. Recipients are notified at their own terminals that they have incoming mail. In addition, the computer allows both the writer and the receiver to establish a file record of correspondence; it is also possible to request and receive a hard copy of the document.

Most electronic mail services use Local Area Networks (LANs) to link workstations within their offices. For example, Fidelity Investments Company in Boston now has more than 850 personal computers spread around nine downtown office buildings. Everyone from salespeople on the phones to analysts who make buy-and-sell recommendations uses those PCs. The network is a kind of "data highway" that enables the PCs to swap information with one another and with the large mainframe computers they are connected to. In essence, it allows people to rapidly extract and share information from data bases both inside and outside the company.

Electronic mail has rapidly gained popularity for several reasons. First, it is a natural extension to word processing. Since word processing stores the document on the computer's disk, it is readily available to be transmitted by electronic mail. Second, electronic mail is a fast, efficient, and cost-effective way to handle interoffice mail. Documents are transmitted and answers received in minutes instead of days. Unlike telephone communication, electronic mail does not require that the recipient be present to receive a complete message. In addition, massive amounts of information can be transferred very cheaply—with hard copy easily available for future reference.

Consistent users of electronic mail systems have noted that these systems tend to make correspondence more frequent and more informal. For memo writers and recipients, this observation suggests both benefits and risks. Obviously, electronic mail systems allow people within an organization to stay more closely in touch with each other. Messages can be "spoken" to the terminal, and because of their transitory nature there is little need to fuss over typos or minute details of style. On the other hand, the extreme ease of sending an electronic memo can tempt "gabby" employees to inundate their co-workers with unimportant mail. Also, some employees are tempted to fall off the deep end of informality, sending out error-ridden, semi-comprehensible documents.

Although today electronic mail systems are chiefly found in comparatively large companies, smaller companies are beginning to use public networks such as GTE's Telenet as their "post office." Such services also frequently make it possible to use the regular office mail to send printed copies of the document to recipients without access to the network.

Besides enabling direct communication between two or more individuals, electronic mail has the capacity to disseminate information among a large number of workers within a company. An example of this service is the "electronic bulletin board." Here, everyone in the system is able to place a message on the computer bulletin board and to read all messages that are present. Electronic bulletin boards are usually developed and maintained by groups of people with common interests, who use the bulletin board to share information, exchange files, and compare ideas. Both the strength and the weakness of electronic bulletin boards is that they provide an extremely open form of communication with virtually no privacy.

## On-Line Information Services (Public Data Bases)

Closely related to electronic mail systems are public data bases, which make a variety of information available for business and research purposes. (Among the most popular public data bases are Compuserve and Dow-Jones News Retrieval.) Originally public data bases primarily contained financial data, such as stock quotations, but today information is stored on diverse subjects such as plane schedules, movie reviews, and college guides. In the future, you will probably find complete libraries of information available through the services of public data bases.

To access a public data base, a user enters a password. The connection is made for a fee based on the time spent on-line and the amount of information received. A user receiving information at a terminal can often convert it to an appropriate format for use with word-processing software or other OA tools. The availability of such data allows business reports to be well substantiated with verifiable data.

## New, Expanded-Service Office Phone Systems

Many companies today have invested in updated internal telephone systems that offer a multitude of new services. These systems are often referred to as PBX (Private Branch Exchange) systems. Among the services they provide are conference calls among three or more parties, call-back systems that ring through when free lines are available, distinctive rings for internal and external calls, call-forwarding to allow phone calls to be received automatically at locales other than that dialed, "speakerphones" that make conversations audible to several people in a room, and memories for storing frequently called numbers.

Some of these services are at best only conveniences, but when combined they make the phone a much more powerful communication tool. If you find yourself working for a company with a sophisticated system, it may take you time to learn to use all of its different features. Try to determine which uses have become a routine part of the corporate environment. For example, do people regularly forward their calls to other locales where they are having conferences, or is this considered discourteous except in an extreme emergency? Are conference calls a common event, or is it generally expected that you will first try to arrange a meeting, and only use a conference call on special occasions?

## "Phone Mail"

Some large corporations have replaced the company telephone operator/receptionist with a computerized "phone mail" system. Working very much like a computerized telephone answering machine, this system records all incoming messages, which can later be received by phone. The major benefit of this equipment is that a receptionist is not needed; therefore, a good deal of human fallibility and expense are eliminated. On the other hand, time is also costly; and many employees complain that these systems waste their time because they must listen to all their messages sequentially to uncover the one or two that are important. It is much faster to scan a pile of written messages and retrieve the critical ones.

## Teleconferences

While an ordinary conference call can bring together three or four people, teleconferences allow 50 or more people in 50 or more cities to communicate. Unless video is used, these conferences are not expensive. In fact, they can save money by eliminating unneeded serial phone calls. A manager can speak to all of his or her employees in one call rather than ringing each one separately. And, obviously, time as well as money is saved.

Teleconferences increasingly are used when a company needs to make a major announcement to executives in its branches or subsidiaries. For instance, a teleconference might be called to introduce a new member of the management team or to announce an important new product. Some geographically dispersed companies even use audio conferences for sales meetings, and in a growing number of cases, video teleconferences are being used on such occasions.

Because coordinating arrangements can be tricky, important teleconferences are frequently managed (for a fee) by private companies. The amount of preparation often has a direct effect on the success of the conference. In many ways, planning a teleconference is like planning a radio or TV program: the agenda must be carefully prepared in advance and opportunities provided for each participant to pose questions and receive answers from the primary speaker and each other.

Differences in time zones can create difficulties in arranging convenient times for a conference; this is particularly true of international conferences, which can also be troubled by

technical difficulties. Satellite calls, which are those most frequently used today, present the problem of dealing with the echo/delay phenomenon; and speakers must learn to speak slowly to avoid stumbling over each other's comments. Still, advanced technology has already found ways to eliminate these problems, and undoubtedly international telephone conferences are becoming routine events in many major companies.

## Facsimile (FAX)

Facsimile, or FAX, uses telecommunication technology to transmit documents from one locale to another—even internationally—in a matter of minutes. (Transmitting a two-page document generally takes less than five minutes.) Although today's FAX technology cannot transmit color, it is possible to send sharp black-and-white charts and high-quality typescript.

Although FAX technology existed as far back as the 1950s, it is only recently that its speed, quality, and cost have made it an attractive alternative to express mail and courier systems. Law firms, traditionally heavy users of FAX equipment, continue to rely on it to send briefs from office to office. But now, engineering companies, ad agencies, architectural firms, and almost any kind of business with dispersed offices may use FAX equipment.

A new trend in FAX technology is to make the equipment portable. A traveling executive or consultant can plug a portable unit into a phone and send or receive documents instantaneously from a hotel room or other locale.

## Where to Now?

Although the technology described in this short article is impressive, this is only an overview of the many different OA products that are available today. Moreover, even while you are reading, today's technologies are being enhanced and new products are being introduced.

To become either overly fascinated or overly intimidated by this new technology is a present danger for communicators. In an attempt to master the technology, it would not be difficult to allow it to master you—to rely on it for tasks for which it is either inappropriate or unnecessary. On the other hand, to attempt to ignore OA equipment in the hope that it may vanish would be equally foolish.

Office automation is here to stay—today, tomorrow, and always. It will not, however, eliminate the need for business people to learn how to speak and write effectively. Business communicators will still have to ensure that their findings are accurate, that their meaning is clear, and that

their audiences are convinced. But, if used with skill and intelligence, OA technology can provide a host of new ways to accomplish these objectives more efficiently and more effectively.

*Previously Product Manager for the "Wang Professional Computer" at Wang Laboratories, Inc., Lowell, MA, Jonathan Newman currently is Director of Product Management at Phoenix Technologies, Ltd., Norwood, MA.*

---

# The Cultural S-T-R-E-T-C-H: Communicating in the Global Marketplace

RUTH G. NEWMAN

In his best-selling book, *Megatrends*, author John Naisbitt declares that the shift from a national to a world economy will be one of the ten most significant trends in our lives. "Yesterday is over," he asserts, "and we must now adjust to living in a world of interdependent communities."[1]

American businesses today are indeed competing in a global marketplace. According to the United States Department of Commerce, over 3500 U.S. firms are multinational; 30,000 U.S. manufacturers export their products; and 25,000 U.S. companies have branchs or affiliates in other countries. Moreover, another 40,000 U.S. firms intermittently do business abroad. It is a fact that roughly a third of U.S. corporate profits are generated by international business. And international business currently is conducted in all corners of the world—not only in Western Europe and Latin America, but also in the Middle East and the Orient. For example, the *Wall Street Journal* (November 18, 1985) reported that at the

end of 1984 U.S. corporations were the biggest foreign investors in China, with a total investment of over $700 million. As for people, over 100,000 American executives and their families are currently stationed abroad; millions more have become frequent international travelers.[2]

In preparing for your business or professional career, you should expect that your firm almost certainly will have transactions in the international arena. And even if you don't have the opportunity to travel abroad, you are likely to have to deal with people from other cultures by phone, by mail, or in person. More and more college graduates in entry-level positions are finding themselves performing tasks associated with furthering foreign trade. One out of every six manufacturing jobs in the United States depends on foreign trade; therefore, you may find that you work for a company that depends heavily on markets in other countries. Also (and this may surprise you), many foreign firms are operating in this country: Howard Johnson's, Baskin-Robbins Ice Cream, Saks Fifth Avenue, and Alka-Seltzer are just a few of the well-known "American" firms with foreign ownership.[3]

Because interacting with non-Americans is becoming inevitable and because many jobs with

---

[1] *Megatrends: Ten New Directions Transforming Our Lives,* John Naisbitt, Warner Books (New York, 1982).

[2] Neil Chesanow, *The World-Class Executive: How to Do Business Like a Pro Around the World,* Rawson Associates (New York, 1985), pp. 28, 46.

[3] Lennie Copeland and Lewis Griggs, *Going International: How to Make Friends and Deal Effectively in the Global Marketplace,* Random House (New York, 1985), p. xviii.

upward mobility will require an aptitude for cultural interchange, you would do well to take stock of your cultural awareness and abilities. To deal successfully with people from other cultures, you will need to be able to understand, acknowledge, and respond appropriately to activities and behavioral norms that are very different from your own.

## "People Are People"—or Are They?

As soon as we attempt to generalize about cultures or nationalities, we face an ever-present danger of ignoring significant differences among the individuals within any one group. No society is totally homogeneous; nor is any stereotype likely to capture all of the multiple facets of a particular human being. On the other hand, history, religious beliefs, geography, and politics do play a critical role in determining the behavior, outlook, and expectations of the various peoples of the world. And to dismiss these cultural differences as unimportant may be even more damaging to relationships than to make too much of them.

When world commerce first began to contract into a global market, a common assumption of American executives trying to deal abroad was "people are people and business is business." Espousing such a belief, however, has been costly to U.S. companies. It is now obvious that many of the very characteristics and attitudes that produced dynamic growth on our own soil are damaging to us abroad. Today, we are losing out in global markets to Japan, South Korea, Taiwan, Brazil, Mexico, and a host of other nations.

By all evidence, this failure to compete successfully was not caused by a lack of business or technical skills. Rather, it stemmed from our inability to transfer our "audience analysis" skills to international markets. To create a successful TV ad, a U.S. firm spends thousands of dollars on market research to understand the attitudes and preferences of potential customers. The same company may invest thousands of dollars negotiating to sell products abroad, but with little attention paid to researching how best to appeal to their foreign counterparts.

To correctly assess how others differ from us, we first need to see *ourselves* more clearly. The values that Americans accept without a second thought are often irrelevant or even threatening to people whose histories, politics, religions, and daily lives differ greatly from our own. And business behavior that we Americans consider right and natural may appear inappropriate and even crude to business people from other cultures.

Let's consider some of the edicts that a young American business person might hear on assuming the responsibility of his or her first important position: "Don't waste time on small talk or generalities." "Get right to the point when you have a message to deliver." "Stick to the facts!" "Deadlines are extremely important." Few American employees would not subscribe to the basic "rightness" of these generalizations about appropriate business behavior. On the other hand, the underlying assumptions of each would be seriously questioned in many other cultures.

As a nation, Americans highly regard rugged individuality, informality, directness, youthful energy, and all-encompassing enthusiasm for hard work and accumulating wealth. And we carry this value system throughout the world as an offering, certain that once others get the hang of it, they inevitably will perceive its rightness. After all, haven't these same values made the United States one of the most affluent and powerful nations in the world?

A basic flaw in this expectation is that, although our wealth is often envied, our energetic dedication to accumulating it is not necessarily seen as a virtue by persons from other cultures. Even when conducting business, sophisticated people from other nations are likely to believe and demonstrate that respect for age, personal honor, trust, family, long-standing friendship, and other intangible values take precedence in their scheme of things.

Certainly, at some level of awareness, most Americans also have a very high regard for these same ideals. But although we perceive their value, we have a difficult time understanding why such intangibles should be allowed to delay or even prevent a profitable business venture. And we find it especially difficult to master and patiently act out the time-consuming protocol that is the visible expression of adherence to such beliefs.

A vivid illustration of our problem is reflected in the slowness with which we have been able to build trade relations with China. Few of our ventures thrive, but even though there is much overt anti-Japanese sentiment in China, Sino-Japanese trade is flourishing—more than doubling in 1985. According to the previously cited *Wall Street Journal* article, experts believe that much of this success is due to the Japanese ability to understand and adapt to Chinese culture and customs. An observant American executive in Peking reports: "U.S. companies are oblivious to things that are important to the Chinese, such as proper seating arrangements at a banquet table. The Japanese would never put anyone in the wrong seat [according to protocol reflecting age or rank], but American businessmen say, 'Sit anywhere—we're all friends.'" Such behavior on our part signals not only a lack of knowledge of Chinese customs and manners but a failure to understand and show respect for their closely held values.

## We–They: The Cultural Stretch

In *The World-Class Executive* (cited above), Neil Chesanow asserts that Americans learning to do business abroad soon discover the following three truths: "Each of the world's business peoples is culturally unique; beneath their differences there are often key similarities; the similarities are not ones that Americans typically share."[4]

If we take a close look at some typical American attitudes and behavior patterns and compare them to those of other nationalities, we can see why the cultural stretch is generally more difficult for us than for others competing in the global arena.

### Family, Friendship, and Business

Whether or not he has actually been introduced to a business acquaintance's wife and children, an American businessman may attempt to show that

[4] Chesanow, p. 17.

he is cordial and friendly by ending a phone conversation with words such as "and by the way, Harry, how are the wife and kids?" Unless the introduction had previously taken place, most Europeans and Latin Americans would consider such a question presumptuous; most Arabs would find it a shocking breach of etiquette.

Few Americans would be late for or entirely miss an established business appointment because of a mildly important family matter. To a Latin American or Arab business executive, such behavior would be considered entirely normal and right.

Most American business executives would select a supplier who promised the lowest prices and fastest delivery over one who was a long-time personal acquaintance. Virtually no Japanese would.

Family is, of course, an important ideal in our own culture, and certainly we esteem friendship. But our formulas for mixing and separating our business and personal relationships often baffle and even annoy acquaintances from other cultures. They believe that family matters are never casual; generally, they also believe that they are extremely private. They feel that the pivotal relationship in a business dealing must be *trust*, which is normally established through careful and often time-consuming attention to personal relationships.

With only a few exceptions (mostly countries in northern Europe), preliminary business encounters abroad are intended to enable the parties to get to know each other better before negotiations begin; also, even during ongoing negotiations, considerable time may be spent getting further acquainted and building relationships.

For instance, newly arrived executives in China are often taken to see the local sights and wined and dined for days before serious negotiations are attempted. In Japan, once negotiations are under way, evenings may be spent drinking and socializing at bars; the purpose is to soften inhibitions and allow relationships to deepen. To a Latin, it is often exceedingly important for prospective business associates to spend time together at a cafe, conversing at length to discover whether they are *simpatico*. Arabs usually spend a few minutes before—and sometimes during—conferences exchanging small talk over coffee. During all these varied interchanges, business, money, and family matters are almost never discussed. The object is to enable the parties to assess each other's trustworthiness, intelligence, common interests, and even cultural attainments.

## Religion and Tradition

Americans have a variety of attitudes toward their religions, and some of us are undoubtedly more religious than others. But for the majority of Americans the practice of religion amounts to a recognition of certain moral and ethical precepts and, at the most, a weekly participation in its rituals. In most cases, the precepts of our religion do not directly specify how we conduct the moment-to-moment details and events of our daily lives. In many other cultures, however, it is otherwise.

To most Arabs, their religion, Islam, is one of the most important and central aspects of life. Not only does Islam shape all moral and ethical beliefs, it also regulates the way Muslims[5] conduct all facets of social and business intercourse—what they can eat and drink, the hours in which they conduct business, their treatment of women, and almost all social interactions. Minor infractions have great significance. For instance, offering an alcoholic beverage to a Muslim is an insult; asking about his wife's health is a serious indiscretion.

Over 2000 years ago, Confucianism was a way of life in eastern Asian countries, and its influence is still deeply felt there. Like Islam, Confucianism is more an ethical code regulating all aspects of life than it is a system of religious beliefs. Perhaps the central tenet of Confucianism is regard for family, especially respect for one's parents and elders. In modern cultures, this respect is often represented by extreme politeness and protocol, such as sending business representatives who are either the age peers of those they will negotiate with or are ready to show visible respect for their elders. Equally important to East

Asians is close attention to rank: subordinates must respectfully demonstrate their awareness of seniority at all times.

In Latin America, Catholicism is as pervasive as Islam is in Arab countries; similarly, it affects all aspects of daily life including business and social intercourse. In fact, both cultures share a strong sense that everything is dictated by God's (or Allah's) will. Therefore, in both, the ability to carry out commitments—and most certainly to carry them out *on time*—rests in God's hands. If family or personal events unfortunately interfere—well, that's destiny.

## Formality and Etiquette

Even this brief look at how religion and tradition govern behavior in other parts of the world suggests another very basic difference between other cultures and our own—the importance placed on the outward forms of behavior, or *etiquette*.

Americans tend to find the minute attention to the details of protocol frustrating and bothersome. In our culture, we are likely to equate good manners with the golden rule. To us, real courtesy is "treating the other guy decently." In some respects, we are even suspicious of extremely formal manners, interpreting them as priggish or phony. But to people of other cultures, the outward forms of courtesy represent much more than good manners. In most cases, manners are closely linked to their ethical underpinnings; equally important, they are pathways that must be followed in order to accomplish both personal and business objectives.

While Americans are result-oriented, most other cultures are performance-oriented. Americans joke "A good loser is still a loser!" But to our global competitors, the way the game is played usually counts as much as the outcome. Moreover, they see winning as a long-term goal: it is the ultimate result of doing things in the right way; not the immediate reward for a clever thrust.

A Japanese, for example, would never directly assert that you are "wrong"—and especially not in the presence of others. In Japan, your personal sense of worth is closely tied to how others perceive your behavior; to dishonor others by di-

---

[5] The religion is Islam. Its practitioners are called Muslims.

rectly refuting their opinion is, therefore, a grave misdemeanor. Equally important, every Japanese operates within the rights and restrictions appropriate to his or her rank and place in the social order. Face-saving protocol both reflects and strengthens this system.

Not only in Japan but in most other cultures besides our own, etiquette has an important place in daily interactions. In Latin American and Arab countries, for instance, the serving of coffee symbolizes the beginning and often the end of a meeting or an engagement. To refuse coffee is grossly ill-mannered; in Arab countries, to accept it with your left hand may be construed as an insult to your host (the left hand is reserved for personal hygiene). Invitations to social occasions, gift giving, thank-you letters, and a myriad of other intricate details of etiquette and protocol oil the machinery that enables personal and business interactions to take place.

A predominant example of etiquette that is critically important in a multinational setting is the exchange of business cards. More frequently than not, if Americans exchange cards at all, they do so casually at the *end* of a conference or meeting. In other parts of the world, the formal exchange of "calling cards" is mandatory at the *beginning* of a transaction. You are expected to present your card immediately to every person you are introduced to and to receive one in return. Courtesy demands that the reverse side of the card bear a translation printed with the same attention to quality as the information printed in the owner's language; good manners also require that the card be offered with the translation uppermost. In some countries (such as Japan), this exchange is done with ritualistic formality and bows. At group meetings, it is common practice to arrange the cards on the table in front of you to reflect the seating order.

Why so much attention to what Americans consider nothing more than a somewhat convenient way to leave an address and phone number? The answer is, of course, that exchanging the information on the cards immediately enables business protocol to be properly enacted. Awkward questions about rank need not be asked; names of people and firms can be referred to correctly.

## Individuality and Conformity

If circumstances forced an American executive to withdraw midway through negotiations for a business deal, it would be construed an unfortunate inconvenience; but a colleague with similar qualifications would quickly be briefed and sent to complete the transaction. However, in most of Europe, Latin America, a good part of East Asia and the Middle East, it is likely that the loss of a key negotiator would gravely damage the progress of negotiations, and perhaps even end them. In these cultures, getting to know and to trust a particular person is basic to successful negotiating. But, ironically, in America, where we hold individuality in very high esteem, we tend to feel that our personal selves are for the most part irrelevant to the way we perform our jobs.

"Individuality" to most Americans represents the ability to make independent decisions and to stand up and fight for opinions that differ from those widely accepted. It's no wonder that we have coined the term "rugged individualist"; the prototype American individualist is a bit of a maverick who can firmly take a stand and defend it.

Compare this rugged individuality to the "personalism" that Latin Americans esteem, and the basic difference becomes clear. A Latin's personal identity is a composite of ancestors, family, and current affiliations; it is often expressed by cultivating a particular art or special branch of knowledge, such as painting or archaeology. In essence, it is what marks an individual as "civilized." Therefore, Latins generally insist on sharing this special kind of individualism with acquaintances before giving and expecting trust.[6]

Individuality in Japan, on the other hand, is tied to one's personal honor, which in turn depends heavily on one's ability to conform to the ideals of Japanese society. The Japanese system of conducting business depends heavily on consensus, which in their case truly means "by consent." In Japan, a tactic or plan is meticulously studied, discussed, and evaluated until all those involved assent to the benefits of implementing it. During this process, direct confrontations are studiously

[6] Chesanow, pp. 268–269.

avoided. The proponent of a viewpoint does not try to establish that others are wrong. Rather, persuasion is accomplished by proving one's personal qualities of trustworthiness, dedication, and sincerity.

## Presentation Tactics: Some Basic Differences

Students in business communication courses at U.S. universities ordinarily are taught four basic tactics in composing written or spoken presentations:

- Know your audience and their needs.
- Know yourself and your purpose.
- Keep your style clear and uncluttered.
- State your position and recommendations as soon as possible.

When dealing with a foreign audience, the first three of these tactics are perhaps even more important than ever. The fourth, however, almost always is inappropriate in other cultures, and frequently it is damaging. Having read this far, you can perhaps perceive why.

It is obviously essential to know as much as you can about your audience and to empathize with their expectations and needs. As you have seen, it is also critical to understand yourself and your own culture well. Moreover, since culture shock can be disorienting, you need a firm grasp on what you hope to accomplish. And, in regard to the third tactic, if you are addressing a foreign audience in English, a simple and clear style is certainly a must; similarly, if your words are to be translated, an accurate translation will require that the original be clear and comprehensible.

But the fourth tactic listed above is another matter. A strong statement of your position, followed by a rapid-fire presentation of the chief issues and relevant facts—the approach that is most likely to win an American audience—is apt to frustrate or even anger business people from other cultures. They see Americans as far too direct and blunt, and they often equate our directness with discourtesy. To them the typical Amer-

ican approach of "Let's set the record straight" or "Let's put it all on the line" is both bad manners and bad business. Whereas we have been trained to move quickly and logically from issue to issue, often presenting our conclusions as we go, they want to consider the presentation holistically and to examine it in the context of their feelings about the person presenting the information and the firm represented.

Spoken presentations abroad are therefore likely to begin with an exchange of factual information about the history and accomplishments of the presenter's company, and courteous affirmations of the pleasure or honor of doing business with the firm represented by the audience. Similarly, as we have seen, office conferences often open with a mandatory interchange of small talk—frequently over coffee. Business correspondence also is often less direct, generalizing on issues under discussion rather than affirming opinions and restating points. And, as might be expected, very formal salutations and closings that would seem stiff and outdated here are common and often expected in other cultures.

## Doing Away with the Stereotype

So what can we do to dispel the harsh stereotype of Americans as overly aggressive, discourteous, and self-centered philistines?

The aggressive American style of doing business, which others so often interpret as rude and bumptious, is almost certainly a direct outgrowth of American confidence and optimism. We take the privilege of speaking our minds virtually for granted whenever an occasion allows an opinion, and especially when competition is in the air. We feel assured that if one "knows his stuff" and "has the goods," success is likely. And this belief in ourselves and our system is something we would not want to change. On the other hand, although not a negative feature in our landscape, our exuberant confidence appears an oddity in cultures where events move slowly and class and rank are immutable. Moreover, when we deal with those societies, aggressive outgoingness is a significant barrier to communication and mutual understanding.

As with our aggressive business style, our self-preoccupation stems directly from the positive qualities of American optimism and pride. In the main we are not an unfriendly people; nor are we uninterested in learning about other peoples and their ways. At bottom, however, we feel assured that any cultural interchange must inevitably result in their being convinced that *our* opinions are right and *our* ways are better. In our eagerness to make this happen, we forget that our measurement of "right" and "better" is apt to be based entirely on the experience of being an American.

America's economic health today depends to a great extent on our ability to strengthen our toeholds in new international markets and to operate successfully in those countries where we already have considerable presence. Both of these objectives can be accomplished without our attempting to shed our special brand of American optimism and confidence. We must, however, discipline ourselves to behave in ways that reflect increased sensitivity to the customs and values of those with whom we wish to do business. For better or worse, cultures other than our own have come down very different pathways and have very different perspectives.

Of course, we may question why *we* should have to make the major effort—why don't *they* try harder to understand us and to learn our ways? But, in fact, there is much to suggest that *they* do.

Perhaps the most obvious evidence is that, even though only 4 percent of the world outside our borders consider it their first language,[7] English has now become the language of international commerce. Foreign visitors show respect and consideration to us by speaking our language, and when we are guests in their country, they courteously greet us in English. Nevertheless, most Americans stubbornly refuse to master foreign languages. Fewer than 8 percent of our col-

leges and universities require knowledge of a foreign language for entrance,[8] and college enrollments in language studies continue to decline. Moreover, very few of our business emissaries even bother to gain a rudimentary knowledge of the native language before attempting to negotiate abroad.

Our attitude of "they speak English, so why should we bother?" not only conveys a lack of courtesy but also limits our effectiveness in other ways. If we fail to translate our thoughts in either a spoken or written engagement, even those who appear to understand us may mistake our meaning. Often, foreigners who speak English fairly well have only a limited understanding of its nuances—especially of the American idiom. A written document is apt to be passed along to persons with no knowledge of English at all. And not to be minimized is the fact that total ignorance of a foreign language can sometimes lead to embarrassment. President Ronald Reagan, for instance, described an incident that took place in Mexico City. After completing his address to an unenthusiastic audience, the President returned to his seat disappointed. When he noted that the next speaker—who spoke to the audience in Spanish—was interrupted at frequent intervals by loud applause, he felt even worse. "So, to hide my embarrassment, I started clapping before everyone else until our ambassador leaned over to me and said, 'I wouldn't do that if I were you. He's interpreting your speech.'"[9]

Additional evidence that people from other nations show more cultural sensitivity than we do is their willingness to learn our ways and to adopt them while transacting business here. Arabs who dress exclusively in native attire in their own countries wear impeccable business suits in the United States; Latin American representatives arrive at their appointments precisely on time; Europeans who at home would not dream of talking shop over lunch cheerfully take part in typical American business lunches.

---

[7] Chesanow, p. 19.

[8] Copeland and Griggs, p. xxii.

[9] "Back-patting Clapping," *Forbes*, June 18, 1984, p. 20. Narrated in Copeland and Griggs, p. 101.

## Becoming Worldly-Wise: Opportunities and Challenges

Multinational corporations based in the United States, foreign-based companies doing business here, and American companies selling our products and services abroad are increasingly seeking help from employees who can exhibit cultural dexterity. Personnel specialists are needed to assist in recruiting and retaining qualified people to work on multinational projects. Marketing and sales departments require assistance in discovering, surveying, and servicing international markets. Planning functions are gearing up to reexamine corporate strategies in the light of new foreign competition and worldwide growth opportunities. And these are only a small portion of the burgeoning needs for qualified assistance.

The global marketplace is not only placing new demands on senior executives, it is also providing new challenges for employees in the start-up phase of their careers. An acquaintance of mine employed in the marketing communications department at a large bank was asked to assist in arranging to have their annual report published in three foreign languages. In another instance, a young colleague assigned to office administration at a high-tech firm was requested to make suitable arrangements for entertaining a group of visiting Japanese executives. And still another colleague in her early twenties, a public relations assistant at a consulting firm, was asked to spend a week in London to interest the British press in publicizing the opening of the firm's new London office.

Taking advantage of such opportunities as they arise will depend on what you already know and how willing you are to go after the knowledge you'll need. Many American colleges and universities are now actively considering adding core courses in international business to their graduate and undergraduate business curricula. A small number have aleady done so.[10]

But whether you are a college student or are already working in your field, you would do well to focus on the following three objectives *before* a specific international project arrives at your doorstep:

- Build your knowledge of American culture, values, social norms, and priorities so that you understand yourself better and are capable of inspiring respect from people from other lands. In essence, this means to cultivate as good a knowledge as you can of our history, politics, and geography, of our achievements in the arts and sciences, and of current happenings in American entertainment and sports.

- In preparing for an international assignment, learn as much as you can about that country's culture; get familiar with at least some of the relevant subject areas mentioned above. If you expect to visit a foreign country, take special care to know the existing rules of etiquette and protocol.[11]

- Become proficient in at least one foreign language. In any case, before traveling abroad, learn the appropriate expressions of courtesy for the countries you will visit.

It has become increasingly obvious that the study of the history, language, and literature of our own and other cultures has more direct relevance to business than we've ever suspected. But without flexibility and a sense of humor, even a good foundation in these subjects may not be sufficient in a world that is changing so rapidly and unpredictably.

For instance, a young oceanographer who was my seat companion on a recent plane trip from Chicago to Boston told me of his experience working on a three-year project with a group of

[10]"Internationalizing the Business School," unpublished keynote address by Tony G. Bonaparte, delivered at the American Assembly of Collegiate Schools of Business (AACSB), at San Francisco State University, March 14, 1985.

[11]The International Trade Administration (ITA) of the U.S. Department of Commerce offers advice and assistance to persons and firms seeking to do business abroad. Also, the U.S. State Department publishes a helpful series of "Facts on . . . ," pamphlets that review local customs and current conditions throughout the world. Foreign trade organizations (their main offices are mostly located in New York and Washington, D.C.) will also willingly supply literature, some of which covers cultural matters.

Chinese scientists. "The Chinese team was composed of two men and a woman," he said. "On their first trip to the United States, the woman wore a Mao jacket and at all times walked about three steps behind the rest of us, maintaining silence throughout our discussions. On their second trip a year later, the woman wore a Mao jacket, and although she now walked alongside us, she seldom made any comments. This year, the same team came over again. Their female colleague was dressed in a smart Western business suit; not only did she walk beside us, but she frequently led the discussion."

**Sources**

*Books*

Chesanow, Neil. *The World-Class Executive: How to Do Business Like a Pro Around the World*, New York: Rawson Associates, 1985.

Copeland, Lennie, and Lewis Griggs. *Going International: How to Make Friends and Deal Effectively in the Global Marketplace*, New York: Random House, 1985.

Naisbitt, John. *Megatrends: Ten New Directions Transforming Our Lives*. New York: Warner Books, 1982.

*Articles*

Bonaparte, Tony H., "Internationalizing the Business School," unpublished keynote address delivered at the American Assembly of Collegiate Schools of Business (AACSB), at San Francisco State University, March 14, 1985.

Miles, Mary. "Business Etiquette Abroad," *Computer Decisions*, January 15, 1985.

Oh, Tai K. "Selling to the Japanese," *Nation's Business*, October 1984.

Zimmerman, Mark. "How to Do Business with the Japanese," *United Magazine*, May 1985.

# VII. Meeting the Media

Although dealing with the media may not be a regular part of your responsibilities, in many jobs media relations do play at least a subordinate role. You may be called on to respond to a press inquiry by phone, to prepare materials for a superior who will be interviewed, or to be your firm's spokesperson in regard to a particular problem or achievement. The following articles will help you with these tasks.

# When a Reporter Calls . . .

## CAROLE HOWARD

When you deal with the news media, any mistake is liable to be very public. Visions of a terrible *faux pas* splashed across the newspaper or on television screens in living rooms throughout the community dance in our heads and make our stomachs churn.

*The Book of Lists* ranks fear of public speaking ahead of death, flying and loneliness—and talking with a reporter for attribution has to be the most "public" of public speaking opportunities.

An anecdote in journalism circles tells of a city editor who called a reporter to the city desk to point out a mistake in a story. "Well," he said, "you have already made 280,000 mistakes today (circulation—280,000) and it is only noon." It impressed the reporter and it should impress a spokesperson.

Yet it does not have to scare you away. Like

so many other talents, the skills required to be an effective spokesperson can be practiced and perfected.

Most reporters are too sophisticated to be impressed by style over substance. Conversely, a fine position can be misunderstood if it is not presented with clarity and confidence. Interviews are not conversations—they are highly structured situations. These techniques should help when you are interviewed by a reporter:

- Prepare and practice. Learn from Mark Twain, who once said it takes three weeks to prepare a good ad-lib speech. Have in mind two or three major points that you want to get across. Ask yourself, "If I could edit the article, what two or three sentences would I like to see?" Well in advance of the interview, write them out, then simplify and shorten them.

  Practice aloud so your words sound natural to the ear. In a phone interview, keep your key points in front of you. At the earliest opportunity, present your main points in answer to questions.

- Place your most important points at the beginning of each response, where they will be clear and isolated. In TV or radio interviews, this is especially important. Responses like, "There are three reasons for that" invite poor editing. Instead say, "Price, performance and reliability are key factors in our decision."

- Refer to the interviewer by name—early and often. In print this is a simple courtesy. In TV it may help get that sentence past the editing process and onto the screen, since stations often like to show that their reporters are well known in the community.

- It is not only what you say but *how* you say it that communicates. The effective speaker is not necessarily polished and perfect. He or she *is* energetic, involved and direct. A forthright, enthusiastic response to a question portrays candor and confidence.

- You should not feel pressured to respond instantaneously to a difficult question on a complex subject. You are making instant history—sometimes instant policy—and you

have the right to be comfortable with the way you articulate your organization's role in it. Take a moment to organize your thoughts.

- Think fast but talk slowly. If the reporter is taking notes, it will help the accuracy. If you are being taped for broadcast it will help your audience's comprehension.

- Never forget your ultimate audience. You are *talking* to a reporter—but you are *speaking* to the people who read the publication or watch the program—your customers, employees, shareholders and suppliers past, present and potential.

  Frame your answers from their point of view, not your organization's. For example, say, "Our customers now have three new colors to choose from," rather than, "We have expanded our color selection." Or, "If this bill becomes law there will be significantly fewer parks for you to take your family to," rather than, "Our industry is opposing this legislation because . . ."

- Try to humanize your responses by giving a bit of your personality as well as the organization's position. Your field is interesting to you. Make it equally interesting to the reporter.

- Don't be embarassed if you do not have a number or a detail at hand. Simply tell the reporter that the person on your staff responsible for media relations will get it.

  Also, don't feel obliged to accept a figure or fact the reporter cites. Say you are not familiar with it and offer to have it checked.

  Never have other staff people besides the media relations person in the room with you. Accompanied by too many advisers, you may appear to be an obedient Gulliver surrounded by Lilliputians. The reporter wants your views and comments.

- Don't let a reporter put words in your mouth. Whenever you hear the phrases, "Are you saying that . . .?," "Do you mean . . .?" or "Isn't it really . . .?" alarm bells should ring in your head. Mishandling this type of question can result in your feeling your words were reflected back by a fun-house mirror when the final story appears.

If you do not like the way a question is stated, do not repeat it in your response—even to deny it. The reporter's question will not appear in print. Your answer will.

For example, if a reporter asks if one of your products is overpriced, don't say, "I wouldn't want to use the term 'overpriced.'" Instead say, "We believe our products provide high value for the price."

- Look for the hidden agenda in questions. If a reporter is probing your recent hiring of sales people proficient in certain skills, the resulting article may say that your company is in the midst of a marketing buildup to launch a new product line.

- Keep your cool. A few interviewers deliberately frame their questions in emotional or accusatory tones. It is just a technique to get you to say something controversial. Don't let it work.

- Avoid tongue-twisters like "specificity."

- When a reporter interrupts with what seem to be basic clarifying questions, it may be that you have unconsciously dropped into obscure professional or industry jargon.

  Look for ways to explain your points with simple illustrations or analogies out of everyday life. "The first transistors looked like top hats on stilts," or, "Today we can put all the intelligence of a room-size computer from the 1950s into a silicon chip the size of a cornflake."

- Avoid negatives. Don't say, "No, we are not discriminating against women." Rather, say, "We have a program to actively recruit more women managers . . ."

- You don't want to be as parochial as Humpty Dumpty, who told Alice, "When I use a word it means just what I choose it to mean—neither more nor less." Frequently the same word can have different meanings to different audiences. A terminal in the computer business is a piece of equipment—but to many people it is a place where you catch a bus.

- Be realistic in your answers. Look at each question from the public's point of view. If a reporter says, for instance, "You don't have many black supervisors, do you?" don't counter with, "Our record on that is terrific. We're doing much better than most companies." That sounds defensive. Instead, be positive in your answers. You might say, "We still don't have enough black supervisors although we are making progress. Such and such percent of our supervisors are black, and we have these specific programs . . ."

- Avoid answering a simple question with 10 paragraphs. Short, simple answers are better than long, complicated ones. A few sentences using simple language give the interviewer less opportunity to misunderstand you.

- Never underestimate the intelligence of your audience—and never overestimate their knowledge. There is no need to adjust your prose to the words used by high school sophomores. But you should take care to explain your terms, especially when you are covering a difficult subject.

- Speak in the first-person, active voice. Avoid the passive. Say, "We will be moving our offices . . ." not "Our offices will be moved . . ." You want to portray your organization as a group of interesting, concerned people who decide and do things, rather than as a faceless, inanimate group. Similarly, don't duck responsibility for difficult actions. Say, "We reluctantly have decided that a layoff of some of our employees is required . . ." not, "The economy has forced a layoff . . ." Companies don't make decisions or establish policies—people do.

- Don't waste your brief time with a reporter by arguing *against* the other side, even to refute their point of view. You may inadvertently end up giving valuable media exposure to their position. Instead, state your case positively, without mentioning your opponents at all.

- Don't be offended by a reporter's questions in what you consider private areas. But don't feel you have to give out the information, either. It is your responsibility to decide how much you want to say in your answer. If the questioning moves into proprietary or confidential areas, simply explain that providing such information would be too helpful to your competitors.

When the questioning gets too personal, wit can be a good defense. Ronald Reagan practices this technique with the best of them: "Our family didn't exactly come from the wrong side of the tracks," he says of his beginnings, "but we were certainly always within the sound of the train whistles."

- Don't respond to narrow questions with an equally narrow answer. Rather, make it one more opportunity to reiterate one of your key points.

    If you are interviewed on a plant closing and are asked how many people will be out of work, don't reply, "about 750." Instead say, "About 750 people, but we are doing everything we can to help ease the employees' transition."

- Don't answer hypothetical questions. Instead, particularize them with, "That's a hypothetical question so it is impossible to know what might happen. But let me tell you exactly what *did* happen in a similar case . . ."

- It should be obvious: Never, absolutely never, lie to a reporter.

- Above all, be yourself. If you like to sit around a conference table when you are meeting with your staff, that is probably a fine place for the interview; you will feel comfortable and the reporter will have a surface on which to write or place a tape recorder. If you prefer to emphasize your points by drawing diagrams on an easel, do it. If you love sports, it is perfectly appropriate to use an analogy from the football field to illustrate your point. If your taste leans more to music, feel free to make a comparison using an orchestra as a metaphor. The reporter wants your perspective—not that of a well-trained but impersonal robot who gives the impression of speaking fluently but formally in a foreign language.

Here are some topics to avoid when you are talking with reporters, since they inevitably cause misunderstandings:

- Don't ask if you can review the story in advance. Just as the reporter cannot expect to see your annual report or latest product plans until you are ready to make them public, you cannot have advance access to reporting of the news.

- Don't mention how much your organization advertises in the reporter's medium. No reputable publication or station permits its editorial judgment to be influenced by advertising, and you may insult both the reporter's personal and professional codes of behavior.

- Don't tell broadcast reporters you think 30 or 60 seconds is too short a time to adequately tell your story. They are no more satisfied with the time constraints they work under than you are.

- Don't tell a reporter you will provide written answers to his questions if he or she will send them to you. The media are not in the business of taking dictation.

- Don't ask a reporter to keep what you say "off the record." We must remember that the sole reason a reporter is interviewing you is for the record—that is, to write and produce a story for publication or airing that gives you and your organization's views on a particular subject.

There are a number of benefits to sharpening your spokesperson skills beyond improving your performance when you are interviewed by a reporter.

Many of these same hints can help you the next time you are asked to give a speech or lead an employee meeting.

## Choosing a Spokesperson

Selecting the right spokesperson is not easy. It is one of the critical elements that will determine the success of an organization's news coverage.

The obvious and frequent choice—the chief executive officer—is not always the best one. CEOs deal with broad, general, policy-making matters. Rarely are they involved in the nitty-gritty of the organization enough to know the details of a specific project or issue. Unless the CEO has a personal desire to be the primary spokesperson, it frequently is better to reserve access to the top for reporters whose assignments require comments on overall policy or strategic direction.

The head of the department involved in the topic is not necessarily the right person. Promotions in organizations are normally based on outstanding technical or professional knowledge and performance. Even the ability to make a presentation at an internal meeting or to the board of directors is not necessarily the same as being able to meet with reporters.

When the spokesperson is from a middle or lower echelon, be mindful of the sensitivities of that person's superiors in the organization. The top manager is usually known as such in the community. Do not make it look as if some whippersnapper has usurped the leadership.

Sex or age of the person usually is not relevant to the decision. Some believe a middle-aged man is a better choice, claiming he projects authority. Others point to a 1981 Boston University study showing women are more trusted than men, thus making them better public spokespersons, particularly in government where there was a dramatic difference in trust between male and female spokespersons in similar positions.

The best advice is simply to pick the person who can do the best job. Here are the characteristics of a good spokesperson:

- Above all, knowledge of the topic. Only with a firm grounding in the facts can anyone speak confidently and positively.

- An understanding of the organization's overall objectives and strategies. The spokesperson should be able to think quickly and also gracefully walk the fine line between being responsive to the reporter's needs and giving away the store.

- An ability to "tell and sell"—in everyday English and from the point of view of the reporter and the publication's or station's audience—not your organization's.

- The confidence of top management. This person will be representing the company or organization to the general public. You do not want to choose someone who is not well respected by those within.

- A desire to do the interview. If a spokesperson demurs beyond what normal modesty and apprehension would explain, back off. Whoever is responsible for the selection should sense when people believe they are poor choices for the assignment.

*Carole Howard is Division Manager, Regional Public Relations, AT&T Information Systems, Morristown, N.J.*

# The Anatomy of an Interview

## JERR BOSCHEE

At Control Data, and many other companies, employees are not allowed to be interviewed without a public relations person present.

Why?

Because reporters are professionals. They conduct hundreds of interviews a year. They know what they are doing.

When it comes to interviews, most business people do not, and this leads to something few journalists understand. As amateurs, business people are taking a significant risk. The stakes are much higher than the questioner may realize—a job, a reputation, a company's well-being. Amateurs make mistakes. They mis-speak, they contradict themselves, they release proprietary information, they speak with confidence about subjects they don't understand. In short, most of them are over-matched, and they know they need an equalizer—so they turn to their public relations people, many of whom are former journalists.

## Develop Mutual Trust

The objective of both the reporter and the public relations person is to develop an accurate, representative story, and the only relationship worth having between them is mutual trust. In a given instance, the public relations person is an advocate and the journalist is an investigator. That tension is recognized by both. But "advocate" and "investigator" need not be pejorative terms.

A public relations person has three major tasks in approaching an interview:

- To minimize misunderstandings—inaccurate information can damage a company.
- To help the person being interviewed achieve his or her objectives.
- And to help the reporter develop a good, accurate story.

When a reporter calls an employee at Control Data, he or she is referred immediately to a public relations person, whose first task is to clarify the reporter's request. In some instances, the public relations department will provide whatever information is desired. In other cases, the request for an interview is declined because Control Data has no information to provide, no position to take on the issue being advanced, or no time to find the information before the reporter's deadline. Whenever it appears that an interview may be appropriate, however, the reporter is promised a return call as soon as spokespersons have been identified and consulted.

It's important here for reporters to understand what they are up against psychologically. Many executives—and the vast majority of interview requests reaching Control Data are directed toward executives—question the need to do *any* interview, much less one suggested by a reporter. In addition, despite the growing sophistication and specialized training of some business reporters, many executives still have a low opinion of reporters and their skills, especially their knowledge of business, finance, management, economics and similar subjects. They also may question the reporter's objectivity, sometimes with good reason. According to a senior editor at a major U.S. business publication, many young reporters don't distinguish between profits and greed. Asked how long it takes to overcome that built-in bias, he says, "Some of them never do."

And there is another point for journalists to remember about executives during an interview session: Most of them are either scared, nervous or overconfident—all of which are dangerous to themselves and their companies. Reporters may not always be able to tell that executives are battling psychological demons during the interview, but most of them are, and this is true even during the most innocuous interviews. As Oscar Wilde wrote, "In the old days men had the rack—now they have the press." A reporter's clever paraphrase, polished on the copy desk, can haunt the source for years.

## Before You Say Yes, Be Prepared

Before they consent to be interviewed, then, executives usually ask for two sets of information: A thorough explanation of what the interview will be about—and as much background as possible about the journalist and the publication or broadcast service he or she represents. Then, if it can be shown that it's in the best interests of the company, most of them will agree to be interviewed. They know the story will appear whether or not they participate, and they know a refusal means they risk not having their side of the story told. Those considerations usually outweigh personal biases and fears.

Once the interview has been formally scheduled, the role of the public relations person as an intermediary accelerates. Just as reporters prepare for an interview by conducting extensive research, so do executives. Public relations people provide as much of a personal portrait of the reporter as possible: Years of experience, previous assignments, personal style. Does he fire staccato questions or put his subject at ease? Will she sit still for a detailed explanation of a key point? What are the toughest questions he's likely to ask? The executive also will request additional information about the interview topic: Statistics, previous statements, names of key individuals. And he will insist that the journalist be fully briefed: Executives resent most of all reporters who presume to interview them without being properly prepared.

If possible, the public relations person will also meet with the reporter to describe the *executive's* background and style: Is he a succinct or wandering responder? Does she take the time to explain complicated ideas? Is he impatient? Are there specific topics she likes to discuss? What areas are likely to be sensitive? And the public relations person will supply the reporter with considerable background material, some of it specifically requested, some elected for its pertinence.

## Have a Mock Interview; Go Over the Rules

Occasionally, depending on the importance of the interview and/or the experience of the executive, a training session is arranged in which public relations people take the roles of reporters and conduct a mock interview session. It's a way for an executive to focus on something not typically part of his or her responsibilities. During the session, public relations people will help crystallize key points and review some basic rules:

1. Prepare thoroughly. Anticipate the questions you may be asked, rehearse your answers, and try them out on somebody else.
2. Don't lose sight of your objectives. Make sure that whatever points you want to make are made.
3. Never go off the record, never agree to be quoted on background only, never provide information to be used without attribution, and never say "no comment."
4. If you do not know the answer to a question, say so and promise to get the answer (this is one of the tasks the public relations person will perform after the interview has been completed).
5. Keep it simple. Avoid technical jargon.
6. Stick to the subject. Don't ramble and waste the reporter's time.
7. Never respond to hearsay.
8. Never provide information or opinions about the competition.
9. Never let the reporter put words into your mouth (for example, hypothetical questions). Challenge illicit presuppositions. Decline to answer any questions preceded by a phrase such as, "Would you say?"

10. Most importantly, tell the truth, without exaggeration or hedging.

All of these rules and other activities are meant to create an atmosphere in which the best possible interview can take place—*an interview free of misunderstandings that satisfies both the executive's need to state his points clearly and the reporter's need to have his questions answered.*

As journalists are painfully aware, the clock is running during all of this. Only rarely can executive interviews be arranged on short notice. Reporters sometimes are willing to "go with what they've got." They'll get another chance tomorrow. Executives probably won't.

The role of the public relations person during the actual interview is relatively unobtrusive. The session belongs to the reporter. At Control Data, public relations people interrupt only to assist, clarify or amplify. Once the interview is concluded, they serve as a follow-up conduit for both the executive and the reporter. If necessary, a second interview can be arranged, but that rarely happens.

Control Data's public relations people followed this process more than 1,000 times last year. We did so because we know the media speaks to our stockholders, our employees, our customers, and other publics important to the corporation. And it is precisely *because* journalists are so important in shaping opinions that we insist upon equalizing the interview situation.

In the final analysis, Control Data expects just three things of reporters:

- That they do their homework.
- That they be objective (and provide Control Data a chance to comment on any potentially negative reports).
- And that they get it right. People's jobs and reputations are at stake.

*Jerr Boschee, formerly general manager of public relations, is now Control Data's loaned executive to a consortium of Fortune 500 companies launching new businesses in the social needs market.*

# INDEX

# W

Word choice
  nonsexist, 245–46
  in oral presentations, 516–17
  style, 232–38
  tone, 57–58
Word order, 238
Word visuals, 448–50
Word-processing, 108–10

Workshops, 500
Writing style, 22, 30–34, 229–46
  clarity, 238–39
  conciseness, 239–40
  emphasis, 244–45
  history, 229–30
  in résumé, 284–85
  vigor, 240–41
  when writing for others, 34–35,
    163

1 2 3 4 5 6 7 8 9 0